ANNUAL REVIEW OF BEHAVIOR THERAPY

ANNUAL REVIEW OF
BEHAVIOR
THERAPY
THEORY AND PRACTICE

VOLUME 8

CYRIL M. FRANKS
Rutgers University
G. TERENCE WILSON
Rutgers University
PHILIP C. KENDALL
Center for Advanced Study in the Behavioral Sciences
KELLY D. BROWNELL
University of Pennsylvania

CALIFORNIA SCHOOL OF PROFESSIONAL PSYCHOLOGY LOS ANGELES

THE GUILFORD PRESS
New York   London

©1982 Cyril M. Franks, G. Terence Wilson, Philip C. Kendall, and Kelly D. Brownell

Published by The Guilford Press
A Division of Guilford Publications, Inc.
200 Park Avenue South, New York, N.Y. 10003

Printed in the United States of America

Library of Congress Catalog Card No. 76-126864
ISBN 0-89862-612-9
ISSN 0091-6595

It is a wretched argument that is supported by custom and tradition. . . . There are but two ways to arrive at knowledge—experience (through personal experiment) and reason.

ROGER BACON (1214–1286)

PREFACE

With the appearance of Volume 8 in this series we resume an old tradition and start what we hope will become a new one. The old and established tradition, of course, is that of the series itself. The inaugural volume saw the light of day in 1973 and Volume 7, up to the summer of 1979, appeared in 1980. For reasons which will shortly become apparent, there was no *Annual Review* in 1981. The present volume, Volume 8, spanning the period from mid-1979 through the summer of 1981, continues this tradition and marks the potential beginning of a new one.

This situation came about as follows. Volume 1 in the series consisted of some 90% reprinted articles and 10% commentary by Cyril M. Franks and G. Terence Wilson. Successive years saw a systematic increase in the ratio of commentary to reprinted material until, with the advent of Volume 7 in 1980, the number of pages of original commentary and the number of pages devoted to articles already in print were approximately equal. It also became increasingly evident that many readers, especially those with ready access to contemporary journals and adequate libraries, were more interested in acquiring the *Annual Review* series for the commentaries than the articles. Reprinting articles seemed to be a largely superfluous activity, and space, time, and energy could better be devoted to commentary. The time was ripe for a reformulation of the *Annual Review* concept in terms of totally original contributions. The problem at issue was, how could this best be accomplished? The two primary editors/authors, Franks and Wilson, were clearly not in a position to provide comprehensive and up-to-date commentaries upon every aspect of the prevailing behavior therapy scene at the level of scholarship that was indicated. The solution was obvious—get help. It was at this stage that Philip C. Kendall and Kelly D. Brownell, both of whom bring specific areas of expertise to the task at hand, came aboard.

The *Annual Review* is no longer a hybrid mixture of commentary and reprints. Commencing with the current year, each volume is to consist exclusively of original commentary and other pertinent material written by the present four-author team. Unlike most annual reviews, even those which do consist of original rather than reprinted material, the new *Annual Review of Behavior Therapy* provides continuity of both theme and thought. This is accomplished by having the same four authors comment, respectively, upon the same subject areas each year. By this means, it is our intent to offer a progressive, integrated critical perspective upon ongoing developments which highlights both accomplishments and deficits in key areas of behavior therapy over the years. Each of us has agreed to be responsible for two broad areas of behavior therapy, as indicated by the Contents, for a three-year period, at the very least. We hope that these changes will meet with your approval and, if not, that you will so advise us. Feedback of any sort, especially with respect to our choice of topic areas, is most welcome. How else can behavior modifiers modify their behavior?

As in the past, this volume would not have materialized so smoothly were it not for the secretarial and other skills of Gloria Johnson at the Graduate School of Applied and Professional Psychology at Rutgers University; Alleen Pusey at the Carrier Foundation, Belle Mead, New Jersey; Barbara Honig at the Rutgers Alcohol Behavior Research Laboratory; and Pat Mitchell at the University of Pennsylvania School of Medicine.

The third author (PCK) is most grateful to the Center for Advanced Study in the Behavioral Sciences, Stanford, California—especially its director, Gardner Lindzey—for the opportunity to complete this volume under ideal working conditions. Financial support for this endeavor was also provided by the National Institute of Mental Health, the John D. and Catherine T. MacArthur Foundation, and the University of Minnesota.

Finally, as always, we acknowledge with love and admiration the critical comments, encouragement, and support of our respective wives, Violet, Elaine, Sue, and Mary Jo.

Cyril M. Franks
G. Terence Wilson
Philip C. Kendall
Kelly D. Brownell

CONTENTS

ANNUAL REVIEW OF BEHAVIOR THERAPY

1

BEHAVIOR THERAPY: AN OVERVIEW

CYRIL M. FRANKS

INTRODUCTION

Stocktaking and soothsaying have long been fashionable in professional circles, and behavior therapists provide no exception. So far, neither the wishful prediction that behavior therapy is riding the wave of the future, soon to replace all other psychological therapies, nor the gleeful anticipation that behavior therapy is sinking to the depths shows signs of becoming a reality. The prevailing mood is probably better described as one of cautious optimism. Thus, Rachman and Wilson (1980) acknowledge behavior therapy's many accomplishments: the phenomenal growth in behavioral medicine, the development of well-established methods for reducing anxiety and fear, the progress made in the treatment of obsessions, compulsions, and sexual disorders, and so on. But they also note weaknesses: the narrowness of vision, the reluctance to give up underlying medical theories, and the lack of a generally accepted theoretical model (see also Barlow, 1980). There is no single element within the field of behavior therapy that can be identified as a focal core, and despite a plethora of pontification there is little agreement about such basics as the proper domain and definition of behavior therapy, the roles of conditioning and learning theory, or the links between behavior therapy and experimental psychology.

Kazdin (1979b) explores in detail some of the "fictions, factions, and functions" of behavior therapy. Foremost among his fictions is the notion that behavior therapy rests upon theory derived from experimental psychology. Systematic desensitization, for example, may be one of the great accomplishments of behavior therapy but its clinical

1

utility almost certainly does not rest upon any commonly proposed theoretical rationale. For many techniques, including some highly effective ones, no clear, predominant, theoretical account, or even supporting data, can be provided. Regrettably, despite a decade of growth, London's 1972 lament that behavior therapy is technique-oriented still hits nearer home than some of us care to admit.

Another "myth" to which Kazdin draws attention is that behavior therapy does not predict symptom substitution. We would be more inclined to argue that the alien notion of symptoms, and hence of symptom substitution, has no place in the behavior therapist's conceptual framework, and that behavior therapy can predict neither symptom substitution nor its absence. Rather, we should be concerned with the observable phenomena upon which "symptom" substitution is based; these *are* amenable to identification and empirical study.

Kazdin's myth that behavior therapy focuses upon overt behavior is a myth. In this cognition-oriented era one would be hard put to find a practicing behavior therapist to stake either reputation or income upon such a contention. Similarly, the myth that behavior therapy places little importance on the therapeutic relationship is a throwback from a bygone era. Kazdin's disagreement with those who make the blanket statement that behavior therapy is more effective than other interventions rests on firmer ground. In the first place numerous investigations attest to the fact that behavior therapy is about as effective as psychotherapy and that, in certain areas, it fails to provide evidence of a clear increment of efficacy over traditional treatments. In the second place, as we repeatedly remind readers of this *Annual Review* series, it is not appropriate to contrast an entity entitled "behavior therapy" with something called "psychotherapy." Each includes a variety of quite different procedures and strategems, depending upon the problem at hand. In every instance, precise statements can be made only about comparative studies of specific procedures applied to specific problem areas. More general conclusions are meaningful only to the extent that they are backed up by such data. Where behavior therapy does score is with respect to methodology. There is probably no other treatment modality which comes even close to behavior therapy in the consistent, rigorous, and systematic application of sophisticated methodology.

Perhaps the most important myth to which Kazdin, this time correctly, draws attention is that behavior therapy is scientific and empirically based. It is only in contrast with other forms of therapy that there is some truth to this statement. Too much in the practice of behavior therapy is based on clinical impression or hearsay rather than empirical research. Another of Kazdin's myths is that behavioral assessment improves upon traditional assessment. As noted and documented time and time again in this series, there is truth to this belief only in comparison with assessment based upon global personality traits and inferences derived from projective tests. Procedures based upon behavioral observation are probably an improvement to these. So-called behavioral questionnaires, for the most part, studiously ignore any but the rudiments of psychometrics and, in so doing, forfeit their claim to superiority. Concern with such matters is a relatively recent development.

When all is said, if not done, behavior therapy in the 1980s offers little that has not been broached in an earlier decade (Franks, 1981b; Franks & Rosenbaum, 1982). Perhaps most of all, behavior therapy needs a coherent theoretical framework, a model of man (in the generic sense, for here "man" embraces woman). As yet, no one has succeeded in developing such a model. Kalish (1981) attempts to document the historical relationships between the knowledge bank of behavior science and the clinical application of behavioral principles. If he fails, it is partly because no such clear-cut relationship exists at this stage. Eysenck has long championed the cause of theory in the evolution of behavior therapy, his not altogether successful attempt to develop a conditioning model of neurosis being a case in point. In his own well-chosen words,

> Theories in science are not right or wrong; they are fruitful or not depending on whether they lead to research with theoretically and practically important results. Judged by this standard, it seems that the conditioning theory of neurosis has been extremely fruitful, leading to extensive research activity both in the animal laboratory and in the clinic. The results of this research have inevitably led to modification of the original theory; no doubt this most recent model, embodying many of these modifications, will in turn give way to a more advanced one. This is as it should be; in science no theory is sacrosanct and no model lasts for very long. All the different parts of the model are open to experimental testing; more cannot be asked of any scientific theory. (Eysenck, 1979a, p. 166)

Despite several attempts to develop an integrative model, diversity prevails at all levels. There are those who argue for the need to bridge the gap between clinical and experimental psychology. Others bemoan the extension of behavior therapy into regions far from the main stream of mental health. Yet others stress the universality of behavior therapy and search for fresh fields to plough.

Gone are the days when behavior therapy could readily be defined in terms of specific stimuli or something called modern learning theory. Gone are the days of reliance upon the clear-cut and unequivocal mechanisms of classical and operant conditioning. The experience of the Brelands is salutary. When Keller and Marion Breland founded Animal Behavior Enterprises in 1947, their faith in the new "Skinnerian" psychology was limitless and their successes many. By 1961 came the realization that, however thorough the shaping, altering, and suppressing of an animal's chain of natural behaviors, sooner or later some form of instinctual (yes, instinctual) drift is going to emerge. It was at this stage, sadder but wiser, that they wrote their then heretically entitled article "The Misbehavior of Organisms." In the 1980s, the matter is still unresolved (Bailey & Bailey, 1980)!

As we advance into the 1980s, so the many seemingly new disciplines in which the term "behavioral" is incorporated dangle enticingly ahead of us: behavioral neurophysiology, behavioral genetics, behavioral pharmacology, behavioral economics, behavioral medicine, and more; the list seems endless. Special interest groups within the AABT (Association for Advancement of Behavior Therapy) abound, with new ones surfacing monthly. From such practicalities as sports psychology (e.g., Fensterheim, 1980; Gravel, Lemieux, & LaDouceur, 1980; Allison & Ayllon, 1980) and nursing (e.g., Barnard, 1980) to such esoteric and "behavioral-alien" doctrines as Zen meditation and Karma Yoga (e.g., Shapiro & Zifferblatt, 1976; Singh & Oberhummer, 1980; Mikulas, 1981) the clarion call for behavioral hegemony resounds. Where will it end?

Attempts to incorporate behavioral principles into a miniframework with clearly testable postulates are fewer in number but, in the long run, more likely to bring about consolidation of knowledge and practice. For example, the calculated use of microcomputer systems within the framework of general behavior therapy is more likely to advance day-to-day practice than any new technique or measuring instrument (e.g., Jernstedt & Forseth, 1980). Another example, at a more operational level, comes out of the pioneering work of B. T. Yates in the application of cost-effectiveness and cost–benefit analyses to behavior therapy (Yates & Newman, 1980a, 1980b). Until 1965, cost–benefit analysis was performed primarily for the United States Corps of Engineers in the evaluation of water resources projects. Only very recently have these principles been applied to more general programs (e.g., Thompson, 1980) and application to mental health is even newer (primarily by Yates and his associates).

Without doubt, accountability is one of the pillars of behavior therapy, and meaningful accountability is impossible without some form of cost–benefit analysis. As in all other areas of human endeavor, mental health resources are not confined to money alone. Therapist and client time, office space, equipment, materials, the capacity to endure psychological suffering are all measurable assets. It is only (and this is a very crucial "only") the units of measurement, and the priorities and weightings given to each that differ—and it is here that Yates comes into his own.

Therapeutic processes are whatever is said or done to clients or whatever the clients may say or do to themselves and others during treatment. Effectiveness, the implicit and explicit values of these processes, has to be measured in terms of multiple outcome units. Cost-effectiveness pertains to the set of relationships between the values of resource consumed and values of therapeutic outcomes produced. Cost-benefit analysis is a somewhat more limited concept usually applied to dollars spent versus dollars produced but equally appropriate to specific nonmonetary units (e.g., Yates, 1980).

As yet, the range of mental health therapies and client populations to which cost-effectiveness and cost-benefit analyses have been applied is limited, and few definitive statements can be made about their utility. Areas for potential application include comparisons of community-based versus institutional therapy for adult schizophrenics, residential versus institutional therapy for problem children, professional versus paraprofessional versus self-directed therapy, and the pros and cons of introducing behavioral procedures into such professions as nursing or medicine.

While still speculative, the merging of the Miller's "new look" in general systems theory with the precepts of behavior therapy offers considerable promise. J. G. Miller's *Living Systems* (1978) is different in three major respects: it is data-based, sympathetic to learning theory principles, and specifically oriented toward *living* systems. A similar if less directly relevant emphasis pervades Boulding's (1978) *Ecodynamics: A New Theory of Societal Evolution*. Contemporary general systems theory could enable us to bring together diverse fields in such a manner as to solve problems that are inherently complex, multiprocessed, and multilevel in nature. Schwartz (1980a) makes this point in terms of behavioral medicine, but it is equally applicable to behavior therapy at large. In Schwartz's own words,

> As we combine more variables in interdisciplinary research and treatment, as we discover and incorporate more parts of a system at a given level, and as we pursue more levels across systems, it seems inevitable that, if total information overload does not occur, then a general theory for organizing and synthesizing this wealth of information will emerge as a new paradigm. The history of systems theory applied to living systems, from Walter Cannon and Norbert Weiner in the 1930s and the 1940s to the recent work of James G. Miller, suggests that information overload can be counteracted by the development of a general theory. If future students in the behavioral or biomedical sciences are exposed to general systems

theory early in their careers as part of their speciality training, the goals of developing a general theory for behavioral medicine may be achieved. (Schwartz, 1980a, p. 30)

It is on this encouraging note that we turn now to discussion of further issues and areas of influence for behavior therapy that have arisen or been reactivated in the very recent past.

COGNITION AND BEHAVIOR THERAPY

In Chapter 4, "Cognitive Processes and Procedures in Behavior Therapy," the implicit assumption is that the cognitive revolution is by now an integral part of the mainstream of behavior therapy. While this position cannot reasonably be faulted, it is equally certain that the cognitive–behavioral debate is still alive and, by its very nature, probably resolvable (if it is resolvable) as much in terms of personal philosophy as appeal to data.

To recapitulate briefly: Ledwidge's (1978) provocative salvo, entitled "Cognitive Behavior Modification: A Step in the Wrong Direction," triggered off many rounds of spirited replies, rejoinders, rebuttals, counterrebuttals, and what have you (e.g., Ledwidge, 1979a, 1979b, 1979c; Locke, 1979; Mahoney & Kazdin, 1979). Ross (1978, cited by Ledwidge, 1979c) characterizes behavior therapy as "a throwback to the psychotherapy of the 1940s that sought to gain contemporary respectability by attaching 'behavioral' to its label." Jaremko (1979a) accuses cognitivists of "a flirtation with mentalism," and Richard Lazarus (1980) senses that "cognitive behavior therapists have been guilty of euphemisms that disguise their movement towards psychodynamic concepts." The cognitive-behaviorists debate extends itself into the area of classical conditioning theory. For example, Hillner's (1979) division of the entire history of conditioning into two categories, traditional (from about 1900 to 1960) and contemporary (since about 1960), uses the advent of cognition as one major point of departure for the old order. While many would take issue with his arbitrary division into two eras, the appearance of this book is a sign of the times.

For Ledwidge (1979c) the position is clear: "Cognitions are not behaviors (they are hypothetical constructs used to account for relationships between environmental events and behaviors) and CBM is not behavior modification" (p. 163). For Locke (1979) the main difference between behavioral and cognitive techniques lies in the kind and degree of emphasis on the cognitive activity. There is no such thing as direct behavior change, and in any event, so it is argued, behavior change is not the essence of therapy. Behavior therapists may be less conceptual in their approach than cognitive-behavior therapists (these arbitrary labels are irksome), but all employ some form of cognition. Even the distinction between methodological behaviorism, espoused by most behavior therapists today, and metaphysical or radical behaviorism, which denies the relevance or even existence of any form of cognitive event whatsoever, is debated by Locke on the grounds that the former makes little sense unless there is an at least implicit belief in materialism and metaphysical behaviorism to back it up.

Wolpe's position is clear (1978, 1980). Cognition is a behavior, a function of specifiable behaviors in the nervous system (cf. Taylor, 1962). Philosophically, freedom is an illusion and thinking is subject to the same laws and the same inevitability as any other class of behavior.

Espousing a preference for cool data rather than heated opinions, Mahoney (in press) surveyed 42 leading contributors to the behavior therapy and cognitive-behavior modification literature. The two factions seem to differ neither with respect to their views about the existence of "mind" nor the importance of experimental rigor in theoretical evaluation. Mahoney and Kazdin (1979) argue convincingly from such data that all therapies are simultaneously cognitive and behavioral to greater or lesser extents, a position with which it is hard to take serious issue. Here we must let the matter rest until the next round of articles appears, which will doubtless be soon. (For a more extended discussion of these matters see previous issues of the *Annual Review*, especially Vol. 7, pp. 119–136.)

THE CONVERGING PATHS OF BEHAVIOR THERAPY AND PSYCHODYNAMICS

In previous years we have devoted considerable space to the heated debate between those who see behavior therapy and psychoanalysis as compatible at philosophic and/or technical levels and those who do not. Our position may be summed up as follows: Behavior therapy and psychoanalysis are conceptually, methodologically, and technically incompatible and an integration of the two at any level will probably be to the disadvantage of both. We therefore suggest that the systems remain incompatible, occupy different worlds, and go about their respective business constructively but independently. Some third position might emerge but that day has not yet arisen and, in our opinion, is unlikely to be speeded by premature integration.

We also reject the concept of technical eclecticism as advanced by Lazarus (1976). Enticing as it may seem to take refuge in the doctrine of demonstrable effectiveness—use anything that works—this strategy has at least two serious deficits. First, the enthusiastic clinician is likely to be less than searching in the quest for evidence that a technique is valid and many of us have different criteria with respect to "validity." Second, out of the vast compendium of techniques which could be "dreamed up" by those who are so inclined, it is virtually impossible to establish a priority for their rigorous investigation. A far more appropriate strategy would be to work within some form of research program in which techniques are generated and selected for investigation upon some rational basis.

There are other positions. Thus Strupp (1979), an unabashed psychodynamicist, and Marmor and Woods (1980) are all convinced that the two systems are complementary. McNamara (1980) seems to think that the real dichotomy is not between behavior therapy and psychoanalysis. It is between those who favor the rational and intellectual study of human behavior (regardless of orientation) and the anti-intellectual forces which endorse personal revelation and a denial of reason as the essential basis for therapeutic intervention. While we sympathize with this position, it does not negate the profound, irreconcilable methodological and conceptual difference between psychoanalysis and behavior therapy. For a more extended discussion of these and related issues, see Chapter 8.

BEHAVIOR THERAPY, APPLIED BEHAVIORAL ANALYSIS, AND TECHNICAL DRIFT

Winkler (1979) makes a useful distinction between behavior therapy and applied behavioral analysis. Behavior therapy takes problems generated historically by the medical model and tries to show how they can be handled more effectively. Applied behavioral analysis has been shaped by methodology rather than by the medical model when defining behaviors to be changed. Similarly, if for different reasons, applied behavioral analysis, with its narrowly conceived notions of objectivity and research methodology, tends to ignore decisions of value and the need to attend to the ideologies and power structures involved in making decisions about change.

Whatever the reason, as Winkler observes, journal pages devoted to applied behavioral analysis research do seem to have a rather deadening similarity. Investigators are trained to think in terms of circumscribed, generally tangible, reinforcers rather than search for new and socially meaningful variables. Wardlaw (1980) discusses the limitations of the Premack principle in this respect and Berger (1979) makes a similar point when he draws attention to the hazards of "mindless technology," the use of techniques divorced from a socially meaningful context.

In 1978, Deitz raised important points concerning what Hayes, Rincover, and Solnick (1980) refer to as the technical drift in applied behavioral analysis. When Hayes, Rincover, and Solnick (1978) examined the first 10 volumes of the *Journal of Applied Behavior Analysis*, their data demonstrated convincingly that applied behavioral analysis is becoming progressively more and more technologically oriented and that interest in conceptual issues is on the decline. The term *applied* is being formalized in the terms of the structural appearance of the research rather than the impact it has on actual problems. Pierce and Epling (1980) make a similar point. Thus, the technological thinking of applied behavioral analysis leads to the mistaken belief that the ability to control the behavior is synonymous with understanding.

The more complex the society, the greater the gap between research and application. If technicians ignore conceptual issues, fundamental research, and social significance, then this gap is going to increase. We view this as one of the potential dangers for behavior therapy in general and applied behavioral analysis in particular in the coming years.

THE GAP BETWEEN THEORY AND PRACTICE

The gap between fundamental research and technological application is paralleled by that between theoretical knowledge and its implementation (see Chapter 8). Translated into the language of clinical practice, what clinicians say they believe in and what they actually do are two different things, and common behavioral procedures are rarely underwritten by substance (Emmelkamp, 1980). Locke (1980), for example, ingeniously compared two independent field studies, both remarkably similar in design, technique, and findings. However, one study confidently evoked a cognitive interpretation to account for the data whereas the other, with equal certainty, employed a behavioristic model. Unlike Komaki (1981), one of the authors scrutinized by Locke, we do not believe that such disputes can readily be resolved by "letting the data speak for themselves."

Techniques which seem successful in terms of theory and practice in journal articles fade away when exposed to everyday clinical exposure. As Mozer (1979) wryly comments, "It is enough to make anyone an ex-behaviorist!" (p. 3). Behavior therapy is supposed to be committed to empiricism but little is known about the impact of this commitment on practice. Kanfer's (1972) survey of some 30 leaders in the field suggests that the relationship between clinical assessment and research is minimal. More recently, Swan and MacDonald (1978) explored the research–practice discrepancy by surveying a representative sample of AABT members. While unequivocal indications of this discrepancy emerged, the trend towards eclecticism which they also found is less readily explained. A sizable percentage of behavior therapists currently label themselves as eclectic, a situation evident in clinical psychology at large (Garfield & Kurtz, 1976). Eclecticism is an elusive concept to define (Swan, 1979), and Swan and MacDonald succeeded in identifying at least four distinct subtypes. Wade, Baker, and Hartmann (1979) likewise report a discrepancy between acknowledged principles and translation into practice. Perhaps, as Ford and Kendall (1979) lament, it is time for behavior therapists to apply behavioral methodology to increasing their own adherence to the espoused tenets of behavior therapy.

Farkas (1980) questions the utility of attempting to maintain rigid distinctions between behavior therapy and other approaches. To appreciate this question, it is important to generate an understanding of the more important divisions within our field. Hayes (1978) attempts to identify and make explicit the possible dimensions of behavior therapy (which for some curious reason he persists in equating with behaviorism). Many classification systems have been suggested: applied versus basic; clinical versus nonclinical; animal versus human; operant versus classical; behavior therapy versus behavior analysis; and so forth. The two fundamental quasi-dimensions described but not statistically isolated by Hayes and Barlow (cited by Hayes, 1978) are the "level of analysis" and the "type of paradigm."

Scientific investigation typically involves certain general ways of making contact with the world and of controlling and assessing that contact. An appropriate scientific methodology leads to the development of specific techniques rooted within a theoretical or conceptual system embedded in an integrating philosophical perspective. These various activities, argue Hayes and Barlow, can be arranged more or less hierarchically into what they term the "level of analysis." Techniques, the lowest level of this hypothetical dimension, need not necessarily involve the use of any particular methodology or reference to other levels. The next level, methodology, typically requires knowledge of certain techniques and may even lead to the development of new ones, but it does not necessarily require the adoption of a particular conceptual system. This emphasis upon conceptualization constitutes the third level. In its turn the formulation of a conceptual system need not necessarily involve the highest level, which rests upon some philosophical position or world view.

Certain clinicians consider themselves "behaviorists," merely because they use behavioral techniques. At this level, it is possible for a psychoanalyst who at times uses selected behavioral techniques to consider himself or herself as an occasional behavior therapist. Those who function at this level may have no knowledge or inclination toward any facet of the levels above. Similarly, a conceptually oriented behavior therapist may have no interest in the philosophical implications of a behavioral view of the world.

The second quasi-dimension hypothesized by Hayes and Barlow pertains to the type of paradigm deployed. (We would prefer to use the term "framework" or "model" rather than paradigm in this context, but that is besides the point.) Hayes and Barlow find it useful to view the field in terms of two rather broad paradigms: behavior analysis and methodological behaviorism. At the technical level, behavior analysis emphasizes straightforward manipulation of antecedent and consequent events. Methodologically, it relies heavily upon single-subject designs, direct observation, and repeated measurements. Its primary concepts include reinforcement, punishment, and generalization. Philosophically, its roots lie in materialism and functionalism, especially Skinner's radical behaviorism. Methodological behaviorism emphasizes group designs, inferential statistics, and intervening variables. Philosophically, this paradigm is closely related to operationalism and logical positivism. The older form of methodological behaviorism attempts to avoid the accusation of mentalism by operationally defining its terms. The new form, as exemplified by the cognitive–behavioral movement, stresses operationalism but makes no attempt to avoid any form of mentalism. Their ensuing two-by-four matrix leads to eight different categories for ordering the activities of behavior therapists. While this is an intriguing concept, its utility at any level, other than the purely descriptive, awaits the accumulation of relevant data and factor analysis.

THE IMAGE OF BEHAVIOR THERAPY

Each year we deplore the image of behavior therapy which seems to prevail among laypersons and professionals alike. Repeated surveys reveal an unfortunate association of behavior therapy with such adjectives as inhuman, mechanistic, and simplistic (e.g., Turkat, 1979). For Wolpe (1981), there is little problem, those images are "false" and, presumably, that is all there is to it. This widespread perception of behavior therapy is at variance with the facts, and there is little need to consider the contributions, possibly inadvertent, of behavior therapists to it. Barling's (1979) more self-searching analysis examines some of the underlying factors: an apprehension regarding behavioral control; the dislike and fear of a deterministic model of human behavior; the unnecessarily offensive and jargonistic terminology employed by many behavior modifiers; the increasing specialization and isolation within behavior modification; the failure of behavior modifiers to communicate the scientific and humanistic substraits of their discipline to others; and so forth.

Many individuals have offered solutions; few have attempted implementation. Turkat (1979) suggests that the AABT develop an "all-out" public relations campaign. Milan (1981) advises behavior therapists to be more cautious and more responsible in their interface with semiprofessionals. As Milan notes, many an inadequately trained semiprofessional has unsuccessfully applied what are thought to be correct behavioral principles in a manner which the world at large rightly views as naive, self-serving, and even cruel. Knapp and Delprato (1980) stress the need to educate elementary psychology students in the basic tenets of behavioral psychology. (In a study of prevailing notions among beginning and more advanced psychology classes, they found a belief in "willpower" to bear no relationship to formal education or the number of psychology courses completed.) As Wolpe (1981) reminds us, people are unlikely to change their opinions unless they have something to gain or lose. Perhaps recent statements from the National Institute of Mental Health and the insurance companies with respect to their unwillingness to go on paying for psychotherapy without evidence of efficacy will generate increasing concern among all therapists with the need for accountability. And, we may hope, this will accrue to our advantage in the eyes of the public.

ACCOUNTABILITY AND GUIDELINES

Accountability may be defined as responsibility. It is also associated with such phrases as "quality care," "quality assurance," and "cost-effectiveness." Like God, flag, and the mother country, all of us pay lip-service to accountability, but few of us think through the complexities involved. Our society is in the midst of a severe and growing crisis, much of it centering around the distressed state of the economy. As part of an emerging conservative reaction, demands for accountability have been proliferating. When public and private agencies call for insurance reimbursements for psychotherapy to be made contingent upon demonstrations of efficacy, this would seem good. But all too often, accountability is based upon an obsolete understanding of systems and how they operate. Accountability is seen within an Aristotelian framework in which cause and effect are linearly related. For example, accountability is used to assign responsibility for cause of an unwanted effect to some person, group, or agency, with a resulting search for scapegoats when the effects are shown to be adverse.

Noting this dilemma, Alger (1980) suggests that the present societal crisis be viewed as a dysfunctional manifestation of a complex system and that attempts to comprehend the operation of the system be made within some framework involving general systems and cybernetics. This would eliminate a simplistic blame assignment of the cause-and-effect thinking embodied in the usual interpretation of "accountability." But at this stage it is difficult to see how these generalities are to be translated into concrete proposals. Therefore our preference is for Yates's cost–benefit analysis model of accountability.

That accountability-minded behavior therapists favor guidelines is only to be expected. Numerous guidelines have been proposed for such diverse situations as the conduct of office practice, institutional programs, the training of professional and lay groups, weekend workshops, and do-it-yourself therapy manuals. Back in 1975 Stein (1975), drawing attention to the ethical considerations involved in behavior therapy workshops which "qualified" participants to engage in independent practice of the workshop's methods after one or two weekend exposures, suggested the need for guidelines. Similarly, Rosen (1981) has outlined detailed guidelines for the review of do-it-yourself treatment books. While most early behavioral guidelines focused upon controversial procedures involving aversion or deprivation, by the end of 1978 the "guidelines notebook" of the Professional Consultation and Peer Review Committee of the AABT had collected no less than 21 different entries (Risley & Sheldon-Wildgen, 1980).

The legal profession offers little help with the formulation of guidelines other than to stress the hazards of attempting to function without them (Coval, 1980). Most ethical codes for professionals are vaguely formulated, difficult to enforce, and therefore rarely enforced. By implication, guidelines can even be potentially harmful if they serve to deny individuals their rights. As Schwitzgebel and Schwitzgebel appropriately put it with respect to the possible long-term consequences of increased legal intervention in mental hospitals, "It is no advance to trade authoritarian treatment for authoritarian nontreatment (1980, p. 3).

The courts fail to realize the full implications of recent legal decisions. The landmark court decision of Wyatt v. Stickney of 1971, together with other relevant rulings, pinpoint the fundamental rights that have to be considered whenever a behavior modification program is implemented (Braun, 1975). But this can raise a variety of problems. For example, if reinforcers such as television and ground privileges are given noncontingently, then patients are likely to revert back to the institutional syndrome of apathy, dependency, and irresponsibility (Berwick & Morris, 1974). As McNamara (1978) points out, it is encumbent upon the behavior therapist to try to persuade the courts to establish evaluative procedures for monitoring the effects of these decisions upon patient care. Until further data are collected, it cannot be assumed that these legal constraints are other than mixed blessings.

Be this as it may, specific guidelines have been enacted or are well under way throughout the English-speaking world (e.g., California—Bazar 1979; Wisconsin—Finesmith, 1979; the United Kingdom—Comments on the Report of a Joint Working Party, 1981). While most of these programs are geared toward aversion therapy or some other socially equivocal form of correction, numerous agencies concern themselves with less hazardous procedures such as guidelines for behavioral parental training (Parrish & Hester, 1980).

Recent pages of *The Behavior Therapist*, an official publication of the AABT, have seen lively and sometimes acrimonious interchange among those who favor and those who disagree with the establishment of guidelines for behavior therapists. According to Griffith (1980a, 1980b), guidelines protect both clients and staff. Stolz (1980a, 1980b) prefers checklists: Guidelines naively assume all participants in the decision-making process to be of good will and in total agreement as to the goals and methods of therapy. Others point to the possibility of guidelines stifling research. Additional resistance stems from a perhaps realistic belief that the establishment of guidelines would result in additional paper work and committee meetings and reduce the time available for direct professional activities. But perhaps the most commonly voiced objection to guidelines is that they might restrict the freedom of therapists to act in their clients' best interests. The reader is referred to *The Behavior Therapist* for further discussion of the intricacies involved in the pros and cons of various forms of guidelines (Coval, 1980; Griffith, 1980a, 1980b; Martin, 1980, Stolz, 1980a, 1980b; Thomas, 1980; Thomas & Murphy, 1981).

TRAINING IN BEHAVIOR THERAPY

Training in behavior therapy falls into two broad categories: intensive, full-time systematic training for behaviorally sophisticated, qualified professionals who plan to function as behavior therapists; and the training of paraprofessionals or those who plan to function at lower levels of behavioral sophistication but nevertheless wish to apply behavioral procedures. For example, Shorkey (1973) reports a behavioral training program for social workers and Miller and Lewin (1980) systematically review the numerous training and management programs which are now available for psychiatric aides. Noting that medical students sometimes become confused by vague theoretical formulations which have little generalization to medical practice, Munford and Wikler (1976) describe a program which specifically utilizes behavioral procedures in the training of medical students in the fundamentals of interpersonal interactions. Numerous individuals have developed appropriate training programs in the elements of behavior therapy for undergraduate students of psychology (e.g., Innes & Owen, 1980; Jason, in press), Goldstein (1978, 1980a, 1980b) devotes considerable attention to the development of systematic training programs in organizational psychology within an industrial setting, and Latham and Saari (1979) examine role modeling as a training device within the organizational environment.

Psychiatric education still deemphasizes behavioral training. Interest in behavioral training still remains confined, in the main, to psychologists. Psychologists have relatively little influence within the medical setting and are therefore unlikely to bring about change. In 1973, despite the reported need for such programs, Brady's survey bore striking witness to the lack of behavioral training programs in medical facilities. The increase in such training since 1973 is modest at best (Brady & Wienckowski, 1978), and a recent survey by Latimer (1980) indicates that the Canadian scene is similar. All these surveys indicate an awareness of the need for training in behavior therapy but little concern with implementation.

While the situation with respect to behavioral training programs for doctoral-level clinical psychologists is much more encouraging, behavioral medicine is less fortunate (Weiss, 1978). In most behavioral medicine programs the emphasis seems to be upon training for research and to reflect whatever definitions of behavioral medicine happen to prevail (Belar, 1978; Swan, Piccione, & Anderson 1980).

With predictable regularity, those involved in training tell us that behavior therapy rests upon a profound appreciation of scientific principles (e.g., Meyer, 1980). In practice, especially in more specialized or intensive training programs, this dictum is often ignored. Ott (1980) draws attention to the dangers of cookbook training in his analysis of various preconvention programs offered by the AABT. A little learning can be extremely dangerous when a professional decides to practice on an intensive basis what has been learned in a four- to eight-hour workshop (Kuehnel, Marholin, Heinrich, & Liberman, 1978). AABT announcements which pander to a belief that usable behavior therapy skills can be so acquired without preparatory training may well, to use Ott's mild admonishment, "generate undue confusion."

Another curious thing about behavioral training is that we still do not practice what we preach. Didactic instruction rather than modeling, role playing, graded practice, and the like is still the rule (Munford, Alevizos, Reardon, Miller, Callahan, Liberman, & Guilani, 1980). Also curious, at least to us, is the way in which certain so-called behavioral programs expect some form of personal "insight-gaining" therapeutic experience as an essential prerequisite of successfully completed training (cf. Ramsay, 1980). We find this lingering psychoanalytic heritage absurd. A personal analysis may be essential for the practice of psychoanalysis but it is not necessary to be factor analyzed to complete a successful factor analysis and the same goes for behavior therapy. At the same time, we recognize that people are not machines. While a personal analysis is, at best, totally inappropriate, it is essential for the therapist to gain some understanding of his or her relationship to other human beings, no matter how this is obtained.

BEHAVIOR THERAPY AND THE BLACK EXPERIENCE

For reasons clearly documented by Turner (1982), the black community in general, and black psychologists in particular, tend to view behavior therapy as suspect. When the adverse experiences of black Americans, controlled by a dominant white population for some three centuries, are combined with a human tendency to be suspicious of control, it can be understood why blacks remain skeptical of behavior therapy despite repeated demonstrations of its advantages.

Behavioral intervention is of relevance to the black community at three levels. First, good behavior therapy is good behavior therapy, regardless. The fact that the recipient is black may be either irrelevant or of secondary significance. For example, token reinforcement programs can be utilized to help remediate educational deficits in black students as with any other individuals (e.g., Miller & Schneider, 1970; Staats, Minke, & Butts, 1970). Further, when Hersen, Turner, Edelstein, and Pinkston (1975) utilized social skills training to help reintegrate a chronic, regressed schizophrenic into the community, the fact that he was black was of secondary relevance.

Second, behavior therapy can help blacks cope with problems arising specifically out of their black experience. For example, Frederiksen, Jenkins, Foy, and Eisler (1976/1977) utilized social skills training to modify abusive explosive, verbal, and other antisocial behaviors in black VA males. And Kandel and Ayllon (1976) reported that achievement in black prisoners increased when a contingency management program was implemented specifically for them. Similarly, Milby, Garrett, English, Fritschi, and Clark (1978) developed a response-outcome program for black addicts in which clients earned Methadone take-home privileges contingent upon clean urine and productive activity. In all of these instances it could reasonably be argued that the deviant behavior arose primarily as a consequence of being black.

Third, behavioral interventions may be utilized with the predominant white population in the struggle against racial prejudice. For example, O'Donnell and Worrell (1973) utilized systematic desensitization to reduce antiblack feelings in white college students. (In this respect, it is probably first advisable to use systematic desensitization to reduce the prevailing anxiety, guilt, and feelings of disquiet in the individuals concerned; Susskind, Franks, & Lonoff, 1971.) And Turner reports two large-scale attempts to alter discriminatory behavior within an interracial group (O'Connor, 1977a) and a then recently mixed government agency (O'Connor, 1977b).

Behavior therapy would seem to offer distinct advantages to blacks in that it is action oriented rather than rooted in putative intrapsychic conflict (Jackson, 1976). One problem is that most black psychologists are trained at white institutions and, as yet, no effective program for the training of behaviorally oriented black psychologists who wish to work with minority clients has been developed (Green, 1981; Hayes, 1972).

Turner and Jones (1982) detail the problems involved in behavior modification with black populations. Green (1982) focuses specifically upon Seligman's (1975) model of learned helplessness. Be it in terms of education, social acceptance, employment, living conditions, the law, or political systems, an impressive case can be made for a learned helplessness model to account for the numerous problems confronting black Americans. The learned helplessness model is eminently testable, readily applicable to any disadvantaged group, and particularly appropriate to the study of community processes involving complex determinants beyond the individual's control (Sue & Zane, 1980). Changes at the societal level are difficult to implement but this is no reason why individual intervention should not be attempted. As Dweck and Reppucci (1973) note, and Jones, Nation, and Massard (1977) demonstrate, when uncontrollable outcomes occur, individuals who have had appropriate prior experience with successes and failures are less likely to show deficits in motivation, cognition, and affect than those who have not.

INSTITUTIONAL BEHAVIOR MODIFICATION

Overview

Most institutional behavior therapists are academically oriented clinical psychologists and therefore likely to be at odds in one way or another with the usual medical milieu (Hersen, 1979; Hersen & Bellack, 1978). Guidelines sometimes enhance harmonious relationships and efficient administration as well as the patient's lot. Accreditation is supposed to serve similar purposes but this is not always so (Repp & Barton, 1980). All too often, specific treatments are contingent upon institutional rather than patient needs. For example, Soloff and Turner (1981) found neither mental status nor diagnosis to be related to the use of seclusion on two acute treatment units of a university hospital. There was no relationship between a precipitating event and the duration of seclusion, nor was there any change in duration or restriction of seclusion with repeated episodes. What were correlated with the incidence of seclusion were legal status on admission and the race of the patient. There is a clinical bias toward seclusion with committed, chronic, and black patients. Such findings are of particular importance to those concerned with accountability and objectivity.

Institutional token economies have come under particular assault within recent years. Despite increasing evidence with respect to the efficiency and general utility of carefully executed programs, it is possible, as Greenberg (in press) sadly notes, that token economies may have "had their day" due to mounting legal difficulties. Alternatively, this could provide the necessary impetus for greater ingenuity in the construction of reinforcement procedures which are therapeutically effective and yet within both the letter and spirit of the law. This may take the form of a more sophisticated concept of reinforcement, perhaps involving peer and group contingencies, self-control procedures, and the teaching of social or vocational skills (e.g., Bedell & Archer, 1980; Matson & Zeiss, 1979).

Administrative and Staff Matters

Understandably, behavior therapists in residential settings focus on direct client care and, despite recent public concern with such matters, pay little attention to the impact of their programs upon the total organizational structure (Christian, 1981). Most staff management and staff–patient studies have involved relatively few staff, limited periods of time, restrictive settings, short-term behavior change with little provision for long-term maintenance, and no concern with spinoff effects. Furthermore, the effects of administrative policy changes as intervention strategies have been generally overlooked.

One of the few studies to examine the application of behavioral management strategies within a large institutional setting in terms of the impact upon staff and staff–patient relationship is that of Prue, Krapfl, Noah, Cannon, and Maley (1980). Their sophisticated design, extending over a 57-week period, points to the utility of performance feedback as a straightforward and inexpensive way of increasing treatment activities and constructive staff–patient interactions.

Staff self-recording has received minimal investigation despite ample documentation of the value of such a procedure as a behavior-change technique. One class of institutional staff behaviors that could be the focus of self-recording and appropriate supervision procedures is the provision of personal interactions with residents by direct-care personnel. Burg, Reid, and Lattimore (1979) were interested in the extent to which a self-recording and supervision program (in which direct staff recorded their interactions with residents with intermittent supervisory monitoring) would increase such interactions. The participants were eight direct-care personnel in one ward of a state residential facility for the developmentally disabled. Clients were 45 severely or profoundly retarded adult males. Following baseline, the staff was provided with instructions with respect to what to self-record, the criteria for how many interactions to record, and given prepared cards on which to make the recording. Throughout the study, the staff supervisor monitored staff–client interactions. When the staff recorded their interactions with clients in a loosely structured day-room setting, the rates of interactions increased noticeably for each staff person. Furthermore, other staff responsibilities, such as maintaining the cleanliness of residents and the physical environment, showed small improvements as social interactions increased. Additionally, small decreases in residents' self-stimulatory and disruptive or aggressive behaviors occurred when the rate of social interactions with staff persons increased. Follow-up measures at seven and eleven weeks indicated that the rates of staff self-recordings were variable but that, when the staff did self-record, the increased rates of staff–client interactions were maintained. Unfortunately, the reliabilities of these self-recordings were not evaluated.

Not only day-to-day interactions are amenable to self-monitoring. Emergencies, such as disaster or fire, usually covered by routine drills, could be studied in such terms. For example, Edelman, Herz, and Bickman (1980) have developed a sophisticated behavioral model which can be applied to the generation of improved fire emergency training for staff and residents as part of the overall behavioral management program for the institution.

The only recent behavioral approach to the reduction of absenteeism, surely a prime example of a lack of staff–patient interaction, is that of Reid, Schuh-Wear, and Brannon (1978), who report successful use of a group contingency program in which a preferred work schedule was implemented contingent on entire work shifts maintaining a level of absence below a predetermined criterion.

The usual approach to absenteeism is to focus on all workers in a given unit. But the majority of absences are usually attributable to a minority of employees and much institutional absenteeism is beyond the individual agency's control. An alternative strategy might therefore be to focus primarily on those workers who have excessive absences. It is within this context that Shoemaker and Reid (1980) set out to reduce absenteeism within a residential facility. Only procedures involving minimal financial investment were selected. These consisted of systematic counseling between supervisor and chronic attendance abuser, written positive feedback, and a reinforcing but low-cost lottery system. As expected, their two-workshift multiple-baseline design demonstrated considerable improvement while the study was in effect. But we know nothing about either the relative contributions of the various components of their program package or what happened following formal termination of the project.

The Institutionalized Schizophrenic

The majority of mental hospital beds are now occupied by chronically disturbed patients, deficit in adaptive skills and generally minimally responsive to conventional treatment. While helpful, antipsychotic drugs do not, in themselves, directly compensate for basic behavioral deficits. Behavior therapists are therefore in a unique position to develop appropriate programs for such individuals. Matson (1980a) reviews progress in the three areas which have been most investigated to date: token economies, training in social skills, and overcorrection. There are many deficits. For example, token economies tend to neglect follow-up and generalization data. Social skills research emphasizes analogue measures at the expense of the more naturalistic setting. Among the positive trends noted by Matson is the development of individualized programs to supplement the token economy; another pertains to the development of social responsiveness and the use of praise as a reinforcer.

Few innovations are evident. Giving a procedure a new name does not, in itself, ensure newness. For example, McGuire and Polsky (1979) refer to their program for the charting of behavioral changes in hospitalized schizophrenics as "an ecological perspective." Despite this pretension, their investigation is not without interest or merit. Most investigations of hospitalized schizophrenics deal with chronic populations. McGuire and Polsky (1979) studied the acute schizophrenic, charting the behavioral differences between patients whose clinical conditions improved as contrasted with those who showed relatively little change. The details of their specific findings, while significant, may be of less importance in the long run than the development of a viable methodology. In particular, there is the possibility of a method which allows for the prediction of the clinical course of such disorders. For example, their data point to the possibility that low frequencies of pathological behavior coupled with high frequencies of receiving stimuli behavior may be indicative of impending improvement. By contrast, behaviors often assigned clinical importance, such as agitation and postural deviance, may be unpredictive of outcome. In a related study, Polsky and Chance (1978) obtained an inverse relationship between the total amount of social behavior seen in chronic schizophrenics on the wards and the amount of social behavior received by these individuals. That is, otherwise asocial individuals tend to be on the receiving end of most social behavior (see also McGuire, Fairbanks, & Cole, 1977; Polsky & McGuire, 1979).

The Mentally Retarded Institutionalized Adult

The bulk of research in institutional settings has been carried out with the mentally retarded. Here we will select three studies which focus exclusively upon the problems of the institutionalized mentally retarded adult. It is particularly important that the right to live in the least restrictive environment possible be especially preserved for those who are not able to protect themselves. To this end, Gruber, Reeser, and Reid (1979) taught four profoundly retarded institutionalized males to walk independently from living area to school and to maintain this accomplishment. The training included instructions, practice, praise, feedback, verbal reprimands, prompts, and edible reinforcers.

The institutionalized mentally retarded tend to utilize their leisure in passive ways, such as lying around or watching television, and it would seem appropriate to develop more active skills. Adkins and Matson's (1980) partly successful attempt to inculcate meaningful leisure-skills activities in six chronically institutionalized mentally retarded females includes six-week follow-up data, the measurement of the generalization effects of training, and the rudiments of a comparison among different treatment methods for training leisure skills.

It is important to know the criteria for application of any procedure, behavioral or otherwise. Time out has repeatedly been found successful in reducing disruptive and aggressive behavior in mentally retarded individuals and offers several advantages over other aversive procedures. But we know little, as yet, about the characteristics of those for whom time out is most effective and under what circumstances. According to Matson, Ollendick, and DiLorenzo (1980), the individual most likely to receive time out is young, institutionalized for a short period of time, in the mild-to-moderate range of intellectual retardation, and medicated. But their data are limited to one institution and bereft of long-term follow-up.

Planning for Rehabilitation

Returning or introducing the chronically institutionalized individual to the community involves many issues. Here we will touch briefly upon two facets of this problem which have attracted recent interest. Several investigators have used interview-skills training to increase the employment potential of newly discharged psychiatric patients (e.g., Furman, Geller, Simon, & Kelly, 1979), but little attention has been given to the mentally retarded. Investigations involving real-life job situations are difficult to carry out, and it is understandable that most studies are of a primarily analogue nature. Thus, Kelly, Wildman, and Berler (1980) used simulated small-group behavioral training to improve the job interviewing skills of mildly retarded adolescents in a short-term residential treatment program; and Kelly, Laughlin, Claiborne, and Patterson (1980) employed a similar procedure with formally hospitalized psychiatric patients.

Individuals long accustomed to a protective, limited institutional environment are likely to be accident prone when subjected to the hazards of everyday living. It is therefore necessary to develop appropriate training programs prior to "exit" into the community. To this end, Matson (1980b) trained five moderately to severely retarded adults in the skills necessary for handling emergency situations. Utilizing classroom training and participant modeling, the program consisted of instructions, modeling, feedback, rehearsal, and social reinforcement, with a seven-month follow-up. In the first study, a method for training adults in escaping from house fires was investigated. However, the data were largely anecdotal in that the subjects were only able to provide spoken reports of correct performance in a hypothetical fire. In a second study a similar procedure was applied to various other possible emergency situations and a similar limitation applies.

BEHAVIOR MODIFICATION GOES INTO
THE COMMUNITY

The Ubiquity of Community Behavior Therapy

In the 1970s, the appearance of a behavioral community psychology text was an event, in the 1980s it is commonplace (e.g., Cone & Hayes, 1980; Glenwick & Jason, 1980; Hamerlynck, 1980a; Martin & Osborne, 1980). The utilization of behavioral principles within a community setting extends from the significant to the trivial. At one end of the spectrum, there are concerted attempts to cope with the energy crisis by the use of behavioral principles (e.g., Battalio, Kagel, Winkler, & Winett, 1979; Geller, 1981a, 1981b; Luyben, 1980; Luyben, Warren, & Tallman, 1979; McClelland & Cook, 1980; Reichel & Geller, 1981; Rothstein, 1980). At the other end of the spectrum, there are the ubiquitous studies of such lesser problems as litter control (e.g., Bacon-Prue, Blount, Pickering, & Drabman, 1980; Geller, Brasted, & Mann, 1979; Reiter & Samuel, 1980; Schnelle, McNees, Thomas, Gendrich, & Beagle, 1980).

One should not sneer at the usually well-designed and invariably well-intentioned attempts to make the "pooper-scooper" a working reality for our genteel surburban communities (e.g., Jason, McCoy, Blanco, & Zolik, 1980). But with all due respect to our canine friends, there are more pressing areas of concern—such as the use of public transport whenever available (e.g., Isaacs, 1980). If this sometimes leads to antisocial destructive behaviors, then they too can be corrected by the application of behavior modification principles (e.g., Barmann, Croyle-Barmann, & McLain, 1980). For those who must use their own cars, a variety of community-based behavioral intervention strategies for the promotion of seat-belt wearing is being investigated (e.g., Geller, Casali, & Johnson, 1980; Geller, Johnson, & Pelton, in press). For those who drink to excess and drive, behavioral procedures are being utilized in various educational programs (e.g., Brown, 1980).

Even those who enforce our traffic laws have been subjected to the grinding attention of the behavioral mill. Sometimes the findings are surprising and perhaps less than encouraging to those who call for more law enforcement in the hope that this will lead to increased order. For example, Carr, Schnelle, and Kirchner (1980) conducted a retrospective, quasi-experimental reversal design to examine the effects of increases and decreases in police traffic enforcement on the frequency of traffic accidents in a metropolitan area. Over a two-month period, police substantially increased the number of citations for moving violations and then decreased all self-initiated activities. The examination of the traffic accident data collected throughout these periods found no change in either the frequency of accident reports or in the distribution of accident types involving property damage, personal injury, or fatalities. While not definitive, findings such as these are useful, to use the delicate phrasing of the authors, "in calling into question the traffic enforcement policies of police departments."

Geller, Eason, Phillips, and Pierson (1980) developed an effective combination of special training and feedback procedures for improving the sanitation practices of kitchen workers. Fridgen (1980) studied leisure behavior and resource management. In 1978, Eysenck and Nias reviewed over 200 studies of the effects of television violence. Contrary to arguments in favor of the cathartic effects of watching violence on the media advocated by many psychodynamic clinicians, virtually all the studies reviewed reported an increase in aggression after watching television scenes of violence. Despite these findings, numerous film producers, clinicians, and even academics dismissed the investigations as trivial, trite, inconclusive, or contrary to intuition. If such studies are meaningful, as we believe them to be, then it should not be beyond the ingenuity of behavioral technologists to develop appropriate ways of convincing society at large of their importance. In this regard, Nias (1979) suggests that by watching violence people become less emotionally disturbed by it. Exposure to media violence may thus serve to make people less sensitive and thereby contribute to the prevailing apathetic attitudes. It may be that, as Nias suggests, due to constant exposure, the citizens of Northern Ireland begin to accept violence and football crowds become more tolerant of bottle throwing.

Research on crowding is characterized by diversity with respect to methodology, technique, concept, and theory (Baum & Epstein, 1978). A feasible strategy for naturalistic investigation has yet to emerge. These limitations notwithstanding, few would reject the proposition that crowding and mental health can be intimately related (cf. Schwab, Nadeau, & Warheit, 1979). Numerous investigators are exploring the parameters of crowding and territoriality in behavioral terms in situations such as city streets or student dormitories (e.g., Mercer & Benjamin, 1980). Karlin and Epstein (1979) developed a simple, objective method for the induction and measurement of crowding stress in the laboratory and a viable procedure for the investigation of the various relevant parameters within these limited terms. However, as these authors are well aware, the extrapolation of these procedures to the real world is another matter. Similar arguments apply to the behaviorally based attempts of Baum and his associates to study the effects of various types of information on the reduction of crowding stress (e.g., Baum, Fisher, & Solomon, 1981; Fisher and Baum, 1980).

Behavior Modification and the Community: Doubts Arise

Approximately a decade and a half ago, when behavior modification first ventured forth into the natural environment, Tharp and Wetzel's (1969) epoch-making text encountered enormous resistance from the mental health establishment. Now that behavior modification is itself the establishment and community behavior therapy well on the way to becoming established, it is fitting that second thoughts and third looks begin to create doubts.

Behavior modification is marching into home, school and community. From the development of a social learning theory model of wife abuse (as opposed to traditional explanations based on the sex structure and traditions of our society; Peterson, 1980) to the application of management-by-objectives to an entire community's mental outpatient service (e.g., Garrison & Raynes, 1980), community behavior therapy has advanced on all fronts. Perhaps the ultimate step in this seemingly all-encompassing advance is reflected in Krasner's (1980) text which succeeds in capturing seven fashionable key words in one title. (*Environmental Design and Human Behavior: A Psychology of the Individual in Society.*) For Krasner, environmental design opens up new horizons for traditional behavior therapists while subscribing to a basic, albeit eclectic, formulation. Unfortunately, or perhaps fortunately in terms of the ability to generate innovative "out of the box" thinking and new testable models, individual investigators began to encounter a diversity of disquieting problems in their attempts to extend tried and true behavioral principles into the community. For example, Schneider, Lesko, and Garrett (1980) found that the hypothesized inhibitory effects of hot and cold temperatures on health behavior which emerged very clearly in the laboratory did not appear in real-life situations. In similar fashion, somewhat to their surprise Turner and Luber (1980) discovered that token economy procedures did not function in the customary manner when applied to chronic day-hospital populations. Token economies were found to take on symbolic and social reinforcement attributes which were related to the setting as well as the nature of the backup reinforcers.

Models and strategies which are effective in the research laboratory or even within the natural environment on a small scale are not necessarily appropriate to large settings. As Hamerlynck (1980b) cautions, professionals involved with human services must recognize that political as well as the more traditionally behavioral contingencies operate. Failure to anticipate these additional parameters can sometimes lead to failure when least expected. The parameters of social policy interact to produce behavioral consequences that are as yet little understood (cf. Agras, Jacob, & Lebedeck, 1980). If the culture, traditions, and social forces operating within the community are either ignored or violated, unexpected consequences are prone to occur (Jason & Zolik, 1980). For example, the thinking underlying much of the prevailing movement toward deinstitutionalization seems to be subsumed within the phrase "the least restrictive environment." Unfortunately, the sociological and semantic implications of this seemingly straightforward term are vast (Bachrach, 1980). The decisions involved in characterizing one treatment setting or treatment modality as less restrictive than another are enormous.

As behavioral community psychologists become increasingly sophisticated, so a variety of innovative approaches emerge. Barker's concept of behavior settings, with its notion of social systems whose components include people and inanimate objects which interact in an orderly and established fashion, is one of the very few in behavioral science that combine both the total ecological environment and human behavior in a single unit of analysis. Developments within ecological psychology include systematic surveys of community and organizational settings, the study of intersetting linkages and the life cycle of settings, and the development of a technology for improving the human environment (Wicker, 1979a, 1979b, 1981).

As examples of the contemporary application of ecological theory, we draw attention to attempts to apply some form of human ecological approach directly to problems pertaining to mental health by Bubolz, Eicher, Evers, and Sontag, (1980) and Catalano (1979), and the new role for community psychologists and identified by Jason and Smith (1980). The Behavioral Ecological Matchmaker's role of Jason and Smith is to identify individuals or groups desiring behavioral change and to link the target participants with networks of settings involving the direct modification of groups of people within a variety of real-life systems. (See Marston, 1979, for a more extended discussion of what he calls behavioral ecology as a more appropriate base for contemporary behavior modification than the still-prevailing specific stimulus–specific response-bound model.)

The ecological model, of course, is not the only current contender for the allegiance of the behavioral community psychologist. If Winkler (1980, 1982) has his way, we will be behavioral economists rather than behavioral ecologists! Until recently, token economies were regarded exclusively as exercises in the application of conditioned reinforcement principles. Winkler's concern is to establish the proposition that total economies are also closed economic systems which function according to the laws of economics. In his most recent explication of behavioral economic theory, Winkler (1980) stresses the essentially systemic nature of his model. Behavioral interventions are viewed as interventions within an interconnected whole (such that changing one part of the system affects behavior in other parts). To account for the complex system effects in the community it is necessary to evoke and to integrate both economic and reinforcement theory (see also Winett, 1981).

Pointing to the all too often observed lack of generalization of maintenance behavior and the less often recognized lack of knowledge about natural settings, O'Donnell and Tharp (in press) contend that the general resolution of these limitations is not likely within the confines of behavioral community psychology as currently conceptualized. Like Winkler, O'Donnell and Tharp think in terms of social networks and other disciplines. By social networks they mean the structure of social relationships among units, individuals, groups, or institutions. Networks are key sources of information, emotional support, and access to desired resources for their members and it is only through such social networks that the environmental context of behavior can be adequately conceptualized. Studies cited by these authors seem to demonstrate the influence of student networks on academic performance, attitudes toward school, and choices of academic fields. Other studies indicate the importance of social networks in delinquency and vocational selection.

Fawcett, Mathews, and Fletcher (1980) also discuss the limitations of behavioral community technology and stress the need to integrate our emerging framework and technology with other theoretical and conceptual systems. Even then, they caution, the contributions of behavioral technology may be limited to what they call first-order changes, changes within a basic social system that itself remains unchanged. The example they cite is that of job-training technologies which may help persons acquire skills to compete for limited wages without promoting second-order changes involving the redistribution of power, wealth and other resources within the social system. However, precisely how behavioral methods can bring about changes in the social system remains less clear.

Finally, we draw attention to an informative survey by Hutchison and Fawcett (1981) arising out of the formation of the Community Research special interest group of the AABT and the ensuing *Network* of individuals interested in applying behavioral methodology to community problems. Two items of potential significance emerged: evidence

of a forward-looking interdisciplinary approach to behavioral community psychology stressing diverse methodology and a resounding
rejection of the notion that the group consider some form of certification
for its members.

BEHAVIOR MODIFICATION AND CRIME

Overview

Nietzel (1979) readily admits that social learning theory alone may not
be adequate to account for the full complexities of crime. Nevertheless,
as his comprehensive text documents, behaviorally oriented techniques
probably provide a much better chance for rehabilitation than any
currently available alternatives. Other relevant new reviews include the
following: Stumphauzer's (1981) overview of behavior modification
with delinquents; Morris's (1980) attempt to apply Baer, Wolf, and
Risley's (1968) basic dimensions of applied behavior analysis to the
practice of criminal justice; Maloney, Fixsen, and Maloney's (1978)
overview of the general practical considerations that therapists and
program developers must face when they attempt to work with antisocial youths; and an entire issue of the *British Journal of Criminology*
(Vol. 19, No. 4, October 1979).

Brantingham and Faust (1976) classify crime prevention measures
in terms of the time at which the measure is applied. The goal of
primary prevention is to modify conditions so that the crime cannot
occur, secondary prevention is concerned with deterrents for those who
might commit crimes, and tertiary prevention pertains to the post-hoc
measures carried out after the crime to prevent further activity. As
Ferguson and Geller (1979) point out, much of the efforts of the criminal
justice system would appropriately be classified as tertiary. By contrast,
most applied behavior modification has focused upon primary and
secondary prevention. Noting the conceptual and methodological limitations of much of this literature, Nietzel offers a prescription of
his own. First, behavioral correction should be delivered in the environments where most crime actually occurs, with rehabilitation focusing
upon deinstitutionalization, decriminalization, and diversion. Second,
there must be an emphasis upon primary prevention and the development of behaviors which decrease the necessity of crime. Third, rather
than the prevailing adjustment model, the emphasis needs to be also
upon system-level changes, changes of the second rather than first
order. Fourth, the behavior correction literature currently reveals the
neglect of techniques aimed at increasing generalized ability and maintenance. Finally, it is essential to consider the role of multiple deter-

minants. These lovely phrases are hard to refute. Translating them into action is another matter.

Another problem stems from the fact that behavior therapists, especially those who call themselves behaviorists, adopt a broadly deterministic view of behavior which can be sharply at odds with the predominant legal ascription of free will. For example, the legal requirement of criminal *intent* is at variance with behavioral thinking, especially since private events are not amenable to investigation other than by the admission of some form of cognitive independence. Behaviorists are further inclined to be skeptical of orientations which shift responsibility for action to putative inner processes, thereby deflecting attention from environmental influences on behavior. This, of course, is not to imply that society should condone unlawful behavior, merely that we search for the external determinants of the undesirable activity. These profound philosophical and conceptual differences between behavior therapists and members of the legal profession present fundamental barriers to a meeting of "minds" (Blackman, 1979, in press).

Many individuals offer ethical objections to what they view as the behavioral intent to impose change upon an individual. Certainly, for rehabilitation to be ethical it must be voluntary, with the offender assuming his or her role as an active, informed, and informative participant (Brodsky, 1973). Another ethical objection pertains to the argument that it is all too easy for behavior modifiers to become agents of the institution rather than of the individuals whose behavior they seek to influence. (There has been much discussion in the recent literature and in earlier volumes in this series pertaining to this issue.) This is especially of importance when the task of the behavior modifier, an employee of some correctional institution, is to develop procedures for increased conformity to rules and regulations. However, as Nietzel (1979) notes, such ethical questions should not remain restricted to adversarial debates between special interest groups, be they prisoners of behavioral psychologists. Legitimate behavior modification programs should cause no qualms about exposure to public or legislative scrutiny, and this includes the informed gaze of those inmates they are intended to serve. To this end, Nietzel advocates a behavioral analysis of the means whereby the public can increase its input into discussions of such matters as one of the most needed "ethical" contributions.

Behavior Modification within the Correctional Institution

Behavior therapists working within residential correctional settings are typically viewed as outsiders who fail to appreciate the intricacies of the situation and the competencies of the insider. The problems, as Milan and Long (1980) note, are further compounded by the overlapping and often conflicting areas of authority and responsibility which bedevil most correctional facilities. Even more regrettable, behavior therapists are still inclined to view themselves as agents of management, so to speak. Typically, programs are developed for "reducing rule violations" (Milan, Throckmorton, McKee, & Wood, 1979), motivating academic achievement within the cell block (Milan, Wood, & McKee, 1979), "motivating the performance of activities that administrators consider important for the orderly operation of their institutions." (Milan, Wood, Williams, Rogers, Hampton, & McKee, 1974, as reported by Nietzel, 1979).

Institutional behavior modification generally takes three forms: remedial education, contingency management programs, and aversion therapy. Token economy programs in penal settings are characterized by high inmate dropout rates, limited and short-term behavior change, and prisoner dissatisfaction as a result of involuntary participation. Furthermore, token economies present particular difficulties due to the large amount of time required for training change agents, the scarcity of appropriate reinforcements, and a tendency on the part of unsupervised prison personnel to revert to punishment procedures. To correct these deficits, Bornstein, Rychtarik, McFall, Bridgwater, Guthrie, and Anton (1980) developed a promising treatment strategy based upon positive principles, similar to those applied within classroom settings for controlling disruptive behavior. But still, their primary goal was the development of an effective approach to the "management" of prison behavioral problems!

Milan (1981) draws attention to the fact that most of the behavioral research reported in the literature was conducted prior to 1975. According to Milan, restrictive regulations governing research with prisoners are in part responsible for this situation; psychologists who would normally conduct applied research in correctional settings are consequently developing new interests. Milan raises the possibility that correction administrators have been intimidated to such a degree that they automatically squash research proposals. The extent to which solutions lie in attempts to modify these regulations and the attitudes of those who promulgate them as contrasted with the development of effective research programs more in accord with these regulations remains a matter for investigation.

In 1940, Clemmer coined the term "prisonization" to describe assimilation to the prison culture. Social ecology provides a potential strategy for the exploration and modification of the total human environment. It would be of interest to see social ecology applied to the correctional environment and the "prisonization" process. Waters (1980) reports the application of a recently developed social ecology scale to the institutional setting but, as yet, his strategies focus primarily upon assessment and evaluation rather than intervention. Finally, we draw attention to the need for what Jeffery (1977, 1978) calls a "biosocial theory of learning and criminal behavior." Based on the principles of behavioral genetics and psychobiology, behavior is viewed as the interaction of a physical organism within a physical environment in which both biological and environmental components are given due consideration. This, of course, is a nice way of presenting all things to all men and, while it is hard to take issue with involving all possible determinants, how to translate this into practice remains to be seen.

Behavior Modification and Juvenile Delinquency

In nonresidential settings the academic performance of youths considered to be high risks for delinquency has been improved. However, whether so doing reduces the likelihood of delinquent behavior is debatable (O'Donnell & Tharp, in press). Similar limitations apply to the development of contracting programs for adolescents. While social skills training programs have generally been shown to be effective, the extent to which these programs are generalized and maintained also remains unresolved (Golden, Twentyman, Jensen, Karan, & Kloss, 1980).

In Achievement Place, teaching "parents" directly supervise small groups of adolescent males in a family-style, token economy, rehabilitative program with the major goals of teaching social, academic, self-help, and prevocational skills. Recidivism rates and measures of various school activities taken up within two years of release demonstrate such youths to be considerably more improved than those placed in large institutions (Fixsen, Phillips, Phillips, & Wolf, 1976). It might also be noted that this has been successfully replicated by investigators in other states (e.g., Liberman, Ferris, Selgado, & Selgado, 1975). See previous issues of the *Annual Review* for more extended discussion.

An alternative strategy involves intervention prior to delinquency, on the debatable assumption that there is a direct relationship between social and academic problems in childhood and subsequent prevalance of juvenile crime (e.g., Burdsal & Buel, 1980). Such projects await systematic investigation. Meanwhile, the evidence suggest that community-based behavior modification group home treatment programs are probably the most effective methods available to date for dealing with juvenile offenders. Nevertheless, there are community situations where it is either not financially possible to provide a community home or where the youths' difficulties are not sufficiently major to require such a placement. To meet this need Gross and Brigham (1980) suggest that these predelinquent and delinquent youths be taught the principles of self-management and related skills.

Our final point in the never ending saga of crime and behavior modification: Which is more reinforcing, the development of new and perhaps more effective methods of crime prevention or the continuation of the present model? Stumphauzer (1981) correctly points out that, if effective, crime prevention would put thousands out of work. Many find their current behaviors of arresting, defending, judging, correcting, · and treating highly reinforcing. Whether behavior therapy can develop a more reinforcing, viable model of crime prevention remains to be seen.

BEHAVIOR MODIFICATION, INDUSTRY, AND THE MARKETPLACE

Despite demonstrable advantages (e.g., Andrasik, Heimberg, & Mc-Namara, in press; Komaki, Collins, & Thoene, 1980; Ritschl & Hall, 1980) and a growing interest in Organizational Behavior Modification (OBM) (e.g., Johnston, Duncan, Monroe, Stephenson, & Stoerzinger, 1978; Komaki, Collins, & Thoene, 1980), the application of behavioral principles in industry, commerce, and government as yet remains sporadic and lacks any well developed theoretical formulation (Andrasik *et al.*, in press). Within recent years, at least four management consultants have written texts based upon operant learning principles (Connellan, 1978; Gilbert, 1978, L. K. Miller, 1978; Potter, 1980). All are directed primarily toward the practicing manager with little or no knowledge of behavioral technology; theoretical foundations are underplayed. All four pay no more than cursory lip-service to the need to utilize scientific knowledge in the management of people. It is those outside traditional behavior therapy who are beginning to produce the necessary research. For example, Brett (1980) skillfully applies behavioral principles to fundamental issues in industrial relations pertaining to union management systems.

The continuing resistance of workers and management alike to behavior modification is reinforced in part by naive interventional strategies, but also by realistic ethical concerns. Like any technology, behavior modification may indeed be misused. Fortunately, there is a reciprocal influence, a so-called controller and the so-called controlled. It is incumbent upon us to understand the many complexities involved, as Andrasik *et al.* put it, the "who, what, when, and where of control"; see also McNamara and Andrasik (1981). It is depressing to note that behavioral intervention is still considered in terms of negative rather than positive consequences in the management of employees. Thus, when Mayhew, Enyart, and Cone (1979) surveyed the 250 members of the National Association of Superintendents of Public Residential Facilities for the Mentally Retarded, 98% of the 130 respondents reported using negative consequences and more than half indicated a preference for such consequences.

With a combination of scholarship and missionary zeal, Lepper and Greene (1978) suggest that the deliberate use of extrinsic rewards can sometimes be dysfunctional. It is too bad that this need for caution in the indiscriminate use of extrinsic reward systems is coupled with an antibehavioral plea for cognitive causal mechanisms. A perhaps more balanced appraisal of the intrinsic versus extrinsic reward controversy stems from the writing of Mawhinney (1979). It is by no means certain that self-reinforcement is a legitimate concept (cf. J. Martin, 1980). As Jones and Mawhinney (1977) point out, this is no academic matter. For example, Deci (1972, 1976) has already prescribed intrinsic motivation by way of increased decision making and job enlargement as a "proven" alternative to contingent payment. Most of us would agree with the prevailing common-sense notion that people prefer to be unhampered by external constraints on their functioning at work. However, whether this can be attributed to an intrinsic *self*-reinforcement or not remains unresolved. But we still need to know precisely how such preferences are to be measured, how stable they are over time, and how and under what circumstances jobs can be rearranged to accomodate such preferences.

Another practical issue pertains to the effective utilization of feedback. Training alone does not seem to be an efficient means of improving and maintaining performance and it is only when feedback is provided that maximum benefits can be obtained (e.g., Komaki, Heinzmann, & Lawson, 1980). Sulzer-Azaroff (1980) systematically investigated the use of written feedback in the reduction of hazardous physical conditions in a university research laboratory. More recently, and with equally encouraging findings, Sulzer-Azaroff and De Santamaria (1980) extended this study to a small industrial setting. Feedback was also used by Komaki, Barwick, and Scott (1978) to improve worker safety within a food manufacturing plant.

In certain occupational settings, safety performance feedback is complicated by the nature of the activity itself. For example, it is difficult to provide direct feedback to police officers and security personnel who patrol large areas. Addressing themselves to this problem,

Larson, Schnelle, Kirchner, Carr, Domash, and Risley (1980) utilized advances in behavioral technology to measure patrol performance. Monitored supervisory feedback by way of an inexpensive tachograph (Kloss, Christopherson, & Risley, 1976) was found to offer distinct advantages in the development of occupational safety programs under the circumstances of even remote job functioning.

Vocational training, especially for the mentally handicapped, and career development are two related areas in which behavioral principles are beginning to receive systematic application (e.g., Albin, Stark, & Keith, 1979; Bellamy, Inman, & Horne, 1979; Bellamy, O'Connor, & Karan, 1979; Crosson & Pine, 1979; Hall, Sheldon-Wildgen, & Sherman, 1980; Koop, Martin, Yu, & Suthons, 1980; Martin & Morris, 1980; Rusch & Mithaug, 1980; Waters, 1979). In 1979, the American Institutes for Research reported the deliberations of a number of nationally recognized career development experts with respect to the impact of social learning theory on the career decision-making process (Mitchell, Jones, & Krumboltz, 1979). Krumboltz (1979) provides us with what is perhaps the first new testable theoretical perspective within the career-decision-making field for many years. Many parameters await resolution. For example, the relevant influences of intrinsic and extrinsic decision factors—an extension of the already discussed intrinsic/extrinsic rewards debate—are still largely undetermined. Recent conclusions that internal rather than external influences are more likely to be associated with increased feelings of satisfaction and attitudinal commitment (O'Reilly & Caldwell, 1980) overlook the possibility that so-called internal reasons for career choice may in themselves be determined by external variables.

A decade ago, behavioral training programs in industry were few and far between. Now, over a half a million supervisors and employees of all kinds are being trained by behavior modeling technology (Robinson, 1980). Whether this is a fad and the extent to which these programs are data-based await resolution. Not all are as firmly rooted in behavior modeling principles as those of such seasoned campaigners as Goldstein and his associates (e.g., Goldstein & Sorcher, 1974).

In the marketplace, good studies are in even shorter supply. The technology of behavior modification is far easier to apply in structured settings such as hospitals, schools, prisons, and factories than within the shopping mall or neighborhood store. No wonder then, as Nord and Peter (1980) point out, that while many current marketing tactics are vaguely consistent with the principles of behavior modification, application of these principles remains ad hoc. Nord and Peter further question both the ends to which the technology is directed and the process by which these ends are determined. Efforts to market products rarely include the subject whose behavior is being modified as a full participant in determining either the use of the technology or the ends to which it is put. Even when otherwise sophisticated investigators such as Warshaw (1980) investigate the functional relationships between intention and behavior in product-related settings, they rarely take into account such factors. Most investigations to date are concerned with practical and very specific components pertaining to the smooth functioning of the marketplace—for example, the use of training in feedback to improve customer service in a large department store (Brown, Mallott, Dillon, & Keeps, 1980), the development of programs to reduce employee theft (McNees, Gilliam, Schnelle, & Risley, 1979; McNees, Kennon, Schnelle, Kirchner, & Thomas, 1980), and the fostering of friendliness in a fast-food franchise (Komaki, Blood, & Holder, 1980).

BEHAVIOR THERAPY AND THE ELDERLY

Prior to this decade, no behavioral text was devoted in its entirety to the elderly. Three such books have just appeared and each, in its own way, has a distinctive contribution to make. Hussian (1981) draws on recent empirical findings to develop an integrative model of aging which takes into consideration biochemical and physiological changes, traditional learning theory, and developmental psychology. Zarit (1980) acknowledges the behavioral and developmental determinants of the aging process but stresses cognitive approaches to intervention. Finally, Sobel (1981) introduces us to the new discipline of behavioral thanatology. As Sobel points out, until recently the mere thought of a *behavioral* thanatology seemed to many to reek of dehumanization and decadence, an evil strategy for "controlling the vulnerable dying patient." For the thanatologist who is not particularly familiar with the principles of behavior therapy, and regrettably this is probably the majority, Sobel does much to dispel prevailing myths about behavior therapy and show how behavioral principles can be applied with dignity to dying patients and their families.

Both Hussian (1981) and Schonfield (1980) conclude that classical and operant conditioning functions are impaired in the elderly. Extrapolating the available data, Hussian concludes that conditional emotional responses take longer to develop in the geriatric individual, need greater reinforcements, and are more easily disrupted. Schonfield speculates that elderly individuals are less generally aroused and therefore less prone to extreme emotional reactions. Jarvik and Cohen (1973) suggest that operant conditioning become the primarily vehicle for behavioral investigation of the aged on the grounds that operant becomes less impaired than classical conditioning with advancing years. Baltes and Barton (1977, 1979) also stress the need to approach the problems of the elderly from a broadly operant model, in which the principles of reinforcement can be utilized to develop environments appropriate for adequate response.

A necessary precursor to intervention is the acquisition of basic normative and descriptive data. For example, there are clear-cut sex differences between the needs, lifestyles, and leisure activities of elderly men and women (Keith, 1980), and there is a difference between actual and desired leisure involvements (McGuire, 1980). The elderly belong to fewer interacting systems than younger people and therefore social interactions become of pivotal concern especially with the institutionalized (e.g., Lopez, 1980; Lopez, Hoyer, Goldstein, Gershaw, & Sprafkin, 1980; Quattrochi-Tubin & Jason, 1980). All in all, recent developments in the application of behavioral principles to the elderly are encouraging both in terms of the emergence of a theoretical model and clinical application.

CONCLUSIONS

It is the custom in this section of the *Annual Review* to chronicle recent developments in behavior therapy and to place them in perspective. Each year, we laud accomplishments and lament failures, pointing with pride to successful new applications while bemoaning the seeming inability of behavior therapy to make a meaningful statement about the nature of man. Once again, we draw attention to the possibility of overcomprehension and nonexclusion leading either to a loss of identity or to the fragmentation of behavior therapy into disparate fields of human enquiry.

The early 1960s was the era of the behavioral pioneer, bristling with unswerving allegiance, naive ideology, and polemical urge to do battle with the common psychodynamic "foe." The late 1960s and early 1970s saw the gradual recognition of behavior therapy within the mental health community, both as an alternative conceptual framework and a respected treatment modality. Given this favorable climate, the emphasis shifted from defensive attack upon outsiders to consolidation within. Missionary zeal and inquisitional fervor were abandoned in favor of a search for new horizons inside our own domain. The intervening years, culminating in a burst of activity around the early 1980s, witnessed a flurry of expansion but little conceptual innovation. Behavior therapy spread outwards to encompass virtually every form of human endeavor: ecology, systems theory, economics, psychopharmocology, genetics, medicine, and more. At the other end of the spectrum, behavior therapy turned inwards to explore that once denied, or at best ignored and despised, realm of the inner person. Cognitivism in its many guises—social learning theory, reciprocal determinism, self-control, cognitive-behavior therapy, consciousness, to name but a few—was heralded in certain circles as a conceptual leap forward which renders traditional behavior therapy obsolete and archaic.

Much has happened since Volume 7 was prepared in the summer of 1979. Advances in technology, methodology, and new ways of viewing data are relatively easy to document. Elegant designs, sophisticated therapeutic strategies, comprehensive outcome evaluations, and new areas for behavioral intervention abound. Behavior therapy is no longer confined exclusively to classical and operant conditioning. But, when all is said if not always done, we have still not developed a substantive and integrative model of man.

Changes in definition over the years mirror the above developments. The disarmingly simple description of behavior therapy as the application of "modern learning theory" which sufficed for the 1960s has become little more than an historical curiosity. In its place, the all-encompassing and long-winded "official" definition of the AABT predominates. It is difficult to find any discipline of even remote social significance which has not been linked to behavior therapy as it is now defined. Such diverse fields of human endeavor as Yoga and meditation, genetics, ethology, economics, industrial organization, and politics have all fallen grist to the behavioral mill. Provided that the findings are data-based, an accommodating catch word, and the methodology in accord with the elastic canons of behavioral science, someone, somewhere, will call the procedure behavior therapy. Whether this is the precursor of a meaningful behavioral model of man or whether it foretells an eventual disintegration of behavior therapy as we know it today remains to be seen.

Two closely related developments appear to be at the core of this dilemma. These are the emergence of reciprocal determinism as an essential component of social learning theory and the influx of cognitivism into almost every facet of contemporary behavior therapy. Those who espouse the doctrine of reciprocal determinism are trying to eat their cake and have it too—and, as we know, it is only in Alice's Wonderland that this is at all possible. On the one hand, it is argued that behavior is determined and regulated in accordance with the well-established principles of reinforcement. On the other hand, it is implied that we can modify our environment by our own volitions. This presents an interesting, unresolved, and perhaps unresolvable philosophical dilemma with which behavior therapists have yet to contend. Are we exclusively reactors to our environments or do we also create our environments? If the latter, what then are the principles which govern the activities subsumed under such non-explanatory labels as self-control or cognition? Do we need some explanatory concept over and above classical and operant conditioning to account for these phenomena? As yet, we have no compelling and comprehensive theory of brain function and behavior to guide our philosophical preferences and hence we can have no adequate behavioral model of man.

It is to such issues that we expect behavior therapists to direct attention in this third decade. Whether this will involve some kind of paradigm shift—in our view of behavior therapy there is, as yet, no paradigm to shift—and whether cognition will be demonstrably identified as a causal factor by the experimental ingenuity of our new wave of behavior therapists awaits resolution. One can only hope that, in conjunction with the tolerance for different ways of thinking which characterizes the present era, the experimental rigor, scientific integrity, and appeal to data that guided our formative years will prevail. The uniqueness of behavior therapy, as contrasted with other treatment modalities, lies not so much in claims to therapeutic success as in our commitment to these objectives.

Despite theoretical controversies, occasional clinical insufficiencies, confrontations from within, and challenges from without, behavior therapy remains alive, well, and in accord with our founding mandate.

BEHAVIORAL ASSESSMENT AND METHODOLOGY

PHILIP C. KENDALL

Behavioral assessment, as a part of the practice of behavior therapy, has been observed recently to have moved in two directions: *a turning inward* and *an expanding outward.* The increasing concern with the precise analysis of observational data, such as questions pertaining to the proper method for determining interobserver agreement, and the more detailed studies of factors affecting self-monitoring are examples of this "internal turn" in behavioral assessment. This aspect of the bidirectional movement is evident in the appearance of two new specialty journals, *Behavioral Assessment* and the *Journal of Behavioral Assessment,* and the special assessment issue of the *Journal of Applied Behavior Analysis* (Winter, 1979), in which more "micro" behavioral assessment concerns are addressed. Moreover, two new texts have appeared, focusing separately on assessment with adults (Barlow, 1981) and children (Mash & Terdal, 1981).

The growing use of self-report measures (their use is second only to direct observation; see Bornstein, Bridgwater, Hickey, & Sweeney, 1980), the application of sociometric assessments (e.g., Foster & Ritchey, 1979), and the inclusion of cognitive–behavioral assessments (e.g., Kendall & Korgeski, 1979) are examples of the widening of the behavioral assessment boundaries. Recent texts evidence this expansion as well. Nay's (1979) *Multimethod Clinical Assessment* includes material not typically found in volumes on behavioral assessment, and Kendall and Hollon's (1981a) *Assessment Strategies for Cognitive–Behavioral Interventions* brings cognitive assessments within the behavioral perspective. A second volume on cognitive assessment is now available also (e.g., Merluzzi, Glass, & Genest, 1981).

Behavioral assessment has become a topic of interest in its own right (Nelson & Hayes, 1979a, 1979b). Indeed, six leading figures have initiated Volume 1 of *Behavioral Assessment* with their discussion of "the nature of behavioral assessment" (Goldfried, 1979; Haynes, 1979; Jones, 1979; Kanfer, 1979; Mash, 1979; O'Leary, 1979). One fairly consistent topic appearing in these discussions was situational specificity. While situational specificity remains an important component of behavioral assessment, and one that might be considered a distinguishing feature, there has been talk of related problems (e.g., Kazdin, 1979d). One might be somewhat surprised, though hopefully not disenchanted, by the basic questioning of situational specificity. Haynes (1979), for example, notes that "in many cases there is evidence that behaviors and behavior classes may be relatively stable across situations" (p. 47). Kanfer (1979) questions whether observable behavior will suffice as a way to gain a full account of human behavior in the social context. Are those involved in behavioral assessment retracting notions of situational specificity? We think not. Rather, as Mash (1979) noted, behavioral assessors are less likely to make *a priori* assumptions regarding cross-situational stability of behavior. Stability may sometimes be the case, but it is not assumed. A few additional concerns appeared in several of the discussions: the need for a guiding theory (Eysenck, 1979b; Goldfried, 1979; Kanfer, 1979) and the need for standardization (Goldfried, 1979; Mash, 1979). These matters will likely be the grist for future research mills.

Now that behavioral assessment has come of age, does it want to become independent of intervention procedures? The increased attention given to assessment is no doubt potentially beneficial. For example, advances in accurate assessment create advances in prescriptive treatment: the more carefully we can examine a client's skills and deficits the more accurately we can take action in intervention (see also Kanfer & Nay, 1982, for discussion of behavioral assessment related to clinical decision making). However, as mentioned in Volume 6 (Franks & Wilson, 1978), "Assessment is an integral part of the process of behavior therapy and such specialization is constructive only as long as this is kept in mind" (p. 167). Watching the maturation of behavioral assessment, one hopes that it does not leave its home prematurely.

TURNING INWARD:
ISSUES OF RELIABILITY AND VALIDITY

The recent research which evidences the concern with more micro questions can be divided into two illustrative categories. The first concerns the debate about the proper procedures for examining the *reliability* of behavioral observations. The second focuses on the *validity* of behavioral assessment procedures. Interestingly, both of these current issues could be comfortably placed under the heading of psychometrics.

Reliability: The Case of Observational Data

For some, the observing and recording of the frequencies of target behaviors *is* behavioral assessment, while for most of us behavioral observations are more accurately perceived as but one, albeit central, part of behavioral assessment. In a recent archival analysis of the assessment methods and settings reported in 951 behavior therapy publications from four journals across nine years, Bornstein *et al.* (1980) point out that a full 72% of all assessments utilized direct observational procedures. Early research with behavioral observations was concerned with functionality, whereas the reliability and validity of measurement was largely assumed. In contrast, much recent research has become increasingly focused directly on these topics. Given the central importance of observational procedures within behavioral assessment, it is not surprising that the reliability of such assessments are the current concern of many researchers.

The typical manner of examining the consistency among two or more observers (interobserver agreement) has been percentage agreement (Mitchell, 1979). However, the general consensus that this was the ideal method has come under scrutiny. In a series of papers in the *Journal of Applied Behavior Analysis* (1977), various authors proposed procedures for documenting interobserver reliability. For instance, Hartmann (1977) discussed correlational statistics; Yelton, Wildman, and Erickson (1977) offered probability-based formulae; Hopkins and Hermann (1977) proposed reporting tables of chance agreement; and Kratochwill and Wetzel (1977) argued that plotting calibrating observer data, reporting special agreement estimates, and employing appropriate correlational statistics were valuable aids for reporting observer agreement data (see also Gottman, 1980, for discussion related to sequential analyses).

The *Journal of Applied Behavior Analysis* continues to highlight issues in assessment. Within the special issue on behavioral assessment (Winter, 1979), the discussion of the relative merits and demerits of the use of percentage agreement reliability for reporting interobserver agreement has resurfaced. In two papers, Birkimer and Brown (1979a, 1979b) addressed two of the major problems. The first paper concerned the problem of the inflation of observer agreement when target behavior rates are very low or very high (the effects of low-rate behaviors on the magnitude of agreements relative to disagreements on occurrences, and the similar problem with high-rate behaviors and the agreements on nonoccurrences). In addition, the problematic existence of "chance" agreements affecting reliability estimates was addressed. In this article Birkimer and Brown (1979a) suggest "that comparing the percentage of disagreements to the percentage of agreements on occurrences and to the percentage of agreements on nonoccurrences is simpler and easier than calculating the three reliability percentages" (p. 536). The authors also describe a procedure for reporting this graphically. Birkimer and Brown (1979a) suggest that the disagreement rate itself be the first measure of agreement examined, and then its magnitude in relation to occurrence and nonoccurrence agreements should be considered. That is, for a given reliability check, the percentage of disagreements is found. This disagreement percentage is a bandwidth or confidence interval around the primary observer's data. The disagreement range is then included in the graphic presentation of the data. Similarly, after applying the data to a formula for calculating chance disagreements, the chance disagreement percentage is presented graphically along with the observational data.

In the second paper, Birkimer and Brown (1979b) consider further the second major problem: what to do about "chance" agreements. Three procedures are outlined for guiding decisions about the likelihood that interobserver agreement is not the result of chance. The first two suggested procedures refer the reader to tabled levels of acceptable numbers of agreements and disagreements (according to sample size). Use of this tabled information would require, for example, that researchers check the table and accept agreement rates as true evidence of agreement only when those rates compare favorably to the number of acceptable disagreements provided in the table.

The third procedure described in what has been referred to as the "easier ways" paper is labeled "the easiest way." Birkimer and Brown (1979b), using a probability level of .01, produced a plot of the acceptable agreement and disagreement percentages for target behaviors and numbers of observation occasions. Although there are numerous factors entering into the figure that they provide and it takes a second reading to follow the entire presentation, they extract from it an essential piece of information: the "50–10–10 (90) rule." Rather than attempt to rewrite their comments and risk loss of clarity on this issue, we quote the authors: "If researchers consistently include at least 50 observation occasions in all reliability checks, obtain disagreement percentages of 10% or less, and have reported rates of target behavior between 10% and 90%, then they and consumers can conclude the obtained observer agreement is evidence of true observer agreement" (p. 541). Since there are typically 50 observation occasions or more in reported research, the rule generally fits. Moreover, it can be used instead of the more burdensome procedures described in the former articles by these authors.

The procedures promoted by Birkimer and Brown are sound methodologies for addressing the concerns of interobserver agreement. Both the graphic displaying of disagreement ranges and the 50-10-10 (90) rule are valuable to the reporter and reader of the behavior therapy literature. However, the procedures are not without limitation, as a series of commentaries indicates. Indeed, the commentaries raise several concerns meriting additional attention. For instance, Kratochwill (1979) points out that while graphic displaying will assist in making determinations about the reliability of observational data, this benefit occurs prior to publication—for if the data are not reliable, the researcher redesigns the observational technology or the intervention. It is highly unlikely that unreliable results would be granted archival space. Thus, the graphing procedure does not benefit the reader of research (the consumer) because only acceptable data would appear in the journals.

Hartmann and Gardner (1979) make an important contribution to the discussions of interobserver reliability methods when they identify as a myth the notion that "scholarly concern with interobserver reliability coincides with the history of applied behavior analysis" (p. 559). Consider, for example, that Fisher's Exact Probability Test (1934) indirectly involved in assessing the significance of two-by-two tabled data. These authors offer praise, noting that Birkimer and Brown's suggested use of statistical devices as judgmental aids is desirable, but they also offer criticism. Why is so much space devoted to "easier methods" when a statistical test, a χ^2 test of independence for two-by-two tables with as few as 20 entries, is already available and easily performed?

It appears that interobserver agreement has noticeably piqued the interest of behavioral assessment researchers, but can it be that this interest has peaked! It is typically not advantageous for methodological disagreements to become fixated at the level of verbal argument. One method should not dominate over another because of the polemical skills and/or craftiness of its proponents. It would be unfortunate if there is not some resolution to the "I've got a better agreement measure" (Cone, 1979) controversy. Consider the researcher who wishes to submit a research manuscript that will eventually, it is hoped, be accepted for publication. What are the most desirable procedures for such an individual to follow? Whatever is decided by the individual, will it not then be a fact that eventual publication depends on who the reviewer is? It seems desirable, then, to resolve the concerns—but not by arbitrary decision, not by vote, and not by force. Cone (1979), in the briefest but perhaps most important commentary on the Birkimer and Brown papers, states, "It seems odd that the requirement of demonstrated control of meaningful behavior has not been applied to papers dealing with agreement measures. Perhaps this omission is part of a general failure to appreciate the applicability of this requirement to the *methodology* of behavior analysis as well as to its contents (p. 571)." In a nutshell, what is needed at the present time is a series of carefully designed studies to examine the relative efficacy of the various proposed methods for determining interobserver agreement. These studies could employ either new or existing data, and could examine both relative accuracy and cost-efficiency. It seems valuable to recall at this point Hartmann and Gardner's historical clarification and to recognize that since this is *not* a new problem, nor a problem that is the sole province of behavioral assessors, much can be gained from an examination of the literatures developed by related fields of inquiry.

Perhaps the best example of how other literatures can make important contributions to observational assessment is provided by a recent article by Mitchell (1979) which provides an explanation of the application of generalizability theory (Cronbach, Gleser, Nanda, & Rajaratnam, 1972) to interobserver agreement and reliability in observational studies (see also Hartmann, Roper, & Bradford, 1979). Mitchell (1979) points out, and we agree, that the study of the reliability of behavioral observations has not received the same degree of attention in psychology as has the reliability of traditional test methods. Mitchell not only recognizes this delinquent state of affairs, but also describes the traditional methods of measuring reliability, considers them in relation to observational data, and examines generalizability theory and its application to the case of observational assessment. Mitchell's presentation is clear and concise, and her analysis is important. Out of respect for her organization and clarity, our review of her contribution will follow closely the flow of her report.

Mitchell (1979) states that there are three ways to think about the reliability of observational data: (1) as the extent to which two independent observers agree, (2) as reliability according to classic psychometric theory, and (3) as an instance for the application of generalizability theory. In the first case, percentage agreement is the typically reported index of reliability. Mitchell uses developmental psychology as an example to illustrate that there is a heavy reliance on percentage agreement reliability in the literature: approximately 50% of the observational studies reported in two volumes of two of the major developmental journals reported *only* percentage agreement reliabilities. Mitchell also expresses concern that percentage agreement can, in practice, be affected by the degree of variability among the subjects, that it treats agreement as an all-or-none phenomenon, and that, as already acknowledged, percentage agreement between independent observers can be spuriously inflated by chance agreements.

Considerations of traditional psychometric theory are sometimes dismissed among behavioral assessors since the theory is closely linked with trait-like conceptualizations of human behavior. (See Chapter 7 for further discussion of this issue as it pertains particularly to children.) However, Mitchell's analysis suggests that the most satisfactory way of considering observational data within psychometric theory is to consider each mutually exclusive category of observed behavior as a separate test. In this manner, each time unit of observed behavior is like an item on a test. For example, observational data on the rate of off-task behavior gathered over intervals of time are intended to measure the same aspect of behavior and would be viewed as different test items intending to measure the same trait. Taking this further, interscorer reliability, split-half (or alternate form) reliability, and test–retest reliability can be proposed as applicable methods for the determination of the reliability of behavioral observations. In the first instance, two or more observers can watch and record the incidences of target events, and a correlation between the two scorers can be calculated. Split-half reliability could be examined via a division of an hour-long observation into odd–even minutes. Last, observational measures taken at different times are essentially a test–retest evaluation (see also Tinsley & Weiss, 1975). Not all of these methods would be warmly received by behavioral assessors, for they may suggest that behavior is largely a function of the individual and less a function of the situational or environmental influences. Mitchell also points out that each procedure identified above in some way confounds measurement error with other sources of variance. Moreover, generalizability theory (Cronbach *et al.*, 1972) offers a more desirable methodology to experimentally examine each of the multiple sources of variation in behavior (e.g., Mash & McElwee, 1974).

Unlike the traditional assumption that individual differences are the sole source (aside from error) of variations in test scores, generalizability theory assumes that there are multiple sources of response variation. Sources of variation other than individual differences are called facets (e.g., assessment occasions, subjects, observers) and, using an analysis-of-variance model, it is possible to independently estimate the contributions of each of the facets. A generalizability study (G study) allows the researcher to estimate the size of the contribution of each facet to the observed scores. A G study produces generalizability coefficients that reflect the partitioning of variance into components that correspond to the facets sampled in the study. A properly designed

G study, such as one that includes the facets of observers, observational methods, and the occasions of observation, would provide estimates of the generalizability of the data along each of these dimensions.

Mitchell details three types of generalizability studies that parallel the three types of traditional reliability: duplicate generalizability corresponds to the traditional interscorer reliability; session generalizability corresponds to split-half (alternate form) reliability; and developmental generalizability corresponds to the test–retest reliability. In a duplicate generalizability study, taped observational data would be scored on two or more occasions by two or more observers using two or more forms of the observational system. Since the data are taped, and therefore do not change, there is no variance attributable to occasions. The occasions variance that is evident, then, can be used as an indication of within-observer stability. In a session generalizability study, different subsections of the observed data (e.g., odd minutes and even minutes of hour-long tapes) would be used as measurement occasions. A session generalizability study would reflect the stability of the behaviors being observed over the interval of time that they were observed. A developmental generalizability study uses two or more periods of observation at different times as the measurement occasions. This type of G study, like test–retest reliability, tells the researcher about changes in behavior over time.

There are hints that the session generalizability study and the developmental generalizability study are more appropriate for behavioral observation studies where the behaviors in question are assumed to be somewhat stable. In contrast, stability over time is not an issue in the session generalizability study, and it is this type of G study that appears to have the most to offer behavioral assessment at this time. The interested reader is referred to Mitchell's recommendations, but suffice it to say here that (1) computation of generalizability coefficients should be conducted on the same data used in the substantive analyses of the reported study (gather reliability data at the same time the rest of the data are gathered, (2) two or more occasions of measurement should be included in studies of generalizability, and (3) recognize that generalizability coefficients are stringently conservative and yield estimates of the lower limits of the dependability of the observational data. Specific to the last point, the observer agreement that we are accustomed to (in the 80s and 90s) will be in the 50s and 60s as generalizability coefficients. Although the size of the coefficient is lower, our standards concerning the way of coefficient was determined have gone up. As noted by Mitchell (1979), we will simply have to adjust our expectations.

Articles by Coates and Thoresen (1978) and by Strossen, Coates, and Thoresen (1979) are also relevant for behavioral assessors interested in generalizability theory and research. Coates and Thoresen (1978) provide an illustrative use of generalizability research with a study of adolescents' eating behaviors. Strossen *et al.* (1979) extend generalizability theory and discuss its application to single-subject designs. The decision on "generalizability studies" is not yet in, but it does appear to be a sophisticated methodology that interested behavioral assessors can adopt for a more compelling analysis of the reliability of their reported data. It appears that generalizability theory has the potential to bridge the gap between traditional psychometric theory and behavioral assessment.

In addition to the recent focus on reliability in observational assessment, questions of the validity of observational assessment are considered important (Foster & Cone, 1980). For example, the validity of a 74-category observation code was examined using records of the classroom behavior of 60 hyperactive children and 60 same-sex normal children (Abikoff, Gittelman-Klein, & Klein, 1977). Hyperactives were reported to have significantly higher scores than comparison children on 12 codes. Although single codes were less than satisfactory in making classification, two-code criteria were relatively successful. Haynes and Kerns (1979) criticized Abikoff *et al.* For instance, Haynes and Kerns noted that Abikoff *et al.* had observed their hyperactive children during their most active periods of the day while nonhyperactives were observed concurrently, but without concern for typical activity level. Abikoff, Gittelman, and Klein (1980), using independent samples of hyperactive and normal children and employing a methodology identical to that of their earlier study, recently reported that they were able to replicate their earlier work. That is, all previously obtained results examining the discriminative ability of the codes were cross-validated.

Validity: The Case of Assertion

Behavioral assessors have now come to consider the psychometric issues that have for some time been of interest to more traditional assessment researchers. Issues of reliability, convergent and discriminant validity, and even construct validity, are becoming crucial topics for research attention. Perhaps this thrust is nowhere clearer than in the assessment of assertion. But since this thrust is relevant to behavioral assessment in general, we hope to see such effort become commonplace in the future.

The importance of reliability and validity of assessments of assertion has been recognized by Kern and MacDonald (1980). In their report, they used both direct observational (behavior sample) and self-report indices of assertion and anxiety, thus working toward a multitrait–multimethod analysis. The behavior sample was scored for assertion and anxiety. The self-report tests of assertion included the Conflict Resolution Inventory (CRI—McFall & Lillisand, 1971), the College Self-Expression Scale (CSES—Galassi, DeLo, Galassi, & Bastien, 1974), and a global measure of assertion. The measures of anxiety that were employed were the Fear of Negative Evaluation Scale (Watson & Friend, 1969), a modified Self-Report Inventory of Anxiousness (Endler, Hunt, & Rosenstein, 1962), Scale II from the Social Reaction Inventory (Richardson & Tasto, 1976), and a global rating of anxiety. Following the intercorrelation of these measures, convergent and discriminant validity can be estimated. Convergent validity is evidenced in the correlation of the same characteristics measured by different methods. All of the assertion measures were reported to reach significant levels of convergent validity. Discriminant validity requires a more complex set of criteria, and only the role-play measure showed meaningful discriminant validity.

Examinations of the validity of role-play assertion assessment procedures have proliferated. In a direct and somewhat prototypic manner, Heimberg, Harrison, Goldberg, Desmarais, and Blue (1979) studied the relationship between self-report on the Rathus Assertiveness Scale (RAS—Rathus, 1973) and role-play behavior using an inmate population. The items on the behavioral assertion role-play test were after Eisler, Miller, and Hersen (1973). Subjects' responses to the role plays were videotaped and rated for (1) response latency, (2) response duration, (3) duration of eye contact, (4) speech volume, and (5) speech inflection. An overall assertiveness rating on a five-point scale was also made. The results of this inquiry did not provide supportive evidence— there was not a linear relationship between self-reported assertiveness and assertive behaviors. The authors did report a curvilinear relationship, but its meaning was not entirely clear and it did not hold for all cases. Additional reservations about the applicability of the construct of assertion with inmates were raised by Heimberg and Harrison (1980). For instance, these authors reported that inmates scored higher on assertion than college students and psychiatric patients, but they felt that this difference was the result of (1) confusing aggression and assertion and (2) the influence of social desirability. The utility of assessments of assertiveness with inmate samples remains in question.

In a more elaborate study of the validity of assertion role plays, Bellack, Hersen, and Turner (1979) had 28 inpatients with a variety of diagnoses perform in role-play situations and undergo a clinical interview. In addition, six staged "naturalistic incidents" took place on the ward, and confederates rated the subject's behavior in each instance. Ratings were provided on variables such as eye contact, latency to respond, smiles, etc. The role-play test was again modeled after Eisler *et al.* (1973). The structured interview included asking subjects what they would do in situations similar to those in the other assessment methods. The subject's responses were audiotaped and subsequently rated for praise, requests, compliance, etc. Ratings were determined to be reliable, and the order of the assessments was not found to alter the results. Unlike some earlier research (e.g., Bellack, Hersen, & Lamparski, 1979), the present study employed identical role-play and *in vivo* situations. Thus, the situational specificity of the assertive response was recognized and the evaluation of the role-play tests was not biased or hampered by situational variance. The main findings, which were consistent with the earlier work, indicated that, in the authors' words, "behavior in the role-play was not highly related to behavior in the naturalistic situations" (p. 676). Moreover, there was a stronger correspondence between data gathered in the interview and the *in vivo* behavior than between interview and role-play assessments. These findings led the authors to suggest that perhaps something about the staged nature of role plays affects a subject's behavior. When you know you're play acting, does your behavior deviate from what would have occurred without such knowledge?

As in the work of Bellack and his colleagues, Higgins, Alonso, and Pendleton (1979) paid attention to the comparability of the role-play situation and the situations in the other forms of assessment used. In addition, Higgins *et al.* (1979) placed direct attention on the importance of the subject's *knowledge about whether or not a role play is taking place*. Fifty-two subjects, divided into high and low assertiveness groups based on scores on the CRI (McFall & Lillisand, 1971), were required to engage in an assertion-eliciting situation. While half of the subjects knew that the interaction would be a role play, the others received no such information. The outcome was most interesting. Subjects who knew it to be a role play made significantly more assertive and fewer passive responses than did uniformed subjects. Role-play subjects also refused more requests and were rated as more assertive on a global rating than the uniformed participants. The different levels of self-reported assertiveness did not produce significant effects. As the authors suggest, it is possible that subjects became more involved as a result of their "playing-the-role" and being an actor.

The correspondence of self-report and role-play measures of assertiveness was also addressed in a French-speaking community. Like their cohorts, Bourque and LaDouceur (1979) recognized the need to be concerned with the similarity of the self-report items and the role-play situations. Ten items were selected from a French version of the Adult Self-Expression Scale (ASES—Gay, Hollandsworth, & Galassi, 1975) and used to identify 20 high-assertive and 20 low-assertive subjects from 250 students. Subjects participated in 10 role-play situations, each corresponding to an individual test item, and the role-plays were coded into the Eisler *et al.* (1973) categories mentioned earlier. Bourque and LaDouceur (1979) found significant relationships between the self-report score and measures of assertiveness content, general assertiveness, anxiety, and self-evaluation of performance, but an absence of significant correlations with eye contact, and affect. Some single self-report items also correlated significantly with corresponding behavioral measures. However, eye contact, response latency, length of response, tone of voice, and affect did not correlate meaningfully. Additional data, reported by Bordewick and Bornstein (1980) indicated that the RAS and an abbreviated behavioral role-play assertion test (McFall & Marston, 1970) failed to converge highly as measures of assertion.

Assumptions of the validity of role-play assessments of assertion and/or social skills are no longer accepted without a fair test. Correspondingly, Williams (1981) questioned whether it is legitimate to assume that role-play behavioral assessments are superior to more traditional standardized objective inventories. In her study, Williams (1981) compared a role-play procedure with the social introversion (Si) scale of the MMPI in predicting several criterion measures. Female undergraduates (151) completed the Si scale and reported the number of high school and college organizations to which they belonged and the number of social activities in which they had participated in the last month. Subjects also participated in a role-play interaction with a male confederate while an observer completed ratings of social skill, anxiety, physical attractiveness, eye contact, and 10 others. A representative subsample (142) was also given a peer telephone interview. The upshot of the results obtained in this study is that there was no evidence of the superiority of behavioral assessment via a role play over an objective assessment instrument (Si scale of the MMPI). While the Si scale had the highest significant correlations with four of the six criterion measures, the role-play measures considered together accounted for a slightly higher proportion of the variance in the criterion measures that did the Si scale. As Williams noted, these results may be weak due to the choice of less than optimal criterion measures, or the choice of less than optimal observations in the role play. Nevertheless, these data suggest that claims of the superiority of one assessment procedure over another be based firmly on investigative outcomes and not on polemical claims. The door to the experimental comparison of assessment strategies appears to have been opened.

The statement that assertive responses are situation specific is far from revolutionary. On the contrary, the large majority of assertiveness researchers have come to implicit agreement on the question: assertiveness is situation specific (e.g., Curran, 1978; Linehan, 1979; MacDonald, 1978). However, as Kolotkin (1980) points out, there has yet to be a study which addresses the difficulty levels of the various situations used in assessing assertiveness. The implications of the failure to address the "levels of difficulty question" pertain to contemporary research on both treatment and assessment. For instance, Kolotkin notes that conclusions about limited generalization following assertiveness training and the limited external validity of role-play assessments may be premature because situational factors (the level of difficulty of the different situations) were not controlled.

To examine the difficulty level of various situations, Kolotkin (1980) applied scaling procedures to a list of general situations that spanned the continuum of possible situations. Subjects in the study were screened psychometrically using two instruments. That is, only subjects who scored above a criterion on the ASES (Gay, Hollandsworth, & Galassi, 1975) and the Assertion Inventory (Gambrill & Richey, 1975) were included. The scaling task required subjects to order the situation along a continuum. Kolotkin used the successive intervals scaling method, which entails having subjects rank-order the stimuli, dividing the dimension into categories, calculating frequency of category assignment, and computing a standard score for each situation.

According to Kolotkin's results, the following sample of situations are in order of difficulty for being assertive: "A person you work with asks you a question. You do not know the answer. You say" (mean difficulty value .33). "You are at a movie and the people behind you are talking loudly. You say" (mean difficulty value 1.61). "At a meeting a person you know often interrupts you when you are speaking. This happens again. You say" (mean difficulty value 2.03). "You are in a supermarket and in a great hurry. You have two items to check out. The person in front of you hasn't started checking out yet and has a whole basket of groceries. You say" (mean difficulty value 2.15). Given that the situations do in fact vary according to level of difficulty, then one must indeed exercise caution in treatment outcome research so that pretreatment role-play situations are not more/less difficult than posttreatment situations. An intervention may in fact be extremely beneficial but fail to show effects on situational role plays if the pretreatment situations are extremely easy while the posttreatment situations are difficult. Kolotkin (1980) offers an example of how his scaled situations can be used in outcome research, and the interested reader is referred to the actual report. Concern about the comparability of the difficulty of the situations used in role-play assessments will likely have direct bearing on future research on assertiveness.

As we have seen, validational studies of the role-play assessment of assertiveness have captured the efforts of numerous researchers. The studies are impressive in both the breadth and depth of analysis. As a result of this series of investigations one must be concerned with the comparability of role-play situations and self-report items (and naturalistic incidents as well), recognize the reactivity associated with knowing that the test is a "role play," and control for the level of difficulty of the situations employed. While these research concerns can now be readily incorporated into future work, we are still left with muddy waters—are role plays valid? A simple-minded answer is not in order, but it does appear that role plays where specific behaviors such as eye contact and response latency are coded do not offer much validity. Other behaviors, perhaps those associated with paralinguistic and nonverbal channels, may prove more so. Indeed, some evidence to support this notion was provided in Romano and Bellack's (1980) application of social validation procedures to the assessment of assertion.

To identify the specific behaviors referred to when one speaks of assertiveness or social skill, a sample of judges, representing a larger group, can observe actual behavior and provide ratings. In the study by Romano and Bellack (1980), 20 women (10 outpatients and 10 non-patients) were videotaped role playing 10 scenes concerning negative assertion. These videotapes were then observed and rated by 13 men and 13 women. Judges provided a list of the cues that they were using in making their judgments. The videotapes were later subjected to categorization by trained observers. The observers scored the occurrences of specific behaviors (e.g., eye contact, smiles, speech duration) and instances of the cues suggested by the judges (e.g., offering alternatives, acknowledging the feelings or position of others). Among the numerous findings, it was reported that the best predictors of an individual's overall performance were found to be paralinquistic and nonverbal behaviors. Variables such as intonation and facial cues emerged as influential factors in accounting for variability in ratings of social skill. The notion that assertiveness is "simply performing certain behaviors" does not appear satisfactory, for more complex individual differences in the manner of performance account for large portions of the variability. The authors point out that the judges viewed accommodation and compromise as important parameters of assertiveness and that this has direct implications for assertiveness training. As the authors note, "assertiveness training programs have emphasized 'sticking up for one's rights,'" but it seems also important to stress the offering of alternatives and the acknowledging of feelings in order to teach the skills that are judged (through social validation) to be most socially skilled.

Factor-analytic studies of self-report measures of assertion have appeared (e.g., Gambrill & Richey, 1975; Gay, Hollandsworth, & Galassi, 1975). With an eye toward population, race, and sex differences, two recent studies have further examined the factor structure of tests of assertion (Galassi & Galassi, 1979; Kendall, Finch, Mikulka, & Colson, 1980). In the Galassi and Galassi report, several large samples of subjects' responses to the CSES were subjected to factor analyses. The samples varied in gender and the geographic region from which they were drawn. Multiple factors were identified, with different factorial structures emerging for different gender subjects and different subject groups. Similar results were obtained by Kendall *et al.* (1980) who examined the factor structure of two tests of assertion (the RAS and the CSES) for black and white subjects.

The consensus of research along these lines is not unequivocal, but it does suggest that there are multiple factors in measures of assertiveness and that each of the factors account for only moderate amounts of the variability. These findings also contribute to the belief that assertion is a construct that should be considered situation-specific, rather than as an individual cross-situational predisposition. However, it must be recalled that factor-analytic methods do not identify hidden causes of behavior nor do they create meaning from confusion. Factor-analytic research essentially helps organize the items of a test into groupings according to the subject's responses to the test items. The fact that the groupings (factors) differ across sexes and races may simply reflect differences in the way these subjects perceive assertion. In a similar vein, different factors emerging from different tests are most likely the result of the different items that comprise the tests. The potential value of the factor-analytic studies may lie in the identification of groupings of items that will allow for differential prescription of intervention procedures or the differential prediction of treatment outcomes.

Before moving on to other topics, a study of the RAS reported by Blanchard (1979) deserves attention because it addresses an important aspect of the validity of the scale. That is, are there meaningful changes in behavior that correspond with significant changes in the self-reported test scores? The results of an earlier assertion training program for dental students were reexamined. The nonassertive students were on probation for, among other problems, not being able to interact effectively with faculty and/or patients. Some interesting evidence appeared when promotion decisions were made. Students who had reported themselves as more assertive on the RAS after the training were judged to be worthy of promotion. A rather compelling corollary also emerged —students who did not self-report change did not pass. Moreover, there were nonoverlapping distributions of direction of change on the RAS and promotion decisions. The subjects who knew, or had learned, how to appear more desirable on the RAS also were able to appear more desirable for the judges.

Other Measures Briefly Noted

A number of recent papers have addressed assessment issues for more circumscribed topics. For instance, Farkas, Evans, Sine, Eifert, Wittlieb, and Vogelmann-Sine (1979) conducted three investigations of the reliability and validity of the mercury-in-rubber strain-gauge measure of penile circumference. The measure was found to be reliable, though more so at the basal end and less so at the maximal end of measurement. The subjective physiological effects resulting from the ingestion of alcohol were assessed by the Sensation Scale (Maisto, Connors, Tucker, & McCollam, 1980), a new measure five of six factors of which discriminated subjects who had or had not drunk alcohol.

Barlow, Hayes, Nelson, Steele, Meeler, and Mills (1979) developed a checklist of sex-role-specific motor behaviors and reported that the checklist discriminated between biological males and females, and between masculine and feminine females, but that it failed to discriminate between masculine and feminine males. This checklist, in conjunction with attitudinal inventories (Bem, 1974), may help to identify characteristics of perceived socially competent behaviors. Barlow et al. (1979) noted that preliminary work suggested that people of either gender are seen as more competent when adopting "masculine" motor behavior. Such findings, however, may be limited to the situations in which the behavior takes place.

A scale designed to measure sleep-incompatible behaviors was developed by Kazarian, Howe, and Csapo (1979). The 20-item scale showed acceptable test–retest reliability and internal consistency, and discriminated insomniacs from noninsomniacs (when insomnia was operationalized as latency to sleep onset). Because sleep recordings are considered an important part of the evaluation of behavioral treatments for insomnia, the work of Coates, Rosekind, and Thoresen (1978) and Coates, Rosekind, Strossen, Thoresen, and Kirmil-Gray (1979) is important. These studies suggest that all-night recordings in the lab produce comparable data to recordings gathered in the home and that the data can be transmitted from the home to the lab by telephone.

Marital satisfaction questionnaires often appear within the behavioral treatment literature, as does some form of the Marital Interaction Coding System (MICS—Patterson, Weiss, & Hops, 1977). Haynes, Follingstad, and Sullivan (1979) employed the Locke–Wallace Marital Adjustment Scale (Locke & Wallace, 1959) and the Stuart Marital Precounseling Inventory (Stuart & Stuart, 1972) along with 10 behaviors from the MICS in a study of the validity of assessments used in marital interaction research. Satisfied and dissatisfied couples participated by completing the questionnaires and being observed at home by behavioral coders. While the observation codes and the questionnaires evidenced only moderate correspondence, both questionnaires were highly successful in discriminating between the satisfied and dissatisfied couples. Six of the 10 behavioral codes also evidenced high levels of discrimination. Surprisingly, dysfunctional subjects emitted a higher rate of eye contact and agreement than functional individuals. The Locke–Wallace Marital Adjustment Scale's published criteria were successfully used to correctly identify 24 of the 26 individuals as clinic or nonclinic cases.

Jacobson and colleagues (e.g., Jacobson, Waldron, & Moore, 1980; Jacobson, Elwood, & Dallas, 1981) have also addressed the behavioral assessment of marital dysfunction. For example, Jacobson *et al.* (1980) reported that daily satisfaction ratings were predicted from displeasing events for distressed couples, whereas the frequency of pleasing events (e.g., shared activities) were more useful predictors for nondistressed couples. These data suggest that distressed couples are more reactive to displeasing behavior. These findings are not the result of different rates of pleasing and displeasing behaviors for distressed and nondistressed couples since the relationships were based on standardized scores.

In yet another factor analysis of the Fear Survey Schedule (FSS-III), Arrindell (1980) used a principal-components procedure on the responses of 703 noninstitutionalized phobics. The somewhat standard factors emerged, with the addition of a factor that the author labeled agoraphobia. The items loading on this factor included being alone, being in a strange place, large open spaces, and journeys by various means of transportation. The use of a sufficiently large sample is important in factor-analytic research (e.g., Comrey, 1974; Gorsuch, 1974), and one is initially impressed with the *n* of 703. However, there were 76 items included, thus making an even larger sample desirable. This problem is often true in factor-analytic studies. Nevertheless, the emergence of an agoraphobia factor from the FSS-III is relevant and supports clinical and theoretical notions.

As each of these studies illustrates, behavioral assessment is no longer limited to one method of data collection nor to a restricted set of topic areas. In contrast, new measures are being developed and the reliability and validity of existing measures are coming under more rigorous scrutiny. It is only reasonable to expect that as behavior therapy expands and enjoys the growth associated with wide application, issues in assessment will expand as well.

EXPANDING OUTWARD:
COGNITIVE–BEHAVIORAL ASSESSMENT

As stated earlier, we believe that, as with behavior therapy at large (see Chapter 1), behavioral assessment has moved in two directions simultaneously. On the one hand, the heartland of assessment has been entered via basic reliability and validity studies of assessment procedures that vary from self-report to naturalistic observation. On the other hand, behavioral assessment has taken a wider cut, expanding into the arena of cognitive–behavioral measurement. As we shall see, there are several methods, numerous contents, and a rather large variety of measures receiving initial research attention. Before we discuss these topics, it seems reasonable to first consider some of the reasons put forth as evidence of the need for cognitive–behavioral assessment.

Several of what might be called basic purposes for cognitive–behavioral assessment have been described elsewhere (Kendall, 1981a; Kendall & Korgeski, 1979). The major purposes are as follows:

1. *To study the relationships among covert phenomena and their relationship to patterns of behavior and expressions of emotion.* The aim is to uncover the relations and possible causal channels among various cognitive constructs and processes and to further discover the connections between these events and observable behaviors and emotions.

2. *To study the role of covert processes in the development of distinct psychopathologies and to examine their role in the behavorial patterns associated with coping.* The aim here is to determine both the cognitive content that differentiates pathological from nonpathological behavior and the types of cognitions associated with specific psychological dysfunctions. Are there cognitive errors associated with maladjustment that are not evident among the adjusted? Going one step further, are specific cognitive problems associated with distinct types of psychological dysfunction? Research and theory describing the covert processes associated with successful coping are also needed.

3. *To confirm the effects of treatment and to study the mechanism of change.* The assessment of cognitive processes is necessary to confirm that a therapy which has been designed to alter cognitions did, in fact, produce changes in the targeted cognitions. For example, an intervention intended to alter self-statements or negative automatic thoughts results in a demonstration of behavioral improvement. In order to confirm the treatment mechanism (the mechanism by which the treatment had its effects), cognitive functioning both before and after therapy would have to be assessed. Behavioral changes, in the absence of changes in the targeted cognitions, would necessitate a cautious interpretation of the data in relation to the role of cognitive phenomena in behavior change. Without the cognitive assessments, little can be learned about the function of cognitive change in relation to behavior change. This is, perhaps, the most important reason for cognitive–behavioral assessment.
4. *To check studies where cognitive factors have either been manipulated or implicated in the effects of the manipulation.* This purpose is important in experimental studies where the investigator, for example, produces different conditions under which the subject's performance is recorded. If the experimenter gave subjects different instructions regarding cognitive information, then the researcher would necessarily have to assess the cognitive factors to check on the experimental manipulation. If subjects were instructed to focus on an intense image, did they in fact create the image? Was it intense? Did they focus on it? Again, methodological rigor requires the assessment of the cognitive phenomenon of interest.

Although we see the coassessment of cognitive functioning and behavioral functioning as an essential mandate for contemporary behavior therapy, no doubt there are others not as enthusiastically inclined. But even if there were agreement on the intrinsic merit of cognitive assessment, we are still far from agreement on exactly how to undertake such measurement. As Meichenbaum and Cameron (1981) note, "In attempting to assess cognition, the investigator is confronted with several important questions concerning what to assess, where and how to assess the subject's cognition, how to score the thought processes in terms of the units and levels of analyses, and most important, how to interpret the data collected" (p. 4). Basic arguments against the assessments of cognition might include the nonobservable nature of cognition, the reliance on verbal self-report, the idiosyncratic quality of thought, and the inaccessibility of cognitive data. Much like the initial controversy surrounding self-efficacy theory (see the special issue of *Behaviour Research and Therapy*), uniform endorsement is not expected for all cognitive–behavioral assessments.

It is beyond the scope of the present review to individually detail the current status of the numerous measures employed in cognitive–behavioral assessment. It would also be inappropriate in the present context simply to summarize the available reviews (Glass & Arnkoff, 1982; Kendall & Hollon, 1981a; Kendall & Korgeski, 1979; Kendall & Braswell, 1982; Merluzzi, Glass, & Genest, 1981). What does seem appropriate, however, is a review of the measures and measurement procedures receiving current research attention within behavior therapy. As will be seen, there is a heavy reliance on verbal self-report. Nisbett and Wilson's (1977) influential article notwithstanding, there do seem to be justifications for our paying attention to individuals' verbal reports (Ericsson & Simon, 1980; see also Mischel, 1981).

Self-Efficacy

Perhaps more than any conceptual framework aside from learning theory, self-efficacy theory (Bandura, 1977a) has captured the interest of behaviorally oriented applied psychologists. The theoretical separation of behavioral procedures and cognitive processes as components of therapeutic change has instigated relevant laboratory and clinical investigation. Yet another sign of behavior therapists' willingness to court self-efficacy theory is the reported invoking of explanations of therapeutic outcome based on self-efficacy. The upshot is that we must be aware that with proper notice must come adequate precaution.

Caution is necessary, for instance, in the assessment of self-efficacy. Bandura (1981) emphasizes that "self-appraisals that occur prior to performance must be distinguished from retrospective conjectures about the causes of past behavior. It is probes of antecedent self-appraisals that are best suited for elucidating the relationship between self-referent thought and action" (p. 223).

Three dimensions of efficacy judgments have been described. Bandura (1981) proposes that they differ in *level*, *strength*, and *generality*. These distinctions are aptly detailed in the following quote:

> They differ in *level*. Thus, when tasks are ordered by level of difficulty, the self-judged efficacy of different individuals may be limited to the simpler tasks, extend to moderately difficult ones, or include some of the most challenging and taxing performances. Efficacy judgments also vary in *strength*. Weak self-percepts of efficacy are easily negated by disconfirming experiences, whereas people who have a strong sense of personal mastery

will persevere in their coping efforts in the face of dissuading experiences. In addition, self-percepts of efficacy differ in *generality*—they may encompass varied domains or only a few. An adequate efficacy analysis therefore requires detailed assessment of the level, strength, and generality of self-efficacy commensurate with the precision with which behavioral processes are measured. The relationship between self-referent thought and action is most clearly revealed by microanalysis of the congruence between efficacy judgment and performance at the level of individual tasks.

More specific examples of the actual procedures employed in assessing self-efficacy are available in Bandura, Adams, Hardy, and Howells (1980). For instance, subjects in this report were given a list of performance tasks and asked to indicate those that they judged that they could perform. For each task, subjects rated their own strength of efficacy on a 100-point scale (10-unit intervals). The level of self-efficacy was the number of tasks subjects expected to perform. Strength of self-efficacy was computed by summing the magnitude scores across tasks and dividing the number of tasks. Generality of self-efficacy was the rated level and strength of perceived efficacy in coping with an unfamiliar task.

Self-efficacy assessments, therefore, require that a specific instrument be designed for each type of investigation. That is, a separate list of performance tasks would have to be generated for inquiries with different foci (e.g., phobics, depressives, children). As a result, efforts to make comparisons across efficacy assessments must be conducted cautiously. One would not be certain that the range of performance tasks used in assessing self-efficacy in one context are comparable on key dimensions (scaling of item difficulty) to the assessment device used in another context.

Kirsch (1980) has expressed concern regarding the range and hierarchy of the performance tasks for which subjects make efficacy judgments. Kirsch (1980) points out that if a subject is expected to succeed on a task then it is presumed that the subject also expected to succeed on a prior task. If this is the case, then Kirsch argues that Bandura's microanalyses of self-efficacy are overstatements. There is also the problem that congruence between efficacy judgments and behavioral performances could result from chance. Bandura (1980), however, pointed out that it is not always the case that all subjects perceive the tasks as a perfectly ordered hierarchical set. Future research should consider these concerns.

Last, there is the question of whether making efficacy judgments in itself can affect performance by creating public commitment and pressure for consistency (Bandura *et al.* 1980). Precautions such as having subjects make judgments of self-efficacy in private and requiring judgments for a variety of activities together in advance of specific behavioral tests are being exercised in current investigations (e.g., Bandura *et al.* 1980).

Self-Statements

Even a disinterested participant must readily recognize the striking increase in behavior therapy's interest in the role of an individual's "internal dialogue," or self-statements, in the development of psychological dysfunctions and the behavior therapy procedures for their treatment. Evidence has appeared to suggest that an internal dialogue of conflict is central to assertion deficits (Schwartz & Gottman, 1976), that modifications of self-statements can affect behavior (Glass, Gottman, & Shmurak, 1976), and that self-statements can be assessed (Kendall & Hollon, 1981b). Indeed, one area where behavioral researchers have begun to assess cognitive data is in the measurement of self-statements. One must keep in mind, however, that self-statements are only one aspect of "cognition" and that cognitive assessment is very complex.

The use of self-report inventories (endorsement method) to assess self-statements was spurred by Schwartz and Gottman's paper (reprinted in Franks & Wilson, 1977) on a task analysis of assertive behavior. Regarding their assessment, these authors developed an Assertiveness Self-Statement Test (ASST) which they had subjects complete after taking part in an assertive situation. Half the items were independently judged to be adaptive and half were judged maladaptive. Subjects read each item and rated it on a scale of 1 to 5 indicating the extent to which they had had the thought, from "hardly ever" to "very often." The scale helped identify the "internal dialogue of conflict" that was found to differentiate subjects of differing assertion levels. It should also be noted that the ASST has been useful in evaluating treatment outcome (Craighead, 1979).

Kendall, Williams, Pechacek, Graham, Shisslak, and Herzoff (1979) developed a Self-Statement Inventory (SSI) to assess the cognitions of patients undergoing an invasive medical procedure (i.e., cardiac catheterization). Twenty items, 10 positive (helpful) and 10 negative (interfering) thoughts, comprised the SSI. Patients retrospectively completed the SSI and physicians and nurses provided independent ratings of each patient's adjustment during the medical procedure. Positive thoughts were not found to be related to ratings of adjustment, but the higher negative self-statement scores were meaningfully related to lower ratings of adjustment.

These two studies are similar in that a similar method was employed in the development of the scales. Both groups of authors produced an initial list of self-statements that were thought to be important for the situation under study. Consensual validation of the items was then conducted using independent samples of normal individuals. Items receiving 90% consensual agreement (Schwartz & Gottman, 1976) or 100% consensual agreement (Kendall *et al.* 1979) were then used in arranging the final scale. Both scales also had a balance of positive and negative self-statement items.

A different approach to the development of a self-statement questionnaire was employed by Hollon and Kendall (1980) in their work on the Automatic Thoughts Questionnaire (ATQ). This 30-item inventory, designed for the study of the negative cognitions associated with depression, was developed via the comparison of known groups. First, 788 students each provided a thought that might come into one's head during depression. The list was pared down by the authors and the resulting list administered to another group of students. Next, based on the dual criteria of high scores on both the Beck Depression Inventory and the MMPI Depression scale, groups of depressed and nondepressed subjects were identified. Items significantly differentiating the criterion groups constituted the ATQ. In order to eliminate chance discriminations, the ATQ was cross-validated on another sample of known groups.

Self-statement inventories, where subjects are required to endorse the degree or extent to which they had certain thoughts, are being developed for each individual study in which they are used. Clearly, the SSI contains items appropriate only to a cardiac catheterization procedure, and the ASST and ATQ are specific to the disorder under investigation. It appears that researchers interested in the assessment of self-statements have recognized the specificity of the types of thoughts to the specific situation or disorder. Unfortunately, researchers have not been fully cognizant of the individual *meaning* of each self-statement but appear to have taken the meaning of each self-statement at face value. That is, researchers have not inquired to identify the meaning that a specific self-statement has for a given subject but have merely assumed that the self-statement has the same personal meaning for all subjects involved.

It seems that both the personal meaning of the self-statement and the degree to which the person actually believes the content of the self-statement are likely to be important pieces of information in an analysis of the role of self-statements in behavior. Consider the following example using the self-statement "I can do it." A client may be told simply to think in a positive manner and to say "I can do it" to himself or herself (by a naive and simple-minded therapist) in order to overcome behavioral problems. But if the client's statement is nothing more than an acquiescent reply, should we expect this self-statement to carry with it the potential of behavioral control? We are inclined to think not. If the meaning of the thought "I can do it" is "Yeah, but not very well," then the mere recording of the existence of the self-statement may not be sufficient for prediction of behavior. Advances in the measurement of self-statements may necessitate the simultaneous assessment of the specific meaning of each self-statement and the degree to which the individual believes the self-statement.

Another potentially valuable consideration in the assessment of self-statements concerns the sequence of the self-statements. Would we not expect marked differences between individuals who self-correct each negative thought with a positive one and persons whose negative thoughts are not followed by retorts! Henshaw (1978), in a study of creative problem solving, had subjects follow a "think aloud" procedure. Among other procedures and findings, Henshaw reported that high-creative subjects were significantly more likely to follow an inhibitive self-statement with a positive (facilitative or creative) one, whereas low-creative subjects followed inhibitive self-statements with another inhibitive self-statement or silence. The high-creative group tended to "counter" their own negative thinking. It is possible that a mere count of negative or positive self-statements may not be as predictive or informative as the sequence of the person's internal dialogue.

The self-statement inventory is but one method to assess an individual's internal dialogue (see Kendall & Hollon, 1981b). Tape recordings of spontaneous speech, videotape reconstruction (e.g., Hollandsworth, Glazeski, Kirkland, Jones, & Van Norman, 1973), thought listing (e.g., Cacioppo, Glass, & Merluzzi, 1979), and "think aloud" procedures (e.g., Genest & Turk, 1981) are examples of some available alternatives. Unfortunately, the relative utility of these and other methods for measuring internal dialogues is as yet not known.

Social Problem Solving

Problem solving has been an active component of behavior therapy since D'Zurilla and Goldfried's paper first appeared (1971), with both assessment (Shure & Spivack, 1972) and treatment (e.g., Bedell, Archer, & Marlowe, 1980; Robin, Kent, O'Leary, Foster, & Prinz, 1977) studies appearing in the literature. Recently, reviews of problem-solving approaches to treatment for children (Urbain & Kendall, 1980) and adults (D'Zurilla & Nezu, 1982) have materialized. An equally extensive literature inspecting the assessment of social problem-solving skills has appeared (e.g., Butler & Meichenbaum, 1981; D'Zurilla & Nezu, 1982; Kendall, Pellegrini, & Urbain, 1981; Krasnor & Rubin, 1981). The reader interested in the details of the reviews of the different methods for assessing social problem solving are referred to these papers. Only a few of the more recent studies employing measures of social problem solving will be mentioned here. In addition, a brief summary of the critical issues facing social problem-solving assessment will be highlighted.

The measures most often mentioned when discussing social/interpersonal problem solving are the various tests developed to assess Interpersonal Cognitive Problem-Solving (ICPS) skills; specifically, the work of Spivack, Shure, Platt, and their colleagues at the Hahnemann Medical College. The measurement of Means–Ends Problem Solving (MEPS), appearing first in the early 1970s (Shure & Spivack, 1972), has received an increasing portion of the research attention. The MEPS procedure involves presenting the subject with a series of stories portraying situations in which a protagonist is having a problem with one or more persons. A resolution to the problem is then presented with the subject's task being to "fill in the middle" of the story. A total MEPS score is often used, though subscores, such as the number of different means enumerated, a relevance ratio (e.g., the number of relevant means to the total number enumerated), obstacles enumerated, and degree of elaboration, sometimes appear. For example, in a study of Platt and Siegel (1976) where they found that male psychiatric patients with low MEPS scores were also more clearly psychotic on the MMPI, it was the number of relevant means and the relevancy ratio that differentiated most often.

The MEPS items are essentially interpersonal. Appel and Kaestner (1979), however, examined both interpersonal and emotional problem solving. Narcotic drug abusers in "good" or "poor" standing in the drug rehabilitation program were compared and found to show the hypothesized relationship for interpersonal problem solving: subjects in poor standing evidenced greater means–ends deficits. They did not, however, differ in terms of relevant means for the emotional problems.

In a study of the problem-solving deficit associated with depression, impersonal (anagram tasks) and interpersonal (MEPS) problem-solving assessments were taken on subjects varying in levels of depression. The authors, Gotlib and Asarnow (1979), found that their depressed and nondepressed subjects did not differ significantly on anagram performance, but the depressed subjects did perform more poorly on the interpersonal problem-solving measure (MEPS) than the nondepressed subjects. Although the use of these results to challenge the learned helplessness model of depression has been criticized (Rohsenow, 1980) and reaffirmed (Gotlib & Asarnow, 1980), the study further illustrates the increased employment of the MEPS procedure in current research.

The MEPS procedure follows a projective assessment format (i.e., subjects are essentially asked to complete a story) and the all too familiar problems of response bias, social desirability, and so on, reemerge. Even if one assumes that valid data are gathered, the scoring of the protocols is not a simple task and acceptable reliabilities do not come without the setting of many scoring rules. Kendall, Pellegrini, and Urbain (1981) noted that scoring differences appeared in the children's MEPS literature. Moreover, the validity of the paper-and-pencil self-report stories does not itself receive wide acceptance. Butler and Meichenbaum (1981) criticize the procedure for lack of "ecological validity" and call for a greater emphasis on the study of social problem solving in the natural environment in which it occurs. D'Zurilla and Nezu (1982) are not as convinced that more behavioral assessments will be the answer, for they warn that we should be careful not to observe behavior and infer cognition. In their opinion we should simply develop better methods to assess the social problem-solving cognitions. Last, use of the MEPS as a treatment outcome measure (in an otherwise successful outcome) led to reduced problem-solving scores (Kendall & Zupan, 1981). These authors argued that the limited number of stories (i.e., six) required repeated assessment with the same materials, thus leading children to give more brief responses over time (as if they thought that, individually, "I've already done this once before"). It is reasonably accurate to state that many current behavioral researchers are involved in the use of problem-solving procedures in their treatment and related research, and it is equally accurate to indicate that most are not yet satisfied with the assessment measures.

Self-Control

One area that witnessed comparable scale developments for both children and adults was self-control. Kendall and Wilcox (1979) reported on the development and validation of a self-control rating scale (SCRS) for children, and Rosenbaum (1980a) provided a schedule for assessing adult self-control (Self-Control Schedule [SCS]). It should be pointed out that, while the topics are similar, the intent of the scales is somewhat different. The SCRS, as a rating scale completed by teachers or parents, provides an indication of the degree to which the child's behavior can be described as self-controlled (vs. impulsive). The SCS is a self-report scale that assesses an individual's tendency to apply self-control methods to the solution of his or her own behavioral problems. These differences aside, the scales are similar in that they both have a cognitive–behavioral underpinning. Kendall and Wilcox's (1979) SCRS is based on a definition of self-control that contains both cognitive and behavioral components (see also Kendall & Williams, 1982), and Rosenbaum's SCS taps self-control behaviors that are also partially cognitive (e.g., use of cognitions and self-statements to control emotions).

Rosenbaum's SCS contains 36 items. These items were the result of judgments made by clinicians and time analyses performed on a larger sample of potential items. The self-control behaviors assessed by the SCS were categorized in the following way: "(a) use of cognitions and 'self-statements' to control emotional and physiological responses, (b) the application of problem-solving strategies (e.g., planning, problem definition, evaluating alternatives, anticipation of consequences), (c) the ability to delay immediate gratification, and (d) perceived self-efficacy" (pp. 110–111.). Sample items include, "When I am feeling depressed I try to think about pleasant events," "When I plan to work, I remove all the things that are not relevant to my work," and "I need outside help to get rid of some of my bad habits" (scored in reverse). Subjects indicate on a scale from +3 to −3 how characteristic or descriptive each statement is of them. Test–retest reliabilities and normative data are provided. Rosenbaum (1980a) also reported that subjects scoring high on the SCS (as compared to low scorers) had an internal locus of control, held fewer irrational beliefs, and were better able to control and tolerate noxious stimuli. In two additional studies (Rosenbaum, 1980b), subjects high on self-control (based on the SCS) tolerated cold-pressor pain longer than low-self-control subjects. Though preliminary, the SCS appears to be a reliable and valid index that can be used to assess individual differences in the tendency to employ self-control. The potential utility of this scale in the identification of optimal clients for distinct treatment procedures merits research attention.

Kendall and Wilcox's Self-Control Rating Scale (1979) requires an observer (the rater) to place the person being rated at a point along a continuum. The continuum is self-control to impulsivity, and there are 33 items requiring a rating. Of the 33 items, 10 are descriptive of self-controlled action, 13 are indicative of impulsivity, and 10 are worded to denote both possibilities. Each item has anchor words attached to the 1-to-7 scale such that the calculation of the total score on the SCRS is the total of the 33 ratings. Higher scores indicate a greater lack of self-control. In the initial scale development, teachers rated 110 randomly selected third- through sixth-grade children, and research personnel administered measures of the children's intelligence, cognitive style (Matching Familiar Figures test—Kagan, 1966), Porteus Maze performance (Porteus, 1955), delay of gratification, and behavioral observations. Children rated as lacking in self-control were also found to show an impulsive cognitive style and to display a greater number of the observed off-task behaviors. This convergent validity was supplemented by evidence of discriminant validity: nonsignificant correlations with intelligence and mental age. Teacher-referred classroom problem children were found to be rated as significantly less self-controlled than matched nonreferred children. Additional validational analyses, employing measures of social cognition and observations gathered in the classroom add support to the SCRS (Kendall, Zupan, & Braswell, 1981). It should be noted that the SCRS has been found to be sensitive to treatment effects (e.g., Kendall & Wilcox, 1980; Kendall & Zupan, 1981) and therefore can be a useful measure in treatment evaluations.

Cognitive–Behavioral Assessment and Treatment Outcome

As stated earlier, perhaps the most important reason for assessing cognitive variables is *to confirm the effects of treatment and study the mechanism of change.* Did a therapy designed to alter cognitions actually alter the targeted cognitions? It is pleasing to report that many therapy outcome researchers now employ measures for just this purpose. Rather than be redundant with some of the material reviewed in Chapter 4 on cognitive processes and procedures within behavior therapy, the present section will include only a few illustrative cases.

The efficacy of various psychological procedures in the treatment of assertion and depression has captured researchers' interest. In two studies, Fleming and Thornton (1980) and Hammen, Jacobs, Mayol, and Cochran (1980), the authors employed general measures of cognition to facilitate an understanding of treatment effects. For instance, Hammen *et al.* (1980) tested the hypothesis that type of assertion treatment would interact with level of dysfunctional cognitions (using Weissman & Beck's Dysfunctional Attitudes Scale [DAS], 1978). Fleming and Thornton (1980) employed a variety of general cognitive and behavioral assessments, with various treatments (cognitive, behavioral, nondirective) producing general reductions in depressive symptomatology. In addition to the more general assessments it may prove enlightening to assess changes in the more specific cognitions associated with depression using an instrument such as the ATQ, or specific cognitions related to diverse psychological dysfunctions, such as self-efficacy.

Assessments of self-efficacy have begun to appear in the treatment outcome literature (e.g., Hammen *et al.* 1980; Kazdin, 1979b). If self-efficacy is to be truly evaluated as a unifying theory of behavior change, then not only must it be assessed in behavioral and cognitive–behavioral therapy outcome studies, but also in the study of the outcome of other forms of therapy. It will prove interesting to include an assessment of self-efficacy in a comparative treatment outcome study such that one can examine the relative changes in self-efficacy across the different treatments. Along these lines it is worth noting that previous research where self-efficacy was assessed as part of treatment outcome has indicated that repeated testing alone produces little or no change in self-efficacy, behavior, or fear arousal (Bandura *et al.* 1980).

While it is essential to include cognitive assessments in the study of treatment outcomes, it should be recalled that such assessments are a part of multimethod measurement procedures. Theoretically, some would argue, the different assessments (e.g., behavioral, cognitive) should show differential change as a result of behavioral or cognitive treatments—that specific types of treatment will have specific effects. In a study by Zeiss, Lewinsohn, and Muñoz (1979) clients were provided with interpersonal skills training, pleasant activities schedules, or cognitive training. Clients were also assessed with measures particularly sensitive to each type of treatment (e.g., Interpersonal Events Schedule, Pleasant Events Schedule, Personal Beliefs Inventory). The authors reported that a major finding of their study was that all of the treatments had nonspecific effects—treatments with a specific focus did not have dominant effects on measures of their respective focus. Zeiss *et al.* noted that the results might have been different had the subjects been assigned to treatments based on pretreatment assessments rather than randomly. Also, the failure to find specific changes may have been the result of the assessments used. Many of the scales employed, such as the measures used to assess cognitive variables, have not been studied on their own and have, as yet, received insufficient psychometric analysis. Zeiss *et al.* discussed their outcomes in terms of self-efficacy theory (Bandura, 1977a), but did not include the assessment of self-efficacy expectations.

In the self-instructional literature, a reexamination of the Kendall and Finch (1978) report was conducted to see if there were treatment-produced changes in children's verbal behavior while performing a task (at pretreatment, posttreatment, and follow-up). The spontaneous verbalizations were recorded and later coded into six categories. It was found that the treated impulsive children increased their total on-task verbal behavior (Kendall & Finch, 1979b). Other researchers have also begun to include cognitive assessments in their treatment evaluations (e.g., Craighead, 1979; Glogower, Fremouw, & McCroskey, 1978), though some studies claiming cognitive changes have used measures typically considered as indices of personality (locus of control) (Spence & Spence, 1980).

One potential problem with employing measures designed to assess cognitive functioning in treatment evaluation has to do with the similarity of the assessment instrument and the treatment content. An example should clarify this concern, which fits many cases. A client participating in a cognitive therapy for depression (e.g., Beck, Rush, Shaw, & Emery, 1979) is taught, among other things, not to distort social situations, not to blame himself or herself for all less-than-perfect events, and not to make himself or herself feel worse through rigid self-evaluation. At posttreatment the client completes a cognitive assessment measure for cognitions associated with depression. After the education of therapy, the client now knows how the therapist wants the measure answered! In a nutshell, we must take care that measures of cognitive change due to treatment are not merely indications that clients have learned how to respond to our questionnaire.

A related concern has to do with increases in self-knowledge that result from therapy and the potential for such self-knowledge to *deflate* treatment effects. Consider, for example, a client participating in a rational–emotive treatment. At the outset, the client is not fully aware of holding any irrational beliefs and may fail to endorse items designed to assess irrationality (see Sutton–Simon, 1981). After several treatment sessions the client becomes increasingly aware of the irrationality of certain personal beliefs and may now, *after therapy*, endorse more of the irrational items. If the treatment is of sufficient duration and effectiveness, one would expect the measure of irrationality to eventually decrease, but measurement of such an outcome can be marred by a deflated pretreatment score due to the client's initial lack of self-awareness.

On Accessibility and Accuracy

Ericsson and Simon (1980) provide an elaborate account of studies of cognition to document their main point: Verbal reports are data. A dissimilar position might be taken by Nisbett and Wilson (1977), whose basic position is that explanations of individuals' behavior based on their own self-reports are often incorrect.

This influential article has triggered a number of comments. For instance, Smith and Miller (1978) and Genest and Turk (1981) contend that while it may not make sense to use subjective cognitive accounts as data in all situations, Nisbett and Wilson do not distinguish between situations where it would and would not make sense. Genest and Turk also argue that Nisbett and Wilson's position refers to the use of verbal self-report in the accessing of the causality of behavior, not in the use of the verbal report as data. One might not be accurate in self-reporting the causes of behavior and yet be quite capable of providing self-reported cognitive data for experimental study. Kendall and Korgeski (1979) argue that accessibility will vary along several dimensions: different types of subjects (e.g., clinical psychologists vs. hysterical clients), different assessment methods (e.g., self-statement inventories vs. thought listing procedures), and the type of cognition being assessed (e.g., transient thoughts vs. belief systems). In certain of these cases cognitive data are readily available, whereas in others such information may not be accurately retrievable.

Two factors may be said to influence the accessibility of cognition: the closeness in time to when the cognitions took place, and the amount of processing of the cognitive data required of the subjects. "Cognitive intransience," as described by Hollon and Kendall (1981), suggests that what a person believes or thinks does not vary as a function of time and place. It is, however, a myth, for temporal and situational influences affect cognition. Recent research into the temporal factor, however, has not provided us with consistent results. Concurrent versus retrospective assessment of cognitions in a test-anxiety situation was investigated by Galassi, Frierson, and Sharer (1980). Subjects of varying levels of test anxiety were asked to complete a checklist of positive and negative thoughts, either during or after an examination. Assessments were gathered at two critical periods: after the test question had been read for the first time, and approximately halfway through the test. The results indicated that the concurrent and retrospective assessment groups did not differ on the number of positive and negative thoughts reported (or on self-reported anxiety). Importantly, concurrent assessment did not affect test performance as measured by final exam grade. In contrast, depressed college students who monitored their mood on an hourly basis provided a less depressed picture than those depressed subjects who provided a retrospective mood summary (Hollon & Evans, 1978). It is, however, entirely possible that the effects of temporal variation in the assessment of cognition vary according to the type of data being assessed. In the case of depression, for instance, it is part of the psychological disorder to exaggerate in the negative direction, so increased time allows for increased distortion: Mood can be said to affect cognitive recall.

Some data are available to support the notion that mood affects recall. Teasdale, Taylor, and Fogarty (1980), for instance, found that extremely unhappy memories were significantly more likely to be recalled while subjects were in a depressed mood than an elated mood. Correspondingly, extremely happy memories were significantly more likely to be retrieved in the elated mood than the depressed mood. As the authors conclude, there appears to be an effect of mood state on the accessibility of different types of cognition (see also Teasdale & Fogarty, 1979).

The amount of cognitive processing required of subjects has been shown to affect verbal reports (see Ericsson & Simon, 1980). These authors conclude that verbalizing information affects cognitive processing only if subjects are required to verbalize information that would not otherwise be attended to. Verbal reports are likely to be valuable data if they require subjects to remember mental events, but less valuable if subjects are asked to make inferences about their mental processes.

One additional assessment topic appears to be emerging as an issue for the future: measurement consistency/terminological clarity in the assessment of attributions. While there are proposed definitions, there is no single, widely accepted measure nor single, widely accepted procedure for assessment. By way of illustration, attributions have been assessed in several different ways (see Krantz & Hammen, 1979; Nasby, Hayden, & De Paulo, 1980; Seligman, Abramson, Semmel, & von Baeyer, 1979; Metalsky & Abramson, 1981); and while the methods of assessment appear to be tapping a similar construct, different terminologies are employed (e.g., Jackson & Larrance, 1979). One person speaks of attributions as disambiguations of the causes of specific behavior while another addresses attributional variance as trait variance. Moreover, some betray an important temporal distinction by speaking of attributions as expectancies for future behavioral outcomes (e.g., expectancies occur before behavioral events, attributions after; Kendall & Braswell, 1982).

ASSESSMENTS WITH CHILDREN

Efforts within the area of behavioral assessment of children have been rewarding. The field has grown rapidly and many clinical settings actively employ behavioral assessment procedures. A new book by

Mash and Terdal (1981) evidences the breadth of application of behavioral assessment with children. Space restrictions limit our review to a few topics particularly popular in the recent past (see also Chapter 7).

Anxiety

An innovative application of behavioral observations was provided in a study of distress in children with cancer undergoing anxiety-provoking medical procedures. Katz, Kellerman, and Siegel (1980) worked with a sample of 115 children with cancer who were scheduled to undergo bone marrow aspiration (BMA). The authors developed a list of the behaviors thought to reflect anxiety among children in this situation and taught observers to independently observe and record the incidences of the target behaviors. To gain additional specificity with respect to time, Katz *et al.* (1980) divided the BMA procedure into four phases: two anticipatory phases, the actual procedure, and a postprocedure rest phase. Observers recorded the occurrence of the target behaviors during each specific phase. Acceptable levels of reliability (both percentage agreement and interscorer correlations) were reported for the full list of behaviors, but the authors report shortening the list by eliminating behaviors for various reasons (e.g., behaviors that never or only rarely occurred, behaviors that did not correlate significantly with other behaviors, or behaviors that correlated negatively with high-anxious items). The result is a 13-behavior list including items such as cry (tears in eyes or on face), cling (physically holds on to parent/nurse), scream (no tears, raises voice, verbal or nonverbal), refusal position (does not follow instructions with regard to body placement on treatment table), muscular rigidity (any of following behaviors: clenched fists, white knuckles, gritted teeth, clenched jaw, etc.), and requests termination (verbally asks/pleads that procedure be stopped).

Interesting age differences in the expression of anxiety were found to be associated with stressful medical procedures. Younger children were consistently more anxious than older children, as measured by the observational system. Moreover, younger children tended to exhibit a greater variety of anxious behaviors than older children. The youngest children expressed anxiety by crying, screaming, and needing restraint, whereas the oldest group of children expressed anxiety via muscular rigidity and verbal expressions of pain. As the authors note, there seems to be a move toward less diffuse protest and activity and greater emphasis on verbal expression and increased muscle tension. Gender effects, with females displaying greater anxiety than males, were also reported.

Katz *et al.* (1980) recognized that their subjects had had different amounts of experience with the medical procedure, and so they examined the possibility of there having been habituation over time. However, the number of prior experiences and the time since the last BMA were not correlated with nurses' ratings of anxiety. Repeated observations of 26 children for two or more occasions also showed no significant pattern of reduction. The authors acknowledge this lack of habituation, and we hasten to add that it speaks strongly for the need for some form of psychological preparation for the stressful nature of the medical procedure.

The complete list of behaviors that were observed in the Katz *et al.* study contain several akin to those observed by Melamed and her colleagues in studies of children's anxiety in dental situations (e.g., Melamed & Siegel, 1975; Melamed, Yurcheson, Fleece, Hutcherson, & Hawes, 1978). They are also fairly consistent with the behaviors that were rated for quality of adjustment among adults undergoing stressful dental (e.g., Auerbach, Kendall, Cuttler, & Levitt, 1976) and medical (e.g., Kendall *et al.*, 1979) procedures. With the rapid increase in the application of behavioral procedures in medical contexts, the Katz *et al.* observations provide a valuable system for quantifying children's anxiety at the behavioral level. Importantly, these observations can be valuable dependent variables in the study of the effectiveness of psychological preparations for stressful medical procedures (see also Kendall & Watson, 1981).

The assessment of anxiety among emotionally disturbed children using self-report inventories (e.g., Children's Manifest Anxiety Scale [CMAS]—Castaneda, McCandless, & Palermo, 1956; State–Trait Anxiety Inventory for Children [STAIC]—Spielberger, 1973) has produced a somewhat enigmatic literature (see discussion in Finch & Kendall, 1979). Specifically, the results of various manipulations seem to have differing effects depending on the self-report measure employed. Moreover, some failure manipulations which should affect state anxiety (while trait anxiety remains relatively stable) have produced changes in trait anxiety (Finch, Kendall, Montgomery, & Morris, 1975). A reasonable conclusion seems to be that self-reports of children's moods, particularly of emotionally disturbed children, do not result in consistent outcomes. One possibility is that the measures are less than adequate.

Reynolds and Richmond (1978) recognized several potential weaknesses of the CMAS (e.g., item difficulty for children, length of administration time, limited range of items) and undertook a revision. The "What I Think and Feel" scale was the result of their efforts. The scale contains 28 anxiety items and 9 lie items (like the CMAS, the revision has a lie scale). In a subsequent study, Reynolds (1980) reports that the revised CMAS correlated .85 with the trait portion of the STAIC, but did not correlate significantly with the state portion. While these data are evidence of concurrent validity, additional validational efforts are required. The importance of situational variance in the assessment of anxiety, which has been recognized among adult anxiety researchers, will also need to be considered.

Depression

In terms of sheer number of studies, it can be said that depression has captured the interest of behavioral and cognitive–behavioral researchers. Depression in children has also been a topic of recent inquiry (Craighead, in press). However, the extension of the interest in depression to the study of depression in children has been hampered by the lack of an acceptable index. What constitutes depression in children? Can it even be said to exist? Answers to these and related questions are not currently experiencing unanimous agreement (see Lefkowitz & Burton, 1978).

Even the existence of depression in children does not appear to be confirmed. Nevertheless, nonexperimental data are cited by some to support the notion of "masked depression." That is, depression in the child exists, but the symptoms are expressed in depressive equivalents such as hyperactivity, aggression, psychosomatic problems, etc. Needless to say, this is a far cry from the behavioral perspective, and the likelihood of the notion of masked depression being endorsed by behaviorists can be dismissed summarily. Still others argue that while depression may exist in children, the behaviors or symptoms associated with the problem are ephemeral, transient, developmental changes (Lefkowitz & Burton, 1978). The answers to numerous basic questions continue to elude us.

Accordingly, it is predicted that studies of childhood depression will show a marked increase in the upcoming years. But while the research efforts will increase, the problem of how to measure childhood depression remains. An overview of recent publications dealing with this topic illustrates the variability in its assessment.

Given the popularity of the Beck Depression Inventory, one might suspect that a children's version would receive unanimous support as an index of depression in children. Though such an instrument exists (Kovacs & Beck, 1977) a consensus regarding its validity has not yet been reached. The Children's Depression Inventory (CDI—Kovacs & Beck, 1977) is a forced-choice self-report inventory. It has been used in several recent projects (e.g., Lefkowitz & Tesiny, 1980; Leon, Kendall, & Garber, 1980), but the reader should be aware that it has been modified in different ways by several of its users.

If self-report has not received wide acceptance, perhaps parent report is the answer. The Personality Inventory for Children (PIC) is an MMPI-type instrument completed by parents which is applicable to the study of children. The PIC (Wirt, Lachar, Klinedinst, & Seat, 1977) contains, among various clinical scales, a scale to assess depression. The PIC D scale is composed of 46 items that were judged by practicing clinicians, using the definition proposed by the Group for the Advancement of Psychiatry (1966), as indicative of childhood depression. Though the PIC may prove useful in the assessment of childhood depression, it follows a more personality–trait conceptualization than is adhered to by many behaviorists and it may not (for some) be the "instrument of choice."

To date, behavioral observations have not been routinely employed in studies of childhood depression. One is struck by the uncertainty that exists regarding which behaviors to observe, though some related data suggest that behavioral frequency counts may not be sufficient. We refer here to the studies of withdrawn and socially isolated children by Gottman and colleagues (e.g., Gottman, 1977; Gottman, Gonso, & Rasmussen, 1975). Without intending to oversummarize, these authors provide strong evidence that the existence of low rates of interpersonal interaction are insufficient in identifying socially withdrawn children. A child with a low rate of interaction may be a child who has tried to interact, but who has been rejected by peers, rather than one who does not or cannot interact with peers. Sociometric assessments have been employed in studies of socially withdrawn children, and their application in studies of childhood depression deserves attention. The exact nature of the behaviors that one would want to observe in studies of childhood depression remains a topic for future inquiry.

In general, sociometric assessments have been on the increase within behavioral research. For instance, sociometrics have been proposed as a part of the measurement of social competence in children (Foster & Ritchey, 1979) and as an important index of therapeutic effectiveness (Kendall, Pellegrini, & Urbain, 1981). One form of sociometric, the peer nomination procedure, has been proposed as a method for assessing depression in children (Lefkowitz & Tesiny, 1980). These authors developed the Peer Nomination Inventory of Depression (PNID). The PNID consists of 13 depression items, 4 happiness items, and 2 popularity items. For instance, "Who often looks lonely" and "Who doesn't have much fun" are depression items. "Who often smiles" is a happiness item and "Who would you like to sit next to in class" is a popularity item. The peer nomination approach requires children to indicate, from among their peers, who fits a certain category or description. For example, Lefkowitz and Tesiny (1980) asked "Who often looks lonely" and required the children (in class groups) to indicate which child on the class list "best fits the question." Employing 452 boys and 492 girls, the PNID was reported to have acceptable reliability and validity. Content validity was determined by experts' judgments. Concurrent validity was evident in the significant correlations between the PNID and self- and teacher ratings. Also, children with high PNID scores "exhibited depressed intellectual functioning, poor social behavior, and diminished ebullience" (Lefkowitz & Tesiny, 1980, p. 43).

The strength of the peer nomination sociometric approach for the assessment of depression in children is evident in the results reported by Lefkowitz and Tesiny. Their report employed large and representative samples, cross-validation, multiple-method measurement, and estimates of reliability and validity. Interestingly, some of their results using the PNID to assess depression in children correspond with results obtained using the PIC to categorize children as depressed or nondepressed (Leon et al., 1980). In both studies, depressed children perceived control of events as external. Lefkowitz and Tesiny reported a significant correlation between the PNID and an external locus of control (Nowicki & Strickland, 1973) and Leon et al. (1980) reported that depressed children attributed positive events to external causes and negative events to internal causes more than nondepressed children did.

It will first be necessary to come to some agreement about the acceptable methodology for the assessment of depression in children, but with some sense of agreement will come an even greater mandate: the study of the etiology, nature, and treatment of the problem. To what extent is childhood depression like adult depression? What role does developmental variability play in the attempt to capture and describe this disorder? How situation-specific is depression among youngsters? We anticipate a lively discussion surrounding these and related topics.

Other Measures Briefly Noted

Goldfried and D'Zurilla's (1969) behavioral–analytic methodology for the development of assessment scales was adopted and applied by Deluty (1979). Unlike various other children's assessment inventories that are more or less tangentially behavioral, Deluty's Children's Action Tendency Scale (CATS) follows a behavioral model more closely. The behavioral–analytic method was employed in the following manner. First, the questions were selected on the basis of an empirical analysis of the relevant problem situations. Because the CATS is designed to assess aggression, assertion, and submission, situations associated with these types of behavior were elicited from 6- to 12-year-old children. A list of possible responses to each situation was generated as the second part of the scale development. Last, children, teachers, parents, and psychologists evaluated each item, and the responses that discriminated the types of behavior most often were used in forming the questionnaire.

The resulting scale employs a forced-choice format. The number of aggressive, assertive, and submissive alternatives a child chooses constitutes his or her aggressiveness, assertiveness, or submissiveness score. The child's score on each dimension can range from 0 to 26, with the sum of the three scores equaling 39 (due to the forced-choice format). Deluty employed subjects from a parochial school and conducted a replication on children from a public school (public school children were from both open and more traditional classrooms). His results indicate that the CATS subscales correlated significantly with peer and teacher ratings of the subject's interpersonal behavior. The replication with a different sample adds additional supportive evidence. Moreover, clinically hyperaggressive children scored significantly more aggressive and less assertive than did the public school boys from either open or closed classrooms. The CATS has also been used in a study of alternative thinking in aggressive, assertive, and submissive children (Deluty, 1981).

One potentially useful application of the CATS will be in the study of assertion (social skills) in children. This topic remains a hotbed of controversy, and the need for multiple method assessments has been recognized. The CATS might well be an important self-report inventory for inclusion in multiple-method assessments of childhood assertion. Should the evidence dictate, it may also prove useful as an outcome measure in treatment evaluations.

A reinforcement survey schedule for special-needs children, containing both food and nonfood reinforcers, has been shown to have test–retest reliability (Dewhurst & Cautela, 1980). When working with children with restricted verbal skills or with children whose parents are not available, the reinforcement survey can help identify the items most likely to have the desired reinforcement effect upon behavior. The lists of reinforcers are somewhat predictable (e.g., foods such as milk shakes, pudding, french fries, and nonfoods such as gym, coloring, a bicycle), but having the list readily available does reduce the likelihood that individual options are accidentally omitted. In order to increase the utility of the survey, Dewhurst and Cautela (1980) provide a breakdown of the ordering of the reinforcers by grade, but the sample is restricted geographically so that the hierarchy has obvious biases (e.g., in Minnesota, as opposed to San Diego, hockey tickets might outrank dinner with Paul McCartney).

Specific fear assessment in children has not paralleled the developments seen with adult instruments. Fear Survey Schedules (FSS) have been employed in behavior therapy for some time, but the scales include both items and vocabulary not appropriate for children. A Children's Fear Survey Schedule was developed and studied by Ryall and Dietiker (1979). These authors sampled 177 kindergarten through sixth-grade children and composed a list of the children's responses to questions about common fears (e.g., loud noises, bugs, fire, the dark, bad dreams). The authors found that the test showed a one-week test–retest reliability of .85 and that it discriminated between clinic (children with anxiety as the presenting symptom) and nonclinic children matched for sex, age, and grade. While such a scale may prove useful for identifying and ordering the stimuli for which children report fear, we are still left with an instrument based entirely on self-report. The scale is somewhat more behavioral than other self-report inventories due to its recognition of specific feared stimuli (specific situations), but it has not gotten away from the dilemma of relying on children's own knowledge and awareness of the emotional state of fear, their understanding of when they experience it, and their self-report of such conditions.

METHODOLOGY

Single-Subject Methodologies

As a methodology that has direct connections with operant psychology and direct application within behavior therapy, single-subject procedures are an important component of what has been labeled as behavior therapy. However, while the methods enjoyed an early burst of interest and application (e.g., Hersen & Barlow, 1976; Kratochwill, 1978) and continue to merit discussion as a means of outcome evaluation (Kazdin & Wilson, 1978; Kendall & Nay, 1979), there are problems that continue to trouble the thoughtful behavior therapist. Single-subject designs have been reviewed in earlier volumes of the *Annual Review* (see Franks & Wilson, 1977), so the present discussion will be limited to two current articles that raise the critical issues of (1) the reliability of visual analysis and (2) the methods for considering generalization.

DeProspero and Cohen (1979) addressed a fundamental issue of single-subject analysis: Is there consistency across researchers and research evaluators in the visual analysis of intrasubject data? I can recall, as perhaps many of us can, reviewing an article for publication where the changes in the rates of behavior were judged by the author(s) to indicate meaningful changes, and where it was my opinion that the changes were not meaningful. But how would I be able to determine who was correct? Were there statistical tests that I could conduct (Kazdin, 1976)?

DeProspero and Cohen (1979) sent 36 different ABAB reversal figures to 250 reviewers of behavioral journals. Each participant was asked to evalute each figure in terms of "experimental control" by providing a rating on a 100-point scale. The figures included variation in each of four areas thought to affect visual analysis: pattern of mean shift across phases, degree of mean shift across phases, variation within phases, and trends within the data. The mean rating for each of the 36 graphs was examined in an appropriate analysis of variance, and the results indicated that pattern and degree of mean shift were the significant factors accounting for the differences in ratings of demonstrated experimental control. The most crucial finding, and one that has been reported by others (Jones, Weinrott, & Vaught, 1978), was that the judges were not particularly reliable. The median interjudge agreement was a modest .61. As DeProspero and Cohen note, except for those figures where the pattern of results were ideal, there was a wide range of ratings for almost every figure. Quoting from DeProspero and Cohen's discussion, "The above variability of opinions suggests that a behavioral researcher seeking corroboration on the interpretation of results would not be likely to get the same answer twice" (p. 578). While the problem may not be as much of a concern for clear-cut instances of experimental control, it is a concern when decisions about the nature of effects are less clear. The reader interested in the discussion of interrupted time-series analysis (ITSA) as an approach to understanding time-series data is referred to an article by Hartmann, Gottman, Jones, Gardner, Kazdin, and Vaught (1980) employing a question-and-answer format.

Assessing generalization using single-subject methodologies was examined in an article by Kendall (1981b). Essentially, a caution raised by Hartmann and Atkinson (1973) has resurfaced. When single-subject designs show a desired change in behavior from, for example, phase A to phase B, and subsequently return to pretreatment levels at the return to baseline (the second phase A), is this state of affairs an instance of treatment control (evidenced by the reversal) or an example of the lack of treatment generalization (also evident in the reversal)? Hartmann and Atkinson aptly referred to this as "having your cake and eating it too." Kendall's paper isolates response generalization and stimulus generalization and examines four single-subject designs to determine whether a researcher can provide single-subject evidence of generalization without contradicting evidence of "experimental control." The proposed methodology involves the use of probes, applied following the demonstration of treatment effects. Variations in the treatment (e.g., new therapist, different setting) are imposed on the time series, and the rates of behavior are examined to see what variations affect the rate. When successive variations in the treatment do not alter the rate, evidence is said to exist for generalization. The methodology is most efficient in multiple-baseline-across-behaviors designs. It should be kept in mind, however, that for most single-subject designs, evidence for generalization often contradicts evidence for "experimental control."

Group Comparison Methodologies

The use of group comparison methodologies and their associated factorial designs continues to be the strategy of choice for most types of therapeutic evaluation. A recent paper by McLean (1980) concerning the impact of the newly required informed consent procedures and the increase in the appearance of "normative comparisons" as part of studies of treatment outcome are two topics we will discuss.

Behavior therapy has witnessed a call for outcomes studies employing both real clients and appropriate control groups. With the fear that psychotherapy researchers would compromise client well-being came standards for informed consent. Before a client is assigned to a treatment (randomly, rather than based on clinical judgment), the client is to be informed of the possible treatment alternatives. As McLean (1980) pointed out, many investigators thought that such a disclosure might lead clients to conclude that the investigator's research interests override his or her clinical interests. During the recruitment of clients for a treatment comparison study, changes occurred in the code of ethics regarding informed consent. McLean was then able to make comparisons of subjects who were informed versus uninformed that their assignment to treatment conditions was random. He reported that knowledge of random assignment did not affect a subject's willingness to participate. This finding is important, for we will all be employing informed consent and it is comforting to know that it does not appear to be affecting external validity. An ancillary point, McLean should be commended for taking advantage of such serendipitous data.

The data used to evaluate the effectiveness of clinical intervention procedures are submitted to statistical tests of significance. Group averages are compared. An outcome is said to be significant, and the treatment efficacious, if the magnitude of the mean treatment difference is beyond that which could have occurred by chance alone. This process provides evidence of statistical significance, but what about clinical significance? Although there have been examples in the extant literature (e.g., Braud, 1978; Meichenbaum, Gilmore, & Fedoravicius, 1971; Patterson, 1974), recent treatment outcome studies appear to have shown more concern with "normative comparisons." One example from each of the adult and child literatures will suffice at this time.

In a study of the effects of imagery elaboration and self-efficacy in the covert modeling treatment of unassertive behavior, Kazdin (1979b) gathered data on subjects who did not consider themselves unassertive and compared the treated subjects to the range of scores of these individuals. The assessments of the normative sample took place at the time of the postassessment of the treated clients. The normative sample provided the data against which Kazdin compared his treated clients. The normative comparison supported the effectiveness of the treatment.

In an examination of the effectiveness of a cognitive–behavioral treatment for non-self-controlled children, Kendall & Wilcox (1980) employed normative comparisons on multiple measures. A random sample of children was rated by their classroom teachers, using the same scales used for treatment evaluation, and these children completed the same battery of tests that the treated children completed at pretreatment. The distribution of scores of the random sample (plus and minus one standard deviation from the mean) were then used as normative comparisons to aid in the evaluation of treatment effects.

In both of these examples assessment data on nondistressed subjects were gathered using the same measure(s) that were employed in treatment evaluation. The range of these scores was then used to determine if the treated clients were brought back to within reasonable limits as defined by the normative group. The use of normative comparisons makes available to the researcher information that can lead to statements about clinical significance. The inclusion of normative comparisons is a methodological step in the proper direction. Moreover, as noted in Volume 7 of this series (Franks & Wilson, 1980), norms can be used to help determine what behaviors require treatment (see also Hawkins, 1979).

Assessment Methodology

While it is fair to say that behavioral assessment has for some time recognized the merits of multimethod assessment, it is equally fair to point out that, to date, behavioral assessors have not employed multiple-method assessments to a sufficient degree. The data reported by Bornstein *et al.* (1980), mentioned briefly at the outset of this chapter, bear on this concern. These authors examined a 50% sample of the experimental studies in four major behavioral journals (*Behavior Therapy*, *Behaviour Research and Therapy*, *Journal of Behavior Therapy and Experimental Psychiatry*, and *Journal of Applied Behavior Analysis*). Assessment methods were categorized (after Cone, 1978) as interview, self-report, rating by other, self-observation, analogue role play, analogue free behavior, naturalistic role play, and naturalistic free behavior (see also Franks & Wilson, 1980). Of the 951 articles surveyed, the majority used only *one* assessment method (61%). Only 25% of the papers included reports with two assessment methods, and only 10% employed three methods.

Why should one be concerned with multiple-method assessment? The answer is quite simple. Data can be more influenced by the method used to collect them than by variations in the topic being assessed. Unless measured via different procedures, one cannot isolate and remove from the total variability that which is due to method variance. The literature on the assessment of anxiety illustrates the point nicely. Anxiety, it is generally argued, has a three-part expression: behavior, cognition, and physiology. Inconsistencies both within and across studies can occur when different researchers assess different components of anxiety. This triple response system is held by most contemporary behaviorists (Nelson & Hayes, 1979a, 1979b) and thus, regardless of the specific topic of interest, behavioral assessment includes the measurement of overt motor behavior, physiological–emotional behavior, and cognitive–verbal behavior. With the expansion of the behavioral assessment arena, we hope to see additional efforts directed toward the application of multiple-method assessment strategies.

Since it is our contention that behavioral assessment plays a most crucial role in studies of the outcome of behavior therapy (and other forms of therapy), the direct implications of multimethod procedures for treatment outcome research deserve mention. For example, subject behavior can be assessed via direct observation in naturalistic settings or in analogue situations. A subject's behavior on different tasks can provide evidence of performance improvements, which is especially relevant when the tasks have already been shown to identify deficits in individuals with the problem being treated. Ratings of improvement, preferably from raters who are blind (though knowledgeable about subtle behavioral differences), are essential. Therapist ratings are also useful. Last, self-report constitutes an important source of outcome data (Hersen, 1978). With such an employment of multiple-method assessment devices, the outcome evaluator avails himself or herself of the optimal data for studying the effects of therapy.

3

FEAR REDUCTION METHODS
AND THE TREATMENT
OF ANXIETY DISORDERS

G. TERENCE WILSON

There is no more active area of theorizing, research, and clinical application in behavior therapy than the investigation and treatment of the anxiety disorders. The past two years bear ample testimony to this fact. Among the more notable developments that have taken place during this short period are the following: the publication of major texts on the nature and treatment of phobic and obsessive–compulsive disorders (Marks, 1981; Mavissakalian & Barlow, 1981; Rachman & Hodgson, 1980); further refinement and critical testing of theoretical viewpoints that depart from traditional conditioning explanations of fear reduction methods such as systematic desensitization and flooding (Bandura, Adams, Hardy, & Howells, 1980; Lang, 1979; Rachman, 1980); the reports of original therapy outcome research on different treatment techniques, their comparative efficacy, and the generalizability and durability of their effects (Munby & Johnston, 1980); and a major conference, sponsored by the National Institute of Mental Health, at which 20 leading clinical investigators working in this general area were asked to review the current status of the field and to make specific recommendations about the future directions of research (Barlow & Wolfe, 1981).

Any serious attempt to cover all of the above-mentioned developments, even briefly, would take something on the order of a book itself. Accordingly, the remainder of this chapter focuses selectively on some of the more significant or influential trends over the last two years.

PHOBIC DISORDERS

Therapy Outcome Research

LONG-TERM FOLLOW-UPS

A glaring limitation of therapy outcome research has been the absence of appropriate long-term evaluations of treatment effects (Kazdin & Wilson, 1978). With the plaintive query of "Where have all the follow-ups gone?" LaDouceur and Auger (1980) examined studies published in seven journals[1] on behavior therapy for evidence of follow-ups of at least six months. The period surveyed was from 1963 to 1979. The results indicated that only 25% of the studies included six-month follow-up data. In their analysis of the growth of clinical research in behavior therapy, Agras and Berkowitz (1980) looked at the contents of *Behaviour Research and Therapy* and *Behavior Therapy* from 1970 through 1978. The findings showed that the average outcome study used a relatively small number of subjects, included a treatment program of approximately six weeks, and reported a follow-up of only four weeks. If we are to be guided by these surveys of the contents of leading behavioral journals, it is apparent that the disappointing lack of long-term follow-ups in behavior therapy that was noted by Kazdin and Wilson (1978) some years ago, has changed little at all.

In light of this situation, the publication of three sets of data on the long-term effects of the behavioral treatment of agoraphobic disorders is particularly welcome. The most informative of these papers is Munby and Johnston's (1980) follow-up of the agoraphobic patients who had been treated by the clinical research group at Oxford University in England. More specifically, the patients were those described in previously published studies by this group, namely, Gelder, Bancroft, Gath, Johnston, Mathews, and Shaw (1973), Mathews, Johnston, Lancashire, Munby, Shaw, and Gelder (1976), and Mathews, Teasdale, Munby, Johnston, and Shaw (1977). (Two of these papers, by Gelder *et al.* and Mathews, Teasdale *et al.*, were reprinted in Vols. 3 and 6, respectively, of this series.) Of the 66 patients treated in these three studies, 95% were interviewed by a psychiatric research worker five to nine years later. Follow-up measures, repeating those used in the original studies, were compared with those obtained prior to treatment and six months after treatment ended. On most measures of agoraphobia the patients

---

1. *Behaviour Research and Therapy, Journal of Applied Behavior Analysis, Journal of Consulting and Clinical Psychology, Journal of Behavior Therapy and Experimental Psychiatry, Behavior Therapy, Behavior Modification,* and *Cognitive Therapy and Research.*

were much better at follow-up than before treatment. The assessor's ratings suggested that there had been little change in the patient's agoraphobia since six months after treatment. Some of the patients' self-ratings showed evidence of a slight improvement over this period. No evidence of any symptom substitution was found. The patients who showed the greatest reduction in agoraphobia were, at follow-up, among the least anxious and depressed. With understated tone, Munby and Johnston concluded that "the widespread acceptance of the behavioral treatment of agoraphobia appears to be justified" (1980, p. 425).

These results are encouraging in view of the epidemiological findings of Agras, Chapin, and Oliveau (1972). They found that among adults with phobias, of those who had not sought nor obtained any treatment during a five-year period, only 43% showed any improvement. Thirty-three percent became worse during this period. Evidence on the natural history of agoraphobia and the pattern of correlations between assessments at the time of therapy and at follow-up, Munby and Johnston suggest, indicate that the behavioral treatment was responsible for the change:

> If the treatment was not a determinant of the patients' current state, then one would expect that the correlations between current state and measures taken before treatment and shortly after treatment would be approximately the same. This was not the case. Behavior six months after treatment was a very much better predictor of current behavior than was behavior immediately before treatment. Since the difference in time between the two earlier measures is trivial compared with the length of the follow-up period, this strongly suggests that the treatments led to a change in the patients' behavior and that this change has persisted. (Munby & Johnston, 1980, p. 426)

Nevertheless, caution must be exercised in interpreting Munby and Johnston's results, as they themselves are quick to point out. First, no fewer than 9 of the 12 patients from the Gelder et al. (1973) study, 21 of the 35 from the Mathews et al. (1976) study, and 1 of the 12 from the Mathews et al. (1977) study received "further treatment in addition to consultations with their general practitioners" over the course of the follow-up. Excluding these patients from the data did nothing to change the outcome, however. Second, at the end of the follow-up period, 8 of the patients from the Gelder et al. study, 25 from the first Mathews et al. study, and 4 from the second Mathews et al. study were receiving unspecified psychotropic drugs.

It is most important to assess patients' functioning during a lengthy follow-up period. Munby and Johnston asked all these patients if they had experienced a relapse, defined as a setback of at least one month, after the end of behavioral treatment. Six of the patients from the Gelder *et al.* study and 15 of their counterparts from the Mathews *et al.* (1976) study reported such a relapse. Intriguingly, none of the patients from the third study (Mathews *et al.*, 1977) reported severe relapse. Although the small number (12) of patients in this study militates against making too much of these data, the finding that they needed less additional therapy and experienced substantially fewer relapses should not go unnoticed. It must be remembered that these patients received an innovative home-based treatment program designed to teach them and their spouses to cope with the agoraphobic disorder with a minimum amount of professional assistance. The promising nature of this home-based treatment is underscored by the recent replication of its findings by Jannoun, Munby, Catalan, and Gelder (1980) discussed below.

In Holland, Emmelkamp and Kuipers (1979) followed up 70 outpatient agoraphobics out of a sample of 81 patients who had received exposure treatment four years previously. Unlike the most reliable procedure used by Munby and Johnston, all information in this study was obtained from questionnaires mailed to patients. The overall findings showed that therapeutic progress at posttreatment had been maintained and on some measures additional improvement occurred. At follow-up, 75% of the patients showed improvement on the main phobia. A reduction in depression (as measured by the Zung Self-Rating Scale) was evident and no new neurotic disturbances developed.

In the third of the long-term follow-ups, McPherson, Brougham, and McLaren (1980), in Scotland, conducted a three-to-six-year (mean = 4.3 years) follow-up of 56 agoraphobic patients who had shown improvment during initial treatment. Information was obtained from questionnaries mailed to patients. The results are consistent with those of the Munby and Johnston and Emmelkamp and Kuipers studies. To quote the authors, "The results of the present follow-up are compatible with the hypothesis that improvement in agoraphobic patients, brought about by behavioral treatment, is maintained over at least 4 years, with no evidence of significant deterioration or of the emergence of new symptoms. This is true of improvement in the main, agoraphobic symptoms, and also in other phobic symptoms, depression and in the patients' social relationships and effectiveness at work" (McPherson *et al.*, 1980, p. 152).

Measurement Problems. Careful analysis of these follow-up studies cannot overlook the fact that the findings are based on clinical ratings of outcome. The limitations of these clinical ratings have been detailed elsewhere (e.g., Kazdin & Wilson, 1978; Rachman & Hodgson,

1980). Changes of one or two points on a five- or nine-point rating scale that assesses phobic anxiety and avoidance on different activities (e.g., a supermarket, public transportation, a busy street, etc.) provide a very limited view of therapeutic progress irrespective of the high reliability among assessors using these scales. Emmelkamp and Kuipers even combined ratings of phobic fear and avoidance, two phenomena that should be separated for both theoretical and clinical reasons. Moreover, the validity of these scales have yet to be firmly established. Williams and Rappoport (1980) found that the nine-point fear questionnaire typically used in many of these studies was only modestly correlated with objective behavioral assessment of agoraphobics' functioning. The rating tended to overestimate subjects' degree of improvement compared to the behavioral test, and the authors concluded that such measures may at times overestimate the value of weak treatments while obscuring real differences in effectiveness existing between treatment methods.

Ideally, evaluation of the treatment of phobic disorders would include multiple objective and subjective measures of outcome, using the triple-response-system framework to analyze changes in fear and avoidance, and including measures of generalized change (e.g., social functioning, marital satisfaction, and so forth) (Rachman & Wilson, 1980). The attempts to use behavioral measures of outcome in the treatment of agoraphobics, and the inherent problems, are discussed by Wilson (1982). Suffice it to note here that a major difficulty is that behavioral measures typically focus on one particular aspect of agoraphobics' functioning. For example, Williams and Rappoport only assessed their subjects' actual driving behavior. The degree to which changes were produced across other areas of functioning is unclear. In their research program, Emmelkamp and his colleagues employed the following measure of behavioral change. The patient had to walk along a certain route from the hospital towards the center of town. He was instructed to stay outside until he began to feel uncomfortable or tense, then he had to come back straightaway. The duration of time spent outside by the patient was measured by the therapist. The maximum time was set at 100 minutes in connection with the calculations to be made. While yielding statistically significant differences, therapists might question the clinical significance of an overall difference between two treatment groups of roughly 30 minutes' time spent walking outside the hospital. In these, as in other studies, one is left to form an overall impression of therapeutic change from the clinical ratings.

In another major research program on the behavioral pharmacological treatment of agoraphobic disorders, Zitrin (1981) and her associates attempted to obtain behavioral measures of their patients' performance, but gave up, claiming that such a measure "proved to be highly unreliable because the patients, in order to please the examiner, put pressure on themselves to do things that they had not done for long periods of time. For example, a patient who had not been in an elevator for years, when taken by the evaluator before treatment to an elevator and asked to go in, could comply" (p. 150). Far from dismissing such a finding as evidence of "unreliability," the contemporary behavioral researcher, guided by the triple-response-system framework, would attach considerable significance to this result. It raises questions about the nature of patients' phobic distress and leaves one to guess at the pattern of results that might have emerged if behavioral measures were gathered consistently.

GENERALIZED TREATMENT EFFECTS:

MARITAL SATISFACTION AND THERAPY OUTCOME

There is now broad agreement that evaluation of therapy outcome must include measures of generalized functioning in addition to specific assessment of patients' fear and avoidance. The findings from the Munby and Johnston (1980), Emmelkamp and Kuipers (1979), and McPherson et al. (1980) long-term follow-up studies are consistent with the results of numerous other investigations showing that positive generalized effects are often obtained and that symptom substitution is the psychoanalytically inspired red herring that it has always been. An apparent exception to this pattern of results was a much-publicized study by Hafner (1976). To examine marital satisfaction in relation to therapy outcome, Hafner interviewed spouses of a large group of agoraphobics and obtained ratings of satisfaction with spouse as well as overall ratings of marital adjustment. After a one-year follow-up, he concluded that a group of subjects with the "poorest" marriages also demonstrated the most symptom reemergence, with a significant number of them becoming worse. Hafner's conclusion was disputed in a previous volume in this series (Franks & Wilson, 1977). More recently, Marks (1981) points out that Hafner based his observations on data from a study by Hafner and Marks (1976), which Marks reexamines. According to Marks, "The evidence is clearly that greatest improvement in phobias was associated with greatest improvement to other areas of function, including marital satisfaction. This result is the opposite of that to be expected from the symptom substitution model or from general systems theory. Patients with poor marriages to start with improved least in all areas" (1981, p. 238).

In another uncontrolled study of agoraphobic women and their husbands, Milton and Hafner (1979) divided 14 couples into those who reported marital satisfaction and those who expressed some dissatisfaction on the basis of a median split on a questionnaire of marital adjustment. A six-month follow-up of these couples after an intensive *in vivo* flooding treatment showed no change in the marital dissatisfaction scores of the dissatisfied group and an improvement in the agoraphobics' ratings of marital and sexual adjustment in the maritally satisfied group. The fears of both groups decreased after treatment, but the maritally dissatisfied group did not improve any more by the six-month follow-up. The maritally satisfied spouses also improved on the psychoneurotic scales, whereas the dissatisfied group did not. Extrapunitiveness and hostility fell for the maritally dissatisfied group, with no significant rise for either group. These data suggest that maritally dissatisfied couples do not continue to improve following therapy. But these data cannot be used to provide support for the allegations of symptom substitution and negative therapy effects.

In the first controlled study of its kind, Cobb, McDonald, Marks, and Stern (1980) assigned phobic obsessional patients and their spouses to one of two treatment groups: (1) *in vivo* exposure directed at reducing the phobias and rituals; and (2) marital therapy designed to improve the relationship. In the *in vivo* exposure treatment no attention was focused on marital issues although the spouses were asked to help the patients comply with their exposure homework assignments. Spouses acted as cotherapists in both conditions, however, to control for simple participation in treatment. All couples had experienced chronic marital dissatisfaction. After a 12-week follow-up all couples received the alternative therapy in another of this research group's well-known crossover designs. The results showed that the exposure treatment not only produced the expected reduction in phobic and obsessional complaints, but also an improvement in the couples' marital relationships. In contrast, the marital therapy improved couples' marital relationships but had little effect on phobias and obsessions.

These findings add to the confidence we can place in exposure treatment of agoraphobics. In the majority of cases this form of treatment appears to have consistently positive effects on measures of specific phobic behavior and related problems. Of course, there will be exceptions, and in clinical practice the therapist will necessarily be guided by assessment of the particular needs of individual clients. For example, a previous clinical report from the same research group at the University of London's Institute of Psychiatry illustrated one such instance in which marital therapy successfully eliminated phobic problems (Stern & Marks, 1973, reprinted in Franks & Wilson, 1975).

In another study that bears importantly on the relationship between marital functioning and response to behavioral treatment, by Barlow, Mavissakalian, and Hay (1981), six agoraphobic women and their husbands took part in a group therapy program consisting of *in vivo* exposure, covert rehearsal of coping, and cognitive restructuring. The husbands acted as cotherapists and both spouses independently completed ratings of marital satisfaction and severity of the phobic complaints throughout the course of treatment and follow-up. The ratings of phobias were the same as those used by Marks and his associates, combining fear and avoidance, and based on a nine-point scale. This rating was completed for each of the 10 items in each patient's hierarchy of phobic situations. Marital satisfaction was assessed using the Marital Happiness Scale (Azrin, Naster, & Jones, 1973).

The results of this informative study could be grouped into two distinctive patterns. In four of the couples, a parallel relationship was observed between improvement in the phobic disorder and marital satisfaction. In the other two couples (Couples 5 and 6, see below) improvement in the agoraphobic condition was accompanied by less marital satisfaction. In both these latter cases, the husbands reported decreases in marital satisfaction correlated with improvements in their wives' phobic conditions. Significantly, 12-month follow-ups revealed that the wives continued to improve despite the decreases in marital satisfaction. These observations refute the clinically popular but empirically unsubstantiated notion that agoraphobia cannot be treated successfully if the interpersonal context is poor. Several other clinical observations by Barlow *et al.* further indicate that it is unwise to accept prevalent clinical stereotypes about "typical" marital patterns of agoraphobics and necessary to conduct individualized assessments of individual patients:

> Contrary to hypotheses of reinforced dependency on the part of husbands of agoraphobic women . . . the husband in Couple 6 did not seem to enjoy his wife's dependency, but rather was dissatisfied with her behavior in general. The husband in Couple 5, however, did seem to enjoy his wife's dependency, although supportive of her improvement in his own quiet way. The husband in Couple 3 actually verbalized the most distress at his wife's increasing independence by noting that she was now taking over many of the duties that he used to enjoy doing with the children. Nevertheless, he reported he was pleased with her progress and his slight deterioration in marital satisfaction during the first six sessions quickly turned around at posttreatment and at the 12-month follow-up. (1981, p. 255)

RELATIVE EFFICACY OF DIFFERENT TREATMENTS

Cost-Effective and Self-Directed Exposure Methods. The therapeutic potential of Mathews *et al.*'s (1977) home-based treatment program for agoraphobics was referred to earlier in this chapter. In a

controlled outcome study that sought to replicate and extend the findings from that study, Jannoun et al. (1980) randomly assigned 28
agoraphobic women to one of two alternative treatments: (1) programmed practice in entering feared situations; and (2) problem-solving
treatment designed to reduce anxiety by resolving life problems. The
exposure treatment, described more fully by Mathews et al. (1977),
emphasized daily practice with the patient's partner reinforcing her
activities. Separate treatment manuals for both partners detailed the
step-by-step instructions for negotiating the feared situations. In the
problem-solving treatment,

> the patient's instruction booklet describes agoraphobia as the result of
> chronic anxiety and undue sensitivity to stress. As such, agoraphobia can
> be treated by lowering the patient's level of arousal by identifying relevant
> life stresses and finding ways of reducing or resolving them. The patient is
> given step-by-step instructions on how to set problem solving targets and
> how to deal with them. No advice is given about going out more. The
> couple is instructed to discuss life stresses and problems for at least an
> hour each day. The partner is instructed on how to assist the patient in
> solving such problems and how to reinforce her own attempts at doing so.
> (Jannoun et al., 1980, p. 296)

The same two therapists conducted both of the treatments, spending an
average of 3.5 hours with each patient, at her home, in each treatment.
Treatment changes were assessed by patient, therapist, and an independent assessor's ratings on a nine-point scale at posttreatment and at
a six-month follow-up.

Several interesting findings emerged from this study. The main
analysis indicated that the programmed exposure method was generally
superior to the problem-solving method. Mathews et al.'s results were
replicated despite the therapists in this study having even less direct
patient contact than in the previous investigation. Nevertheless, the
problem-solving treatment produced substantial therapeutic benefit,
and in the case of one of the therapists, the treatments were equally
effective. Another potentially significant finding was the tendency of
the patients who had received the problem-solving treatment to continue to improve following after therapy ended. Commenting on their
results, Jannoun et al. have the following to say: "These findings do
not support the hypothesis that systematic practice in entering the
feared situations is an essential part of the treatment of agoraphobia.
Our patients began to go out more following a treatment aimed at
anxiety reduction by solving life problems, even without specific
instructions to do so. It is not clear why this happened" (1980, p. 304).
The significance of this observation is elaborated upon below in the
section on theoretical mechanisms.

Finally, the differential success of the two therapists in this study warrants mentioning. Jannoun *et al.* provided data to indicate that the therapist who was successful with the problem-solving method did not achieve these effects by unwittingly encouraging patients to go out and practice. Rather, it seemed that this therapist was more successful than the other in reducing the patients' general level of anxiety, which led to behavioral improvement. These results, not to mention clinical experience, suggest that some therapists are better than others in achieving specific treatment goals. The importance of the therapist's contribution to effective behavior therapy is discussed in greater detail in Chapter 8. Let it be noted here, however, that the presence of a therapist effect on treatment outcome has been reported by this group of clinical researchers at Oxford University before (Mathews *et al.*, 1976).

Self- as opposed to therapist-guided exposure was the core of the home-based treatments of Mathews *et al.* (1977) and Jannoun *et al.* (1980). In a brief study by McDonald, Sartory, Grey, Cobb, Stern, and Marks (1979), 20 agoraphobics were assigned to either a self-exposure or nonexposure discussion group. Patients in both conditions met with their therapists for 20–30 minutes on each of four occasions over a six-week period. In the *in vivo* exposure treatment therapists planned patients' self-exposure assignments whereas in the control condition they discussed general life difficulties and gave advice for coping with them.

The results of this study indicated that the self-exposure treatment had a modest effect in reducing phobic anxiety and avoidance, although these therapeutic effects were less than those obtained with therapist-guided exposure in other studies by this research group. Patients' self-monitoring records confirmed that those in the self-exposure condition did attempt more activities than their counterparts in the control group. No correlation was found between ratings of family involvement or patients' willingness to work hard and treatment outcome. The superior results obtained by the Oxford group are plausibly attributed to more systematic planning, the use of a detailed manual, limited but possibly crucial therapist involvement in treatment, and the active role of the spouse in the procedure.

The therapist's involvement in guided exposure treatment was also examined in a study by O'Brien and Kelley (1980). Using snake phobic subjects, they compared the efficacy of four *in vivo* practice conditions: a self-directed condition, a predominantly self-directed condition, a predominantly therapist-directed condition, and an exclusively therapist-directed condition. All four treatment conditions resulted in reduced fear on behavioral and self-report measures. The predominantly therapist-directed subjects showed more improvement than subjects in the exclusively self-directed and predominantly self-directed conditions, but not more improvement than subjects in the exclusively therapist-directed condition.

Varying degrees of direct therapist involvement in performance-based exposure treatment for acrophobics were compared in a study by Bourque and LaDouceur (1980). The five treatment groups were as follows: participant modeling, as described by Bandura (1977b), involving maximal therapist contact and guidance; participant modeling without direct therapist contact; modeling-plus-response rehearsal, involving no performance aids except for therapist presence and social reinforcement; therapist-controlled exposure, that is, the former treatment but without prior modeling of the behavior by the therapist; and self-directed exposure, in which the subject was given the rationale behind exposure treatment and told to practice without the therapist ever being present. Treatment effects were assessed using multiple measures including behavioral performance, heart rate, and self-reported fear. The results? All treatments effectively reduced subjects' fear and avoidance of heights, but there were no between-group differences. Although it would be well not to generalize too widely from the treatment of this specific phobic population, the success of the self-directed exposure treatment in equalling the therapeutic effects of more extensive and expensive methods stands out.

Another cost-effective means of treating phobic disorders has been the use of former phobics as "therapists." J. Ross (1980) has described one program that employs former phobics to assist patients (mainly agoraphobics) in carrying out their therapeutic assignments in the course of *in vivo* exposure treatment. A professionally trained therapist is responsible for the overall supervision of the treatment. Controlled evaluations of the efficacy of this variation of *in vivo* exposure therapy, together with formal analyses of cost-effectiveness, seem clearly warranted at this stage.

To conclude this section, with the single exception of the O'Brien and Kelley results with snake phobics, treatments featuring extensive self-directed exposure on the part of clients themselves, aided in some instances by the use of a detailed therapy manual and spouse support or that of a former phobic, have chalked up some noteworthy successes. The limits of these cost-effective methods and the clients for whom they are appropriate need to be established so that informed decisions can then be made about which patients should receive more extensive treatment at the hands of a professional therapist.

Supplementing In Vivo *Exposure Treatment.* Despite the consensus that *in vivo* exposure methods are effective in treating phobic disorders (Mavissakalian & Barlow, 1981; Marks, 1981), it goes without saying that the results often leave something to be desired. In one of the more somber appraisals of overall therapeutic success, Barlow *et al.* (1981) reached the following conclusion:

> Although summary statements are difficult, due to differing methods of assessment and lack of follow-up in some studies, it appears that the dropout rate from exposure *in vivo* treatments ranges between 8 and 40%, with a median of about 22%. Similarly, the improvement rate among those who complete treatment seems to average between 60 and 75% and this is without specifying the degree of improvement. Thus, the number who are unimproved or perhaps worse off, as the result of this procedure, is as high as 40% of those who complete treatment. (p. 246)

In evaluating appraisals of this kind it is important to remember that it is the efficacy of a specific treatment technique (i.e., *in vivo* exposure) that is at issue. In many instances, research requirements militate against individual assesment of each patient's problems as would be standard clinical practice. Such individual assessment, a cardinal feature of clinical behavior therapy, would in all likelihood have led to multifaceted interventions in many cases. *In vivo* exposure would have been supplemented with such diverse strategies as assertion training, behavior rehearsal, marital therapy, self-regulatory procedures, and combined behavioral and pharmacotherapy methods.

The effect of combining marital therapy with *in vivo* exposure was discussed earlier in this chapter (Cobb *et al.*, 1980). Although the addition of marital therapy did little to enhance improvement in that study, alternative forms of marital therapy and attention to other interpersonal issues are likely to play an important role in behavioral treatment of agoraphobia. Another therapeutic method that would appear appropriate to combine with *in vivo* exposure is cognitive restructuring. Williams and Rappoport (1980) compared a therapist-guided exposure treatment with exposure plus cognitive restructuring in the treatment of 20 agoraphobics. The target behavior in this study was the inability of these subjects to drive alone. All subjects received a performance-based treatment in which the therapist accompanied them while they attempted to drive increasingly greater distances. The 10 subjects who received cognitive restructuring were given the typical rationale that goes with this method together with intensive practice in how to alter their maladaptive thoughts under actual driving conditions. As Williams and Rappoport describe this treatment, the cognitive strategies the subjects were taught fell into five classes: attending to nonthreatening cues; distraction techniques; more benign relabeling of perceived arousal; replacing negative expectations with more positive anticipation; and task-relevant self-instructions à la Meichenbaum's (1977a) approach. A welcome feature of this methodologically sophisticated study was the direct assessment of the extent to which subjects in the cognitive condition complied with the therapist's instructions to use specific cognitive strategies during behavioral performance. Analysis of these data showed that subjects in the combined cognitive–behavioral condition used cognitive coping strategies significantly more than their counterparts in the exposure-alone group. In short, Williams and Rappoport established the integrity of their independent variable, a rarely achieved goal but a nonetheless critical precondition for comparative outcome research.

The results of this study provide no comfort for those who emphasize the importance of cognitive treatment strategies. There were no differences between the two treatments across multiple measures of self-reported anxiety and behavioral performance although both methods produced improvement in subjects' functioning. These results, calling into question as they do the value of cognitive methods in the treatment of phobic disorders, are consistent with other negative findings in this regard (Biran & Wilson, 1981; Biran, Augusto, & Wilson, 1981; Emmelkamp, Kuipers, & Eggeraat, 1978).

Cognitive restructuring treatment was also found to be essentially ineffective in a study by Woodward and Jones (1980). This study is of importance not only because of the treatment comparisons it entailed but also because the subjects had been diagnosed as suffering from anxiety neuroses in the absence of any specific phobia symptoms. Overwhelmingly, the evidence on behavioral treatment of anxiety disorders is based on studies of simple phobics and agoraphobics (Wilson, 1982). Controlled evaluations of anxiety neuroses are a rarity, and Marks (1981) has asserted that this is one area in which behavior therapy cannot be said to be the recommended treatment. Four treatment groups were compared: (1) cognitive restructuring consisting of elements of rational–emotive therapy and Meichenbaum's self-instrucional training; (2) modified systematic desensitization with the emphasis on coping rather than mastery imagery; (3) a combination of (1) and (2), referred to as cognitive-behavior modification; and (4) no-treatment control. Woodward and Jones found that the combined group was significantly more successful than any of the other groups in reducing anxiety. Cognitive restructuring alone produced no noticeable improvement on any of the dependent measures. Commenting on this apparent ineffectiveness of their cognitive restructuring method, the authors stated that it

> may reflect many factors, but the choice of subject group seems particularly important. General anxiety patients are "difficult customers," not often used as subjects in studies of treatment efficacy. They display a high level

of physiological arousal, together with rather nebulous symptomatology. Perhaps this experiment has in fact demonstrated that a multidimensional approach to treatment, for example, cognitive behavior modification, is more likely to succeed with this type of patient than treatments comprising one element only, as does cognitive restructuring. (Woodward & Jones, 1980, p. 407)

(See also Emmelkamp, van der Helm, van Zanten, & Plochg's [1980] failure to find any incremental value for cognitive restructuring methods in the treatment of obsessive–compulsive disorders as discussed below.)

Taken at face value, some of the most persuasive evidence for the efficacy of using pharmacotherapy in the treatment of agoraphobics comes from the research of Zitrin (1981) and her colleagues. In the first of two studies, they compared imipramine plus systematic desensitization, imipramine plus supportive psychotherapy, and systematic desensitization plus a placebo in the treatment of chronic agoraphobics, mixed phobics, and simple phobics. Both drug treatments were superior to desensitization plus placebo treatment for the agoraphobics but not the simple phobics. Systematic desensitization was not significantly different from supportive psychotherapy with any of the groups of phobics. However, among the simple phobics, 60% treated with systematic desensitization were rated by the independent assessor as markedly improved compared to 29% of patients treated with supportive psychotherapy. This difference appears more impressive when it is realized that 42% of the patients treated with supportive psychotherapy plus imipramine dropped out of therapy. The comparable figures for behavior therapy plus imipramine and placebo, respectively, were 29% and 10%. This differential attrition rate can be seen as artifactually inflating the success of the supportive psychotherapy treatment. Two other findings are important. The attrition rate was higher for patients treated with imipramine than with the placebo. Similarly, during a one-year follow-up, the relapse rate is greater (but statistically nonsignificant) among patients treated with imipramine than with placebo.

Several shortcomings with this study complicate interpretation. All results are based on global clinical ratings, the limitations of which have been noted above. Furthermore, debatable differences between the behavior therapy and supportive psychotherapy treatments (Kazdin & Wilson, 1978) and the absence of a direct comparison between imipramine and behavioral treatments (Hollon & Beck, 1978) tend to obscure the findings.

In a second study, Zitrin, Klein, and Woerner (1980) treated 75 agoraphobic women in groups using *in vivo* exposure. Half of the patients received imipramine, the other half a placebo. Following an initial four weeks of drug treatment, *in vivo* exposure sessions were begun that lasted for an additional 10 weeks. Thereafter imipramine treatment was continued for another three months. The same limited, global clinical ratings once again indicated the greater efficacy of imipramine compared to placebo. The attrition rate was a high 29% in both conditions.

Zitrin (1981) observes that in both of these studies, "the vast majority of patients were moderately to markedly improved both globally and in relation to the primary phobia at the completion of the treatment" (p. 166). Zitrin also notes that over 60% of these patients had previously been treated unsuccessfully with traditional psychoanalytic psychotherapy. However, the inadequacy of the dependent measure calls for caution in interpreting these results. Finally, consistent with other behavioral outcome studies, Zitrin found no evidence of either symptom substitution or therapy-induced negative effects. On the contrary, she comments,

> We found a significant improvement in the quality of their lives: better functioning at home and at work, increased social life, expanded interests and activities, and improved interpersonal relationships. In general, there was a greater richness in the fabric of their lives. With stresses and traumas, there often was a recurrence of the old phobic behavior, rather than the emergence of new symptoms. (p. 169)

Flooding in imagination, with the concurrent administration of Brevital, a quick-acting barbiturate, was compared to flooding only and an attention-placebo control condition by Chambless, Foa, Groves, and Goldstein (1979). The purpose of this study was to examine the effect on treatment outcome of the degree of anxiety patients experience during *in vivo* exposure treatment. Marks (1978), in his comprehensive summary of the available research evidence, concluded that "it is not crucial whether patients are relaxed, neutral, or anxious during exposure." Other reviewers (Levis & Hare, 1977) have similarly agreed that the original rationale for flooding treatment, which emphasized the importance of eliciting maximal anxiety during exposure to feared situations, has gone unsupported. Nevertheless, on the basis of their model of agoraphobia, Goldstein and Chambless (1978) predicted that the experience of intense anxiety during exposure would be therapeutic because this would allow for the neutralization of interoceptive stimuli that are presumed to be responsible for the "fear of fear" phenomenon in agoraphobics. Accordingly, Chambless *et al.* sought to control the degree of anxiety their subjects experience through the controlled administration of Brevital.

The subjects in this investigation were all agoraphobics, and treatment consisted of eight two-hour sessions. Anxiety-eliciting stimuli were continually introduced during the first 75 minutes of each session in order to evoke fear arousal. The authors add that "the remaining 30 min. of each 2-hr session was spent in supportive psychotherapy, discussing events that had occurred since the last session and inquiring about contact with phobic situations. Therapists were enjoined from introducing other behavioral techniques and from suggesting clients enter feared situations. Clients who reported entering formerly avoided situations, however, were praised" (Chambless *et al.*, 1979, p. 245). The attention-placebo group received supportive psychotherapy and training in progressive relaxation plus the use of pleasant, relaxing imagery. Subjects in this group were also praised for any attempts they made to confront their phobic situations although therapists did not explicitly instruct them to make such attempts.

Based upon the familiar nine-point rating scales introduced by Marks and his group, the results provided some sketchy support for Chambless *et al.*'s hypothesis about the importance of patients' experiencing anxiety during flooding, which necessarily led to the prediction that the best results would be achieved by flooding without the anxiety-suppressant effects of Brevital. As the authors summarized the data, "Though differences between the drug group and the nondrug group were significant only on clients' ratings of fear, a consistent pattern emerged on most measures. The nondrug group improved most followed by the drug group, with the attention-control group improving least. Moreover, only the nondrug group improved significantly more than the attention-control group on both clients' and therapists' ratings" (Chambless *et al.*, 1979, p. 249).

Some additional findings of this carefully conducted study are of interest. First, none of the treatments had much of an effect on patients' reported panic attacks. Chambless *et al.* were not surprised by this finding since in the Goldstein and Chambless model, panic attacks are related to interpersonal conflict that would require more extensive therapeutic intervention (e.g., marital therapy). Whether this is so remains to be demonstrated. Of course, other investigators would argue that it takes pharmacotherapy to control panic attacks (e.g., Zitrin, 1981). Second, the inclusion of behavioral and physiological measures of outcome failed to serve as useful outcome markers. The behavioral test consisted of asking each patient to spend a maximum of 30 minutes in his or her most feared situation. Yet 9 of the 27 subjects were able to do this at the pretest. This puzzling finding raises questions concerning the selection of these tasks. It is commonplace for agoraphobics to show variability in their pattern of avoidance, but completing their *most* feared item is surprising. Even if patients forced themselves to do this, it would have been useful to know what their subjective or physiological responses were *while* entering such anxiety-provoking situations. These measures might prove to be sensitive indicators of therapeutic effects. The physiological measures were not helpful since subjects failed to show greater reactivity to phobic images than to neutral ones on the pretest. This finding should not pass unnoticed. It suggests that more attention should be paid to the sort of phobic image that the phobic patient is asked to generate, a point taken up in great detail by Lang (1979) as discussed in the following section.

THEORETICAL MECHANISMS IN FEAR REDUCTION

As we have indicated in this series in previous years, our knowledge about specific treatment procedures and the outcomes they produce far outstrips our understanding of the theoretical mechanisms involved in the fear reduction process. Against this background, it is encouraging to report that the past two years have seen increased attention to theoretical issues. In addition to the conceptual analyses and empirical research sparked by Bandura's (1977a) self-efficacy theory, the concept of emotional processing has been advanced. This line of thinking seems rich in theoretical leads. Moreover, the so-called triple-response-system framework for analyzing the effects of different fear reduction methods has been further discussed and elaborated with specific implications for alternative unifying theoretical models.

Before turning to these developments, it should be pointed out that the ordering of observations about the parameters of imaginal and *in vivo* exposure methods does not constitute an explanation of these procedures. Consider, for example, Marks's (1981) recent proposal that we abandon conditioning theory (what he calls the "conditioning paradigm") in favor of a "clinical paradigm." According to Marks,

> Laboratory models of conditioning are inadequate because they simulate neither onset nor extinction of most phobias or obsessions. For clinical work it is preferable to use the simpler notation ES (evoking stimulus) and ER (evoked response of psychopathology) rather than the traditional US, UR, CS, and CR. The ER-ER paradigm indicates a therapeutic strategy without the dubious etiological connotations of conditioning models. It also focuses on the theoretical conditions that differentiate therapeutic from sensitizing exposure; in time this may lead to better ideas about etiology. (1981, p. 233)

Marks's emphasis on ferreting out the antecedants of neurotic reactions is a cardinal feature of behavioral assessment, and is necessarily central to the clinician's endeavors. But this ER-ER paradigm does not take us beyond the limitations of the conditioning model. It does not help to understand the critical question in the use of behavioral fear reduction methods, which, as Marks points out, is how do different methods eliminate avoidance behavior and reduce fear reactions? There is a consensus that these diverse behavioral methods have as their common denominator of therapeutic efficacy repeated, typically prolonged exposure to the threatening stimuli. This is a description of the necessary (and often sufficient) condition for successful treatment; it is not an explanation. In using the term "exposure theory" Marks is referring to the procedure of systematically exposing a patient to his or her feared stimuli according to what we currently know about this method's optimal parameters (e.g., prolonged exposure until anxiety diminishes). He presents no theory that details the process involved in this procedure, although he presents a full analysis of the experimental and clinical phenomena that any acceptable theory will have to accomodate. Put somewhat differently, we have refined a workable extinction procedure that more often than not produces a successful treatment outcome that we also call extinction. But we lack an adequate theory of extinction.

Self-Efficacy Theory. Bandura's (1977a) presentation of his self-efficacy theory was reprinted in the 1978 volume of this series. In 1980 we reprinted Bandura's reactions to a broad range of commentaries on his theory, expressing our firm belief that his bold proposals would lead to the initiation of numerous research efforts and inevitable theoretical controversy. Events have swiftly borne out this prediction, and it is with Bandura's own research on the concept of self-efficacy and fear reduction that this discussion begins.

One of the questions about the studies on which Bandura (1977a) based his self-efficacy theory concerned the possible influence on the data of any reactive effects of the making of efficacy judgments. As Lang (1978), for one, put it, "It would be good to have control subjects in these experiments who were not asked to estimate performance. To what extent does the verbalization of one's intentions formulate them and control what occurs? Would performance levels and variances have been different without this self-generated social pressure?" (p. 191).

To evaluate the potential motivational effects of asking subjects to make efficacy judgments, Bandura, Adams, Hardy, and Howells (1980) completed a study in which snake phobics received treatment with or without assessment of their self-efficacy, and subsequent changes in their fear and avoidance behavior were compared. The treatment was covert modeling, or what Bandura *et al.* chose to designate as cognitive modeling "to indicate its principal modality of operation" (p. 40). To test the theory that cognitive rehearsal of effective coping with feared situations improves performance by increasing perceived efficacy, efficacy expectations were measured prior to, and after, the cognitive modeling treatment. The methodology was the same as that used by Bandura and his students in previous studies of the treatment of snake phobic subjects.

Making efficacy judgments had no effect on avoidance behavior or fear arousal. Treatment increased both efficacy ratings and approach behavior; the higher the self-efficacy, the greater the approach behavior. Congruence between perceived efficacy and behavioral avoidance at the level of individual tasks (what Bandura calls a "microanalysis") reached 81% for both similar (the same snake that was used during the pretreatment test) and dissimilar (a different snake) threats. In other words, self-efficacy was an accurate predictor of performance that ranged from 3% to 100% of the tasks. Combining these results with those of previous studies from the same laboratory, Bandura *et al.* concluded that "perceived self-efficacy is an equally accurate predictor of individual task performance, regardless of whether efficacy is enhanced by enactive mastery experiences, by vicarious performance attainments, by eliminating emotional arousal to threats, or by cognitive coping" (1980, p. 48). An analysis of the relationship between self-efficacy and self-reported fear led these authors to a similar conclusion. In this study fear arousal declined as efficacy increased, and comparing these data with those from previous studies Bandura *et al.* argue that the relationship between efficacy and fear is the same regardless of the source of the self-efficacy. This is an important prediction from the theory and it will be important to see if future studies of additional treatment methods replicate this finding.

Another objection to Bandura's (1977a) theory of self-efficacy was that it was based on studies of snake phobic subjects. As such, its external validity has been challenged in the now predictable criticisms of this methodology. In a study designed to demonstrate the generality of self-efficacy theory, Bandura *et al.* evaluated the treatment of 11 agoraphobics. These clients participated in an intensive 10-day, therapist-guided *in vivo* exposure treatment program described by Hardy (1976). Behavioral measures of avoidance behavior were obtained before and after therapy, and efficacy scales tapping various activities agoraphobics find distressing were also obtained at these assessments.

Overall the clients showed considerable improvement. The results of interest here, however, are those that bear on the congruence between efficacy expectations and behavioral performance. Self-efficacy proved to be an accurate predictor of performance in the behavioral tests on 79% of the tasks for the pretest phase of the study, and in 88% of the tasks in the posttreatment assessment. Moreover, efficacy ratings were significantly more accurate in predicting posttreatment performance than their actual behavior during the course of treatment. These findings provide further support for the utility of self-efficacy theory.

In a study referred to earlier, by Bourque and LaDouceur (1980), efficacy expectations were assessed together with measures of the effects of the different exposure-based treatments that were used. These efficacy ratings were consistently correlated with behavioral performance across different tasks, under similar and dissimilar threats, and for different treatments. Bandura's theory also predicts that the greater the self-efficacy, the more clients will persist in coping with threatening situations. Bourque and LaDouceur found that the length of time subjects spent in attempts to master the situation, as measured by the total therapy time, was correlated significantly with strength of self-efficacy. These results are consistent with an important prediction from the theory and also add to its generality in that the subjects were all acrophobics.

Emotional Processing. The emphasis on behavior *qua* behavior in the assessment and treatment of clinical disorders helped to define behavior therapy as it emerged as a systematic alternative to the psychodynamic model in the late 1950s. This emphasis continues to be a distinguishing characteristic of the field and it has been one of behavior therapy's signal contributions to clinical psychology. In the 1970s, the cognitive connection was made, although the controversy surrounding this development in behavior therapy is still lively. Perhaps inevitably, if the focus is on overt behavior and cognition, can *affect* be far behind? Of course, clinical behavior therapy with neurotic patients has always emphasized conditioned emotional responses. They were the raw matter of Wolpe's (1958) pioneering concepts and procedures. Furthermore, it might be pointed out that the triple response system, by definition, stresses the importance of taking physiological arousal into account in the analysis of fear and its modification. But the recent concern with affect or feelings goes far beyond simple S-R formulations of "emotional habits" or unexceptional assertions that physiological arousal, self-report of fear, and avoidance behavior should all be assessed in planning treatment and measuring its outcome.

In a weighty and provocative paper that requires more extended discussion than the brief comment directed to it here, Mahoney (1980) takes his fellow cognitive–behavioral therapists to task for allegedly ignoring the role of feelings in the therapeutic process, and for viewing them as the mere by-products of thought. He lists several arguments for the primary importance of feelings, suggestions that are being borne out in current research showing the reciprocal influence between mood and cognition (e.g., Bower, 1981; Kihlstrom & Nasby, 1981).

In a related vein, Zajonc (1980) has challenged cognitive theories that assume that affect is largely "postcognitive," namely, that emotional reactions occur after perceptual and cognitive processing of information. The evidence suggests otherwise. Affective responses may be more fundamental, more rapid, and independent of cold cognitive judgments. According to Zajonc, "Affect and cognition are under the control of separate and partially independent systems that can influence each other in a variety of ways, and that both constitute independent sources of effects in information processing" (p. 151).

Although some current cognitive–behavioral therapies exalt the primacy of rationality in determining affective responses, as Mahoney (1980) suggests, this is not a criticism of self-efficacy theory, or the broader framework of social learning theory (Bandura, 1977b). According to Bandura (1977a), affective arousal is a major source of the cognitive appraisal that produces specific efficacy expectations. In turn, level, strength, and generality of self-efficacy influence affective reactions. In his 1969 book, Bandura emphasized that fear reactions and other emotional responses may be functions of two different stimulus sources. The first is emotional arousal that is self-generated by distressing thoughts or images. The second is the emotional arousal that appears to be more directly elicited by the conditioned stimulus. Many phobics, for example, respond instantaneously to situations or objects they fear before they have time to think about the possible dangers involved. One of the advantages of viewing learned fear reactions in this manner is that two stimulus sources of emotional responses suggest different therapeutic interventions. In the first case of self-generated arousal through thoughts and images, treatment methods known as cognitive restructuring seem indicated. In the second case of the more direct elicitation of fear, behavioral procedures, such as flooding that extend prolonged nonreinforced exposure to the feared situation or object, are required.

Despite this early emphasis in social learning theory on differential cognitive and emotional sources of arousal, Lang (1978) faults self-efficacy theory for failing to take better account of the triple-response-system view of fear, an issue taken up below. Noting that Bandura relies upon self-report for information about people's cognitive processes, Lang points out the possible limitations of self-report as a "window into men's cognitions." As he puts it, "We should also be open to the possibility that the best integrating theories in psychology may not be isomorphic with phenomenology, that the deep structure of cognitive processing may not be directly accessed by verbal report, and that our concept of the mind may someday no more resemble our internal experience than the world of atoms, neutrinos, and quarks conforms to our experience of physical reality" (1978, p. 191).

Lang (1979) has attempted to index cognitive processes not through self-report, but through physiological measurement. In doing so, he has proposed a bioinformational theory of emotional imagery that is directly relevant to fear reduction treatment methods. In this propositional analysis, an image is seen as a conceptual network, the cognitive structure of which controls specific physiological responding and serves as a prototype for overt behavioral expression. Lang stresses that an image is not an internal stimulus to which the person responds (the former S-R conception of imagery in the behavior therapies). Rather, the person generates a conceptual structure that contains both stimulus and response propositions. Behavior change "depends not on simple exposure to fear stimuli, but on the generation of the relevant affective cognitive structure, the prototype for overt behavior, which is subsequently modified into a more functional form" (Lang, 1979, p. 501).

One of the advantages of this theory is that it provides an explanation for the variable effects of exposure therapies in the treatment of phobic and obsessive–compulsive clients. Only those who generate the relevant affective stimulus and response propositions will respond successfully (Lang, Melamed, & Hart, 1970). Those who are unable (or unwilling?) to accomplish this primary processing of affective information will show poorer outcomes.[2] Since Lang (1979) has been able to train subjects to improve their generation of affective response propositions, a direct test of this assumption of the theory seems feasible.

Two other aspects of the theory warrant comment here. Lang (1979) has stated that "once you have [emotional processing] it is not clear whether the next step is to modify the structure of related behavioral acts, the visceral responses, or the semantic information in the network" (p. 15). The evidence, as pointed out above, clearly indicates that phobic disorders are most effectively treated using performance-based techniques. How Lang's bioinformational theory would predict this remains to be shown. Finally, if one of the implications of this theory is that generating the greatest amount of arousal (anxiety)

2. It has long been noted that a client's inability to react with some anxiety during imaginal systematic desensitization limits the use of this method. For example, Bandura (1969) noted that "individuals who are unable, for one reason or another, to visualize threatening stimuli vividly, or for whom imagined scenes fail to evoke emotional reactions, will most likely derive little benefit from an exclusively cognitive form of counterconditioning treatment" (p. 473). And Wolpe (1978) has observed that systematic desensitization does not benefit that "considerable number of people" who "do not have fear when they imagine the things they fear."

during therapy should produce the most behavioral change, as Barlow and Mavissakalian (1981) suggest, the theory is inconsistent with treatment outcome data showing no such relationship (Marks, 1978).

There is little research evidence that bears directly on Lang's theory. One of the predictions from the theory is that imagery that includes both stimulus elements and response components of the fear reaction will be more successful in activating the full propositional framework and hence increase the extent of fear reduction through a method such as imaginal systematic desensitization. Recent work in Lang's own laboratory, cited by Anderson and Borkovec (1980), confirms this prediction. In their own attempt to explore this prediction, Anderson and Borkovec had speech-anxious subjects repeatedly imagine scenes described by either stimulus or stimulus plus response scripts. The predicted effects of the different scripts were not found on either physiological or self-report measures of fear. However, content analysis of subjects imagined scripts indicated that response components were included in both conditions, thereby clouding interpretation of the results. In line with Lang's theory, changes in response component detail over repetitions of the imaginal scripts did correlate significantly with both heart rate and self-reported fear.

In the course of a study on synchronous and desynchronous changes in subject's responses during fear reduction, Grey, Sartory, and Rachman (1979) failed to find support for the prediction that high-heart-rate responders would show greater posttreatment fear reduction than low-heart-rate responders. These results held true for both nonpsychiatric (volunteer phobic subjects) and psychiatric patients.[3] Grey et al. hasten to point out that they used an in vivo fear reduction method rather than the imaginal techniques Lang and his associates have analyzed: "It must be noted that we did not set out specifically to replicate the observation and indeed our procedures could not provide a full and direct test. It does mean, nevertheless, that it is desirable to replicate the basic finding before proceeding too far" (Grey et al., 1979, p. 146). Sound advice.

The concept of emotional processing is also advanced by Rachman (1980) in a paper that we believe will prove to be both controversial and influential in the years to come. The concept is defined as

> a process whereby emotional disturbances are absorbed, and decline to the extent that other experiences and behavior can proceed without disruption. If an emotional disturbance is not absorbed satisfactorily, some signs

---

3. Although these findings based on a small n must be viewed cautiously, they do not support the view that carefully chosen subjects in analogue research are somehow intrinsically different from patients seen in clinical practice (see Rachman & Wilson, 1980).

become evident. These signs are likely to recur intermittently, and may be direct and obvious, or indirect and subtle. The central, indispensible index of unsatisfactory emotional processing is the persistence or return of intrusive signs of emotional activity (such as obsessions, nightmares, pressure of talk, phobias, inappropriate expressions of emotion that are out of context or out of proportion, or simply out of time). Indirect signs may include an inability to concentrate on the task at hand, excessive restlessness, irritability. (p. 51)

Ambitious in scope, the concept is said to encompass the following apparently unrelated phenomena within a single, workable framework: "obsessions, the return of fear, incubation of fear, abnormal grief reactions, failures to respond to fear-reducing procedures, nightmares" (p. 52). Regardless of the many dissimilarities among these phenomena, they are viewed as instances of incomplete emotional processing.

In putting forward this concept of emotional processing, Rachman has in mind the same goal that motivated Bandura (1977a) and Lang (1979) in developing their theories: the need to find unifying concepts that can incorporate the disparate findings of behavioral research on fear and its reduction through such diverse means as imaginal methods, *in vivo* flooding, vicarious learning, problem-solving training, cognitive restructuring, appropriate pharmacotherapy, and so on. What is intriguing is Rachman's deliberate analogy to Freud's treatment of the famous Anna O (or Bertha Pappenheim, as she should perhaps be known [Ellenberger, 1972]). His point is to focus attention on emotional events that are "stored" and return at some later point in time to disrupt normal behavior.[4]

Many traditional psychodynamic therapists and some researchers have developed the penchant of finding in innovative cognitive-behavioral treatment strategies "euphemistic" reappearances of time-honored psychodynamic concepts" (e.g., Lazarus, 1980). Lest someone conclude that Rachman has "rediscovered" the psychoanalytic notion or "working through" emotional conflicts that entered the psyche in early childhood years, it would be well to indicate some of the differences. One difference lies in *what* is to be "worked through." The

4. Rachman's thesis takes on added significance in the context of Mahoney's critique of prevailing concepts and strategies in the cognitive–behavioral therapies. "In most contemporary cognitive approaches, feelings are viewed as the products (or by-products) of thoughts. As such, they are to be controlled by the appropriate modification of the latter. In addition, there is a clear bias against 'evocative' therapies, the concept of catharsis, and the idea that feelings are somehow 'stored' or retained by the persons. . . . It is interesting to note that the cognitive therapist seems comfortable with the 'storage' of information, but is reluctant to extend the storage metaphor to feelings" (1980, pp. 164–165).

emotional processing Rachman refers to covers a broad range of experiences that might befall the individual at any stage in his or her life. Conditioned emotional reactions, vicarious learning of fear responses, and verbally transmitted information about fearful events (see Rachman, 1977) are the sort of experiences that are referred to in this context, as opposed to the standard psychoanalytic fare of sexual and aggressive impulses.

How incomplete emotional processing can continue to exert an influence is a second difference. There is no need to invoke discredited notions of autonomous unconscious mechanisms that give rise to highly obscure symptoms (symbolic expressions) that are the filtered residue of an unremitting and devious psychic censor. Although he does not draw out the possibilities, Rachman's concept, as with Lang's version of emotional processing, falls squarely within the emerging mainstream of experimental cognitive psychology that seeks to relate affective experiences to information processing (e.g., Bower, 1981). Finally, it requires little emphasis here that the contemporary behavior therapist uses different means of facilitating desired emotional processing or "working through" examples of incomplete processing (e.g., *in vivo* exposure methods) than psychoanalytically oriented therapists who are still wedded to the allegedly critical importance of resolving the therapeutic transference (see Chapter 8 for a discussion of this difference).

Of the several observations rich in theoretical and therapeutic potential that Rachman makes, two can be mentioned briefly here. The first concerns the question of how to assess completeness of emotional processing. Rachman suggests the use of test probes: "After an emotional disturbance has subsided, the extent of emotional processing can be estimated by presenting relevant stimulus material in an attempt to reevoke the emotional reaction. The degree to which the test probes are successful in provoking the reaction provides a measure of emotional processing. For example, six months after successfully completing a fear-reducing training course, a subject is re-presented with the phobic stimulus. Or, a former griever may be reminded about or asked to speak about the dead person some time after he has ceased to show overt signs of grief" (1980, p. 55).

In many ways this is what is often done in multiple measurement of treatment effects. Nevertheless, the emphasis on information processing in the Rachman and Lang conceptions suggests assessment methods (test probes) that go beyond methods of evaluating therapy outcome in behavioral studies. More specifically, well-established measures of the processing of information from experimental cognitive psychology would seem to be a useful first step in this direction (e.g.,

Burgess, Jones, Robertson, Radcliffe, & Emerson, 1981; Kihlstrom & Nasby, 1981).

The second set of observations involves an initial charting of those factors that facilitate and those that impede desired emotional processing. Rachman suggests that "the transformation or neutralization of emotion-provoking stimuli is facilitated by repeated presentations, by stimuli presented for certain minimal durations, by piecemeal presentations, by minimizing distractions, by inducing a low level of arousal. The transformation can be impeded by brief presentations, excessive stimulus intensities, unduly complex, ambiguous or large stimulus inputs, excessively high levels of arousal" (1980, p. 57).

The source for these suggestions is the accumulated findings of the treatment of phobic and obsessive–compulsive disorders with different behavioral methods. Many critical questions still have to be answered. As indicated earlier in this chapter in connection with the Chambless *et al.* (1979) study, it is still unclear precisely what level of arousal is facilitative during exposure treatments. Consistent with the thrust of theoretical concepts such as those proposed by Bandura, Lang, and Rachman, and by Wilson and O'Leary (1980) have noted that the success of exposure methods will depend not only on the intensity of the fear arousal, but also the informative function of the cues. We shall be hearing more of emotional processing in the next few years.

Is Exposure a Necessary Condition for Fear Reduction? This thought-provoking question was posed by DeSilva and Rachman (1981) in a paper that examined the necessary and sufficient conditions for successful reduction of fear. Their conclusion is straightforward. Exposure[5] is undoubtedly the most powerful means of treating phobic fear and avoidance and it is often sufficient; however, it cannot be said to be necessary as is increasingly assumed in the literature.

Several strands of evidence of fear reduction occurring in the absence of exposure to the feared stimulus are combed by way of documenting this position:

1. There is considerable experimental and anecdotal evidence showing that fears can be established by simply informing some-

5. Exposure here is defined as "planned, sustained and repetitive evocations of images/ image sequences of the stimuli in question. Mere thoughts or fleeting images do not constitute imaginal exposure in this sense" (DeSilva & Rachman, 1981, p. 227). In an important corollary to their main argument in this paper, DeSilva and Rachman issue the following caveat: "With regard to both imaginal and *in vivo* exposure, we should like to draw attention to the dubious assumption that any form of exposure is likely to be efficacious in fear-reduction. . . . A case can be made for distinguishing between passive and active exposure" (1981, p. 227). The nature of this active or "engaged" exposure (Rachman & Hodgson, 1980) will very likely hold one of the keys to the explanation of exposure-based treatment methods.

one that a situation/object is dangerous (Rachman, 1977). By extension, it must follow that fear can be reduced by the same verbal transmission of information.

2. There is some evidence, albeit tentative (Rachman & Wilson, 1980), that cognitive restructuring treatment methods can reduce fear (e.g., Meichenbaum, Gilmore, & Fedoravicius, 1971). DeSilva and Rachman hasten to point out that "we know of no experimental analysis of the effects of cognitive–behavioral therapy of fear reductions in which care has been taken to ensure that the subjects who received such therapy were dissuaded from or even shielded from coming into contact with fear-evoking stimulus. However, there are studies in which fearful subjects were successfully treated with a cognitive-based technique that did not include contact with the fear stimuli" (1981, p. 228). They conclude quite reasonably, however, that it is improbable that uncontrolled exposure was responsible for all reported instances of successful cognitive treatments.

3. The well-established phenomenon of spontaneous remission of neurotic disorders provides further indirect support for the thesis, unless it is argued, perhaps implausibly, that all cases of spontaneous remission are due to repeated exposure, be they incidental or deliberate.

4. Fears have been reduced as a result of attention-placebo treatments and nonbehavioral forms of psychotherapy that do not involve planned, repeated exposure to feared situations.

5. Fears have been reduced by nonexposure behavioral treatments. The Jannoun et al. (1980) study on problem solving in the treatment of agoraphobics, discussed earlier in this chapter, is one example. Another that is mentioned by DeSilva and Rachman is Emmelkamp and van der Heyden's (1980) successful treatment of obsessional patients using assertion training. And to these observations of DeSilva and Rachman's could be added the occasional successes of pharmacotherapy in reducing fears.

The implications of this analysis for behavioral research and practice are varied. DeSilva and Rachman suggest that a premature focus on exposure as a necessary condition of fear reduction might discourage the search for new techniques. They also relate their analysis to the triple-response-system model of fear discussed below. Their suggestion is that "long-lasting reductions of fear in subjects who show strong physiological reactions can be achieved only after repeated engaged exposures [whereas] subjects whose fears are not accompanied by strong physiological reactions are more likely to respond to nonexposure types of intervention" (1981, p. 231). Finally, DeSilva and Rachman speculate that an adequate theory of fear reduction will probably have to accomodate the success of both exposure-based and nonexposure treatments. Self-efficacy theory, in which one of the sources of information that determines the client's perceived ability to cope with feared situations—verbal persuasion—is not based on exposure, is one such possibility.

The Three-Systems Model of Fear. According to this model, the major architects of which have been Lang (1969) and Rachman (1978), fear is viewed not as an entity or single system, but as a set of loosely coupled components, namely, avoidance behavior, physiological arousal, and verbal report. These three components may be differentially affected by different treatment methods and may change at different speeds. Hodgson and Rachman (1974) described the ways in which changes across these components were either synchronous or desynchronous, and were able to spell out testable hypotheses about conditions under which changes would be synchronous or not. Among the factors which have received experimental and clinical support are intensity of emotional arousal, level of demand for change, the type of treatment technique, and the length of follow-up. It is important, however, to recognize that these contributions are largely descriptive in nature, and not an explanation of interdependent processes.

In an analysis of the three-systems model, Hugdahl (1981) addresses himself to the causal links between the three components and observes that the focus of the model is on "independence rather than interdependence" (p. 77). As such, he points out how this model differs from Schachter's (1964) theory of emotion that stresses interdependence between physiological arousal and cognitive labeling. He might also have added that the model also differs from Bandura's (1977a) self-efficacy theory. Commenting upon the view that the three response systems are loosely coupled components, Bandura (1978a) has argued:

> If indeed they are only loosely linked, they might be better treated as partially independent response systems regulated by different determinants rather than as a disjointed triadic family. . . . In the social learning view, thought, affect and action operate as reciprocally interacting factors rather than as loosely linked components or as conjoint events. While recognizing the role of labeling processes in emotional expressions, this approach acknowledges that thought creates physiological arousal as well as provides cognitive labels for it. Arousal can, in turn, influence thought. The relative influence exerted by these three sets of interlocking factors will vary in different individuals for different activities performed under different circumstances. (p. 257)

Among the other issues Hugdahl raises in his analysis of the three-systems model are the manner in which the different components are defined and the implications the model has for the etiology and treatment of phobic disorders. With respect to definition, he points out how the so-called subjective or cognitive component of fear is variously characterized by different workers. Regarding implications for treatment, Hugdahl suggests that if clients "load differentially" on different fear components, then treatment should be tailored to the precise patterning of the fear response. In short, a client with high physiological arousal and few anticipatory negative self-statements would be predicted to show little benefit from cognitive restructuring, whereas another client with the reverse "loading" would be helped. At this level there is a marked similarity between Hugdahl's position and the multimodal treatment approach of Lazarus (1981), as discussed in Chapter 8. Hugdahl, however, goes further in his analysis. By way of illustration he suggests that the reader consider three agoraphobics. Client 1 is a "behavioral responder"; Client 2 is a "physiological responder"; and Client 3 is a "cognitive responder." Assuming that one could quantify agoraphobics in this manner, a very debatable proposition, Hugdahl proceeds to match treatments to fear-response patterning: *in vivo* exposure for Client 1, systematic desensitization for Client 2, and cognitive restructuring for Client 3.

The problems with this analysis, which are also touched on in Chapter 8 in an analysis of multimodal therapy, include the following. First, why choose cognitive restructuring as the preferred means of treating Client 3? There is no acceptable evidence for an assumption of an isomorphic relationship between the way in which a problem is expressed and the form of its treatment. If anything, it could be argued that a performance-based treatment is the most effective means of altering phobic cognitions as well as actual behavior. The available evidence clearly supports this position (Marks, 1981; Wilson, 1982). Moreover, this is what self-efficacy theory, which attempts to go beyond the notion of coupling of independent components, predicts. Second, there are few data to suggest that systematic desensitization is the best means of treating "a physiological responder." Here Hugdahl appears to be accepting Wolpe's original reciprocal inhibition rationale as the basis for such a choice. Yet the precise explanation of systematic desensitization is still unclear. What if one were to accept the self-efficacy explanation? Would this then qualify desensitization for the "cognitive responder?" There is also evidence that a performance-based method reduces physiological arousal as effectively as imaginal desensitization—perhaps more effectively. In short, the current evidence on therapeutic process and procedure is at odds with the straightforward predictions from the three-systems model that Hugdahl makes. Indeed, in the ultimate analysis, Hugdahl would seem to concur with the choice of a performance-based method for all three agoraphobics despite the previous predictions. Noting that all phobias include a behavioral component, he suggests that "treatment methods are probably best 'tailored' to the individual needs of every patient if they also include an exposure-based response prevention. This is further supported by Marks (1978), who concluded after a review of the literature, that exposure is the only overall effective mechanism for the extinction of phobic anxiety" (1981, p. 83).

The point of the foregoing commentary is that the three-sytems model is a descriptive one that does not provide the basis for making specific decisions about treatments of choice (a problem shared by multimodal therapy; see Chapter 8). Nonetheless, one study that does indicate some support for Hugdahl's position was reported by Ost, Jerremalm, and Johansson (1981). Following participation in a structural social interaction test, 40 social phobics were classified as either "behavioral" or "physiological" responders. The former were rated as high on behavioral indices of social anxiety, and showed low physiological arousal. The latter displayed the opposite pattern. Subjects within each of these experimentally structured groups then received either relaxation training or social skills training (a similar procedure to that used by Shaw, 1979). In sum, Ost et al. compared a treatment that corresponded to the subjects' response pattern with a treatment that did not.

Treatment consisted of 10 individual sessions. The within-group comparisons showed that both treatments yielded improvements on most measures. The between groups comparisons showed that for the behavioral reactors, social skills training was significantly better than applied relaxation on most of the measures, and for the physiological reactors relaxation was significantly better than social skills training on some of the measures. Ost et al. concluded that these data indicate that superior treatment effects are obtained when the method meshes with the patient's response pattern.

OBSESSIVE–COMPULSIVE DISORDERS

Obsessive–compulsive disorders have always been among the most difficult clinical problems to treat. Therapists who have wrestled with these recalcitrant disorders will find themselves drawn to Aubrey Lewis's grand assertion that "it may well be that obsessional illness cannot be understood altogether without understanding the nature of man" (cited in Rachman & Hodgson, 1980, p. 1). If obsessive–compulsive disorders, let alone the nature of man (and woman), have not yielded all their secrets during the past two years, it nonetheless can be said with some confidence that significant steps have been made toward the effective treatment of obsessions and compulsions.

Preeminent among the developments in behavioral research and therapy on obsessive–compulsive disorders during this period was the publication in 1980 of Rachman and Hodgson's book *Obsessions and Compulsions*. This scholarly and comprehensive text reviews the natural history of these disorders, what is known about their etiology and maintenance, the results of conventional therapy, the development of different behavioral treatments, and the current evidence on therapy outcome. It concludes with an incisive analysis of possible theoretical mechanisms in the treatment of obsessions and compulsions with behavior therapy. Rich in clinical detail, empirical documentation, and innovative theorizing, the book is a call to action that will influence all serious researchers in this area.

Other developments include the emergence of controlled clinical studies, clinically useful analyses of therapeutic failures, and the evaluation of combined behavioral and pharmacological treatments.

Specific Behavioral Treatments

As different reviewers have indicated, the most effective treatments for obsessive–compulsive disorders appear to be *in vivo* exposure and response prevention (Foa & Tillmanns, 1980; Rachman & Hodgson, 1980). The specific effects of each of these treatments were evaluated by Foa, Steketee, and Milby (1980) in a study of eight obsessive–compulsives with washing rituals. The exposure treatment was designed to produce prolonged, continuous exposure to discomfort-eliciting stimuli. Daily treatment sessions were two hours, and subjects were asked to expose themselves to these stimuli for four hours each day as homework assignments. Subjects were free to wash or clean as often as they wished during this treatment, with the exception that they had to reexpose themselves to the stimuli immediately after washing during the exposure sessions and homework. Response prevention was continuous and strictly supervised. Any contact with water was prohibited with the exception of one supervised 10-minute shower every fifth day. Subjects were allowed to avoid contact with discomfort-inducing stimuli during this period. Half of the subjects received 10 days of exposure treatment alone followed by 10 days of combined treatment, while the other half received 10 days of response prevention alone followed by the combined treatment. In the combined treatment, subjects were asked to touch their discomfort-eliciting stimuli and were prevented from washing. The frequency and duration of washing rituals were measured during four-day periods before treatment, after the first 10 days, and after the combined treatment.

Exposure alone reduced subjects' self-reported anxiety significantly more than response prevention, whereas the opposite pattern prevailed for self-recorded duration of actual handwashing. The addition of the other treatment during the second 10 days of combined treatment erased any differences between the two groups on anxiety and handwashing. Exposing compulsives to the stimuli that evoke their rituals and preventing any avoidance response (i.e., the compulsive ritual) is confirmed as the optimal treatment for this type of disorder, although, as Foa *et al.* hasten to point out, the small *n* and the use of subjects' self-recording of their behavior warrant caution in generalizing from these results.

In discussing the theoretical implications of their results, Foa *et al.* point out that the data are inconsistent with the view that response prevention is effective because it involves prolonged exposure to the aversive stimuli (Marks, 1978). Their study involved six hours of daily exposure to the perceived contaminants (a total of 60 hours), which reduced anxiety but failed to eliminate the rituals. In proposing an explanation of their findings, Foa *et al.* hearken back to Walton and Mather's (1963) formulation of obsessive–compulsive disorders and suggest that rituals become functionally autonomous from the drive that initially evoked them. By functional autonomy they mean that "ritualistic activity is also maintained by multiple environmental stimuli other than contaminants (second-order stimuli) that signal the emission of this behavior" (Foa *et al.*, 1980, p. 77). Exposure alone fails to elicit the full range of cues that come to control compulsive rituals. Foa *et al.* summarized their view of compulsive rituals in the following manner: "We propose that ritualistic responses are maintained by decreasing the drive induced by first-order stimuli (contaminants) and second-order stimuli (stress, mood state, environmental cues). Prolonged exposure reduces the drive evoked by contaminants, and response prevention serves two roles: (a) prolongation of the exposure to first-order stimuli and (b) dissociation of second-order stimuli from ritualistic behavior, allowing new responses to these stimuli to occur and thus extinguishing their drive induction and discriminative stimulus properties" (1980, p. 78). As Walton and Mather (1963) and then Bandura (1969) emphasized, this formulation draws attention to the importance of whether the compulsive rituals are of recent onset or are chronic in nature. Different treatments seem required depending on this determination.

Given the growing cognitive connection in behavior therapy it was merely a matter of time before serious attempts were initiated to introduce cognitive restructuring methods into the treatment of obsessive–compulsive disorders. The first controlled study of this possibility was reported by Emmelkamp, van der Helm, van Zanten, and Plochg (1980), who compared *in vivo* exposure treatment to a method that combined *in vivo* exposure with a cognitive restructuring procedure closely resembling that used by Emmelkamp *et al.* (1978) in the treatment of agoraphobics. The details of this study are described by Kendall in Chapter 4. Suffice it to note here that Emmelkamp *et al.* (1980) found no benefit from adding cognitive restructuring (an amalgam of rational–emotive therapy and self-instructional training) to *in vivo* exposure. As Kendall observes, proponents of cognitive restructuring might argue that the method received less than a fair test because of the relative brevity of the treatment and the overall amount of time allotted to cognitive therapy. This is a reasonable objection, and controlled evaluations of more extensive cognitive treatment are definitely called for. Nevertheless, when viewed in the context of the failure of cognitive restructuring methods to facilitate the behavioral treatment of phobic disorders (e.g., Biran *et al.*, 1981; Emmelkamp *et al.*, 1978; Williams & Rappoport, 1980; Wilson, 1982), it seems entirely possible that cognitive restructuring is ineffective in the treatment of rituals.

Future research on this topic might well be guided by the theoretical analyses outlined by Rachman and Hodgson (1980). For example, in a discussion of the relevance of the three-systems model of fear and obsessions, these authors suggest that specific features of the presenting problem will dictate different treatments. Thus a method such as cognitive restructuring would be recommended for a client whose problem is one of unwanted and intrusive thoughts. It would be inappropriate and hence predictably ineffective if used to treat a compulsive whose excessive fear of contamination is characterized by intense autonomic arousal. (As described in Chapter 8, multimodal therapy makes much the same point.) Whether or not this is so remains to be put to the empirical test. However, the argument is made earlier in this chapter (and in Chapter 8) that it is unwise to assume an isomorphic relationship between problem and procedure. This promises to be a fruitful line of research.

Behavioral Treatment and Drugs

Of the different types of drugs that have been used to treat obsessive–compulsive disorders, the tricyclics have seemed to show the most encouraging results (Marks, 1981). Moreover, given the frequent association between obsessions and depression (Rachman & Hodgson, 1980), antidepressive drugs seem indicated. In view of the therapeutic promise of tricyclics, the publication of a major controlled outcome study that examined the separate and joint effects of clomipramine and behavioral treatment is of considerable interest (see reports by Marks, Stern, Mawson, Cobb, & McDonald, 1980; Rachman, Cobb, Grey, McDonald, Mawson, Sartory, & Stern, 1979).

The patients were 40 obsessive–compulsives with handicapping rituals at least one year in duration. Five had had previous psychosurgery for their problems. The design of the study was 2×2 factorial design arranged as follows. For the first four weeks patients received either oral clomipramine or a placebo on an outpatient basis. At the end of the four-week period patients receiving clomipramine were on a mean dose of 164 mg. At this point they were admitted to the hospital where each group was randomly split into subgroups that received either relaxation training or *in vivo* exposure treatment plus self-imposed response prevention for the next three weeks. During weeks 7–10 all patients received *in vivo* exposure plus response prevention. Several patients received additional treatment at different points following the end of this planned therapy stage. Marks *et al.* (1980) described this as follows: "Domiciliary sessions were carried out when necessary (mean of 2.5 sessions per patient for the whole group), and in cases where the patient lived a long way from hospital a local therapist was enlisted to provide treatment cover after discharge. During follow-up only essential psychological treatment was given, and 12 patients brought their families to a six-weekly therapeutic group for a mean of four sessions" (p. 4). Furthermore, Marks *et al.* report that during the two-year follow-up eight patients had to be readmitted to the hospital four each from the drug and placebo conditions and that "extra counseling and support was given to five clomipramine and four placebo patients, to a mean of five sessions" (p. 17). From week 36 medication was tailed off over four weeks so that patients were off all capsules by week 40.

Asessments were carried out at weeks 0, 4, 7, 10, 18, 36, 44, 62, and 114. Measures of therapy outcome included ratings of patients' four main target rituals, a compulsive activity checklist, a behavioral avoidance test in which patients were asked to carry out five tasks that usually triggered compulsive rituals, ratings of depression, general anxiety, and social adjustment. The results up to week 18 are reported by Rachman *et al.* (1979), with Marks *et al.* (1980) describing the follow-up findings.

The *in vivo* exposure plus response prevention treatment was significantly superior to relaxation training with respect to compulsive rituals, consistent with previous results from this group of investigators

(Rachman & Hodgson, 1980). There were no differences between these two groups, however, on measures of mood. In other words, the behavioral treatment produced specific changes in behavior. Rachman *et al.* comment that "such specificity, although it is moderately disappointing for clinicians, is of theoretical significance. It encourages the view that there is a direct connection between the treatment provided and the effects observed; the specificity discourages explanations which rest on the operation of nonspecific factors such as, for example, the influence of the therapist–patient relationship" (1979, p. 476). Clomipramine had a significant effect on rituals and mood, but this effect was restricted to depressed patients. This finding shows that the drug has a useful antidepressive effect but does not seem to possess direct antiobsessive properties as has been believed.

The one-year follow-up showed that the effects of clomipramine were greatest at 18 weeks and declined thereafter. When patients stopped taking the drug they often relapsed and improved one more upon resuming the drug. There was no interactive effect between behavioral and pharmacological treatment. Rather, each treatment had its own specific effects on different aspects of functioning. An interesting finding was that clomipramine facilitated compliance with the behavioral treatment. In general, these results provide additional support for the use of behavioral treatment methods in the treatment of severe obsessive–compulsive disorders and suggest that multifaceted treatments will be necessary to cope with cases in which depression plays a role.

When Therapy Fails

It is a mark of the continuing development of behavior therapy that with documented clinical successes an established fact, attention has been focused on instances of therapeutic failure. Both Rachman and Hodgson (1980) and Foa (1979) have provided informative discussions of the clinical and theoretical implications of the failure to modify obsessive–compulsive disorders.

Reviewing the results of the several controlled outcome studies completed at the Institute of Psychiatry in London, Rachman and Hodgson concluded that the gross failure rate was roughly 20–28%. Indeed, a failure rate figure of approximately 30% probably describes the behavioral treatment literature in this area in general (Rachman & Wilson, 1980). Rachman and Hodgson discuss treatment failures in terms of patients' failure to adhere to either the exposure or the response prevention components of treatment. Their suggestions for facilitating adherence to *in vivo* exposure include the following:

1. The use of drugs to reduce anxiety or depression that might interfere with behavioral treatment requirements. (Note that in the therapy outcome study discussed above, comparing behavioral and pharmacological treatments, clomipramine did increase compliance with behavioral methods [Marks *et al.*, 1980].)
2. Increasing patients' motivation by more intensive and thorough preparation for treatment. (Typically, this vitally important "preparation" for specific behavioral treatment would be indiscriminately lumped into the catch-all category of "nonspecific" therapeutic factors, a most unsatisfactory way of proceeding.)
3. Adopting a more graduated approach.
4. Using modeling procedures to improve adherence. (Bandura, 1977b, would describe this function as one of several "response induction aids.")

For patients who fail to improve because they are unable to complete the response prevention part of behavioral treatment, Rachman and Hodgson recommend strictly enforced, externally imposed response prevention. In many studies, such as that reported by Rachman *et al.* (1979) and Marks *et al.* (1980), response prevention was client-controlled. Its success depended on the willingness of the patient to comply with the therapist's instructions. It should be noted that in their treatment program, Foa and her associates use strict response prevention procedures. Since this group has reported the most impressive therapy outcome results to date, it is tempting to infer that such a procedure, despite the taxing demands it makes on hospital staff and its added expense, is the preferred one.

Parenthetically, the use of externally supervised response prevention raises an important practical and theoretical concern. In their analysis of self-efficacy theory and the treatment of obsessive–compulsive disorders, Rachman and Hodgson point out that an externally imposed method of this kind could hardly be expected to increase a patient's sense of *self*-efficacy. As these authors imply, such a procedure would not be likely to foster the self-attribution of therapeutic change that is essential to the development of self-efficacy. This is the reason for including self-directed activities following externally supervised practice, whether it be in the treatment of phobic disorders using therapist-assisted *in vivo* exposure or therapist supervised response prevention in the treatment of obsessive–compulsive problems (see Bandura, 1977a).

Finally, Foa (1979) addressed the nagging question of why some patients fail to improve even when they comply with the requirements of behavioral treatment. This subgroup appears to be different from those discussed above and will probably require alternative treatment methods. Specifically, the two categories of patients identified by Foa are those who are severely depressed, and those who believe that their fears and obsessions are appropriate or realistic. In a further intriguing observation on these two subgroups of patients Foa reported that severely depressed obsessive–compulsives failed to show habituation (of their subjective distress) either during or between treatment sessions. Those who believed that their fears and obsessions were justified showed habituation during sessions but not between sessions. Future research on these and related issues relevant to reducing therapeutic failures of this kind is likely to be rewarding.

SUMMARY

Treatment of the anxiety disorders and the theoretical analysis of fear reduction treatment methods continues to be one of the most productive areas in behavior therapy. Major developments in the treatment of phobic disorders have included the publication of long-term follow-up studies, ranging from four to nine years, that confirm the value of behavioral treatment; the beginnings of a careful analysis of the effects of *in vivo* exposure treatment of agoraphobics on their marital satisfaction; and the further examination of the relative cost-effectiveness of different exposure treatments. At present, client-controlled *in vivo* exposure, with the aid of a detailed treatment manual, a cooperative spouse, and some minimal direction by the therapist appears to be a particularly promising treatment approach.

In vivo exposure is the preferred treatment of phobic disorders, but overall therapy outcome results still leave much to be desired. Accordingly, *in vivo* exposure treatment needs to be supplemented by different behavioral and possibly pharmacological methods in some cases. The incremental value of adjunctive marital therapy, cognitive restructuring, and drug therapy is critically discussed.

Although exposure treatments are usually effective to one degree or another, the reasons for their success remain to be identified. The past two years have been rich in research and ideas on possible theoretical mechanisms in fear reduction. Further support for self-efficacy theory has accumulated, while both Lang and Rachman have published influential papers on the concept of emotional processing. This latter line of thinking is likely to spur innovative research programs based on different conceptual models from traditional conditioning theory.

It is increasingly assumed that exposure, be it in imaginal, vicarious, or *in vivo* form, is a necessary component of fear reduction.

DeSilva and Rachman take issue with this assumption, showing on the basis of several lines of evidence and inference that exposure may often be sufficient but that it is not a necessary condition of fear reduction.

The three-systems model of fear and fear reduction holds that fear is not a single entity but a set of loosely coupled components. Hugdahl provides a critical discussion of this model and addresses the causal links among the components. This model is contrasted with Bandura's self-efficacy theory, and predictions from the three-systems model evaluated in the light of available evidence on fear reduction.

Obsessive–compulsive disorders are among the most difficult of all clinical problems to remedy. Significant developments in the behavioral treatment of these disorders include the publication of Rachman and Hodgson's definitive book on the subject, the publication of a major outcome study from the University of London's Institute of Psychiatry in which the joint and separate effects of behavioral treatment and pharmacotherapy were systematically evaluated, and initial analyses of the reasons for the rather consistent failure rate of roughly 30% in the behavioral treatment of obsessive–compulsive problems.

CHAPTER

4

COGNITIVE PROCESSES AND PROCEDURES IN BEHAVIOR THERAPY

PHILIP C. KENDALL

The increasing interest in the cognitive processes and procedures within behavior therapy has been documented in earlier volumes of the *Annual Review*. As noted in greater detail in Chapter 1, the trend continues. An informal information-providing newsletter by Dowd is in its third year, Meichenbaum's most recent research–review newsletter is Volume 4, and the journal *Cognitive Therapy and Research* has spanned half a decade. The special interest group of AABT remains active, and numerous papers, panels, and symposia at the recent AABT convention dealt with "cognitive" topics and issues. At least two books on cognitive–behavioral interventions are now available (i.e., Foreyt & Rathjen, 1978; Kendall & Hollon, 1979) as are two volumes on assessment for cognitive-behavioral interventions (Kendall & Hollon, 1981a; Merluzzi, Glass, & Genest, 1981). Other volumes, on cognitive–behavioral stress management (Meichenbaum & Jaremko, in press) and cognitive-behavior therapy with children (Meyers & Craighead, in press), are scheduled to appear in the near future. A serial publication, *Advances in Cognitive–Behavioral Research and Therapy* (Academic Press), will begin with Volume 1 in 1982 and provide an outlet for contemporary research, theory, and therapy pertinent to the study of the interaction of cognition and behavior and related therapeutic applications. There have also been two reviews of cognitive–behavioral and social-cognitive interventions with children (Hobbs, Moguin, Tyroler, & Lahey, 1980; Urbain & Kendall, 1980). If cognitive–behavioral therapy had come in for an annual checkup, the physician would be quite comfortable in offering an optimistic prognosis.

Finding that the organism is alive and without disease, however, does not further indicate that all systems are totally without weakness or that some systems could not be improved. In fact, there are several questions that continue to puzzle contemporary cognitive-behavior therapists. What is the proper role of emotional arousal and discharge? What guidelines can be used in deciding which cognitive techniques to employ and when to employ them? What does one do about client resistance or noncompliance? What alternatives exist for clients with limited cognitive abilities? Furthermore, while self-efficacy theory has generated enthusiasm and research, a wider range of investigations will be necessary to see if it will survive as a unifying theory of behavior change.

There exists the need for an understanding of common change principles across schools of therapy (Goldfried, 1980b). A related conceptual problem concerns "insights." A look into "insight" revealed that while it has been posited as a cognitive conceptualization for traditional therapies, an accurate assessment of it has decidedly been lacking. Further, insight has often been sidelined as the less than optimal outcome of treatment. While these truths are not challenged, one can question whether current cognitive intrusions into behavior therapy are leading to another bout with "insight." A number of the major proponents of cognitive–behavioral therapy have avoided mention of the term, but each has tended to underline the importance of the client's coming to accept the cognitive rationale for the disorder, coming to understand the importance of negative self-talk, and coming to realize the cognitive causes of behavior problems. Are these not insight issues? Are they (Roberts & Kendall, 1981)? One final question: Is insight anything more than the client's learning the language and conceptual system of the therapist (e.g., meaning of concepts) and becoming capable of expressing the problem in these new ways?

As illustrated in the preceding paragraphs, there are many conceptual questions. What appears to be needed, in addition to carefully conceived and carried out treatment outcome research, is the development of conceptual models (e.g., Beutler, 1979; Rachman, 1980) and theoretical systems (e.g., Bandura, 1977b; McFall & Wallersheim, 1979) to guide cognitive–behavioral procedures. There have been worthwhile efforts to describe the criteria for such conceptualizations (e.g., Arnkoff & Glass, 1982) and to consider cognitive psychological theory and its specific ramifications (e.g., Arnkoff, 1980; Marzillier, 1980), but we choose to point out that further developments are required (see also Mahoney & Arnkoff, 1978).

THE PROCESS OF THERAPY

For years, behavior therapists and researchers have been attentive to and concerned (perhaps overly concerned) with treatment *techniques* and therapy *outcomes*. The early claims of the superior efficacy of behavior therapy in comparison to other therapeutic approaches was based in part on a "techniques" argument (as well as presenting the pertinent data). Return for a moment to the mid- to late 1960s, when behavioral therapy was in its infant stage. Psychotherapy was being studied by other investigators, such as those with the perspective of client-centered therapy. Research into therapy *process* was quite active at that time (see Kiesler, 1973). One of the ancillary effects of the burgeoning interest in cognition within behavior therapy has been the reemergence of interest in the therapeutic process.

Three current sources illustrate the reemergence of process as a priority. First, the journal *Cognitive Therapy and Research* published a special issue on psychotherapy process (guest-edited by Goldfried, 1980c). Second, a semidialectical edited text by Mahoney (1980) places psychotherapy process as the keystone for discussion. Third, behavior therapy researchers have begun to investigate the role of process variables within behavior therapy (e.g., Ford, 1978, reprinted in Vol. 7, Franks & Wilson, 1979). In each case the reader comes to recognize the new involvement with what actually transpires in the course of therapy and how this ongoing process affects treatment outcome.

Goldfried's introduction to the special issue of *Cognitive Therapy and Research* suggests that therapists become more similar with increasing experience and that the well-seasoned therapists are likely to have "commonalities" that contribute significantly to the effectiveness of therapy (see also Goldfried, 1980b). He hastens to add that it would be an error to conclude that "we all do the same thing," but that the search for common underlying principles is not misguided. Toward this end, 13 therapists of differing theoretical perspectives each addressed five specific questions:

1. What is the role played by new experience provided to the patient/client in facilitating change?
2. To what extent does offering patients/clients feedback on their thinking, emotions, and behavior facilitate therapeutic change?
3. In what way do you see the therapist–patient/client relationship as contributing to the change process?
4. How have you used language/cognition/awareness in facilitating change within the therapeutic setting?
5. What clinical strategies or principles of change do you believe to be common across all therapeutic orientations? (Goldfried, 1980a, p. 272)

In one sense, providing the questions to be answered both details and perhaps limits the likely commonalities that will be identified. The latter might be considered restrictive, but it can also be directive, for the questions themselves help us to index the important commonalities. The first three questions have to do with the roles played by new experiences, feedback, and relationship issues. Here, embedded in the very questions, are three central commonalities! Effective psychotherapies provide new experiences, with guided feedback, in the context of a trusting relationship.

The fourth question was perhaps worded a bit too broadly, with the exact meaning of "language/cognition/awareness" open to discussion. For instance, psychoanalytically oriented responses dealt with "interpretations," behaviorally flavored answers mentioned cognitive change following performance-based procedures, while Gestalt comments tended to focus on increasing client awareness. Interestingly, the clear majority of responses, although sometimes superficial, expressed the opinion that some form of cognition was important within therapeutic change.

The final question directly asked each respondent to identify the strategies or principles believed to be common across therapeutic orientations. The answers to this query, in part, reaffirmed the importance of new experiences, guided feedback, and the therapeutic relationship. In addition, the majority of respondents addressed "expectations" or "beliefs" about positive outcomes as key to the benefits of therapy. Not all authors chose these specific terms, although it does seem reasonable to categorize "hope" and "changing misconceptions" within the same context as "expectations" and to draw the tentative conclusion that therapy provides an experience that alters the client's view of the future. Indeed, many of the responses also spoke of enhancing self-mastery and self-awareness, both of which would affect the client's ensuing expectations. Noteworthy by their absence, the client's past history and its reanalysis were seldom mentioned as a part of the core therapeutic principles. The implication here is that active participation in current experience is more powerful than reliving earlier experiences.

Self-identified behavior therapists may find only select portions of the special "psychotherapy process" issue to be reinforcing to their own beliefs. Similarly, readers with other theoretical persuasions will find only delimited endorsements of their positions. But we must keep in mind that it was the purpose of the special issue to take an eclectic look at therapy process and to avoid jargon. Seeking comfort in common terminology will not be possible. However, a synthesizing of the essential ingredients is possible and will likely promote an understanding of therapeutic strategies across theoretical lines. On the disappointing side, precious few of the commentaries attempted to make statements that used testable terminology.

It is of interest to return to an article published in 1972 to consider the three types of process studies that were then being conducted. According to Hertel (1972) the three basic designs included: (1) using pretherapy and posttherapy tests, (2) counting the occurrence of various categories of behavior within therapy, and (3) obtaining the contingencies between various categories of behavior. At the time of the publication of Hertel's paper, pre–posttreatment comparisons were sometimes used to operationalize process. Today we know these efforts as outcome studies, but when they were considered process studies they were subject to criticism—the fact that something happened between pre and post could not confirm the existence of any specific process. This approach, Hertel pointed out, treats process as one large unit rather than an unfolding series of smaller units.

The second way in which process was investigated involved the categorizing of events that happened in therapy and the operationalizing of process as the frequency of these events. This approach was criticized for relying solely on frequencies and failing to take into account the ordering of events. However, some clarity could be added by dividing therapy into sections or units of time and examining the frequency of events across these time units. Hertel's third design counted the contingency of two events—how often does a certain client's behavior follow a specific therapist behavior? This method operationalizes process as a series of one-step contingencies.

In addition to the merits of the categorization proposed by Hertel (1972), what can be learned from a reconsideration of process? The reader awaiting a single clear-cut answer will likely be disappointed, for, as yet, there is no such conclusion. We must point out, however, that there is nothing more foolish than the rediscovery of a crooked wheel: behavior therapists interested in "process" would be wise to acquaint themselves with the methodologies, problems, and suggested solutions that have already emerged from our earlier colleagues' efforts to untangle therapy process (e.g., Kiesler, 1973).

In a recent exposition, Kiesler (1980) offers direction to the psychotherapy process researchers of the 1980s. His sage prescriptions begin with the call for a synthesis of process and outcome research: "Outcome researchers must integrate process measures into their investigations, and process researchers must include measures of in-therapy and extra-therapy outcome" (p. 82). Topics that warrant attention include the analysis of nonverbal messages between therapist and client and the investigation of the evolving interpersonal transactions between therapist and client. Last, Kiesler (1980) identifies yet another crucial uniformity myth. Measures of therapy process are exceedingly general— investigators must develop process measures for particular homogeneous groups of clients. No one measure of process will uniformly serve the diversity of types of treatments and client disorders.

COGNITIVE PROCEDURES

A great many questions regarding the efficacy of cognitive–behavioral intervention procedures continue to require attention. Nevertheless, there have been increasing numbers of studies and added methodological sophistication, all buttressed by clarifications in the therapy procedures. Advances have been made, although interesting questions remain.

To provide some form of organization to our review of the literature pertinent to cognitive–behavioral procedures, we have divided the literature according to the treatment procedures employed. We considered an organization that focused on the type of disorder treated, but such an arrangement would have closely approximated the present organization and would have been open to redundancy in descriptions of procedures. We are, perhaps, not dividing the literature as each of our readers might prefer. There is no magic to our categories. Rather, they were selected to systematize the large bulk of research relevant to cognitive procedures within behavior therapy.

Cognitive Therapy of Depression

Enthusiasm has been spurred by the appearance of *Cognitive Therapy of Depression* (Beck, Rush, Shaw, & Emery, 1979), a book which provides the most detailed presentation of Beck's therapy to date. The enthusiasm is evident in the bulk of research that has recently appeared dealing with this and related treatment procedures.

While it is beyond the scope of the present chapter to describe the entire intervention, it is worthwhile to take a closer, albeit brief, look at what is entailed. As will be evident from a select citing from two chapters of the Beck *et al.* (1979) book, cognitive therapy for depression may more aptly be labeled cognitive–behavioral therapy for depression. We can readily accept Beck *et al.*'s tendency to retain the original label and their desire to place emphasis on cognitive changes as being the key factors in the treatment, but we prefer for the sake of clarity that the reader recognize the procedures as cognitive–behavioral. The felicity of this latter title is evident in the following excerpt from Beck *et al.* (1979):

The cognitive *therapy* of depression is based on the cognitive *theory* of depression. By working within the framework of the cognitive model, the therapist formulates his therapeutic approach according to the specific needs of a given patient at a particular time. Thus, the therapist may be conducting cognitive therapy even though he is utilizing predominantly behavioral or abreactive (emotion releasing) techniques. . . .

Specifically, engaging the patient's attention and interest the therapist attempts to induce the patient to counteract his withdrawal and to become involved in more constructive activities. . . .

The ultimate aim of these [behavioral] techniques in cognitive therapy is to produce change in the negative attitudes so that the patient's performance will continue to improve. Actually, the behavioral methods can be regarded as a series of small experiments designed to test the validity of the patient's hypotheses or ideas about himself. As the negative ideas are contradicted by these "experiments," the patient gradually becomes less certain of their validity and he is motivated to attempt more difficult assignments. (pp. 117–118)

And in the next chapter, on cognitive techniques, Beck *et al.* (1979) state:

The specific cognitive techniques are aimed at providing points of entry into the patient's cognitive organization. The techniques of questioning, of identifying illogical thinking, of ascertaining the rules according to which the patient organizes reality, are employed to help both the therapist and the patient to understand the patient's construction of reality. . . .

Since there is more verbal interchange during the "cognitive phase" of treatment, this aspect of the therapy is likely to be much closer to a joint enterprise than the earlier phase, which emphasizes behavioral techniques. (pp. 142–143)

In a nutshell, Beck's cognitive–behavioral therapy seeks to uncover, to examine through "experimental tests," and to correct the client's dysfunctional cognitions. A rather impressive literature has already appeared in support of the treatment (e.g., Rush, Beck, Kovacs, & Hollon, 1977; Shaw, 1977; Taylor & Marshall, 1977; see also Hollon & Beck, 1979), with some positive one-year follow-up data (Kovacs, Rush, Beck, & Hollon, 1981). Also, several recent reviews of the extant literature on the treatment of depression have appeared (see individual contributions in Rehm, 1981). A number of the reviewers have suggested that a combination of behavioral *and* cognitive intervention strategies offers considerable promise. In addition to this largely American group of authors, Whitehead, in England, offered a similar summary. Whitehead (1979) concluded that psychological treatment can be effective in alleviating depression and that therapies involing both behavioral and cognitive elements appear the most promising.

It is interesting to note, though the following data are not intended to serve as empirical support, that subjects who were asked, "When you are depressed, what sorts of things can make you feel worse?" responded "being alone" (24%), "inactivity" (20%), and "thinking about the problem that was getting them down" (18%) (Rippere, 1980). The things that cognitive–behavioral therapists do in treatment address these concerns.

A major outcome study in which four modes of treatment for clinically depressed outpatients were compared was reported by McLean and Hakstian (1979). One-hundred-ninety-six depressed patients were screened for level of depression (according to acceptable standards) and randomly assigned to treatment conditions. The four conditions were: (1) short-term psychotherapy, (2) relaxation therapy, (3) behavior therapy, and (4) drug therapy. The short-term psychotherapy sought to restore the client's functioning through insight into psychodynamic forces concerning the current depression and through the recognition of personality problems related to past experiences and current depression. Relaxation therapy focused on teaching the client to appreciate the relation between muscle tension and depression and to develop a significantly increased ability to relax. Sessions were largely devoted to practicing progressive muscle relaxation and reviewing homework assignments. The clients receiving the behavior therapy condition were informed that their depression was the result of ineffective coping techniques, and the treatment emphasized teaching effective ways to cope with stress. The task of therapy was to help clients to avoid their negative cognitive habits by engaging their environments. Clients were exposed to models, graduated practice exercises, and the monitoring of achievements. Last, those clients in the drug treatment were administered amitriptyline daily, with four physician appointments over the course of treatment. In all treatment conditions, spouses were included in some sessions when deemed appropriate, and each of the 10 sessions lasted approximately one hour.

McLean and Hakstian (1979) evaluated outcome via a large number of dependent variables. However, these measures were entirely self-report. The measures included the Beck Depression Inventory, Depression Adjective Checklist, Eysenck Personality Inventory, and a questionnaire prepared specifically for their study. The authors performed a factor analysis and derived seven factors, which (along with the Beck Depression Inventory, number of complaints, and personal treatment goals) constituted 10 outcome indices. On nine of the 10 measures, the behavioral treatment was superior at the end of treatment and marginally superior at three-month follow-up. The short-term psychotherapy fared most poorly, and there were no significant differences between relaxation and drug treatments (this is only the second study to report superior effects from a psychological rather than a pharmacological treatment).

Although this study leans more on the behavioral strategies that exist within cognitive–behavioral therapy, it can be said to share some common emphases with cognitive–behavioral procedures. As a result, while it clearly provides supportive evidence for behavioral therapy of depression, it may also be suggestive of the merits of the cognitive–behavioral perspective.

Methodologically, McLean and Hakstian (1979) included a few procedures that are worth mentioning in the hope that others will follow. First, therapist experience was taken into account by having therapists of different experience levels within each treatment condition. Second, the therapists were experts in the treatment that each provided. Both of these procedural niceties, while not the only method for controlling the related factors, are highly desirable characteristics of their study. Third, as we mentioned in Chapter 2, the use of normative comparisons in the evaluation of treatment provides data against which to compare the posttreatment levels of the treated clients. McLean and Hakstian included data on 55 normal subjects within their comparisons. Last, these authors categorized their clients according to pretreatment scores into one of four groupings and attempted to isolate types of clients for whom the treatment was most effective. Although this effort did not produce clear-cut differences, it is a desirable and laudable procedure and helps substantiate the meaningfulness of the therapy for clients in general.

Another major study (Zeiss, Lewinsohn, & Muñoz, 1979) reported on an evaluation of three different types of therapy for depression when applied to depressed individuals who responded to an announcement of the therapy research project. Sixty-six clients participated after having been screened using the Minnesota Multiphasic Personality Inventory (MMPI) and a clinical interview. The three treatment conditions were: (1) interpersonal skills training, (2) pleasant events scheduling, and (3) cognitive therapy. Patients receiving the interpersonal skills training worked on assertion, interpersonal style of expressive behavior, and social activity. Covert modeling was applied to overcome assertion problems and included instruction, modeling, rehearsal, and feedback. The same sequence of strategies was applied using specific goals related to interpersonal expressiveness. Last, increasing goals for social activity rounded out this treatment condition.

Clients receiving pleasant events scheduling monitored both pleasant events and mood. Based on these data, specific target activities were selected and patients began increasing target activities. Patients were also taught muscle relaxation and a systematic format for organizing their time and activities.

Cognitive therapy patients received treatment designed to change the way they thought about reality. Kelly's (1955) fixed-role therapy was adapted such that each client was instructed to take on a role, or characterization, as prepared by the therapist. Patients received a rationale stressing the importance of working with thoughts, and patients were taught to identify, categorize, and count certain thoughts. Self-monitoring of thoughts occurred each day. In addition, Zeiss *et al.* (1979) stated:

> A number of cognitive self-management techniques were used, including thought stopping and Premacking of positive thoughts (Mahoney, 1974) and Meichenbaum's (1974) self-talk procedure. Rational–emotive concepts were covered, and a procedure for disputing irrational thoughts was presented (Ellis & Harper, 1961; Kranzler, 1974). All techniques were presented as skills to be learned and practiced to become maximally useful. (p. 433)

The authors identify several factors that were common to all treatment modalities. First, treatment was brief and intense—all 12 sessions took place over a one-month period. The treatments were structured, but there was time to discuss individual issues raised by each client.

A wide variety of assessments were employed to evaluate the treatments. The assessments included self-reports, behavioral observations, and ratings by others. Self-report measures included an Interpersonal Events Schedule, a Pleasant Events Schedule, a Personal Beliefs Inventory, a Subjective Probability Questionnaire, and the *D* scale of the MMPI. Behavioral observations were taken, with coders rating levels of social skill and cognitive style. Peers also rated social skills and cognitive style.

The outcome of the Zeiss *et al.* (1979) study was summarized as follows: "Results indicated that all treatment modalities significantly alleviated depression. However, no treatment modality had specific impact on the variables most relevant to its treatment format" (p. 427).

Two related studies deserve mention. In a study by Fleming and Thornton (1980), behavioral, cognitive, and nondirective treatments were applied in workshop groups. In the cognitive workshop, clients were taught to modify depressive thoughts and irrational assumptions according to the manual by Shaw (1977). Self-monitoring, self-evaluation, and self-reward, as in the self-control therapy of Fuchs and Rehm (1977), constituted the behavioral workshop. The nondirective workshop was essentially a client-centered treatment (i.e., therapists focused on maintaining genuineness, accurate empathy, and unconditional positive regard). These authors reported "significantly decreased depressive symptomatology as measured by general, cognitive, and self-report behavioral measures of depression" (Fleming & Thornton, 1980, p. 652). Like Zeiss *et al.*, not all of the treatments in the Fleming and Thornton study involved skills training. This pattern of results led Fleming and Thornton to question whether or not skills training is the key component in altering depression.

Dunn (1979) treated a sample of psychiatric outpatients who were neither suicidal nor organic, but who were suffering from depression (and maintained on medications). Twenty patients participated in either a cognitive–behavioral intervention or a waiting condition consisting of medication and support. The goals of the intervention, in the words of Dunn, were "to elicit patients' maladaptive, rigid, punitive self-report related to five target cognitive processes, and to challenge and confront the depression-prone self-report patterns, while modeling and reinforcing the use of more precise, adaptive cognitive processes in depression management situations" (pp. 308–309). Treatments occurred twice weekly for eight weeks. Dunn collected data using the Beck Depression Inventory, a frequency count of adaptive, nondepressive verbalizations, and a rating of depression. The last two measures were based on videotapes of the patients' behavior. The outcome supported the cognitive–behavioral therapy since treated patients reduced their expressed and observed level of depression as well as increased their adaptive, nondepressive verbalizations.

Beyond the apparent support for the psychological treatment of depression, two topics of concern emerge from our review of these important studies. First, evaluation of the procedures for the treatment of depression will not be capable of cumulative examination until the researchers clarify the existing *semantic dilemma*. The problem is one of imprecise terminology. There are several treatment strategies relevant to the problems of depression, and outcome researchers are trying, with much to be said in their support, to compare the different treatment approaches. However, one researcher's "cognitive therapy" is not another's "cognitive therapy." One researcher's "behavioral approach" is "cognitive–behavioral," yet another researcher's "cognitive therapy" is also "cognitive–behavioral." Undoubtedly, a confusing state of affairs! In still other cases, what has been labeled "cognitive therapy" by title has in only limited fashion any resemblance to Beck's "cognitive therapy." For instance, recall that Zeiss *et al.*'s (1979) "cognitive therapy" was a conglomerate of fixed-role, thought-stopping, and rational–emotive strategies. The comparative studies of the treatments for depression are at a stage where clarification of what is meant by each treatment modality is essential.

Second, evaluations of treatments for depression, including behavioral, cognitive–behavioral, and related therapies, must employ cognitive and behavioral assessments. In addition to the already well-recognized limitations, the sole reliance on self-report data does not allow for an examination of whether or not cognitive change corresponds with behavioral change. Similarly, one cannot determine whether or not behavioral changes occur in the absence of cognitive change and whether or not cognitive changes occur as a result of other forms of therapy. Whereas McLean and Hakstian placed too much emphasis on self-report, Zeiss *et al.* made the laudable effort to measure behavioral and cognitive changes. Zeiss *et al.* deserve credit for assessing not only the frequency of positive and negative thoughts, but also the perceived emotional impact of these thoughts on their subjects. Unfortunately, the measures employed in the Zeiss *et al.* study to assess cognitive variables were instruments that have not been systematically examined with psychometric (reliability and validity) considerations in mind. This unwanted state of affairs reflects more on the current need for studies of the assessments of cognition than it does on Zeiss *et al.*

Correspondingly, self-efficacy, the critical cognitive variable which Zeiss *et al.* invoke in their explanation of their outcome, was not measured. Again, this reflects more on the current need for measurement methodologies than on any neglect on the part of the researchers. It will be wise, nonetheless, for future research to include a measurement of self-efficacy to determine if the hypothesized change on this variable did in fact occur as a result of treatment. It will also be valuable to include an assessment of self-efficacy in studies designed to compare different treatments to determine if self-efficacy changes are related to improvements produced by *non*behavioral and *non*cognitive interventions.

Rational–Emotive Therapy (RET)

The question of whether or not RET is aptly categorized as a part of behavior therapy remains a topic of discussion. Zettle and Hayes (1980) noted that RET differs from most cognitive–behavioral therapies because it is not rooted in behaviorism. These authors also pointed out that while RET was not mentioned in some behavior therapy texts, it has received expanded discussion in recent editions of other behavior therapy texts. Despite considerable reservations explored each year, RET continues to be included in this *Annual Review* series.

Initial sentiments expressed by Ellis (1973) suggested that RET was different from cognitive–behavioral approaches, and Ellis (1980) has recently offered a more detailed account of the similarities and differences between RET and cognitive behavior therapy, as he sees them. Ellis (1980) proposes that RET can be subclassified into general or *nonpreferential RET* and specialized or *preferential RET*. According to this dichotomy, cognitive–behavioral therapy is synonymous with general or nonpreferential RET, but it is not synonymous with specific or preferential RET. The choice of these adjectives suggests that Ellis may have taken a less pejorative position, for an earlier dichotomy referred to the distinctions as "general" RET versus "elegant" RET. General RET or cognitive-behavior therapy is considered the more generic descriptor, whereas preferential RET, which is potentially but not necessarily included under the generic term, has special meaning. Ellis offers his distinctions under the headings of cognitive, emotive, and behavioral, and these distinctions *as seen by Ellis* are outlined in Table 4-1.

TABLE 4-1.

Summary of the Similarities and Differences between RET (Preferential RET) and CBT (General RET) *According to Ellis* (1980)

	Type of therapy	
Dimensions	Rational–emotive therapy	Cognitive-behavior therapy
Cognitive		
*Philosophical	Profound philosophical perspective	Does not stress a philosophical outlook
Humanistic	Humanism is intrinsic	Usually humanistic, but does not have to be
Goals and purposes	A new philosophical outlook	
Self-ratings	Does not espouse positive self-ratings	
Use of humor	Stresses, but does not mandate, the use of humor	May include humor
Antimusturbatory techniques	Attacks the "must" or "should" premise	Often employs empirical arguments to show clients
Disputing techniques	More actively disputes client irrationality and teaches the client to self-dispute; also employs other methods	Employs other methods, with less disputing
Recognition of cognitive palliative methods	Relies less on these and more on underlying philosophies	Cognitive distraction methods (e.g., relaxation)

TABLE 4-1. (*Continued*)

Dimensions	Type of therapy	
	Rational–emotive therapy	Cognitive-behavior therapy
*Problem solving	Discourages problem solving until after irrationality is confronted	Employs problem solving
Discomfort anxiety	Looks for and disputes reasons for discomfort anxiety	Deals with anxiety, but to a lesser extent
Secondary symptoms	Looks more for secondary symptoms	Is less concerned with secondary symptoms
Selectivity of techniques	Eclectic, but more selective	Eclectic
Emotive		
Discriminating appropriate from inappropriate	Favors some emotive techniques, but not others; accepts emotions, but tries to alter related self-defeating aspects	Less selective; tries to alter emotions
Work on emotion	Emotion-evocative exercises	Emotion-evocative exercises
Relationship procedures	More selective, emphasizes therapist's accepting and teaching of self-acceptance	Concerned with relationship
*Forceful emotive interventions	Important for therapists to use a great deal of force in interrupting client's philosophies	Less forceful
Behavioral		
*Operant conditioning	Skeptical view of social reinforcement, but, for practical reasons, adopts Skinnerian methods	Less selective, uses a wider range of behavioral techniques
Penalization	Often utilizes self-penalization	Emphasis on reinforcement methods
In vivo desensitization	Favored more than imaginal	Uses desensitization
Flooding/implosive therapy	Much more use of these procedures	Less often used
Skill training	Used, but only with changing basic irrationality	Used

Note. Asterisk (*) indicates a somewhat more fair distinction in our opinion.

Ellis may have changed the titles he assigned to the types of RET ("preferential" RET rather than "elegant" RET), but the bulk of the differences he points out still reflects the basic idea that cognitive-behavior therapy is somehow less elegant. This implication is perhaps most clearly visible in Ellis's consistent use of the term "more selective" to describe RET in relation to cognitive–behavioral approaches (see Table 4-1). A list of distinctions that is somewhat more fair may be constructed by including only those items marked by an asterisk in Table 4-1.

A second concern readily emerges from an analysis of Ellis's article. He assumes that cognitive-behavior therapy is a single treatment approach. This assumption is not justified. Stress-inoculation training, cognitive therapy of depression, rational restructuring, self-instructional training, and covert modeling, to name several, are not equivalent. Furthermore, one could also argue that there are preferential (elegant) and nonpreferential (inelegant) forms of each of these treatment modalities. For example, self-instructional training in which clients are simply taught to say certain things to themselves is "inelegant." When clients are provided a sequence of experiences where they learn to adapt or modify their internal dialogue and are given opportunities for guided practice in increasingly distressing situations, then the procedure becomes more "elegant." It might also be mentioned that Ellis's proposed distinction based on RET's greater use of punitive methods would be inaccurate in self-instructional training with children where the method is typically accompanied by response-cost contingencies (Kendall & Finch, 1979c; Kendall & Wilcox, 1980).

An encouraging aspect of the Ellis paper lies in the concluding section where he first states specific hypotheses about the effectiveness of RET and cognitive–behavioral procedures, and then goes on to encourage the systematic examination of these notions. While not everyone will agree with the hypotheses as stated, they do provide a basis for empirical questioning.

Writers who are involved with cognitive-behavior therapy (Meichenbaum, 1977b; Mahoney, 1977) and RET (DiGiuseppe, Miller, & Trexler, 1977) have not stated that RET is a *proven* therapy. Quite the contrary, these authors recognize the limited nature of the data offered in support of the utility of RET. Perhaps the most current and complete review offers an accurate summary: "Because the effectiveness of RET is unknown, both by itself and as it is usually practiced in the treatment of nonassertiveness, any generalizations to its clinical efficacy in this area should be made with considerable reservation" (Zettle & Hayes, 1980, p. 160). To provide this caveat is not to say that there are no studies that support the effectiveness of the treatment, but rather that the studies are less than optimal for various reasons. One of these reasons pertains to the types of subjects studied. Carefully controlled evaluations of RET with *clinical* samples are quite rare.[1] For this reason, a recent study by Lipsky, Kassinove, and Miller (1980) is especially noteworthy.

Lipsky *et al.* (1980) studied the effectiveness of RET using 50 adults who were applying for psychotherapy at an outpatient clinic. The clients were described as either "neurotic" or "adjustment reaction of adulthood." Psychotics, addicted personalities, children, and adults with IQs less than 80 were excluded. Clients were then randomly assigned to one of five treatment groups and one of two therapists. (Treatment effects did not differ across therapists, and the data were combined.) The five treatment groups were: (1) RET (clients were taught the RET conceptualization of maladjustment and were given bibliotherapy and behavioral homework assignments); (2) RET plus rational role reversal (same as RET with a total of 10 rational role reversal experiences); (3) RET plus rational–emotive imagery (same as RET with 10 experiences practicing imagining rational thinking, feeling, and acting); (4) an attention–alternate treatment control (supportive therapy and deep muscle relaxation); and (5) a no-contact control. The dependent variables included measures of rational thinking, anxiety, depression, and neuroticism and were administered before and after the 12-session therapy.

Lipsky *et al.* (1980) reported that "on each dependent variable used, RET, either alone or in combination with rational role reversal or rational–emotive imagery, was superior to both no–contact and a realistic alternate treatment condition" (p. 371). They further noted that both rational role reversal and rational-emotive imagery were useful adjuncts to RET, with large proportions of the dependent variables evidencing superior results for the "RET plus" conditions.

While this study is to be commended for undertaking the careful evaluation of RET and several of its components with a clinical population, it was limiting to have employed only verbal self-report measures. The authors themselves recognized this limitation. However, it would have been highly desirable to have acquired and analyzed videotapes of role plays, for example, as an additional index of outcome. Ratings by others (e.g., spouses) would also have been advisable. In the absence of such data, conclusions about the effects of RET are restricted to clients' statements about themselves.

One additional thought about the Lipsky *et al.* study. The clients were outpatients in a county just outside New York City. We are all

---

1. It should be noted that a study of the treatment of stuttering by Moleski and Tosi (1976), in which the effects of RET and systematic desensitization were compared, could be considered an instance of a clinical sample—stuttering is a real problem. Also, an unpublished paper by Brandsma, Maultsby, and Welsh (1978; see also Franks & Wilson, 1980) reports on an application of RET to problems of alcoholism.

familiar with the confrontive quality of RET and the verbal exchanges required to dispute irrational thinking. We are all also familiar with the greater tolerance for and experience with verbal bantering that is said to characterize the New York City environs. Would an RET or RET-like treatment be equally effective with outpatients in Charlotte, North Carolina?

Before we leave the topic of RET, there is an aside we would like to mention briefly. Many of the beliefs individuals come to hold have been quietly but forcefully imposed upon them by the world in which they live. Common "pop" expressions, television scripts, family background, and popular music influence our clients' thinking. For instance, consider the lyrics of the 1980 Grammy-award-winning song by the Doobie Brothers:

> What a fool believes he sees
> No wise man has the power to reason away. . . .
> —*lyrics by M. McDonald/K. Loggins*

Those who employ RET as a method for changing belief systems must recognize and accept this challenge.

Stress Inoculation

The stress inoculation procedures for the treatment of fears and stress developed by Meichenbaum and his colleagues (e.g., Meichenbaum & Cameron, 1973; Meichenbaum & Turk, 1976) have been examined at the procedural and outcome levels (Jaremko, 1979b) and have been applied to the stress of psychiatric hospitalization (Holcomb, 1979) and invasive medical procedures (Kendall, in press). A collection of contributions on the current application of stress-inoculation procedures to stress management and prevention is soon forthcoming (Meichenbaum & Jaremko, in press).

A nicely prepared review by Jaremko (1979b) details the procedures for stress inoculation and provides a review of the literature on their effectiveness. Consistent with the original conception of stress inoculation, Jaremko addresses each of the treatment's three components: education, rehearsal, and application. The educational phase consists of the presentation of a rationale and the examination of stress as a series of events. Jaremko noted that "a stringent test of the contribution of the educational rationale of SI [stress inoculation] has yet to be undertaken" (p. 37).

The rehearsal (or skill training) phase was distinguished by Jaremko as that which was considered most important by a number of researchers (Novaco, 1976; Horan, Hackett, Buchanan, Stone, & Demchick-Stone, 1977; Hussian & Lawrence, 1978). In this phase of treatment the client is taught the coping skills that are to be used to deal with stress. A surprisingly diverse list of skills have been included: relaxation, cognitive restructuring (in this context meaning a collaborating with the client to identify and modify negative self-statements), self-instructions, and other cognitive strategies such as distraction and attention focusing.

In the final phase, application, the client is given practice in the use of the coping skills taught in the earlier stages. Differences exist in the literature, with some studies using imaginal stressors (e.g., Novaco, 1976) and others employing actual exposure (e.g., Horan *et al.*, 1977). Jaremko also pointed out that there are variations in the amount of practice provided and in whether or not clients teach the coping skills to other clients. Variability also exists around the degree to which "modification of self-talk" can be said to be an operationalization of stress-inoculation (e.g., Girodo & Roehl, 1978). Jaremko's analysis of the stress-inoculation literature provides evidence of the utility of the treatment, but it also identifies notable fluctuations in the manner in which the treatment is applied across studies. Importantly, Jaremko avails his reader of the current questions facing stress inoculation and provides an integrated summary of the procedure.

The argument often goes, "OK, but the true test is with clinical patients!" Furthermore, in some circles, the agrument further asks, "Is it better than medications?" A recent report by Holcomb (1979) offers some valuable, though limited, data on the efficacy of stress inoculation procedures in relation to chemotherapy with clinical cases. Holcomb evaluated stress-inoculation procedures with patients hospitalized for severe stress reactions. These "stress reactions" covered a wide range of diagnoses. Twenty-six acute patients were randomly assigned to one of three groups: (1) stress-inoculation training, (2) stress-inoculation training and chemotherapy, and (3) chemotherapy. Subjects received the stress-inoculation training in an average of eight one-hour sessions from the therapist (who was also the experimenter). The stress-inoculation training included autogenic training as a relaxation coping skill, cognitive restructuring as a cognitive change procedure, and rehearsal and modeling as performance-oriented behavioral procedures. Dosage level and type of drug for chemotherapy patients were determined by each patient's physician. Seven measures of distress (e.g., MMPI Depression and Psychasthenia scales and subscores on the Symptom Checklist 90, and the State–Trait Anxiety Inventory) were combined via multivariate methods to produce one dependent measure called "subjective distress" (this factor accounted for 93% of the variance).

Patients were assessed within two days of their arrival at the hospital, again after five days, and finally after the intervention was over.

There was no significant difference on the Subjective Distress factor across the groups at pretreatment. All three groups showed some decrease in Subjective Distress over the first pretreatment week, but the group that received only stress inoculation was significantly superior to the chemotherapy-only group in reducing Subjective Distress assessed after treatment. These data provide support for the merits of stress inoculation for clients with severe stress and suggests the superiority of this treatment over medications. These data are, however, limited by a number of shortcomings in the study. First, the outcome data were obtained by self-report. Second, the therapist was the experimenter. Last, no follow-up data were included. Nevertheless, as an initial demonstration of the application of stress inoculation to severe stress reactions the Holcomb study appears quite promising.

Using an analogue pain situation, Klepac, Hauge, Dowling, and McDonald (1981), conducted an examination of three components of stress inoculation. Seventy-two students with strong fear of going to the dentist were randomly assigned to eight experimental conditions. The eight experimental conditions represented factorial combinations of three components of stress inoculation: relaxation training, instruction in cognitive coping skills, and exposure to a stressor. Measures of arm shock tolerance, tooth shock tolerance, pain, and anxiety were employed. The treatment sessions consisted of a general orientation, using Melzack and Wall's (1965) gate control therapy to describe pain as a complex experience which can be controlled, and *two half-hour sessions* where the treatment components were dispensed. For the relaxation intervention, Benson's (1975) relaxation procedure was employed since it is intended to be brief. A cafeteria-style array of coping skills (after Meichenbaum, 1977a) were described, modeled, and discussed, with each subject practicing his or her preferred strategy(ies). In the exposure condition, subjects were administered tolerance levels of electrical stimulation to the arm (improvements in tolerance were praised). At first glance, it seems that the cognitive treatment may have tried to accomplish too much in too little time.

The authors report that each of the treatment components increased arm-shock tolerance, but none of the strategies generalized to a second stressor not available during training (tooth shock). The combination of relaxation and exposure led to a greater tolerance than either alone. It was pointed out by Klepac *et al.* that the exposure condition repeatedly took subjects to tolerance levels of pain, that improvements were visible as a result of plotting tolerance levels, and that improvements were reinforced. There seems to have been more to the exposure condition than just exposure.

The conclusions drawn from this otherwise solid study are limited by the brevity of the cognitive intervention and by the absence of cognitive assessments. That is, it remains possible that the subjects in the "exposure" condition were actually using some of their own cognitive strategies to control the pain. Only when measures of such cognitive functioning are included can we begin to make statements about the role of these processes in tolerance or adjustment.

The stress-inoculation model has been extended to the treatment of anger (Novaco, 1979). The three treatment phases (i.e., cognitive preparation, skill acquisition, and application training) remain generally intact, with the modifications of the procedures relating most directly to the target problem—anger. Previously reported evidence supports the effectiveness of the cognitive–behavioral control of anger (Novaco, 1975, 1976, 1977) and recent evidence adds further corroboration.

One area where the lack of control of anger has potentially disasterous effects is child abuse. Meichenbaum has repeatedly called for the study of intervention procedures that have applicability to the treatment and prevention of child abuse. A cognitive–behavioral treatment was applied with child-abusing parents by Denicola and Sandler (1980). These authors worked with two families referred by criminal justice and social service agencies for actual incidences of child abuse. The treatments (provided in 12 sessions ranging from 60 to 90 minutes) were complex, including parent training (reading a text, discussing the material, observing videotaped demonstrations, modeling, role playing, and rehearsal) and coping-skills training (relaxation, self-instructions, and problem solving).

The effects were evaluated by examining the rates of observed behaviors gathered over eight half-hour sessions. Examinations of these data showed a reduction in total aversive behavior and an increase in prosocial behaviors. Though limited by the type of single-subject design used and the small number of families treated, Denicola and Sandler have begun to make application of anger control procedures in a place where they are sorely needed.

Cognitive Restructuring

The phrase "cognitive restructuring" means different things to different people! At the most general extreme it is synonymous with "cognitive therapy" and can be said to refer to any treatment that seeks to modify behavior by altering the client's pattern of thought. At the most specific extreme, cognitive restructuring refers to a technique developed by Goldfried, Decenteceo, and Weinberg (1974) called systematic rational restructuring. Unfortunately, the cognitive–behavioral outcome literature is replete with reports of other studies where the authors are not clear in what they mean by "cognitive restructuring." Insufficient explication of the treatment procedures, sometimes the result of authors resorting to the use of a descriptive title, can leave one uncertain as to the exact procedures that were followed.

Unlike the more delimited meaning associated with labels such as RET, cognitive therapy for depression, and self-instructional training, cognitive restructuring appears to be used as a descriptive term referring to interventions that employ "RET-like," "Meichenbaumish," and "Goldfriedian" strategies. The treatments are no less organized, but they do seem to draw from various sources rather than a single source. The literature evaluating cognitive restructuring interventions has burgeoned, with applications for assertion and anxiety appearing in the recent past.

Hammen, Jacobs, Mayol, and Cochran (1980) report on an interesting comparison of cognitive restructuring methods and skills training procedures in the treatment of assertion difficulties. A waiting-list control was also employed. The skills training groups did homework exercises, practiced assertive behavior in sessions, set goals, imagined assertive behavior, role played, and received feedback. Mastery of the assertive response was described to clients as the crucial factor. For the subjects in the cognitive behavioral groups, a discussion of personal rights was followed by lecture and demonstration of cognitive restructuring. Group members were taught to identify problem situations and to develop a list of the interfering thoughts and appropriate coping statements for that situation. Group members discussed these written materials, and trainers emphasized the importance of thinking differently about the problematic situations.

The results of the Hammen et al. (1980) study suggest that skills acquisition and cognitive restructuring are equally effective: both treatment conditions improved self-report and behavioral indices of assertion more than the waiting-list controls. One of the hypotheses initially put forth by Hammen and her colleagues was that the client's level of dysfunctional attitudes would interest with the types of treatment provided. Such an interaction was not found, but the level of dysfunctional attitudes did predict response to treatment in general. Those clients with low levels of dysfunctional attitudes showed more improvement than those with high levels of dysfunctional attitudes. An interesting problem emerges here, as Hammen *et al.* suggested—it is the highly dysfunctional clients that present the real treatment challenge.

In an outpatient setting, patients suffering from general anxiety problems were randomly assigned to cognitive restructuring, a form of systematic desensitization, a combined treatment (called combined cognitive behavior modification by the authors), or a no-treatment control. The researchers, Woodward and Jones (1980), provided the treatments for 27 subjects (seven per group, six in the combined group). A number of self-report assessments were taken, including self-reported anxiety (e.g., Fear Survey Schedule [FSS]), and a detailed cognitive diary that was later scored for subjective anxiety and thinking time.

The cognitive restructuring intervention consisted of three phases. The first phase entailed the presentation of a rationale in which the nature of self-defeating self-statements and irrational beliefs were discussed. The second phase concerned the identification of negative self-talk in the problems presented by the clients, while the third phase encouraged clients to modify maladaptive and utilize adaptive self-statements in anxiety-provoking situations. Imaginal exercises, with self-instructions for preparation, confrontation, coping, and reinforcement during the imagined scene, were also included. The systematic desensitization condition was similar to the cognitive restructuring condition except that the manner of coping was relaxation—no mention was made of thinking style of negative self-statements. Individualized hierarchies were formed and clients imagined coping while relaxed. The combined treatment condition initially emphasized the cognitive restructuring component, with relaxation stressed during the latter sessions. Woodward and Jones (1980) reported that "the combined cognitive behavior modification group improved significantly more than the other two active treatment groups and control group in terms of FSS intensity score. The CBM group and modified SD group were also significantly better than the cognitive restructuring group in terms of lowered subjective anxiety diary score" (p. 405).

While this study is to be commended for its use of clinical cases, a few limitations should be considered. First, the authors report that improvement scores were greater for those patients who began treatment with higher levels of problems. For example, treatment responders, as defined by FSS scores, had higher initial FSS scores than nonresponders. The possibility of regression effects cannot be eliminated. The authors also noted that their sample may have been of a lower level of intellectual ability and therefore not the proper candidates for the cognitive restructuring intervention. A lowered level of functioning could certainly affect the outcome of these types of treatments, and it may be wise for future studies to include indications of the level of intelligence of the patients. One of the interesting findings, though only suggestive, was that subjects who spent a lot of time thinking about their problems (think time from the cognitive diary) also tended to report the most anxiety.

Cognitive restructuring had a more specific meaning in the case of the study reported by Kanter and Goldfried (1979). These authors compared "systematic rational restructuring" with self-control desensitization, a combination of the two procedures, and a waiting-list control. The 68 clients were community members who responded to an ad announcing a treatment for social anxiety. Those clients receiving the systematic rational restructuring were taught to recognize the unrealistic and self-defeating nature of thoughts that led to anxiety and to substitute more reasonable cognitive analyses. Clients were taught to use anxiety as a signal to identify unrealistic thoughts. Imagery was used to move up an anxiety hierarchy. Homework assignments and the resultant client descriptions of their actions and thoughts were discussed in therapy. The self-control desensitization treatment followed Goldfried (1971). The combined treatment received both intervention strategies.

Kanter and Goldfried's (1979) results indicate that all three treatment conditions led to significant decreases in anxiety at posttreatment, and these results were either maintained or improved upon at followup. The overall pattern of results led Kanter and Goldfried to conclude that the rational restructuring condition was more effective than desensitization in reducing anxiety and irrational beliefs, and that it produced more within-group improvements than desensitization. The authors point out, however, that while the findings are supportive of the efficacy of the systematic rational restructuring procedure, the findings for the behavioral checklist and pulse rate measures failed to differentiate among conditions. An ancillary hypothesis, that treatment effects would differ for subjects with varying degrees of anxiety, was not confirmed. This study can be added to the list of recent studies that have failed to find an interaction between type of treatment and level of anxiety/assertiveness.

In contrast, client anxiety level was found to function as a moderator variable on the effectiveness of treatment in a study by Safran, Alden, and Davidson (1980). Safran et al. evaluated behavioral skills training and cognitive-restructuring procedures in the treatment of assertion problems. Behavioral skills training included modeling, feedback, and rehearsal. Cognitive restructuring included identifying maladaptive self-statements and employing cognitive coping. Subjects were divided into high-anxious and low-anxious groups on the basis of the discomfort scale of the Assertion Inventory (Gambrill & Richey, 1975). The low-anxious subjects evidenced comparable improvements as a result of both treatments, whereas the high-anxious subjects benefited more from skills training on behavioral measures. There was also a trend for the high-anxious subjects to benefit more from rational restructuring as measured by the self-report scales.

The search for interactions between types of treatments and types of clients is no doubt a key, yet formidable, question facing clinical researchers. Kiesler's (1971) research model for therapy outcome studies clearly endorses the search for "what works best for what specific type of client." Yet one must approach the search for interactions carefully. While it may seem especially pertinent at the beginning level of research on this question to include several client typologies and examine each to see if any one single dimension can separate treatment responders from nonresponders, one must keep an eye on theory. Why, for instance, should high- and low-anxious clients respond differently to different types of treatment for assertion? One important place for theory within behavior therapy is in the development of an understanding of the interactions between treatment types and client types.

The identification of an interaction between anxiety level and type of treatment has not received consistent support in the recent literature. As mentioned, Kanter and Goldfried did not find an interaction, whereas Safran et al. did. As Safran et al. suggested, it may be that the different types of treatment that were contrasted with rational restructuring (i.e., self-control desensitization and behavioral skills training, respectively) or the different assessment instruments used to identify high and low subjects account for the inconsistency.

Although the procedures of treatment implied by the label "cognitive restructuring" have typically been employed with adult clients, Forman (1980) reported on an application with aggressive elementary school children. In her study, 18 referrals for aggression in school were assigned to either cognitive restructuring, response-cost, or placebo control conditions. The 12 30-minute sessions of cognitive restructuring (in groups with two therapists) consisted of describing aggression-provoking situations, stating what each person was likely thinking in the situation, developing a script of thoughts that would not have led them to get angry, and having the children close their eyes and imagine the aggression-inducing situation while thinking the nonaggressive thoughts. The response-cost treatment was set up such that children in this condition were fined for exhibiting aggressive behavior in the classroom (these children also met with the therapist to control for attention). Children in the placebo control condition met with the therapist but did not receive treatment.

Forman (1980) collected teacher ratings, teacher incidence reports (incidences of aggression), and independent observations of the childrens' behavior in the classroom. The analyses of these data indicated that both cognitive restructuring and a response-cost program were significantly more effective than the placebo control in reducing aggressive behavior, and the results add to the support of cognitive training in the modification of childhood behavior problems. As we will discuss next, the literature on self-instructional training suggests that a cognitive-training *plus* behavioral contingencies treatment is superior to either treatment alone. In the case of aggression in children, it seems reasonable to propose that a similarly combined strategy might maximize therapeutic benefit.

Self-Instructional Training

Of the cognitive-behavior therapies, self-instructional training is most closely associated with interventions in the domain of child clinical psychology (see Chapter 7). Indeed, most of the interventions appearing in the literature have focused on the training of *thinking processes* in order to modify child behavior problems. Self-instructional training is not the only cognitive-behavior therapy for children; social-cognitive problem-solving training and social perspective-taking training would be two examples of approaches that teach thinking strategies to modify behavior (Kendall, 1981c). Nevertheless, the large majority of research reports on cognitive behavioral interventions with children have emphasized self-instructional training, with the target disorders typically being impulsivity/hyperactivity, non-self-control, and aggression. These target problems are typical since theoretical guides suggest that these types of problems are associated with deficits in internal, mediational processing (Kendall, 1977). Of late, however, the applications of self-instructional procedures have broadened beyond impulsivity/hyperactivity to include reading and math difficulties and attention problems. Self-instructional procedures have also expanded to adult disorders, with some reports using self-instructions almost exclusively while others include it as one component of a multifaceted cognitive–behavioral procedure.

An example of a cognitive–behavioral treatment employing self-instructions with children (i.e., Kendall & Finch, 1978) was reprinted in the previous volume of the *Annual Review* (Franks & Wilson, 1980). Since that time, a number of directly related commentaries and studies have appeared. For instance, Abikoff and Ramsey (1979) reanalyzed part of the Kendall and Finch (1978) data and suggested that initial (pretreatment) differences between groups should have been used as covariates in an analysis of covariance. Kendall and Finch (1979a) replied, indicating that tests conducted to determine the appropriateness of covariance were counterindicative and that, due to the direction of the differences, covariance was likely to inflate rather than detract from the results. Because of an unlikely negative relationship between measures, Abikoff and Ramsey's reanalysis reduced the group differences.

Additional analyses of data from the Kendall and Finch (1978) outcome study focus on further changes resulting from treatment. For example, the Matching Familiar Figures test performance of the impulsive children (treated and controls) was tape-recorded and examined along with performances by children classified as reflective (Kendall & Finch, 1979b). The verbal behavior was recorded at pretreatment, posttreatment, and follow-up. Codes for the verbal behavior were developed, and the taped data were coded into categories. The results indicated nonsignificant effects for several specific codes, but the impulsive children that had received treatment evidenced a significant increase in total on-task verbal behavior at posttreatment. This finding adds to the support for the treatment.

As noted by Franks and Wilson (1980 and further discussed in Chapter 7), the evidence that self-instructional procedures can produce treatment generalization is equivocal (see also Meichenbaum & Asarnow, 1979). One factor that has been hypothesized to affect treatment generalization was the *type* of self-instructions that the children are taught (Kendall & Wilcox, 1980). Should children be instructed to use self-guiding talk that is *specific* to each task that they work on, or should the emphasis be on the use of general, *conceptual* self-instructions? Notions of metacognition (such as thinking about thinking) would suggest that conceptual training would be more effective than concrete training. In the Kendall and Wilcox (1980) experiment, 33 non-self-controlled, teacher-referred classroom problem children were randomly assigned to either a concrete training group, a conceptual training group, or an attention-placebo control group. The intervention was generally akin to that employed in Kendall and Finch (1978): self-instructional training via modeling, with a response-cost contingency for errors. The treatment was expanded, however, to 12 sessions entailing a wider array of training materials. Since it has been suggested that generalization from self-instructional training is likely to occur to conditions similar to the training tasks, interpersonal tasks, social problems, and opportunities to engage in role play were included as part of the treatment materials.

Assessments included task performance, self-report, teacher blind ratings, and therapist ratings of improvement. Although self-report data did not indicate significant change, and several performance measures evidenced improvements for all subjects, the teacher blind ratings of both self-control and hyperactivity indicated that the desired change had occurred at posttreatment and follow-up. Importantly, the treatment effects were stronger for the conceptually trained group. Normative comparisons indicated that the teachers' blind ratings of self-control and hyperactivity for the conceptually treated children were within the normal limits as defined in Kendall and Wilcox (1980).

It is noteworthy that the self-instructional procedures examined in the Kendall and Wilcox (1980) and Kendall and Finch (1978) studies were not self-instructions alone. Rather, the procedure also includes modeling, response-cost contingencies, and, in Kendall and Wilcox, role playing of problem situations. The evidence for treatment generalization produced by these studies supports a combined cognitive *and* behavioral treatment for self-control.

The superiority of the combination of cognitive and behavioral strategies over cognitive or behavioral strategies alone was illustrated by Barabash (1978). Four treatment groups were compared: self-instruction training, token fading, a combination of self-instruction and token fading, and control. Observations in the childrens' classroom were taken as assessments of behavioral impulsivity, and task performance on two tests were used as indications of cognitive impulsivity. The treatments took place in groups: eight half-hour sessions were provided. The results indicated that the most effective treatment for modifying both behavioral and cognitive impulsivity was the combined treatment. There was also considerable improvement on behavioral impulsivity for the self-instructionally trained children, while the token fading was only slightly more effective than the control condition in modifying behavioral impulsivity.

Very much related to problems associated with a lack of self-control is the concept of hyperactivity. Indeed, several of the studies already mentioned found somewhat parallel changes in teachers' blind ratings of self-control *and* hyperactivity (e.g., Kendall & Wilcox, 1980). It should not come as a surprise, therefore, that self-instructional training has been increasingly applied to children identified as hyperactive (HA). Interestingly, in a report by Cameron and Robinson (1980), a combination of self-instructional training and self-monitoring and self-reinforcement was effective in improving math accuracy and, to a lesser extent, in increasing on-task behaviors of HA children. Evidence for generalization was provided by an increase in self-correction of oral reading. Combinations of self-instructions, self-monitoring, and self-reinforcement were also reported to have desirable effects on academic performance in HA boys (Varni & Henker, 1979). Many of us would be very interested in the outcomes of further investigation of the effectiveness of the integrated cognitive plus behavioral treatment with HA youngsters (see also our discussions of hyperactivity in Chapters 5 and 7).

In a study with institutionalized adolescents (Snyder & White, 1979), a cognitive self-instruction procedure, a contingency-awareness procedure, and an assessment control were compared. The dependent measures were rates of observed behaviors taken during two-week periods at pretreatment, posttreatment, and at two-month follow-up. Some of the behaviors observed included absence from class, failures to complete responsibilities, and the frequency of certain impulsive behaviors (e.g., stealing or destroying property). The self-instructional training intervention resulted in significant improvements in performance of daily living requirements and a decrease in impulsive behaviors after treatment. The authors further report that the beneficial effects were either maintained or augmented at follow-up. These data are particularly impressive in that they pertain to clinical cases, include observed behavioral changes, and evidence the maintenance of improvement. Institutionalized adolescents are not an easy sample to work with, yet this report is quite encouraging.

The expansion of the application of self-instructional training methods to a wider variety of childhood problems has also provided some encouraging outcomes. Children identified as "poor readers" were provided six hours of training using a self-instructional (self-management) strategy or a modeling (control) condition (Malamuth, 1979). Based upon performance on a reading task, the self-instructional group attained higher reading scores. Based upon an audiovisual checklist assessment of attention, the self-instructional group prolonged their attention and showed an overall increase in self-restraint (based on total errors and errors of commission, respectively). An interesting ancillary result emerged from an examination of the treated children's peer-teaching behavior. The children who had been taught the self-management/self-instructional procedures tended to use the task clarification and cognitive rehearsal elements of their training when instructing other children.

Attentional focusing was also modified by a self-instructional intervention with retarded children (Burgio, Whitman, & Johnson, 1980). The children were taught to employ self-instructions to focus their attention during math and printing tasks, and a multiple-baseline across-subjects design was used to evaluate the treatment outcome. The authors reported that the training resulted in a decrease in off-task behavior during tasks, and that the children were actually employing the self-instructions. That is, the child's performance was observed and incidences of self-verbalization were recorded, with the treated children evidencing use of the self-instructional components that had been taught. Meaningful changes in academic tasks, however, did not occur. Nevertheless, the application of the treatment to attentional problems in retardates is novel, and the effects are encouraging. The assessment of the children's use of self-instructions (obviously only those self-statements at the overt level) was also a novel aspect of the research project.

Given the utility of self-instructional training in reducing impulsive responding, and building from the evidence that self-statement modification reduces anxiety, the application of self-instructional training to mathematics performance in young women seems quite appropriate. Genshaft and Hirt (1980) worked with 36 seventh-grade females who received low math achievement scores (and above grade level reading achievement scores). Tutoring in mathematics occurred for eight weeks, with 40-minute sessions twice per week. One group of young women received conventional remedial tutoring, a second group received self-instructional training intended to help focus attention, reduce self-deprecatory comments, reinforce effort, and decrease arousal. The third group was essentially no treatment. Support for this educational application of self-instructions was evident in improved performance on a diagnostic mathematics test. Specifically, all groups improved on the applications section of the test, but only the tutoring plus self-instructions group showed significant improvement on the computational section. The assessment of the childrens' attitudes toward math allowed the researchers to show that these attitudes were improved as a result of treatment. Unfortunately, there was no measure of anxiety to determine whether or not there were meaningful anxiety reductions, and there was no assessment of the subject's actual use of any of the self-statements that were taught. Nevertheless, the Genshaft and Hirt (1980) report is but one example of the many applications of self-instructional training in educational contexts (see also discussions by Meichenbaum & Asarnow, 1979; Roberts & Dick, in press; a study by Kim, 1980; and a forthcoming special issue of the *School Psychology Review*).

At this time, having overviewed the recent literature on self-instructional training with children, it would be of interest to reflect on the critical issues facing the researcher and therapist. An article by Cole and Kazdin (1980) and a chapter by Kendall and Finch (1979c) outline some of the important issues that will require future attention. For instance, application with clinical cases, further study of the most efficacious manner of producing generalization, employment of a broader range of outcome measures (such as specifying and general impact level assessments; Kendall, Pellegrini, & Urbain, 1981), and normative comparisons to assess the clinical significance of change must be addressed. Research also needs to be directed toward the analysis of the treatment components that are actively contributing to therapeutic success. Judging from the recently published research, many of these points are being recognized and some relevant information is available with additional data forthcoming.

Before closing our discussion of self-instructional training procedures, we turn to two studies where adult clients have been treated with cognitive–behavioral strategies that emphasized self-instructions. Although the recent literature on self-instructions with adults consists of fewer studies than the corresponding literature with children, Barrios and Shigetomi's (1979) review of earlier published work concluded that "research data support self-statement modification techniques as effective over no-treatment and attention placebo in reducing anxiety, as measured by self-report and behavioral techniques" (p. 510).

Craighead (1979) employed self-instructional training for clients with assertion problems. In addition, Craighead examined the role of two factors from the literature on attitude change (see Craighead & Craighead, 1980) that were identified as important for self-statement modification: degree of attitude discrepancy and involvement. The forty unassertive participants in the study were randomly assigned to one of four groups: high-assertion self-instructions, moderate-assertion self-instructions, placebo, and a delayed-treatment control. The discrepancy factor had to do with the discrepancy between the therapeutic attitude and the client's initial attitude. The attitude change literature would suggest that moderately discrepant communications should result in more attitude change than extremely discrepant communications. This distinction corresponded to Craighead's high-assertion and moderate-assertion groups. The involvement factor was examined as a within-subjects factor, with two situations employed: one that had to do with friends and was conceived as highly involving and one that had to do with acquaintances and was thought to be less involving.

Craighead reported that the self-instructional training regime was significantly superior to no-treatment or placebo controls on behavioral tests, self-reported behavior, and self-reported thoughts. Craighead employed Schwartz and Gottman's (1976) Assertiveness Self-Statement Test and found increases in positive self-statements for all groups relative to no-treatment, with negative self-statements decreasing in a somewhat similar pattern. Two subscales of the Irrational Beliefs Test also evidenced improvement for the two self-instructional training conditions superior to that of the controls.

The attitude change factors, discrepancy and involvement, did not result in as clear-cut a set of results as did those for the self-instructional training. In most instances the demonstrated effectiveness of the self-instructional training was comparable for both moderate- and high-discrepancy groups, with one exception: high assertion was superior to moderate assertion on the behavioral test. Few significant differences were reported for the level-of-involvement factor, perhaps due to the less-than-influential nature of this factor (or perhaps due to the manner in which it was operationalized in this particular study). A measure of involvement taken before the subjects participate might be a potentially useful methodology for separating and evaluating levels of involvement. Craighead did assess this dimension, and although situations with friends were seen as more involving than those with acquaintances, *both* situations were considered by the subjects to be important.

In an effort to examine the effectiveness of self-instructional methods with clinical cases, and in order to assess whether self-instructions would enhance the effectiveness of gradual exposure *in vivo*, Emmelkamp, van der Helm, van Zanten, and Plochg (1980) randomly assigned obsessive–compulsive patients to either (1) exposure *in vivo*, or (2) self-instructions and exposure *in vivo*. The intervention was of substantial duration (in relation to the typically brief treatments reported in the literature)—three pretest/interview sessions, two relaxation training sessions, and ten 120-minute sessions of (1) relaxation and exposure or (2) relaxation, self-instructions, and exposure. Exposure accounted for 90 minutes of the session while relaxation for one group and relaxation and self-instructions for the other group occupied only 30 minutes. It seems reasonable to mention that this may not be the most sensitive test of self-instructions since such a small portion of the treatment focused specifically on the self-instructional strategy.

The Emmelkamp *et al.* results indicate significant improvements for all subjects, with no enhancing effects for self-instructional training. Dependent variables were self-report scales of anxiety, depression, and obsessions, and therapist and assessor ratings of patient anxiety and depression. One cannot dismiss these data *ad hominem*. Moreover, it might appear cavalier to attempt to discount these findings for having relied too heavily on self-report and nonblind raters. After all, many studies are comparably restricted. A more meaningful tack might be to accept the negative results and ask what is it about obsessive–compulsive clients that precludes "cognitive" interventions. One possibility is that the nature of the pathology is too similar to the intervention strategy—obsessive–compulsive clients are already engaging in excessive self-talk, rumination, and self-doubting, and a treatment that feeds into this pathological system may not be desired. Equally reasonable is the notion that since these patients were involved to an extended degree in ruminative thinking, the time allotted to the self-instructional component of treatment was simply insufficient. In any case, one cannot eliminate the finding, and so it can also be thought that self-instructional training is not effective or desirable in the case of obsessive-compulsive disorders.

One final point. Self-instructional training procedures have been appearing at a rapidly increasing rate within the behavior therapy literature. In many of these cases they are employed within a "cognitive-behavioral" therapy that also involves several other procedures (such as in certain cases of cognitive restructuring). Before any firm conclusions can be drawn about the efficacy and relative efficacy of self-instructions per se, additional research that is designed to dismantle complex treatment packages will be necessary.

Covert Modeling

Although performance-based treatments have been considered the core of behavior therapy, an increase in the employment of imagery-based interventions has been evident among behavior therapists. One of the "cautions" related to imagery techniques is their lack of observability and the difficulty of verification. Do we know what clients are imagining? Are they imagining what we instruct them to? However, as Kazdin (1979c) notes, a client's tendency to elaborate on imagery instructions, while first considered a therapeutic and methodological problem, may be an important dimension of treatment that is to be encouraged. Within covert modeling, a cognitive–behavioral procedure where a client imagines a model engaging in desired behaviors, Kazdin has reported two studies that addressed the issue of imagery elaboration.

In the first Kazdin (1979c) study, 48 unassertive participants were randomly assigned to one of four groups. Each of the treatments was administered in four sessions over a three- to four-week period. Initially, subjects received a rationale and imagery practice. Assertion training, via covert modeling, followed the initial experiences. In the training scenes, subjects were instructed to imagine scenes and narrate what was being imagined out loud. The following four groups were compared: (1) covert modeling alone, in which subjects imagined persons (same sex and age) in each treatment scene twice, (2) covert modeling plus elaboration, where, rather than imagining the scene twice, subjects were instructed to elaborate the scene the second time, (3) covert modeling plus yoked elaborations, where subjects imagined the elaborated scenes produced by the subjects in the covert modeling plus elaboration group (control for scene content), and (4) scene plus elaboration, in which subjects imagined the scene in which an assertive response would be appropriate but the model did not make the assertive response.

The outcome of this elegantly designed study indicated that covert modeling led to improvements on self-report and behavioral measures of assertiveness. In addition, covert modeling led to increases in self-reported self-efficacy. Covert modeling plus elaboration resulted in the greatest amount of change. Several additional results should be noted: the effects were maintained at six-month follow-up, and the treatment brought the treated clients to within a range of scores obtained by a sample of persons who regarded themselves as socially appropriate and not in need of treatment. The Kazdin (1979c) study indicated that elaborations of scenes in covert modeling interventions are not methodological problems but therapeutic enhancements!

In a similar investigation, Kazdin (1980) further examined the role of imagery elaboration in the treatment of assertion problems. In this report, Kazdin manipulated the type of rehearsal (either overt or covert) and the instructions for elaboration (either elaboration or no elaboration). The treatments again led to improved self-report and behavioral indices of assertiveness and self-efficacy. The manipulation of the type of rehearsal did not result in differential treatment effects—both covert and overt rehearsal strategies were comparably effective. In contrast, the elaboration of scenes resulted in greater effects for both types of rehearsal. Again, treatment effects were favorable in terms of normative comparisons and were maintained at six-month follow-up.

Kazdin's investigations offer both evidence in support of covert modeling procedures and hypotheses for further inquiry. At the first level, it appears that the cumulative data indicate that covert modeling is an effective intervention. It is indeed impressive to read complimentary studies where the intervention, brief as it was, resulted in long-term effects that were sufficient to place the treated clients among subjects without the problem. Further investigation of the utility of the covert modeling procedure for other psychological distresses seems warranted.

At the second level, one wonders what was taking place cognitively during the scene elaborations? Do clients take the therapist's instructions to elaborate as evidence that they can do it themselves (efficacy enhancing communication)? Also, what are the characteristic contents of the elaborations? Further attention needs to be directed toward the examination of the most enhancing types of elaborations. It would be of interest to know whether or not beneficial elaborations were scene-related, interpersonally focused, or confidence-building expansions centered on easy situations. Judging from the Kazdin reports (subjects were tape-recorded) and the record of the Kazdin lab (systematic productivity), we can look forward to manuscripts describing the types of elaborations related to the enhancement of covert modeling.

In addition to assertion problems, difficulties with interfering anxiety have also been treated by an application of covert modeling. For example, test-taking anxiety has been treated with covert modeling combined with study-skills training and compared to self-control desensitization combined with study-skills training and to study-skills training alone (Harris & Johnson, 1980). Students meeting specific criteria ($n = 48$) were randomly assigned to the conditions. Treatments were conducted in groups (eight one-hour sessions). The assessments included self-reported anxiety and achievement, and grade point average. On one or more of the measures, all treatments were significantly better than waiting-list controls. Self-reported test anxiety was substantially reduced by covert modeling and self-control desensitization, but only the covert modeling group showed improvement on academic performance during the academic quarter subsequent to treatment. While this study relied quite heavily on self-report (there were four self-report scales of anxiety), it did include a replication. The waiting-list controls participated in the covert modeling plus study-skills training treatment, and the improvements paralled those reported in the primary study. This replication adds methodological sophistication and empirical support.

Social-Cognitive Problem Solving with Couples

Problem-solving approaches to treatment have been a part of behavior therapy for over a decade, with some very positive reports appearing in the early literature (e.g., Alexander & Parsons, 1973; Klein, Alexander, & Parsons, 1977). The literature has grown to the point that it now offers sufficient data for reviews which consider children and adults separately. As problem-solving approaches to treatment have taken a greater proportion of the behavioral literature, there has also been a greater recognition of the cognitive components of the problem-solving process. It is beyond the scope of the present chapter to cover all of the literature on social-cognitive problem solving, but the interested reader is referred to several recent reviews (D'Zurilla & Nezu, 1982; Heppner, 1978; Urbain & Kendall, 1980).

Jacobson's work with problem-solving treatment of distressed couples has received worthy attention from marriage and family therapists. The approach makes use of behavioral contingency contracting and cognitive problem-solving skills training (e.g., defining the problem, generating solutions, considering consequences) and has been demonstrated to have positive effects with moderately distressed (Jacobson, 1978) and more severely distressed (Jacobson, 1979) couples. The reader interested in pursuing these procedures further is referred to Jacobson and Margolin's (1979) recent book on marital therapy.

Interest in the dismantling of treatment packages has been on the rise, and the marital therapy approach of Jacobson is no exception. In a report by Jacobson and Anderson (1980), the effects of the behavior/ rehearsal and feedback components were independently examined. Forty-eight couples who responded to a newspaper advertisement participated in the study. The couples were only moderately distressed, in terms of psychometric criteria (Spanier, 1976), but the couples' level of distress was consistent across treatment groups. Couples were treated in groups of three, in weekly 90-minute treatment sessions. Each of the sessions focused on teaching a different set of problem-solving skills (e.g., defining the problem, brainstorming solutions, formulating agreements). All of the treatment sessions followed a similar sequence, but they differed in terms of the presence or absence of feedback and behavioral rehearsal. As outlined by Jacobson and Anderson (1980), one group received instructions alone, a second group received feedback about pretest problem-solving performance and instructions, a third group rehearsed the skills included in the instructions, but without feedback, and a fourth group received feedback, behavioral rehearsal, and instructions. Treatment evaluation was based on comparisons of pretest and posttest interactions that were videotaped and coded (specific behavioral codes and a general rating).

Since the level of distress of the couples was less than clinically severe, the study is an analogue. This does not, however, detract from the meaningfulness of the findings. Essentially, the results demonstrated that the combination of instructions, feedback, and behavioral rehearsal was superior to the separate conditions alone. Thus, interventions with couples would be wise to include more than instructions: feedback about performance and opportunities for practice seem to contribute meaningfully to beneficial outcomes. An assessment of the relative credibility of the treatment procedures (total of credibility measures taken following sessions one and two) indicated no significant differences across groups and reduces the likelihood that a demand effect accounted for the outcome.

A BRIEF QUIZ

According to an old bon mot, an optimist is a man who says of a bottle that it is half full while a pessimist complains that it is half empty— and yet, both mean the same bottle and the same quantity of wine. The difference involved here is based on their different views of the same reality, but it should be at once clear that neither view is more "correct," "saner" or more "reality-adapted" than the other. Similarly, when Alexander the Great simply cut through the knot by which Gordius, the King of Phrygia, had tied the yoke to the shaft of his chariot, he obviously acted on a different view of the problem; how to separate the cart from the yoke, not how to untie the Gordian knot (which many people before him had tried unsuccessfully). And five centuries later the Greek stoic philosopher Epictetus made his famous statement: "It is not the things themselves that trouble us, but the opinions we have about the things." (p. 119)

Can you guess the author of the above? Ellis? Meichenbaum? Asking the question in this manner no doubt sensitizes you to the fact that it may not be whom you expect. The answer: It was the introductory paragraph of a chapter by Paul Watzlawick. If you feel a sense of sympatico with its content, you may wonder what comments followed this introductory material.

Watzlawick (1976) contends that effective psychotherapy consists of a change in the client's frame of reference—a change in the meaning and value that a person attributes to a particular aspect of reality. *Reframing* is a technique used to change the client's viewpoint in relation to a problematic situation such that another frame of reference, one that fits equally well or even better, will have an entirely different meaning (see also Watzlawick, Weakland, & Fisch, 1974). Admittedly, the procedural guidelines for implementation of reframing and the empirical data to support its effectiveness are quite limited. Nevertheless, this is but one example of the psychotherapy efforts of nonbehavioral practitioners that has the potential for behavioral investigation. The methodologies of behavior therapy have a great deal to offer the delineation of the procedures for and the evaluation of the effects of cognitive–behavioral techniques such as reframing.

Before closing, a few general comments are in order. First, an argument against the effectiveness of cognitive–behavioral procedures based upon the sole employment of nonclinical cases is no longer justifiable. Many of the investigations reviewed herein have treated clinical clientele. A more compelling argument, however, concerns the relative absence of cognitive and behavioral assessments such that we can confirm *the mechanisms of change* (see Chapter 2). For instance, do the targeted cognitions change as a result of the intervention? A final thought for persons who mistakingly think that cognitive approaches are undermining their favorite behavioral technique—we never lose a good therapy until we find one that is better, and then the loss is a gain.

CHAPTER

5

BEHAVIORAL MEDICINE

KELLY D. BROWNELL

INTRODUCTION

Depending on how behavioral medicine is defined, the field can be enormous or very small. Taylor (1980), in the first issue of *Behavioral Medicine Abstracts*, states that the field should be overinclusive rather than underinclusive, to allow cross-fertilization by researchers and clinicians in different disciplines. The issue of defining behavioral medicine is discussed below, but it is clear that a broad definition is currently in favor. The consequence has been tremendous growth in a field that appeals to professionals with widely varying interests, training, and professional responsibilities.

The past four years have seen a remarkable increase in interest on behavioral medicine. A special interest group on behavioral medicine, formed in the Association for Advancement of Behavior Therapy (AABT), now publishes a newsletter. The Society of Behavioral Medicine (SBM), at first closely aligned with AABT, is now an independent organization with growing membership. SBM publishes a newsletter/journal (*Behavioral Medicine Update*), as well as a quarterly journal with abstracts from more than 100 journals in fields as diverse as epidemiology, sociology, dentistry, cardiology, pediatrics, animal learning, social work, nursing, and psychophysiology (*Behavioral Medicine Abstracts*). SBM also holds an annual convention. The Academy of Behavioral Medicine Research, a group of 100 invited scientists, is dedicated to fostering interdisciplinary research on behavioral medicine. This group also holds regular meetings. The *Journal of Behavioral Medicine* has been an important outlet for articles in the field since its first issue appeared in 1978. The American Psychological Association's Division of Health Psychology (Division 38) publishes a newsletter (*The Health*

Psychologist) and will soon launch a new journal. Journals in psychology, psychiatry, and medicine are beginning to publish position papers on behavioral medicine (Matarazzo, 1980; Pomerleau, 1979b; Pomerleau, Bass, & Crown, 1975; Schwartz & Weiss, 1977, 1978). There are now many books on the subject of behavioral medicine (Davidson & Davidson, 1980; Ferguson & Taylor, 1980; McNamara, 1979; Melamed & Siegel, 1980; Pomerleau & Brady, 1979; Williams & Gentry, 1977). There is even special interest in Washington; the National Heart, Lung, and Blood Institute has formed a study section to review research grants and training programs in behavioral medicine.

The field of behavioral medicine is so broad, that no single chapter can do justice to all the work in all its areas. At the expense of being able to cover only a fraction of all the exciting developments, we choose each year to do an extensive analysis of several key areas rather than a cursory analysis of many topics. In this volume of the *Annual Review*, we will cover four main areas. The first will be definitions and issues involved in the emergence of a new field. The second and third areas, epidemiology and work-site health programs, are two areas currently receiving much attention. The fourth area, hyperactivity, is important in applications with children.

Origins, Definitions, and Boundaries

Melamed and Siegel (1980) state that "any new discipline achieves its identity through what the pioneers in the field actually do" (p. 7). It is not surprising, therefore, that the origins, definitions, and boundaries of behavioral medicine tend to mirror the interests of prominent scientists. We will discuss the origins of behavioral medicine and then attempt to show how its philosophical roots in psychology and psychiatry have determined its definition.

ORIGINS

There are two predominant views on the origins of behavioral medicine; one traces the field to the biomedical discipline of psychosomatic medicine, and the other points to the general area of behavior therapy. In part, the question is whether behavioral medicine began in psychiatry or psychology.

Ferguson and Taylor (1980), both psychiatrists, present the history of psychosomatic medicine in explaining the development of behavioral medicine. They argue that the field owes its philosophical and conceptual foundation to the body–mind interaction of psychosomatic medicine, but that the technology for behavior change has come from behavior therapy. Melamed and Siegel (1980), two psychologists, give a detailed description of the principles of behavior therapy in their book on behavioral medicine. They note that the field was born when behavior therapists began investigating physical problems. Pomerleau and Brady (1979), a psychologist and a psychiatrist, strike a compromise! They claim that behavioral medicine is a synthesis of ideas and practices developed by researchers in behavior therapy (predominantly psychologists) and psychosomatic medicine (predominantly psychiatrists). We agree with Pomerleau and Brady and feel that such an approach leads to a fruitful interaction between scientists not only in psychology and psychiatry, but in many related disciplines.

DEFINITIONS AND BOUNDARIES

There is great variation in different authors' definitions of behavioral medicine. Early definitions were broad and all-inclusive; the most recent definitions are more narrow. Paradoxically, the field itself seems to have moved from narrow interests in certain techniques and problems (e.g., biofeedback and hypertension) to a broader interest in virtually anything in which health and behavior are related.

The first widely cited definition of behavioral medicine resulted from the Yale Conference on Behavioral Medicine held in early 1977. The following definition was issued by Schwartz and Weiss (1978b):

> Behavioral medicine is the field concerned with the *development* of *behavioral science* knowledge and techniques relevant to the understanding of *physical health* and the *application* of this knowledge and these techniques to prevention, diagnosis, treatment and rehabilitation. Psychosis, neurosis, and substance abuse are included only insofar as they contribute to physical disorders as the endpoint. (p. 6)

As Gentry (1982) observes, the Yale Conference emphasized behavioral medicine as a field of endeavor rather than a specific discipline, theoretical approach, or set of techniques. Figure 5-1, from the Yale Conference, shows how behavioral medicine involves the study of each facet (prevention, diagnosis, treatment, etc.) of many disorders approached by many disciplines. Schwartz and Weiss then noted that, by excluding the mental disorders unless they were related to physical health, the original definition fostered a disconcerting mind–body dualism. They offered an amended definition:

> Behavioral medicine is the *interdisciplinary* field concerned with the development and *integration* of behavioral *and* biomedical science knowl-

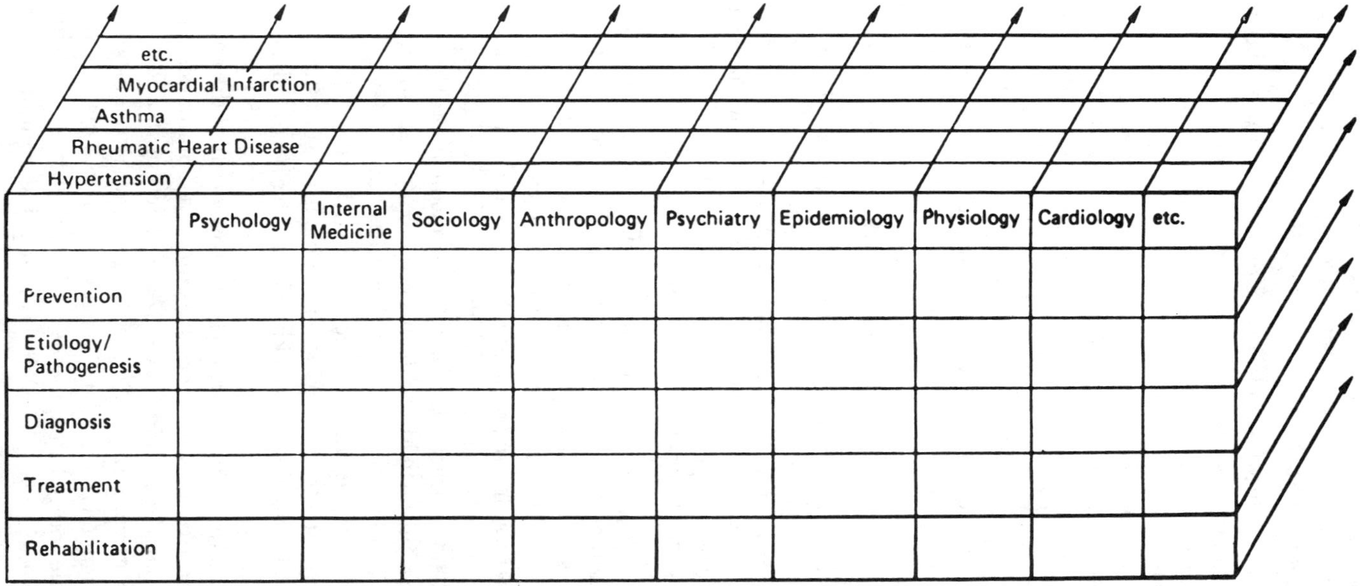

FIG. 5-1.

A matrix of diseases, disciplines, and areas for intervention in behavioral medicine. (From "Yale Conference on Behavioral Medicine: A Proposed Definition and Statement of Goals" by G. E. Schwartz and S. M. Weiss, *Journal of Behavioral Medicine*, 1978, *1*, 3–12. Copyright 1978, Plenum Publishing Corp. Reprinted by permission.)

edge and techniques relevant to health and illness and the application of
this knowledge and these techniques to prevention, diagnosis, treatment
and rehabilitation. (Schwartz & Weiss, 1978a, p. 250)

Matarazzo (1980) has also adopted a broad definition, classifying behavioral medicine as the "broad interdisciplinary field of scientific
inquiry, education and practice which concerns itself with health and
illness or related dysfunction" (p. 807).

Other authors choose to define behavioral medicine more narrowly, as the application of techniques or principles of behavior therapy
to health problems. Ferguson and Taylor (1980) define behavioral
medicine as "systematic application of applied behavior analysis and
behavior therapy techniques to medical problems." Blanchard (1977)
offers an almost identical definition: "By behavioral medicine I mean
the systematic application of the principles and technology of behavioral psychology to the field of medicine, health, and illness" (p. 2).
Pomerleau and Brady (1979) define behavioral medicine as

> (a) the clinical use of techniques derived from the experimental analysis of
> behavior—behavior therapy and behavior modification—for the evalua-
> tion, prevention, or treatment of physical disease or physiological dys-
> function; and (b) the conduct of research contributing to the functional
> analysis and understanding of behavior associated with medical disorders
> and problems in health care. (p. xii)

We feel that defining behavioral medicine in terms of the application of behavioral techniques restricts the field and gives it a much too
narrow focus. Such a definition suggests that behavioral medicine is
little more than a subspecialty within behavior therapy, that is, that
behavior therapy for medical problems is similar to behavior therapy
for sexual problems, anxiety problems or social skills problems. But
this would not attract members of the medical professions and the
social sciences to a field much in need of interdisciplinary efforts. In
addition, it implies that behavior therapists have a major contribution
to make to medicine and that persons in other disciplines should see
how powerful the technology can be. This is presumptuous for a field
in its infancy and does not acknowledge the need to learn from our
colleagues in other disciplines as well as convey our principles and
procedures to them. Interestingly, the proponents of the narrow definition cannot live within their self-imposed boundaries. The edited
books by Pomerleau and Brady (1979) and Ferguson and Taylor (1980)
contain chapters on subjects (e.g., exercise physiology and epidemiology)
not even remotely related to applied behavior analysis or behavior
therapy. The journal *Behavioral Medicine Abstracts,* in which Taylor
and Pomerleau have played important roles, contains relatively few

articles which fall within the domain of these authors' definitions of behavioral medicine. For all of these reasons, we favor a broad definition, as proposed by Schwartz and Weiss (1978a).

Caution for a Growing Field

Any new field is greeted by legions of followers enthusiastic about the promise of something novel. This enthusiasm generates many ideas and much controlled research, but there are dangers in having so many eager persons jump on the behavioral band-wagon. It is common during the early development of a field for the most respected scientists to issue statements of caution. These scientists see an early demise of a field which cannot deliver what it promises. Neal Miller, one of the important figures in behavioral medicine, has issued such a statement:

> The increasing interest in Behavioral Medicine opens up significant opportunities for research and applications. But there is a danger that overoptimistic claims or widespread applications without an adequate scientific base and sufficient evaluation by pilot testing can lead to failure and disillusionment. Such disillusionment could block the promising developments in this new area for another generation. (Miller, 1979, p. 5)

Miller's caveat, that we should not outdistance our data, comes from a person who has seen the rise and fall of many new trends in the health disciplines. We feel his words are valuable. Unfortunately, the field already shows signs that the caution is not being heeded.

The signs are predictable and they are clear. We see two such signs already: disputes over credit for "pioneering" work in the field, and the invention of subspecialties. There is already discussion of who first coined the term "behavioral medicine," who made the first important contributions, and who has the right to invent a new jargon. Matarazzo (1980), for example, suggests that "behavioral medicine" should be distinguished from "health psychology," and furthermore, that there is a need for yet another term: "behavioral health." The field is searching for an identity and must rely on evidence from quality research. It is this research, and not disputes over terminology and credit, which will strengthen the field.

There is also a tendency for persons to invent subspecialties in behavioral medicine. With no justification other than an interest in a specific medical problem, people feel licensed to preface any medical speciality with "behavioral." We now see established professionals, graduate students, and applicants for professional schools list their interests in "behavioral pediatrics," "behavioral cardiology," and even "behavioral gynecology." This trend is troublesome for two reasons. First, behavioral medicine itself is not well defined, so naming sub-specialties is premature. Second, the cavalier use of medical terms may alienate the very professionals needed for collaboration. Imagine the dismay of a cardiologist or gynecologist who has studied for years in his or her specialty, when a psychologist or psychiatrist who knows relatively little about these fields uses terms like "behavioral cardiology" and "behavioral gynecology." How would behavioral researchers react if a cardiologist used some common practice (e.g., exhorting patients to stop smoking) and labeled it "cardiovascular behaviorism?" This is not to say that behavioral researchers will not contribute to these fields— we are the first to agree that an important contribution can be made. However, we cannot pretend to know more than we do. To do so suggests that we know very little, even about our own specialty. (For a more extended discussion of the problems raised by a promiscuous use of the prefix "behavioral," see Chapter 1.)

EPIDEMIOLOGY AND BEHAVIORAL MEDICINE

Epidemiology is the study of the prevalence, etiology, and consequences of disease in humans (MacMahon & Pugh, 1970). It differs from most clinical research in that large groups of subjects are studied, with an emphasis on the determinants and natural history of disease. This necessarily involves the study of persons with and without disease and includes investigation of a wide range of characteristics in the subjects and their environments (Mausner & Bahn, 1974; Sexton, 1979). There are several detailed texts on the field of epidemiology (Lilienfeld, 1976; Mausner & Bahn, 1974; MacMahon & Pugh, 1970; Morris, 1975; Sussner, 1973). We will focus here on the application of epidemiological findings to the study of behavioral medicine, a topic also recently addressed by Sexton (1979).

The Importance of Epidemiology

The study of epidemiology is focal to behavioral medicine. Most be-havioral researchers proceed on the assumption that specific patterns of behavior influence physiological factors which, in turn, increase the risk of serious disease. All this information is derived from epidemiol-ogy. Cigarette smoking is a good example. Smoking cessation programs are based on several assumptions: that smoking damages health; that not smoking is better than smoking; and that stopping smoking will improve health, or at least retard further deterioration. As we discuss below, there is not always evidence to support common beliefs about behavior and health, yet these beliefs direct the research and clinical efforts of many scientists in behavioral medicine. Here are but a few of these beliefs:

1. Diet and heart disease—consumption of saturated fat increases serum cholesterol which contributes to heart disease.
2. Smoking and cancer—smoking damages the lungs and increases the risk of cancer, and smoking cessation leads to reduced risk.
3. Seat-belt usage and traffic deaths—chances of death are increased in persons who do not wear seat belts, so encouraging nonusers to wear seat belts will decrease their chances of death.
4. Exercise and heart disease—physical inactivity is associated with hypertension, elevated serum cholesterol, and obesity, so increased activity in sedentary persons will decrease risk for heart disease.

It is common clinical practice to ask patients to stop smoking, exercise more, lose weight, eat nutritiously, wear seat belts, drink less alcohol, and so forth. We believe these changes will improve health. It seems reasonable to hold such beliefs because we are convinced that people who do not follow these practices die earlier than people who do. By making these inferences, we use epidemiological data to justify violation of a rule that epidemiologists believe firmly—that finding an association between behavior and disease is much different from knowing that the alteration of that behavior will remedy the disease. For this reason alone, it is important that researchers and clinicians in behavioral medicine appreciate the basic concepts of epidemiology.

Some Basic Concepts in Epidemiology

We will define several epidemiological terms which relate to behavioral medicine and then discuss the ways in which epidemiology can identify behaviors which are likely to make people healthier. The following definitions have been adapted from Morris (1975).

1. *Annual incidence* = (Number of persons in a population at risk during a given year who newly manifest the disease/Average number in that population in the year) $\times$ 1000. Incidence, therefore, is a measure of the new cases in the population.
2. *Prevalence* = (Number of persons in a population at a stated time who manifest the disease/Number in the population at

that time) $\times$ 1000. Prevalence represents volume across all cases. A cross-sectional measure, it depends on the frequency of the disease and its duration. When the disease has a short course (e.g., infections) or when death is quick (e.g., some cancers), there is little difference between incidence and prevalence. In the chronic diseases like heart disease, diabetes, and obesity, incidence and prevalence are quite different.

3. *Morbidity* is the presence of a specific disease. Incidence and prevalence are measures of morbidity.

4. *Mortality* (*death rate*). The overall death rate is the proportion of the population at risk dying from all causes in a given period (typically one year). The death rate for a particular disease is: (Number in a population who die of the disease in the year/Midpoint population in that year) $\times$ 1000. The diseases are defined by the World Health Organization's International Classification of Disease (ICD).

5. *Case fatality* is the number of persons with a particular disease who die in a certain period.

6. *Individual risk*. A person's risk of developing a disease over a certain time is calculated by summing the incidence rates for the successive intervals during that time. Risk is usually expressed as a 1 in x chance of developing the disease within the stated period.

More detailed definitions and examples of these epidemiological terms are available elsewhere (Lilienfeld, 1976; Morris, 1975). The most important terms for behavioral medicine are "individual risk, incidence, and prevalence." Most behavioral researchers have a notion of relative risk, but incidence and prevalence are often confused. Morris (1975) discusses this issue:

> In studying morbidity, information on the incidence and some measure of prevalence are wanted, and I hope it is beyond doubt by now how different these are. The *incidence rate* is essential: to give the rate at which the population is being affected and, therefore, the risk on average to an individual, in seeking risk factors—causes and precursors—which lead up to the onset of disease, and in judging the outcome of attempts at primary prevention; to describe the appearance of a new condition and its spread among the population. . . . Since the *prevalence* includes all the cases it is a measure of the burden of a given disease on the community at large and on particular groups. . . . Prevalence data thus are useful for describing the natural history of chronic conditions. They are less helpful in seeking causes and precursors. (p. 266)

Morris (1975) has listed seven uses for epidemiology. We list the seven below, than add an eighth—the use we consider most important for behavioral medicine. Morris's seven uses are:

1. To study the history of health of populations, to measure the rise and fall of disease, and to make future projections about a disease.
2. To diagnose the health of the community; to define the relative importance to various diseases.
3. To study the working of health services.
4. To estimate individual risk from the group experience.
5. To identify syndromes by describing the association of diseases.
6. To describe the natural history of diseases; to follow the course of relapse and remission; to identify opportunities for prevention.
7. To search for causes; to describe the mode of operation of diseases, either singly or together; to describe the relative risk of those exposed.

Researchers in behavioral medicine are likely to be most interested in the prevalence of a disease, individual risks, the natural history of a disease, and the search for causes. Most importantly, however, they are interested in the effects of specific behavior changes on health. We feel this is the eighth factor: *the study of behavior changes and their effects on rates of morbidity and mortality.* Data of this nature will determine the impact of treatment programs and help health professionals assess the cost-effectiveness of programs aimed at altering specific behaviors. For instance, smoking and hypertension are both risk factors for heart disease. One may contribute more to morbidity, but the other may yield more easily to treatment. In which area is it wisest to devote resources?

Behavior and Health

The entire field of behavioral medicine is based on the supposition that behavior contributes to ill health and that changes in health-related behaviors can improve a person's physical status. Few would question those assumptions. Sexton (1979) has done a comprehensive review of studies relating behavior to disease. Changes in the causes of death during this century highlight this relationship, and explain the interest in "lifestyle."

Figure 5-2 presents the leading causes of death in 1900 and 1973. The main causes of illness and death in 1900 were the infectious

Death Rates Per 100,000

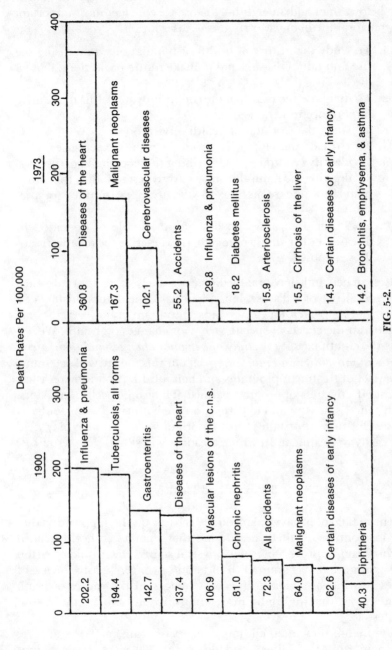

FIG. 5-2.

A comparison of the leading causes of death in 1900 and 1973. Data taken from U.S. Census statistics. (From "Behavioral Epidemiology" by M. M. Sexton, in O. F. Pomerleau and J. P. Brady, Eds., *Behavioral Medicine: Theory and Practice*, Baltimore: Williams & Wilkins Co., 1979. Copyright 1979, Williams & Wilkins Co. Reprinted by permission.)

diseases. With the advent of improved public health methods, people are living longer and are subject to chronic diseases (conditions whose progression is insidious and may last many years). By the time symptoms appear and the condition is diagnosed, chances for control are greatly decreased (Sexton, 1979). The chronic diseases are influenced by many of the behaviors considered part of the modern lifestyle. Seventy-three percent of total mortality is accounted for by the four leading causes of death, and each is influenced by patterns of behavior. The four causes and some of the contributing factors are as follows: diseases of the heart (diet, exercise, smoking, stress); malignant neoplasms (diet, smoking); cerebrovascular disease (smoking, diet); and accidents (drinking, seat-belt use).

There has been great interest in lifestyle modification and disease prevention in recent years. Prominent public health figures have trumpeted the glories of prevention. The Surgeons General and the Secretaries of Health and Human Services in both the Carter and Reagan administrations have vowed to increase federal support for efforts to prevent disease, yet only a tiny fraction of the health dollar is devoted to this cause. Leaders in the public health field feel that the priorities must be changed.

> One's lifesytle, including patterns of eating, exercise, drinking, coping with stress, and the use of alcohol and drugs, together with environmental hazards, are the major known modifiable causes of illness in America today. Medical care, on which we spend so much has, in comparison, only a weak effect on health. In addition, the way people use health services for both acute and chronic sickness is often inappropriate, costly and ineffective. Education to alter personal lifestyle and illness behavior has quite naturally been advocated with increasing frequency as an idea whose time has come. (Haggerty, 1977, p. 276)

Breslow (1978) feels that the risk factors for disease should receive a higher priority in health services than the diseases themselves, and that interdisciplinary efforts between researchers in the epidemiological, medical, and behavioral sciences may lead to major gains in health improvement. The potential benefits from such efforts may be enormous, judging, for example, from data from the Alameda County study in California (Belloc, 1973; Belloc & Breslow, 1972; Breslow & Enstrom, 1980; Wiley & Camacho, 1980).

> The pattern of daily living, including eating, physical activity, use of alcohol and cigarettes, largely determines both health and how long one lives. One study in California showed the significance of just seven habits: eating moderately, eating regularly, eating breakfast, no cigarette smoking, at least some exercise, moderate or no use of alcohol, and seven to eight

hours of sleep. Men at age 45 who followed only three or fewer of these habits had a further longevity of 22 years; those following four to five of the habits, 28 years; and those following six to seven habits, 33 years. (Breslow, 1979, p. 2094)

As Breslow (1979) notes the 11-year increase in longevity associated with specific habits is impressive, considering that during the period from 1900 to 1960, during which many advances were made in surgery, drug therapy, and other medical interventions, the average man at 45 gained only four years in longevity.

The epidemiology literature contains encouraging news about the benefits of altering behavior. Research on smoking indicates that a smoker of two packs per day will halve their risk for coronary heart disease by halving the number of cigarettes consumed (Bain, Hennekens, Rosner, Speizer, & Jesse, 1978). Gordon and Kannel (1976) estimate that if everyone were of optimal weight, there would be 25% less coronary heart disease and 35% fewer episodes of congestive failure and brain infarctions. Prescribing changes in smoking, diet, and other health habits seems sensible. Is there evidence to justify these efforts?

Sexton (1979) notes that "in behavioral epidemiology, the ultimate goal is to produce scientifically sound evidence that a change in behavior produces a change in morbidity or mortality" (p. 17). As we show below, it cannot be assumed that behavior changes will produce the desired effect. Even if behavior changes and health were nicely related, encouraging these behavior changes is a difficult task. In the words of Dubos (1961), "Men as a rule find it easier to depend on healers than to attempt the more difficult task of living wisely." Or, as Morris (1975) puts it, "What so often prevents prevention is people: we refuse to be bullied, won't be persuaded, are slow to learn."

Problems with Inference

Why should people be encouraged to decrease fat consumption, stop smoking, exercise more, and so forth? The answer seems simple enough—these changes will improve health. This facile statement, rarely questioned by professionals and almost never by the public, guides much of the clinical and research activity in behavioral medicine. For example, studies are appearing on the use of behavioral procedures to increase adherence to exercise programs, to change dietary practices, and to investigate adherence patterns to medication regimens.

Many assumptions about desired lifestyle practices are drawn unknowingly from weak data; that is, few of the inferences we make can be supported by evidence from controlled studies. The absence of these data stems from practical matters. A series of complex and very costly studies must be carried out to establish the relationships between behavior change and changes in health. Figure 5-3 shows the five stages of study necessary for this task. Observational evidence usually begins the process. This is followed by large- and small-scale studies, both prospective and retrospective, to finally provide the necessary evidence for determining which behaviors should be changed and how much change is necessary for health to improve.

THE DIET–HEART HYPOTHESIS—AN EXAMPLE

The relationship between diet, serum cholesterol, and coronary heart disease began to interest scientists in the 1950s. In a very short time, physicians were telling their patients to alter their diet in hopes of reducing the risk for heart disease. Mann (1977) noted that practicing physicians were being bombarded with this notion from the public as well as from fellow professionals.

> In a few years some combination of the urgent needs of health agencies, oil–food companies and ambitious scientists had transformed that fragile hypothesis into treatment dogma. Physicians were overwhelmed by this assault, arising from both their waiting rooms and their professional journals. A low fat, low cholesterol diet became as automatic in their treatment advice as a polite goodbye. (p. 644)

This advice is still being given today. The American Heart Association (1980b), in its "Statement for Physicians," makes very specific recommendations for dietary habits:

> The diet prescribed must be nutritionally adequate, economical, and pleasureable. Calorie intake should be adjusted to achieve and maintain lean body weight. Calories from fat should be reduced to 30%–35% of the total calories, with less than one-third of these calories coming from saturated fat; up to 10% of the calories coming from polyunsaturated fats and oils, and the remainder from monosaturated sources. Reduction in saturated fat to less than 10% of calories should be accompanied by reduced dietary cholesterol intake of under 300 milligrams per day. Severe hypercholesterolemia may require even greater restriction of saturated fat and cholesterol. To make up for the calories lost through fat restriction, consumption of carbohydrates (other than refined sugar) may be increased to 50% or more energy intake. (pp. 4–5)

Is there sufficient evidence to draw such conclusions? Let us examine each of the five stages of epidemiological study to answer this question.

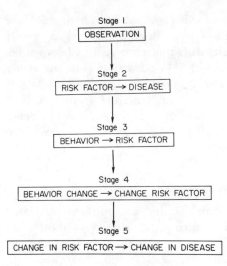

Stage 1
OBSERVATION

Stage 2
RISK FACTOR → DISEASE

Stage 3
BEHAVIOR → RISK FACTOR

Stage 4
BEHAVIOR CHANGE → CHANGE RISK FACTOR

Stage 5
CHANGE IN RISK FACTOR → CHANGE IN DISEASE

FIG. 5-3.
Stages of study necessary to establish a cause-and-effect relationship between behavior change and changes in health.

Figure 5-4 presents the stages with information regarding the diet–heart hypothesis.

Stage 1: Observation. In 1950, Gofman and colleagues described a method for characterizing lipoproteins in blood serum, and suggested that cholesterol was a useful index of atherogenesis and that diet could alter cholesterol (Gofman, Hanig, & Jones, 1956). Keys (1953) followed with a study of coronary disease in six countries. Heart disease was correlated with available fat in the diet.

Stage 2: Risk Factor–Disease. The next step was to establish a relationship between serum cholesterol and risk for coronary disease. Many epidemiology studies, both cross-sectional and longitudinal, established such a relationship, so that there is no dispute that persons with high cholesterol are at increased risk (Carlson & Bottiger, 1972; Gordon, Castelli, Hjortland, Kannel, & Dawber, 1977; Kannel, McGee, & Gordon, 1976; Keys, 1980; Rhoads, Gulbrandson, & Kagen, 1976; Shekelle, Shryock, Paul, Lepper, Stamler, Liu, & Raynor, 1981).

Stage 3: Behavior–Risk Factor. This step involves examination of the relationship between dietary practices and serum cholesterol. There have been cross-cultural investigations, large-scale epidemiological studies, and studies of special dietary practices (e.g., vegetarianism), and there is the suggestion that dietary cholesterol and saturated-fat intake are related to serum cholesterol (Glueck, 1979; McGill, 1979; Stamler, 1978). There are, however, epidemiological studies which show no relationship between diet and serum cholesterol (Frank, Berensen, & Webber, 1978; Nichols, Ravenscroft, Lamphiear, & Ostrander,

GENERAL SCHEME

DIET – HEART EXAMPLE

Observation

Stage 1

Diet, serum cholesterol, and heart disease related

Risk Factor → Disease

Stage 2

Elevated cholesterol relates to increased incidence of heart disease

Behavior → Risk Factor

Stage 3

Dietary practices predict variations in serum cholesterol

Behavior Change → Risk Factor Change

Stage 4

Altering diet can modify levels of serum cholesterol

Risk Factor Change → Disease Change

Stage 5

Lowered cholesterol associated with decreased morbidity and mortality

FIG. 5-4.

An example of the inferences linking behavior (diet modification) to changes in health (coronary heart disease).

1976). There is still doubt that dietary practices relate to serum cholesterol levels, even in a correlational manner (Mann, 1977; McGill, 1979).

Stage 4: Behavior Change–Risk Factor Change. Animal studies and dietary intervention programs suggest that changes in the dietary intake of cholesterol and saturated fat can alter serum cholesterol (Stamler, 1978). Grande (1980) concludes that these dietary changes make predictable changes in the serum cholesterol levels in a population. McGill (1979) feels that dietary cholesterol causes modest increases in serum cholesterol. Mann (1977), however, feels that the evidence is not as clear as it may seem, and that bold conclusions are drawn from weak studies. As Cornfield and Mitchell pointed out back in 1969, the better the study design, the less well dietary treatment appears to lower serum cholesterol.

Stage 5: Risk Factor Change–Disease Change. Prospective studies with very large samples are necessary to determine whether changes in cholesterol will actually reduce morbidity and mortality from heart disease. These studies are rare because of the expense and the lack of reliable methods to alter dietary practices and, in turn, lower cholesterol. There are two large trials now underway which may provide an answer to this question. Both are multicenter studies with thousands of subjects. The first is the Coronary Primary Prevention Trial, a double-blind trial of a cholesterol-lowering drug (cholestyramine) and placebo in 3810 healthy male volunteers with hypercholesterolemia. The trial is part of the Lipid Research Clinics Program funded by the National Heart, Lung, and Blood Institute, and is being carried out in 12 centers in the United States and Canada. The second is the Multiple Risk Factor Intervention Trial (MRFIT). This is a six-year intervention program aimed at hypertension, hypercholesterolemia, and smoking in men at risk for heart disease. The study is also funded by the National Heart, Lung, and Blood Institute and it involves 20 centers. Half of the 12, 866 men meeting the criteria for the study were assigned to intervention groups and the remaining half received standard medical care. These studies may yield valuable information, but even studies as intensive as these can only estimate behavior–disease relationships in groups, not individuals.

What can be concluded from studies in each of these five stages? It is apparent that changes in diet cannot be related to decreased morbidity or mortality from heart disease. Mann (1977) concludes that "no diet therapy has been shown effective for the prevention or treatment of coronary heart disease" (p. 646). McGill (1979) agrees: "We lack direct evidence that the reduction of dietary cholesterol decreases the incidence of atherosclerotic disease in humans" (p. 2635). Should we or should we not ask our patients to alter their diet? Mann (1977) is cautious and suggests the evidence is too weak to prescribe specific changes. Stamler (1978) and McGill (1979) and the American Heart Association (1980b) feel that the cautious approach is to recommend a low-fat, low-cholesterol diet, because it cannot hurt and it may help. They acknowledge making an inferential leap not completely justified by the data but feel that it is safest to prescribe altered diets while waiting for the conclusive evidence. We agree, and feel that the weight of indirect evidence is considerable. It is clear, however, that much more research is necessary in this area.

We present the diet–heart controversy as an example of the process of epidemiological evaluation. The diet–heart question could have just as easily concerned the relationship between stress and heart disease, smoking and cancer, exercise and heart disease, and so forth. Careful examination of the literatures in these areas suggests that we do not have firm evidence to support the notion that the "healthy" behaviors we prescribe will actually make people more healthy.

PSYCHOLOGICAL AND PHYSIOLOGICAL ASPECTS OF EXERCISE

Despite the fanfare surrounding jogging, tennis, and other forms of physical activity, most persons in industrialized countries exercise very little. Furthermore, levels of physical activity have been decreasing markedly since the turn of the century. The extent of this decrease is suggested by a twofold increase in the prevalence of obesity since 1900 despite a 10% decrease in daily caloric consumption (U.S. Department of Agriculture, 1962; Van Itallie, 1977).

Decreased physical activity is usually ascribed to mechanization and the use of labors saving devices. One can imagine the increase in energy expenditure of a person in 1900 who did not use an automobile, washing machine, elevator, electric knife, riding lawnmower, garage door opener, and so forth. Some persons now feel they exercise sufficiently because they are busy at work or because they play a round of golf or tennis on weekends. Others feel they must exercise vigorously every day to achieve any benefits.

Do most people exercise enough? What types of exercise are beneficial? Is exercise good, or is lack of exercise bad? What physiological factors improve with exercise? What methods can be used to increase physical activity in sedentary persons? These are some of the questions addressed in the past several years in the literatures of exercise physiology, internal medicine, cardiology, sports medicine, psychology, and so on. We will review these studies because physical activity is a classic example of a challenging topic for researchers in behavioral medicine. Specific activity patterns have a powerful effect on both physical and psychological functioning, and there is a high likelihood that behavioral principles can be used to study the modification of exercise habits.

The Epidemiology of Exercise

In 1873, in a book entitled *University Oars,* John Edward Morgan discussed the longevity of Cambridge and Oxford oarsmen and found that members of the crews survived longer than their sedentary classmates. Since that time, much has been written about the virtues of exercise. For example, Paul Dudley White (1957), President Eisenhower's physician, claimed that "exercise of almost any kind . . . can and does play a useful role in the maintenance of both physical and mental health (p. 71). Few people dispute this claim, and base their opinion on personal experience. What evidence is there that physical activity protects against disease?

In 1953, Morris and colleagues found that drivers of London's double-decker buses were more likely to die of coronary thrombosis than the conductors, and that government clerks fell victim to rapidly fatal cardiac infarction more than postmen (Morris, Heady, Raffle, Roberts, & Parks, 1953). Morris and Crawford (1958) evaluated postmortem examinations on 5000 men and found that mortality was greater in men with "light" physical activity at work than in men with "active" jobs, who in turn had greater mortality than men in jobs with "heavy" physical activity. Taylor, Kleptar, and Keys (1962) studied American railroad workers and found a similar relationship between light, medium, and heavy work.

Recent studies have confirmed the earlier reports on activity and heart disease. In a study of civil servants in Britain, vigorous leisure-time activity was associated with reduced risk of coronary heart disease (Morris, Adam, Chave, Sirey, & Sheehan, 1973). Paffenbarger, Hale, Brand, and Hyde (1977) did a 22-year study of 3686 San Francisco Longshoremen, and found that higher energy output on the job reduced the risk of fatal heart attack. Table 5-1 shows different physical activities which predicted rates of heart disease in 16,936 Harvard male alumni, ages 35-79 years, studied by Paffenbarger, Wing, and Hyde (1978). Morris and colleagues recently published a follow-up on British civil servants they first studied in 1968-1970. Men with vigorous physical activity have less than half the incidence of coronary heart disease

TABLE 5-1.

Age-Adjusted Rates and Relative Risks of First Heart Attack among 16,936 Harvard Male Alumni in a 6–10 Year Follow-Up, by Measures of Energy Expenditure

Physical activity in 1962 or 1966	Person-years of observation	Number with heart attack	Number with heart attack per 10,000 person-years of observation	Relative risk of heart attack[a]	p
Stairs climbed daily					
<50	37,946	222	56.5	1.25	.008
50+	76,064	329	45.1		
City blocks walked daily					
<5	24,996	140	57.8	1.26	.016
5+	85,345	385	45.7		
Light sports play					
No	50,606	288	59.8	1.08	.501
Yes	16,032	102	55.3		
Strenuous sports play					
No	66,688	390	54.1	1.38	.001
Yes	45,724	148	39.3		
Physical activity index (kcal/week)					
<2000	56,459	307	57.9	1.64	<.001
2000+	38,027	122	35.3		
Undetermined	23,194	143	47.6		

Note. From "Physical Activity as an Index of Heart Attack Risk in college Alumni" by R. S. Paffenberger, A. L. Wing, and R. T. Hyde, American Journal of Epidemiology, 1978, 108, 161–175. Reprinted by permission.

[a]Rate for less active divided by rate for more active.

than did sedentary men (Morris, Everitt, Pollard, Chave, & Semmence, 1980).

From these data it appears that both work-related activity and leisure-time exercise reduce the risk of coronary heart disease. There is even some suggestion that not much activity is necessary to incur these advantages. Leon and Blackburn (1977) state, "A sedentary individual might have to increase his activity by no more than 100 kilocalories per day to be placed in a more favorable intermediate activity group" (p. 571). Paffenbarger *et al.* (1978) found that walking more than five city blocks per day or climbing more than 50 stairs each day were related to reduced risk. There are, however, studies which do not support this relationship. For example, Keys (1980) presented results from a seven-country study of heart disease, and found that physical activity did not explain variations in heart disease.

It is enticing to say that exercise is associated with reduced risk for heart disease and that the exercise causes the reduced risk. It is probably safe to say that exercise promotes health and certainly does not hurt. However, cause and effect is another matter. It could be that coronary heart disease (or susceptibility for disease) influences exercise (job assignment, leisure activities), rather than vice versa. Also, exercise and heart disease may be related to a third factor, say body constitution. A series of studies, similar to those described in the section on epidemiology in this chapter, must be done to answer these questions. In the meantime, studies on the physiological consequences of exercise may be instructive.

The Physiology of Exercise

Much work has been done on the effects of physical training on physiology. Extensive discussions of this work are contained in volumes in the exercise physiology literature (Astrand & Rodahl, 1977; Katch & McArdle, 1977; McArdle, Katch, & Katch, 1981; Pollock, Wilmore, & Fox, 1978). Specific applications to coronary heart disease can be found in other texts (American Heart Association, 1980a; Naughton, Hellerstein, & Mohler, 1973; Wenger, 1978). We will discuss a few of the relevant findings.

There are several ways that researchers have attempted to demonstrate the effects of exercise on physical condition. The first is the cross-sectional evaluation of persons at different levels of training. Highly trained people tend to score higher on measures of coronary conditioning (McArdle *et al.*, 1981; Pollock *et al.*, 1978). Second, many prospective studies have evaluated the effects of conditioning on both trained and untrained persons. Aerobic regimens combining adequate intensity, duration, and frequency reliably improve conditioning (Astrand & Rodahl, 1977; McArdle et al., 1981; Pollock et al., 1978). The figures generally used indicate that a person must exercise at approximately 70% of maximum heart rate, for 15–20 minutes each session, at least 2–3 times per week.

The third type of research involves the study of exercise on specific physiological factors (blood pressure, insulin sensitivity, etc.) which may relate to specific diseases (heart disease, diabetes, etc.). Reviews of these topics can be obtained elsewhere (Brownell & Stunkard, 1980; McArdle et al., 1981; Naughton et al., 1973; Pollock et al., 1978). We will discuss this area briefly to give a picture of the effects of physical activity.

The most prominent effects of exercise appear to be on blood pressure, plasma insulin levels, plasma lipid and lipoprotein levels, and coronary efficiency. Active persons generally have lower blood pressure than do sedentary persons (Morris & Crawford, 1958). In addition, regular exercise can decrease blood pressure (Boyer & Kasch, 1970; Kiveloff & Huber, 1971), especially in hypertensive patients (Hanson & Neede, 1970). A decrease in plasma insulin is one of the earliest and most pronounced changes seen in physical training, in both humans and animals (Ahrens & Koh, 1971; Bjorntorp, Fahlen, Grimby, Gustafson, Holm, Renstrom, & Schersten, 1972; Bjorntorp, Sjostrom, & Sullivan, 1979; Hermansen, Pruett, Osnes, & Giere, 1970).

Exercise has also been cited as a method for improving lipid and lipoprotein patterns and coronary efficiency. Trained athletes generally have lower triglyceride, cholesterol, and LDL-cholesterol levels, with higher HDL-cholesterol levels than do more sedentary persons (Adner & Castelli, 1980; Hartung, Foreyt, Mitchell, Vlasek, & Gotto, 1980; Wood, Haskell, Klein, Lewis, Stern, & Farquhar, 1976). There is also evidence from prospective studies that exercise can lead to beneficial changes in these factors (Haskell, Taylor, Wood, Schrott, & Heiss, 1980; Lewis, Haskell, Wood, Manoogian, Bailey, & Periera, 1976; Lopez, Vial, Balart, & Arroyave, 1974). However, Brownell, Bachorik, and Ayerle (1982) found that moderate exercise produces much more favorable lipid changes in men than in women. Exercise in sufficient amounts has been shown to improve nearly every function of the cardiovascular system (Scheuer & Tipton, 1977). These improvements include changes in exercise tolerance, electrocardiographic abnormalities in cardiac patients, myocardial vascularity, and coronary efficiency in general (American Heart Association, 1975; Naughton, Hellerstein, & Mohler, 1973; Oberman & Kouchoukos, 1978; Scheuer & Tipton, 1977).

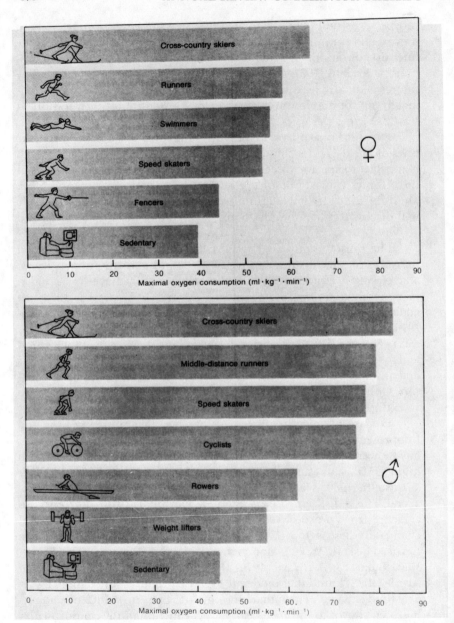

FIG. 5-5.
Maximal oxygen consumption of male and female olympic-caliber athletes and healthy sedentary subjects. Data taken from Saltin and Astrand (1967). (From *Exercise Physiology: Energy, Nutrition, and Human Performance* by W. D. McArdle, F. I. Katch, and V. L. Katch, Philadelphia: Lea & Febiger, 1981. Copyright 1981, Lea & Febiger. Reprinted by permission.)

The Psychology of Exercise

Popular lore has it that exercise makes people feel better. Some feel intuitively that exercise provides extra energy, while more avid proponents cite the exercise "high" and claim that self-concept improves or deteriorates with increases or decreases in activity. As far as hard data are concerned, Folkins and Sime's exhaustive review of the literature (1981) on physical fitness training and mental health leads to the conclusion that as yet, little definitive evidence exists in this area. Nevertheless, numerous uncontrolled studies suggest that activity does relate to mental factors. We will present some of the evidence below. More detailed reviews are available from several sources (Buffone, 1980; Folkins & Sime, 1981; Hammet, 1967; Layman, 1974; Morgan, 1974; Scott, 1960; Suinn, 1980).

Many studies have attempted to evaluate the association between physical activity and psychological functioning (Folkins & Sime, 1981). There is evidence that physical training improves cognitive/ intellectural functioning in children, adults, and geriatric patients (Gruber, 1975; Gutin & DiGennaro, 1968; O'Conner, 1969; Powell, 1974; Weingarten, 1973; Young, 1979). However, there are discrepant results also (Gutin, 1966), and the positive data are not always from sound studies (Folkins & Sime, 1981; Harris, 1973). There are studies suggesting that exercise improves perception, but again, final conclusions are premature (Layman, 1974).

The evidence is stronger that exercise has a positive effect on behavior and affect (Folkins & Sime, 1981). In a review of exercise and work performance, Donoghue (1977) found that exercise was associated with decreased absenteeism, fewer errors and improved output, and self-reports of better performance. Physical activity appears to be related to sleep (Baekeland, 1970; Folkins, Lynch, & Gardner, 1972) and social behavior (Stevenson, 1975). There are suggestions that exercisers report an improved sense of well-being (Carter, 1977; Morgan, Roberts, Brand, & Feinerman, 1970; Morris & Husman, 1978). One study has shown beneficial mood changes in depressed patients who exercise (Greist, Klein, Eischens, Faris, Gurman, & Morgan, 1979).

Physical activity may have applications for the rehabilitation of many physical disorders. The obvious example is physical therapy, but there are others. Physical training has been a standard prescription for patients recovering from myocardial infarction (American Heart Association, 1975, 1980a; Naughton et al., 1973; Wenger, 1978). There is also a suggestion that exercise may bring some relief from headaches (Atkinson, 1977) and asthma (Marley, 1977). These physical changes may bring corresponding changes in mental functioning (Folkins & Sime, 1981).

To summarize the data on physiological and psychological changes with exercise: Definitive evidence is not yet in on whether exercise causes reduced risk for serious disease and improved psychological functioning. The weight of the imperfect evidence is impressive, but to place our faith in such evidence is to assume that weak data multiplied many times over constitutes strong evidence. At the risk of falling prey to this temptation, we must face the choice of encouraging exercise in sedentary persons or waiting for conclusive data which may be years in coming. We choose the liberal path and feel that exercise is probably beneficial. Therefore, studies on improving exercise patterns are important to the field of behavioral medicine.

The Problem with Adherence

Poor adherence is a difficult problem in the treatment of many medical disorders (Dunbar & Stunkard, 1979; Haynes, Taylor, & Sackett, 1979), and exercise programs are no exception. Nonadherence is an often overlooked problem. This is unfortunate because any treatment is useful only to the extent it is followed. Researchers in behavioral medicine are now confronting this issue (Brownell & Stunkard, 1980; Epstein & Wing, 1980b).

Attrition from exercise programs averages at least 50% after six months. Taylor, Buskirk, and Remington (1973) carried out a three-state cardiovascular fitness program for men at high risk of coronary disease. Fifty percent had terminated by six months. In a six-month fitness program for healthy volunteers in Scotland, one-third of the patients conformed to the prescribed regimen, one-third made a "rather half-hearted effort," and the remaining third made no effort at all (Ballantyne, Clark, Dyker, Gillis, Hawthorne, Henry, Hole, Murdock, Semple, & Stewart, 1978). Mann and colleagues conducted a comprehensive, six-month exercise program for men at risk for coronary disease, and even though the authors claimed good adherence, only 59% of the sample remained in treatment at six months (Mann, Garrett, Farhi, Murray, & Billings, 1969). Gwinup (1975) found that only 32% of obese women completed a one-year program requiring only modest exercise (walking).

Adherence is poor even among persons who should be especially motivated to improve their physical condition. In a long-term rehabilitative program in Sweden for men who had suffered myocardial infarctions, 70% of the patients had dropped out by three years (Sanne, 1973). In a similar trial, 39% of 112 cardiac patients remained in a training program after one year (Wilhemsen, Sanne, Elmfeldt, Grimby, Tibblin,

& Wedel, 1975). In a Canadian program with 163 male cardiac patients, 57% remained in a physical training program after one year (Oldridge, Wicks, Hanley, Sutton, & Jones, 1978). Oldridge (1979) provided supplementary information on patients in the Ontario Exercise–Heart Collaborative Study. After a follow-up of 23 months, 55% of the patients remained in the program. Kentala (1972) reported that only 13% of male cardiac patients attended at least 70% of the training sessions scheduled during a one-year program. One study did find good adherence; 31 of 38 cardiac patients attended at least 85% of weekly sessions during a two-year program (Kavanaugh, Shephard, Doney, & Randit, 1973).

A recent study reported a careful analysis of dropout rates in 203 male and female patients referred to a cardiac rehabilitation program conducted by the YMCA in Portland, Oregon (Carmody, Senner, Malinow, & Matarazzo, 1980). Figure 5-6 shows the number of patients remaining in the program over the 40 months of the study. Only 18.7% of the group completed 40 months of training. The shape of the curve,

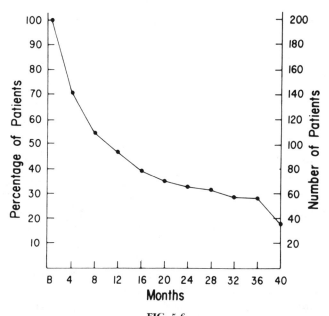

FIG. 5-6.
Rate of compliance to an exercise program in 203 patients with coronary heart disease. (From "Physical Exercise Rehabilitation: Long-Term Dropout Rate in Cardiac Patients" by T. P. Carmody, J. W. Senner, M. R. Malinow, and J. D. Matarazzo, *Journal of Behavioral Medicine*, 1980, *3*, 163–168. Copyright 1980, Plenum Publishing Corp. Reprinted by permission.)

a downward-sloping negatively accelerated function, shows that the majority of dropouts occurred within the first three months of training. This bears a striking resemblance to the dropout curve for patients in programs for smoking, alcoholism, and heroin addiction (Hunt, Barnett, & Branch, 1971) (see Chapter 6, "The Addictive Disorders"). Sutton (1979) has cautioned against inferring changes in individuals from group relapse curves, but it is still striking that relapse patterns are so similar across different health problems.

We can only speculate about why people drop out of exercise programs. The large dropout rate in the first three months may be an artifact of several phenomena. First, research programs may charge no fee or modest fees, so "half-hearted" patients may enter and then drop out in the first months of the program. Second, many patients may enter with a burst of enthuiasm prompted by a recent myocardial infarction, coronary bypass surgery, or another compelling influence. This motivation apparently fades rapidly. Third, some patients may not realize that vigorous exercise is necessary, and those who were not athletically inclined before a program are not likely to be so inclined simply because they enter a program. Attrition after the first months may also be attributable to learning factors (Carmody et al., 1980; Hunt et al., 1971) or by loss of the population to moves or to death.

Methods for Increasing Programmed Activity

The word "exercise" conjures up images of running, strenuous calisthenics, swimming, tennis, or any number of activities which tend to be programmed (scheduled regularly, require dressing, showering, etc.). These include the activities required to produce measurable changes in cardiovascular fitness (running, cycling, swimming, rope jumping, rowing, etc.), and are the types of exercise used in most fitness programs and cardiac rehabilitation programs. The adherence data presented above deal with exercise regimens of this nature.

Several recent studies have tested behavioral procedures designed to improve adherence to exercise programs. Wysocki, Hall, Iwata, and Riordan (1979) studied adherence to an aerobic exercise program in seven male and five female college undergraduates. The subjects deposited items of personal value which were returned for earning aerobic points (Cooper, 1970). This contracting procedure also involved the subjects observing and recording each others behavior. A multiple-baseline design was used, and the contracting procedure was successful in increasing the subjects' activity. Questionnaire data collected one year after the 10-week program indicated that most of the subjects continued to earn more aerobic points than they had during baseline.

Epstein, Wing, Thompson, and Griffen (1980) assigned 37 female college students to three contracting groups, a lottery group, or a no-treatment control group. The subjects were instructed to run one or two miles per day for the five weeks of the program. The contract involved the return of $1 each week from a $5 deposit for attendance at sessions. Subjects in the lottery condition earned access of a $21 drawing at the end of the program. All treatment groups showed better attendance than the control group; the contracting and lottery groups did not differ from each other.

Keefe and Blumenthal (1980) tested a behavioral program for encouraging increased activity in three middle-aged, overweight men. The program included stimulus control instruction for structuring the antecedents of exercise (time and setting), along with self-reinforcement for providing positive consequences for exercise. The three men increased their exercise, and sustained a higher level of exercise for as long as one year.

These studies show several promising approaches for improving adherence to exercise programs. The studies report either short-term programs or long-term follow-up with weak measures, but they are a start. Since much of the attrition in exercise programs may occur in the first few months (Carmody et al., 1980), it is encouraging to see even short-term results. It is likely that the results of such programs will improve even further as our analysis and modification of activity patterns become more sophisticated. The measurement of physical activity has been discussed in several articles (Brownell, 1981; Epstein & Wing, 1980b; McArdle et al., 1981). Developing better measures may not only help in evaluating exercise programs, but may provide researchers with new tools for giving immediate feedback to subjects. One potential avenue for increasing participation may be through the use of social support from sources such as family, peers, and coworkers (Brownell & Stunkard, 1980, 1981; Colletti & Brownell, in press). Epstein and Wing (1980b) give a detailed discussion about using behavioral principles to alter exercise patterns. The combination of behavioral and social support interventions may be a fruitful avenue for research.

Methods for Increasing Lifestyle Activity

Lifestyle exercise refers to activity undertaken in the day-to-day routine of walking, using stairs, standing, moving objects, and so forth. As mentioned earlier, labor-saving devices have greatly decreased the lifestyle activity of most persons. We distinguish programmed and routine exercise because the two may differ in their appeal to certain individuals. Programmed activity for some may be poor because of a vigorous regimen, but adherence for others may be poor because of discomfort, boredom, embarrassment, or the inability to exercise regularly. Although programmed activity will pay the greatest physical dividends, lifestyle activity may be beneficial for some people because adherence might be better. This might be particularly true of persons who cannot or will not engage in vigorous activity (e.g., obese or elderly persons).

Behavioral programs for obesity often prescribe lifestyle activity (Brownell & Stunkard, 1980; Wilson & Brownell, 1980). These activities might include using stairs rather than elevators or escalators, disembarking from a bus before one's destination, parking some distance from the entrance of stores, and so forth. Initially, these activities were encouraged because few clinicians expected obese persons to be capable of strenuous activities. These activities have now found favor outside of the obesity arena because of the potential for increased adherence. It is possible to view lifestyle activities as a regimen which could prepare individuals for more vigorous activities.

Several recent studies have evaluated lifestyle activity patterns in the natural environment. Brownell, Stunkard, and Albaum (1980) examined the choice of stairs or escalators in public places where stairs and escalators were adjacent. More than 45,000 persons were observed in a shopping mall, train station, and bus terminal. Only 5% of the subjects used the stairs; the rate of stair use was only 1% for obese persons. These results were consistent with those from a similar study by Meyers, Stunkard, and Coll (1980). Brownell *et al.* (1980) then positioned a sign (Figure 5-7) at the base of the stairs and escalators and nearly tripled the frequency of stair use. A second study in the same paper found that the effect of the sign endured for one month after the sign was removed, but the effect had disappeared by three months.

These investigations of stair climbing are interesting for several reasons. First, stair use is one of the few physical activities which Paffenbarger *et al.* (1978) found associated with decreased risk of heart disease. Morris *et al.* (1973) also found that regular stair use was related to reduced risk for heart disease. Second, there is evidence from the exercise physiology literature that stair use can have positive physiological effects (Oldenberg, McCormack, Morse, & Jones, 1979), although the effects are not consistent (Ilmarinen, Ilmarinen, Koskela, Korhonen, Fardy, Partanen, & Rutenfrantz, 1979). Third, stair climbing expends more calories per minute than almost any other activity (Brownell & Stunkard, 1980). Fourth, this type of activity is readily available, does not require special equipment or extra time, is not painful, and can be done at one's own pace. This may encourage some individuals to take the next step—a walking program. This also can be beneficial (Astrand

FIG. 5-7.
Sign used to encourage use of stairs in a study of more than 45,000 persons in public locations. (From "Evaluation and Modification of Exercise Patterns in the Natural Environment" by K. D. Brownell, A. J. Stunkard, and J. M. Albaum, *American Journal of Psychiatry*, 1980, *137*, 1540–1545. Copyright 1980, the American Psychiatric Association. Reprinted by permission.)

& Rodahl, 1977; McArdle *et al.*, 1981; Schoenfeld, Keren, Shimoni, Birnfeld, & Sohar, 1980). As people can accomplish this, they may be able to increase their activity to more strenuous levels.

There has been only one study comparing programmed and lifestyle activity. This recent paper, by Epstein, Wing, Koeske, Ossip, and Beck (1981), reported fitness and weight loss data on obese children who were to do scheduled activities 5–7 days each week (programmed exercise) or who were to do any lifestyle activity for at least 10 minutes each day. After the eight-week program, the children in the programmed exercise condition showed greater changes in fitness (recovery pulse from a step test) than did the children in the lifestyle condition. However, after a three-month follow-up, the programmed exercise group had returned to baseline while the lifestyle exercise group had continued to improve. Presumably, this occurred because of better long-term adherence in children who did lifestyle exercise.

HEALTH PROMOTION AT THE WORK PLACE

There has been tremendous interest in occupational health programs in the past decade. The lead has been taken by industry and, in more recent years, the topic has caught the interest of the federal government and academic researchers. The new field has been greeted with enthusiasm, and grand claims have been made for the potential benefits of encouraging healthy behaviors at the work place. This is an exciting time for researchers in behavioral medicine, because it is only now that strict evaluations of these programs are being called for (Chesney & Feuerstein, 1979; Fielding, 1980). In addition, it is an opportunity for researchers to learn from health professionals in occupational settings, and to test the generalizability of clinical programs to the work place.

Growth in Work-Site Health Programs

Health programs in industry have existed from the first days of the company nurse or company physician. However, health promotion at the work place has become popular only recently. Given its recent development, it is surprising that the programs have spread to industries both large and small. A survey by the Washington Business Group on Health (1978) found that a majority of companies responding to the inquiry had some type of health education or health promotion program in operation. An article in *The New York Times* (August 24, 1981) reported that at least 300 companies have health programs for their employees. More than 300 companies employ full-time fitness directors (Fielding, 1979), and there is a national organization for those directors, the American Association of Fitness Directors in Business and Industry. Health promotion is now being considered by some personnel managers to be a desirable employee benefit, by others to be a means of enhancing morale, and by others as a way to reduce health costs.

Work-site programs are achieving high visibility. In January of 1979, the Surgeon General's Office of Health Information and Health Promotion sponsored The National Conference on Health Promotion Programs in Occupational Settings (McGill, 1979). The March–April 1980 issue of *Public Health Reports* was devoted to the proceedings of this conference. In June 1980, Healthy America, a nonprofit group in Washington, D.C., sponsored a conference on The Corporate Commitment to Health. Dozens of businesses were represented, from large companies like Xerox to companies with fewer than 100 employees. The Institute of Medicine held a conference on Evaluation of Health

Promotion at the Workplace in June 1980. This conference was designed to spur interest in rigorous evaluation of hundreds of existing programs. The armed services are also interested in health promotion at the work place; the Department of Defense organized a consultant conference on fitness and health in June 1980.

There are now health programs which deal with a multitude of problems. The Surgeon General's conference in 1979 produced a recommendation that the following problems be considered (McGill, 1979):

- smoking control
- weight control
- nutrition/healthy dietary practices
- hypertension control
- exercise/fitness
- drug/alcohol abuse control
- stress management
- accidents/self-protective measures against hazards

There are only a few industries trying programs for all areas (Naditch, 1980; Wilbur, 1980), but many industries have at least one program in each area. There is great variation in approaches to the problems, evidence for their effectiveness, and rationales for choosing one program over another. For instance, exercise programs are very popular, even though a smoking program or hypertension program would be much more likely to reduce health costs.

Types of Health Programs

There are several ways to approach health programs at the work place. Fielding (1979, 1980) has reviewed these approaches and given examples of each. We will mention only a few examples to document Fielding's categories.

SCREENING AND INTERVENTION

Screening the employees of a company may lead those with health problems to enter the medical system, even if the company itself does not offer a special program. An example would be hypertension screening, in which all employees could be screened by a nurse and then referred for treatment. Alderman and Schoenbaum (1975) conducted a blood pressure screening program for members of the United Storeworkers Union in New York. Sackett and colleagues also carried out a blood pressure screening program in a Canadian foundry

(Sackett, Haynes, Gibson, Hackett, Taylor, Roberts, & Johnson, 1975). Some companies are now using one of the many Health Hazard Appraisal forms to screen employees. These self-report forms inquire about health factors such as smoking, diet, exercise, and family history of chronic diseases. The forms are scored by computer and individuals receive a profile of their risk relative to people of the same age and sex. Some forms even project the change in life expectancy if a person alters a behavior which contributes to risk. The assumption behind large-scale screening is that enough persons who are at-risk seek care to justify the costs of the program. The effects of screening, however, may not always be positive. Haynes and coworkers found that employees diagnozed as hypertensive by a screening showed an 80% increase in absenteeism, compared to a 9% increase in the general employee population (Haynes, Sackett, Taylor, Gibson, & Johnson, 1978).

IN-HOUSE MEDICAL DEPARTMENTS

Some companies have taken the responsibility of providing health promotion and rehabilitative services to their employees via their own medical departments. Fielding (1979) cites the Gillette Company as an example. An interdisciplinary staff provides treatment of both acute and chronic illness, health education, health appraisals, rehabilitation of cardiac patients, alcoholics, and physically and mentally handicapped employees. The staff consists of internists, a hematologist, an endocrinologist, surgeons, dermatologists, opthalmologists, an allergist, and nurse practitioners. The physicians are available 24 hours each day, and the employees can obtain care at the work place, at the doctor's office, or at a hospital. As discussed below, the savings for Gillette are impressive. Similar savings have been made by General Mills in Minneapolis and the Continental Bank and Trust of Chicago, among others (Fielding, 1979).

CONTRACTING FOR HEALTH PROGRAMS

Many companies are choosing to have outside consultants establish specific programs for their employees. One of us (KDB) has worked with several companies using the method. The Sun Oil Company of Radnor, Pennsylvania, has hired a consulting firm to establish and conduct an exercise program for its employees. Bell Telephone of Pennsylvania and the Colonial Penn Life Insurance Company have arranged for their employees to attend fitness classes at a nearby YMCA. Alderman and Schoenbaum (1975) and Stunkard and Brownell (1980) carried out work-site programs for hypertension and obesity for the

United Storeworkers Union in New York. Considering that some of the outside consultants are researchers, we may see those programs produce experimental tests of treatment effectiveness.

FINANCIAL INCENTIVES OR ENVIRONMENTAL DIRECTIVES

Fielding (1979) notes several examples of companies which offer incentives for changes in health behavior. Other companies simply forbid unhealthy behaviors at the work place. Typically, such companies offer no treatment programs. The Mobil Corporation divided its 27,000 U.S. employees into 10 medical experience groups, and employees with below average medical costs were given an annual bonus. Cybertek Computer Products offered a $500 health bonus to employees who stopped smoking, and the New York City branch of Sears, Roebuck and Company gives tuition rebates to any employee who attends smoking cessation classes and remains abstinent for six months. Some companies do not allow smoking during work periods, and the Johns Manville Company does not hire smokers to work in its 14 plants which produce asbestos because of the synergistic effect on cancer of smoking and asbestos exposure.

ESTABLISHING IN-HOUSE FACILITIES

Companies interested in exercise programs usually consider building their own facility. Some business leaders question the cost-effectiveness of so large an investment, but others have chosen to build. The Xerox Corporation in Leesburg, Virginia, established a modern exercise facility for its employees, and has a large fitness staff. The Pepsico Company in suburban New York has a similar program with a track, exercise bicycles, treadmills, universal gyms, and the like. Northern Natural Gas in Omaha, Nebraska, purchased a building which had been used as a YMCA to use for exercise activities. The Kimberly–Clark Company in Wisconsin has carried out an ambitious program in its own exercise facility.

These are only a few examples of the many programs used by industry. It is evident that businesses vary greatly in their commitment to health, in their choice of risk factors to confront, and in their methods for achieving changes in health. This diversity is due partly to the lack of objective information which could guide business leaders in their choices. We share Fielding's (1979) cautious optimism about work in this area.

> Whether from a sense of social responsibility or a conviction that savings are to be realized through such programs, top managers have been picking

up the theme of public health advocates (that prevention does pay) and
instituting programs which some do claim can reap economic gains for
the company. The verdict isn't quite in yet, but there are enough parties
claiming cost savings from industrial health promotion programs that the
issue warrants examination. (p. 79)

Costs and Benefits: The Issue of Evaluation

A cost–benefit assessment of work-site programs implies an analysis of
the funds spent to develop and implement the program, and the estimates of dollars saved through improved health. The initial reports
from occupational settings were impressive, even though neither the
costs nor benefits were quantified. The president of the Speedcall
Corporation, an electronics firm in California with 36 employees,
offered a $7 bonus each week for employees who did not smoke at work.
The number of on-the-job smokers declined from 24 to 4, and the
president reported improved productivity and morale, and fewer days
lost in illness. The Colonial Bank and Trust of Chicago challenged
two other banks to a weight reduction contest; the employees of the
three banks lost a total of 2½ tons. Jesse Bell, the President of Bonne
Bell Cosmetics, offered his employees $5 for every pound lost, $1 for
every mile run, and $250 for quitting smoking. Absenteeism declined
50%, and in the program's first year, the company was given an insurance rebate of $36,000.

Fielding (1979) has done a survey on some of the costs and benefits
of employee health programs. A few illustrative cases show that evaluation may be more complex than a simple comparison of dollars spent
and dollars saved. Kristein (1977) used data from the Framingham
Heart Study to estimate the benefits of screening and counseling
employees. For every 1000 employees, at least 100 will have two or more
coronary risk factors. This 10% of the company's population will
account for 40–60% of annual medical care for the company. If 25% of
these 100 high-risk employees could alter their risk factors, the company's medical spending would decline 15%.

The in-house medical department provided by the Gillette Company (described above) cost $710,000 in 1976, but the total savings to
the company were $1,210,000. The Firestone Tire and Rubber Company
evaluated a counseling and referral service for employees with alcohol
and drug-abuse problems (Fielding, 1979). The analysis included work
attendance, accident and sickness benefits, and hospital/surgical and
medical costs. The annual savings per employee were $2350. General
Mills, Inc. reported that its in-house medical program for 2000 em-

ployees saved $45,000 after administrative costs of $160,000. The Continental Bank and Trust of Chicago added health promotion activities to its traditional occupational medicine department, and found that the turnover of 101 of 7671 employees due to illness and death in 1973 declined to 78 of 8071 employees in 1978.

There are many possible reasons for a company to implement a health promotion program. Saving health dollars is one reason of course, but there are other important reasons. Fielding (1980) listed some of the objectives typically mentioned by corporate managers:

- to improve health of the employees
- to help people help themselves
- to decrease the inflation of health insurance premiums
- to improve morale
- to keep ahead of unionized companies vis à vis benefits
- to improve productivity
- to educate employees about how their habits influence their health

The methods and targets for the evaluation of a work-site program will vary depending on the evaluator. A business manager is likely to want some measure of savings, a program administrator is likely to want an index of how favorably the program is received by the employees, and an academic researcher may want to assess the functional relationship between specific components of the program and changes in behavior. Each of these objectives is crucial to a comprehensive evaluation, and this issue highlights the need for collaborative work between researchers, health care professionals, and business and labor leaders. In the meantime, it is important for outside evaluators to be sensitive to the needs of the company.

> Given the diversity of objectives, evaluation issues will differ from site to site. To a company who developed a program to improve morale the most satisfying result might be ascertaining that a majority of employees who participated felt "better" about their job and work environment. To a company whose immediate aim is a workforce better informed about health habits, the objectives against which to measure outcomes might be improved recognition of the value of exercise, and knowledge about the effect of salt on blood pressure and the effects to tobacco and alcohol on the fetus. More and more, however, program objectives are being articulated in terms of modifying behavior, improving health and increasing productivity with favorable benefits/cost ratios. (Fielding, 1980, pp. 1–2)

To describe each of the many aspects of evaluation is beyond the scope of this chapter. We refer the reader to Fielding (1980), McGill's (1979) report of the Surgeon General's Conference, the chapter by Chesney and Feuerstein (1979), and *Public Health Reports* (March–April, 1980) for extensive discussions of these issues. We do feel that the initial enthusiasm surrounding work-site programs will fade eventually, and the programs will be judged according to information collected in careful evaluations. Considering the stakes, adequate evaluations is essential.

Research on Work-Site Programs

Work-site health promotion programs have been used for many target behaviors and populations. We will summarize the state of the field in the areas of smoking, diet/weight control, hypertension, stress management, and physical activity. Some companies are using comprehensive programs to target many risk factors (Naditch, 1980; Wilbur, 1980), but no results are available yet.

SMOKING

There are several means of approaching smoking cessation at the work place (Chesney & Feuerstein, 1979; Danaher, 1980). These include in-house smoking cessation programs, programs administered by outside consultants, incentive programs, educational programs from voluntary health organizations (e.g., American Cancer Society), and educational programs done by industry representatives. Danaher (1980) noted the presence of many smoking programs in industry, but the lack of rigorous evaluation of almost all the programs.

Incentive programs were the first used to reduce smoking in industry. The Dow Chemical Company's Texas Division implemented an incentive program after discovering that the company lost $500,000 due to missed workdays by smokers (Danaher, 1980). Smokers were able to earn one chance for each month of nonsmoking to win a boat and motor worth $2400. An award program was also held in which smokers earned $1 for each week of abstinence along with a chance to win $50 quarterly. The Dow program offered incentives for employees who recruited smokers into the program. The recruiters earned one chance toward a boat and motor for each month of nonsmoking reported by one of his or her recruits. Twenty-four percent (400 employees) were recruited into the program. Self-reports of smoking after the one-year program showed a remarkable abstinence rate of 76%.

Intermatic Incorporated of Detroit developed an innovative incentive approach (Chesney & Feuerstein, 1979). The company established a parimutuel betting window where employees bet up to $100 on their ability to stop smoking for a year. The company also contributed $1000 to be divided among successful participants. For employees who forfeited their bets, the money went to the American Cancer Society. The Aluminaire Standard Glass Company in Phoenix deducts an amount equivalent to what smokers would spend on cigarettes from employees' paychecks. After one year, the company matches the paycheck deduction and pays the entire amount to the workers if they are not smoking.

Danaher (1980) also lists some of the outside consultant programs and the in-house programs, but again, there is almost no information on program evaluation. The Campbell Soup Company of Camden, New Jersey, worked with the University of Pennsylvania's Center for Behavioral Medicine to implement a series of smoking cessation workshops. The consultant was a clinical assistant from the university. The employee and the company split the fee of $50. The preliminary data indicate that 25% of the participants were abstinent at a six-month follow-up. Boeing Aircraft sponsored a program conducted by the Seventh Day Adventist Church. Of the 35 employees in the program, 30% reported not smoking at a three-month follow-up. The most ambitious in-house program was established by the Ford Motor Company. Almost 40% of the smokers in the corporate cardiovascular health program were enrolled in groups to test three approaches: aversive smoking and self-control, abrupt withdrawal with contingency contracting and self-control, and gradual withdrawal with contingency contracting with self-control. There were problems with data collection, but 20% of participants were reportedly abstinent after six months (Danaher, 1980).

Many innovative approaches to smoking cessation have been tried at the workplace. Most have not been evaluated, but some have reported encouraging results. There is great potential in this area for collaborative efforts between researchers and business leaders. Two topics for research which may yield important information are methods of recruitment, and methods for exploiting the social support which exists in the work place (Danaher, 1980).

WEIGHT CONTROL AND NUTRITION EDUCATION

Work-site programs for obesity and nutrition have been reviewed by Colletti and Brownell (in press) and by Foreyt, Scott, and Gotto (1980). The most commonly used programs are general counseling programs, contingency systems, outside consultant programs, and in-house programs. For the most part, results from work-site programs fall short of those from clinical programs. In most cases this is not surprising because the work-site programs have consisted of little more than a few lectures by someone who is not trained in the area. There are, however, examples of adequately implemented behavior programs in work settings, and the results are not very positive.

Foreyt *et al.* (1980) have listed some of the programs in industry. General Foods, Inc. in White Plains, New York, conducted a pilot project with 12 overweight employees in 1977. The participants deposited $100 which was returned if they attended classes. There were 19 meetings which were used to cover topics such as nutrition, exercise, and behavior modification. The participants lost an average of 16 pounds after 19 sessions, but 9 of the 12 had regained their losses by a six-month follow-up. The U.S. Public Health Service conducted a three-day training program for nurses, who then administered group weight reduction classes for 8–12 sessions. Weight losses were reported to be ½–2½ pounds per week.

The armed services have instituted plans for weight control. Information on each of the four services was presented at the Department of Defense Conference on Fitness in the Military in June of 1980. The Navy does nutrition counseling for moderately overweight persons and refers heavier persons to Overeaters Anonymous. There are no contingencies for losing weight. The Air Force demands a yearly test of physical fitness, and overweight persons are given nutrition information and dietary guidelines from medical personnel. The Army also requires regular fitness training, and overweight soldiers receive extra physical fitness workouts. The Marines have the strictest requirements. Every Marine must pass a fitness test each year; the test involves sit-ups, pull-ups, and running. Marines with more than 18% body fat (16% is normal for males) are enrolled in a mandatory exercise program. If ideal body fat is not attained in six months, the commanding officer can grant a six-month reprieve, but after one year of excessive fatness, the person is processed out of the Marines due to "apathy." The only evaluation of service programs was done at the Tinker Air Force Base in Oklahoma (Reppart & Shaw, 1978). Weekly sessions were held for overweight persons. Participants lost 6–10 pounds in 1–4 months, and were allowed to stop the program only after attaining ideal weight.

There have been several attempts to adapt the behavioral program used in clinical settings (see Chapter 6, "The Addictive Disorders") for use in industrial settings. Stunkard and Brownell (1980) conducted the first controlled trial of an obesity program at the work site. The study was done with employees of the Bloomingdales and Gimbels retail department stores in New York City and was coordinated through the United Storeworkers Union. The weight control program followed a successful hypertension program in the same union by Alderman and Schoenbaum (1975). The program tested work-site versus medical-site treatment, one versus four meetings per week, and lay therapist (union members) versus professional therapist. These conditions did not differ in weight loss after treatment at a six-month follow-up, and the average subject lost 2.6 pounds. The most interesting and discouraging aspect of the Stunkard and Brownell program was the high attrition. The dropout rate (greater than 50%) was comparable to attrition from self-help groups, but was far higher than would be expected from a behavioral program (Wilson & Brownell, 1980).

Abrams, Follick, and Thompson (in press) conducted a work-site program at Miriam Hospital in Providence, Rhode Island. Abrams *et al.* used the same treatment program (Brownell, 1979) as Stunkard and Brownell (1980). The hospital program reported weight losses of 10–12 pounds, and the authors reported encouraging findings from a relapse prevention program used during a maintenance period. The attrition, however, was 50%. Foreyt *et al.* (1980) reported preliminary results from a program they implemented at the Gold King Company in Houston, Texas. Subjects receiving the behavioral program lost an average of 6½ pounds in eight weeks. There were no data on long-term dropout rates. Another hospital program in Milwaukee provided nutrition education to employees, and 50% of the participants dropped out after six months (Sanger & Bichanich, 1977).

Two findings stand out from these studies: Weight losses are somewhat less than those obtained in clinical settings, and 50% or more of program participants tend to drop out of treatment within six months or less (Abrams *et al.*, in press; Foreyt *et al.*, 1980; Sanger & Bichanich, 1977; Stunkard & Brownell, 1980). Both may result from several factors. First, the lack of a program fee in most instances, and the ease with which patients receive treatment, might attract participants who are less motivated than persons who seek out a clinical program. Second, the potential benefits of social support need to be weighed against the potential drawbacks. For instance, Stunkard and Brownell (1980) assumed that employees in their program would encourage each other to attend sessions, so that any partnerships and friends would be as strong as their stronger members. However, employees may influence each other to drop out, so that some partnerships may be only as strong as their weakest member. These issues deserve careful attention in future work-site programs.

HYPERTENSION

Hypertension programs may be the most cost-effective means of lowering risk of heart disease at the work place. Hypertension is a primary risk factor for coronary heart disease, it is remedied in most cases with medication or lifestyle changes, and the costs of screening and intervention programs are not great. Alderman, Green, and Flynn (1980) have reviewed both published and unpublished reports of programs, and conclude that the results from most programs are impressive.

The two main approaches to hypertension control are screening and referral to outside professionals, and screening and intervention at the work site. The former programs were the first to be used, and the first of these programs was done by the Chicago Heart Association (see Alderman et al., 1980). More than 37,000 employees of 84 industries were screened. Approximately 19% were hypertensive, but only 15% of these were controlled. A later program by the same group involved a one-hour class with a health educator and laboratory tests which were to be discussed by the employees with their family physicians. This was not effective in increasing blood pressure control. The University of Michigan instituted a hypertension program in several industrial settings in collaboration with labor unions and management. Every effort was made to keep contact with the workers and the family physicians. Fully 88% of identified hypertensives consulted a physician, and after two years, more than 80% of the successfully referred employees maintained blood pressure control.

The second type of program, screening and in-house treatment, has been quite successful in one case and not as successful in another. Alderman and Schoenbaum (1975) screened and treated employees of the Gimbels and Bloomingdale's stores in New York. The program was conducted through the 15,000-member United Storeworkers Union. After screening at each of the stores, treatment was offered at one of 11 locations. The program used a health team approach, with a nurse and a supervising physician offering care. The employees paid nothing for treatment or medication. Attrition was less than 10% each year of the program, and blood pressure control was achieved in 80% of active participants. Sackett et al. (1975) carried out a hypertension program for Canadian Steelworkers. In a 2 × 2 design, these authors tested augmented convenience (seeing a physician at work during work hours) versus traditional family physician treatment, and an educational program versus no education. Neither the augmented convenience or the educational program boosted blood pressure control.

Poor compliance with treatment is a major problem with hypertension (Haynes et al., 1979). A recent report revealed that funds would be better spent on improving compliance in detected hypertensives than on screening for new cases (Stason & Weinstein, 1976). Behavioral methods have been useful in improving compliance in laboratory settings (Dunbar & Stunkard; Epstein & Masek, 1978). Haynes and colleagues used a behavioral program to improve compliance in 38 subjects from the Sackett *et al.* (1975) study who were noncompliant (Haynes, Sackett, Gibson, Taylor, Hackett, Roberts, & Johnson, 1976). These authors used home blood pressure monitoring, tailoring of regimens to individual needs, medication charting, and stimulus control methods. In addition, the participants met every other week with a paraprofessional who reinforced changes and gave credit toward ownership of the home blood pressure device. The average compliance of participants in the behavioral program increased 21%, compared to a decrease of 1.5% in a control group.

The issue of compliance is crucial to the prospect of controlling blood pressure at the work site. The program of Alderman and Schoenbaum (1975) was very successful, probably because of the social support and careful follow-up of all the participants. Alderman *et al.* (1980) recommend that programs increase the time spent with the patient, the number of contacts, the participation of the participant in the treatment process, the amount of social support available, and the ability to self-monitor blood pressure. These ideas need to be tested, but based on the experience of many work site programs, they hold great promise.

STRESS MANAGEMENT

It has been long recognized that job-related stress influences both physical and mental health (Cobb, 1976; Kasl, Gore, & Cobb, 1975; McLean, 1974). Specific studies have linked job stress with a variety of problems in white-collar workers in a financial institution (Weiman, 1977), firefighters and paramedics (Dutton, Smolensky, Leach, Lorimer, & Bartholomew, 1978), German sea pilots (Zorn, Harrington, & Goethe, 1977), and other workers in a variety of settings (Schwartz, 1980). Reviews of this area have been done by Schwartz (1980b) and Chesney and Feuerstein (1979), whose articles agree that very little evidence exists on whether stress management programs at the work place are effective.

One controlled program was carried out with the Converse Rubber Company (Peters, Benson, & Peters, 1977; Peters, Benson, & Porter, 1977). One-hundred-twenty-six corporate-level volunteers received eight weeks of one of three approaches: (1) Benson's (1975) technique for producing relaxation; (2) instructions to sit quietly and relax in any way; and (3) no instructions. Changes on every index, including blood pressure, illness days and symptoms, showed the greatest improvements in the first group, followed by the second, and then by the third group. Based on the work of Manuso (1977), the Equitable Life Assurance Society of the United States established an Emotional Health Program for employees (see Schwartz, 1980b). Troubled employees are referred to professionals who treat the employees on company time. The program is staffed by a clinical psychologist, a physician, a psychology intern, and a counselor. Data on this program are not available. A similar counseling/referral service is being offered by the Kennicott Copper Company in Utah, but again no data are available (the company does claim large savings).

Stress management programs in industry are only now being developed. Partly this reflects the state of the field, but it also reflects a greater interest among industry leaders to target smoking, obesity, and other factors before considering stress. Model programs for stress management in occupational settings have been described by Schwartz (1980b), by Chesney and Feuerstein (1979), and by McLean (1979). These programs deserve rigorous evaluation.

PHYSICAL ACTIVITY

Many industries are instituting physical activity facilities and programs, perhaps because of the current interest in jogging and other forms of exercise. The benefits of exercise are indisputable (see the section on exercise in this chapter), and Haskell and Blair (1980) note that exercising during the work day may improve job performances as well as health. Unfortunately, there have been few controlled tests of exercise programs at the work place. The available information is reviewed by Haskell and Blair (1980).

Durbeck *et al.* (1972) evaluated the effects of a one-year exercise program for 237 male employees of the National Aeronautics and Space Administration. Participants reported better mental and physical job performance, and less boredom and more enjoyment from their job. Heinzelmann and Bagley (1970) reported similar changes in a jogging-type program for 239 men from several communities who worked at a variety of jobs. Bjurstrom and Alexiou (1978) tested the effects of a five-year coronary disease prevention program for employees of the New York State Education Department. This program, primarily an exercise class, may have been responsible for a decrease in sick leave for participants.

As with work-site programs in other areas, the exercise programs have not been around long enough to be well developed and adequately tested. The preliminary results are positive (Haskell & Blair, 1980). Long-term adherence is a problem in exercise programs. Haskell and Blair (1980) have described a number of possible methods to improve adherence. They provide useful guidelines for establishing and evaluating a program. We expect to see much more research in this areas in the next few years.

HYPERACTIVITY

The past 10 years have seen a storm of controversy over the treatment of hyperactive (HA) children. O'Leary (1980), in a Presidential Address before Section III of the Clinical Division of the American Psychological Association, traced the development of this furor. He noted three events which brought national attention to the problem: (1) *The Washington Post* reported incorrectly that 5–10% of all children in the Omaha, Nebraska, schools were given psychostimulant drugs for hyperactivity (Maynard, 1970); (2) Schrag and Divoky (1975), two free-lance writers, published an account of pharmacological treatments for hyperactivity, and singled out the drug industry for producing irreversible damage in these children; and (3) Steven Box, a sociology lecturer from England, wrote an article condemning drug treatments for the *American Educator*, the professional publication of the American Federation of Teachers.

It is clear why the treatment of hyperactivity generates alarm in parents, educators, and health care professionals. The problem affects hundreds of thousands of children, the long-term consequences of poor school performance and disturbed social relations can be very serious, and the available treatments are controversial. The topic is of particular interest to behavioral medicine because it provides a classic confrontation between proponents of medical and psychological treatments. We present some of the most recent information; for more extensive reviews, we refer the reader to other sources (Cantwell, 1975; O'Leary, 1980; Ross, 1976; Ross & Ross, 1976; Safer & Allen, 1976; Sprague & Gadow, 1976; Whalen & Henker, 1976). (See also our discussion of recent "behavioral" developments in this area in Chapter 7.)

Definition, Assessment, and Prevalence

Many definitions have been proposed for hyperactivity. Safer and Allen (1976) state that hyperactivity is characterized by short attention span, excessive and purposeless motor activity, distractibility, impulsivity, overexcitability, and aggressiveness. O'Leary (1980) feels this definition to be problematic because children with other behavioral disorders exhibit these symptoms. His suggestion is not to view hyperactivity as the presence of some symptoms or the absence of others, but rather as a judgment of magnitude and character of certain key behaviors.

At present, it appears most reasonable to regard hyperactivity as a set of behaviors—such as excessive restlessness and short attention span—that are qualitatively and quantitatively different from those of children of the same sex, mental age, and SES.

Ross and Ross (1976) assembled a list of behavioral characteristics exhibited by HA persons across different age periods (Table 5-2). These authors, along with O'Leary (1980), note that few HA individuals display all the characteristics at any age period, but the cumulative effect of many behaviors is what leads parents to seek professional guidance.

Given the range of behaviors in HA children, and the fine distinction between normal and abnormal degrees of each behavior, differential diagnosis can be very important. The Conners Teacher Rating Scale (Conners, 1969) has been the most commonly used measurement device to distinguish HA children from their classmates. Similar rating scales have been developed by Davids (1971), Blunden, Spring, and Greenberg (1974), and Zukow, Zukow, and Bentler (1978). The problem with these scales is that they yield false positives—children are misdiagnosed as being HA (O'Leary, 1980). It is difficult to distinguish hyperactivity from aggressive conduct. The Conners Scale, for example, yields a correlation between an HA factor and an aggressive conduct factor of .77 (Werry, Sprague, & Cohen, 1975). Loney, Langhorne, and Paternite (1978) did a psychometric analysis of ratings by trained raters of psychiatric, psychological, and social work reports. They felt that aggression and hyperactivity factors should be separated, confirming suggestions by Werry (1978).

Lahey, Green, and Forehand (1980) used direct observational measures, teachers ratings, and peer evaluations to assess conduct problems and hyperactivity in 109 third-grade children. They found high correlations between conduct scores and hyperactivity scores, and argued against separate classification of hyperactivity. The argument for this lack of distinction is that both hyperactivity and conduct problems are associated with similar etiological factors, are more common in boys than in girls, show little evidence of neurological impairment, do not respond differently to pharmacological treatment, and have the same prognosis (Lahey et al., 1980; Sandberg, Rutter, and Taylor, 1978; Shaffer & Greenhill, 1979). Two recent studies have evaluated a scale which correlates well with parent ratings and scores from the Conners Scale (Abikoff, Gittelman-Klein, & Klein, 1977; Abikoff, Gittelman, & Klein, 1980). This scale, however, does not distinguish conduct problems from hyperactivity.

It is apparent that defining and measuring hyperactivity are thorny issues. It is not clear whether "hyperactive" behaviors are different from conduct problems, or even whether the issue matters. If the

TABLE 5-2.
Behavioral Characteristics of Hyperactive Persons at Different Ages

Age	Description of child
Infancy	Difficult and unpredictable Apoplectic to calm Querulous, irritable Rarely smiles Erratic sleep
Preschool	Sharp temper Strong willed Excessively demanding Light sleeper Short attention span
Middle childhood	Extremely active Difficulty sitting still Unable to remain seated during meal Distractible Light sleeper Often sad or depressed Poor school performance
Adolescence	Poor self-image Poor school performance Lack of social skills Rejection by parents and sibs Decrease in activity level Agressiveness
Adulthood	Personality disorders Explosive personality Alcoholism

Note. Adapted from Ross and Ross (1976).

treatment and prognosis for the two syndromes are similar, what use is differential diagnosis? However, if one problem is to be treated pharmacologically and the other psychologically, then a distinction is of the utmost importance. More work in this area is urgently needed.

Determining the prevalence of hyperactivity depends on how the problem is defined and measured. Estimates of prevalence come from different sources using different measures and definitions, so great ranges in the estimates are to be expected. Minskoff (1973) estimated that as many as 20% of all school children have some problems with hyperactivity. A government report in 1971 listed the prevalence of hyperactivity as 5%, while other surveys suggest that 30% of cases seen in psychological clinics and 10% of cases seen in pediatric clinics are due to hyperactivity (O'Leary, 1980). The exact prevalence is not known, but it is a widespread problem. Safer and Allen (1976) noted, "The most common child psychiatric disability is hyperactivity."

Pharmacological Treatment

The most commonly used medication for hyperactivity is methylphenidate (Ritalin), although a more recent drug, pemoline (Cylert), is also being used. O'Leary (1980) estimates that 600,000–700,000 children take psychostimulants for hyperactivity during the school year. The use of these drugs has increased dramatically since the early 1960s, but the frequency of usage began to level off several years ago (Sprague & Gadow, 1976; Whalen & Henker, 1976). O'Leary (1980) feels that the widespread use of these drugs is at least partly due to aggressive marketing efforts by the pharmaceutical firms, but there are other ways to explain this phenomenon (see Chapter 7).

The psychostimulant drugs have reliably beneficial effects on social behavior in HA children (Cantwell & Carlson, 1978; Conners & Werry, 1979; O'Leary, 1980). These factors have been studied in crossover studies, double-blind trials, and other experimental evaluations. Children on these drugs, according to teacher ratings, show increases in attention, cooperation, and compliance. The precise behaviors which respond to psychostimulants have only been studied recently (O'Leary, 1980). Barkley (1977) used an observational code and found that children changed movement, fidgeting, attention, and compliance. The drugs are associated with improved social activities, yet one study found that children on the drugs initiate less social contact (Whalen, Henker, Collins, Finck, & Dotemoto, 1979). One recent study found that methylphenidate significantly improved attention and behavior, and that its withdrawal led to worsening of these measures (Charles, Schain, Zelniker, & Guthrie, 1979). Brown and Sleator (1979) found that a low dose of methylphenidate (.3 mg/kg) in HA children reduced impulsivity whereas a high dose (1 mg/kg) did not. However, another recent study found that a higher dose (.75 mg/kg) had a better effect for on-task behavior than did a lower dose (.25 mg/kg) (Pelham, Schnedler, Bologna, & Contreras, 1980).

The effects of pharmacological treatments on academic behaviors are less clear. It was expected that the drugs would have a positive effect on achievement simply because attention would increase (O'Leary, 1980; Rie & Rie, 1977). Most studies do not show an advantage of the psychostimulants over no treatment (Barkley & Cunningham, 1978; Riddle & Rapoport, 1976; Weiss, Kluger, Danielson, & Elman, 1975).

The psychostimulants seem to help HA children in some areas and not others, as has been captured nicely by O'Leary (1980):

Psychostimulants have been shown repeatedly and consistently to influence social behavior in classrooms and attentional behavior in laboratory

situations on a short-term basis. Ratings and objective measures of attention and concentration almost always show salutary changes. Given the
academic achievement measures used in most short-term classroom studies
to date (6 to 8 weeks), one would not expect, nor does one find, significant
changes in academic achievement over these brief intervals of treatment
with psychostimulants. However, in the studies of 4 to 6 months duration
where academic achievement gains might be expected, positive results
have not been obtained either. (p. 199)

Several authors have raised one additional concern about drug
therapy for hyperactivity—that of attributional effects (Ross, 1976;
Whalen & Henker, 1976). The use of a powerful exogenous treatment
like a medication may cause children to attribute change to external
factors rather than to their own efforts. Bugental, Whalen, and Henker
(1977) studied this issue and concluded that "many children taking
medication are learning to attribute behavioral improvement to causes
beyond their personal control and to devalue their own personal contributions to problem solutions" (p. 882).

Behavioral Treatment

Behavioral treatments for hyperactivity fall into two categories—those
using parent training, teacher consultation, and school-based reinforcement for appropriate behavior, and those using self-instructional
training. An example of the former approach is a program by O'Leary,
Pelham, Rosenbaum, and Price (1976). This program used teacher
praise for appropriate academic and social behavior, and home rewards
based on a daily report card tailored to specific behaviors for each child.
This study and others have led to changes in attention, completion of
assignments, cooperation, and disruptiveness (Ayllon, Layman, &
Kandel, 1975; Gittelman-Klein, Klein, Abikoff, Katz, Gloisten, & Kates,
1976; O'Leary & Pelham, 1978). The studies using self-control or self-
instructional methods have not found changes in social behavior
(Douglas, Parry, Marton, & Garson, 1976; Friedling & O'Leary, 1979;
Bugenthal et al., 1977).

The effects of behavioral programs on academic performance have
not been consistent. Some studies of the school and home-based programs have shown some improvement in academic achievement (Ayllon
et al., 1975; Wolraich, Drummond, Solomon, O'Brien, & Sivage, 1978).
However, there are problems with assessing these factors in programs
of such short duration (O'Leary, 1980). The self-instructional programs are divided between those showing improvement in academic

performance (Douglas *et al.*, 1976) and those showing no change (Friedling & O'Leary, 1979). O'Leary (1980) acknowledges the lack of conclusive information, but feels there is reason to believe that the behavioral programs may produce lasting changes.

> Given that daily and weekly assignment-completion have increased with behavioral programs for hyperactive children, given that improvements on standardized achievement tests have occurred with self-instructional training, and given that we have found changes on standardized tests with children labeled Conduct Disorder (Kent & O'Leary, 1976), it seems very likely that a behavioral treatment program for hyperactive children could lead to long-range academic and social changes. (p. 200)

Combining Behavior Therapy and Pharmacological Therapy

When two forms of therapy prevail in an uncertain field, there is a natural tendency to compare the two, to find a winner. This has occurred in the field of hyperactivity, a field dominated by drug therapy and behavior therapy. For example, Gittelman-Klein *et al.* (1976) used a between-groups design to compare methylphenidate and behavior therapy, and found the drug treatment to be more effective over the eight-week study. Despite these results, there is great reluctance to rely on pharmacological interventions. These drugs produce side effects such as elevated heart rate and blood pressure, and the possibility of suppressed growth rates (cf. O'Leary, 1980). There is some evidence that memory and learning suffer because of drug therapy (Sprague & Sleator, 1977; Swanson, Kinsbourne, Roberts, & Zucker, 1978). In addition, the effects of chronic drug use are not known.

Recent sentiment among researchers in hyperactivity has been to acknowledge that both drugs and behavior therapy have their places. Safer and Allen (1976) feel that parent training is important because physicians who prescribe psychostimulants generally recommend that the child take the medication only during school hours to avoid side effects. Ross (1976) has another reason for using behavior therapy:

> Drug treatment of hyperactive children should, when used, be combined with behavior therapy so that the child can come to view his increased ability to sit still and to attend as something *he* is learning to master. It might be that with such a combination of approaches (chemical and psychological), the improvement could be maintained when the drug is withdrawn after a relatively short time. (p. 103).

O'Leary (1980) gives several circumstances in which drugs may be a useful adjunct to behavior therapy. The first is when a child does not respond to behavior therapy. In this case, the drug may permit the child to learn the behavioral procedures. The second is when parents are so troubled by their own marital or personal difficulties or are so preoccupied with the problems of their child, that they cannot assist in a behavioral program. The improvement in the child's symptoms produced by the drug might motivate the parents to participate in a behavioral program. The danger with this approach is the attribution of success to the drug. O'Leary (1980) notes that parents or teachers may see little need for a psychological program if the behavior seems to improve with medical intervention. Implicit in O'Leary's suggestions is the preference for behavior therapy; that is, drug therapy should be used only when behavior therapy does not work or needs a boost. Given the evidence on both approaches, we agree with O'Leary's stand.

Several recent reports have discussed using behavior therapy and drug therapy in combination. Pelham *et al.* (1980) found that the combination of methylphenidate and behavior therapy was more effective than either alone. Satterfield, Cantwell, and Satterfield (1979) reported results from the first year of a three-year prospective study of 84 hyperactive boys. They report "unexpectedly good outcome" with "the combination of a clinically useful medication with appropriate psychological treatments simultaneously directed to each of the child's many disabilities." We feel that combining treatments is an especially promising form of research. There is much to learn, however. For instance, it is not clear whether behavior therapy and drug therapy will interact additively, synergistically, or not at all. The attributional processes involved in combining these two treatments may provide the answers to these questions.

Dietary Treatment

There has been great interest in the role of dietary factors in the etiology and treatment of hyperactivity. With the publication of a book by Feingold in 1975, the issue came to public attention, so that now as many as 200,000 children may be following a special diet for their hyperactivity (O'Leary, 1980). The Feingold approach involved the removal from the diet of artificial food coloring, particularly red and yellow dyes. The diet also eliminates the preservative butylated hydroxytoluene (BHT) and natural salicylates contained in foods such as tomatoes, cucumbers, and apricots. Feingold (1975) claimed that 30% of the children on his salicylate-free diet showed "dramatic" improvement and another 18% responded "favorably." The issue has been confronted by researchers, but there is still the need for conclusive evidence (Spring & Sandoval, 1976; Williams & Cram, 1978).

The Feingold diet has been tested in many studies, some well controlled and others not. The uncontrolled studies generally support the Feingold hypothesis (Brenner, 1977; Cook & Woodhill, 1976; Rapp, 1978). Single-case reports offer a mixed picture (Mattes & Gittelman-Klein, 1978; Rose, 1978; Stine, 1976). The controlled studies also present inconsistent results. Conners and colleagues conducted a double-blind crossover study with 15 hyperkinetic children between the ages of 7 and 10 (Conners, Goyette, Southwick, Lees, & Andrulonis, 1976). Teachers' ratings showed a beneficial effect for the diet but parents' ratings did not. Harley and colleagues carried out a study in which the parents were actually supplied with foods (Harley, Ray, Tomasi, Eichman, Matthews, Chun, Cleeland, & Traisman, 1978). Parents, teachers, and observers were all kept blind to the food conditions in this crossover trial. The parents' ratings showed an effect on the diet, but teacher ratings, observational measures, and achievement tests showed no effect. Another study compared the diet with drug treatment, and found that both parent and teacher ratings could detect changes in the diet (Williams, Cram, Tausig, & Webster, 1978).

Two recent studies provide even more evidence on dietary practices in hyperactivity. Swanson and Kinsbourne (1980) admitted HA children to the hospital so a carefully controlled dietary manipulation could be done. Children were given either food dye (in normal daily amounts) or placebo and were tested for cognitive functioning with a paired-associate learning task. Performance on the learning task was significantly worse after the dye than after the placebo. Prinz, Roberts, and Hantman (1980) used seven-day dietary records to correlate the ingestion of food additives and salicylates with hyperactivity. The percentage of these foods in the diet did not correlate with observed hyperactivity.

There is some suggestion that sucrose ingestion may contribute to hyperactivity. Rapp (1978) noted sugar sensitivity in some HA children. Langseth and Dowd (1978) administered a five-hour glucose tolerance test to 261 HA children, and found that 74% had abnormal tolerance curves. Prinz et al. (1980) found a significant positive correlation between reports of sugar intake on seven-day dietary records and observed hyperactivity. They found that activity level in general was not related to sucrose intake, but agitated behavior was related. This correlational study does not prove cause and effect, but combined with data from other studies, the results suggest that more research is needed on the relationship between sucrose intake and hyperactivity.

The existing evidence does not warrant bold claims about the role of dietary factors in hyperactivity. The studies do not agree, and even those with positive findings have inconsistent results among different measures of hyperactivity. We suspect that dietary treatment may be very useful for some children. It will be a challenging task for researchers to identify those children.

CHAPTER

6

THE ADDICTIVE DISORDERS

KELLY D. BROWNELL

INTRODUCTION

Research on the addictive disorders continues to grow at a remarkable pace. It is unusual to read a psychology, public health, or related journal without encountering at least one article on some aspect of the addictions. There are journals devoted entirely to these issues, namely, *Addictive Behaviors* and the *International Journal of the Addictions*. Conferences have been called to assemble researchers in the various areas of the addictions (Krasnegor, 1979; W. Miller, 1980b). These efforts are not in vain; there have been important advances in our understanding of the development and treatment of the addictions.

The Direction of the Field: Away from Outcome Research

The past two years have brought a striking change in the emphasis of research on the addictions. The movement has been away from treatment outcome studies to investigations aimed at *understanding* the disorders we are treating. The research questions are changing from technique-oriented comparisons of treatment procedures to process-oriented evaluations of the social, behavioral, and physiological determinants of the addictive disorders. For example, studies are appearing on the effects of exposure to a model who eats, drinks, or smokes to excess; on the consequences of showing drinkers, smokers, or overeaters on prime-time television, on the aggregation of an addiction within families, and on the addicting properties of nicotine, alcohol, and food.

This new emphasis follows more than a decade in which three major accomplishments have been made: (1) a basic behavioral package has been developed for the treatment of obesity, smoking, and alcoholism; (2) the methodology for evaluating treatment outcome has been improved greatly; (3) the behavioral programs have been compared to many alternative forms of treatment. The results from this research have, in part, contributed to the decreased emphasis on outcome studies.

There are several possible reasons for the shift away from treatment outcome research:

1. Treatment effectiveness has plateaued, and further refinements of the familiar package promise to add only minimally to the effects of a complex group of procedures.
2. There is enormous variability in the response of different patients to treatment, and very few variables predict who will profit from treatment and who will not. Researchers and clinicians wish to know *why* this happens.
3. Some researchers feel it is important to understand a behavior pattern prior to attempting to change it. For example, it may be necessary to study the relationships between patients and their spouses before involving both persons in a treatment program.
4. Professional rewards (publications, tenure, etc.) do not encourage long-term treatment studies (Wilson, 1978b). Conducting a treatment outcome study of any consequence is a major undertaking, and most professional critics (journal reviewers) are satisfied only with studies in which treatment effects are monitored for at least six months after the initial program. The researcher risks disapproval of a project if the initial results are not spectacular or if the results do not last a very long time.
5. Most researchers are concerned about the clinical utility of their findings. It is no longer sufficient to show that a treatment is more effective than a comparison treatment; the professional audience wants to know that a treatment is *very* effective.

The case of obesity highlights this movement within the behavioral field. In the late 1960s and early 1970s, a group of behavioral procedures brought new promise to a discouraging area. In the next 10 years, well over 100 studies showed that the behavioral program was better than any treatment to which it was compared. Most studies tested variations of the basic program, and the weight losses began to be very consistent. There was a call for the demonstration of long-term maintenance, so studies with lengthy follow-up periods appeared. Presently, reviewers for journals routinely reject studies with the same weight losses that were applauded earlier, and impressive initial results are not published unless they are maintained. Researchers are also beginning to question whether the average weight losses reported (10–11 pounds) are clinically significant. It is not surprising, therefore, that more researchers are moving away from treatment outcome studies.

General Issues: Basic Assumptions and New Developments

COMMONALITIES

The "addictive disorders" generally include alcoholism, smoking, obesity, and sometimes drug abuse. We will focus on the first three because behavior therapists have concentrated their efforts in these areas.

There have been some attempts to join obesity, smoking, and alcoholism in a conceptual fashion, that is, to explain similarities among the behavior patterns and to show why they should be known collectively as the "addictive disorders." Are the disorders really similar, and why are other compulsive forms of behavior (gambling, sexual deviation, etc.) not considered addictive? In his recently edited volume on the addictive behaviors, William Miller (1980a) notes that the disorders share four characteristics: (1) short-term indulgence results in long-term difficulty; (2) no treatment has shown superior efficacy in any area; (3) there is no simple model of etiology; and (4) pattern adversely affects health. The first and fourth characteristics represent true attributes of the disorders, while the second and third are based on our ability to understand and treat the disorders.

Peter Miller (1980) also discusses commonalities among the addictive behaviors. He claims that the disorders belong together because they share a negative impact on health, a tendency to trigger each other (e.g., drinking can promote smoking), and an interrelationship when changes are made (persons who stop smoking may gain weight). Health risks for a combination of the disorders can be far greater than the sum of the individual risks. For example, a person who smokes and is overweight has triple the risk for coronary heart disease of the thin smoker (Heyden, Cassel, Tyroler, Hames, & Cornoni, 1971). As Miller (1980) points out, there is a high correspondence among the addictive disorders. Heavy drinking and heavy smoking are closely correlated (Walton, 1972).

We agree that there is much to be gained from grouping obesity, smoking, and alcoholism. A search for common ground may lead to new discoveries about the etiology and treatment of the addictions. Researchers may profit from learning about developments in each area of the addictions, because the addictive behaviors have been studied as separate entities, with too little effort to formulate general theories (P. Miller, 1980).

RESISTANCE TO TREATMENT

There is general agreement that the addictive disorders do not easily yield to treatment. Miller and Hester (1980) reviewed the alcoholism literature and found that 26% of problem drinkers who receive treatment remain abstinent or improved after one year. Smoking cessation clinics report quit rates of 20%, and behavior therapy programs have improved the success to approximately 50% (Lichtenstein & Brown, 1980). The case with obesity is the most discouraging. Fewer than 5% of obese persons will reduce to ideal weight and maintain that weight for more than one year (Bray, 1976; Stunkard, 1980; Van Itallie, 1977).

Without disputing the refractory nature of the addictions, we feel that "success" rate statistics must be viewed cautiously. First, the numbers are based on reports from clinical programs. It is likely that the most seriously distressed people seek professional assistance, and that other persons may establish control on their own. It would be helpful to study the rates of success among persons who do not need outside help. Some data do exist on this issue. For example, 19% of problem drinkers learn to control their own drinking (Miller & Hester, 1980). More than 30 million people have stopped smoking since the first Surgeon General's Report in 1964 (USDHEW, 1979), but it is not clear how many quit on their own, or how many attempts failed before these people finally succeeded. Second, it may be helpful to study *how* these people managed to conquer such a difficult problem. It is possible that some personality characteristics make it possible for some people to succeed, but it may also be possible that the successful persons use specific methods to control their behavior. Perhaps these methods could be used to strengthen clinical programs. The study of this group of persons may pay nice dividends.

RELAPSE

Relapse, more than any single issue, has captured the recent interest of researchers in the addictions. This movement owes a great debt to Marlatt and his colleagues at the University of Washington for developing a model which explains why relapse occurs and how to prevent inevitable transgressions from becoming debilitating relapse (Cummings, Gordon, & Marlatt, 1980; Marlatt, 1980; Marlatt & Gordon,

1980). Marlatt's model is achieving widespread attention in each area of the addictions, and we predict that the next few years will bring many controlled trials of the application of this model. We eagerly await these studies, because this model of relapse prevention is a promising method of improving the long-term maintenance of behavior change.

Relapse is an important problem in each area of the addictions, and this issue has assumed a prominent place in the writings of many researchers. Reviews of the smoking literature suggest that relapse may be *the* most important issue facing researchers (Bernstein & Glasgow, 1979; Lichtenstein & Brown, 1980; Pechacek & McAlister, 1980). Maintaining weight loss has been called the "new frontier" for obesity researchers (Stunkard & Penick, 1979; Wilson, 1980b; Wilson & Brownell, 1980). Relapse is also a crucial issue in the treatment of alcoholism (W. Miller & Hester, 1980; Nathan & Goldman, 1979; Sobell & Sobell, 1980).

Temporal patterns of relapse appear quite consistent across the various addictions. Figure 6-1, published in the early 1970s, shows the patterns of relapse for smokers, alcoholics, and heroin addicts (Hunt, Barnett, & Branch, 1971). Two-thirds of the relapses occurred within three months after treatment.

Marlatt (1980) points out that the similarity in patterns of relapse for the different addictions has been interpreted to mean that the

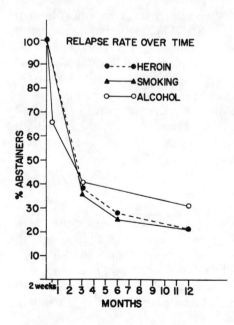

FIG. 6-1.
Temporal pattern of relapse among smokers, alcoholics, and heroin addicts. (From "Relapse Rates in Addiction Programs" by W. A. Hunt, L. W. Barnett, and L. G. Branch, *Journal of Clinical Psychology*, 1971, *27*, 455–456. Reprinted by permission.)

various substances have equivalent addictive potential. Such an approach would lead to investigations of the properties of the substances, or to a search for an underlying addictive personality. Marlatt proposes an alternative notion to explain these data. There may be cognitive, affective, and behavioral factors associated with relapse, independent of the substance being abused (Marlatt, 1980; Marlatt & Gordon, 1980). This conceptual approach would lead to the study of situational and attitudinal factors associated with relapse, and to the development of specific cognitive techniques to prevent relapse from occurring.

Cummings, Gordon, and Marlatt (1980) have assembled information on the determinants of relapse in alcoholics, smokers, opiate addicts, compulsive gamblers, and uncontrolled eaters. The alcoholics were males from two inpatient hospital programs, the smokers were male and female graduates of an outpatient smoking cessation program, the opiate addicts were males from two outpatient drug dependency programs, the gamblers were males from Gamblers Anonymous chapters in eight cities, and the uncontrolled eaters were female graduates of an outpatient dieting program. The 327 subjects were asked open-ended questions regarding the situations, feelings, and other factors surrounding relapse.

The results of the Cummings *et al.* (1980) survey are presented in Table 6-1. The responses were grouped into intrapersonal and interpersonal categories. The intrapersonal determinants consist of all factors within the individual and all reactions to nonpersonal environmental events. These include coping with negative emotional states, coping with negative physiological states, enhancement of positive emotional states, testing personal control (testing one's "willpower"), and giving in to temptation or desire. The interpersonal determinants include those events in which other individuals were present or were part of a contributing event: coping with interpersonal conflict, social pressure, and the enhancement of positive emotional states.

The results combined across all groups show an almost even split between intrapersonal (52%) determinants and interpersonal (48%) determinants. Fully 72% of all the relapses could be accounted for by three categories: negative emotional states (30%), social pressure (27%), and interpersonal conflict (15%). Cummings *et al.* (1980) point out that 72% of all relapses were associated with negative situations, and that relapse may be a response to stress. Only 12% of the relapses were attributed to positive states. The uncontrolled eaters and smokers showed the same even division of intrapersonal and interpersonal determinants as the entire sample, but the alcoholics tended to report more intrapersonal factors.

TABLE 6-1.

Analysis of Relapse Situations with Alcoholics, Smokers, Heroin Addicts, Gamblers, and Uncontrolled Eaters

Situation	Alcoholics (n = 70)	Smokers (n = 64)	WS addicts (n = 129)	VA addicts (n = 16)	Gamblers (n = 19)	Uncontrolled eaters (n = 29)	Total (n = 327)
Intrapersonal determinants	61%	50%	45%	75%	79%	46%	52%
Negative emotional states	38%	37%	19%	19%	47%	33%	30%
Negative physical states	3%	2%	9%	50%	—	—	7%
Positive emotional states	—	6%	10%	6%	—	3%	6%
Testing personal control	9%	—	2%	—	16%	—	3%
Urges and temptations	11%	5%	5%	—	16%	10%	6%
Interpersonal determinants	39%	50%	55%	25%	21%	52%	48%
Interpersonal conflict	18%	15%	14%	6%	16%	14%	15%
Social pressure	18%	32%	36%	19%	5%	10%	27%
Positive emotional states	3%	3%	5%	—	—	28%	6%

Note. From "Relapse: Prevention and Prediction" by C. Cummings, J. R. Gordon, and G. A. Marlatt, in W. R. Miller (Ed.), *The Addictive Behaviors: Treatment of Alcoholism, Drug Abuse, Smoking, and Obesity*, New York: Pergamon Press, 1980. Copyright 1980, Pergamon Press, Ltd. Reprinted by permission.

Marlatt (1980) has developed a manual on relapse prevention which describes the process underlying relapse and strategies for decreasing the probability that relapse will occur. A schematic diagram of the relapse model is shown in Figure 6-2. Marlatt's description of the model is as follows:

> The model proposes that the probability of relapse will increase in a high-risk situation if the individual fails to cope adequately with the problem. Failure to cope effectively leads to decreased self-efficacy in which the person feels less capable of dealing with forthcoming events. If the subsequent situation involves the availability of the taboo substance (e.g., alcohol), the probability increases that a relapse will occur, especially if the individual harbors positive outcome expectancies for the effects of the substance or activity. Should a lapse occur under these conditions, the individual will experience a pronounced cognitive–affective reaction that we call the Abstinence Violation Effect (AVE). The AVE is characterized by two components: a sense of conflict and guilt (cognitive dissonance) associated with the transgression of the abstinence rule, and a tendency to attribute the lapse to personal failure (lack of willpower, etc.). This combination of guilt and self-blame increases the probability that the lapse will escalate into a full-blown relapse. (1980, p. 30)

Marlatt and colleagues take the model even further in proposing specific areas for intervention and specific interventions for each area of the cognitive–behavioral process of relapse. Figure 6-3, from Cummings *et al.* (1980), shows the points of intervention for the prevention of relapse. The model predicts that an individual may be a candidate for relapse if there are deficits in any of the steps in the chain, and that treatment must bolster the individual's repertoire of self-control skills to prepare him or her to deal with difficulties in many situations.

Most behavioral programs have not trained subjects in specific methods to deal with relapse. There are philosophical and historical reasons for this. First, only recently have long-term evaluation of treatment programs been done, so the extent of the relapse problem was not clear. Second, inherent in the behavioral approach is the assumption that our clients are learning permanent changes in behavior. There is some question about whether the clients actually follow requests to change their behavior, and even less is known about how permanent the changes are (Brownell, 1980; Wilson & Brownell, 1980). Third, there has been a trend for behavioral programs to include more and more components, presumably because each new procedure will make the overall package more powerful. In Marlatt's (1980) words, "All of this is heavy artillery—yet all it may do is project the cannonball a little bit further before it hits the ground."

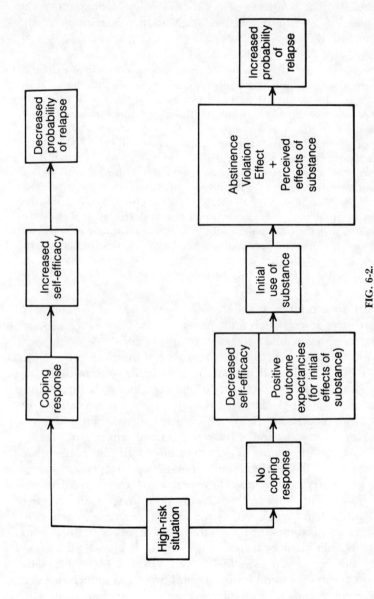

FIG. 6-2.

A schematic representation of the cognitive–behavioral model of the relapse process. (From *Relapse Prevention: A Self-Control Program for the Treatment of Addictive Behaviors* by G. A. Marlatt, Seattle: University of Washington, 1980. Reprinted by permission.)

The relapse prevention model raises several important clinical and experimental questions. For example, are subjects with specific skills deficits most likely to relapse at predictable places in the model? Do all subjects need to learn all the skills (Figure 6-3), or if not, how do we assess strengths and weaknesses? Will relapse training during treatment endure into the months and years that follow treatment? Should relapse training occur when the clients are most likely to relapse (during follow-up)? We expect these questions to be the subject of much research in the coming years.

THE FOCUS ON LONG-TERM RESULTS—A TRAP?

The past five years have brought an increasing emphasis on the long-term maintenance of changes produced during treatment. This is a positive movement because long-term results are necessary to help our clients in a meaningful way, and because relapse is so common among persons treated for the addictive disorders. The aim of this movement is a useful one—to evaluate and improve long-term results. However, there are several untoward side effects of this emphasis on long-term results.

Emphasis on long-term results brings with it changes in the criteria for professional rewards (favorable peer review). There is an increasing tendency for reviewers to reject journal articles, grant applications, dissertation proposals, and so forth if maintenance of behavior change has not been demonstrated or will not be evaluated. These criteria for professional behavior have several dangers:

1. This movement obscures the fact that different processes may be responsible for initial change and the maintenance of that change (Bandura, 1977b), or that completely different behaviors may be necessary early in treatment and years after treatment has ended. Since articles must show that the effects of treatment last many months, researchers may be forced into a search for a single procedure that will produce both initial and long-term results.
2. The movement may discourage researchers from pursuing innovative treatments that produce good results, because they will be criticized if they cannot prove that maintenance occurs. The failure of a treatment to produce long-term results is no reason to abandon it. Perhaps some other treatment will be necessary to *sustain* the promising results.
3. Studies with poor short-term results, for example, failures to replicate results from earlier studies, should not be required to

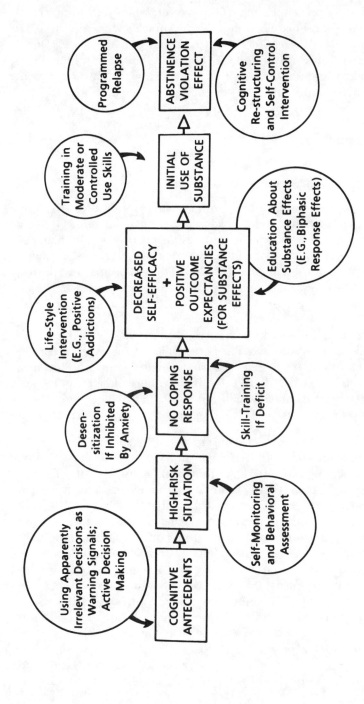

FIG. 6-3.

Points of relapse for each stage in the process of relapse. (From "Relapse: Prevention and Prediction" by C. Cummings, J. R. Gordon, and G. A. Marlatt, in W. R. Miller, Ed., *The Addictive Behaviors: Treatment of Alcoholism, Drug Abuse, Smoking, and Obesity,* New York: Pergamon Press, 1980. Copyright 1980, Pergamon Press, Ltd. Reprinted by permission.)

include long-term follow-up periods, unless there is some reason to expect that a procedure will be more effective in the long-run than it was initially. Relieving researchers of this requirement could allow more time for productive research.

4. The necessity of long-term follow-up increases the logistic problems of doing treatment outcome research, and lengthens the time between the initiation of a study and releasing the results. This time lag may deter graduate students who cannot devote an extra year to a study as well as young researchers who must make their mark in a brief time.

5. There are problems with causal inferences when people are followed for an extended period of time. If an alcoholic is still abstinent 10 years after treatment, can we conclude that the treatment program is responsible? During such a long period, clients will have many important life experiences, they may enter other treatments, and there may be periods of both relapse and perfect adherence. An obese person may lose and regain 50 pounds or more dozens of times in a 10-year period. If he or she happens to be assessed after a bout of weight loss, there is the danger of assuming that the treatment is effective. The same uncertainty pertains to follow-up periods of five years, two years, one year, and perhaps even shorter intervals. How long can we expect a treatment to last?

6. The focus on maintenance assumes there is something to maintain. This is somewhat presumptuous in a field that cannot guarantee that most patients will profit substantially from treatment, or that the persons who will profit can be identified in advance. Long-term maintenance may be a secondary issue until initial change is both consistent and clinically meaningful.

OBESITY

Few medical or psychological problems can match obesity for its seriousness, prevalence, and resistance to treatment (Bray, 1976; Brownell, 1982; Stunkard, 1980; Van Itallie, 1979). Obesity is related to many serious health problems (Bray, 1976; Van Itallie, 1979), but its most important health consequence may be its association with coronary heart disease (Lew & Garfinkel, 1979; Kannel & Gordon, 1979; Sorlie, Gordon, & Kannel, 1980). For most overweight persons, the social and psychological hazards of obesity are even more important than the physical hazards (Brownell, 1982; Stuart & Jacobson, 1979; Stunkard,

1975). At least 30% of adult Americans are heavy enough to justify weight reduction (Van Itallie, 1977). Finally, obesity is a most refractory condition. If "recovery" from obesity is defined as reduction to ideal weight, and maintenance of that weight for five years, a person is more likely to recover from almost any form of cancer than from obesity (Brownell, 1982; Van Itallie, 1977).

In spite of the difficult nature of obesity, the field has seen much progress in recent years. Behavioral researchers have expanded their avenues for investigation. The result has been a refreshing influx of new ideas into a field which, a few years ago, was "spinning its wheels."

Recent Trends

HOW FAT IS FAT? IS OBESITY DANGEROUS?

Defining obesity has been a problem for many years. Most studies define obesity by deviation from some criterion for ideal weight, usually insurance company actuarial statistics. However, "overweight" connotes variation in body weight; obesity is variation in body fat. There are a number of ways of estimating body fat (Bray, 1976; Brownell, 1981), yet most studies rely on body weight. In most cases, body weight and body fat are correlated, but there are exceptions. For example, a football player may have greater body weight but less body fat than a more sedentary person. Using body weight as the primary dependent measure is acceptable in most behavioral studies, but in studies where there is a dramatic manipulation of diet or exercise, measures of body fat may be important. Both diet and exercise can alter body composition (the ratio of lean to fat tissue), so changes in body weight may be deceiving (Katch & McArdle, 1977). A person who exercises may decrease body fat and yet not change in body weight, because the muscle tissue is more dense than the fat tissue it replaces. There has been a call for the use of body fat measures in lieu of body weight measures (LeBow, 1977; Wilson, 1978b), but it is body weight, not body fat, that has been related to health problems, so the simple height–weight norms may actually be the most useful index of ideal weight (cf. Brownell, 1981).

The most commonly used norms for determining ideal body weight are from the Build and Blood Pressure Study of 1959 (Metropolitan Life, 1960). These norms provide a range of ideal weight rated by sex, height, and frame size. A new Build and Blood Pressure Study was conducted recently, and the new norms (several pounds higher in most categories) will probably replace the previous ones. There is still the problem, however, of determining *how* overweight a person must be to be considered obese. Most behavioral studies use arbitrary criteria, say 15%, 20%, or 30% above ideal weight. The lower limit for defining obesity has several implications for interpreting the results of studies. First, subjects 15% overweight are not very heavy, and their treatment may follow a different course from subjects who may be 50% or more overweight. Second, mildly overweight subjects may be better off than their thinner counterparts, an issue discussed below. We feel that studies should use a minimum of 25% overweight for inclusion of subjects in studies. With such a definition, the mean percentage over-weight for a group of subjects will probably be 50–60%, and they should be representative of the population of overweight persons who seek clinical programs for their problem.

It may be most sensible to define obesity as the point at which increases in weight lead to increased risk for psychological and/or medical problems. The psychological area has received little attention, but such is not the case with the medical area. Many studies have been published in the medical and epidemiology literatures in which varia-tions in body weight have been related to morbidity and mortality. Morbidly obese persons (more than 100% above ideal weight) are clearly at risk for major health problems (Drenick, Bale, Seltzer, & Johnson, 1980; Van Itallie, 1979). The relationship between body weight and disease is not so clear in persons 0–30% overweight.

The "ideal" weights from the first Build and Blood Pressure Study were determined by estimating the weight at which least mortality occurred (Metropolitan Life, 1960). Most people presume that "thinner is better" and that risk increases in a linear fashion with body weight. Unfortunately, the relationship is not so simple. Keys (1979, 1980) has done a prospective study of coronary heart disease in seven countries. Gross obesity was related to increased risk, but so was marked leanness. For all other weight categories, there was no direct relationship between body weight and heart disease. Men slightly above the average (not ideal) weight had the lowest risk, and men over 40 years old were not at increased risk at up to 20% above average weight. Data from the Framingham study indicate that the lowest mortality is at the *average* weight, not the ideal weight (Sorlie *et al.*, 1980), but that risk increases with increases in body weight (Kannel & Gordon, 1979). Kannel and Thom (1979) even feel that leaner weights in women are partially responsible for the decrease in the prevalence of heart disease during the past 20 years. Lew and Garfinkel (1979) studied weight and mortality in 750,000 men and women as part of the American Cancer Society

Study from 1959 to 1972. They found that the lowest mortality was among persons close to or 10-20% below average weight, that mortality in persons 30-40% above average weight was increased 50%, and in those heavier than 50% above ideal weight, mortality was increased 90%. Coronary heart disease was the major contributor to mortality, but rates of cancer were increased for those 40% or more above average weight. Andres (1980) has reanalyzed data from several of the major epidemiology studies, and has reported that there is no clear link between body weight and mortality anywhere below 30% overweight.

There is no definite answer to the question of how strongly obesity is related to morbidity and mortality in people who are 20-30% or less above average weights. There is little doubt that heavier people are at greatly increased risk. Since many clinical programs treat subjects who average 50-60% overweight, the health reasons for treating these subjects are compelling. Weight reduction for subjects who are 10-30% over-weight may actually move the subjects to a category of higher risk. There are no prospective studies showing this to be the case, but the issue is important to consider when selecting subjects for study.

RECOGNIZING THE COMPLEXITIES OF OBESITY

It is interesting to scan the references of obesity studies published in the behavioral literature. In the past several years, the trend has been for authors to cite studies from the work of physiologists, nutritionists, epidemiologists, and so forth. Wooley, Wooley, and Dyrenforth (1979) published a superb paper describing the psychological and cultural aspects of obesity, metabolism, hunger and satiety, and many important factors associated with obesity. Recent reviews of the physiology litera-ture have shown the role of physical activity in the treatment of obesity (Brownell & Stunkard, 1980; Epstein & Wing, 1980a). Stunkard (1980) has edited a landmark book on obesity which includes chapters on fat cells, dietary obesity in animals, the regulation of body weight from a physiological perspective, restrained eating, externality, dietary treat-ments, pharmacological treatments, behavioral treatments, exercise, childhood obesity, and so forth. A look at Stunkard's book or Bray's (1976) earlier volume readily indicates that the behavior therapy studies are only a part of the massive literature on obesity. We may profit from reviewing the nutrition literature when prescribing diets, the exercise physiology literature when prescribing increased activity, the physi-ology literature when we try to explain hunger and satiety, and the psychiatry, sociology, and psychology literatures when attempting to understand the psychology of obesity.

Several trends discussed earlier for the addictions in general apply especially to obesity. These include a movement away from outcome research and toward research on the topography of eating behavior, a focus on the maintenance of weight loss, and a demand for long-term studies with large samples, impressive weight losses, and good follow-up results. We will discuss each issue in the sections presented below.

Assessment

There is general and increasing interest in assessment within the field of behavior therapy (see Chapter 2). Within the area of obesity, assessment has become an important issue mainly because of the increased emphasis on the evaluation of treatment outcome (Wilson, 1978b) and on adherence to the program components (Brownell & Stunkard, 1978; Johnson, Wildman, & O'Brien, 1980; Lansky, 1981). Researchers have branched out from these areas so that many of obesity's complex aspects are now the subject of assessment.

Brownell (1981) describes a comprehensive assessment plan for obesity and anorexia nervosa in Barlow's (1981) recent book on behavioral assessment. The chapter describes assessment in the following areas: (1) defining and measuring obesity (body fat vs. body weight); (2) assessing genetic and biological determinants (body weight set points, adipose cellularity); (3) evaluating eating behavior (eating style, food preferences, external control); (4) measuring physical activity; (5) assessing independent variables; and (6) measuring treatment outcome. A few of these issues have been explored by behavioral researchers and show the topics of greatest importance within the field of behavior therapy.

ASSESSING TREATMENT OUTCOME

The most thorough method of measuring the progress of treatment is to combine measures of body weight and body fat (Brownell, 1981), but interpretation of the results may be difficult when the two measures do not correspond (Rogers, Mahoney, Mahoney, Straw, & Kenigsberg, 1980). Since measures of body weight are most commonly used, then the researchers must still choose between several available methods of presenting the data.

The options for presenting data on body weight are absolute weight change, body weight indices, percentage overweight, categorical weight loss, and the weight reduction index (Brownell, 1981; Wilson, 1978b). Merely presenting the number of pounds lost is the most frequently used method. These data are important to include in research reports simply to allow comparison with other studies in which the same measure has been used. However, the same weight loss in two people of different weights may not represent the same degree of treatment effectiveness. The two weight indices are the body mass index (weight/height^2) and the ponderal index (height divided by the cube root of weight). These are used in the epidemiology literature and are designed to equate for differences among subjects in height. Both are difficult to interpret and offer no particular advantage to the measures mentioned below. Change in percentage overweight is calculated by subtracting ideal weight from actual weight, then dividing by actual weight. It is a useful measure because it accounts for frame size, height, and sex. Categorical weight loss, the number of persons who lose 20, 30, 40 pounds, has been used in some studies. Hanna, Loro, and Power (1981) recommend using weight categories to classify obese persons: 10–20% over ideal weight, slight; 21–30%, mild; 31–50%, moderate; 51–75%, severe; 76–100%, massive; 101% or more, morbid. This system is helpful to the extent that we need to consider differences in initial weight, but the categories themselves are not based on any evidence that people within the categories differ. Hanna *et al.* (1981) report their heavier patients lost the most weight, but this is a common finding (Brownell, Heckerman, & Westlake, 1979; Murray, 1975), and it is probably due to the simple matter of the heavier people losing more weight when they have the same number of calories as leaner people. The final measure, the weight reduction index (Feinstein, 1959), is a function of the percentage of surplus weight lost times the relative initial overweight. This method accounts for height, degree overweight, the number of pounds lost, and is one good means of reporting weight change data (Wilson, 1978b).

ADHERENCE TO THE TREATMENT PROGRAM

In 1975, Mahoney questioned whether obese and normal weight persons actually differ in their eating behaviors, and whether changes in these behaviors contribute to weight reduction. Brownell and Stunkard (1978) reviewed the literature and found that behavior change was related to weight loss in some studies and not others, and that the studies with the most extensive measures of weight change were the ones to find no relationship (Brownell, Heckerman, Westlake, Hayes, & Monti, 1978; Jeffery, Wing, & Stunkard, 1978; Stalonas, Johnson, &

Christ, 1978). Lansky (1981) carefully examined the studies in which measures of behavior change had been reported, and concluded that many were beset by methodological problems, and that Brownell and Stunkard's (1978) conclusions about behavior change and weight change may have been premature. Johnson *et al.* (1980) reviewed studies in the behavioral literature from 1969 to 1979 and found a steady increase in the number of studies in which program adherence was considered. However, these authors found many problems with the studies reporting adherence data: assessment during follow-up is rare, assessment is based entirely on self-report, and only a small number of requested behavior changes are measured. Johnson *et al.* (1980) call this issue the "Achilles' Heel" of behavioral research on obesity, and suggest that careful measurement of adherence be undertaken routinely because there are many ways subjects can lose weight.

Wilson and Brownell (1980) note that measuring treatment adherence will bring us one step closer to examining the functional relationship between prescribed behavior changes and weight changes, but that much more detailed measurement will be necessary before this issue can be resolved. Wilson and Brownell (1980) suggest that behavior change and weight change are only two components in a complex chain which includes therapeutic instructions, eating and exercise behaviors, energy balance, and weight change:

$$\text{Therapeutic instructions} \xrightarrow{1} \text{Eating and exercise behaviors} \xrightarrow{2} \text{Energy balance} \xrightarrow{3} \text{Weight change}$$

The failure of a program to produce weight change could occur from an interruption at any point in the chain. At arrow 1, eating and exercise behaviors may not change if patients do not comply with program guidelines. Weight change may still occur, if patients undertake nonprogram practices (e.g., so-called crash diets). There is the possibility (arrow 2) that changes in eating and exercise behaviors may not alter energy balance. Subjects may eat more slowly, but may eat longer and consume the same number of calories. Subjects may report more physical activity during scheduled periods, but may expend less total energy if their movement throughout the remaining hours decreases. Finally, arrow 3 shows that energy intake may decrease and physical activity may increase, but subjects may still not lose weight due to metabolic factors (Bray, 1976; Wooley *et al.*, 1979). Theoretically, a subject may have perfect adherence to behavioral procedures and may lose weight, but the weight loss may not be due to the behavior changes. This area is one that challenges our interest in assessment.

THE ACCURACY OF SELF-REPORTED WEIGHTS

Several studies have appeared recently on whether subjects are accurate in reporting their weights. If subjects are accurate, or if the error is predictable, then data could be collected more efficiently. Long-term follow-up of subjects in weight loss programs could be done with telephone interviews; fewer data would be lost due to subject attrition. Collecting weights via telephone or mail would be especially pertinent for large-scale epidemiological surveys in which thousands of subjects may be involved.

Charney and colleagues found a correlation of .96 between measured and reported weight in 50 adults, ages 20–30 (Charney, Goodman, McBride, Lyon, & Pratt, 1976). However, correlational statistics may be misleading. If, for example, every subject overestimated his or her weight by 30 pounds, the correlation would be perfect. Charney et al. did report that their average subject underestimated weight by approximately 5%. Wing, Epstein, Ossip, and LaPorte (1979) reported two studies on self-report and observers' reports of weight. In the first study of 78 college students, 68% of the subjects were accurate within five pounds and 86% were accurate within 10 pounds. The second study of 118 adults attending a health fair found that 66% of the subjects were within five pounds of actual weight and 91% were accurate within 10 pounds. Another study on self-reported weight was conducted on 3407 subjects who were part of the Lipid Research Clinics Program Prevalence Study in Minnesota (Pirie, Jacobs, Jeffery, & Hannan, 1981). They found differences in reported weights among men and women. Women in all weight categories tended to underestimate their weights; heavier men also underestimated their weights, but lighter men overestimated their weights. Combining subjects across all weight categories, women underestimated their weights by 4.17 pounds and men underestimated theirs by .89 pounds. The errors were larger in some categories (women aged 20–39 who weighed between 170 and 189 pounds underestimated their weights by 10.6 pounds). Pirie et al. conclude that persons make significant errors in reporting their weights, and that the errors depend on sex, age, and weight. Wing et al. (1979) make no particular judgments about self-reported weights, but they do conclude that self-reports are more accurate than observer reports.

Stunkard and Albaum (1981) evaluate the accuracy of self-reported weights in 1302 subjects at seven sites in the United States and one site in Denmark. The error was less than 2.2 pounds for 52% of the subjects and less than 4.4 pounds for 70% of the subjects. The subjects from Denmark made greater errors than the American subjects. The average across the American sites was an underestimate of 2.6 pounds, with a standard deviation of 6.8 pounds. Stunkard and Albaum also found that heavier subjects tend to underestimate their weights more than thinner subjects. Schlichting, Høilund-Carlsen, and Quaade (1981) analyze the Danish data also reported as part of the study by Stunkard and Albaum (1981). They found that tall and heavy subjects underestimated their weights and small and thin persons overestimated their weights.

Do data from these studies show that people are accurate or inaccurate? The answer depends on the purpose of the information being collected. For large-scale epidemiological studies relating body weight to health indices, the errors may not be important because they are spread across hundreds or thousands of subjects. In addition, data from the studies by Stunkard and Albaum (1981) and Schlichting *et al.* (1981) could be used to form an equation to correct for the expected errors. Stunkard and Albaum feel their data "may obviate the need for measured weights in epidemiological investigations."

The case is different for clinical trials of weight loss programs. The errors in weights may vary as a function of sex, age, weight, and other factors (Pirie *et al.*, 1981). The heterogeneity of subjects in most studies, combined with small sample sizes, would make it very difficult to assume that self-reported weights were accurate, or that any error was consistent across subjects within the sample. In addition, the magnitude of error, even the 2.6 pounds that Stunkard and Albaum (1981) feel to be surprisingly accurate, is very high given the differences in weight loss being detected in most studies. In treatment studies where the average weight loss is 10 pounds, relying on self-reported weights would mean that the error in measurement (2.6 pounds) is more than 25% of the measurement itself (and the 2.6 pounds is from the most encouraging study). Pirie *et al.* also note that the standard deviations must be considered. Assuming a normal distribution, the standard deviation of 6.8 pounds reported by Stunkard and Albaum means that 95% of the subjects (two standard deviations) would vary from an underestimate of 11 pounds to an overestimate of 16.2 pounds. We feel, therefore, that the call for actual weights rather than self-reported weights must prevail in treatment outcome studies and in other studies in which extremely large samples are not available.

Studies on the Process of Eating

Obesity researchers in the behavioral area have been increasing their emphasis on *understanding* the determinants and process of eating. For reasons discussed in the first section of this chapter, there has been a striking movement away from outcome research and toward more specific research on smaller and more definable questions. These studies can be grouped into the areas of eating style and food choice, modeling, and externality.

EATING STYLE AND FOOD CHOICE

Much of the behavioral program for obesity is based on the assumption that obese persons have a distinct eating style which contributes to their obesity. Mahoney (1978) notes that the assumption has several components, including (1) that obesity is a simple, learned disorder; (2) that obese persons eat more than thin persons; (3) that the obese eat rapidly; (4) that obese persons are extremely responsive to external food cues; and (5) that teaching obese persons to adopt the "thin eating style" will result in weight reduction. Behavioral programs teach subjects to eat more slowly, to decrease exposure to food cues, and to focus much more on energy intake than on energy output.

The initial studies comparing the eating styles of obese and nonobese persons produced mixed results. For example, LeBow, Goldberg, and Collins (1977) studied patrons at a quick-service diner and found that overweight, compared to nonoverweight subjects, took fewer bites, chewed their food less, spent less time in nonchewing activities, and finished sooner. Rosenthal and Marx (1978) found no differences in eating style between obese and nonobese persons. Stunkard and Kaplan (1977) reviewed 13 studies on the direct observation of eating. They conclude:

> Eating is affected by so many and such diverse factors that the difficulty in uncovering differences between obese and nonobese persons is not surprising. The old notion of a distinctive obese eating style gives way to the idea that there are, at best, a variety of obese eating styles. And it is now clear that no single study of eating under one set of circumstances will be sufficient to describe these obese eating styles. (p. 98)

Stunkard and Kaplan did, however, feel that two factors may differentiate obese and nonobese persons: the amount of food chosen and the rate of eating. Stunkard and his colleagues proceeded to test both questions.

Coll, Meyers, and Stunkard (1979) observed 5291 persons at nine different eating sites. Obese persons choose more food only at one site—that serving the food with the highest caloric content. The site of eating was a far stronger predictor of food choice than body weight. Coll et al. did not feel justified in concluding that obese and nonobese persons eat the same amount of food, because only a small portion of eating is done in public places. Furthermore, there may be less than a perfect relationship between food chosen and food eaten. Krassner, Brownell, and Stunkard (1979) studied obese and nonobese persons in a college cafeteria and found that the obese persons were significantly more likely to clean their plates. Ballard, Gipson, Guttenberg, and Ramsey (1980) followed with a similar study with children. They found that obese and nonobese children differed only slightly in the amount of food left on their plates, but that interesting differences existed when the palatability of the food was considered. The obese and nonobese subjects did not differ in the amount of unpalatable food left on the plate, but nonobese subjects left almost twice as much palatable food. Coll *et al.* also suggest that palatability and body weight may interact to predict food consumption.

Stunkard, Coll, Lundquist, and Meyers (1980) made unobtrusive observations of 30 obese women and 37 matched controls at a fast-food restaurant. The size of the meal was controlled by giving each subject a coupon for a free meal of either 985 of 1800 calories. Obese and nonobese subjects did not differ on 11 of 12 measures of eating style, including eating rate. Furthermore, providing the large meal had similar effects on both groups. Stunkard *et al.* split the meal into three equal intervals and found that eating rate increased between the first and second intervals, but then decreased drastically during the last third. The decreases in rate were more pronounced for nonobese than for obese subjects.

There have been no successful attempts at defining an obese eating style. Many factors appear to influence food choice and eating style, including location and palatability of the food. It still may be useful to search for eating styles in individuals, and to structure a treatment program accordingly, but global differences between obese and non-obese persons are not likely to be discovered.

MODELING

Eating in the presence of other persons may be a powerful determinant of how a person eats. Four recent studies, three in laboratory settings and one in a naturalistic setting, address this issue. Rosenthal and McSweeney (1979) had female college students eat with a female confederate who ate either rapidly or slowly. The subjects increased their rate of eating with the fast model. Rosenthal and McSweeney then used male and female subjects, and male and female models. Male and female subjects both modeled the male model but not the female model. Rosenthal and Marx (1979) tested successful dieters, unsuccessful dieters, and nondieters who were exposed to models who ate much food or an appropriate amount of food, or to no model. Subjects ate more food when exposed to the model who consumed the most food. Subjects in both dieter groups ate less than subjects in the nondieter group. Wing and Jeffery (1979) tested college students during an evening snack. The students ate alone, with a friend, or with a stranger. Even though the three groups did not differ in the total amount eaten, more than 60% of the variance in the calorie intake in subjects eating with a partner could be accounted for by knowing the intake of the partner. Krantz (1979) observed obese subjects and matched controls in a university cafeteria to determine whether the food they chose would vary depending on whether they ate alone or with another person. Normal-weight subjects ate more with others than when alone. In contrast, the obese subjects ate more alone than with others, presumably because the obese subjects were self-conscious about how much they were eating.

These strong modeling effects have two implications for the study of obesity and its treatment. First, it adds yet another factor to the list of variables that influence eating behavior, and further complicates any attempt to find specific eating styles for obese and nonobese persons. Second, it may be important to evaluate the eating patterns of the persons in the dieter's immediate social environment. If they are "inappropriate" models, then direct training of these persons may be helpful.

EXTERNALITY

Schachter (1971) hypothesized that obese persons are extraordinarily responsive to food cues in their environment. Schachter, Nisbett, and others conducted a series of studies which indicated that obese and nonobese persons differed greatly in their externality under a variety of circumstances (cf. Rodin, 1981; Schachter & Rodin, 1974). One major component of the behavoral program for obesity was based on this assumption that obese persons were highly "external" and that decreasing the salience of external cues would help these persons control their weight (Brownell, 1980; Ferguson, 1975; Jeffrey & Katz, 1977; Jordan, Levitz, & Kimbrell, 1977; Mahoney & Mahoney, 1976; Stuart & Davis, 1972).

Much of the recent evidence does not indicate that obese and nonobese persons differ in their external responsiveness. For example, Meyers, Stunkard, and Coll (1980) manipulated the accessibility of high- and low-calorie desserts in a hospital cafeteria, and found that obese, overweight, and normal-weight groups were equally responsive to the alteration of food cues. Milich and Fisher (1979) also found no relationship between body weight and cue salience. There are many more studies which disconfirm the externality hypothesis (Rodin, 1978, 1980, 1981).

Rodin (1981) reviews the literature on the externality theory and asks, "What went wrong?" She concludes that (1) externality occurs in persons in all weight categories; (2) internal sensitivity is not uniquely characteristic of thin persons; (3) external and internal cues can influence each other; and (4) weight gain and weight loss depend on much more than external responsiveness. Based on the theories of Nisbett (1972), Herman and his colleagues have proposed that external responsiveness (and propensity to eat excessively) depends on whether a person is restraining his or her eating (Herman, 1978; Herman & Polivy, 1980). This restraint factor may be a stronger predictor of external responsiveness and success at dieting than body weight.

Treatment Outcome Studies

The past several years have seen the publication of many treatment outcome studies, as well as several major reviews of the literature on behavior therapy for obesity (Brownell, 1979b; LeBow, 1981; Stuart, 1979; Stunkard, 1979; Stunkard & Brownell, 1979; Stunkard & Penick, 1979; Wilson, 1980a, 1980b; Wilson & Brownell, 1980). We will discuss the short-term results first, then the long-term results, then the issue of attrition, and finally present our conclusions.

SHORT-TERM RESULTS

Wilson and Brownell (1980) note that most behavioral programs aspire to weight losses of 1–2 pounds per week and are 8–10 weeks in duration, so it is not surprising that average weight losses tend to be approximately 11 pounds. What *is* surprising is the remarkable consistency of outcome across the many published studies. Jeffery, Wing, and Stunkard (1978) reviewed 21 behavioral studies, and found the mean posttreatment weight loss to be 11.5 pounds. The same authors reported a mean weight loss of 11.04 pounds for 125 patients in the Stanford Eating Disorders Clinic. Brownell *et al.* (1979) found a mean weight loss of 11.01 pounds in 100 patients in a clinic at Brown University. Wilson and Brownell (1980) calculated the mean posttreatment weight loss in 17 long-term studies and found it to be 10.4 pounds. Each of these figures is averaged across many subjects, but the consistency is striking considering that the programs were in different parts of the country, subjects paid varying treatment fees, there was a wide variation in the degree of obesity of the subjects, the therapists in the programs varied widely in their training, and so forth. The behavioral program has predictable results across large numbers of subjects.

The trend in recent outcome studies has been to combine the familiar behavioral package with another form of treatment with the result of improving weight losses. Dahlkoetter, Callahan, and Linton (1979) found a mean loss of 13.3 pounds in eight weeks of treatment in subjects who took part in an exercise program in addition to receiving behavior therapy. Brownell *et al.* (1978) reported 19.6-pound losses in 10 weeks for subjects who entered treatment with their spouses. Pearce, LeBow, and Orchard (1981) reported 14.3 pound losses from a similar study, as did Brownell and Stunkard (1981) (19.6 pounds). Craighead, Stunkard, and O'Brien (1981) reported 33.9-pound losses in a 25-week program in which subjects received behavior therapy and an appetite suppressant drug (fenfluramine), and Brownell and Stunkard (1981) reported 22.9-pound losses with a similar treatment over 16 weeks. Part of the increased weight loss is probably a simple matter of treating subjects longer. The 6–8 week programs have given way to programs of 10–16 weeks. It also appears that combining behavior therapy with other treatments may be promising, an issue discussed below.

Recent outcome studies using behavior therapy alone have helped to refine the basic behavior therapy program. Loro, Fisher, and Levenkron (1979) found that a self-initiated behavioral program individualized self-control strategies) was more effective than stimulus control or eating behavior control. Chapman and Jeffrey (1979) found that subjects adhered better to procedures aimed at altering the eating environment than to standard setting procedures. Carroll and Yates (1981) also found that stimular control procedures facilitated weight loss. Jeffery and Wing (1979) evaluated frequent contact (three times per week, in person and by telephone) with the traditional once-weekly format. Frequent meetings were more effective.

LONG-TERM LOSSES

Some of the recent literature reviews have focused on the long-term results of behavior therapy (Stunkard & Penick, 1979; Wilson & Brownell, 1980). Stunkard and Penick (1979) are pessimistic:

> Clinically important weight losses achieved by behavioral treatments for obesity are not well maintained. (Whether they are better maintained than weight losses achieved by other—nonsurgical—treatments is impossible to determine because of insufficient information on the long-term results of these other treatments). This is an important and disappointing conclusion, for we initially hoped that the first generation of behavioral treatments might produce enduring changes in weight-related behaviors and, as a consequence, long-term weight loss. (p. 805)

We feel that this negative view is not entirely justified.

Wilson and Brownell (1980) review the 17 studies with follow-up periods of one year or longer. After one year, the mean weight loss for the combined studies was approximately 10 pounds, only a slight decrease from the 10.4 pounds lost at posttreatment. Even Stunkard and Penick (1979) found good maintenance in the studies they reviewed, with the exception of their own, which had a five-year follow-up. A careful examination of the data from individual studies reveals that the mean weight loss is upheld over time, but the variability increases steadily as the length of follow-up increases. This reflects the fact that some subjects continue to lose and finish with a large loss, with others regressing toward their baseline weights.

What can be concluded from these unruly results? It depends, in part, on one's perspective. Taking a positive perspective, one could argue that no other treatment has demonstrated long-term results as well as behavior therapy, and given the refractory nature of the disorder, mean weight losses of 10–11 pounds after one year may be no small accomplishment. In addition, the results of the behavioral program are obtained from relatively short treatment periods, most treatments are administered in groups, and the program is not very costly. Being more pessimistic, it could be argued that weight losses of 11 pounds are of little value for patients who average 60% overweight. Furthermore, the large variability in most studies suggests that a few large losers boost the mean weight loss while the majority of subjects lose little weight. We feel that behavior therapists have made great strides in evaluating and facilitating maintenance, but that there is much to be learned.

RESULTS FROM UNCONTROLLED PROGRAMS

Wilson and Brownell (1980) report the results from eight papers, each on programs with no special experimental evaluation. Although the results await further testing, they are helpful in generating ideas and in testing the application of the behavioral programs in clinical situations. The weight losses tended to follow the same pattern as the losses in the controlled studies. For example, Foreyt (1979) found mean weight losses of 11 pounds in an eight-week program, and Levitz, Jordan, LeBow, and Coopersmith (1980) report an 18.6-pound loss in 20 weeks of treatment.

There were two reports of residential programs, one at Hilton Head Island (Miller & Sims, 1981) and one at Duke (Roseman & Nelius, 1980). Both programs involve daily meetings, supervised meals, a 700-calorie diet, structured exercise regimens, and intensive contact with professionals and other participants, and all involve sizable fees. The results are impressive. Miller and Sims report a mean loss of 17.2

pounds after the four-week program. At a one-year follow-up, the mean loss had increased to 29.2 pounds. Roseman and Nelius find an average loss of 22.8 pounds after a treatment period which averaged 48 days. The follow-up, after an average of 18 months, showed a mean loss of 27.2 pounds. Programs of this nature are worth pursuing, especially considering the large weight losses during follow-up—a time in which no treatment was administered.

ATTRITION

Whether or not a person joins and stays in a treatment program is the first, and perhaps most critical, index of adherence. "Large weight losses become less impressive if the program appeals to few or if most of the participants drop out" (Wilson & Brownell, 1980, p. 58). Very little is known about attrition. For example, it is assumed that the least successful patients drop out of treatment. It is hard to dispute this clinical intuition, but some patients may leave treatment because they have reached goal weight or because they have profited all they will from the procedures being employed. Behavior therapists are sensitive to this issue because of the high dropout rates in traditional treatments (Stunkard, 1975) and in self-help and commercial groups (Stunkard & Brownell, 1979; Volkmar, Stunkard, Woolston, & Bailey, 1981).

The only review of attrition rates in behavioral studies was conducted by Wilson and Brownell (1980). The mean attrition rate during initial treatment in the 17 studies they examined was 13.5%. This is remarkable considering the 50–80% attrition in other settings. These authors then computed attrition separately for groups using a deposit-refund system versus those with no deposit. The deposit-refund studies had a mean attrition rate of 9.5%, compared to 19.3% for studies without the deposit. These support the experimental findings of Hagen, Foreyt, and Durham (1976). It appears that some component of the behavior therapy program reduces attrition, and that a deposit-refund procedure can reduce attrition even further. If the least successful subjects do drop out of treatment, behavioral programs undergo careful scrutiny because of low dropout rates.

CONCLUSIONS

After their review of the literature, Wilson and Brownell (1980) come to the following conclusions:

1. The mean weight loss in behavioral programs is approximately 11 pounds, or 1–2 pounds per week. Since clinical programs

have subjects who average 50–60% overweight, few subjects attain their goal weight.

2. The average weight loss is fairly well maintained for follow-ups of one year or less. Too little is known about longer follow-up periods to reach definite conclusions, but for reasons discussed earlier, information collected after very long periods is difficult to interpret.

3. Even when weight loss is maintained, few subjects continue to lose weight after the initial treatment period. The number of subjects who continue to lose may be somewhere around 25%.

4. There is great interindividual variability in outcome during initial treatment, and even greater variability during follow-up. Wilson and Brownell (1980) note, "Variability of this sort is never a good sign and suggests that the critical variables governing weight loss have yet to be identified or that the current behavioral methods are appropriate only for selected eating disorders in certain individuals" (p. 60).

5. Attempts to identify variables which predict outcome have been unsuccessful. Cooke and Meyers (1980) reviewed this literature and found only that social support, cognitive factors, and ability to self-reinforce could predict outcome. There are others such as initial weight and early weight loss, but no variable has consistently predicted outcome.

6. Some components of the behavioral program may be more helpful than others at improving maintenance. For example, several studies have shown that spouse support can improve long-term results (Brownell et al., 1978; Pearce et al., 1981) and others indicate that exercise may be helpful (Dahlkoetter et al., 1979; Miller & Sims, 1981; Stalonas et al., 1978).

7. The comparative long-term effects of behavior therapy cannot be determined because of the lack of well-controlled studies on other approaches (Stunkard & Penick, 1979).

8. Weight reduction via behavior therapy seems to bring improvement in psychological functioning, in contrast to the deterioration found with other forms of dieting (Stunkard & Rush, 1974). Several studies have shown this improvement (Brownell et al., 1978; Brownell & Stunkard, 1981; Craighead et al., 1981; Taylor, Ferguson, & Reading, 1978).

9. Only about half of behavior therapy programs use specific techniques to improve maintenance. Booster sessions are most frequently used.

10. Compared to other treatments, behavior therapy has drastically reduced attrition. Attrition is approximately 12% in behavioral

programs compared to 80% in traditional treatments and 50% in self-help and commercial groups. A deposit-refund system appears to reduce attrition even further.

Expanding the Scope of Behavioral Treatments

In a search for methods to improve both short-term and long-term weight loss, behavior therapists have been moving into several new areas with encouraging initial results. These new directions also promise to bring the interdisciplinary effort that will lead to a fruitful exchange of ideas.

THE SOCIAL ENVIRONMENT

Eating and exercise behaviors may be responsive to social influence, and support from family, friends and others may give the obese person the motivation necessary to adhere to a long-term regimen. Behavior therapists have begun to explore the role of social support in two settings—the home and the work place.

Wilson and Brownell (1978) were the first to evaluate systematically family involvement in a behavioral program. They found that having spouses attend treatment sessions did not improve weight losses in the dieters. Brownell *et al.* (1978) followed with a more involved study in which the spouses were given a step-by-step program of behavioral procedures, and in which the spouses and dieters monitored their own behavior and that of their partner. Subjects in the spouses group averaged 19.6 pounds lost after 10 weeks of treatment, and nearly 30 pounds after a six-month follow-up. The positive results from the Brownell *et al.* study were complemented by findings from two other studies conducted at about the same time. Rosenthal, Allen, and Winter (1980) assigned obese women to husband involvement and no involvement. Spouse involvement had a significant effect at posttreatment and a six-week follow-up, but the effect had disappeared at a three-year follow-up. Saccone and Israel (1978) found that having a spouse reinforce the dieter for weight loss or behavior change could improve maintenance during a one-year follow-up.

Several recent studies have shown that the effect of spouse involvement may not be as simple as it seemed. Pearce *et al.* (1981) found that a couples group was significantly better than three control conditions at three-, six-, and 12-month follow-ups, but this group did not differ from a group in which the husbands were simply informed not to interfere in their wives' efforts to reduce. Weisz and Bucher (1980) reported that subjects in a spouse condition showed the most improvement in marital adjustment and depression, but the spouse condition had no advantage for weight loss. Another study found that subjects who chose to attend treatment sessions with a spouse did not lose weight more successfully than subjects who attended alone (O'Neill, Currey, Hirsch, Riddle, Taylor, Malcolm, & Sexauer, 1979). Fremouw and Zitter (1980) found a positive effect for spouse involvement.

The studies on spouse involvement have mixed results. Brownell (1979b) felt that the degree of spouse involvement determined the outcome. Studies in which spouses were merely spectators seemed to find no effect (O'Neill *et al.*, 1979; Weisz & Bucher, 1980; Wilson & Brownell, 1978). Studies in which spouses were given specific behavior change requirements seemed to have more favorable results (Brownell *et al.*, 1978; Pearce *et al.*, 1981; Rosenthal *et al.*, 1980; Saccone & Israel, 1978). However, Brownell and Stunkard (1981) set out to replicate some of the earlier findings by using a large sample of subjects ($n = 120$) followed for one year after treatment. The spouse program was very similar to that used by Brownell *et al.* (1978), but the results were much different. The couples group did no better than control groups either at posttreatment or follow-up. Brownell and Stunkard (1981) have concluded that more study must be done on the relationships between obese persons and their spouses and that no single program is likely to work with all couples.

The work place may provide another source of social support. Health programs in occupational settings are becoming enormously popular. Several large corporations such as Control Data and Johnson & Johnson are planning to market health programs to other industries. There is a National Association of Corporate Fitness Directors, there are consulting firms which construct health programs for industry, and there have been at least five conferences on health promotion at the work place. An entire issue of *Public Health Reports* was devoted to the subject in 1980. We feel there is great potential here, but there is also the danger of building enthusiasm before effective programs have been developed. We do not have reliable and powerful health programs in clinical settings, much less in the less structured environment of the work place.

One of us (KDB) was asked to consult for a large corporation (the Sun Oil Company) which was establishing an expensive exercise program for its employees. Based on the exercise and physical education literatures, it was projected that fewer than 50% of the participants (not employees) would adhere to the program for more than six months. The corporate people were adamant that this would not happen because there was so much enthusiasm when the program was announced. It did happen, and the corporate leaders are having second thoughts about whether the program was worth the cost.

This area of adherence and behavior change is one where behavior therapists may have a valuable role to play in work-site programs. It is a new area with many exciting things to learn about employee relations, the economics of corporate sponsored programs, and so forth. There have been only a few forays into this area. Stunkard and Brownell (1980) carried out a behavioral program for a group of employees at the Gimbels and Bloomingdale's department stores in New York. The weight losses were in line with those from clinical programs, but attrition (50%) was much higher than expected. There have been similar reports, mainly from programs for hospital employees (cf. Colletti & Brownell, in press). Stunkard and Brownell (1980) attribute this problem to the inclusion of noncommitted subjects who would otherwise not join a program which cost more or was more inconvenient. Foreyt, Scott, and Gotto (1980) reported uncontrolled findings from several work site programs. They also concluded that there is great potential to this approach, but that we must be cautious with our claims.

COMBINING BEHAVIOR THERAPY WITH OTHER TREATMENTS

There are treatments which produce rapid and substantial weight losses (e.g., fasting), but the almost certain relapse renders such treatments useless for nonemergency attempts at dieting. Perhaps behavior therapy could be used to sustain the weight losses produced by more dramatic methods, thus taking advantage of the best qualities of both treatments. This was exactly the intention of the studies mentioned below.

Craighead et al. (1981) used behavior therapy in conjunction with fenfluramine, a sympathomimetic amine with sedative properties. The most important conditions in the study were a drug-only group, a behavior-therapy-only group, and a combined group. After 25 weekly sessions, the behavior therapy group lost 24 pounds, the drug group lost 30 pounds, and the combined group lost 32 pounds (Figure 6-4). The results, however, were quite different at one-year follow-up. The behavior therapy group had rebounded only slightly (to 20 pounds), the drug subjects remained 14 pounds below baseline, and the combination group had gained back all but 10 pounds of their lost weight. Brownell and Stunkard (1981) followed with a program in which fenfluramine was combined with the couples training program used by Brownell et al. (1978). Again, drug subjects lost weight initially, but these subjects (including those with spouse training) regained their weight rapidly. These two studies showed that certain drugs can boost

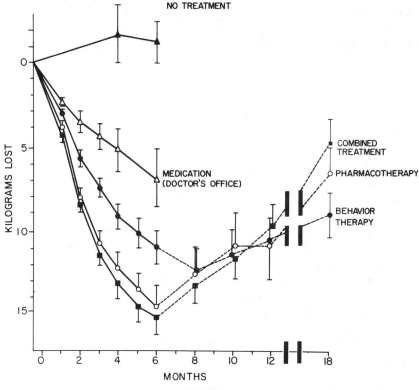

FIG. 6-4.
Weight loss in kilograms for subjects receiving behavior therapy, fenfluramine, the combination of behavior therapy and fenfluramine, or two control treatments. (From "Behavior Therapy and Pharmacotherapy for Obesity" by L. W. Craighead, A. J. Stunkard, and R. O'Brien, *Archives of General Psychiatry*, 1981, *38*, 763–768. Copyright 1981, American Medical Association. Reprinted by permission.)

weight loss, but not even behavior therapy and a couples training program could prevent the relapse.

Radical diets are another possible companion for behavior therapy. One such diet is the Protein Sparing Modified Fast (PSMF). This involves an outpatient fasting regimen supplemented by small amounts of high quality protein designed to "spare" the protein lost by the body during fasting. The PSMF appears to be relatively safe when administered under tightly controlled circumstances, although Van Itallie (1980) suggests that a hypocaloric diet (400 calories per day) is safe and just as effective as the PSMF. Bistrian (1978) and Lindner and Blackburn

(1976) report impressive weight losses, even over the long-term, in uncontrolled programs in which behavior therapy has been added as a component along with the fasting.

SMOKING

Smoking and Health

The recent Surgeon General's Report (USDHEW, 1979) indicted smoking as the largest preventable cause of death in the United States. There is little doubt anymore that smoking is related to heart disease, cancer and other serious medical problems. Studies in the last few years have refined our knowledge on the exact boundaries of these relationships. A 22-year study of 6194 female British physicians found a strong association between smoking and ischaemic heart disease, lung cancer, and chronic obstructive lung disease (Doll, Gray, Hafner, & Peto, 1980). This confirms the Surgeon General's contention (USDHEW, 1979) that women who smoke like men will die like men. Friedman, Dales, and Ury (1979) assessed mortality in an 11-year study of 4004 men and women. The smoker to nonsmoker mortality ratio was 2.6 for death from all causes and 4.7 for coronary heart disease. This powerful association remained even when the authors accounted for 48 other factors in their analysis, suggesting that the increased risk with smoking is not secondary to some underlying characteristic. The Coronary Drug Project Research Group (1979) found that smoking greatly reduced the chance for survival in men recovering from myocardial infarction. Furthermore, the health hazards of smoking may extend far beyond the individual smoker. There is evidence that children in families with smokers tend to be less healthy than children from nonsmoking families (Tager, Weiss, Rosner, & Speizer, 1979). Bonham and Wilson (1981) found that children in families with no smokers had fewer restricted-activity days and fewer bed-disability days than did children in families with two smokers. Children in families with one smoker fell in between. Bonham and Wilson (1981) also found a relationship between the number of cigarettes used by the smokers and the health of the children.

Most smokers want to quit. One survey found that 90% of smokers have made a serious attempt to stop or would do so if an easy method were available (USPHS, 1975). The health risks of smoking are well known, so many smokers believe that a reduction in smoking would improve their health. There is some support for this latter point. Two epidemiology studies have related the decline in mortality from coronary heart disease in the past 20 years to decreases in smoking in men

(Kannel & Thom, 1979; Kleinman, Feldman, & Monk, 1979). Another study suggested that heavy smokers could halve their risk of death from coronary heart disease by reducing their consumption to an intermediate level, and that smokers of two packs per day could halve their risk by halving the number of cigarettes consumed (Bain, Hennekens, Rosner, Speizer, & Jesse, 1978).

There are many treatment options available for the smoker. Commercial programs, self-help books, medical clinics, and psychotherapeutic approaches (e.g., hypnotism) are widely used (Lichtenstein & Brown, 1980). The three major national voluntary agencies all have antismoking programs (American Cancer Society, American Heart Association, American Lung Association). The Council on Scientific Affairs of the American Medical Association (1980) reports that "most smokers consider the physicians' advice the most effective way to get smokers to quit" (p. 781). The Council also reported, however, that only 8% of former smokers could even recall receiving medical advice to stop smoking. Russell and colleagues in England have evaluated the effectiveness of physicians' advice to stop smoking (Russell, Wilson, Taylor, & Baker, 1979). The 2138 patients of 28 general practitioners were given four levels of intervention during a four week period. The patients were followed one month and one year after the program. The best of the interventions, a combination of doctors' advice, leaflets with suggestions, and a warning that the patients would be followed up, produced a 5.1% quitting rate during the one-year period. This is a very low quitting rate, but Russell *et al.* argue that the intervention is inexpensive, and if the efforts were spread across all general practitioners, the overall effect on public health would be substantial.

Wynder and Hoffman (1979) reviewed the literature on smoking and health and concluded that antismoking efforts should take several forms. They suggest a three-pronged approach: (1) smoking prevention programs for children; (2) smoking cessation programs; (3) development of a safer cigarette, or switches in the type of cigarette, for persons who cannot quit smoking. Behavior therapists have been working in each area.

Trends in Smoking Patterns

During the period from 1968 to 1974, the percentage of adult smokers declined from 42% to 33%, but the number of teenage smokers rose almost 30% (USDHHS, 1980). The reduction in smoking among teenagers since 1974 has been as dramatic as the rise in preceeding years, although the decline seems confined to boys. Bachman, Johnston, and

O'Malley (1981) reported smoking rates in a nationally representative sample of 15,000 high school seniors. Between 1975 and 1979, the number of males who smoked at least one-half pack of cigarettes per day declined from 20% to 15% while the rates for females increased from 16% to 17%. There has been a trend, in both adults and teenagers, for smoking rates to drop, but the trend seems to have leveled off. It still remains that one-third of adults and 15% of children smoke regularly. The costs of this fact are staggering. The estimated economic impact of smoking each year is $26 billion; this is 11.3% of the economic cost of all disease, and is 2.5% of the Gross National Product (Haggerty, 1977; Kristein, 1977; Pechacek & McAlister, 1980).

Many social and demographic factors influence the prevalence of smoking. Divorced or separated persons are more likely to smoke than single persons, who in turn are more likely to smoke than married persons (USDHEW, 1979). Smoking rates are associated with education, family income, and occupation (USDHEW, 1979). Social factors may be most important in the decision to begin smoking. Adolescents who have two parents who smoke are twice as likely to smoke themselves as those whose parents are nonsmokers. Families in which one parent smokes fall between the two extremes (USDHHS, 1980). A teenager with an older brother or sister who smokes is extremely likely to smoke, and a teenager with both an older sibling and a parent who smokes is four times more likely to smoke as someone with no smokers in the immediate family (USDHHS, 1980). Pechacek and McAlister (1980) point out that the students themselves report that peer pressure is even more important than family influences.

Why People Smoke

Many factors contribute to the initiation, maintenance, and cessation of smoking. Furthermore, the factors appear to change as the smoker progresses from one stage to another (Leventhal & Cleary, 1980; Pechacek & McAlister, 1980; Pomerleau, 1979a). Leventhal and Cleary point out that most treatments for smoking are based on the assumption that smoking is a simple manifestation of a single stimulus, and that such treatments are bound to have discouraging effects. Lichtenstein (1971) called for the study of the processes which underlie smoking. It is only recently that this has begun to happen. There is a great deal of interdisciplinary information available on smoking, and behavior therapists are venturing beyond the confines of their own studies to search for more information on this complex problem. There are several excellent reviews which discuss the complicated nature of smoking and the implications for treatment (Bernstein & Glasgow, 1979; Leventhal & Cleary, 1980; Lichtenstein & Brown, 1980; Pechacek, 1979; Pechacek & McAlister, 1980; Pomerleau, 1979a).

Lichtenstein and Brown (1980) feel that smoking has four stages—starting, continuing, stopping, and resuming. Figure 6-5 lists the main factors involved in each stage. Lichtenstein and Brown suggest that psychosocial factors determine whether smoking will begin, and that a combination of the pharmacological effects of nicotine and learned psychosocial factors are crucial in the continuation of smoking. Quitting is a psychosocial matter, and although little is known about resuming smoking, stress and social pressure are thought to be important.

Leventhal and Cleary (1980) have written an important theoretical paper on the determinants of smoking, and have collected information from an array of sources on social, psychological, cultural, and physio-

Starting⟶	Continuing⟶	Stopping⟶	Resuming
Availability	Nicotine	Health	Stress
Curiosity	Immediate positive consequences	Expense	Social pressure
Rebelliousness	Signals (cues) in environs	Social pressure	Abstinence violation effect
Anticipation of adulthood	Avoiding negative effects (withdrawal)	Self-mastery	Alcohol consumption
Social confidence		Aesthetics	
Modeling: peers, siblings, parents		Example to others	
Psychosocial	Physiological+ psychosocial	Psychosocial	Psychosocial

FIG. 6-5.
Stages in the natural history of smoking and determinants in each stage. Adapted from Danaher and Lichtenstein (1978). (From "Smoking Cessation Methods: Review and Recommendations" by E. Lichtenstein and R. A. Brown, in W. R. Miller, Ed., *The Addictive Behaviors: Treatment of Alcoholism, Drug Abuse, Smoking, and Obesity*, New York: Pergamon Press, 1980. Copyright 1980, Pergamon Press, Ltd. Reprinted by permission.)

logical aspects of the smoking problem. They state that the developmental history of the smoker moves through the following stages: (1) preparation; (2) initiation; (3) becoming a smoker; (4) maintenance of smoking; (5) dissatisfaction; (6) decision to quit; and (7) adoption and maintenance of the self-image of nonsmoker. Each stage itself can be influenced by a number of factors. For example, in the preparation stage, Leventhal and Cleary note that "smoking has a long and complex developmental history, beginning well before the first cigarette is smoked and extending sometimes over 5 or 10 years" (p. 382). They note that this history can be conceptualized in stages and processes, and that a prevention program should incorporate different procedures to deter smoking at each step in the process.

We agree with the notion that smoking reduction programs need to include many procedures which can be targeted specifically at the stages and processes of the individual smoker. The Leventhal and Cleary (1980) paper provides a valuable conceptual approach for viewing these stages and processes, and also gives many suggestions for altering existing treatment programs. We hope that efforts like this will appear more frequently in the literature, and that researchers from the different disciplines will integrate their work into a cohesive body of evidence.

Assessment

The measurement of smoking itself is difficult, and when one considers the many factors which influence smoking, the task of assessment seems monumental. Frederiksen, Martin, and Webster (1979), in their comprehensive discussion article on the assessment of smoking behavior, concluded that "the importance of a thorough behavioral analysis of the variables relevant to smoking behavior and health risk due to smoking cannot be overestimated" (p. 661). Yet, Frederiksen et al. found that assessment in multiple risk areas occurred in only 20% of the studies published in four journals they reviewed between 1975 and 1978. They note, "The assessment of smoking behavior is clearly an area in need of considerable refinement" (p. 662). Some of this refinement has happened in the past several years.

THE ACCURACY OF SELF-REPORT AND SELF-MONITORING

Self-report is the most commonly used method of evaluating smoking rate (Frederiksen et al., 1979; Pechacek & McAlister, 1980). This technique typically involves asking subjects to estimate the number of cigarettes they smoke per unit time. There is considerable disagreement about the accuracy of these reports. Lichtenstein and Brown (1980) are "more optimistic than many" because they feel the rates of false self-reports is low in programs where rapport has been established between the counselor and participants (Glasgow, 1978). Frederiksen *et al.* feel that the self-reports are open to "bias, distortion, or deliberate falsification." Pechacek and McAlister cite many studies showing that self-reports are not accurate in adults or teenagers (e.g., Brockway, 1978; Ohlin, Lundh, & Westling, 1976; Sillett, Wilson, Malcolm, & Ball, 1978). There are, however, several studies which indicate that self-report may be accurate (e.g., Petitti, Friedman, & Kahn, 1981).

This issue is complicated by the use of imperfect standards against which to judge self-report. The physiological measures of smoking, usually serum or saliva thiocyanate and expired carbon monoxide, are not perfect indicators of smoking behavior (Frederiksen *et al.*, 1979; Pechacek & McAlister, 1980; Petitti *et al.*, 1981). Petitti *et al.* (1981) used physiological and self-report measures to assess smoking in 276 members of a prepaid medical care plan. They found that the physiological measures gave false positives and could not detect small differences in smoking rates among subjects. They conclude, "Questionnaire response appears to be the standard against which physiologic tests of smoking must be judged, not vice versa" (p. 309).

Self-monitoring is the most frequently used method to measure smoking rates prospectively in behavioral studies. Frederiksen *et al.* (1979) feel that self-monitoring is potentially accurate, but that its reactivity (McFall, 1970) may decrease its accuracy. Pechacek and McAlister also feel that self-monitoring should not be the sole form of data collection. As with self-report, there is some evidence that self-monitoring records may be accurate (Colletti & Supnick, 1980).

It appears that a combination of measures may be the most sensitive means of measuring smoking. Combining physiological measures may increase their accuracy (Petitti *et al.*, 1981). Informing subjects that physiological measures will be taken can increase the validity of self-report (Evans, Hansen, & Mittlemark, 1977). There is also evidence that confronting subjects with physiological data which disagrees with their self-report can increase the accuracy of self-report (Ohlin *et al.*, 1976). Pechacek and McAlister (1980) conclude from these findings that uncorroborated self-reports may lead researchers to overestimate success.

PHYSIOLOGICAL MEASURES

The two most common physiological measures of smoking are expired carbon monoxide and thiocyanate (Pechacek & McAlister, 1980). Recent reviews have been written about each of these measures.

Frederiksen and Martin (1979) have reviewed the literature on carbon monoxide and smoking. Elevated carbon monoxide levels are associated with increased risk of coronary heart disease and reduced rates of survival once coronary disease has been diagnosed (Aronow, 1973; Goldsmith & Aronow, 1975; USDHEW, 1979). Carbon monoxide levels depend on several factors, including an ambient CO level determined primarily by automobile exhaust. Smoking accounts for the most variance in CO level (Wald & Howard, 1975). The simplest way to measure CO is by measuring CO concentration in expired air samples (Hughes, Frederiksen, & Frazier, 1978). Henningfield, Stitzer, and Griffiths (1980) measured CO levels in eight heavy smokers who smoked varying amounts of cigarettes over an eight-hour period. CO levels increased in an orderly fashion within the subjects as smoking increased, but there was large variability in CO across the different subjects. Using CO is also hampered by the fact that it has a short half-life (two to six hours), is affected by environmental sources, and has high diurnal variability (Pechacek & McAlister, 1980; Stewart, 1975). Despite these drawbacks, Frederiksen and Martin (1979) feel that CO assessment is "an objective, sensitive, and easy to use measure which can be used either on a macroscopic or microscopic level" (p. 29).

Thiocyanate levels are also an important measure of smoking. This area has been reviewed recently by Prue, Martin, and Hume (1980), who note that thiocyanate, the body's end product of the detoxification of cyanide compounds, can be measured in urine, blood, or saliva. Thiocyanate can distinguish smokers from nonsmokers, correlates moderately well with smoking rate, and has the advantage of a long half-life (10–14 days) (Pechacek & McAlister, 1980; Prue et al., 1980). It cannot be confounded by nonsmoking sources. Prue et al. conclude that measuring thiocyanate in saliva is the easiest and most accurate method of determination, and that saliva thiocyanate assessment "shows the most promise for smoking research."

It appears that the optimal measurement of smoking would include self-report, expired carbon monixide, and saliva thiocyanate. The presence of the physiological measures can enhance the accuracy of self-report (Evans et al., 1977; Ohlin et al., 1976). The discrimination power of CO and thiocyanate can be greatly increased when the two measures are used together (Petitti et al., 1981; Vogt, Selvin, Widdowson, & Hulley, 1977).

THE TOPOGRAPHY OF SMOKING

The Surgeon General's Report states that the health hazards of smoking depend on the dose of carbon monoxide, tar, and nicotine introduced into the body (USDHEW, 1979). Frederiksen et al. (1979) point out that most researchers use smoking rate as the sole measure of smoking behavior, presumably because the number of cigarettes smoked is considered the only important factor. Frederiksen *et al.* note that dose depends on *rate*, substance (qualities of the cigarette), and *topography* of smoking (e.g., puff volume). Substance is relatively easy to evaluate with self-report or observational measures; that is, the subject needs to be observed or asked about the brand of cigarette smoked. Measuring smoking topography is much more challenging.

Frederiksen, Miller, and Peterson (1977) described the complexities of smoking topography, and suggested that smokers may reduce their rate, and perhaps use a less harmful substance, but these actions may have no impact on health if the smoker makes compensatory changes in topography. For instance, a smoker may smoke fewer and less harmful cigarettes, but may take more puffs per cigarette or may draw harder with each puff. Some of the topographical characteristics already defined are puff frequency, puff duration, interpuff interval, amount of tobacco used, cigarette duration, puff volume, puff intensity, and puff distribution (Frederiksen *et al.*, 1979). It is likely that individual patients will require specific treatment procedures depending on their specific methods of smoking. Moody (1980) studied smoking topography in 517 adult patients in a medical center in the Southeast. Patients from lower socioeconomic groups had a greater number of puffs, shorter intervals between puffs, larger puff duration, shorter cigarette butts, and more daily tar and nicotine than patients from higher groups. Sex and age were also related to topography. Frederiksen *et al.* (1979) have discussed the benefits and disadvantages of various methods of measuring the topographical characteristics of smoking.

The Process of Smoking

MODELING

Social factors, particularly the presence of other smokers, may influence many facets of smoking behavior. If the presence of other smokers increases the probability of smoking in a person attempting to quit, then it may be helpful to teach patients to cope with these situations. Glad and Adesso (1976) found that exposure to other smokers in a small group setting increased smoking more in light smokers than in heavy smokers. This is consistent with Herman's finding (1974) that light smokers were responsive to both internal and external cues, whereas heavy smokers were responsive only to internal cues. Several recent studies provide additional evidence on this issue.

Miller, Frederiksen, and Hosford (1979) had heavy and light smokers sit alone or with two nonsmoking confederates for 30-minute sessions. Light smokers took more frequent and longer puffs when alone than with confederates. Heavy smokers were not affected by the social manipulation. Antonuccio and Lichtenstein (1980) had heavy and light smokers exposed to high- and low-rate smoking confederates. The high-rate model increased smoking and changed smoking topography in both groups; there were no differences between the heavy and light smokers in their response to the modeling condition. From these two studies it would appear that light smokers smoke less in the presence of nonsmokers and more in the presence of smokers. Heavy smokers seem influenced by smoking models but not by nonsmokers. However, these findings are not entirely consistent with those mentioned above, and this question requires more research before the picture is complete.

OTHER PROCESSES

Epstein and colleagues have carried out a series of studies on factors which influence smoking. Marshall, Epstein, and Green (1980) measured smoking in coffee-drinking smokers who were given 0, 1, 2, or 3 cups of coffee during two-hour sessions while they worked on crossword puzzles. Subjects who had any amount of coffee smoked more than subjects who had no coffee. A second study used a similar design with coffee, a coffee substitute, decaffeinated coffee, water, or no drink. Subjects receiving caffeinated or decaffeinated coffee smoked more than subjects in the other conditions, suggesting that caffeine or liquid are not the important components in the effect of coffee on smoking. These same authors conducted another study in which urinary pH was manipulated (Marshall, Green, Epstein, Rogers, & McCoy, 1980). Coffee increased the smoking, and urinary pH was not related to smoking behavior. Marshall *et al.* suggest that smoking and coffee drinking are related by stimulus control, not by a basic physiological process. Ossip and Epstein (1981) found that coffee drinking increased smoking only slightly, and also that subjects required to smoke two cigarettes in the 30 minutes prior to the experimental session smoked less during the session than subjects who had no preload. These studies suggest that coffee drinking may increase smoking, and that breaking the discriminative power of coffee drinking may be a useful component of therapy.

Treatment Outcome Issues

Research on treatment outcome has slowed considerably in recent years, probably due to the factors discussed in the beginning of this chapter. The effectiveness of two basic treatment packages has been established, and researchers are turning to the issue of maintenance. We review these two packages because only recently have their uncertain effects become certain. Several authors have made extensive reviews of treatment procedures (Bernstein & Glasgow, 1979; Danaher, 1977b; Lichtenstein & Brown, 1980; Pechacek, 1979; Pechacek & Danaher, 1979; Pechacek & McAlister, 1980).

RAPID SMOKING: EFFECTIVENESS AND SAFETY

The vast majority of research on the effectiveness of rapid smoking was completed before 1979. In the past two years, there have been more papers published on the safety of rapid smoking than on its efficacy.

Rapid smoking is only one of many aversive procedures used for smoking cessation. These include satiation, the use of warm smoky air, electric shock, covert sensitization, and others. Several reviews, however, determined that rapid smoking was the most promising technique because of its effectiveness and ease of administration (Danaher, 1977b; Lichtenstein & Penner, 1977). Lichtenstein and Penner evaluated the long-term results of a number of studies on rapid smoking conducted earlier by Lichtenstein and colleagues. They found 36–47% of the subjects abstinent two to six years after treatment. The short-term abstinence rates for rapid smoking are at least 50% (Lichtenstein & Brown, 1980). Danaher reviewed more recent studies on rapid smoking and calculated the abstinence rate to be approximately 30% at six months. Bernstein and Glasgow (1979) feel that the lower rates in the studies reviewed by Danaher are due to a standardized treatment with less emphasis on therapist–client factors.

The overall evaluation of rapid smoking differs from author to author. Surprisingly, one of the pioneers with the approach (Lichtenstein) is most cautious. Lichtenstein and Brown (1980) feel it can be used only under limited circumstances because it "greatly intensifies the naturally harmful effects of smoking." Danaher (1977b) claimed rapid smoking to be the single most effective option available for treatment. It is apparent that the safety of rapid smoking and the atmosphere in which it is administered are crucial to its value.

> Rapid smoking, when employed with proper safeguards and combined with strong therapist support and positive expectations (and when continued at least until subjects are abstinent) is one of the more powerful treatment techniques available. In the absence of these features, it is not clearly superior to other approaches. (Bernstein & Glasgow, 1979, p. 241)

The safety of rapid smoking has been a controversial matter. The absence of serious problems in the early trials suggested that rapid smoking was a benign, although unpleasant procedure. Then reports appeared on the dangers of rapid smoking, as investigators began to examine the physiological effects of the procedure (cf. Franks & Wilson, 1978). With the publication of several recent papers showing that rapid smoking is safe, the field has come full circle.

The first note of caution about rapid smoking came in 1977. A study with six subjects found that rapid smoking produced increases in systolic blood pressure and depth of inhalation (Hackett, Horan, Stone, Linberg, Nicholas, & Lukasi, 1977). A subsequent study by these authors found that rapid smoking led to significant rises in heart rate, blood pressure, carboxyhemoglobin, and even to cardiac abnormalities (Horan, Hackett, Nicholas, Linberg, Stone, & Lukasi, 1977). Horan, Linberg, and Hackett (1977) concluded from these data that rapid smoking can produce nicotine poisoning. These studies received great attention in clinical circles, even though two carefully conducted studies done about this time found no adverse consequences (Miller, Schilling, Logan, & Johnson, 1977; Sachs, Hall, & Hall, 1978). Lichtenstein and Glasgow (1977) reviewed the literature and concluded that rapid smoking is not dangerous for healthy subjects, but that subjects should be screened for a history of coronary disease, hypertension, emphysema, and so forth.

Recent studies provide much-needed data on the safety of rapid smoking. Hall, Sachs, and Hall (1979) did extensive monitoring of 24 healthy male smokers during rapid smoking. They found no EKG abnormality; there were elevations in heart rate, respiratory rate, and systolic blood pressure after *both* normal smoking and rapid smoking. Rapid smoking did produce elevated arterial pH and relative hypoxemia, but Hall *et al.* conclude that rapid smoking is safe for healthy subjects and of unknown risk for persons with cardiopulmonary disease. A paper from Australia found some cardiac abnormalities in patients undergoing rapid smoking, but the authors felt that none were serious enough to exclude patients from treatment (Poole, Sanson-Fisher, German, & Harker, 1980). Another study evaluated subjective reactions to rapid smoking, and found that it was more aversive than normal smoking initially, but no more aversive during later sessions (Glasgow, Lichtenstein, Beaver, & O'Neill, 1981).

Sachs, Hall, Pechacek, and Fitzgerald (1979) completed an extensive review of the literature on rapid smoking. These authors conclude that earlier studies which stressed the dangers of rapid smoking were not based on firm evidence, and that any estimate of risk must include consideration of benefits. Sachs *et al.* conclude that rapid smoking is both safe and effective, and that the risk–benefit ratio is very favorable. In response to the earlier negative comments about rapid smoking, Sachs *et al.* note, "Such statements could cause therapists and clients not to use this technique, thus leaving the client exposed to a much greater risk, namely, disability or premature death secondary to cancer or heart disease" (p. 1058). The evidence presented by Sachs *et al.* is compelling. With appropriate subject screening, rapid smoking carries far more benefits than risks.

SELF-MANAGEMENT PROCEDURES

A collection of self-management techniques forms the second widely used behavioral approach (Bernstein & Glasgow, 1979; Lichtenstein & Brown, 1980). Each part of the package is based on the clinical experience of many investigators. As with the treatment packages for obesity and alcoholism, not all parts of the package have been tested, and it is not clear which parts are critical. Lichtenstein and Brown (1980) give a clinical description of their program, and the reader can refer to this or other sources for more detailed guidelines (Danaher & Lichtenstein, 1978; Pomerleau & Pomerleau, 1977). We will discuss only the new developments in the various parts of the program that have occurred recently.

Self-monitoring is the hallmark of most behavioral programs (see Chapters 1, 2, and 7). Lichtenstein and Brown recommend that subjects not be asked to quit immediately to allow time for recording of baseline smoking rate, the situations associated with smoking, frequency of urges, and so forth. Abrams and Wilson (1979) used a 2×2 design in which subjects monitored nicotine versus cigarettes and in which subjects received health hazard information versus no information. Self-monitoring of nicotine was more effective than monitoring of cigarettes; the health hazard information had no effect. The Abrams and Wilson (1979) study is consistent with earlier findings which indicate that self-monitoring has reactive effects if subjects are motivated to reduce their smoking (McFall, 1970; McFall & Hammen, 1971).

Contingency contracting is also commonly used as a component of behavioral programs. Danaher and Lichtenstein note that "contingency contracting appears to offer a simple and economical method of producing cessation and may be grafted on to other methods" (1978, p. 198). Several controlled studies have shown promising results for this method (Spring, Sipich, Trimble, & Goeckner, 1978; Winett, 1973). Two studies by Paxton (1980, 1981) address some of the issues associated with implementing a contingency contract. Paxton (1980) used a deposit contract with half of his subjects, while the other half received no contract (both groups received a self-management program). The contracting group had greater reductions in smoking during initial treatment, but the two groups did not differ at a six-month follow-up.

Paxton (1981) carried out three studies in which the frequency and amount of deposit were manipulated. Increasing the frequency and amount of the deposit improved initial smoking rates, but again, there were no effects over the long-term. It appears that contingency contracting may be helpful in the early stages of treatment.

Covert sensitization came on the scene with great fanfare in the early 1970s, but most authors now conclude that it is not useful in the treatment of smoking (e.g., Bernstein & Glasgow, 1979; Danaher & Lichtenstein, 1978; Lichtenstein & Brown, 1980). This view is supported by recent findings that covert sensitization added nothing to the basic self-management program (Lowe, Green, Kurtz, Ashenberg, & Fisher, 1980). Covert sensitization produces impressive reductions in smoking if administered in intensive sessions and if real stimuli are used, but the results disappear by a two-month follow-up (Lichstein & Sallis, 1981). The weight of evidence seems to argue against the use of covert sensitization.

One new development merits special attention: nicotine fading. There is some evidence that nicotine produces dependence and that cessation of smoking creates specific withdrawal symptoms (Russell, 1971). This hypothesis is not fully documented, but it does suggest a technique that may be very helpful for some smokers. Foxx and Brown (1979) found very encouraging reductions in nicotine and tar in subjects who received a combination of self-monitoring and nicotine fading. The nicotine-fading procedure required subjects to switch to successively lower-nicotine cigarettes, until they were ready to quit altogether. At an 18-month follow-up, 40% of these subjects were abstinent and all who had not stopped smoking were smoking cigarettes with lower tar and nicotine.

The controversial aspect of this study is that brand switching may not have the desired consequences. Hammond, Garfinkel, Seidman, and Lew (1976) note three possibilities in which reduced tar and nicotine cigarettes would not benefit health: (1) smokers would simply smoke more cigarettes per day; (2) smokers may inhale more deeply on the new cigarettes and increase their exposure to the harmful gases in cigarette smoke; (3) the reduction in tar and nicotine could create an increase in exposure to carbon monoxide, and could actually *increase* health risk. Foxx and Brown (1979) marshal some evidence that these possibilities may not occur. First, Foxx and Brown, Hammond *et al.*, and Goldfarb and Jarvik (1972) found that smoking low-tar-and-nicotine cigarettes was not associated with increased consumption, although two studies did find an inverse relationship between tar and nicotine and consumption (Firth, 1971; Schachter, 1977). Second, a recent study suggests that smoking low-tar-and-nicotine cigarettes leads to decreased intake of these substances (Forbes, Robinson, Hanley, & Colburn, 1976). Third, there is no firm evidence about the intake of poisonous gases with the use of reduced-tar-and-nicotine cigarettes.

The nicotine-fading procedure has great promise, although it must be approached cautiously. Gori (1976) has recommended the use of cigarettes lower in tar and nicotine, and Hammond *et al.* found that smokers of lower-tar-and-nicotine cigarettes were less likely to die of lung cancer and coronary heart disease than were smokers of high tar and nicotine cigarettes. It is likely that the switch to "safer" cigarettes does not lead to increases in the numbers of cigarettes smoked (Foxx & Brown, 1979; Jaffe, Kanzler, Cohen, & Kaplan, 1978). The important issue is whether the switching changes topographical behaviors enough to increase the intake of toxic gases (Schachter, 1978).

MAINTENANCE STRATEGIES

It is widely recognized that relapse is a common problem among smokers, yet relatively little attention has been paid to specific techniques to improve maintenance (Bernstein & Glasgow, 1979; Lichtenstein & Brown, 1980). Fortunately, the picture is changing. Bernstein and Glasgow feel that "researchers are at last recognizing that, if they are to reach the goal of long-term maintenance of nonsmoking behavior, that point at which a person stops smoking must mark the beginning of a new intervention phase, not the onset of follow-up" (p. 245). The relapse prevention model developed by Marlatt and colleagues may be a very important advance in this area (Cummings *et al.*, 1980; Marlatt, 1980; Marlatt & Gordon, 1980). This model was discussed in detail earlier in the chapter, but it has not yet been applied to smoking in a systematic investigation.

The model for improving maintenance has been to extend treatment into the follow-up period, usually by scheduling periodic meetings (booster sessions) of programming some regular interaction between therapist and client (continued contact). Booster sessions have not been effective (Relinger, Bornstein, Bugge, Carmody, & Zohn, 1977). Continued contact has met with mixed results. The early studies showed that continued contact had no effect (Bernstein, 1970; Danaher, 1977a; Schmahl, Lichtenstein, & Harris, 1972). This led Bernstein and Glasgow (1979) and Lichtenstein and Brown (1980) to conclude that continued contact does not improve long-term results. There are, however, some positive studies. Dubren (1977) reported that recorded telephone messages with tips and encouragement had promising results. Colletti and Kopel (1979) found that a group which had posttreatment contact with the therapist and also self-monitored smoking behavior had better rates of maintenance than several comparison groups. A two-year follow-up of this study showed that the results persisted (Colletti & Stern, 1980). Colletti and Supnick (1980) followed with a study which showed that a minimal contact condition improved maintenance at six months but not at one year.

Leventhal and Cleary (1980) criticize the current approach to smoking cessation among behavioral researchers. They maintain that the behavioral approaches address only one of many aspects of smoking behavior (the learned component) and that further refinements of the same sort of treatment will add only minimally to overall effectiveness. We agree that refinements of the basic behavioral package will not improve treatment results. Such research may make theoretical contributions, but will probably not be clinically useful. The behavioral approaches have much to offer as *part* of a smoking cessation program; these approaches can even stand alone for some subjects. However, we have gone far enough with the same procedures. We are throwing balls at a target we can already hit; perhaps we need to search for new targets. We feel that Leventhal and Cleary have made some useful suggestions about broadening the base of our treatment approaches. Furthermore, we feel that maintenance is an issue distinct from initial treatment, and that the answer to long-term results will not be discovered by using the same procedures used to reduce smoking early in treatment.

SOCIAL SUPPORT

Nearly everyone agrees that social support is important, but surprisingly little research has been done in this area. Most researchers feel that social support should be structured into a treatment program (Bernstein & Glasgow, 1979; Colletti & Brownell, in press; Lichtenstein & Brown, 1980; Pechacek & McAlister, 1980). Colletti and Brownell have reviewed the literature on social support in obesity, smoking, alcoholism, and disease in general. They conclude that social support is *the* area of most promise for improving the maintenance of treatment gains.

There is both direct and indirect evidence that social support may be helpful in smoking reduction. One study of smokers with chronic obstructive pulmonary disease found "psychosocial assets" to be one factor, albeit a weak one, associated with ability to quit (Daughton, Fix, Kass, & Patil, 1980). Dudley, Aicken, and Martin (1977) reported that psychosocial assets were the main variable underlying the ability to stop smoking.

The first direct evidence of the effects of social support came from Janis and Hoffman (1970). They found that subjects paired with a "buddy" maintained better smoking rates than subjects without such a partner. Hamilton and Bornstein (1979) used a buddy system and found that subjects with a buddy achieved significantly greater abstinence than subjects with no buddy at a three-month follow-up, but not at a six-month follow-up. Lichstein and Stalgaitis (1980) reported interesting findings from a reciprocal aversion procedure used with couples. Each time one partner smoked, the other had to smoke a consequent cigarette. Five of the six couples completed the program and three of five had at least one abstinent member at a six-month follow-up.

We follow other researchers in being cautious about the effects of social support on smoking (Bernstein & Glasgow, 1979; Colletti & Brownell, in press; Lichtenstein & Brown, 1980). There simply are not sufficient data to warrant the enthusiasm this approach might otherwise evoke. We know from research on obesity that social interactions are complex and that it may be necessary to understand these interactions before attempting to make modifications (Brownell & Stunkard, 1981). Colletti and Brownell discuss many of the processes involved in social support.

ALCOHOLISM

Research continues at a remarkable pace on what Nathan and Goldman (1979) have characterized as the nation's number one public health problem. Alcoholism draws more attention in the literature than the other addictive behaviors, and few issues provoke more heated discussion in both public and academic circles. The decade of the 1970s revolutionized a field which had been plagued by "a limited biomedical model and pseudopsychological concepts of dubious validity" (Wilson, 1978a), "opinion, unproven hypothesis, and conjecture" (Nathan & Goldman, 1979), and "unsupported suppositions" (Sobell & Sobell, 1980). The result has been the development of a possible new treatment goal (controlled drinking) and the study of many factors which influence drinking. As with obesity and smoking, research on alcoholism is no longer focused entirely on treatment outcome. Paradoxically, this shift in emphasis may improve treatment effectiveness more rapidly because it may generate new interventions based on knowledge of the disorder itself, rather than on borrowed techniques from the general field of behavior therapy.

Challenging Basic Assumptions

The treatment of alcoholism, as practiced by most professionals, is guided by presumed answers to several basic questions. These questions pertain to the effectiveness of treatment, who is best equipped to treat alcoholics, and so forth. Miller and Hester (1980) have addressed this issue in their extensive review of the literature:

> These are questions that face any mental health practitioner who comes into contact with problem drinkers—which means virtually every mental health professional. There have been standard accepted answers to these questions. How effective is treatment for alcoholism? Not very. Are some approaches better? No—all treatments are equally ineffective. Do some respond better to treatment than others? Yes—those alcoholics who have "bottomed out" or gone through enough suffering to be motivated for treatment. Who is best qualified to treat alcoholics? Another alcoholic, who's been through it.
>
> These are the easy answers. They continue to be passed down from one year to the next and appear in the most recent writings of some of the most respected professionals in the field. But what support is there for these statements from scientific research? After reading more than 500 treatment outcome studies and writing this chapter, we believe that there is ample reason to question every one of these commonly accepted answers. (p. 12)

As Miller and Hester note, dealing with the alcoholic requires knowledge of many treatment techniques, and any single approach is unlikely to be useful for the majority of individuals. Treatment outcome studies will answer these questions, but there are other important issues which need to be studied in new ways. For instance, why does the drinker drink? Are there specific moods which are the cause or the consequence of drinking? Does it hurt the alcoholic to be around other drinkers? Do drinkers vary in the way they drink, and does this necessitate different treatments? These factors are now becoming the subject of well-controlled research.

Controlled Drinking

Interest in moderation rather than abstinence began in the early 1970s (Lovibond & Caddy, 1970). In the following decade, the issue was at the center of a stormy debate between adherents and opponents. Now that the smoke has cleared, it is possible to take an objective look at the objective evidence on controlled drinking. We will cover the area briefly here. More detailed reviews are readily available elsewhere (Franks & Wilson, 1980; Lloyd & Salzberg, 1975; Miller, 1976; Miller & Hester, 1980; Nathan & Briddell, 1977; Nathan & Goldman, 1979; Pattison, 1976; Pattison, Sobell, & Sobell, 1977; Sobell, 1978; Sobell & Sobell, 1978, 1980).

The suggestion that controlled drinking may be a viable alternative to abstinence may have been prompted by reports that some alcoholics were moderating their drinking either spontaneously or after completing a program with abstinence as the goal (cf. Pattison *et al.*, 1977). There was, however, tremendous opposition to the notion of controlled drinking (Block, 1976; Fox, 1967). Fox claimed, "Among my own approximately 3000 patients not one has been able to achieve [moderate drinking], although almost every one of them has tried to" (p. 777). What evidence is there on either side?

Lovibond and Caddy (1970) found that many subjects could be trained to limit their drinking with a treatment package consisting of behavioral counseling and blood alcohol discrimination training. Sobell and Sobell (1973) carried out a controlled test of controlled drinking versus abstinence goals in chronic alcoholics in a state hospital. The subjects were taught to control their drinking with a multifaceted program which involved experimental intoxication, videotaped replay of drunken behavior, and a variety of other behavioral procedures. These subjects showed more improvement than their controls, and spent more time abstinent than all other subjects. By 1977, Pattison *et al.* found 74 studies or reports on the goal of controlled drinking. In studies where abstinence was the goal but controlled drinking rates were reported, approximately 12% of 10,000 patients were drinking in a controlled fashion at follow-up. Miller and Hester (1980) note that the controlled drinking rates in the Pattison *et al.* study are actually much higher when examining the 17 studies in which controlled drinking was the goal. The rates were either 30% or 63%, depending on the inclusion of several studies with very high rates.

The publication of the controversial Rand Report (Armor, Polich, & Stambul, 1978) brought this issue to the attention of the public, and quickly forced professionals into "taking sides." The Rand Report was a national survey of 14,000 clients at 44 federally funded alcoholism treatment centers. Nathan and Goldman (1979) point out that the major finding of the study was overlooked—that 70% of the clients who completed treatment improved their drinking status at either six-month or 18-month follow-ups. Great attention was paid to the following:

> The improved clients include only a relatively small number who are long-term abstainers. About one-fourth of the clients interviewed at 18 months have abstained for at least 6 months . . . the majority of improved clients are either drinking moderate amounts of alcohol—but at levels far below what could be described as alcoholic drinking—or engaging in alternating periods of drinking and abstention. (Armor *et al.*, 1978, p. 98)

The Rand Report has some weaknesses (Nathan & Goldman, 1979), but its dissemination to the popular press led to fears that abstinent alcoholics would feel they could drink with impunity. This does not seem to have occurred (Hingson, Scotch, & Goldman, 1977).

There is still some controversy about whether controlled drinking is a viable goal for treatment, and if it is, which clients should be encouraged to limit their drinking rather than abstain. In reviewing the literature, Miller and Hester (1980) conclude that "an average of 33% of clients achieve moderation when this is the goal of treatment, with an additional 31% abstinent or improved as of one year follow-up. This overall improvement rate of 64% is at least comparable to that from abstinence programs" (p. 64). These authors feel that controlled drinking is not only a viable goal, but the preferred goal for some clients. Miller & Caddy (1977) have proposed seven criteria for the goal of abstinence:

1. Evidence of progressive liver disease or other serious medical or psychological problems related to drinking.
2. A commitment or strong external demand for abstinence.
3. Pathological intoxication.
4. Physiological addiction with severe withdrawal symptoms.
5. Use of medication which is dangerous when combined with alcohol.
6. Current successful abstinence following severe problem drinking.
7. Prior failure of competent moderation-oriented treatment.

They list the following contraindications of abstinence:

1. Refusal to consider abstinence as a goal.
2. Strong external demands to drink, or lack of external support for abstinence.
3. Early-stage problem drinking without history of physiological addiction.
4. Prior failure of abstinence-oriented treatment.

Miller and Hester (1980) note three types of data that address the issue of selecting the goal of treatment. The first data pertain to the client's preferred treatment goal. The second area is the prediction of who will be a controlled drinker following abstinence-oriented treatment, and the third is the prediction of outcome in moderation-oriented studies. Miller and Hester review the studies in each area, and draw the following conclusions about controlled drinkers:

The picture that emerges is clear: individuals who will become successful controlled drinkers show less resemblance to the classic diagnostic picture of alcoholism. They have fewer problems related to drinking and have had them for a shorter period of time, have fewer symptoms and less family history of alcoholism, and drink less. They are more likely to be women, to be younger, and not to regard themselves as alcoholics. It appears that social stability increases the probability of controlled drinking, although this is also a prognostic factor for abstinence. (p. 102)

Nathan and Goldman (1979) are more cautious in their recommendations for abstinence or controlled drinking. They claim, "Abstinence ought to be the initial goal of treatment for alcoholism. . . . Abstinence-oriented treatment clearly works for some patients while the success rate on controlled drinking-oriented treatment is less certain" (p. 266). These authors also feel that sober alcoholics must be convinced that they can never drink in moderation, and that controlled drinking is a suitable goal only for "alcoholics who have repeatedly tried and failed to achieve abstinence, who despair of ever doing so, and who are nonetheless physically able to drink moderately."

Sobell and Sobell (1980) feel that the evidence is "unequivocal" that controlled drinking can and does occur. They propose a flexible treatment goal to avoid the artificial dichotomy of controlled versus abstinent behavior and suggest that all alcoholics should be helped to "reduce drinking to a nonproblem level." Sobell and Sobell acknowledge that the difficult task is targeting individuals for a specific goal. They have proposed guidelines for this process (Sobell & Sobell, 1978, 1980) similar to those used by Miller and Caddy (1977).

We feel that controlled drinking must be undertaken cautiously, but that it has a definite place in the treatment of problem drinkers. We anticipate that controlled drinking will occupy a more and more important position in the alcoholism literature in the 1980s. We hope that many more studies will be devoted to refining methods of encouraging controlled drinking, and that the technology improves for selecting in advance the best candidates for drinking in moderation or not drinking at all.

Assessment

Assessment in the alcoholism field has matured greatly in recent years. Whereas "assessment" used to be no more than asking alcoholics how much they drank, it now involves the measurement of behavioral, psychological, and physiological factors associated with drinking. P. Miller (1980) has done a comprehensive analysis of assessment methods in alcoholism that highlights the complexity of this essential part of research and treatment. Miller lists six major areas in which

assessment should take place: (1) consummatory behavior; (2) physiological monitoring and health; (3) social–psychological functioning;
(4) motivation; (5) life problems associated with abuse; (6) specific
therapeutic procedures employed by the patient. We refer the reader to
Miller's detailed information on these issues. We will focus here on one
topic that has generated much interest recently—the accuracy of self-
reports of drinking.

VALIDITY OF SELF-REPORTED DRINKING

Self-reports of drinking behavior are the most common, and the most
practical means of assessing how much an alcoholic drinks. Special
forms have been developed for this purpose, such as Sobell and Sobell's
(1973b) Alcohol Intake Sheet and Marlatt's (1977) Drinking Profile.
These forms help develop some consistency across investigations, but
how accurately do they assess drinking—that is, do subjects incorrectly
(perhaps inadvertently) record what they drink?

Recent studies on the accuracy of self-reports have focused on
subjects' experience of past drinking and their experiences with ongoing
drinking. Miller, Crawford, and Taylor (1979) used significant others
to corroborate reports of drinking in 145 subjects who participated in
four earlier studies. The product–moment correlations between subjects'
and significant others' reports were .48 at intake, .66 at posttreatment,
and .79 at a three-month follow-up. Miller et al. (1979) conclude that
these data "generally support the validity of clients' self-report of
drinking behavior," but they do question whether the accuracy would
decline if subjects were not informed that significant others would be
contacted.

Maisto, Sobell, and Sobell (1979) collected data from 52 alcoholics
and their collateral informants six months after hospitalization. Correlations between these reports ranged from .46 to .97 for measures of
days abstinent, days of limited drinking, days drunk, days hospitalized,
and days jailed. Maisto et al. feel that self-reports are "generally reliable," that collateral informants provide a useful standard against
which to judge the accuracy of subject reports, and that the agreement
does not depend on the number of days the subjects are in contact with
the collaterals.

Sobell, Sobell, and VanderSpek (1979) studied current drinking by
using self-reports, breath analysis, and clinical judgments. They found
that self-reports were valid when subjects had not been drinking, but
that subjects who were drinking were likely to underreport their consumption. The incidence of inaccurate self-reports did not vary with

level of intoxication. Sobell *et al.* feel that combining observers' judgments with self-reports increases the chances of identifying when a subject has been drinking, though there are still many false negative evaluations.

What can be concluded about the accuracy of self-reports? Sobell *et al.* (1979) claim that reports of current drinking are often inaccurate, but that reports of past drinking experiences are generally valid. Miller *et al.* (1979) and Maisto *et al.* (1979) agree with the conclusion about past drinking experiences. We agree that these reports are more accurate than one might expect considering that alcoholics often hide how much they drink. However, we do *not* feel that self-reports are sufficiently accurate to form the sole source of assessment for treatment outcome studies.

An example may demonstrate how inaccurate the average self-report may be. Miller and Taylor (1980) conducted a study on controlled drinking and found a significant decrease in the number of days subjects had more than five Standard Ethanol Content units (2.5 ounces total alcohol). The decrease was from 1.7 days per week during the first week of treatment to .81 days per week during a week at a 12-month follow-up. In the Maisto *et al.* (1979) study, subjects and collateral informants estimated the number of days the subjects had less than three ounces of alcohol. The mean collateral estimate was 2.72 days per week and the mean subject estimate was 1.46 days per week (86% difference). The error in the Maisto *et al.* study was 1.26 days per week— more than the mean change (.89 days) in the Miller and Taylor study! Furthermore, the standard deviations in the Maisto *et al.* study were at least three times the mean change, so the number of subjects whose error would be less than reported change would be quite small.

Admittedly, it is difficult to compare error rates from one study with outcome rates from another. Also, the comparison is complicated by the fact that the change in days of controlled drinking in the Miller and Taylor (1980) study would have been greater if pretreatment drinking rather than first-week drinking had been the baseline. There were also differences in definitions of drinking. Miller and Taylor included days abstinent in their definition of controlled drinking, while Maisto *et al.* (1979) included abstinent days in a separate category. In spite of these qualifications, the comparison of these studies does highlight an important point. When the changes being detected in treatment studies are relatively small, only a very small error in self-report can be tolerated if this form of measurement is to be the dependent variable. We do not feel the error is sufficiently small to justify reliance on self-reports as a valid measure of drinking.

The Process of Alcohol Consumption

MODELING

Social factors may be important determinants of alcohol consumption, and one of the most important social determinants may be the observation of others who drink. This issue has received much attention in the alcoholism literature. Studies in this area began as observational investigations of drinking in natural settings (barrooms). Analogue studies began to appear in the mid-1970s, and now there are more observational reports appearing again.

Sommer (1965) observed drinkers in a barroom setting and found that group drinkers consumed about twice as much beer as persons drinking alone. Several subsequent studies replicated this finding (Cutler & Storm, 1975; Kessler & Gomberg, 1974). Caudill and Marlatt (1975) then studied modeling effects in the laboratory. Male college students (heavy social drinkers) were exposed to a high-consumption confederate, a low-consumption confederate, or no model in an analogue drinking situation (wine tasting). Each modeling condition was subdivided into "warm or cold" interactions with the model. Subjects exposed to the high-consumption model drank significantly more than subjects in the other two conditions; the warm and cold distinction made no difference. Two studies by Sobell and colleagues showed that a heavy drinking model would increase drinking in college students regardless of the sex of either the subjects or confederates (Cooper, Waterhouse, & Sobell, 1979; Hendricks, Sobell, & Cooper, 1978). Two additional studies in a simulated barroom setting found that subjects would increase or decrease their consumption depending on the consumption of a model (Dericco & Garlington, 1977; Garlington & Dericco, 1977). Reid (1978) concluded that drinking with another may increase total consumption because it increases the amount of time spent in a drinking setting.

Recent studies confirm the notion that the social setting has an important impact on drinking. Tomaszewski, Strickler, and Maxwell (1980) found that subjects drank more rapidly and consumed more alcohol when with a drinking partner than when alone, but exposure to a drinking model did not differ from exposure to a nondrinking model. Foy and Simon (1978), however, found that a drinking model had no effect. Lied and Marlatt (1979) used the wine-tasting test in the laboratory to study modeling factors in a $2 \times 2 \times 2$ design (male vs. female subjects; light vs. heavy drinking history; light vs. heavy consumption models). The heavy-drinking model, compared to the light-drinking model, produced a twofold increase in the consumption of the heavy drinking subjects. The same model produced only a slight increase in the light drinkers. In another observational study, Rosenbluth, Nathan, and Lawson (1978) evaluated beer drinking in a college pub. Both males and females drank more in groups than in dyads. Opposite-sex dyads were related to more rapid consumption than same-sex dyads.

Collectively, these studies show very clearly that exposure to other drinkers increases drinking. This has been demonstrated by experimental manipulation in analogue settings and by observation in barroom settings. The size of the group also seems to matter; subjects in groups drink more than subjects in dyads (Rosenbluth *et al.*, 1978). These data support the use of stimulus control procedures in the treatment of problem drinkers, as well as social skills training so patients can avoid drinking situations or refuse drinks if the situations cannot be avoided.

DRINKING AND ANXIETY

The tension-reduction hypothesis has been influential in guiding the work of many behavioral researchers (Nathan & Goldman, 1979). This hypothesis maintains that alcohol reduces tension in problem drinkers, thereby reinforcing drinking among persons thought to be chronically anxious. For instance, Farber, Khavari, and Douglass (1980) classified 2496 respondents to a questionnaire into subjects who drank for social reasons (positive reinforcement) and those who drank to escape unpleasant feelings or situations (negative reinforcement). Negative-reinforcement drinkers scored higher than positive-reinforcement drinkers on all measure of alcohol consumption; 93% of all alcoholics were classified as escape drinkers. It is clear that the tension-reduction hypothesis is too simple a model to explain complex behavior (Nathan, 1980), but anxiety is still a topic of great appeal to researchers.

The studies on alcohol and anxiety have posed several questions involving the way anxiety is induced, how anxiety is measured, and whether anxiety interacts with subject characteristics. In addition, some studies have measured alcohol consumption in response to anxiety while others have investigated anxiety in response to alcohol consumption.

Studies on alcohol intake following stress yield mixed findings. Higgins and Marlatt (1973) reported that subjects did not drink more in response to the threat of physical pain (shock), and Holroyd (1978) found that subjects who received negative interpersonal feedback drank *less* than control subjects. Higgins and Marlatt (1975) found that college males drank more when told they would be evaluated by college females. Similar findings were reported by Miller, Hersen, Eisler, and

Hilsman (1974) for alcoholics but not for social drinkers. A recent study by Tucker, Vuchinich, Sobell, and Maisto (1980) found that social drinkers drank more before and after exposure to a high-stress intellectual task compared to exposure to a low-stress task.

Research on stress following alcohol intake is also not conclusive. The results depend on how anxiety is measured. Steffen, Nathan, and Taylor (1974) found that alcohol reduced tension as measured physiologically, but not as measured subjectively or behaviorally. A recent study reported that alcohol had a dose-related effect (decrease) on physiological and observational measures of anxiety, but not on self-report measures (Wilson, Abrams, & Lipscomb, 1980). Bradlyn, Strickler, and Maxwell (1981) gave subjects high or low doses of alcohol and then asked them to give a speech. The alcohol (high dose) reduced self-report and observational measures of anxiety, but the subjects showed an *increase* in the physiological measure of anxiety (skin conductance). Lipscomb, Nathan, Wilson, and Abrams (1980) gave subjects high and low doses of alcohol and then had them interact with a silent female confederate to induce anxiety. The high dose of alcohol decreased one physiological measure of anxiety (heart rate), but showed no effect on another physiological measure (skin conductance), a self-report measure, or an observational measure.

There exist many well-controlled studies on the relationship between anxiety and alcohol consumption. Unfortunately, the picture is still very confusing. For every study showing that anxiety increases alcohol consumption, there is another showing that it does not. The studies investigating whether alcohol consumption reduces anxiety agree that such an effect may exist, but there is remarkable inconsistency in behavioral, subjective, and physiological measures of anxiety. It is not so surprising that there is disagreement among the measures within most of the studies, because anxiety is a multidimensional construct (Lipscomb et al., 1980). It *is* surprising that there is little agreement within the same measure across studies. This area may be a fruitful one for research in upcoming years, because the results have implications for understanding the etiology of problem drinking and for developing methods for treatment.

Treatment Outcome Issues

The past several years have marked the publication of several important reviews of the literature (Miller & Hester, 1980; Nathan & Goldman, 1979). These along with Sobell and Sobell's (1980) review of the evidence on controlled drinking and two major books on the treatment of alcoholism (Miller, 1976; Sobell & Sobell, 1978) cover the literature in extraordinary detail. We will summarize these chapters and books at the end of this section, after we discuss the findings of the most recent studies on treatment outcome issues.

SOCIAL SKILLS TRAINING

There is almost universal agreement that alcoholics will profit from direct training in skills to deal effectively with interpersonal situations. This training generally includes instruction in assertiveness, refusing alcohol, relapse prevention (see the first section of this chapter), and methods for obtaining reinforcement by methods other than drinking. Most behavioral programs for alcoholics include training of this nature (Miller, 1976; Miller & Muñoz, 1976; Sobell & Sobell, 1978). Early behavioral programs included training in these areas (Sobell & Sobell, 1973a; Hunt & Azrin, 1973), but this was before the time when "social skills training" became a popular topic in behavior therapy. Aside from the convincing intuitive support for this emphasis in treatment, there is indirect support from several studies. Hamilton and Maisto (1979) found that male alcoholics and matched nonalcoholic drinkers did not differ on tests of assertive behavior, but the alcoholics reported more discomfort in the situations. Earlier, Miller and Eisler (1977) found just the opposite—that alcoholics described themselves as assertive, but behavioral measures indicated deficits in assertion. Sturgis, Calhoun, and Best (1979) reported that alcoholics who rated high on a self-report assertiveness scale were better adjusted than those who scored low. The clinical evidence and indirect research evidence is convincing. What about controlled studies on social skills training?

The early evaluations of social skills training were encouraging. One study found that assertiveness training seemed to help alcoholics, except that a control group was not used (Adinolfi, McCourt, & Geoghegan, 1976). Two subsequent studies suggested that alcoholics could be trained in assertiveness and problem-solving skills, but there was the question of whether the skills were useful (Hirsch, Von Rosenberg, Phelen, & Dudley, 1978; Intagliata, 1978). Chaney, O'Leary, and Marlatt (1978) carried out the first controlled test of skills training. Male alcoholics from a VA hospital were assigned to a skills training group, a discussion group which focused on feelings, or a control group which received the standard hospital program. The skills training involved rehearsal and feedback on interpersonal situations selected by the subjects. At a one-year follow-up, the skills training group was significantly lower on several measures of drinking behavior than the two control groups. In addition, Chaney *et al.* found that response latency for assertive behaviors predicted outcome as well as fairly good predictors such as drinking history. Another study, using single-case methods, found that alcoholics could be trained to refuse drinks (Foy, Miller, Eisler, & O'Toole, 1976). Based on the available evidence, Van Hasselt, Hersen, and Milliones (1978) concluded that social skills training is an important part of the treatment of alcoholics.

Two recent studies add to our knowledge about skills training. One study reported that hospitalized alcoholics showed significant improvements in ratings of skills when given training in refusing drinks and in positive assertion (Greenwald, Kloss, Kovaleski, Greenwald, Twentyman, & Zibung-Huffman, 1980). A treatment outcome study by Oei and Jackson (1980) compared a social skills training program to traditional supportive therapy. These authors measured both skills and drinking. One year after treatment, the social skills group consumed less alcohol and scored higher on measures of skills than did the group receiving supportive therapy.

We are inclined to yield to the indirect evidence that social skills training is important for alcoholics. Certainly, our clinical experience compels us to do so. However, there is little direct evidence that a multifaceted behavioral program for alcoholics will increase in effectiveness with the inclusion of social skills training. Furthermore, it is not completely apparent that alcoholics lack these skills more than persons with no drinking problem. These issues will require much more investigation before the final answers are available. In the meantime, we suspect that skills training will remain part of the treatment for alcoholics.

RECENT TREATMENT STUDIES

As with obesity and smoking, the number of treatment studies in the alcoholism area has declined in recent years because researchers have moved into the investigation of factors associated with drinking. The studies that have been done in the past several years are informative.

A multifaceted treatment program for alcoholics, using either abstinence or controlled drinking as the goal, has been evaluated by many researchers (Caddy & Lovibond, 1976; W. Miller, 1978; Pomerleau, Pertschuk, Adkins, & d'Aquili, 1978; Vogler, Compton, & Weissbach, 1975; Vogler, Weissbach, Compton, & Martin, 1977). Several investigators have used a program requiring less time and fewer resources—an approach labeled "behavioral self-control training" (BSCT). The BSCT program includes goal setting, self-monitoring, training in rate control, self-reinforcement, functional analysis of drinking behavior, and instruction in alternatives to alcohol abuse (W. Miller, 1978; Miller &

Muñoz, 1976). Using this focused program (not concentrating on general life problems, W. Miller found an overall improvement rate of 82% at a 12-month follow-up. A similar program tested by other investigators has produced equally impressive results; Caddy and Lovibond had 64% improvement at one year, Pomerleau *et al.* had 72% improvement at one year, and Vogler *et al.* (1977) had 65% improvement at one year.

The studies with a direct comparison of the multimodal and focused programs have produced mixed results. These studies are divided between those showing a slight advantage for the multimodal programs (Caddy & Lovibond, 1976; Vogler *et al.*, 1975) and those showing no differences (W. Miller, 1978; Vogler *et al.*, 1977). Two studies by W. Miller and colleagues provide more information on this issue. Miller, Taylor, and West (1980) assigned 56 problem drinkers to one of four groups: (1) bibliotherapy (subjects received self-help materials only); (2) BSCT consisting of six weekly sessions; (3) BSCT plus 12 sessions of relaxation, communication, and assertion training; and (4) BSCT plus 12 weeks of individually tailored broad-spectrum modules. At the one-year follow-up, all groups showed significant reductions in drinking. There were no differences among the four treatment conditions, with the exception that bibliotherapy subjects spent more hours per week intoxicated than did the other subjects. Miller and Taylor (1980) carried out a study very similar to the Miller *et al.* (1980) report. A self-help manual was compared to the BSCT program and to the BSCT program with relaxation training. All groups showed significant improvement, but there were no differences among the groups.

It would appear that the BSCT program is as effective (and is less costly) than a more extensive multimodal program. Miller and Hester (1980) calculated average improvement rates at three-month and six-month follow-ups of 79% for BSCT and 68% for multimodal programs. If the multimodal programs were to have any advantage, we would expect it to appear during follow-up. Marlatt (1980), for example, discusses the importance of "lifestyle balancing," that is, developing positive activities to replace drinking. We agree with Miller and Hester that simple and inexpensive treatments are likely to work with some patients, and more extensive treatments will be necessary for others. The problem lies in pairing individuals with treatments, an issue discussed below in the section of predictor variables.

Several other recent studies have addressed treatment outcome issues. Craigie and Ross (1980) testing two programs to encourage male detoxification patients to seek treatment. The "pretherapy" training programs were (1) a videotaped modeling procedure with subsequent discussion and (2) a control procedure of commercially available films and discussion. Subjects in the experimental group were more likely to follow through on treatment referrals, and once involved in treatment, they were more likely to remain longer and to complete the program. Brown (1980) evaluated two strategies for drunken drivers who were required to enter a program. He tested the standard driver's education course and a controlled drinking program in which subjects were taught self-control skills. These were compared to a no-education control condition. Both treatment groups showed significant improvements in psychosocial adjustment at a 12-month follow-up, but only subjects in the controlled drinking program had a reduction in the number of days of uncontrolled drinking.

PREDICTORS OF TREATMENT OUTCOME

The search for predictors of treatment outcome has had a long history. This area has been reviewed by others, so we refer the reader to several sources for a detailed examination of this issue (Armor et al., 1978; Gibbs & Flanagan, 1977). We will briefly characterize the status of the field and will present data from recent studies.

The most obvious source of variance in treatment outcome is the type of treatment delivered. There is, of course, a massive literature on the comparison of various treatments (see next section). One critical variable in treatment research is the length of the treatment program. Miller and Hester (1980) question the commonly held notion that if treatment helps, more treatment will help more. Correlational studies yield mixed data on this question. Several studies show a positive correlation between length of treatment and outcome (Armor et al., 1978; Smart & Gray, 1978), some studies show no correlation (Penk, Charles, & Van-Hoose, 1978; Ritson, 1968), and another shows a negative correlation (Gunderson & Schuckit, 1978). Miller and Hester conclude from their review of this issue that inpatient treatment offers no advantage over outpatient treatment, that length of time within a method of treatment does not predict outcome, and that extensive treatments are no better than simpler treatments.

There have been many attempts to relate subject variables to treatment outcome (e.g., Armor et al., 1978; Bromet, Moos, Bliss, & Wuthmann, 1977; Cronkite & Moos, 1978). Cronkite and Moos found that interactions between subject and treatment variables could account for 23–40% of the variance in treatment outcome, but these same authors conclude from their findings and others that the explained variance is between 10% and 30% (Cronkite & Moos, 1980). Again, no variables consistently predict outcome. Gibbs and Flanagan (1977) attribute this to the heterogeneity among studies in subject populations, treatment methods, choice of predictor variables, definitions of alcoholism, and measures of treatment outcome.

There is some indication that life events and a person's ability to cope with these events may explain part of the variance in treatment outcome (Foster, Horn, & Wanberg, 1972). Hore (1971) found an association between stressful life events and relapse in 14 alcoholics. Longitudinal evidence has shown that subjects who experience negative life events show the poorest treatment outcome (Finney, Moos, & Mewborn, 1980). Cronkite and Moos (1980) found that posttreatment stressors and the resulting coping responses could double the variance explained by pretreatment subject variables. These findings support the emphasis of Marlatt and his colleagues on training subjects to cope with stressful events in hopes of preventing relapse (Cummings et al., 1980; Marlatt, 1980; Marlatt & Gordon, 1980). The survey reported by Cummings et al. found that both intrapersonal and interpersonal factors were related to the majority of relapse episodes in subjects they studied (see the first section of this chapter). These are exciting developments, but the majority of the variance in outcome has yet to be explained (Cronkite & Moos, 1980).

Research on predictor variables will bear fruit when specific treatment approaches can be targeted to specific individuals. Progress toward this goal has been made in studies of variables which predict success in adherence to controlled drinking or abstinence goals. Miller and Joyce (1979) evaluated client characteristics in 141 problem drinkers who were treated using controlled drinking as the goal of treatment. The comparisons these authors made were between controlled drinkers and abstainers. Controlled drinkers had less severe symptoms and less family history of alcoholism. Women were more likely to be controlled drinkers and males were more likely to abstain. Lower income and education were associated with success at both moderation and abstinence. Maisto, Sobell, and Sobell (1980) studied predictors of outcome two years after treatment in 69 male alcoholics. They found that drinking behavior tended to stabilize between one and two years after treatment. There was a strong relationship between controlled drinking goal and controlled drinking outcome, but not between abstinence goal and abstinence outcome. Consistent with Miller and Joyce's findings, Maisto et al. found that less severe symptoms were related to success at controlled drinking (measured by pretreatment hospitalizations and by drinking in the six months prior to the follow-up assessment). Results of this type are important, because the overall effectiveness of either controlled drinking or abstinence programs may be greatly enhanced if appropriate patients can be selected in advance.

TREATMENT RECOMMENDATIONS

Guidelines for the treatment of the problem drinker have been described in detail (Miller, 1976; Miller & Hester, 1980; Nathan & Goldman, 1979; Sobell & Sobell, 1976, 1980). We will discuss several global issues regarding treatment in an attempt to conclude which treatment(s) are likely to be effective. We will focus on behavioral treatments because they have been the most extensively evaluated. Miller and Hester and Nathan and Goldman have reviewed alternative approaches, such as hypnosis, electrical and chemical aversion, self-help groups (AA), psychotherapy, group therapy, and family therapy.

Miller and Hester (1980) conclude that when problem drinkers receive treatment, one-third will be abstinent and one-third will improve. These are short-term data, and when follow-up is as long as one year, only 26% remain abstinent or improved. For drinkers who receive no treatment, approximately 19% are abstinent or improved after one year. It is clear that "behavior therapy" can improve these rates, particularly over the long-term. Even this conclusion, however, must be based partly on faith. As Miller and Hester point out, "No treatment method has been shown to be consistently superior to the absence of treatment or to alternative treatments in a sufficient number of well-controlled studies to warrant 'established' status" (p. 108). What is even less clear is which among the options offered by behavior therapists is the treatment of choice?

The assessment and treatment of the problem drinker is a multi-dimensional task (P. Miller, 1980; Miller & Hester, 1980; Nathan & Goldman, 1979). Evaluation of drinking behavior is only part of the task, because problem drinking occurs in a complex system of feelings, interactions with others, and environmental events. There is a tendency to assess what is easiest to assess—drinking behavior. Nathan and Goldman note that behavioral researchers must not "go beyond their data" and risk the "transgression of their own fundamental precept":

> Behavioral clinicians who proclaim preemptively that controlled social drinking is the best goal for all alcoholics, who concentrate their behavior change efforts on maladaptive drinking because it can be readily quantified, instead of including the alcoholic's associated behavioral deficits and excesses in a treatment package, or who contrast a new behavioral procedure with an old and ineffective one, thereby proving the superiority of the former—all have forsaken a precious birthright. (p. 274)

Miller and Hester (1980) also argue for a flexible approach which can be tailored to the needs of the individual. W. Miller and his colleagues are the first to argue that we may be administering too much treatment rather than too little. Miller's studies suggest that a focused

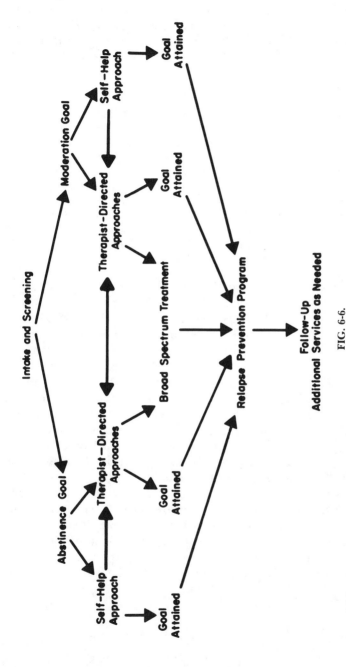

FIG. 6-6.

A model for the outpatient treatment program for problem drinking. (From "Treating the Problem Drinker: Modern Approaches" by W. R. Miller and R. K. Hester, in W. R. Miller, Ed., *The Addictive Behaviors: Treatment of Alcoholism, Drug Abuse, Smoking, and Obesity*, New York: Pergamon Press, 1980. Copyright 1980, Pergamon Press, Ltd. Reprinted by permission.)

behavioral self-control program may be as effective as a more extensive multimodal program, and further, that a program which is almost completely self-administered may be as effective as more costly therapist-administered procedures. Sobell and Sobell (1976, 1980) along with Miller and Hester feel that controlled drinking is a viable goal for some problem drinkers. According to Miller and Hester,

> If a program intends to offer comprehensive treatment services for problem drinkers, it seems clear that a range of alternative interventions must be offered. Predictive data, for example, suggest that for early-stage problem drinkers, moderation-oriented methods may be optimal, whereas more advanced alcoholics may be best served by effective abstinence-oriented approaches. The consistent finding that extensive and intensive interventions are no more effective than are more minimal treatments suggests that it would be unwise policy to routinely provide multimodal, long-term, or broad-spectrum treatment for *all* clients. Rather, both minimal and more intensive alternatives should be available, with the latter used selectively. (pp. 109–110)

Miller and Hester have developed a scheme to describe their integrated outpatient program for alcoholics (Figure 6-6). It is clear from this scheme that Miller and Hester feel that controlled drinking is the preferable goal for some patients, that the least expensive treatments (self-help or focused self-control approaches) should be used first, and only after a patient's failure should broad-spectrum approaches be used, and that all patients should receive a relapse prevention program.

We feel that Miller and Hester's scheme is a useful one for heuristic reasons, and is helpful for clinical reasons to the extent it informs clinicians that many treatment approaches are available. However, the model must be considered very tentative because of lack of information at almost every important decision-making point in the diagram (at each arrow). For example, there are no definitive studies on which to judge who should be assigned to controlled drinking treatments and who should enter an abstinence-oriented treatment. Even less is known about who would profit most from self-help, minimal treatment, and extensive treatment approaches. Finally, not a single study has proven that Marlatt's relapse prevention procedures will prevent relapse (although we join those enthusiasts who hope for the best).

BEHAVIOR THERAPY WITH CHILDREN AND ADOLESCENTS

CYRIL M. FRANKS

INTRODUCTION

In 1979, the first behavior journal devoted exclusively to young people appeared under the seemingly straightforward title *Child Behavior Therapy*. Consistent with the prevailing *zeitgeist*, behavior was held to incorporate any "verbal and nonverbal elements of social interaction, overt motor activity, sensation, imagery and cognition, affect, and intra-organismic biological activity" as long as it pertained to children (Franks & Diament, 1979). In 1982, it is argued that a comprehensive, truly contemporary child behavior therapy must take into account the family or family surrogate and the title of this new journal has accordingly been changed to *Child and Family Behavior Therapy* (Franks & Diament, 1982).

As many a recent critic has correctly noted, unbridled expansion is not without hazard. Phillips and Ray (1980) draw attention to the loss in precision that can occur when distinctions between diverse models become blurred. Without clearly articulated conceptual and contextual boundaries we run the risk of losing what Kuhn (1977) terms that "essential tension" between competing models which is necessary for knowledge to advance. As if to underscore this point we note the recent emergence of a new series entitled *Advances in Behavioral Pediatrics: A Research Annual* (Camp, 1980). For the most part methodologically sound and data-based, the contents of this inaugural volume augur well for its future. But we fail to discern any commonality between the subject matter and conceptual framework of the various chapters and "behavior therapy," as we define this term. Judging from the sample offered to us in this first volume, virtually any experimentally sophisticated article dealing with measurable entities would fit into this series as long as it pertains to children.

Doubts have also been expressed about the practical utility of expanding the domain of child behavior therapy at this stage, the eagerness with which certain clinicians embrace "cognitive child behavior therapy" being very much a case in point. In the words of Hobbs, Moguin, Tyroler, and Lahey (1980), "No single dependent measure has been demonstrated to improve in a consistent manner as a result of cognitive–behavioral intervention" (see also Franks, 1981a, 1981b; Franks & Rosenbaum, 1982).

Throughout this *Annual Review* series and elsewhere we have repeatedly stressed both the hazards of fuzzy overinclusion and the need to integrate sensitivity to current developments with the rigor, if not the content, that characterized the formative years of behavior therapy. This, in a sense, is still our raison d'être, a point of view shared by authors of recent major texts in this field (e.g., Ollendick & Cerny, 1982; Ross, 1981).

Child behavior therapy becomes *comprehensive* when it systematically takes into account the unique needs, special considerations, and problems of young people. As such, it rests, not always firmly, upon six interlocking and partially overlapping foundations: (1) the principles of child development, including the concomitant acquisition of longitudinal data and the generation of norms; (2) classical and operant conditioning; (3) the methodology of behavioral science in general and of applied behavioral analysis in particular; (4) an intervention model which goes beyond the traditional one-to-one confines of the therapist's office to a multidimensional data-oriented structure involving interacting systems, groups, and communities; (5) a recognition that it is appropriate clinical practice or relevant field intervention that makes perfect; armchair or even laboratory formulations cannot be substituted for disciplined experience and learning by doing; and, finally, (6) an active appreciation of the inalienable right of the child, no longer to be considered as either a puppet on a string or a little adult.

Children are less structured, less rigid, more malleable with respect to their nervous systems, and, in this sense, progressively evolving and more amenable to change than adults. Developmental psychologists and psychometricians, if not certain Skinnerian behavior therapists, have long been acutely aware of this proposition. The development of assessment scales in behavior therapy is still characterized by rudimentary standardization and, even if psychometric sophistication is on the increase, we have a long way to go. Factor analysis, complex reliability measurement, normative studies, and appropriate cross-validation remain relatively rare. (For a more extended discussion of problems relating to assessment with children, see Chapter 2.)

In the formative years of child behavior therapy, maturational data were acquired primarily for physiological and sensorimotor activities such as bladder control and tying shoelaces. Perhaps because of problems in measurement or perhaps because of a still lingering antipathy toward "mentalism" among data-based investigators, cognitive and affective maturation have not been subjected to such scrutiny. Whether we think in terms of simple motor activities, socialization rating scales, Piagetian cognitivism, Luria's neurological maturation, Lovaas's operant progression, or the many investigators who have mapped out the complex developmental parameters of verbal learning and problem-solving ability, the conclusion remains the same: Whatever the framework, developmental differences and longitudinal data cannot be overlooked in working with children. Child behavior therapy bereft of such data is like a ship without a rudder. It is of equal importance to recognize that, if the classical and operant conditioning of traditional S-R learning theory remains necessary, it is not sufficient. Our complex physical, biological, psychological, and socioeconomic environment is determined by many systems and reciprocal interactions. According to Bandura (1978b), the environment is as much shaped by the behavior of the organism as vice versa.

The child's rights to "integrity as a person, privacy and self-determination" (Ross, 1981) are primary and much has been written on this topic (e.g., Kazdin, 1979a; Martin, 1975; Rosen, Rekers, & Bentler, 1978; Rothman & Rothman, 1980; Vardin & Brody, 1979). To what extent the rights of the child include the right to treatment or no treatment and the right to have an adult speak for him or her, and under what circumstances, remain matters of current debate. What is not debatable is that the contemporary child behavior therapist has to adopt new perspectives and acquire new behaviors including diverse disciplines, different role models, and methodologies more appropriate to the complexities involved (Christopherson & Gleeson, 1980; Peterson, Hartmann, & Gelfand, 1980). Perhaps what is required is a fresh perspective on the nature of the child. In his discussion of the ecology of human development, Bronfenbrenner draws attention to Leontiev's perhaps idealized distinction between American and Soviet researchers. In the Soviet Union, the concern is not so much with how the child came to be what he is as how he can become what he not yet is (Sampson, 1981). In similar vein, I am reminded of a conversation with the late A. R. Luria in which he good-humoredly drew my attention to the fact that, in the United States, the primary focus was upon "depth psychology" and the attempt to explore the innermost recesses of the child's being whereas his goal was a determination of the *heights* to which the child might rise. It is with this frame of reference in focus that we turn now to a review of recent developments in certain key areas of child behavior therapy.

BEHAVIOR MODIFICATION IN THE SCHOOL SYSTEM

Overview

Especially in earlier years, much of the behavioral input into the educational system has come from clinical rather than school psychologists. But behavior therapy transported to the school milieu does not constitute behavioral school psychology. Behavior within the school setting is the result of complex interactions among peers, teachers, the physical environment, and a diversity of administrative, political, and program influences (Maher & Barbrack, 1979).

For behavioral school psychology to be effective it must be competency-based and stress clearly defined goals (Kratochwill & Bergan, 1978). Target behaviors need to be selected on a theoretical or empirical rather than subjective basis (Drabman & Furman, 1979). For example, disruptive behavior is typically targeted on the assumption that this is one indirect cause of achievement deficiency. But reducing disruption does not necessarily, in itself, improve school work and direct academic intervention may be an equally primary strategy. However, a simplistic allegiance to behavioral objectives can be harmful. There are many reasons why students do not learn, some quite unrelated to the teacher (Bosco, 1980), and school systems are more complex than simple teacher–pupil interactions. For example, most studies in education concentrate on students and teachers, with little attention given to the reinforcement systems which motivate administrators, school principals, and those concerned with funding (Isherwood & Tallboy, 1979).

Behavior Modification in the Classroom

Effective classroom behavior modification must be part of the more sophisticated consultative process noted above (see also Glynn, 1981; Lahey & Drabman, 1981). Ruggles and LeBlanc (1982) make the related point that, while many behavioral texts help teachers maintain classroom discipline (e.g., Clarizio, 1980), a way to arrange the learning environment so that all children can learn at a pace commensurate with their abilities is a neglected topic. When the behavioral technology of how to teach reaches the level of sophistication of the behavioral technology of discipline and motivation, teachers will be able to concentrate upon teaching. This is particularly important when dealing with disadvantaged children (e.g., Bushell, 1978; McLaughlin, Big Left Hand, & Cady, 1979).

External rewards are important but so may be knowledge of success. The systematic use of feedback to magnify and channel feelings of success offers several advantages. It directly involves the learning material; it employs natural reinforcers that generalize well to new settings where learning is involved; it costs nothing to implement; it is relatively easy to show students how to generate their own feedback reinforcement systems with respect to their successes; and it requires little effort and teacher–pupil time. Furthermore, there is no reason why systems of learning through feedback should not be combined with more traditional reinforcement procedures (Van Houten, 1980).

Many programs have attempted to enroll the home as an ally in the campaign against classroom problems. Barth (1979) reviews critical studies of 24 such programs. While much remains unknown—for example, what methods are best suited to which parents—the data suggest that most parents can be trained to structure the home environment to help modify their children's school behavior. But sometimes the problem and the solution are literally within the school setting. For example, a child's academic performance can be a direct function of seating distance from the teacher. But whether more able and more interested students select front seats or whether being placed in the front generates academic interest awaits investigation (Levine, O'Neal, Garwood, & McDonald, 1980; Stires, 1980).

It is usually assumed that teachers determine classroom learning behavior. For Doyle (1978), the teacher is but one, albeit powerful, facet in the classroom learning complex. Teaching behaviors are as likely to be the products of pupils' actions as their causes (Copeland, 1980). This calls into question much of the teacher effectiveness literature and its assumption that classroom conditions are primarily matters of direct teacher influence. Variables cannot be simply labeled as dependent or independent in such studies. (See also Randhawa's [1980] study of verbal teacher–pupil relationships across 117 classrooms.)

The Disturbed Child in the Classroom

Childhood problems in the schools encompass a diversity of deviant behaviors of varying severity and clinical significance. While many therapeutic classroom techniques have been suggested, few have been researched. Both classroom maintenance of benefits after the procedure is withdrawn and transfer of the new behavior to fresh settings remain problematic. Another difficulty is that most programs are in effect for a single term or a single classroom (Jones & Kazdin, 1981).

Within the above constraints some ingenious coping strategies have been formulated. For example, Israel, Pravder, and Knights (1980) trained peers to ignore inappropriate and praise appropriate behavior, thereby producing reductions in the disruptive behavior of the target child. Regrettably, maintenance and generalization data are conspicuously absent. The impact of the program upon the teacher and the school as a social system also remains unaddressed.

What do teachers think constitutes a problem child and how valid are their perceptions? Green, Beck, Forehand, and Vosk (1980) found third-grade teachers well able to identify children having difficulties but less able to differentiate between different types of problem behavior (e.g., conduct and withdrawal problems). In general, little is known about the characteristics, training, or other requirements within specific teacher–classroom environments which favor successful recognition and differentiation of such problems.

Prevention in the Schools

Primary prevention is instigated before the disease occurs, secondary prevention pertains to the early diagnosis and treatment of disease, and tertiary prevention to rehabilitation after the disease has occurred or is under control. Cowen (1977) focuses upon the child's social environment and the establishment of social skills for potentially effective behavioral intervention at the primary level, and Jason (1980) delineates a sophisticated person-centered, primary-level behavioral technology for the school system. But for the most part, intervention takes place at the second or third levels and involves few support systems outside the immediate target area.

The more comprehensive the model, the further reaching the implications of our endeavors. An intervention planned to involve parents, administrators, politicians, and funding agencies raises nagging ethical questions. To what limits are we willing to go in terms of mass primary prevention? Should we "license" parenthood? Is genetic selection to be tolerated and even encouraged? What are the limits of the rights of the child as contrasted with the integrity of the family structure? The extreme nature of these questions should not lead to facile dismissal of either the questions or their implications.

PARENT TRAINING

Each year seven or more million Americans take a step that will significantly change their own lives and profoundly influence the coming generation. They will have children. How they raise their youngsters is going to affect virtually all of us in one way or another. Can parenting skills be acquired, and if so, how? 1980 saw the emergence of the first comprehensive multiauthored *Handbook on Parent Education* (Fine, 1980), but no clear answer to the latter part of this question. Even more regrettable, from our point of view, is this book's superficial and dated discussion of behavioral training (Simpson, 1980) (as contrasted with Gordon & Davidson's [1981] model overview of this important topic).

Parental opinions obtained through questionnaires, a parent-recorded frequency of child behavior problems, and an independently measured frequency of child behavior problems have all been used to measure outcome. To determine agreement among these measures, Atkeson and Forehand (1978) surveyed some 24 outcome studies. Parent reports seem to be associated with positive outcome, and conclusions about outcome depend upon the measure used. Which measure should serve as our primary criterion? Atkeson and Forehand suggest multiple outcome measures, with the final selection dependent upon the presenting problem. If the child is obviously deviant, the outcome measure should focus on the child's behavior. If the problem is more one of parental perception of the child as deviant, then parental questionnaires may be more appropriate. Unfortunately, as Gordon and Davidson note, no way of differentiating or even clearly identifying these two categories has, as yet, been established.

Generalization and maintenance studies yield equally inconclusive findings (Forehand & Atkeson, 1977). Three types of generalization need to be evaluated: setting generalization from clinic to home and school; generalization to new behaviors not targeted in treatment; and generalization to the targeted child's siblings. Of these, probably the most crucial, and certainly the most intensely investigated, is that of generalization to the home. Regrettably, the literature pertaining to the ability of parents to generalize their acquired skills to modify destructive behaviors other than those targeted during treatment is sparse and discouraging (Patterson & Fleischman, 1979).

According to O'Dell, Mahoney, Horton, and Turner (1979), direct behavioral training is more effective than the customary written material. Such studies, and there are more, argue for the decreased use of written material in favor of behaviorally based intervention. Scovern,

Bukstel, Kilman, Laval, Busemeyer, and Smith (1980) found no advantage in the use of behaviorally based techniques, but since they failed to employ behavioral assessment measures little credence can be placed in their findings.

Christensen, Johnson, Phillips, and Glasgow (1980) carried out a well-designed comparison of group and individual parent training and minimal-contact bibliotherapy in which assessment procedures were exemplary and unobtrusive (Christensen, 1979). When compared with the bibliotherapy condition, parents in both treatment groups reported significantly lower frequencies of target behaviors. This was true at termination and at a two- to ten-week posttherapy assessment (a time span unfortunately too short). Even within a behavioral framework, different parent samples are likely to require different training strategies. Tavormina (1975) worked with parents of mentally retarded children, Hampson and Tavormina (1980) with foster parents, and Diament and Colletti (1978) with parents of learning disabled children.

It is usual to instruct parents in behavioral principles and techniques for general application. Forehand and his associates take a somewhat different approach, preferring to focus upon a specific problem area, for example, noncompliance (Forehand & King, 1977; Forehand, Sturgis, McMahon, Aguar, Green, Wells, & Breiner, 1979; Forehand, Wells, & Griest, 1980). Eyberg and Matarazzo (1980) compared these direct specific treatment programs with the more usual general problem approach. Both of their treatment groups showed significant improvement on four out of five attitude scales whereas the waiting-list controls remained largely unaffected. But it should be noted that their child population was not a clinical one. Also, parents were not randomly assigned to groups, the control group children were two years older than the others, and there was no follow-up.

All in all, we know little about the long-term efficacy of such training programs, control for nonspecific factors is usually neglected, and assessment measures have been less than adequate. With the exception of the Scovern et al. (1980) study, parental attitudes and feelings have been largely neglected. We also know little about the influences of race, social class, or the nature of the specific problem. Most of Forehand's children were mildly disturbed. Hargis and Blechman (1979) examined the socioeconomic status of parents treated in 138 parenting studies over the years 1959–1973. Only 9% of these were in the lowest social class as compared with 22% of the general population. Furthermore, most investigators worked with children under 10 years old, and no study to date has trained fathers or examined the effects of both parents participating as opposed to just one. Tavormina's (1975) study is one of the few to compare different models of parent training.

Books are frequently used as part of the parent training instruction, yet few studies have examined the intrinsic validity of these manuals. Bernal and North (1978) suggest that the more circumscribed the problem, the more likely it is that a manual for parents is likely to be helpful. Thus, Christensen *et al.*'s (1980) minimal-contact bibliotherapy condition had parents read Patterson and Gullion's (1971) *Living with Children* and then apply the principles to more general problems. They fared poorly when compared with those receiving professional contact and over half of the families in the bibliotherapy group used punishment inappropriately.

The behavioral training package typically comprises a mélange of didactic material, behavioral rehearsal, modeling, feedback, coaching, and more. Systematic dismantling studies of the active components remain to be carried out. Parents who are psychotic or have poor marriages are often excluded on little basis other than hearsay, clinic facilities, or staff interests, and this is characteristic of the training field.

O'Dell's (1974) review of some 70 studies of behavioral parent training programs led, in essence, to the conclusion that data lag far behind potential. We doubt if a 1982 update of this review would document any significant advances. Investigators still focus upon specific models rather than comparative studies (e.g., Gordon, Lerner, & Keefe, 1979; Sharpley & Poiner, 1980). Gordon *et al.* modified Hall and Copeland's (1972) Responsive Teaching to develop the interesting concept of Responsive Parenting. But no comparison was made with either waiting-list control groups, groups which control for specific factors, or other treatment modalities. Furthermore, there was no long-term follow-up and neither problem nor setting generalization was considered. Authier, Sherrets, and Tramontana (1980) offer a possible schema for the grouping of parental training programs according to their applicability to specific target populations, the unique characteristics of the community, and resources available for program delivery. However, these observations remain as yet in the realm of conjecture.

Wahler (1980) uses the term "insular" to describe those mothers who report themselves to be both isolated from and harassed by their own community. Such mothers seem to be poor candidates for parent training. By contrast, noninsular, self-referred, middle-income, community-active mothers evidence much improvement in child–parent interactions during training and maintain these gains in the home. Insular mothers may show equal improvement during training but fail to maintain these gains in other situations (Wahler & Afton, 1980).

As far as specific populations are concerned, most attention has been given to parents of mentally retarded, hyperactive, and autistic children. (Parental training for autistic children is discussed in a subsequent section.) Parental training for the mentally handicapped is beginning to shift from an impairment to a developmental deficit basis, with the family viewed as a resource rather than a source of pathology (e.g., Baker, 1981; Baker & Clark, 1980; Brightman, Ambrose, & Baker, 1980; Baker, Heifetz, & Murphy, 1980). With noninsular parents, home-based programs which utilize family resources in addition to other facilities are probably ideal (e.g., Boyd, 1979). Families that do less well are characterized by lower socioeconomic status, less education, and fewer life experiences. Not surprisingly, they are more likely to be single-parent families or to have less well-adjusted marriages.

Parents of hyperactive children in such programs seem to be somewhat different. Children and parents who remain in treatment tend to be older and more intelligent than those who drop out. Families of female children drop out more frequently than families of male children. Somewhat surprisingly, single female parents are not more likely to drop out of training than two-parent families (Firestone & Witt, in press).

Behavioral training programs for hyperactive children are frequently complicated by the concomitant use of medication. Firestone, Kelly, Goodman, and Davey (in press) failed to find evidence of significant benefit from the addition of parent training to the administration of medication. Parental behavioral training with the child given a placebo, training plus methylphenidate, or methylphenidate alone all yielded improvement in home and school behavior. However, only with medication were there gains in attention, impulse control, school achievement, and classroom behavior. Probably, as the authors conclude, effective intervention should include medication, parent training, and educational services.

Parental training stems from two major streams: behavior modification and reflective communication (e.g., Parent Effectiveness Training—Gordon, 1970). Dubey, O'Leary, and Kaufman (in press) found both systems effective in reducing hyperactivity ratings, problem severity ratings, and daily problem occurrence, with behavior modification training being generally better received by the hyperactive children's parents. Bernal, Klinnert, and Schultz (1980) carried out a somewhat similar study of children with conduct problems and their parents. The superiority of behavioral training observed in the short run was not substantiated at follow-up in terms either of children's conduct or parental satisfaction. Because most families resisted home observation, follow-up had to be carried out by telephone, and the extent to which parental perceptions reflect behavioral change remains unknown.

We conclude this discussion with a brief return to the vexing problem of self-help programs and parent training manuals. The parent-training book market is replete with grandiose promises and it remains questionable to what extent parents left to their own devices could successfully implement the simplistic interventions offered (e.g., Schaefer & Millman's [1981] compendium of "look it up for yourself" childhood problems). Bernal and North (1978) evaluated 26 readily available manuals for parents. Their conclusion is that the more specific and circumscribed the child's problem, the more likely is the manual to be useful.

Each year in this series we lament the plethora of unvalidated parent-training manuals and this year is no exception. McMahon and Forehand (1980) come to a similar conclusion and, in a later publication, spell out what is needed for effective evaluation: large and well-defined samples; appropriate control groups; multiple outcome measures; behavioral observation of both parent and child by independent observers; assessment of procedures and consumer satisfaction; cost-effectiveness analyses; and, finally, at least a six-month follow-up using the same dependent measures. If these proposals seem extravagant, as the authors note, the potential cost–benefit ratio in terms of overall advantages would seem to be well in their favor.

SELF-REINFORCEMENT

Self-control research used to be confined primarily to laboratory studies of children, with therapeutic application reserved for adults. In 1977, Karoly rightly criticized the quality of this research and, in 1979, Meichenbaum came to similar conclusions. With the advent of cognitively oriented social learning theory, well-researched strategies for therapeutic intervention with children are at last beginning to emerge (see Chapter 4).

Self-control in children offers many advantages: Independent action is expected and valued in our society; meaningful others may not always be capable of successfully implementing external controls; self-control frees adults to teach the child other skills; the self-controlling child is able to learn to behave more effectively when adult supervision is not available (O'Leary & Dubey, 1979).

With the exception of criterion setting (in which children set their own standards of performance), self-control procedures are probably as effective as similar, externally imposed procedures. When comparative maintenance effects have been assessed, the results are usually positive. Much more is now known about the intricacies of how and under what circumstances self-controlling behaviors can be effectively taught and implemented. Telling a child to self-instruct does not necessarily ensure implementation and, in this respect, O'Leary and Dubey (1979) recommend a return to the principles of shaping and modeling.

Developmental and cognitive psychology may broaden the basis for understanding self-instructional training more than clinical research alone (Cole & Kazdin, 1980; Glenwick & Barocas, 1979; Meichenbaum & Asarnow, 1979). How we proceed will depend in large part upon our personal frame of reference and our notions about the concept of "self" (cf. Masters & Mokros, 1974).

What is the role of external variables? The majority of studies reviewed by Jones, Nelson, and Kazdin (1977) have been conducted in classroom settings where the self-administration of consequences is the crucial behavior-change event. But simple self-delivery of consequences is insufficient for a behavior to be termed self-reinforcement. Self-reinforcement involves free access to reinforcers and self-selection of the contingencies for reinforcement in addition to self-administration of reinforcing stimuli (Bandura, 1976, 1978b). In many of the studies reviewed by Jones *et al.* these criteria were not met. External factors may well be playing a major role in results attributed to self-reinforcement alone (Jones & Evans, 1980).

Be this as it may, the utilization of "self-control" procedures in the classroom overcomes the many obvious disadvantages noted by Kazdin (1975) in having to rely upon external agents to design and administer classroom contingencies. Rosenbaum and Drabman (1979) evaluate self-control classroom training procedures and offer the following sequential suggestions: Pupils should first be taught how to self-observe, matching their records with those of the trainer and then gradually fading out the matching process. At this stage, externally determined contingencies for desirable behavior changes can be introduced. The control of these contingencies can then be transferred to the pupils. At this time, pupils can be taught to provide the necessary guiding instructions and praise for themselves. When reliable control of academic and social behaviors is apparent, explicit contingencies can be gradually withdrawn in the hope that natural contingencies will become fully operative. Finally, students can be taught the major principles of self-control for application in future situations. The cynic will doubt the practicality of these proposals, the behavioral scientist will ask for data, and the clinician for the relevant conditions. We question these suggestions on all three accounts.

Workman and Hector (1978) draw attention to the advantages of gradually transferring adult administered token reinforcement contingencies to the children themselves. Most programs begin with external token reinforcement contingencies. But as Noland, Arnold, and Clement (1980) demonstrate in their case report of the successful treatment of two underachieving, undercontrolled sixth-grade girls by training in self-reinforcement, this is not always necessary. What we find most extraordinary about their study is not so much its understandable methodological limitations as their naive conclusion that "self-reinforcement is not a myth; it is a meaningful, psychological reality." Would that we could all be so certain!

SOCIAL SKILLS TRAINING IN NORMAL AND HANDICAPPED CHILDREN

Overview

The 20th century has witnessed remarkable achievements in the mastery of technical skills. Sophisticated but elegantly simple training procedures are now routine. But even in the helping professions, the emphasis still tends to be upon the acquisition of technical competence rather than social and interpersonal skills. Competent physicians, teachers, and senior executives who know their subject matter well but who do not interact constructively with patients, students, or employees are commonplace. Most mental health practitioners are psychodynamic in orientation and focus on alleged underlying bases to maladaptive behavior rather than teaching effective coping skills. Some therapists even believe that the teaching of social competencies is destructive to the subtleties of the patient–therapist relationship and hence to the implicit values of nonintrusive psychodynamic therapy (see Franks, 1981a).

Contemporary social learning theory subscribes neither to the early behaviorist belief that man is a passive recipient of external stimuli nor to the psychodynamic notion that intrapsychic influences are primary. Rather, there is a reciprocal interactional process whereby each individual can modify the social behavior of others and this, in turn, serves to modify his or her own behavior. As social skills training extends this repertoire of behavioral competencies, so the individual learns to feel comfortable with himself or herself, with his or her environment, and in his or her relationships with others (Rathjen & Foreyt, 1980). Social skills may be conceptualized as part of a broader construct known as social competence (Foster & Ritchey, 1979) or, more narrowly, in terms of specific dimensions (Gresham, in press-b).

Social Skills Training and the Normal Child

Combs and Slaby (1977) review social skills training with children and some methods for improving research. Asher, Oden, and Gottman (1977) focus upon children's friendships in school settings and some of the reasons why interventions with isolated children are relatively ineffective. Cartledge and Milburn (1980), Foster and Ritchey (1979), and Greenwood, Walker, and Hops (1977) discuss problems of assessment. Cartledge and Milburn (1978) highlight the close relationship between social behaviors and school achievement. Social skills training goes on all the time in the classroom as a "hidden curriculum" even when formal teaching is directed elsewhere. Cobb and his colleagues (e.g., Cobb & Hops, 1973; Hops & Cobb, 1973; Walker & Hops, 1976) identify the specific social "survival" skills related to academic achievement. Improvement in academic achievement may either result from or bring about improvement in social skills. In most instances the relationship is a reciprocal one.

Peer relationships contribute significantly to psychosocial adjustment. Modeling and coaching procedures have often been successfully employed to facilitate adaptive social behaviors through improved peer relationships. With the notable exception of Gresham and Nagle (1980), who worked with third and fourth graders, most studies of social skills training in the classroom have either used much younger children or employed analogue dependent measures. A recent multiple-measure study by La Greca and Santagrossi (1980) points to the value of group social skills training in the elementary school classroom. Thelen, Fry, Fehrenbach, and Frantschi (1979) stress the value of multiple measures in outcome studies of social skills training.

One might expect the development of effective peer relations to feature prominently in most school programs. Howeer, as Hargrave and Hargrave (1979) note, this is not so. Recognizing this deficit, the Hargraves designed a study to investigate the effects of incorporating a preadolescence socialization group into the normal school program. An additional concern was the feasibility of teachers functioning as temporary group therapists. The encouraging results also yielded one serendipitous finding which warrants investigation. Although the focus was on improving general social skills, the major change (at least as perceived by the teachers) was an increase in classroom adjustment.

Finally, in our discussion of social skills training within the normal classroom, we draw attention to a large-scale five-year study of a group-oriented social skills training program by Filipczak, Archer, and Friedman (1980). The PREP (Preparation through Responsive

Educational Programs) project is a multifaceted education and training program for students in public junior high and middle schools who demonstrate sizable academic or social deficits. Working within the regular classroom, the curriculum consists of over 200 instructional units. The core unit focuses on behavioral management skills for students, family living, careers, and study skills. Additional units cover decision making, verbal and nonverbal communication, drug facts, teenagers' rights and responsibilities under the law, and how to observe and report behavior.

It is understandable that such an ambitious program encountered many problems, both of a methodological and sociological nature. (See Filipczak, Friedman, & Reese, 1979, for a more detailed description of the experimental design and the measures used on a year-by-year basis.) There were always specific students, teachers, or parents more than willing to complain about the nature of specific content materials or programs. An additional problem was the need to tailor extracurricular examples of interpersonal behavior to the particular sociocultural milieu. But despite all limitations, the PREP training model does succeed in demonstrating beyond refute that a social skills curriculum can be generally well received, implemented, and measured effectively in a public school system on a cost-effective basis.

Social Skills Training and the Handicapped Child

Public Law 94-142 has mandated special educators to provide handicapped children with free, appropriate education in an environment that is as nonrestrictive as possible. Most agencies take this to mean that exceptional students are to be mainstreamed into regular classrooms to the maximum extent possible. The underlying assumption is that physical placement of handicapped children in the presence of their nonhandicapped peers will somehow automatically result in increased mutual social interaction and social acceptance between the two groups. But as Gresham (in press-b) notes, the research data suggest otherwise. Handicapped children are poorly accepted by their nonhandicapped peers, they do not automatically emulate or interact with them, and they do not acquire social skills by vicarious observation of their nonhandicapped peers. To place handicapped children in the regular classroom without providing them with the necessary social skills is to invite increased social isolation and an even more restrictive social environment. An alternative approach is for handicapped children to be taught the requisite social skills for effective social interaction and peer acceptance. To this end, Gresham (in press-a) suggests a variety of social skills curricula for use by both special and regular education teachers.

Gresham (in press-a) reviews the literature pertaining to social skills training in handicapped children in detail. Despite the "usual" methodological deficits and the lack of any coherent model of social skills training, the results are moderately encouraging. What we need to know now is what social skills, for which types of handicaps, in which settings, results in what predictable effects with which non-handicapped groups. Additionally, we do not have adequate evidence concerning the impact of social skills training on "socially valid" measures of social competence. By way of a beginning, Cartledge and Milburn (1980) document the development and application of social skills training programs to a variety of deviant as well as normal populations, Farkas (1981) reminds us of the special social skills needs of sensory-deprived children such as the blind, and Elder, Edelstein, and Narick (1979) report the successful use of social skills training with psychiatric hospitalized adolescents.

Finally, we draw attention to social skills training with juvenile delinquents. The treatment of juvenile offenders through institutionalization and probation is disappointing. Community behavior modification programs, parent training in contingency management, negotiation tactics, and contracting skills training for the families have all been tried and found wanting. Getting parents to participate in such programs is usually a major problem at the onset (Gross, Brigham, Hopper, & Bologna, 1980). And once again, we know remarkably little about the characteristics of those delinquents who respond favorably to social skills training. Ollendick and Elliott (1978) found internally oriented delinquents to be more compliant and ready for discharge in a shorter period of time than their externally oriented counterparts. At one-year follow-up, the internally oriented delinquents had a 26% recidivism rate, contrasted with 58% for the externally oriented. The externally oriented delinquents evidenced a "near absence" of basic interpersonal skills. Although Ollendick and Hersen (1979) later demonstrated the value of this approach in the treatment of incarcerated juvenile delinquents, its general utility remains to be seen.

CHILD ABUSE AND NEGLECT

The Parameters of Child Abuse

The reported tenfold increase in child abuse during the last decade reflects better reporting as well as greater incidence. In 1973, Light estimated a national annual incidence of 200,000 to 500,000. By 1979,

Straus, Gelles, and Steinmetz revised this figure upward to an awesome 1.4–1.9 million. The journal *Child Abuse and Neglect* is in its seventh year of publication. The first International Congress on Child Abuse and Neglect was convened in 1976 and 1981 saw the fifth meeting in the United States of the National Conference on Child Abuse and Neglect. The National Center on Child Abuse and Neglect of the Department of Health and Human Services is now firmly established and funds many projects (e.g., Felt, Montes, Irueste-Montes, & Eichengreen, 1981). Recent years have also witnessed numerous books and reviews of child abuse (e.g., *Four Perspectives on the Status of Child Abuse and Neglect Research*, 1975; Friedman, 1975; Green, 1978; Helfer & Kempe, 1974; Parke & Collmer, 1975; Williams & Money, 1980).

Of the several attempts to provide a strategy of behavioral assessment, Friedman, Sandler, Hernandez, and Wolfe (1981) probably provide the most comprehensive and practical. Direct observation is rarely possible, and serious inferential difficulties are presented by the measurement of frequently occurring behaviors presumed to bear some discernible relationship with the problem behavior (Wolfe, Sandler, & Kaufman, in press). Situation-specific self-report measures may also be utilized to supplement observational data. Other appropriate strategies include the collateral report of changes in attitude, perceptions, knowledge, and skills in situation-specific child-rearing functions.

Data which define the characteristics of abusing parents or parent surrogates, the children themselves, and the situations in which they occur are beginning to accumulate. For example, children who are exposed to overly punitive parenting models are more likely to abuse their own children (Steele & Pollock, 1974; Straus, Gelles, & Steinmetz, 1979). Interest is shifting from abusive parents toward functional analyses of family interactions (Burgess, 1979; Friedman, Sandler, Hernandez, & Wolfe, 1981; George & Main, 1980; Sandler, Van Dercar, & Milhoan, 1978). Social isolation of mother and child may be contributing to certain child abuse situations (McAuley, 1980). Abusing parents tend to be unmotivated, overtly hostile to the suggestion that they may suffer from emotional difficulties, and cooperative only because there is little or no alternative. They also tend to exhibit a stubborn tendency to repeat in the therapeutic situation their frustrating and humiliating interactions with their own parents and spouses. Under these circumstances, it is not surprising that, despite the best of intentions and insight, negative attitudes and feelings are sometimes elicited in those who attempt to treat these parents (Green, 1978).

Then there are the characteristics of abused children. While we concur that a functional analysis of specific contingencies is of greater significance than any generality about so-called personality structure, *behavioral* observations of such children do report them to exhibit tendencies toward manifest stubbornness, unresponsivity, negativism, and depression (Johnson & Morse, 1978). According to Galdston (1965), they are often fearful, apathetic, and unappealing, with a blunted appetite for food and human contact. But which is cause and which is effect in any particular case is another matter.

Dubanoski, Evans, and Higuchi (1978) offer a "set of behavioral propositions" for the investigation of the circumstances whereby specific acts of physical abuse become more probable. They suggest measures to define operationally the factors related to abusive incidents such that individual cases of abuse can be objectively analyzed and the propositions rigorously tested, but once again sketch little more than a blueprint for the future. In terms of immediately applicable guidelines, their propositions are of limited valued.

The Treatment of Child Abuse

Once child abuse occurs, it tends to be maintained by a lack of knowledge about children and parenting and by mounting feelings of self-contempt and unworthiness. Removal of the child, if this becomes unavoidable, is therefore but one facet of the therapeutic strategy. Within this context, Otto and Smith's (1980) cognitive–behavioral model utilizes the group process, in addition to cognitive restructuring and other behavioral accoutrements, to provide the necessary support system for building self-esteem and healthier family relationships. Parents alone are unlikely to receive steady home support for contemplated behavior change. Spouse and siblings tend to react to the abusive behavior by manipulation followed by guilt. For these reasons, though attempting to stop abusive behavior might seem a commendable first step, the family is likely to experience it as upsetting and respond accordingly.

Several studies of parent training programs for child abusers have recently been reported (e.g., Crozier & Katz, 1979; Mastria, Mastria, & Harkins, 1979). In most intances, formidable practical difficulties lead to serious methodological flaws. The one exception is a new study by Wolfe, Sandler, and Kaufman (in press) which draws attention to the need to incorporate individual socioeconomic determinants into the overall group program. As in other investigations, their abusive parents suffered from a learning, or perhaps performance, deficit with respect to child management skills (see also Denicola & Sandler, 1980; Sandler, Van Dercar, & Milhoan, 1978). What does seem to have been learned is an escalation toward abuse based upon reciprocally destructive parent–child interactions (Mulhern & Passman, 1979). What is less clear are the contingencies which prevent the large majority of problem families in our society with similar social problems from degenerating into abuse.

Abusive parents may prefer to view themselves, and be viewed, as uninformed or misinformed rather than pathological. Ambrose, Hazzard, and Haworth (1980) present their eight-week program to parents as educational. The curriculum consists of four consecutive models: child development, teaching skills, behavior problems management, and anger control. Each model builds upon input from preceding models and a variety of methods is used to present group content. These include didactic questioning, modeling, role playing, video presentation, group discussion, and problem solving. Furthermore, parents are given weekly homework assignments which involve putting behavioral principles discussed "in class" into action in the home. While seemingly effective, it is important to note that their subjects were probably not typical of abusive parents and that, in any event, no long-term outcome data are reported.

While such a program is cost-effective and seemingly of value in bringing about short-term changes in cognitive behavior, appropriate and controlled empirical assessment is lacking. In view of the potential advantages of such a program, it is to be hoped that appropriate control and outcome evaluation will be conducted in the coming years.

AUTISM

Concepts and Issues

There is still no generally accepted operational definition of early infantile autism, and its etiology remains unclear (Margolies, 1981). Although there is a recognizable cluster of syndromes manifest in the predominantly male majority of children with this disorder (Ross & Pelham, 1981), not all autistic children are likely to evidence all the symptoms (Schreibman & Koegel, 1981). Psychodynamic, biochemical, neurological, and behavioral formulations have all been advanced, examined, and found wanting in various respects. The three primary contenders—psychoanalytic, sensory deficit, and behavioral—have recently been compared and contrasted by Egel, Koegel, and Schreibman (1980). Even though the behavioral literature is by far the most sophisticated methodologically, serious deficits are still evident. More to the point, in practice the cost–benefit ratio in terms of progress obtained for energy expended is disadvantageous. In most instances, the repertoire of the treated child approximates grossly, imperfectly, and inconsistently at best those of normal children. For recent, primarily behavioral, reviews see Lovaas, Ackerman, and Tauoman (1982); Lovaas, Young, and Newsom (1978); Ross and Pelham (1981); Rutter and Schopler (1978); Schreibman, Koegel, Charlop, and Egel (in press); and Schreibman and Mills (in press).

A popular behavioral overview for teachers and special educators is provided by Dunlap, Koegel, and Egel (1979). For educational researchers, this material is renewed in more scholarly fashion by Egel, Koegel, and Schreibman (1980). Parents seeking an introduction to early childhood autism which demystifies without oversimplifying should read Morgan (1981). At the more professional level, in a text which could be read with benefit by parents and professionals alike, DeMyer (1979) traces the problems faced by the family of an autistic child from infancy through adolescence and adulthood. Neither dismissing nor glorifying the role of the parent, DeMyer clearly articulates what it means to be the parent of such a child. Most importantly, she refutes, with data, the still-voiced claim that these parents are somehow "to blame" for their children's disease. Parents of autistic children are far from the uncaring or unresponsive individuals they are sometimes reported to be. Many, in fact, devote so much time to their autistic children that other aspects of family life suffer. Confused and bewildered by a multitude of problems, they are desperately in need of the advice and support that DeMyer provides.

Koegel, Gluhn, and Nieminen (1978) showed that, without special training, adults are not likely to be effective teachers of their own autistic children. Mere observation of a trained therapist is not effective since the adult observer can then only teach the specific skills observed. Most autistic children can acquire at least the rudiments of communicative speech, and parents are in an ideal position to facilitate the generalization of their children's newly acquired skill. As Harris, Wolchik, and Weitz (1981) demonstrate, such generalization is more likely to occur when the "teacher" plays a major role in the child's experiences than when speech is taught in a special setting by a special person not part of the daily routine. Unfortunately, although gains were maintained at one-year follow-up, despite the high motivation of the parents their well-controlled study provided no evidence of significant improvement beyond that achieved at the end of training. But even with this limitation, home training offers many cost–benefit advantages in addition to improvements in parent morale (Luiselli, 1980a).

Until recently, most autistic children had to be institutionalized before reaching the age of 12. As a result of recent legislation, classrooms for autistic children in the United States are mandated by law. However, as Schreibman, Koegel, Charlop, and Egel (in press) note, mandating such classrooms and bringing them into existence do not necessarily ensure quality. To develop an effective classroom program for autistic children, two skills must be established: the ability to learn in a large group and the ability to work on an individual task without constant teacher supervision. Behaviors acquired in a one-to-one situation often fail to generalize to the group setting. Koegel and Rincover (1974) found that individually taught autistic children perform more poorly when even one other child is added. Nevertheless, the shaping procedure developed by these investigators led eventually to the design of classroom procedures specifically appropriate to the autistic child (see also Meyers & Craighead, 1979). The ultimate goal, of course, is the progression of the child into the normal classroom (Russo & Koegel, 1977) but this is easier said than done.

There are many autistic children who, for a variety of reasons, cannot live in their natural homes. Parental age, separation, mental illness, economic factors, or the presence of other children sometimes intercede. For whatever reasons, many autistic children have to be institutionalized, and this leads to a different set of problems. Behaviors appropriate to a hospital rarely facilitate the rehabilitation process. Institutionalization creates psychological as well as geographical distance between child and parent. To cope with such problems, Lovaas and his associates evolved the concept of community-focused "Teaching Homes," based on the successful Achievement Place model for the treatment of delinquents (see Schreibman, Koegel, Charlop, & Egel, in press).

New Behaviorally Related Developments

Behavioral researchers are continually endeavoring to understand the variables that might influence generalization in order thereby to develop procedures for its promotion. Numerous authors suggest that severely disturbed children may be bound to the specific physical elements of the stimulus situation and consequently become restricted in their abilities to transfer learning from one situation to another. Recent attention has been directed toward the issue of stimulus overselectivity and the effects that this pattern of responding might have on both generalization and learning (Koegel, Egel, & Williams, 1980; Lovaas & Koegel, 1979). Treatment gains do not generalize from school or home automatically and it is important to train in a variety of physical locations (Handleman, 1979, 1980).

Taken together, such investigations point to the beginning of an appropriate technology for programming stimulus and response generalization over time and setting. The behavioral treatment of autism is customarily evaluated in terms of specific, objectively measured targets.

But with Schreibman, Koegel, Charlop, and Egel (in press), one may justly ask what these changes mean in terms of more global recognition of progress. Can objective measures of improvement be correlated with subjective judgments of change as provided by naive observers? Does the child "look" more normal or more "likable"? According to data accumulated by Mills, Burke, Schreibman, and Koegel (1979), there is a strong relationship between the two types of measures. This is encouraging.

Autistic children tend to be unmotivated. They respond less or with much longer latencies to environmental stimuli than normal children. Typically, they fail to explore new environments, to test alternative responses, or even to seek out food and comfort not readily available. They show little curiosity or drive in any but the most mundane portions of their environments. Autistic children are particularly lacking in motivation for learning. One way to increase motivation is to design procedures which prompt responding until the task is successfully completed (Dunlap & Koegel, 1980; Koegel & Egel, 1979).

Learned helplessness is the label given by Seligman and his associates to the behaviors that result from the recognition that responding and reinforcement are independent (Miller & Seligman, 1975). According to Koegel and Egel (1979), the behavior of subjects in the learned helplessness studies was strikingly similar to that reported in their investigations. Certainly, both research programs seem to generate similar treatment strategies. For Seligman, a treatment procedure designed to force exposure to the response–reinforcement contingency would correct the maladaptive behaviors associated with learned helplessness. Similarly, the treatment procedures used by Koegel and Egel were designed to force their autistic children to experience a response–reinforcement contingency for perseverance.

It is tempting, as with schizophrenia, to believe that the autistic child is going to improve if only the magic key can be found. After all, the schizophrenic child may once have been normal and could be normal again, and so it is to be with autism! The data offer no encouragement for this fantasy. No "breakthrough," behavioral or otherwise, is imminent. What we do have is the beginning of a viable behavioral technology for slow, painstaking improvement.

MENTAL RETARDATION

Whether we agree or not, the law (PL 94-142) asserts that, without exception, all children are educable. In calling for free "appropriate education for every child and youth," it challenges long-held assumptions about the capabilities of persons with severe mental disabilities, the responsibilities of the public education system, the nature of the educative process, the limits of habilitation technology, and prevailing community feelings. A recent issue of the journal *Analysis and Intervention in Developmental Disabilities* is devoted exclusively to the pros and cons involved but no resolution is as yet in sight or likely for a while (Kauffman, 1981).

Data educed by Ellis (1979) fail to support the contention that all clients can benefit from formal training. Hawkins (1981) argues that education for severely retarded children should be home-oriented and Wetherby and Baumeister (1981) stress training in adaptive behavior. As Bailey (1981) puts it,

> Our enthusiasm to train greatly exceeds our expertise, and at this point we need to recognize the place of "stimulation programming" with the unresponsive profound (profoundly disturbed) individual. Lack of a (well) functioning central nervous system is a limiting condition of habilitation, and our resources to provide such training are also severely limited. It is time to recognize these limiting conditions and to adjust our expectations accordingly. Stimulation programming, as opposed to teaching programming is, I believe, most appropriate with these clients and this shift in emphasis represents an advance in our understanding of the right-to-treatment model. (parenthetic words added)

If formal learning is to occur, highly instructable students must somehow learn to sustain attention to school-related materials and activities. Unfortunately, while the teacher is expected to cope with the problem, he or she is not provided with the tactical wherewithal, and no demonstrably effective solution to this dilemma seems to be in the offing. The self-instructional package of Burgio, Whitman, and Johnson (1980) is geared toward increased attending behavior in a training situation followed by generalization to one-to-one and classroom situations. But as yet the data are equivocal and the methodology of this and related studies questionable (see also Friedling & O'Leary, 1979).

Institutions for the mentally handicapped are notoriously austere and, despite a lack of empirical data, it would seem reasonable to assume that this has adverse effects upon the development of such children. One way to achieve an enriched environment is through an active training program. Unfortunately, in many instances, implementation of such programs requires effort and financial resources beyond both the ability and the inclinations of those who make the decisions (Horner, 1980).

Another regrettable consequence of institutionalization for profoundly handicapped young people is the minimal contact which these children have with their parents. To this end, Shoemaker and Reid (1980) describe a potentially promising program geared to increasing such contacts. The program includes structured special activities for parental involvement on the institutional grounds, the encouragement of parental attendance rather than telephone calls, and support for attendance via personal interactions and letters. Mentally handicapped children, and other profoundly handicapped institutionalized individuals for that matter, do not have to remain alienated from parents and meaningful others in their lives.

RECENT DEVELOPMENTS IN HYPERACTIVITY

Hyperactivity is reviewed in detail by Brownell in Chapter 5. For additional specifically behavioral reviews see Dubey (in press); Gittelman (1979); Kauffman and Hallahan (1979); Lahey, Delamater, and Kupfer (1981); Ross and Pelham (1981); and Whalen and Henker (1980). Dubey and Kaufman's (1978, 1979) documentation of their extensive experience in the development of behavioral training programs for parents of hyperactive (HA) children also merits attention.

It is of interest to observe how treatment strategies closely follow notions about etiology. For example, a medical orientation leads to the supposition that hyperactivity is a disease entity resulting from some form of minimal brain damage and should be treated accordingly. Another spin-off from the medical model is the use of medication in the treatment of hyperactivity. Brownell's chapter reviews the evidence with respect to utility. Here, we draw attention to a recent observation by O'Leary (1980) which speaks for itself: "The burgeoning number of children diagnosed as hyperactive has been at least partly spurred by the pharmaceutical industries." Further, there are those who view disorders in perception as primarily responsible for hyperactivity and thereby focus upon improving academic performance by treatment of the presumed underlying perceptual dysfunction. More recent theories stress cognitive and attentional factors in hyperactivity, and elaborate methods for investigation have been developed (e.g., Firestone & Martin, 1979). In 1972 Winett and Winkler wrote a much-quoted paper which criticized procedures whose apparent goal was the production of a model child—silent, attentive, and docile. Sparked by such considerations, behavior therapists now tend to think in terms of academic performance as the major target for intervention. Backman and Firestone (1979) believe that behavior therapy and medication modify different aspects of HA behavior and that this accounts for many of the observed differences in the effects of the two treatment modalities. In any event, effective treatment programs require a range of procedures such as medication, behavior therapy, family counseling, parent training, and educational intervention in a mixture and under circumstances as yet undetermined.

The rest of this section will consider selected aspects of the hyperactivity literature from the above perspectives. Overlap with the material presented by Brownell will be reduced to an unavoidable minimum.

Self-management is a topic closely related to the subject matter of Chapter 4. Self-instruction involves "higher-order" variables such as cognitive style, approach to the task, and information processing, and "lower-order" behaviors through self-monitoring and self-reward. With HA children in particular, the requisite procedures would seem to be difficult to implement and to require repeated training sessions as well as persistence on the part of both child and trainer. Furthermore, generalization across both task and time have been consistently weak (Cameron & Robinson, 1980; Lahey, Delamater, & Kupfer, 1981). Self-instructional training appears to influence the impulsive behavior of children on laboratory tasks, but the extent to which it attributes to academic improvement is less certain. Friedling and O'Leary (1979) failed to find any evidence for the utility of self-instructional training with HA children on such tasks. As O'Leary (1980) notes, there is a critical need for replication with follow-up for at least 12 months. For the present, we fail to discern any significant advances in the application of self-management principles in the treatment of the HA child.

Somewhat more encouraging, there are a variety of as yet not systematically explored "behaviorally compatible" interventions on the horizon. Lahey, Delamater, and Kupfer (1981) draw attention to the numerous and potentially rewarding psychophysiological studies of the autonomic correlates of hyperactivity currently in progress. The "immature" cortical functioning of many HA children is believed responsible for the selective attention deficits held to underlie their learning and activity problems. Direct modification of these inferred attentional deficits usually involves some form of biofeedback training.

To reduce motor activity in HA children, Schulman, Stevens, and Kupst (1977) invented the biomotometer. A small plastic box worn at the waist measures activity and provides simultaneous auditory feedback to the HA child. The child monitors his or her own activity level through a crystal earphone connected to an adjustable audiofeedback circuit inside the apparatus. When an agreed number of activity counts are exceeded during a preset time interval a tone is provided through the earphone. Activity level was shown by these authors to increase in free-play settings and decrease within the classroom. In a later study, Schulman, Suran, Stevens, and Kupst (1979) successfully combined the use of the biomotometer and material reinforcers to reduce the activity levels of HA children within the classroom.

Most theories of hyperactivity assume that this is a disorder of overstimulation and that treatment necessitates a reduction in environmental input. Zentall (1975) comes to a quite different conclusion. HA behavior may result from a homeostatic mechanism that functions to increase stimulation for a child who is experiencing *insufficient* sensory stimulation. Both medication and behavior therapy are effective, argues Zentall, to the extent that they epitomize sensory input and homeostatic equilibrium (Zentall, 1980; Zentall & Shaw, 1980). HA children are actually underaroused and their repetitive attention-demanding behavior in low-stimulation environments really represents stimulation-seeking activity. When provided with sufficient stimulation, they no longer need to create their own. Behavior becomes calm and performance improves. As yet, due primarily to a paucity of data, conclusions based upon comparative studies and follow-up are of limited value. We await further investigation of this potentially promising new direction.

Finally, we draw attention to a paper which deserves much wider publicity than it will probably receive. Pollack and Gittelman (in press) note that, while the hyperactivity literature is extensive, reports about everyday difficulties are usually omitted. The reader is led to anticipate regular, smooth process with little variation in the practicalities of treatment. As Pollack and Gittelman caution, this is misleading. Their very readable paper outlines common obstacles encountered in the behavioral treatment of HA children: parental attitudes, marital conflict, teacher resistance, school obstructiveness, lack of space, and more. Frank discussion of such matters is rare. We hope it will lead to a more realistic alliance between therapist, parent, and teacher.

USE AND ABUSE OF PUNISHMENT: A PERSPECTIVE

General Issues

Technically, punishment is defined as a response-suppressing procedure that may involve the delivery of an aversive stimulus or a response-weakening procedure whereby a stimulus is removed or postponed contingent upon the omission of a specific response. The latter procedures tend to go under the general term of "time out from positive reinforcement" or, more simply, "time out" (Azrin & Holz, 1966).

A continuous schedule of a relatively intense punishment stimulus seems more likely to be effective. But it would be unwise to proceed on the assumption that this is always so. For example, punishment applied on an intermittent rather than a continuous basis could offer certain advantages in terms of staff time required, reduced discomfort for the child, and the decreased amount of time in which the child is removed from the academic environment. While cautioning against the utilization of punishment at all, except as a last resort, Luiselli and Townsend (cited by Marholin, Luiselli, & Townsend, 1980) advocate the use of intermittent rather than continuous punishment whenever possible. However, they were able to locate only five studies which adequately compared the effects of continuous and intermittent punishment in applied settings. Here, we focus upon three topics, all relevant to the use of punishment in both clinic and classroom: punishment in the treatment of self-injurious behavior; overcorrection; and vicarious punishment.

Self-Injurious Behavior

In what may be the first experimental demonstration that self-injurious behavior (SIB) can be eliminated by operant means, Carr and McDowell (1980) successfully treated the self-injurious scratching behavior of a normal 10-year-old child by a combination of time out for scratching plus tangible reinforcement for reduction in the number of body sores. A reversal design with nine-month follow-up was used to demonstrate the efficacy of treatment.

In their review of SIB in children, Picker, Poling, and Parker (1979) draw attention to the diversity of disorders and punishing stimuli encountered in the SIB literature. While the data are complex and at times in conflict, it seems well established that no other form of treatment for SIB is likely to be more lasting than electric shock. There are, however, numerous limiting constraints. The suppressive effects may be restricted to the environment in which the shock is delivered; that is, SIB may come under the control of discriminative stimuli associated with the delivery of the shock. This may be corrected by arranging for the treatments to be in effect across a variety of times, administering individuals and settings. A more difficult problem is that of maintenance. Long-term follow-up studies are the exception rather than the rule and, in any event, such data as do exist are inconsistent. The suppressive effects of punishment seem more likely to endure when the child is reinforced for appropriate behavior during and after exposure to punishment. In planning the use of electric shock the possibility of side effects, such as aggression or avoidance of those delivering the shock, and the locale where shocks are delivered must be considered. Of equal importance are ethical and legal considerations. No matter how convincingly ends seem to justify means, inflicting severe pain on a child is both abject and illegal. The complex scientific, professional, and ethical issues involved in the use of aversive stimuli in therapy have been discussed at length in previous volumes in this series and, doubtless, will continue to be. There is no facile solution.

Time out can be an effective procedure in the treatment of SIB (Frankel & Simmons, 1976). However, in practice, certain factors restrict its utility. First, time out controls SIB slowly, with extended treatments being required. During this time, severe injury might occur. Second, the use of time out makes considerable staff demands in terms of time, vigilance, and facilities. Third, under certain circumstances time out could serve as a positive reinforcer. Fourth, even though time out is not directly aversive, it is restrictive and therefore has to be deployed with full awareness of possible ethical and legal constraints.

To sum up: Positive punishment should be utilized in the treatment of SIB only after consideration of all circumstances, alternatives, and limiting factors. If at all possible, negative punishment procedures should be utilized rather than positive, preferably as part of a total therapeutic program and even then only with due caution and as a last resort.

Overcorrection

In 1972, Foxx and Azrin introduced overcorrection (OC) as a response-deceleration technique that combined educative and suppressive treatment components with the goal of punishing deviant behavior while simultaneously providing training in more adaptive forms of response. Restitutional OC requires the person to return the environment to a condition better than that which existed prior to the inappropriate behavior, whereas positive practice OC requires the practice of correct, topographically similar behaviors contingent upon the inappropriate behavior (Foxx & Martin, 1975; Matson, Ollendick, & Martin, 1979).

Since 1950 over 75 reports of the use of OC have appeared (Luiselli, 1980b). However, as Marholin, Luiselli, and Townsend (1980) note, neither theory not procedure is as straightforward and well established as its advocates would have us believe (see also previous volumes in this series). In 1972, Foxx and Azrin issued the following directives: OC should be (1) directly related to the misbehavior, (2) applied immediately following the misbehavior, (3) extended in duration, and (4) applied in an "active, effortful manner." The reasons for topographically matching OC with the misbehavior is to reeducate the offender. Marholin et al. conclude that the educative function of OC is not as Foxx and Azrin suggest. The OC need not be directly related to the misbehavior.

And even if OC is matched topographically to the target behavior, the goal of achieving independent contingent control over responding is not necessary for suppression to occur.

Immediate rather than delayed application of OC is based on the principle that reinforcement procedures are most effective when they immediately follow the behavior. But delayed application can also be effective (Bornstein, Hamilton, & Quevillon, 1977; Schwartz & Hawkins, 1970). They found only one comparative study of the effects of immediate and delayed application (Azrin & Powers, 1975). Both conditions were equally effective. Foxx and Azrin (1972) suggest that OC should be extended in duration, as long as 30 minutes. Marholin *et al.* conclude that OC can be effective when performed for periods as short as 30 seconds or as long as two hours. Finally, exactly what constitutes application in an "active, effective manner" and how this can be maintained and measured in both subject and therapist remain unanswered questions.

While both positive and negative side effects have been reported at various times, the evidence conflicts with respect to their nature and circumstances of occurrence. Whether these side effects are unique to OC or common to punishment per se remains unknown. With certain autistic children, there is some reason to believe that positive side effects such as appropriate smiling can occur. Which of the two OC procedures to employ—or both or neither—and the circumstances determining such a decision are also unknown at this time (Marholin *et al.*, 1980; Matson, Horne, Ollendick, & Ollendick, 1980). Follow-up data are equally equivocal (e.g., Matson, Ollendick, & Martin, 1979).

Interestingly enough, self-reports indicate that some children actually prefer OC to other forms of punishment (Matson, Horne, Ollendick, & Ollendick, 1979). There is by now mounting evidence to suggest that OC, of whatever variety, is effective in the rapid elimination of disruptive behaviors in relatively normal children. In one study reported by Matson, Stephens, and Horne (1978), OC was found to be a more effective treatment of minor disruptive behavior in normal nursery school children than extinction–reinforcement. Trainers preferred extinction–reinforcements because the process is more familiar, easier to learn, and therefore requires less effort on their part. Both treatments were considered feasible and effective, and recommended for future use. Interestingly enough, the children who were treated did not consider either method as particularly unpleasant and preferred it to such punishments as time out, being yelled at, or being spanked. The children also reported that the treatments did not make them dislike either themselves or the trainers.

The effects of many behavioral treatment programs tend to be specific to the responses treated, the individuals doing the treatment, and the settings in which the treatment is applied. When treatment is discontinued, it is not uncommon for behavioral frequencies to return to baseline levels. This is especially true of OC. While specificity is desirable for research, from the clinical perspective this is of little value to the client.

Cross-setting generality research can be divided into two categories: implementation of OC in controlled treatment settings to determine whether the effects of treatment generalize to other settings; and the monitoring of behavior in two or more settings or the application of OC in a multiple-baseline across-settings design. According to Marholin et al., when cross-setting generalization is reported, it appears to be influenced by the similarities between treatment and nontreatment environments. Relatively few studies have assessed the generalization effects of OC across behavior but here too generalization appears to be the exception rather than the rule.

Follow-up reports on the suppressive effects of OC range from one month to one year. The studies surveyed by Marholin et al. fall into three general categories: those in which OC reduced responding to zero or near-zero levels and responding did not recover over time even in the absence of the OC contingency; those in which suppressed responding was accompanied by continued use of OC; and those in which suppressed responding was maintained by a verbal warning established as a conditioned aversive stimulus during OC treatment. Here again, the findings are highly equivocal. In a recent study by Matson, Ollendick, and Martin (1979), eight chronic institutionalized patients successfully treated with response-contingent OC for self-stimulatory behavior were reexamined one year later. For two of the subjects, response suppression was maintained. For the other six subjects, the frequency of self-stimulatory behaviors approached pretreatment rates.

To facilitate generalization and maintenance, Marholin et al. advocate application of treatment over a wide variety of stimulus conditions. Ideally, OC should be applied in as many settings and at as many times of the day as possible, whenever or wherever the target behavior might occur. The number of practitioners who apply OC should also be maximized. Another strategy is to combine verbal stimuli with administration of OC in the hope that they can later be used as CS to help maintain low rates of responding. This is especially effective when OC programs employ lengthy procedures which cannot readily be expanded to the natural environment. A final strategy noted by Marholin et al. is to develop or concurrently increase the incidences of certain behaviors that are likely to be reinforced in the natural environment. By and large, Marholin et al. conclude that OC is an effective procedure for reducing and eliminating a wide range of maladaptive behaviors in both normal and disturbed children.

Luiselli's advice to the practitioner is as follows: Apply the procedure immediately following each occurrence of the target response. Initial application should be for three to four minutes and subsequently modified as the situation dictates. If two or more behaviors are targeted, try to apply an OC procedure topographically related to each behavior. Finally, practitioners should not expect positive effects to speed vicariously to those children who merely observe the intervention. Practitioners must be prepared to apply OC directly to each child concerned and, in view of the limited findings with respect to maintenance, to reapply OC should a previously suppressed problem behavior reappear.

Vicarious Punishment

Unlike vicarious reinforcement, vicarious punishment is an "iffy" phenomenon which has received little attention outside the laboratory and hardly any in the classroom. This, in itself, is curious since teachers often justify punishment on the basis of its deterrent effects on others. As Kazdin (1981b) observes, opportunities for vicarious classroom reinforcement or punishment are great because all children are in a position to observe and react to the consequences in one way or another. To neglect vicarious processes in the classroom can create or exacerbate existing problems in a complex manner which resists evaluation.

Kazdin is able to locate only two studies of vicarious punishment. The first, by Kounin and Gump (1958), was a naturalistic investigation of 26 kindergarten classes designed to evaluate the effects of reprimands delivered to selected children on the behaviors of their peers. In general, teacher punishment of one child tended to influence the behavior of other children, a phenomenon which the authors term a "ripple effect." However, this was an uncontrolled investigation and it is difficult to rule out extraneous influences that may have had a direct impact on the nontarget children. Then, in 1979, Wilson, Robertson, Herlong, and Haynes utilized time out to suppress aggressive behavior in a 5-year-old boy. Of particular interest is the fact that, even though one of the peers was included in the time-out contingency, the aggressive acts of the child's classmates also decreased.

CONCLUSIONS

Despite numerous methodological problems and "unfinished business," child behavior therapy is alive, well, and living lustily in the domain of behavioral science. As expected, emerging issues and new developments parallel those in behavior therapy at large. Horizons are expanding, data are being accumulated, and theory is struggling hard to make practice scientifically respectable. The extent to which practitioners truly practice what they preach still remains an open question. The merging integration of data derived from related disciplines and other ways of viewing data, such as systems theory and community psychology, without loss of the essential "behavioral approach" is particularly encouraging. No longer are child behavior therapists throwing out the baby with the proverbial bath water. We hope to chronicle this progress further in future volumes in this series.

CHAPTER

8

CLINICAL ISSUES AND STRATEGIES IN THE PRACTICE OF BEHAVIOR THERAPY

G. TERENCE WILSON

INTRODUCTION

A striking impression that one gains from surveying the varied clinical practice of behavior therapy is its ambitious scope. Breadth and boldness characterize the applications of behavioral methods to diverse problems in clinical psychology and psychiatry, community psychology, education, and even medicine. These broad-ranging applications, varying in both success and sophistication, provide ample testimony to the inventiveness and optimism of behavior therapists. Clearly responding to Neal Miller's oft-quoted charge to his fellow biofeedbackers to be "bold in what they try," some behavior therapists have not always heeded Miller's further call to be "cautious in what they claim." Critical evaluation of the therapeutic efficacy of behavioral treatment methods is pursued in the preceding chapters in this volume and elsewhere (e.g., O'Leary & Wilson, in press; Rachman & Wilson, 1980). This chapter focuses on the application and practice of behavior therapy. These matters are closely related to issues raised and discussed at length in Chapter 1.

Another salient feature of contemporary behavior therapy is its vitality and rapid growth. Clinical strategies continue to evolve, becoming more sophisticated and complex. Existing methods are being modified and refined. Fewer new techniques[1] have been added in the

1. Unless one considers the increasingly widespread use of cognitive–behavioral procedures such as those of Beck's (1976) and others as "new."

past couple of years than previously, but innovative techniques are still being described (e.g., Marshall, 1979). The basic principles of classical and operant conditioning have been extended to new problems in enterprising and rewarding ways (e.g., Josephson & Rosen, 1980; Redd & Andresen, 1981). In the latter case, Redd and Andresen drew on their knowledge of the development and modification of conditioned aversive reactions to help alleviate chemotherapy-related nausea and vomiting in cancer patients. Their extension of behavioral techniques to the modification of what oncologists view as some of the most distressing side effects of chemotherapy is not only a singular therapeutic contribution but also a splendid example of interdisciplinary research in behavioral medicine. Parenthetically, the careful clinical documentation of anticipatory nausea as a powerful conditioned aversive reaction also has obvious theoretical importance (Seligman & Hager, 1972; Wilson & Davison, 1969). For the most part, such conditioned aversive reactions were linked directly to olfactory or gustatory stimuli. Nevertheless, Hacker (1981), a gynecologic oncologist, notes:

> Stimuli that elicit the nausea may vary and may include doctors and nurses. This can at times lead to social embarrassment. Our oncology nurse recalls an unexpected meeting in a grocery store with a chemotherapy patient who said, "The minute I laid eyes on you I wanted to vomit!" To what extend such conditioned aversion is related to compliance with cancer therapy is unknown, but would be of considerable interest. (p. 2)

Several major issues in the clinical practice of behavior therapy that have been addressed in this section in previous volumes of this *Annual Review* series continue to be important foci of consideration and controversy. Among these issues are the following: (1) the relationship between experimental research and clinical practice; (2) the possibility and desirability of any rapprochement between behavior therapy and alternative psychotherapeutic approaches; and (3) the nature and efficacy of Lazarus's (1977, 1981) multimodal therapy and its overlap with behavior therapy. The remainder of this chapter is devoted to an analysis of the foregoing issues, together with a discussion of such a hardy perennial as the therapeutic relationship.

EXPERIMENTAL RESEARCH AND CLINICAL PRACTICE: TAKING THE GAP

To a clinical psychologist, it often seems that not only are death and taxes always with us, but also discussions about the relationship between experimental research and clinical practice. One becomes inured to the invincible obstinacy of those fringe psychotherapists who deny or denigrate a scientific approach to the development and evaluation of treatment methods and hence have little knowledge of and still less interest in experimental psychology. One also becomes familiar with those more ready to bemoan the complexity of psychotherapy than to actually try to test the value of the concepts and methods of experimental psychology in clinical practice. More surprising is that many behavior therapists appear to concur with the view that a significant gap exists between research and practice even in behavior therapy. In his thoughtful and provocative Presidential Address to the Association for Advancement of Behavior Therapy (AABT), Barlow (1980) suggested:

> If you examine the behavior of practicing clinicians, few, if any, of our clinical procedures are guided by the scientific training we received. And despite the recent advances in behavioral assessment, I doubt if even a small minority of behavior therapists administer more than an occasional questionnaire or a short period of self-monitoring to determine the effectiveness of their interventions, an impression confirmed in recent surveys by Ford and Kendall (1979) and Swan and MacDonald (1978). (p. 323)

Assuming Barlow to be correct,[2] this conclusion is striking. More than any other treatment approach, behavior therapy, at least in principle, has been committed to integrating research and therapy within the context of the scientist–practitioner model of clinical training. What then are the reasons for this gap, and what are we to do about it?

The New Look Empirical Clinician?

Boldly, Barlow diagnoses the problem and discusses the cure. The main reason for the failure of research to influence the day-to-day functioning of clinical practitioners is said to be too great a reliance on the wrong experimental methodology or science, one that "emphasizes factorial designs, multivariate statistics, and the .05 level of probability. For these will never be used in the private office or clinic" (1980,

---

2. A survey of behavior therapists (actually members of the Association for Advancement of Behavior Therapy) by Wade, Baker, and Hartmann (1979) showed that in comparison to an earlier survey of clinical psychologists in 1977, behavior therapists reported devoting somewhat less time to therapy, more time to research, and approximately the same time to teaching. Wade et al. went on to conclude that "fears regarding a potential imbalance between clinical practice and research in clinical psychology are apparently not as applicable to behavior therapists as to clinicians in general" (p. 5). Nevertheless, Barlow's concern is not allayed by these findings. There is no indication from this survey that those respondents in practice are particularly influenced by research findings.

p. 323). Although Barlow is quick to acknowledge that between-groups experimental designs using inferential statistics have their place in research, his contention, shared by many other behavior therapists, is that group designs that emphasize average effects lose sight of the individual and discourage a searching analysis of treatment failures. His proposed solution? "A fine-grained analysis of an individual's behavior, or a series of individuals' behavior, with attention to technique building, repeated measurement, and social rather than statistical significance; and approach to science that in its very nature attends to our failures" (1980, p. 322). In short, through the wider use of single-case experimental designs, clinical practitioners will not only become more responsive to research evidence but also produce some of that evidence themselves.

Barlow goes on to argue that two recent developments might make this goal attainable. The first is the development of valid outcome measures and assessment techniques that can be easily adopted by the practitioner. The second is pressure from the federal government and society at large for all therapists to be accountable for the management of each case. This second factor is discussed later in this chapter. Our immediate attention is turned towards the dependent measures that the practitioner can use to carry out single-subject research.

The question of realistic dependent measures for clinical use is addressed by Nelson (1981) in her paper in the informative series of articles entitled *Empirical Practice and Realistic Research: New Opportunities for Clinicians*, edited by Barlow and published in the *Journal of Consulting and Clinical Psychology*. A variety of measures are discussed, including self-monitoring, self-ratings, card sorts, questionnaires, observations in the clinic, observations in the natural environment, physiological recordings, and behavioral indices. Nelson's conclusion is that "systematic measurement is possible with most, if not all, clients. Although the preparation and implementation of measurement procedures does require time and effort, similar measures can often be used with several clients, thereby eventually lessening the required effort" (p. 178).

In another paper from the same series on empirical clinical practice, Hayes (1981) asserts that the use of single-case experimental designs will do away with the schism between researcher and clinician. Practicing clinicians, he suggests, "may not be lacking a dedication to research, just tools for the task" (p. 193). Hayes then gives a most useful analysis of single-case experimental designs, or what he prefers to call time-series methodology, advancing the thesis that the "goodness of fit" between the logic and implementation of this time-series methodology and the clinical decision making of the therapist in individual cases "is remarkable." However, particularly conspicuous in this paper, directed to the practitioner, is the virtual absence of concrete (realistic) examples of actual therapy with a "real" client with a "real" problem. According to Hayes, the use of time-series methodology by practitioners could create a "true revolution in clinical psychology." He also raises the awesome spectre that a "flood of information could emerge from the many thousands of practicing clinicians. Where would it be put? Who would publish it? Would it be simple-minded research anyway?" (p. 209). Perhaps knowingly, these questions are left unanswered.

Although Hayes foresees revolutionary consequences attendant on the adoption of time-series methodology by practitioners armed with the realistic dependent measures described by Nelson (1981) and imbued with concern for accountability and respect for research, the issue is not new to this *Annual Review* series and the argument is not necessarily true. In the 1977 volume of this series, Franks and Wilson (pp. 176–178) took issue with the notion that the advent of single-case experimental designs would result in the merging of the role of the scientist and the practitioner. Those objections are very relevant to the current concept of the empirical clinician as described above.

To summarize, we argued that there were methodological, ethical, and practical problems to be contended with. Methodologically, completing well-controlled single-case experimental design studies that permit one to establish cause–effect relationships is usually as demanding and requires as much experimental control as more traditional group outcome research. This is not to say that on occasion the practitioner will be able to conduct a single-case experimental study with sufficient control to make causal analyses, but these are likely to be relatively rare.

Ethically, the problem is that the client be fully informed as to whether he or she is participating in a research project or receiving therapy. The therapist's activities must be identified as one or the other. If it is therapy that the client is receiving, many of the critical requirements of single-case experimental designs are difficult, if not impossible, to meet. In essence, all single-case experimental designs necessitate baseline observations, holding certain conditions constant at different times, and intervening selectively in a limited manner at any one point. This conflicts with the priority in any service delivery setting, which is to treat the client's problems in as effective and efficient a manner as possible. Clinically relevant change, produced at the least possible cost (in terms of time, effort, money, and emotional stress), is the goal of clinical practice. Identifying the determinants of behavior change is of little relevance to the therapist or the client in this setting. The latter is a scientific concern that need have no immediate bearing on the behavior of the practitioner. It must be admitted that Hayes's expert presentation of a variety of time-series designs goes well beyond the more obvious limitations of a simple reversal design and potentially provides the practitioner with increased flexibility. Nonetheless, the fundamental objection, we believe, still holds. Until specific clinical examples are reported, demonstrating the "goodness of fit" that Hayes refers to, the argument will not be substantially advanced.

On the practical side a number of difficulties are encountered by the practitioner who would complete single-case experimental research. Consider some of the characteristics of single-subject methodology. One is the observation of overt behavior. Behavior is assessed directly either in the situation of interest or in simulated circumstances where the behavior is sampled under laboratory conditions. Daily observations of this nature are usually reported. In 1977 we concluded that these demands "exceed the capabilities and resources of the practitioner." Neither Nelson's comprehensive coverage of dependent measures a practitioner might use, nor Hayes's argument appear to warrant any substantial revision of this conclusion.

To the methodological, ethical, and practical considerations we raised in 1977 must be added personal factors that make the merging of the roles of scientist and practitioner unlikely. One must agree with Strupp (1981), who in his commentary on the empirical clinician series in the *Journal of Consulting and Clinical Psychology*, offers the following observation:

> Research in psychotherapy has become a highly specialized and demanding discipline that is not easily mastered and calls for dedication and commitment of a rather special kind. By the same token, the personal and professional requirements for responsible clinical practice are equally stringent . . . as has often been pointed out, there are temperamental and philosophical differences that underscore the basic incompatibility of the two functions. (p. 217)

To argue that practitioners do not necessarily lack the interest in and dedication to research but simply the right "tools," is to misread a fundamental and critical issue in the field of clinical psychology. Anyone familiar with the mainstream of clinical psychology in the United States today knows that the movement toward professionalism, for better or worse, is well under way. The decade of the 1970s marked a significant swing toward the aggressive implementation of the professional model of clinical psychology training in the United States (Caddy, in press). (Peterson, 1976, provides an informative summary of the rationale for this development.) The new practitioner trained according to this professional model receives either a PhD or a PsyD

(Doctor of Psychology) degree that takes the usual 4–5 years of graduate study. Already, there are 21 PsyD programs in operation (Peterson, Eaton, Levine, & Snepp, 1980) while professional schools that offer the PhD appear to have become one of California's growth industries. One of the major reasons students attend these schools is the virtual absence of exposure to serious research or training and a nearly exclusive focus on the practice of whatever therapy is in vogue at a particular institution. As the number of applicants to more traditional, scientist–practitioner model PhD training programs in clinical psychology appears to be decreasing around the country, the applications to at least some of the new professional schools of clinical and school psychology are increasing.

Two of us are intimately acquainted with the functioning of the Doctor of Psychology (PsyD) professional training program at Rutgers University, one of the comparatively few university-based practitioner training programs with a full set of academic and scholarly requirements. Nevertheless, research training is not a mandatory part of the curriculum nor are students required to complete any experimental research as part of a doctoral dissertation.[3] Of course, the choice to become involved in research is always open to the student. Yet despite the presence of fellow research-oriented PhD students completing a scientist–practitioner training program and the diverse clinical research activities of a wide range of faculty members, very few of the roughly more than 100 PsyD students who have graduated from the program have ever conducted any experimental research. It should be realized that this assessment holds true for the behaviorally oriented students as much as for their psychodynamic counterparts. Moreover, we have often been all too painfully aware of the disfavor with which the vast majority of these students greeted the minimal didactic instruction in experimental design and research analysis. For the most part, psychoanalytically trained students, not surprisingly, either ignore or reject the advances in behavioral research and therapy that have taken place over the past two decades or more. In sum, sadly, a reading of the clinical psychology literature, combined with clinical and teaching experience, leaves no illusions about the "dedication" of most students in schools of professional psychology or of full-time practitioners to research.

One final point in connection with the notion of the empirical clinician that is being proposed bears mention. The training model and the methodology have been around for some time without any of

3. For some "all-but-dissertation" students this is one of the major reasons for their interest in the program.

the effects that are now being predicted for the future. Why have these promised consequences not materialized and what will ensure that the future will see anything different?

Developing as a serious alternative to the then prevalent psychodynamic approach in the 1960s, behavior therapy had a major impact on training programs in clinical psychology. The Boulder conference had reaffirmed the ideal that the clinical psychologist should be a scientist–practitioner. However, there were those who felt that clinical training programs predicated upon this model were producing neither scientists nor practitioners; students were falling between two stools, emerging from their graduate training relatively unskilled and inexperienced in the practice of psychotherapy and uninterested, if not antagonistic, to research activities. Behavior therapy, its proponents argued, would infuse new vigor into the moribund scientist–practitioner model.

The argument was simple. How could one train a clinician to be a scientist–practitioner unless his or her training was based upon a scientific approach to clinical behavior change? Unlike the speculative and heavily criticized psychodynamic model, behavior therapy purportedly derived from scientific psychology. Not only was behavior therapy said to be based upon scientific theory and research, but it also brought with it the methodological means of integrating therapy and research. The methodology for the merger was single-case experimental design derived from animal operant research (Sidman, 1960). Unlike group outcome research with its statistical analyses of mean performance across subjects, single-case experimental designs address the individual case, which happens to be the practicing therapist's concern. One of the reasons for the apparent fit between behavior therapy and the Boulder model was the assumption that for the behavior therapist, armed with this newfound methodological flexibility, therapy was research and research therapy. Critics of the Boulder model were informed that it was not that it was inappropriate—the problem was that it had never been really tried. The advent of behavior therapy was to fulfill the dream of producing this happy hybrid.

Obviously, this behaviorally retreaded Boulder model did not produce large numbers of full-time practitioners who have actively used single-case experimental designs in their therapy. If they had, there would be no need for the current advocacy of the empirical clinician (a scientist–practitioner by any other name?). Possible reasons for this apparent "failure" are given above—it is neither feasible nor necessarily desirable for the practitioner to complete experimental research. Nevertheless, Hayes (1981), while acknowledging the "underutilization" of time-series methodology in applied settings, offers an alternative and more optimistic explanation.

Hayes give six reasons for the underutilization of time-series methodology by practitioners. (1) Single-case experimental methodology is simply not taught enough in our training programs. This point seems well taken. Experimental design courses almost always favor the teaching of group designs and inferential statistics. (2) Single-case experimental methodology has "not been aimed at the practicing clinician . . . methodological niceties have often been overemphasized . . . and it may be rejected because it is seemingly impractical to do it right" (1981, p. 194). Here Hayes is arguing that the impracticality that we and others have emphasized as an objection to his thesis is merely perceived, a simple problem of overconcern with "methodological niceties." We disagree. Completing high-quality, controlled research is impractical for practitioners for the most part. If the result is merely to encourage more "simple-minded" research that does not quite meet adequate scientific standards, a clear probability in our view and a possibility Hayes himself voices some concern about, science will not have been served. (3) Single-case experimental methodology is associated with behaviorism and may often be rejected for this reason. This point begs the question. The phenomenon to be accounted for is why behaviorally trained and behaviorally oriented therapists now in clinical practice in one setting or another clearly have not carried out the research Hayes and others are calling for. (4) Research is identified with between-groups studies with the result that the baby (single-case experimental designs) is thrown out with the bathwater (the dismaying rejection of research findings in clinical psychology). Our view is that practitioners will not feel differently about rigorous single-case experimental methodology than they do about traditional research. (5) Single-case experimental studies are rejected by journals that fail to take into consideration the "realities of clinical practice." Again, this translates into an appeal for journals to change their scientific standards to accept less than adequately controlled studies. Causal relationships will not be established if this path is taken and there are more acceptable alternatives for ensuring that practitioners have the opportunity to influence research and therapy. (6) Treatment agencies infrequently provide support for scientific activities. Nor is it at all likely that they will, or should, in the future. Hayes adds, "Fortunately, third-party payments are beginning to create counterpressures for clinical evaluation" (1981, p. 194). However, as we discuss below, evaluation of treatment effects, a feasible and necessary goal, is one thing; scientific research often quite another.

An Integrative Framework for Research and Practice

By virtue of its demanding nature, controlled research undertaken to identify specific cause–effect relationships, using either between-groups statistical designs or single-case experimental methodology, will necessarily be the province of the clinical researcher trained in the scientist–practitioner tradition. With rare exceptions, practitioners will be unable (and unwilling) to conduct such experimental studies, a conclusion that Barlow (1980) endorses. This position should not imply that the full-time practitioner does not have a vital and continuing role to play in the overall clinical research enterprise. The practitioner has an invaluable and unique role to play, providing the clinical researcher with novel hypotheses, unusual observations, and theoretical leads, as well as participating in field tests of experimentally tested methods (see Agras, Kazdin, & Wilson, 1979, and Agras & Berkowitz, 1980, for further details on the role of practitioners in field-testing treatment methods). Recently, Geiss and O'Leary (in press) creatively tapped the clinical needs and interests of practitioners in the field of marital therapy by surveying a selected sample about what issues they thought needed to be researched but were being neglected by clinical researchers. One way to keep clinical research "honest" is by addressing real clinical concerns; it might have reciprocal benefits in making the practitioner more amenable to the influence of research findings.

THE CASE STUDY

Although the practitioner will not complete analytic research, he or she can contribute detailed case studies that achieve at least two important purposes. First, provided that the treatment methods are precisely described so that they are replicable, and are applied to clearly identified problems in well-described clients, they illustrate clinical practice. Second, if adequate measures of outcome are reported, they can be used to evaluate overall efficacy of service even if the determinants of those effects cannot be disentangled. The latter is the task of the clinical researcher.

The clinical case study (as opposed to single-subject experimental design) has been central to the study and development of clinical psychology. One has only to think of such classics as Little Hans, Anna O, Little Albert, Mary Cover Jones's Peter, and the boy called Noah, among many others, to see the enormous influence that case studies or clinical reports have had on the field. This influence has not always been desirable, as in the case of Little Hans, the uncertain details of which lent such impetus to the development of questionable psychoanalytic procedures.

Aside from individual case reports, collections or series of case studies have often had a decisive impact on the field as Barlow (1980) points out. In behavior therapy, for example, the early series of clinical cases reported by Wolpe (1958) and Lazarus (1963) constituted the basis for the initial clinical practice of this treatment for adults with anxiety disorders. In 1970, Masters and Johnson's report of their innovative treatment of 790 cases of sexual dysfunction became a national best-seller and ushered in the era of the "new sex therapy." The massive influence of Masters and Johnson's findings, causing even psycho-analytically oriented therapists to adopt their methods (e.g., Kaplan, 1974), went well beyond their data, which were, after all, a collection of uncontrolled case studies.

Inevitably, Masters and Johnson's work has come under critical review. Thus Zilbergeld and Evans (1980) have issued the following charge: "Our conclusion is brief: Masters and Johnson's sex-therapy research is so flawed by methodological errors and slipshod reporting that it fails to meet customary standards—and their own for evaluation. This raises serious questions about the effectiveness of the 10-year-old discipline they created" (p. 30). Among the several methodological difficulties with the first Masters and Johnson (1970) report on the treatment of sexual dysfunction in heterosexual men and women and their second volume, in 1979, on similar disorders in homosexual men and women, is the imprecision with which treatment outcome is de-fined. Masters and Johnson reported only failure rates, arguing that it is easier for therapist and patient to agree on what constitutes failure than success. The reader is therefore left without any operational definition of therapeutic success—or failure, for that matter. Masters and Johnson define failure as indication that the two-week rapid-treatment phase has failed to initiate reversal of the basic symptomatol-ogy of sexual dysfunction. Yet as Zilbergeld and Evans point out, "initiating reversal" is subject to different interpretations.

> An anorgasmic woman, for example, might feel less guilty about sex, become less performance-oriented during sex, enjoy sex more, have an orgasm with masturbation, or have an orgasm in intercourse. . . . The need for specificity is illustrated in this example. Treatment for anorgasmic women often teaches patients to have orgasms with masturbation. This method is highly successful as long as success is defined as ability to have orgasms with self-stimulation. However, if the standard of success is the ability to have an orgasm via the partner's manual or oral stimulation, the success rate drops significantly. It takes an even greater plunge if the

criterion is orgasm in intercourse. The results of therapy may differ
tremendously depending upon which standards of success or failure are
used. (Zilbergeld & Evans, 1980, p. 33)

Other problems include the lack of independent evaluation of the
results and some vagueness with which part of their treatment, that
having to do with what we might call the maintenance phase of the
program, is described. Yet in their critical zeal, Zilbergeld and Evans go
too far in not only questioning Masters and Johnson's results but in
casting doubt on sex therapy as a whole, ignoring much of the solid
controlled research in the field (see Franks & Wilson, 1977, 1980, in
earlier volumes in this series; Wilson, 1982).

The point of the foregoing example of Masters and Johnson's
landmark collection of clinical case studies is to show both the advantages and the potential hazards of uncontrolled clinical reports. (Reasons
for the unusually influential nature of clinical case reports are discussed
below.) In an important paper in the series on the empirical clinician
in the *Journal of Consulting and Clinical Psychology*, Kazdin (1981a)
makes clear how case studies can be reported so as to increase the
likelihood that we can draw valid inferences about treatment effects.
Kazdin's thesis is that while case studies can never have the analytic
power of formal experimental methodology, they need not be dismissed
as an inadequate basis for drawing scientific inferences. According to
this argument, case studies and experiments can be ordered along a
continuum of scientific adequacy. Specifically, several types of uncontrolled case studies can be identified that vary in the degree to which
they allow valid inferences to be drawn:

> Case studies encompass several types of demonstrations that may differ in
> the extent to which inferences can be drawn. The issue is not whether a
> particular report is a case study. The focus on classifying reports on the
> basis of their lack of experimental design detracts from the more pertinent
> issue. Drawing inferences, whether in case studies, quasi-experiments, or
> experiments, in a matter of ruling out rival hypotheses that could account
> for the results. In case studies, by definition, the number of rival hypotheses
> and their plausibility are likely to present greater problems than they
> would in experiments. However, it is possible to include features in the
> case study that help decrease the plausibility of specific rival hypotheses.
> (Kazdin, 1981a, p. 191)

The dimensions that are said to determine the degree to which
scientific inferences can be drawn from uncontrolled case studies include
the type of data collected, the number of assessment occasions, past and
future projections of performance, the type of effect demonstrated, and
the number and heterogeneity of the patients described in case studies.

Case studies can include objective as well as subjective information on therapeutic change, as Nelson (1981) has described. Kazdin, correctly, in our opinion, underscores the necessity of objective information if the case study is to serve much of a purpose. All too often, case studies report anecdotal information of little practical or scientific value. As Kazdin and Wilson (1978) have pointed out, the inclusion of inadequate measures and the failure to obtain unambiguous objective information has rendered many otherwise well-controlled experiments uninterpretable, let alone vitiating the usefulness of an uncontrolled report.

Single assessments of the patient's problem(s) before or after therapy are the least secure basis for inferring treatment efficacy since these isolated measures are most vulnerable to a host of influences aside from the particular technique in question. Repeated or continuous measurement over time before and after therapy allows one to rule out several sources of extraneous influence and increases the confidence with which we can interpret treatment-specific change.

By past projections of the patient's problem Kazdin refers to the question of whether the history of the disorder has been stable or chronic as opposed to acute or episodic. Consider, on the one hand, the case of an exhibitionist who has been exposing himself regularly for several years despite arrests, fines, imprisonment, and lengthy spells of expensive psychotherapy at the hands of recognized expert practitioners. Should an alternative form of therapy (e.g., behavior therapy) immediately produce a cessation of exposure incidents (presumably assessed with reliable and objective measures), it is not unreasonable to attribute the successful outcome to the behavioral methods. (Of course, even this demonstration would not be definitive; for example, the role of the particular therapist using the behavioral techniques could not be totally discounted.) Now, on the other hand, consider a client suffering from depression of recent onset. Assume too that this client has had a history of episodic depressive spells which have passed without the benefit of formal therapeutic intervention. Evidence that the depression lifts while the client is receiving therapy, of any variety, would not be very convincing. A most plausible rival hypothesis is that history repeated itself with therapy an unrelated concomitant of more basic change.

Projections about the future, natural course of clinical problems, based upon empirical evidence of the particular disorder, similarly affect the inferences one can draw from treatment effects. That "most remarkable of providences," spontaneous remission, becomes particularly significant in cases of neurotic disorders, despite the inexcusable neglect of this robust phenomenon by many traditional psychotherapists (see Rachman & Wilson, 1980).

The type of effect obtained with treatment powerfully influences our interpretation of case studies. Therapeutic change that is immediately coincident with specific interventions makes it more likely that the effect is due to the treatment. It will be recalled that the absence of any discernible relationship between treatment and behavioral improvement in the case of Little Hans was one of the many damning criticisms leveled at Freud's highly speculative interpretation of that enormously influential case report by Wolpe and Rachman (1960) in their classic critique. Magnitude of effect similarly lends credence to the presumed potency of therapeutic interventions.

Finally, Kazdin emphasizes the value of demonstrating therapeutic effects across large numbers of heterogeneous clients:

> If change is demonstrated across several clients who differ in various subject and demographic characteristics and the time that they are treated, the inferences that can be drawn are much stronger than if this diversity does not exist. Essentially, different persons have different histories and rates of maturation. As the diversity and heterogeneity of the clients and the conditions of treatment increase, it becomes increasingly implausible that the common experience shared by the clients (i.e., treatment) accounts for the changes. (1981a, pp. 187–188)

One final point about clinical case studies must be made. Their decisive influence on psychotherapeutic approaches from Freudian analysis to behavior therapy is widely accepted. A significant majority of psychotherapists would probably claim that controlled group outcome research with sophisticated statistical analyses has had relatively little impact on therapeutic practice (see Barlow, 1980, for examples). The intriguing question is why should this be so?

Quite obviously one answer is that group outcome research using factorial designs are irrelevant to the clinician's task. Aside from the arguments considered above, Bergin and Strupp (1970), Strupp and Hadley (1977), and Meehl (1978)—the latter with more verbal flourish than substance—have all expressed this opinion. Regardless of the merit of this particular position, one strongly contested by other clinical psychologists, the remarkable fascination with clinical case studies is still left unexplained. I suggest that there are good reasons for the disproportionate influence of uncontrolled clinical case studies on thinking and practice in psychotherapy, reasons that can be studied scientifically rather than simply guessed at.

In their recent book on human inference, Nisbett and Ross (1980) discuss the manner in which people, including social scientists, assign weights to different data or sources of information. Among the many valuable points they make that are relevant to current cognitive-behavioral approaches to assessment and treatment, is their conclusion that people give inferential weight to information in proportion to its vividness. To quote them:

> Research indicates that highly probative, data-summary information sometimes is ignored while less probative, case-history information has a substantial impact on inferences. Although people's responsiveness to vivid information has a certain justification and confers occasional advantages, the policy of weighting information in proportion to its vividness is risky. At best, vividness is associated imperfectly with probativeness. Consequently, highly probative but pallid information sometimes will be ignored, and conversely, evidentially weak but vivid information sometimes will have an undue impact on inferences. (p. 62)

In short, they explain the success and popularity of those charismatic therapists who rely upon the time-honored tactic of discounting "pallid" but more "probative" evidence with the seemingly inevitable response of "But I had a patient who . . . ." Is there little wonder that the Paul and Lentz (1977) tome will be less salient and probably prove to be less influential than the therapeutic success of Sybil and all her selves (Schreiber, 1974)?

Elsewhere (Wilson, 1981b) I have proposed a framework for what I regard as the different levels of analysis along the continuum from basic scientific research to clinical practice (see Table 8-1). This framework emphasizes that each level has its unique and necessary place in the overall development of an applied clinical science. The actual flow of treatment-related research within this framework is outlined by Agras *et al.* (1979) (see Figure 8-1). I have also argued that the relative

TABLE 8-1.

Different Levels of Scientific/Clinical Analysis along the Continuum from Basic Research to Clinical Practice

Level 1	Basic laboratory research on mechanisms of change behavior.
Level 2	Analogue treatment research to identify effective ingredients of therapeutic procedures under controlled laboratory conditions.
Level 3	Controlled clinical research with patient populations. Two subtypes can be distinguished: (1) studies of specific techniques with detailed process and outcome measures; (2) studies designed to show optimal treatment effects using multicomponent therapy packages.
Level 4	Clinical practice. Therapists may measure outcome in case studies or clinical series (an AB design), or, in rare instances, conduct single-case experimental designs.

Note. From "Some Comments on Clinical Research" by G. T. Wilson, *Behavioral Assessment*, 1981, *3*, 217–226. Copyright 1981, Association for Advancement of Behavior Therapy. Reprinted by permission.

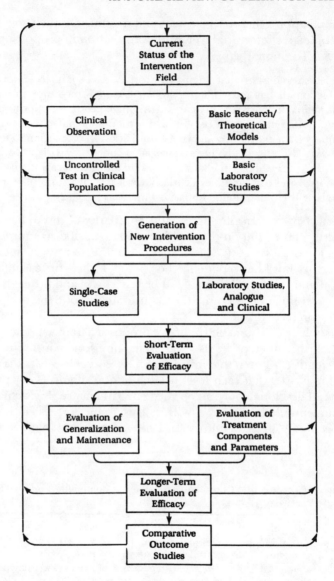

FIG. 8-1.

The flow of therapeutic research. (From *Behavior Therapy: Towards an Applied Clinical Science* by W. S. Agras, A. E. Kazdin, and G. T. Wilson, San Francisco: W. H. Freeman, 1979. Copyright 1979, W. H. Freeman Co. Reprinted by permission.)

paucity of clinical or level 3 research has been a problem in this country and one of the reasons for the less than ideal influence of research on practice, this despite the encouraging trend toward an increase in clinical research noted by Agras and Berkowitz (1980). Confronted with substantial changes of obvious clinical relevance obtained with "real" patients by using clearly described and replicable methods under realistic conditions of clinical practice, the practitioner is more likely to take notice. Too often he or she is required to make the inferential leap from level 2 to level 4 without the benefit of clinical research at the intervening level. (No wonder they look for a soft place to land.) The reasons for the lack of clinical research can be identified and, together with remedial actions that can be taken to correct the imbalance, are discussed elsewhere (Agras *et al.*, 1979; Wilson, 1981b). The point I wish to single out here is one that has aroused the ire and anxiety of many psychotherapists.

From a behavioral perspective it is easy to lament the fact that procedures that are grounded in empirical research are used sparingly, if at all, in general clinical practice. Numerous examples could be cited. Thus agoraphobics are subjected to questionable long-term psychodynamic therapy instead of receiving demonstrably effective and efficient exposure treatment (Marks, 1981). Obsessive–compulsives are mistreated with futile psychotherapy, major tranquilizers, electroconvulsive therapy, and even psychosurgery when there is growing evidence that exposure and response prevention methods are the treatments of choice in many cases (Rachman & Hodgson, 1980). Then there is the compelling example of Paul and Lentz's (1977) splendid demonstration of the superiority of social learning methods in the treatment of chronic, institutionalized mental hospital patients. Despite the unprecedented evidence of efficacy and cost-effectiveness, the program itself was terminated when government funding was withdrawn and similar programs elsewhere have not been established.

The lesson that we should learn from these events has been cogently detailed by Liberman (1980). To quote him:

> After almost 20 years of behavioral analysis and therapy, workers in the field must realize that political, personal, and social factors determine upwards of 90% of the success and survival of technical procedures. . . . Implementation, survival, and dissemination of empirically validated interventions require much more than data and journal publications. . . . If we want our work to live beyond a library bookshelf, we will have to jump into the political mainstream and get our feet wet as administrator researchers. (pp. 370–371)

Liberman is right in noting that the quality and clinical relevance of our research alone will not suffice to influence clinical practice. Data do not speak for themselves. They need to be interpreted and forcefully presented to the public, professionals, and funding sources alike.

In a related vein, Inouye (1981), in his recent remarks to non-physician health providers in *The Behavior Therapist*, suggested:

> It is up to you to take the time to educate your own elected officials as to the specifics of your professional training and the types of clinical services that you deliver. You have to sell your own case, you have to convince the elected officials from your state that Medicare is important to you, and to your clients. It would definitely be helpful if your senators would agree to "co-sponsor" the various measures that I have introduced during our present Congress, the relevant bills are: S.123, for the psychologists; S.1238, for the nurses; and S.2176 for the social workers. Next session, I plan to combine these measures into one omnibus bill that would feature the term "qualified mental health professional." I have already arranged for it to be designated Senate Bill 123. But the absolutely crucial issue is whether it is important enough to you to take the time to meet personally with your representatives. Now is the time for you to develop "grassroots" support for your eventual inclusion under national health insurance. (p. 10)

Behavior therapists have a vested interest joining with other concerned organizations in supporting any reasonable legislation that seeks to make only those mental health services that are safe and effective be reimbursable, and to guarantee the appropriate recognition of psychologists and other professionals as independent health providers.

COMMON CLINICAL STRATEGIES ACROSS DIFFERENT THERAPIES: RAPPROCHEMENT RECONSIDERED

The theme that behavioral treatment might be integrated with more traditional psychodynamic therapy has been sounded throughout the brief but boisterous history of behavior therapy. The various proposals along these lines, together with the inevitable rebuttals from the more behaviorally inclined, have featured prominently in the commentary in previous volumes in this series (Franks & Wilson, 1973–1980). Hardly had we entered a new decade before another variation on this theme hinted at the harmonious coming together of diverse therapeutic approaches (Goldfried, 1980b).

Goldfried's thesis is straightforward:

> The argument has been advanced by several writers in the field that with increased experience, therapists tend to become more similar in their actual clinical practice. It has been suggested that there exists a "therapeutic underground," which may rarely appear in the literature, but

which nonetheless reflects some common observations among well-seasoned clinicians as to what tends to be effective. If this indeed is the case, then such commonalities are likely to shed light on some very significant principles of change, as they have managed to emerge in spite of the theoretical biases inherent in each of our varying orientations. (1980b, p. 992)

In support of this contention, Goldfried (1980b) mentions Fiedler's (1950) finding that greater similarity was to be found among experienced clinicians of different therapeutic schools than among beginning therapists of varying orientations. Although Goldfried's argument does not depend on the validity of Fiedler's finding, it would be well to put this oft-quoted study into its proper perspective. When Fiedler conducted this study the psychodynamic school of practice dominated the clinical scene. So-called differences in orientation were relatively trivial and thus the results cannot be generalized to the genuinely different orientations, including behavior therapy, that emerged during the 1950s and later. Not surprisingly, empirical evidence directly contradicts this tired testimony. To take only one example, the data from the Sloane, Staples, Cristol, Yorkston, and Whipple (1975) comparative outcome study clearly showed differences between behavioral and psychoanalytically oriented therapists despite the inclusion in the study of only expert, very experienced exemplars of these two treatment approaches. In a separate analysis of the way these therapists acted, Staples, Sloane, Cristol, Yorkston, and Whipple (1975) concluded:

> Differences between behavior therapy and analytically oriented psycho-therapy . . . involved the basic patterns of interactions between patient and therapist and the type of relationship formed. Behavior therapy is not psychotherapy with special "scientific techniques" superimposed on the traditional therapeutic paradigm; rather, the two appear to represent quite different styles of treatment although they share common elements. (p. 1521).

The behavior therapists were more directive, more open, more genuine, and more disclosing than their psychoanalytically oriented counterparts. Both sets of therapists used similar numbers of interpretations during therapy, but the quality of these interpretations differed predictably, with the psychotherapists focusing psychodynamically on feelings and the behavior therapists concentrating on behavior. Similarly, well-controlled research has shown that Beck's cognitive therapy is reliably discriminable from an alternative psychotherapeutic method (DeRubeis, Hollon, Evans, & Bemis, 1981).

According to Goldfried, "Although the therapeutic underground . . . may always have been there, we now seem to be at a point in time when clinicians are starting to acknowledge its existence more openly and are beginning to recognize the contributions from orientations other than their own" (1980b, p. 992). As evidence of this development he cites sundry comments from psychoanalysts, the "humanistically" oriented, and some identified with behavior therapy. The degree to which this scholarly scanning of the psychotherapeutic literature reflects actual practice is debatable, and the case can be made that traditional psychodynamic therapists have done little to acknowledge the contribution of demonstrably effective cognitive–behavioral methods (Wilson, in press). Be this as it may, Goldfried provides a new twist to the rapprochement argument by proposing the way in which this is likely to be achieved.

Influenced by findings from contemporary cognitive psychology on the formation of natural categories of events and encoding processes, Goldfried conceptualizes therapy as an activity comprising different levels of abstraction. The highest level consists of overall theoretical frameworks, a level that he rejects as useful for any rapprochement. The lowest level involves specific therapeutic techniques, a level at which Goldfried feels any commonalities would be "trivial." Instead, Goldfried suggests that the level between theory and practice, which he calls clinical strategies, offers the possibility of a consensus among different approaches. He gives two examples of such clinical strategies.

The first clinical strategy that Goldfried suggests might be common to all theoretical orientations is providing the client with new, corrective experiences. In support of this view, isolated statements by Freud himself, Fenichel, Alexander and French, and other psychoanalytic authorities[4] about the desirability of having patients try new ways of

---

4. Parenthetically, Goldfried cites Horwitz's report of the Menninger Foundation Psychotherapy Research Project as showing that corrective experiences provide as much "long-lasting therapeutic change as did more traditional psychotherapy." Again, while Goldfried's thesis stands or falls irrespective of the Menninger Psychotherapy Project's findings, it is dismaying to see such totally flawed research introduced into serious analyses of treatment process and procedure. It must be remembered that Kernberg and his colleagues (1973), in their final report of this Project, concluded that the "most severe limitation of their study was its "lack of formal experimental design" (p. 76). They point out that it was not possible: "(i) to list the variables needed to test the theory; (ii) to have methods of quantification for the variables, preferably existing scales which would have adequate reliability and validity; (iii) to be able to choose and provide control conditions which could rule out alternative explanations for the results . . . (iv) to state the hypotheses to be tested; or finally (v) to conduct this research according to the design" (p. 75). Commenting on the Menninger Project, Rachman and Wilson (1980) state that "this astonishing conclusion can have few equals. If we then add to their list of frank self-criticism, some of the faults already mentioned (e.g., contamination, nonrandom allocation, etc.) one is left with a study that is so flawed as to preclude any conclusions whatsoever" (p. 73).

behaving in the extratherapeutic environment are cited. Gestalt therapy, encounter groups, and other approaches are similarly said to include an emphasis on corrective experiences. Behavior therapy, of course, as Goldfried notes, places great emphasis on performance-based methods and explicit homework assignments, as in the treatment of anxiety disorders. Yet these carefully culled comments establish only the most superficial commonality among diverse therapeutic approaches.

It would be sheer fantasy to imagine that the average psychodynamic practitioner recommends anything in the way of direct, systematic exposure to anxiety-eliciting situations in treating anxiety disorders, irrespective of Freud's fleeting fancy to this effect. It may be that some unconventional psychodynamic therapists, particularly those who practice short-term treatment, do, on occasion, recommend some form of extratherapeutic experience outside of the transference relationship but to allege that this can be likened seriously to the highly structured, explicitly scheduled, and systematically checked technique- and even problem-specific nature of *in vivo* homework assignments in behavioral assessment and therapy is to go too far. Moreover, as Wilson (1981a) has observed:

> It is not just the structure and systematic nature of homework assignments in behavior therapy (e.g., daily self-monitoring records of operationally defined target thoughts, feelings, or behaviors that must be returned to the therapist by a certain date) that makes it distinctive. The substantive nature of these assignments is also characteristically different. Consider, for example, the highly specific nature of behavioral assignments in sex therapy, such as sensate focus exercises, the "squeeze" or "stop–start" technique to eliminate premature ejaculation, masturbatory programs for primary orgasmic dysfunction, and so on. These procedures have revolutionized the treatment of sexual dysfunction and deviance. There had not been anything like this before Masters and Johnson (1970), building on the prior work of Wolpe and Lazarus (1966) and others, developed their methods. Nor had there been anything like the success that is now routinely recorded. This is the telling point. (p. 157)

The second common clinical strategy in Goldfried's view consists of giving the client direct feedback to help them "become more aware of what they are doing and not doing, thinking and not thinking, and feeling and not feeling" (1980b, p. 995). Self-monitoring, a backbone of so much assessment and treatment in behavior therapy, is viewed as one aspect of this common clinical strategy. Yet self-monitoring is not comparable to the therapist reflecting back to clients their thoughts in client-centered therapy, or the feedback people receive in other humanistic–existential therapies such as Gestalt therapy or encounter groups. Behavioral research has shown that it matters a great deal precisely *what* people self-monitor, . . . *when* they self-monitor, . . . and *how*. . . . The conceptualizations that spurred this research, the methodology that facilitated it, and the clinical imperative of specifying antecedent and consequent variables that result in the significant use of self-monitoring in clinical practice are the dimensions that are important, and they serve to differentiate among competing therapeutic philosophies, despite what may appear to be surface similarities in approach. (Wilson, 1981a, pp. 157–158)

Pursuing the goal of searching for common principles of effective psychotherapy, Goldfried (1980a) asked a varied group of 13 therapists from different theoretical orientations to draw on their "own personal experiences and observations as clinicians" in stating what they believed to be common underlying principles in therapeutic change. Those associated with the cognitive–behavioral tradition were John Paul Brady, Gerald Davison, Arnold Lazarus, and Julian Rotter. Each therapist was asked to respond to the same set of five questions about the therapeutic process: (1) What is the role of new experiences? (2) How does feedback about client behavior affect change? (3) How important is the therapist–patient relationship? (4) How did they use "language/ cognition/awareness" in promoting change? (5) What are the common principles that underlie treatment success?

Several unsurprising themes characterize the therapists' answers to these questions. First, all of them, psychoanalysts, "humanists," behavior therapists, and eclectics alike, agreed that new experiences, feedback to the client about his or her thoughts/feelings/behavior, and the therapist–patient relationship were all vitally important to facilitating therapeutic change. Second, different therapists viewed new experiences, feedback and the therapeutic relationship quite differently. And third, these differences of opinion could have been reliably predicted by the therapists' theoretical orientation.

Consider the role of new experiences. Brady, Davison, and Lazarus, in keeping with behavioral research and practice, emphasize the importance of performance-based methods that promote new thoughts, feelings, and behavior. For example, Lazarus, noting the limitations of purely verbal methods, states that he "deliberately provides a series of performance-based 'new experiences' for my clients to transact or put into effect. At the start of each session I customarily ask, 'What new or different things have you done this week?' If the answer is 'None!' one can be quite certain that little (if any) progress will have been made" (Goldfried, 1981a, p. 277). Responding to Goldfried's questions, DeWald, a psychoanalyst, agrees that new experiences are crucial but quickly asserts that the experience occurs primarily "in the two-person field of patient and analyst, and the analyst maintains a relatively circumscribed and constant form of neutral participation. The therapeutic situation and technique are designed to promote a return for the patient of earlier and at times forgotten forms, organization, and levels of behavior previously experienced toward key persons during the patient's earlier life and development. Progressively, these are reactivated and are felt and expressed toward the analyst (transference and transference neurosis)" (Goldfried, 1980a, p. 277).

Several other examples of this pattern could be given, but the point has been made. Given the *fundamentally different* views of representatives of different theoretical orientations on so many *basic issues*, their apparent consensus on the issues raised by Goldfried is trivial. We shall have to look to other means of identifying these putative common clinical strategies. Alternatively, we might resist the temptation to begin what is likely to prove a futile search and devote our energies to developing replicable, testable, and effective methods of therapeutic change within the social learning framework of behavior therapy and invite other theoretical orientations to do the same (Wilson, in press). There will be time enough to discuss common principles of change when different approaches can show convincing evidence of what they can and cannot accomplish.

BEHAVIOR THERAPY AND MULTIMODAL THERAPY

As Erwin (1978), Kazdin (1979b), and Wilson (1978c), among others, have pointed out, there is no simple, universally agreed upon definition of behavior therapy. The field is marked by a diversity of views, heterogeneous methods that often have different rationales, frequently conflicting debate about theoretical mechanisms, and varying appraisals of therapeutic efficacy. Nevertheless, it is possible to identify the common core characteristics that make behavior therapy a distinctive approach (see Wilson & O'Leary, 1980) and to describe the major conceptual positions currently encompassed by this term. Thus Kazdin and Wilson (1978) and Wilson and O'Leary (1980) suggested that the different approaches within behavior therapy included applied behavior analysis (e.g., Baer, 1982), neobehavioristic S-R model (e.g., Eysenck, 1982), cognitive–behavior modification (e.g., Meichenbaum & Cameron, 1982), social learning theory, (e.g., Bandura, 1977a; Rosenthal, 1982), and multimodal behavior therapy (Lazarus, 1976). While including Lazarus's multimodal therapy under the general rubric of behavior therapy, Kazdin and Wilson noted that this approach had drawn severe criticism from some behaviorists as a form of eclecticism that departed fundamentally from behavior therapy as they viewed the meaning of this term (e.g., Wolpe, 1976, 1978). Lazarus (1977) himself had placed his multimodal approach beyond behavior therapy by asserting that "behavior therapy is a small but significant part of the multimodal approach" (p. 553). In their own analysis, Kazdin and Wilson concluded that although there is "some historical connection and considerable overlap in terms of therapeutic techniques, multi-modal therapy departs from behavior therapy on both conceptual and methodological grounds" (p. 2). Lazarus has issued the most complete statement of his position in his 1981 book entitled *The Practice of Multimodal Therapy*. The omission of the word "behavior" is pointed. In sum, Lazarus argues that multimodal therapy is both bigger and better than behavior therapy.

Before attempting any comparative analysis of relative efficacy, it is imperative to establish the precise operational differences between the two approaches. One way to do this is to examine Lazarus's list of the 39 most frequently used techniques in multimodal therapy. At least 30 of these techniques seem to be the standard fare of routine behavior therapy (e.g., modeling, reinforcement, behavior rehearsal, biofeed-back, and aversive imagery). The remaining methods require some interpretation. Consider, for example, hypnosis, meditation, and para-doxical strategies. Hypnosis is not widely used by behavor therapists, although its carefully limited application as a form of self-control training designed to induce relaxation or reduce pain would not represent a significant conceptual or procedural departure from current behavioral treatment methods such as relaxation and self-regulatory training. Stripped of any mystique, meditation is used broadly by behavior therapists as another form of relaxation training. Paradoxical strategies certainly were not derived from a learning-based approach, but these techniques have been frequently described in the practice of broad-spectrum behavior therapy, as Lazarus (1971) formerly docu-mented. Most recently, in their handbook of behavioral interventions for the clinician, Goldstein and Foa (1979) saw fit to include a detailed chapter by Asher on paradoxical intention. Then there is the "step-up" technique in which clients are asked to anticipate the worst consequence that may befall them in an anxiety-eliciting situation and to imagine coping with such adversity. Procedurally, it is hard to see how this could differ from the range of imaginal exposure methods that are part of the demonstrably effective behavior therapy approach for treating anxiety disorders (Goldstein & Foa, 1979; Marks, 1981).

The other techniques clearly receive no attention in the behavior therapy literature and probably equally little use in practice. These include the empty-chair technique, focusing, and time projection (forward or backward). It is unclear how frequently these methods are used or how central they are to the practice of multimodal therapy, but the use of any technique from any therapeutic approach is consistent with Lazarus's notion of technical eclecticism and does differ from behavior therapy.

All in all the listing of the principal techniques of multimodal therapy does not indicate that this approach is appreciably different from behavior therapy. Does the eclectic use of those techniques that would be disregarded by the broadly trained behavior therapist make multimodal therapy more effective? We do not know since at present there are no controlled studies or even acceptable uncontrolled clinical trials to help decide the issue. This points up one of the central problems for multimodal therapy, as we have observed in earlier volumes of this series (Franks & Wilson, 1978, 1980): How are techniques selected by the therapist in the absence of any empirical support?

In behavior therapy, the therapist draws upon a broad range of principles and procedures within the general framework of social learning theory in designing specific treatment interventions (see Wilson & O'Leary, 1980). Inevitably, although this particular theoretical framework is broad enough to incorporate recent advances in personality, social, and cognitive psychology and allows the creative therapist considerable flexibility, it is necessarily limited. Behavior therapy does not try to do everything, and it is a truism that effective, nonbehavioral methods might be developed within alternative theoretical perspectives. Despite the continuing lack of compelling evidence of the therapeutic efficacy or efficiency of most traditional psychotherapeutic treatment methods (Rachman & Wilson, 1980), it would be most surprising if some strategies from some approaches are not shown to be useful in the course of future outcome research.

For the practitioner, a great advantage of the multimodal approach outlined by Lazarus is the technical flexibility and breadth of clinical vision that it promises. In view of the parochial and partisan positions that have hindered the development of effective treatment methods in the past, a willingness to be responsive to different therapeutic approaches and to go beyond narrowly defined theoretical boundaries must be welcomed. It would seem impossible to fault this overall goal. Yet the problem that is immediately encountered is precisely *how* the technical eclectic is to proceed. What are the principles that guide conceptualization of problems and the selection of appropriate treatment techniques from the bewildering array of currently available psychotherapeutic methods?

The point at issue here is the importance of operating within an explicit conceptual framework that allows for critical testing and self-correction. Either therapists are guided in their formulations and treatment of different problems on the basis of clearly stated principles or they act as a result of personal preference and intuition. Behavior therapy represents an attempt to move beyond the latter unsatisfactory but regrettably common state of affairs and to base clinical practice on more secure scientific foundations. Of course, this does not mean that the clinical practice of behavior therapy is always based on solid empirical evidence. As I have discussed elsewhere (Wilson, in press), behavior therapists have of necessity and common sense borrowed concepts and treatment methods from other therapeutic approaches that are not directly connected with experimental psychology and might not be supported by data from controlled research. Moreover, behavior therapists, not unlike therapists from other approaches, have developed their own clinical lore, much of which owes nothing to experimental research. Lacking sufficient information and guidelines from scientific research, behavior therapists frequently are obliged to adopt an informed trial-and-error approach to difficult or unusual problems. This, quite literally, is the current state of the art—and science—in behavior therapy. Nonetheless, the practice of behavior therapy is clearly linked to a specifiable and testable conceptual framework. Multimodal therapy allows greater flexibility in this trial-and-error process that is part of treatment, at the cost of less conceptual clarity. Whether this increases efficacy remains to be seen. All therapists have their particular conceptual assumptions (biases) whether they acknowledge them or not. These biases come into play from the moment the therapist begins the often arduous task of making sense of a client's problem, in the questions asked or not asked, in the choice of assessment methods, in the framing of goals, and in the selection of treatment strategies. The real issue reduces to an analysis of the nature of these different conceptual sets and the implications they carry for treatment and the development of the field. And in this analysis, as in therapy itself, success hinges upon uncovering, recognizing, accepting, and working through distorted assumptions and hidden agendas.

What then are the guiding concepts and principles of multimodal therapy? According to Lazarus (1981), "In multimodal therapy, the selection of techniques and the focus on different problem areas is not based on intuition and random guesswork, as Franks and Wilson (1980) have averred. The choice of techniques often follows logically from issues and points of emphasis that arise during the course of therapy" (p. 151). To illustrate this contention, Lazarus describes the multifaceted treatment of a complex case in the course of which he postponed the direct modification of the client's premature ejaculation problem in favor of first addressing compulsive rituals that were interfering with sex therapy. The technique chosen? Response prevention—with contingency contracting used to facilitate compliance. The rationale? Empirical research findings (e.g., Rachman & Hodgson, 1980). This is precisely what a behavior therapist would do, since exposure and response prevention have been shown to be effective and were derived directly from the principles of avoidance conditioning. But what "follows logically" in this instance would be viewed very differently by psychoanalysts, most family therapists, and so on. And some of the assessment and treatment techniques Lazarus prescribes, having neither empirical backing nor following from social learning theory, are rejected by behavior therapists.[5] The point is that any therapist's specific conceptual assumptions dictate treatment strategies that might diverge drastically from methods deriving quite logically from other frameworks. This underscores the necessity of making explicit, and hence testable, the nature of these conceptual assumptions.

"What," asks Lazarus, "are the terms, concepts, theories, constructs, and principles necessary for the implementation of multimodal therapy?" The answer: "classical and operant conditioning, modeling and vicarious processes, private events, nonconscious processes, and defensive reactions" (1981, p. 40) plus an understanding that in some cases, the notion of a family or interpersonal *system*. For the most part, there is little here to unsettle the behavior therapist who adopts a broad social learning perspective, although behavior therapy does not share many of the assumptions made by some family or systems approaches. The precise role of a systems model in multimodal therapy is difficult to gauge. Finally, as he has consistently made clear, Lazarus rejects any rapprochement between behavior therapy and psychoanalysis and is careful to indicate what he means by "nonconscious processes" and "defensive reactions." To quote him: "When I refer to 'nonconscious processes,' I mean simply that people are not necessarily aware of certain connections between past and present events, and that these connections can influence ongoing behaviors, perceptions, and emo-

5. An example is the deserted-island-fantasy technique. The reliability, validity, and utility of this "structured projective test" remain to be shown. To what extent does this technique add to the clinical insights a skilled therapist would derive from the interview itself? There seems to be no reason to differentiate the deserted island fantasy from the variety of fantasy techniques that have been studied so intensively over the past 30–40 years, and no reason to think that it will improve on the well-known inadequacies of this genre of personality assessment device (Mischel, 1968).

tions. No additional psychic mechanisms or dynamic forces are implied. We are not closet analysts!" (1981, p. 40). The literature on behavior therapy traditionally has said little about unconscious processes and their influence on behavior, undoubtedly due to the reaction against psychoanalytic thinking. Yet as Lazarus points out, therapeutic investigation of unconscious processes can proceed without the intrusion of psychoanalytic theory, and his clinical approach is at the forefront of cognitive–behavioral efforts in this regard. It seems clear that in behavior therapy the attention to the concepts and procedures of cognitive psychology will increasingly lead to a rigorous examination of unconscious (and affective) influences on behavior (e.g., Bower, 1981; Mahoney, 1980; Rachman, 1980; Wilson, in press).

Although the preceding comments do not establish a genuine difference between behavior therapy and multimodal therapy, Lazarus includes a table spelling out the similarities and differences between the two approaches as he sees them. The ten similarities cover basic conceptual, methodological, and clinical matters. The seven differences are reproduced in Table 8-2 and call for some comments.

The first assertion places an emphasis on seven modalities of human functioning. But to what is this contrasted? Behavior research

TABLE 8-2.
Proposed Differences between Behavior Therapy and Multimodal Therapy

1. In multimodal therapy, personality is specifically and systematically divided into seven discrete but interactive components (modalities) represented by BASICI.D.

2. Multimodal therapists deliberately construct Modality Profiles (BASICI.D. Charts) as a "blueprint" for therapy.

3. Second-order BASICI.D. Profiles are employed to overcome treatment impasses and to elucidate significant areas of "personality" and "psychopathology."

4. The *goodness of fit* in terms of the client's expectancies, therapist–client compatibility, matching, and the selection of techniques is examined in much greater detail by multimodal therapists.

5. The multimodal therapist determines interactive effects across the BASICI.D. in order to establish the Sequential Firing Order of specific modalities. (This procedure is called *tracking.*)

6. Multimodal therapists tune into the client's preferred modalities to enhance communication before delving into other areas that seem clinically more productive. (This procedure is called *bridging.*)

7. The amount of depth and detail that is entailed in examining sensory, imagery, cognitive, and interpersonal factors and their interactive effects, goes beyond the confines of the usual stimulus and functional analyses conducted by behavior therapists. (Thoresen, 1980, has edited a stimulating and provocative book that tries to answer the question, "What does it mean to be a behavior therapist?")

Note. From *The Practice of Multimodal Therapy* by A. A. Lazarus, New York: McGraw-Hill, 1981. Copyright 1981, A. A. Lazarus. Reprinted by permission of McGraw-Hill Book Co.

and therapy for many years now have focused intensively on the inter-actions among behavioral, physiological, and verbal response systems. This analysis and the research it has inspired, dating back to Lang's (1969) view of emotion, have become increasingly sophisticated and complex. Today we have the well-known three-systems analysis of phobias and obsessive–compulsive disorders that generates an expand-ing conception of these problems, gives rise to numerous predictions about therapeutic change, and provides a basis for a new strategy on which to base outcome research (e.g., Hugdahl, 1981; Rachman & Hodgson, 1980). It can be safely argued that this line of research in behavior therapy has resulted in fundamental changes in the manner in which fear and fear reduction methods are viewed. It is now widely accepted that assessment of treatment outcome must include these three dimensions, and specific theories have sought to describe the inter-actions among systems. A case in point would be Bandura's (1977a) self-efficacy theory, the details of which have been presented and dis-cussed in previous volumes in this series (Franks & Wilson, 1978, 1980).

Multimodal therapy emphasizes the interpersonal dimension, but so does contemporary behavior therapy. Behavior therapists appear increasingly to involve the client's spouse or family members in the overall treatment process, examples of which include the treatment of alcoholism, agoraphobia, and obesity. Then there are also the recent developments in behavioral marital therapy. As I have indicated before, traditional formulations of behavior therapy have fallen far short of providing an adequate conceptualization of interpersonal influences in the assessment and modification of behavior. Current behavioral treat-ment techniques for marital interpersonal conflict have a mixed pedi-gree, deriving variously from the operant conditioning model, cognitive restructuring concepts, and even communication analyses of inter-personal interactions. In short, behavioral marital therapy is a technol-ogy in search of a integrative theoretical framework—a conclusion that applies to multimodal therapy as well.

The second claim in Table 8-2 holds that a multimodal or a BASICI.D. (Behavior, Affect, Sensation, Imagery, Cognitive, Interper-sonal, and Drugs) profile provides a "blueprint" for therapy. By ensuring that the therapist casts a comprehensive eye over the client's problems, such profiles or charts undeniably serve a useful function. But a blue-print for therapeutic intervention requires much more. What is needed, as Lazarus points out and illustrates in his own clinically creative case analyses, is a functional analysis of the factors that maintain particular problems. What are the immediate causes, concomitants, and consequences of the problem(s)? In other words, the very stuff of which behavioral assessment is made (e.g., Barlow, 1981; Kanfer & Nay, 1982).

In behavior therapy, a functional analysis governs the selection and use of therapeutic techniques in addition to the identification of the factors that maintain the client's problems. At first blush, it would appear that multimodal therapists assume isomorphic relationships between modality-specific problems and the therapeutic techniques needed to modify them. For example, a problem in the cognitive modality (e.g., a preoccupation with "musts" and "shoulds") would be treated by a cognitive procedure (e.g., rational disputation à la Albert Ellis). Similarly, a problem in the affective modality (e.g., physiological manifestations of anxiety) might be treated with a technique such as progressive relaxation that presumably is appropriate for such a disorder. Note that this tendency to see one-to-one connections between locus of the problem and nature of the procedure has also been characteristic of some of the three-systems analyses of anxiety-related disorders (e.g., Hugdahl, 1981). Yet there is persuasive evidence that a cognitive procedure is not necessarily the best way of changing maladaptive cognitions, let alone behavior. Rather, performance-based methods consistently appear to be the most effective means of altering phobic behavior and cognitions[6] (Bandura, 1977a; Wilson & O'Leary, 1980). Recognition that behavioral procedures are usually the most powerful means of changing cognitive processes does not vitiate the value of BASICI.D. profiles, but it does call for more detailed theoretical analyses.

The third item in Table 8-2 refers to "second-order" BASICI.D. profiles. Whereas the overall BASICI.D. profile is said to provide a "macroscopic" view of the client's problems, the second-order profile allows a "microscopic" analysis. Lazarus has the following to say:

> To illustrate: The item "tension headaches" appears on a client's Modality Profile under the sensory modality. Relaxation and biofeedback training have been applied with minimal success. (Our rule is first to treat problems with the most logical and obvious procedures. If these fail to remedy the situation, a reevaluation, such as a second-order BASICI.D., may be warranted.) As the term implies, a "second-order BASICI.D." consists simply of subjecting any item on the initial Modality Profile to a more detailed inquiry in terms of behavior, affect, sensation, imagery, cognition, interpersonal factors, and drugs or biological considerations. "When you experience these tension headaches, what do you usually do? How do they affect your behaviors? What emotions do you typically experience when suffering from one of your headaches? Can you describe the type of pain and its location? Apart from the pain in your head, what other sensations do you experience at the time? Are there any pictures or images that come to mind when you have a severe headache? What sorts of thoughts go

6. Lazarus (1981) himself underscores this point.

through your mind when you are having a really severe tension headache? How do your headaches interfere in your dealings with other people? Do you take any medications other than those already listed? Are there biological disruptions such as vomiting or insomnia?" (1981, pp. 85–86)

To the behavior therapist, this second-order profile looks like the routine assessment of possible maintaining factors across potentially relevant dimensions of functioning. The attempt to construct a specific (microscopic) picture of the current causes of a client's disorder is the hallmark of behavioral assessment as Lazarus (1971), among others, has often observed. Another cardinal feature of behavioral assessment is its continuous nature. A therapeutic impasse immediately prompts a reevaluation of the treatment plan just as Lazarus illustrates in the foregoing excerpt. Consider the following example.

A successful, independent business woman consulted one of the present authors complaining of debilitating tension headaches. Organic causes had been ruled out, and the headaches seemingly attributable to reported stress. Progressive relaxation training was quickly introduced for the same reasons Lazarus spells out. In addition, cognitive restructuring was begun because of its usefulness in treating stress and tension headaches (Holroyd & Andrasik, 1978). Minimal success during the first two weeks of therapy was easily traced to a spotty compliance record. Therapeutic attention then shifted to analyzing the reasons for this lack of compliance. A clear theme emerged. Professionally successful and independent, the client felt guilty about taking time out from her family to practice the relaxation in private at home. She experienced personal conflict about merging the two roles of professional and homemaker. Discussion of this issue in the context of assertion training resolved the conflict. The client practiced relaxation, reported a marked decrease in stress, and her headaches disappeared. The point of this fairly typical sequence of events is that the behavior therapist often uncovers relevant maintaining variables in seeking to overcome a therapeutic impasse. The similarity between this strategy and second-order BASICI.D. profiles is obvious, although a possible difference is that the behavior therapist would not necessarily assume, as a matter of course, that he or she would have to intervene in all seven areas of functioning as multimodal therapy requires.[7] For the behavior therapist

7. Although multimodal therapy seems to be predicated on the treatment of all seven modalities, there are exceptions: "With some clients, the introduction of more than one or two tactics may cause them to feel overwhelmed and confused. Problem areas that may respond better to specialized procedures include some phobias, compulsive disorders, sexual problems, eating disorders, some cases of insomnia, tension headaches, and the management of oppositional children (Agras, Kazdin, & Wilson, 1979). Assessment should always be multimodal, but treatment may sometimes be narrowly focused— especially when a BASICI.D. profile reveals no significant network of interrelated problems" (Lazarus, 1981, p. 162).

the extent of any therapeutic intervention will depend on the specific functional analysis of the individual case. In actual practice, the same seems to be true of multimodal therapy.

The fourth point in Table 8-2 is an unsubstantiated assertion. Suffice it to say here that other therapists, including behavior therapists, would endorse the importance of clients' expectancies and therapist–client compatibility and claim that they try to be sensitive to these issues. Multimodal therapy is distinctive by virtue of offering a means for determining therapist–client compatibility. According to Lazarus, "The most elegant treatment outcomes often depend on a reasonable degree of similarity between the client's BASICI.D. and the therapist's BASICI.D." (1981, p. 142). "Structural profiles" are created of both therapist and patient by rating of them on each of the seven modalities using 10-point scales. It is unnecessary to belabor the problems with this sort of procedure. Suffice it to note the inherent limitation of personality typologies as significant predictors of behavior (e.g., Mischel, 1968), the questions of reliability and measurement of such profiles, and the existence of a substantial literature on prior attempts at matching therapists with clients. In short, the findings from these studies have proved inconsistent and discouraging (Parloff, Waskow, & Wolfe, 1978). Indeed, the results of previous work on matching would suggest that "structural profiles" are a most unpromising way to approach the issue of therapist–client compatibility. Moreover, while Lazarus recommends similar BASICI.D. profiles for increasing treatment efficacy, he also, correctly in our view, indicates that "outcome is as much a function of creative differences as a product of comforting agreement" (1981, p. 142). Our current knowledge of therapy process and outcome does not permit much more than this still unsatisfactory conclusion.

The fifth point in Table 8-2 raises a little understood but clinically important issue: the best way to sequence different treatment interventions. The "firing order" that Lazarus speaks of continues the therapeutic metaphor of Heller (1963), who spoke of "precision rifles" in lieu of "therapeutic shotguns" as the way to avoid "the patient uniformity myth" (Kiesler, 1966) and to individualize treatment. But how do multimodal therapists determine the appropriate firing order? Lazarus gives the example of two phobic clients, one of whom reports that panic attacks suddenly begin as a sensory reaction, while the other indicates that specific thoughts initiate panic. In commenting on the implications of this difference for treatment, Lazarus states:

> If both cases were treated by relaxation training, the second one would be far less likely to derive benefit than Case 1. Our clinical findings point to the need for techniques to be fitted to the initiating stimuli: to treat sensory reactions with sensory techniques, cognitive reactions with cogni-

tive techniques and so on. Case 2 would probably respond favorably to thought-stopping, coping or positive imagery, and rational disputation. Of course, a multimodal therapist would not stop there, but the point under consideration is how to select an initial technique. (1981, p. 96)

The problem with this analysis has been referred to above. Even if it can be reliably determined that individual clients' panic attacks are triggered by different stimuli in the sensory and cognitive modalities respectively, an interesting clinical observation, the rules or guidelines for selecting corresponding treatment methods are not clear. In Case 1, for example, why choose relaxation training? First, clinical research indicates that it has little lasting effect on agoraphobic disorders. Second, why not choose pharmacotherapy (e.g., imipramine) that has been shown to be of some value in the treatment of panic attacks (e.g., Zitrin, 1981)? In Case 2, there is no evidence that thought stopping has any beneficial effect, while the available evidence on rational disputation is negative (e.g., Biran, Augusto, & Wilson, 1981; Wilson, 1982), although in conjunction with exposure-based treatment it might be useful. It is precisely this lack of what might be called rules of correspondence that renders BASICI.D. profiles not so much a blueprint for therapy as a first survey of potential problems.

If Lazarus does not provide the answer, it is because the state of the art does not permit one at this juncture. In some instances it seems clear what the sequencing of intervention should be. For example, Beck *et al.* (1979) note that in cases of severe depression they begin with concrete behavioral tasks and then move to the cognitive procedures in their approach as the depressed client starts to make progress. Or it might be necessary to work to improve a couple's relationship before succeeding in the use of a specific method for the reversal of a problem of sexual dysfunction (e.g., Brady, 1976). But for the most part we suspect that decisions about the sequencing and timing of specific interventions within multifaceted programs is determined primarily by the therapist's intuitive feel or on a more prosaic trial-and-error basis. The behavior therapy literature is dotted with intriguing examples of the apparent importance of sequencing methods, as in the Barlow, Reynolds, and Agras's (1973) classic study of a transsexual client. Their creative use of single-case experimental methodology graphically revealed how aversion therapy aimed at sexual arousal patterns first failed and then subsequently proved successful following successful interventions in other areas of the client's functioning.

It is not without interest that the clinical issues that Lazarus refers to in his discussion of a "firing order" of treatment techniques have become an increasingly prominent focus of research in cognitive psychology. The issue here is the interaction between mood (affect) and cognition. Much of the research in cognitive psychology on memory processes has ignored the role of affect in the encoding, storage, and retrieval of information. Yet recent research has shown the decisive influence of affect on memory processes (Bower, 1981; Zajonc, 1980). Relating these research findings on the reciprocal influence of affect and cognition to the task of refining cognitive–behavioral treatments, Kihlstrom and Nasby (1981) make the following observation:

> While moods are created cognitively . . . [they] affect cognitive processes —thus leaving open the possibility for a vicious cycle that can be highly maladaptive. Consider the case of a clinician who attempts to alter the "depressive triad" of negative cognitions (Beck, 1967)—about one's self, one's past, and one's future—by leading the client to focus on positive rather than negative features of percepts and memories. This will be difficult to do if the client's mood is having just the opposite effect. The clinician must find some way to break the vicious cycle of affect and cognition before treatment can hope to be successful—either by means of a physiological manipulation (drugs or ECT) or, better, by teaching the client a self-regulatory strategy by which he or she can learn to modulate the affect of mood. (p. 298)

For those who continue to seek to relate clinical practice to laboratory research this apparent concordance between innovative therapeutic ideas and developing experimental investigation will be encouraging.

In the sixth and seventh points Lazarus refers to procedures that do set off multimodal therapy from the usual practice of behavior therapy. The critical question then becomes whether the expanded range of techniques referred to in the seventh point results in greater therapeutic efficacy. Presumably, the multimodal approach could be described in a way that would be replicable and allow it to be discriminated from alternative therapies, the first step in interpretable comparative research as discussed above in connection with Beck's cognitive therapy. At present, there is no evidence for judging the relative efficacy of multimodal therapy.

THE THERAPIST–PATIENT RELATIONSHIP

Despite unflattering and inaccurate stereotypes to the contrary, behavior therapy usually places great importance on the role of the therapeutic relationship, although the social learning or behavioral conceptualization of this relationship differs from the traditional psychodynamic perspective (Wilson & Evans, 1977). It will be recalled that one of Goldfried's (1980a) five questions concerned the role of the therapist–

patient relationship. The behaviorally oriented therapists who responded to this question all reaffirmed the importance of the therapeutic
relationship. Brady's comments in this connection bear reprinting:

> There is no question that qualitative aspects of the therapist–patient
> relationship can greatly influence the course of therapy for good or bad.
> In general, if the patient's relationship to the therapist is characterized by
> belief in the therapist's competence (knowledge, sophistication, and train
> ing) and if the patient regards the therapist as an honest, trustworthy, and
> decent human being with good social and ethical values (in his own
> scheme of things), the patient is more apt to invest himself in the therapy.
> Equally important is the quality and tone of the relationship he has with
> the therapist. That is, if he feels trusting and warm toward the therapist,
> this generally will facilitate following the treatment regimen, will be
> associated with higher expectations of improvement, and other generally
> favorable factors. The feelings of the therapist toward the patient are also
> important. If the therapist feels that his patient is not a desirable person or
> a decent human being or simply does not like the patient for whatever
> reasons, he may not succeed in concealing these feelings and attitudes
> toward the patient, and in general they will have a deleterious effect.
> There are some exceptions to these generalizations, however. Some pa
> tients will feel frightened and vulnerable with a therapist toward whom
> they feel attracted, particularly if from past experience they perceive such
> relationships as dangerous (danger of being hurt emotionally). With such
> a patient, a somewhat more distant and impersonal relationship may in
> fact be more desirable in that it will facilitate the patient's involvement in
> the treatment, following the treatment regimen, etc. (Goldfried, 1980a,
> pp. 285–286)

Among the many points Brady touches upon in this excerpt are
the concern for the therapist's and client's respective feelings for each
other,[8] the importance of the therapist being flexible in adjusting to
different clients' varying personal needs, the developing of trust and
appropriate therapeutic expectations, and the impact of the quality of
the relationship on the client's compliance with treatment prescriptions. This latter point it taken up in greater detail by Wilson (1980a).

Additional evidence showing that behavior therapists recognize
the importance of the therapeutic relationship comes from Swan and
MacDonald's (1978) survey of behavioral practitioners. Data from this
survey indicate that the treatment procedures most frequently used in

---

8. Stereotypes, however false, die hard. It is both discouraging and astonishing to find no
less a figure than Marmor (1980) declare that the major emphasis in behavior therapy is
on "removing the presenting symptom . . . by behavior modification; and the patient's
subjective problems, feelings, or thoughts are considered essentially irrelevant to the
psychotherapeutic process" (p. 410). So much for the much publicized tilt of behavior
therapy toward cognitive processes and procedures in the 1970s!

behavioral interventions were relationship enhancement methods. More specifically, relationship enhancement methods were reported as being applied in 58% of all cases. Commenting on this finding, Ford and Kendall (1979) state that "it is of some concern that relationship enhancement methods are not used in 42% of all cases. Greater attention seems warranted to the integration of specific behavioral techniques with the relationship enhancement methods in behavioral research, texts, and training programs" (p. 38).

Curiously, Turkat and Brantley (1981) take issue with Ford and Kendall's (1979) concern that slightly less than half of the therapists whom they surveyed did not use relationship enhancement procedures: "Our position is that such advocacy does not have a supportive data base (for widespread clinical use), is inconsistent with the tenets of behavior therapy, and can only impede the advancement of efficacious clinical practice. Before anyone can claim that nonspecific factors such as warmth and empathy should be utilized with all cases, these factors must be operationalized, evaluated in terms of their outcome and mechanisms, and demonstrated to be indicated by the formulation of each individual case" (Turkat & Brantley, p. 16). It would be unfortunate if, unwittingly, this assertion were to further the erroneous impression that behavior therapy emphasizes impersonal precision at the expense of warmth, wit, and humanity.

It would seem clear that behavior therapists, including Ford and Kendall, recognize the importance of flexibility on the part of the therapist in adjusting his or her style to the particular needs of individual clients. Brady's comments in the excerpt referred to above are representative. Other sophisticated discussions of the therapeutic relationship in cognitive–behavioral therapy can be found in Beck *et al.* (1979) and Lazarus (1981). For example, Beck *et al.* view factors such as warmth as necessary but not sufficient conditions of therapeutic improvement. Yet these authors issue the following caveat:

> The therapist is well-advised to exercise caution and vigilance in displaying this warm attitude. If the therapist is too active in demonstrating a warm, caring concern (or more importantly, if the patient thinks the warm attitude is too intense), the patient may react negatively. For example, the patient may think, "I am undeserving of such caring," or "I am deceiving the therapist because he appears to like me and I know I am worthless." Or the patient may misconstrue the therapist's motives: "He's insincere," or "How can he like a worthless person like me?" . . . In essence, the therapist must strike an appropriate balance in displaying warmth. The patient may construe minimal warmth as rejection, while too hearty a display of caring may be misinterpreted in either a negative or overly positive way. Thus, the therapist must carefully attend to signs that suggest that his attitudes are counterproductive. (pp. 46–47)

Turkat and Brantley underscore the inadequacy of a single mode of therapist–client interaction in all cases. But to be warm and to display empathy for one's clients need not tie one to a rigid, unimodal interpersonal demeanor. For example, one could be directive or relatively nondirective in therapy while showing warmth, empathy, and genuineness. By the same token, one can use attention contingently, challenge assumptions and actions vigorously, and offer constructive criticism and still rate high on the Rogerian triad. Recall that in the Sloane *et al.* (1975) study the behavior therapists were not only significantly more directive than their psychoanalytically oriented counterparts but also showed higher levels of accurate empathy, interpersonal contact, and congruence. O'Leary, Turkewitz, and Tafel (1973) found that virtually all parents whose children were treated at the Stony Brook Child Guidance Clinic rated their behavior therapists as understanding, warm, sincere, and interested.

Similarly, in a study of marital therapy by Turkewitz and O'Leary (in press), clients' ratings of their behavior therapists were very positive: Using a seven-point scale, wives' ratings averaged 6.8 and the husbands' average was 6.7 across the four personal characteristics of empathy, concern, likableness, and competence.

There is no evidence that "nonspecific" factors such as warmth and empathy hinder effective behavioral treatment and there are data confirming that they help (e.g., Goldstein, 1971; Morris & Suckerman, 1974). Behavior therapy stresses the necessity of using demonstrably effective techniques within the context of a facilitative therapist–patient relationship. The great Rogerian hope that the personal qualities of the therapist and the helping relationship he or she established with clients were the necessary and sufficient conditions of therapeutic change has been dashed. Warmth, empathy, and genuineness do not ensure treatment success. Lambert, de Julio, and Stein (1978) reached the following well-founded conclusion:

> The best conclusions that can be drawn based on the existing data are as follows: . . . despite more than twenty years of research and some improvements in methodology, only a modest relationship between the so-called facilitative conditions and therapy outcome has been found. Contrary to frequent claims for the potency of these therapist-offered relationship variables, experimental evidence suggests that neither a clear test nor unequivocal support for the Rogerian hypothesis has appeared. (p. 486)

So-called "nonspecific" factors, including the therapist's contribution to effective therapy can be explicitly described and measured, and their effects on treatment outcome evaluated (Wilson, 1980c). Particularly helpful in this respect has been the specification and evaluation of Beck's cognitive therapy (Beck *et al.*, 1979). Consistent with previous descriptions of the therapeutic relationship in behavior therapy (e.g., Goldfried & Davison, 1976; Lazarus, 1971; Wilson & Evans, 1977), Beck *et al.* emphasize the importance of warmth, empathy, genuineness, as well as trust, rapport, and active collaboration between therapist and client. Concrete suggestions are made about how the therapist goes about promoting these conditions. Moreover, these qualities are specified in a competency checklist for cognitive–behavioral therapists.

Not unlike Gaul, the checklist consists of three parts. The first describes general interview procedures, such as collaboration and mutual understanding, establishing an agenda, eliciting reactions to the therapist and therapy, and structuring therapy time efficiently and so on. The second part covers the use of specific cognitive–behavioral techniques. The third focuses on the therapist's personal and professional characteristics. For example, under the subheading of rapport, the therapist is rated on the following dimensions: "a. Patient and therapist seemed comfortable with each other. b. Eye contact maintained. c. Good affective interaction (e.g., when one smiles, the other smiles). d. Flow of verbal interchanges was smooth. e. Neither patient nor therapist appeared overly defensive, cautious, or restrained" (Beck *et al.*, 1979, p. 407).

DeRubeis *et al.* (1981) have developed and tested a scale (The Minnesota Therapy Rating Scale) that included items from the Beck *et al.* checklist, for discriminating cognitive–behavioral therapy from psychotherapy and for evaluating whether the differences that are detected are related to those that would be expected by experts associated with cognitive–behavioral therapy. Initial findings have been positive. Procedural differences have been shown to exist between cognitive–behavioral treatment and psychotherapy, differences that can be reliably assessed. Moreover, there is some promise that the use of specific techniques linked to particular theoretical orientations can be distinguished from general therapist skills and styles. Consistent with the Sloane *et al.* (1975) findings, DeRubeis *et al.* report that cognitive–behavioral therapists were rated more highly on some nonspecific relationship skills than a small group of nonbehavioral psychotherapists. Not too much can be made of such findings since no generalization to the full population of therapists in the respective "schools" are possible. The data may be of some value, however, in discrediting uninformed views of cognitive–behavioral therapy as necessarily "less human" than psychodynamic approaches.

The potential significance of the foregoing research is obvious. To yield interpretable findings, comparative therapy outcome studies must be able to show that rival treatments are procedurally different and that they are implemented in accord with the requirements of each approach

(Kazdin & Wilson, 1978). If the therapist's personal skills can be reliably differentiated from the specific techniques associated with a particular theoretical approach, resolution of some enduring controversies in therapy outcome research will be greatly facilitated. On the practical level, if therapist skills that might be shown to be related to treatment outcome are operationalized, the task of training effective therapists in the future will have been greatly aided.

SUMMARY

A striking feature of the clinical practice of behavior therapy is the wide range of diverse problems to which behavioral strategies are applied. Behavior therapists are bold in what they try although not always cautious in what they claim. Few novel therapeutic techniques or clinical strategies were introduced over the past two years, but well-established principles of behavior change were extended in creative fashion to new areas.

Among the most significant and salient issues that dominated the clinical scene in behavior therapy were several that we have addressed in previous volumes of this series. This chapter focused intensively on four of these much discussed issues: (1) the gap between experimental research and clinical practice; (2) the possibility of a rapprochement between behavior therapy and traditional psychotherapeutic approaches; (3) the similarities and differences between Lazarus's multimodal therapy and behavior therapy; and (4) the role of the therapist–patient relationship in behavior therapy.

A thoughtful paper by Barlow has led to a reexamination of the relationship between research and practice in behavior therapy. Arguing that the distance between laboratory and clinic is in large measure due to the undue reliance upon group outcome studies that lose sight of the individual client, Barlow has recommended what might be done to improve the impact of research on clinical practice. Practitioners, using versatile single-case experimental methodology, must involve themselves in the research and evaluation process. In elaborations of this theme, Nelson has described handy dependent measures that practitioners could realistically employ, while Hayes has tried to demonstrate a "goodness of fit" between routine clinical practice and the logic of time-series methodology. Yet a combination of personal, practical, and methodological problems make it unlikely that practitioners will be able to carry out experimental research that establishes causal relationships except in rare instances. Controlled clinical research, using either between-groups or single-case experimental designs, will be conducted mainly by specialists who are clinical researchers and who have been trained in the scientist–practitioner model.

The unique and crucial contributions of the practitioner include making careful clinical observations about the nature and treatment of disorders, generating hypotheses that can guide and spur relevant research, and field-testing the adequacy of research-based methods. The clinical case study continues to play an important role in the transmission of therapeutic knowledge, although its influence on practitioners is usually incommensurate with its probative value. Case studies can be more or less useful, and Kazdin has outlined the ways in which they might be improved so as to yield more valid inferences about treatment effects.

A much discussed paper by Goldfried suggests that the time is ripe for a rapprochement among different therapeutic approaches. His thesis is that principles of effective therapeutic change common to alternative approaches can be identified not at the abstract level of theoretical frameworks or the concrete level of specific therapeutic techniques, but at the intermediate level of what he calls clinical strategies. An example of a clinical strategy is the emphasis in therapy on creating new learning experiences. A critical analysis of this argument shows that despite some surface similarities, for alternative treatment approaches such as behavior therapy and psychoanalysis fundamental differences on basic conceptual and practical issues still divide the approaches. In contrast to Goldfried's proposal that therapeutic advances will be made once we identify common principles, it is suggested here that progress is more likely to result from rigorous attempts by different therapeutic approaches to describe their methods in replicable fashion and to link those discriminable methods to measurable treatment outcome.

Lazarus, a pioneer of behavior therapy, has launched an approach called multimodal therapy that he claims is bigger and better than behavior therapy. A careful analysis of treatment concepts and procedures indicates relatively minimal differences between the two approaches. The value of some of the non-behavior-therapy techniques used in multimodal therapy is questionable. Whether or not the approach yields more durable effects than all alternatives as is claimed must await overdue empirical tests. Despite statements that multimodal profiles provide a blueprint for treatment, categorizing clients' problems in this global manner appears to have little connection to treatment unless the functional analyses that are the hallmark of behavior therapy are conducted.

The importance of the therapist–client relationship in behavior therapy has been strongly reemphasized by behavioral practitioners in response to questions and surveys about the critical ingredients of therapeutic change. Among other issues the importance of flexibility in adjusting to particular clients' individual needs is stressed. Positive therapeutic relationships require, among other personal qualities, warmth and empathy of the therapist, attributes that behavior therapists possess according to their clients' reports in studies of the clinical practice of behavior therapists. Beck and his colleagues have devised a competency checklist for cognitive–behavioral therapists that helps to operationalize the therapist's personal and technical skills. Emerging research that detects differences between cognitive therapy and psychotherapy and allows evaluation of the adequacy with which that treatment is implemented promises a significant advance in clinical research and training.

REFERENCES

Abikoff, H., Gittelman-Klein, R., & Klein, D. F. Validation of a classroom observation code for hyperactive children. *Journal of Consulting and Clinical Psychology*, 1977, *45*, 772–783.

Abikoff, H., Gittelman, R., & Klein, D. F. Classroom observation code for hyperactive children: A replication of validity. *Journal of Consulting and Clinical Psychology*, 1980, *48*, 555–565.

Abikoff, H., & Ramsey, P. P. A critical comment on Kendall and Finch's cognitive-behavioral group comparison study. *Journal of Consulting and Clinical Psychology*, 1979, *47*, 1104–1106.

Abrams, D. B., Follick, M. J., & Thompson, C. B. Work site weight loss intervention: Procedures, problems, and potentials. In T. J. Coates (Ed.), *Behavioral medicine: A practical handbook*. Champaign, Ill.: Research Press, in press.

Abrams, D. B., & Wilson, G. T. Self-monitoring and reactivity in the modification of cigarette smoking. *Journal of Consulting and Clinical Psychology*, 1979, *47*, 243–251.

Adinolfi, A. A., McCourt, W. F., & Geoghegan, S. Group assertiveness training for alcoholics. *Journal of Studies on Alcohol*, 1976, *37*, 311–320.

Adkins, J., & Matson, J. L. Teaching institutionalized mentally retarded adults socially appropriate leisure skills. *Mental Retardation*, 1980, *18*, 249–252.

Adner, M. M., & Castelli, W. P. Elevated high-density lipoprotein levels in marathon runners. *Journal of the American Medical Association*, 1980, *243*, 534–536.

Agras, W. S., & Berkowitz, R. Clinical research in behavior therapy: Halfway there? *Behavior Therapy*, 1980, *11*, 472–487.

Agras, W. S., Chapin, H., & Oliveau, D. The natural history of phobia. *Archives of General Psychiatry*, 1972, *26*, 315–317.

Agras, W. S., Jacob, R. G., & Lebedeck, M. The California drought: A quasi-experimental analysis of social policy. *Journal of Applied Behavior Analysis*, 1980, *13*, 561–570.

Agras, W. S., Kazdin, A. E., & Wilson, G. T. *Behavior therapy: Towards an applied clinical science*. San Francisco, Calif.: Freeman, 1979.

Ahrens, R. A., & Koh, E. T. The effect of dietary carbohydrate source in controlling body composition changes due to forced exercise in rats. *Journal of Nutrition*, 1971, *101*, 885–888.

Albin, T. J., Stark, J. A., & Keith, K. D. Vocational training and placement: Behavior analyses in the natural environment. In G. T. Bellamy, G. O'Connor, & O. C. Karan (Eds.), *Vocational rehabilitation of severely handicapped persons: Contemporary service strategies*. Baltimore: University Park Press, 1979.

347

Alderman, M. H., Green, L. W., & Flynn, B. S. Hypertension control programs in occupational settings. *Public Health Reports*, 1980, *95*, 158–163.

Alderman, M. H., & Schoenbaum, E. E. Detection and treatment of hypertension at the work site. *New England Journal of Medicine*, 1975, *293*, 65–68.

Alexander, J. F., & Parsons, B. V. Short-term behavioral intervention with delinquent families. *Journal of Abnormal Psychology*, 1973, *81*, 219–225.

Alger, I. Accountability: Human and political dimensions. *American Journal of Orthopsychiatry*, 1980, *50*, 388–393.

Allison, M. G., & Ayllon, T. Behavioral coaching in the development of skills in football, gymnastics, and tennis. *Journal of Applied Behavior Analysis*, 1980, *13*, 297–314.

Ambrose, S., Hazzard, A., & Haworth, J. Cognitive–behavioral parenting groups for abusive families. *Child Abuse and Neglect*, 1980, *4*, 119–125.

American Heart Association, Committee on Exercise. *Exercise testing and training of individuals with heart disease or at high risk for its development: A handbook for physicians*. Dallas: American Heart Association, 1975.

American Heart Association. *The American Heart Association heartbook: A guide to prevention and treatment of cardiovascular diseases*. New York: Dutton, 1980. (a)

American Heart Association. Risk factors and coronary disease: A statement for physicians. *Circulation*, 1980, *62*, 1–8. (b)

Anderson, M., & Borkovec, T. Imagery processing and fear reduction during repeated exposure to two types of phobic imagery. *Behaviour Research and Therapy*, 1980, *18*, 537–540.

Andrasik, F., Heimberg, J. S., & McNamara, J. R. Behavior modification of work and work-related problems. In M. Hersen, R. M. Eisler, & P. M. Miller (Eds.), *Progress in behavior modification*. New York: Academic Press, in press.

Andres, R. Influence of obesity on longevity in the aged. In C. Borek, C. M. Fenoglio, & D. W. King (Eds.), *Aging, cancer and cell membranes*. Stuttgart: Thieme, 1980.

Antonuccio, D. O., & Lichtenstein, E. Peer modeling influences on smoking behavior of heavy and light smokers. *Addictive Behaviors*, 1980, *5*, 299–306.

Apolloni, T., Cappuccilli, J., & Cooke, T. P. (Eds.). *Target excellence: Achievements in residential services for persons with disabilities*. Baltimore: University Park Press, 1980.

Appel, P. W., & Kaestner, E. Interpersonal and emotional problem solving among narcotic drug abusers. *Journal of Consulting and Clinical Psychology*, 1979, *47*, 1125–1127.

Armor, D. J., Polich, J. M., & Stambul, H. D. *Alcoholism and treatment*. New York: Wiley, 1978.

Arnkoff, D. B. Psychotherapy from the perspective of cognitive theory. In M. J. Mahoney (Ed.), *Psychotherapy process: Current issues and future directions*. New York: Plenum, 1980.

Arnkoff, D. B., & Glass, C. R. Clinical cognitive constructs: Examination, evaluation, and elaboration. In P. C. Kendall (Ed.), *Advances in cognitive–behavioral research and therapy* (Vol. 1). New York: Academic Press, 1982.

Aronow, W. S. Smoking, carbon monoxide, and coronary heart disease. *Circulation*, 1973, *48*, 1169–1172.

Arrindell, W. A. Dimensional structure and psychopathology correlates of the Fear Survey Schedule (FSS-III) in a phobic population: A factorial definition of agoraphobia. *Behaviour Research and Therapy*, 1980, *18*, 229–242.

Asher, J. R., Oden, S. L., & Gottman, J. M. Children's friendships in the school setting.

In L. G. Katz (Ed.), *Current topics in early childhood education* (Vol. 1). Norwood, N.J.: Ablex, 1977.

Astrand, P. O., & Rodahl, K. *Textbook of work physiology.* New York: McGraw-Hill, 1977.

Atkeson, B. M., & Forehand, R. Parent behavioral training for problem children: An examination of studies using multiple outcome measures. *Journal of Abnormal Child Psychology*, 1978, *6*, 449–460.

Atkinson, R. Physical fitness and headache. *Headache*, 1977, *17*, 189–191.

Auerbach, S. M., Kendall, P. C., Cuttler, H. F., & Levitt, N. R. Anxiety, loss of control, type of preparatory information, and adjustment to dental surgery. *Journal of Consulting and Clinical Psychology*, 1976, *44*, 809–818.

Authier, K. J., Sherrets, S. D., & Tramontana, M. G. Methods and models of parent education. *Journal of Clinical Child Psychology*, 1980, *9*, 38–40.

Ayllon, T., Layman, D., & Kandel, H. J. A behavioral educational alternative to drug control of hyperactive children. *Journal of Applied Behavior Analysis*, 1975, *8*, 137–146.

Azrin, N. H., & Holz, W. C. Punishment. In W. K. Honig (Ed.), *Operant behavior: Areas of research and application.* New York: Appleton-Century-Crofts, 1966.

Azrin, N. H., Naster, B. J., & Jones, R. Reciprocity counseling: A rapid learning-based procedure for marital counseling. *Behaviour Research and Therapy*, 1973, *11*, 365–382.

Azrin, N. H., & Powers, M. Eliminating classroom disturbances of emotionally disturbed children by positive practice procedures. *Behavior Therapy*, 1975, *6*, 525–535.

Bachman, J. G., Johnston, L. D., & O'Malley, P. M. Smoking, drinking, and drug use among American high school students: Correlates and trends, 1975–1979. *American Journal of Public Health*, 1981, *71*, 59–69.

Bachrach, L. L. Is the least restrictive environment always the best? Sociological and semantic implications. *Hospital and Community Psychiatry*, 1980, *31*, 97–102.

Backman, J., & Firestone, P. A review of psychopharmacological and behavioral approaches to the treatment of hyperactive children. *American Journal of Orthopsychiatry*, 1979, *49*, 500–504.

Bacon-Prue, A., Blount, R., Pickering, D., & Drabman, R. An evaluation of three litter control procedures—trash receptacles, paid workers, and the marked item technique. *Journal of Applied Behavior Analysis*, 1980, *13*, 165–170.

Baekeland, F. Exercise deprivation. *Archives of General Psychiatry*, 1970, *22*, 365–369.

Baer, D. M. Applied behavior analysis. In G. T. Wilson & C. M. Franks (Eds.), *Contemporary behavior therapy: Conceptual and empirical foundations.* New York: Guilford, 1982.

Baer, D. M., & Wolf, M. M. The entry into natural communities of reinforcement. In R. Ulrich, T. Stachnik, & J. Mabry (Eds.), *Control of human behavior* (Vol. 2). Glenview, Ill.: Scott, Foresman, 1970.

Baer, D. M., Wolf, M. M., & Risley, T. R. Some current dimensions of applied behavior analysis. *Journal of Applied Behavior Analysis*, 1968, *1*, 91–97.

Bailey, J. S. Wanted: A rational search for the limiting conditions of habilitation in the retarded. *Analysis and Intervention in Developmental Disabilities*, 1981, *1*, 45–52.

Bailey, R. E., & Bailey, M. B. A view from outside the Skinner box. *American Psychologist*, 1980, *35*, 942–946.

Bain, C., Hennekens, C. H., Rosner, B., Speizer, F. E., & Jesse, M. J. Cigarette consumption and deaths from coronary heart disease. *Lancet*, 1978, *1*, 1087–1088.

Baker, B. L. Training parents as teachers of their developmentally disabled children. In

S. Salinger, J. Antrobus, & J. Glick (Eds.), *The ecosystem of the "sick" child.* New York: Academic Press, 1981.

Baker, B. L., & Clark, D. B. *The family setting: Enhancing the retarded child's development through parent training.* Paper presented at NICHD/UCLA Conference, Impact of specific settings on the development and behavior of retarded persons, Los Angeles, September 1980.

Baker, B. L., Heifetz, L. J., & Murphy, D. M. Behavioral training for parents of mentally-retarded children: One-year follow-up. *American Journal of Mental Deficiency,* 1980, *85,* 31-38.

Ballantyne, D., Clark, A. Dyker, G. S., Gillis, C. R., Hawthorne, V. M., Henry, D. A., Hole, D. S., Murdock, R. M., Semple, T., & Stewart, G. M. Prescribing exercise for the healthy: Assessment of compliance and effects on plasma lipids and lipo-proteins. *Health Bulletin,* 1978, July, 169-176.

Ballard, B. D., Gipson, M. T., Guttenberg, W., & Ramsey, K. Palatability of food as a factor influencing obese and normal weight children's eating habits. *Behaviour Research and Therapy,* 1980, *18,* 598-601.

Baltes, M. M., & Barton, E. M. New approaches toward aging: A case for the operant model. *Educational Gerontology: An International Quarterly,* 1977, *2,* 383-405.

Baltes, M. M., & Barton, E. M. Behavioral analysis of aging: A review of the operant model and research. *International Journal of Behavioral Development,* 1979, *2,* 297-320.

Bandura, A. *Principles of behavior modification.* New York: Holt, Rinehart & Winston, 1969.

Bandura, A. Self-reinforcement: Theoretical and methodological considerations. *Behaviorism,* 1976, *4,* 135-155.

Bandura, A. Self-efficacy: Toward a unifying theory of behavioral change. *Psychological Review,* 1977, *84,* 191-215. (a)

Bandura, A. *Social learning theory.* Englewood Cliffs, N.J.: Prentice-Hall, 1977. (b)

Bandura, A. Reflections on self-efficacy. *Advances in Behaviour Research and Therapy,* 1978, *1,* 237-269. (a)

Bandura, A. The self-system in reciprocal determinism. *American Psychologist,* 1978, *33,* 344-358. (b)

Bandura, A. Gauging the relationship between self-efficacy judgment and action. *Cognitive Therapy and Research,* 1980, *4,* 263-268.

Bandura, A. Self-referent thought: A developmental analysis of self-efficacy. In J. H. Flavell & L. D. Ross (Eds.), *Cognitive social development: Frontiers and possible futures.* New York: Cambridge University Press, 1981.

Bandura, A., Adams, N. E., Hardy, A. B., & Howells, G. N. Tests of the generality of self-efficacy theory. *Cognitive Therapy and Research,* 1980, *4,* 39-66.

Barabash, C. *A comparison of self-instruction training, token fading procedures and a combined self-instruction/token fading treatment in modifying children's impulsive behavior.* Unpublished doctoral dissertation, New York University, 1978.

Barkley, R. A. The effects of methylphenidate on various types of activity level and attention in hyperkinetic children. *Journal of Abnormal Child Psychology,* 1977, *5,* 351-369.

Barkley, R. A., & Cunningham, C. E. Do stimulant drugs improve the academic performance of hyperkinetic children? *Clinical Pediatrics,* 1978, *17,* 85-92.

Barling, J. Image of behaviour modification: A critical analysis. *South African Journal of Psychology,* 1979, *9,* 98-103.

Barlow, D. H. Behavior therapy: The next decade. *Behavior Therapy,* 1980, *11,* 315-328.

Barlow, D. H. (Ed.). *Behavioral assessment of adult disorders.* New York: Guilford, 1981.

Barlow, D. H., Hayes, S. C., Nelson, R. O., Steele, D. L., Meeler, M. E., & Mills, J. R. Sex role motor behavior: A behavioral checklist. *Behavioral Assessment*, 1979, *1*, 119–138.

Barlow, D. H., Mavissakalian, M., & Hay, L. R. Couples treatment of agoraphobia: Changes in marital satisfaction. *Behaviour Research and Therapy*, 1981, *19*, 245–256.

Barlow, D. H., Reynolds, E. J., & Agras, W. S. Gender identity change in a transsexual. *Archives of General Psychiatry*, 1973, *28*, 569–576.

Barlow, D. H., & Wolfe, B. Behavioral approaches to anxiety disorders: A report on the NIMH-SUNY research conference. *Journal of Consulting and Clinical Psychology*, 1981, *49*, 448–454.

Barmann, B. C., Croyle-Barmann, C., & McLain, B. The use of contingent-interrupted music in the treatment of disruptive bus-riding behavior. *Journal of Applied Behavior Analysis*, 1980, *13*, 693–698.

Barnard, M. V. Behavioral approaches to viewing. *The Behavior Therapist*, 1980, *3*, 11–12.

Barrios, B. A., & Shigetomi, C. C. Coping-skills training for the management of anxiety: A critical review. *Behavior Therapy*, 1979, *10*, 491–522.

Barth, R. Home based reinforcement of school behavior: A review and analysis. *Review of Educational Research*, 1979, *49*, 436–458.

Battalio, R. C., Kagel, J. H., Winkler, R. C., & Winett, R. A. Residential electricity demand: An experimental study. *The Review of Economics and Statistics*, 1979, *61*, 180–189.

Baum, A., & Epstein, Y. M. (Eds.). *Human response to crowding*. Hillsdale, N.J.: Erlbaum, 1978.

Baum, A., Fisher, J. D., & Solomon, S. K. Type of information, familiarity, and the reduction of crowding others. *Journal of Personality and Social Psychology*, 1981, *40*, 11–23.

Bazar, J. California institutes guidelines for behavioral techniques. *APA Monitor*, 1979, July–August, *4*, 14.

Beck, A. T. *Depression: Clinical, experimental and theoretical aspects*. New York: Hoeber, 1967.

Beck, A. T. *Cognitive therapy and the emotional disorders*. New York: International Universities Press, 1976.

Beck, A. T., Rush, A. J., Shaw, B. F., & Emery, G. *Cognitive therapy of depression*. New York: Guilford, 1979.

Bedell, J. R., & Archer, R. P. Peer managed token economies: Evaluation and description. *Journal of Clinical Psychology*, 1980, *36*, 716–722.

Bedell, J. R., Archer, R. P., & Marlowe, H. A. A description and evaluation of a problem solving skills training program. In D. Upper & S. M. Ross (Eds.), *Behavioral group therapy: An annual review*. Champaign, Ill.: Research Press, 1980.

Belar, C. D. Training the clinical psychology student in behavioral medicine. *Professional Psychology*, 1980, *11*, 620–627.

Bellack, A. S., Hersen, M., & Lamparski, D. Role-play tests for assessing social skills: Are they valid? Are they useful? *Journal of Consulting and Clinical Psychology*, 1979, *47*, 335–342.

Bellack, A. S., Hersen, M., & Turner, S. M. Relationship of role playing and knowledge of appropriate behavior to assertion in the natural environment. *Journal of Consulting and Clinical Psychology*, 1979, *47*, 670–678.

Bellamy, G. T., Inman, D. P., & Horne, R. H. Design of vocational habilitation services for the severely retarded: The specialized training program model. In L. A.

Hamerlynck (Ed.), *Behavioral systems for the developmentally disabled: II. Institutional, clinic, and community environments.* New York: Brunner/Mazel, 1979.

Bellamy, G. T., O'Connor, G., & Karan, O. C. (Eds.). *Vocational rehabilitation of severely handicapped persons: Contemporary service strategies.* Baltimore: University Park Press, 1979.

Belloc, N. B. Relationship of health practices and mortality. *Preventive Medicine,* 1973, *2,* 67–81.

Belloc, N. B., & Breslow, L. Relationship of health status and health practices. *Preventive Medicine,* 1972, *1,* 409–421.

Bem, S. L. The measurement of psychological androgyny. *Journal of Consulting and Clinical Psychology,* 1974, *42,* 155–162.

Benson, H. *The relaxation response.* New York: Morrow, 1975.

Berger, M. Behaviour modification in education and professional practice: The dangers of a mindless technology. *Bulletin of the British Psychological Society,* 1979, *32,* 418–419.

Bergin, A. E., & Strupp, H. H. New directions in psychotherapy research. *Journal of Abnormal Psychology,* 1970, *76,* 13–26.

Bernal, M. E., Klinnert, M. D., & Schultz, L. A. Outcome evaluation of behavioral parent training and client-centered parent counseling for children with conduct problems. *Journal of Applied Behavior Analysis,* 1980, *13,* 677–691.

Bernal, M. E., & North, J. A. A survey of parent training manuals. *Journal of Applied Behavior Analysis,* 1978, *11,* 533–544.

Bernstein, D. A. The modification of smoking behavior: A search for effective variables. *Behaviour Research and Therapy,* 1970, *8,* 133–146.

Bernstein, D. A., & Glasgow, R. E. Smoking. In O. F. Pomerleau & J. P. Brady (Eds.), *Behavioral medicine: Theory and practice.* Baltimore: Williams & Wilkins, 1979.

Berwick, P., & Morris, L. Token economies: Are they doomed? *Professional Psychology,* 1974, *5,* 436–439.

Beutler, L. E. Toward specific psychological therapies for specific conditions. *Journal of Consulting and Clinical Psychology,* 1979, *47,* 882–897.

Biran, M., Augusto, F., & Wilson, G. T. A comparative analysis of cognitive and behavioral methods in the treatment of scriptophobia. *Behaviour Research and Therapy,* 1981, *19,* 525–532.

Biran, M., & Wilson, G. T. Treatment of phobic disorders using cognitive and exposure methods: A self-efficacy analysis. *Journal of Consulting and Clinical Psychology,* 1981, *49,* 886–899.

Birkimer, J. C., & Brown, J. H. A graphical judgmental aid which summarizes obtained and chance reliability data and helps assess the believability of experimental effects. *Journal of Applied Behavior Analysis,* 1979, *12,* 523–534. (a)

Birkimer, J. C., & Brown, J. H. Back to basics: Percentage agreement measures are adequate, but there are easier ways. *Journal of Applied Behavior Analysis,* 1979, *12,* 535–544. (b)

Bistrian, B. R. Clinical use of a protein-sparing modified fast. *Journal of the American Medical Association,* 1978, *21,* 2299–2302.

Bjorntorp, P., Fahlen, M., Grimby, G., Gustafson, A., Holm, J., Renstrom, P., & Schersten, T. Carbohydrate and lipid metabolism in middle-aged, physically well-trained men. *Metabolism,* 1972, *21,* 1037–1044.

Bjorntorp, P., Sjostrom, L., & Sullivan, L. The role of physical exercise in the management of obesity. In J. F. Munro (Ed.), *The treatment of obesity.* Lancaster, England: MTP Press, 1979.

Bjurstrom, L. A., & Alexiou, N. G. A program of heart disease intervention for public employees. *Journal of Occupational Medicine,* 1978, *20,* 521–531.

Blackman, D. E. Ethical standards for behaviour modification. *British Journal of Criminology,* 1979, *19,* 420–445.

Blackman, D. E. On the mental element in crime and behaviourism. In S. Lloyd-Bestock (Ed.), *Law and psychology: Papers presented at meetings of the SSRC Law and Psychology Seminar Group, 1979–1980.* Oxford: Centre for Sociological Studies, in press.

Blanchard, E. B. A note on the clinical utility of the Rathus Assertiveness Scale. *Behavior Therapy,* 1979, *10,* 571–574.

Block, M. A. Don't place alcohol on a pedestal. *Journal of the American Medical Association,* 1976, *235,* 2103–2104.

Blunden, D., Spring, C., & Greenberg, L. M. Validation of the classroom behavior inventory. *Journal of Consulting and Clinical Psychology,* 1974, *42,* 84–88.

Bonham, G. S., & Wilson, R. W. Children's health in families with cigarette smokers. *American Journal of Public Health,* 1981, *71,* 290–293.

Bordewick, M. C., & Bornstein, P. H. Examination of multiple cognitive response dimensions among differentially assertive individuals. *Behavior Therapy,* 1980, *11,* 440–448.

Bornstein, P. H., Bridgwater, C. A., Hickey, J. S., & Sweeney, T. M. Characteristics and trends in behavioral assessment: An archival analysis. *Behavioral Assessment,* 1980, *2,* 125–133.

Bornstein, P. H., Hamilton, S. B., & Quevillon, R. T. Behavior modification by long distance: Demonstration of functional control over disruptive behavior in a rural classroom setting. *Behavior Modification,* 1977, *1,* 369–380.

Bornstein, P. H., Rychtarik, R. G., McFall, M. E., Bridgwater, C. A., Guthrie, L., & Anton, B. Behaviorally specific report cards and self-determined reinforcements: A multiple-baseline analyses of inmate offenses. *Behavior Modification,* 1980, *4,* 71–81.

Boudin, H., Valentine, V., Ingraham, R., Brantley, J., Ruiz, M., Smith, G., Catlin, R., & Regan, E. *Contingency contracting with drug addicts in the natural environment.* Unpublished manuscript, University of Florida, 1976 (cited by Nietzel, 1979).

Boulding, K. *Ecodynamics: A new theory of social evolution.* Beverly Hills, Calif.: Sage, 1978.

Bourque, P., & LaDouceur, R. An investigation of various performance-based treatments with acrophobics. *Behaviour Research and Therapy,* 1980, *18,* 161–170.

Bourque, P., & LaDouceur, R. Self-respect and behavioral measures in the assessment of assertive behavior. *Journal of Behavior Therapy and Experimental Psychiatry,* 1979, *10,* 287–292.

Bower, G. H. Mood and memory. *American Psychologist,* 1981, *36,* 129–148.

Box, S. Hyperactivity: The scandalous silence. *American Educator,* 1978, Summer, 22–24.

Boyd, R. D. Systematic parent training through a home-based model. *Exceptional Children,* 1979, *45,* 147–450.

Boyer, J. L., & Kasch, F. W. Exercise therapy in hypertensive men. *Journal of the American Medical Association,* 1970, *211,* 1668–1671.

Bradlyn, A. S., Strickler, D. P., & Maxwell, W. A. Alcohol, expectancy and stress: Methodological concerns with the expectancy design. *Addictive Behaviors,* 1981, *6,* 1–8.

Brady, J. P. The place of behavior therapy in medical student and psychiatric resident training. *Journal of Nervous and Mental Disease,* 1973, *157,* 21–26.

Brady, J. P. Behavior therapy and sex therapy. *American Journal of Psychiatry,* 1976, *133,* 896–899.

Brady, J. P., & Wienckowski, L. A. Update on the teaching of behavior therapy in medical student and psychiatric resident training. *Journal of Behavior Therapy and Experimental Psychiatry*, 1978, *9*, 125–127.

Brandsma, J. M., Maultsby, M. C., & Welsh, R. *Self-help techniques in the treatment of alcoholism.* Unpublished manuscript, University of Kentucky, 1978.

Brantingham, P. J., & Faust, F. L. A conceptual model of crime prevention. *Crime and Delinquency*, 1976, *22*, 284–296.

Braud, L. W. The effects of frontal EMG biofeedback and progressive relaxation upon hyperactivity and its behavioral concomitants. *Biofeedback and Self-Regulation*, 1978, *3*, 69–89.

Braun, S. H. Ethical issues in behavior modification. *Behavior Therapy*, 1975, *6*, 51–62.

Bray, G. A. *The obese patient.* Philadelphia: Saunders, 1976.

Breland, K., & Breland, M. The misbehavior of organisms. *American Psychologist*, 1961, *16*, 681–684.

Brenner, A. A study of the efficacy of the Feingold diet on hyperkinetic children. *Clinical Pediatrics*, 1977, *16*, 252–656.

Breslow, L. Risk factor intervention for health maintenance. *Science*, 1978, *200*, 908–912.

Breslow, L. A positive strategy for the nation's health. *Journal of the American Medical Association*, 1979, *242*, 2093–2095.

Breslow, L., & Enstrom, J. E. Persistence of health habits and their relationship to mortality. *Preventive Medicine*, 1980, *9*, 469–483.

Brett, J. M. Behavioral research on unions and union management systems. *Research in Organizational Behavior*, 1980, *2*, 177–213.

Brightman, R. P., Ambrose, S. A., & Baker, B. L. Parent training: A school-based model for enhancing teaching performance. *Child Behavior Therapy*, 1980, *2*, 35–47.

Brockway, B. S. Chemical validation of self-reported smoking rates. *Behavior Therapy*, 1978, *9*, 685–686.

Brodsky, S. L. *Psychologists in the criminal justice system.* Urbana: University of Illinois Press, 1973.

Bromet, E., Moos, R. H., Bliss, F., & Wuthmann, C. The posttreatment of alcoholic patients: Its relation to program participation. *Journal of Consulting and Clinical Psychology*, 1977, *45*, 829–842.

Brown, M. G., Malott, R. W., Dillon, M. J., & Keeps, E. J. Improving customer service in a large department store through the use of training and feedback. *Journal of Organizational Behavior Management*, 1980, *2*, 251–265.

Brown, R. A. Conventional education and controlled drinking education courses with convicted drunken drivers. *Behavior Therapy*, 1980, *11*, 632–642.

Brown, R. T., & Sleator, E. K. Methylphenidate in hyperkinetic children: Differences in dose effects on impulsive behavior. *Pediatrics*, 1979, *64*, 408–411.

Brownell, K. D. *Behavior therapy for weight control: A treatment manual.* Unpublished manuscript, University of Pennsylvania, 1979. (a)

Brownell, K. D. Obesity and adherence to behavioral programs. In *National Institute on Drug Abuse Research Monograph.* Washington, D.C.: U.S. Government Printing Office, 1979. (b)

Brownell, K. D. *The partnership diet program.* New York: Rawson-Wade, 1980.

Brownell, K. D. Assessment of eating disorders. In D. H. Barlow (Ed.), *Behavioral assessment of adult disorders.* New York: Guilford, 1981.

Brownell, K. D. Obesity: Behavioral treatments for a serious, prevalent, and refractory disorder. In R. K. Goodstein (Ed.), *Eating and weight disorders: Current developments.* New York: Springer, 1982.

Brownell, K. D., Bachorik, P. S., & Ayerle, R. S. Changes in plasma lipid and lipoprotein levels in men and women after a program of moderate exercise. *Circulation*, 1982, *65*, 288–297.

Brownell, K. D., Heckerman, C. L., & Westlake, R. J. The behavioral control of obesity: A descriptive analysis of a large-scale program. *Journal of Clinical Psychology*, 1979, *35*, 864–869.

Brownell, K. D., Heckerman, C. L., Westlake, R. J., Hayes, S. C., & Monti, P. M. The effect of couples training and partner cooperativeness in the behavioral treatment of obesity. *Behaviour Research and Therapy*, 1978, *16*, 323–333.

Brownell, K. D., & Stunkard, A. J. Behavior therapy and behavior change: Uncertainties in programs for weight control. *Behaviour Research and Therapy*, 1978, *16*, 301.

Brownell, K. D., & Stunkard, A. J. Exercise in the development and control of obesity. In A. J. Stunkard (Ed.), *Obesity*. Philadelphia: Saunders, 1980.

Brownell, K. D., & Stunkard, A. J. Couples training, pharmacotherapy, and behavior therapy in the treatment of obesity. *Archives of General Psychiatry*, 1981, *38*, 1224–1229.

Brownell, K. D., Stunkard, A. J., & Albaum, J. M. Evaluation and modification of exercise patterns in the natural environment. *American Journal of Psychiatry*, 1980, *137*, 1540–1545.

Bubolz, M. M., Eicher, J. B., Evers, S. J., & Sontag, M. S. A human ecological approach to quality of life: Conceptual framework and results of a preliminary study. *Social Indicators Research*, 1980, *7*, 103–136.

Buffone, G. W. Exercise as therapy: A closer look. *Journal of Counseling and Psychotherapy*, 1980, *3*, 101–115.

Bugental, D. B., Whalen, C. K., & Henker, B. Causal attributions and motivational assumptions in hyperactive children with two behavior change approaches: Evidence for an interactionist position. *Child Development*, 1977, *48*, 847–884.

Burdsal, C., & Buel, C. L. A short term community based early stage intervention program for behavior problem youth. *Journal of Clinical Psychology*, 1980, *36*, 226–241.

Burg, M. M., Reid, D. H., & Lattimore, J. Use of a self-recording and supervision program to change institutional staff behavior. *Journal of Applied Behavior Analysis*, 1979, *12*, 363–375.

Burgess, I., Jones, L., Robertson, S., Radcliffe, W., & Emerson, E. The degree of control exerted by phobic and nonphobic verbal stimuli over the recognition behaviour of phobic and non-phobic subjects. *Behaviour Research and Therapy*, 1981, *19*, 233–244.

Burgess, R. L. Child abuse: A social interactional analysis. In B. B. Lahey & A. E. Kazdin (Eds.), *Advances in clinical child psychology* (Vol. 2). New York: Plenum, 1979.

Burgio, L. D., Whitman, T. L., & Johnson, M. R. A self-instructional package for increasing attending behavior in educable mentally retarded children. *Journal of Applied Behavior Analysis*, 1980, *13*, 443–459.

Bushell, D. An engineering approach to the elementary classroom: The behavior analysis follow-through project. In A. C. Catania & T. A. Brigham (Eds.), *Handbook of applied behavior analysis: Social and instructional processes*. New York: Irvington, 1978.

Butler, L., & Meichenbaum, D. H. The assessment of interpersonal problem-solving skills. In P. C. Kendall & S. D. Hollon (Eds.), *Assessment methods for cognitive-behavioral interventions*. New York: Academic Press, 1981.

Cacioppo, J. T., Glass, C. R., & Merluzzi, T. V. Self-statements and self-evaluations: A cognitive response analysis of heterosexual social anxiety. *Cognitive Therapy and Research*, 1979, *3*, 249–262.

Caddy, G. R. The development and current status of professional psychology. *Professional Psychology*, in press.

Caddy, G. R., & Lovibond, S. H. Self-regulation and discriminated aversive conditioning in the modification of alcoholics' drinking behavior. *Behavior Therapy*, 1976, *7*, 223–230.

Cameron, M. I., & Robinson, V. M. J. Effects of cognitive training on academic and on-task behavior of hyperactive children. *Journal of Abnormal Child Psychology*, 1980, *3*, 405–419.

Camp, B. W. (Ed.). *Advances in behavioral pediatrics: A research annual* (Vols. 1 & 2). Greenwich, Conn.: JAI Press, 1980/1981.

Cantwell, D. P., & Carlson, G. A. Stimulants. In J. S. Werry (Ed.), *Pediatric psychopharmacology: The use of behavior modifying drugs on children*. New York: Brunner/Mazel, 1978.

Cantwell, D. P. *The hyperactive child*. New York: Spectrum, 1975.

Carlson, L. A., & Bottiger, L. E. Ischaemic heart disease in relation to fasting values of plasma triglycerides and cholesterol. *Lancet*, 1972, *1*, 865–868.

Carmody, T. P., Senner, J. W., Malinow, M. R., & Matarazzo, J. D. Physical exercise rehabilitation: Long-term dropout rate in cardiac patients. *Journal of Behavioral Medicine*, 1980, *3*, 163–168.

Carr, A. F., Schnelle, J. F., & Kirchner, R. E. Police crackdowns and slowdowns—a naturalistic evaluation of changes in police traffic enforcement. *Behavioral Assessment*, 1980, *2*, 33–41.

Carr, E. G. The motivation of self-injurious behavior: A review of some hypotheses. *Psychological Bulletin*, 1977, *86*, 800–816.

Carr, E. G., & McDowell, J. J. Social control of self-injurious behavior of organic etiology. *Behavior Therapy*, 1980, *11*, 402–409.

Carroll, L. J., & Yates, B. T. Further evidence for the role of stimulus control in facilitating weight reduction after behavior therapy. *Behavior Therapy*, 1981, *12*, 287–291.

Carter, R. Exercise and happiness. *Journal of Sports Medicine and Physical Fitness*, 1977, *17*, 307–313.

Cartledge, G., & Milburn, J. F. Teaching social skills in the classroom: A review. *Review of Educational Research*, 1978, *1*, 133–156.

Cartledge, G., & Milburn, J. F. (Eds.). *Teaching social skills to children: Innovative approaches*. New York: Pergamon, 1980.

Castaneda, A., McCandless, B. R., & Palermo, D. S. The children's form of the Manifest Anxiety Scale. *Child Development*, 1956, *27*, 317–326.

Catalano, R. *Health behavior and the community: An ecological perspective*. New York: Pergamon, 1979.

Caudill, B. D., & Marlatt, G. A. Modeling influences in social drinking: An experimental analogue. *Journal of Consulting and Clinical Psychology*, 1975, *43*, 405–415.

Chambless, D., Foa, E., Groves, G., & Goldstein, A. Flooding with Brevital in the treatment of agoraphobia: Counter-effective? *Behaviour Research and Therapy*, 1979, *17*, 243–252.

Chaney, E. F., O'Leary, M. R., & Marlatt, G. A. Skill training with alcoholics. *Journal of Consulting and Clinical Psychology*, 1978, *46*, 1092–1104.

Chapman, S. L., & Jeffrey, D. B. Processes in the maintenance of weight loss with behavior therapy. *Behavior Therapy*, 1979, *10*, 566–570.

Charles, L., Schain, R. J., Zelniker, T., & Guthrie, D. Effects of methylphenidate on hyperactive children's ability to sustain attention. *Pediatrics*, 1979, *64*, 412–418.

Charney, E., Goodman, H. C., McBride, M., Lyon, B., & Pratt, R. Childhood antecedents of adult obesity: Do chubby infants become obese adults? *New England Journal of Medicine*, 1976, *295*, 6–9.

Chesney, M. A., & Feuerstein, M. Behavioral medicine in the occupational setting. In

J. R. McNamara (Ed.), *Behavioral approaches to medicine: Application and analysis.* New York: Plenum, 1979.

Christensen, A. Naturalistic observation of families: A system for random audio recordings in the home. *Behavior Therapy,* 1979, *10,* 418–422.

Christensen, A., Johnson, S. M., Phillips, S., & Glasgow, R. E. Cost-effectiveness in behavioral family therapy. *Behavior Therapy,* 1980, *11,* 208–226.

Christian, W. P. Behavioral administration of the residential treatment program. *The Behavior Therapist,* 1981, *4,* 3–6.

Christopherson, E. R., & Gleeson, S. Research in behavioral pediatrics. *The Behavior Therapist,* 1980, *3,* 8–11.

Clarizio, H. F. *Toward positive classroom discipline* (3rd ed.). New York: Wiley, 1980.

Clemmer, D. *The prison community.* New York: Holt, 1940.

Coates, T. J., Rosekind, M. R., Strossen, R. J., Thoresen, C. E., & Kirmil-Gray, K. Sleep recordings in the laboratory and home: A comparative analysis. *Psychophysiology,* 1979, *16,* 339–346.

Coates, T. J., Rosekind, M. R., & Thoresen, C. E. All night sleep recordings in clients' homes by telephone. *Journal of Behavior Therapy and Experimental Psychiatry,* 1978, *9,* 157–162.

Coates, T. J., & Thoresen, C. E. Using generalizability theory in behavioral observation. *Behavior Therapy,* 1978, *9,* 605–613.

Cobb, J., McDonald, R., Marks, I., & Stern, R. Marital versus exposure therapy: Psychological treatments of co-existing marital and phobic–obsessive problems. *European Journal of Behavioural Analysis and Modification,* 1980, *4,* 3–17.

Cobb, J. A., & Hops, H. Effects of academic survival skills training on low achieving first graders. *Journal of Educational Research,* 1973, *67,* 108–113.

Cobb, S. Social support as a moderator of life stress. *Psychosomatic Medicine,* 1976, *38,* 300–314.

Cole, P. M., & Kazdin, A. E. Critical issues in self-instructional training with children. *Child Behavior Therapy,* 1980, *2,* 2–23.

Coll, M., Meyers, A., & Stunkard, A. J. Obesity and food choice in public places. *Archives of General Psychiatry,* 1979, *36,* 795–797.

Colletti, G., & Brownell, K. D. The physical and emotional benefits of social support: Application to obesity, smoking, and alcoholism. In C. Twentyman, L. H. Epstein, E. B. Blanchard, & J. P. Brady (Eds.), *Progress in behavioral medicine.* New York: Plenum, in press.

Colletti, G., & Kopel, S. A. Maintaining behavior change: An investigation of three maintenance strategies and attributional processes in the long-term reduction of cigarette smoking. *Journal of Consulting and Clinical Psychology,* 1979, *47,* 614–617.

Colletti, G., & Stern, L. A two-year follow-up of a nonaversive treatment for cigarette smoking. *Journal of Consulting and Clinical Psychology,* 1980, *48,* 292–293.

Colletti, G., & Supnick, J. A. Continued therapist contact as a maintenance strategy for smoking reduction. *Journal of Consulting and Clinical Psychology,* 1980, *48,* 665–667.

Combs, M. L., & Slaby, D. Social skills training with children. In B. B. Lahey & A. E. Kazdin (Eds.), *Advances in clinical child psychology* (Vol. 1). New York: Plenum, 1977.

Comrey, A. L. *A first course in factor analysis.* New York: Academic Press, 1973.

Cone, J. D. The Behavioral Assessment Grid (BAG): A conceptual framework and a taxonomy. *Behavior Therapy,* 1978, *9,* 882–888.

Cone, J. D. Why the "I've got a better agreement measure" literature continues to grow:

A commentary on two articles by Birkimer and Brown. *Journal of Applied Behavior Analysis*, 1979, *12*, 571.

Cone, J. D., & Hayes, S. C. *Environmental problems/behavioral solutions*. Monterey, Calif.: Brooks/Cole, 1980.

Connellan, T. *How to improve human performance*. New York: Harper & Row, 1978.

Conners, C. K. A teacher rating scale for use in drug studies with children. *American Journal of Psychiatry*, 1969, *126*, 884–888.

Conners, C. K., Goyette, C. H., Southwick, M. A., Lees, J. M., & Andrulonis, P. A. Food additives and hyperkinesis: A controlled double-blind experiment. *Pediatrics*, 1976, *58*, 154–166.

Conners, C. K., & Werry, J. S. Pharmacotherapy of psychopathology in children. In H. D. Quay & J. S. Werry (Eds.), *Psychopathological disorders in childhood* (2nd ed.). New York: Wiley, 1979.

Cook, P. S., & Woodhill, J. M. The Feingold dietary treatment of the hyperkinetic syndrome. *Medical Journal of Australia*, 1976, *2*, 85–90.

Cooke, C. J., & Meyers, A. The role of predictor variables in the behavioral treatment of obesity. *Behavioral Assessment*, 1980, *2*, 59–69.

Cooper, A. M., Waterhouse, G. J., & Sobell, M. B. Influence of gender on drinking in a modeling situation. *Journal of Studies in Alcohol*, 1979, *40*, 562–570.

Cooper, K. H. *The new aerobics*. New York: Bantam, 1970.

Copeland, W. D. Teaching–learning behaviors and the demands of the classroom environment. *Elementary School Journal*, 1980, *80*, 163–177.

Cornfield, J., & Mitchell, S. Selected risk factors in coronary heart disease: Possible intervention effects. *Archives of Environmental Health*, 1969, *19*, 382–394.

Coronary Drug Project Research Group. Cigarette smoking as a risk factor in men with a prior history of myocardial infarction. *Journal of Chronic Diseases*, 1979, *32*, 415–425.

Council on Scientific Affairs, American Medical Association. Smoking and health. *Journal of the American Medical Association*, 1980, *243*, 779–781.

Coval, T. E. Personal liability in the conduct of behavior modification professionals. *The Behavior Therapist*, 1980, *3*, 24.

Cowen, E. L. Baby-steps toward primary prevention. *American Journal of Community Psychology*, 1977, *5*, 2–22.

Craighead, L. W. Self-instructional training for assertion–refusal behavior. *Behavior Therapy*, 1979, *10*, 529–542.

Craighead, W. E. Cognitive–behavioral treatment of depression in children. In A. Meyers & W. E. Craighead (Eds.), *Cognitive behavior therapy with children*. New York: Plenum, in press.

Craighead, W. E., & Craighead, L. W. Implications of persuasive communication research for the modification of self-statements. *Cognitive Therapy and Research*, 1980, *4*, 117–125.

Craighead, L. W., Stunkard, A. J., & O'Brien, R. Behavior therapy and pharmacotherapy for obesity. *Archives of General Psychiatry*, 1981, *38*, 763–768.

Craigie, F. C., Jr., & Ross, S. M. The use of a videotape pretherapy training program to encourage treatment-seeking among alcohol detoxification patients. *Behavior Therapy*, 1980, *11*, 141–147.

Cronbach, L. J., Gleser, G. C., Nanda, H., & Rajaratnam, N. *The dependability of behavioral measurements: Theory of generalizability for scores and profiles*. New York: Wiley, 1972.

Cronkite, R. C., & Moos, R. H. Evaluating alcoholism treatment programs: An integrated approach. *Journal of Consulting and Clinical Psychology*, 1978, *46*, 1105–1119.

Cronkite, R. C., & Moos, R. H. Determinants of the posttreatment functioning of alcoholic patients: A conceptual framework. *Journal of Consulting and Clinical Psychology*, 1980, *48*, 305–316.

Crosson, J. E., & Pine, A. L. The application of experimental behavior analysis in vocational training for the severely handicapped. In G. T. Bellamy, G. O'Connor, & O. C. Karan (Eds.), *Vocational rehabilitation of severely handicapped persons: Contemporary service strategies*. Baltimore: University Park Press, 1979.

Crozier, J., & Katz, R. C. Social learning treatment of child abuse. *Journal of Behavior Therapy and Experimental Psychiatry*, 1979, *10*, 213–220.

Cummings, C., Gordon, J. R., & Marlatt, G. A. Relapse: Prevention and prediction. In W. R. Miller (Ed.), *The addictive behaviors: Treatment of alcoholism, drug abuse, smoking, and obesity*. New York: Pergamon, 1980.

Curran, J. P. Comments on Bellack, Hersen, and Turner's paper on the validity of role play test. *Behavior Therapy*, 1978, *9*, 462–468.

Cutler, R. E., & Storm, T. Observational study of alcohol consumption in natural settings: The Vancouver beer parlor. *Journal of Studies on Alcohol*, 1975, *36*, 1173–1183.

Dahlkoetter, J., Callahan, E. J., & Linton, J. Obesity and the unbalanced energy equation: Exercise vs. eating habit change. *Journal of Consulting and Clinical Psychology*, 1979, *47*, 898–905.

Danaher, B. G. Rapid smoking and self-control in the modification of smoking behavior. *Journal of Consulting and Clinical Psychology*, 1977, *45*, 1068–1075. (a)

Danaher, B. G. Research on rapid smoking: An interim summary and recommendations. *Addictive Behaviors*, 1977, *2*, 151–166. (b)

Danaher, B. G. Smoking cessation programs in occupational settings. *Public Health Reports*, 1980, *95*, 149–157.

Danaher, B. G., & Lichtenstein, E. *Become an ex-smoker*. Englewood Cliffs, N.J.: Prentice-Hall, 1978.

Daughton, D. M., Fix, A. J., Kass, I., & Patil, K. D. Smoking cessation among patients with chronic obstructive pulmonary disease (COPD). *Addictive Behaviors*, 1980, *5*, 125–128.

Davids, A. An objective instrument for assessing hyperkinesis in children. *Journal of Learning Disabilities*, 1971, *4*, 499–501.

Davidson, P. O., & Davidson, S. M. (Eds.). *Behavioral medicine: Changing health lifestyles*. New York: Brunner/Mazel, 1980.

Deci, E. L. Intrinsic motivation, extrinsic motivation, and inequality. *Journal of Personality and Social Psychology*, 1972, *22*, 113–120.

Deci, E. L. Notes on the theory and metatheory of intrinsic motivation. *Organizational Behavior and Human Performance*, 1976, *15*, 130–145.

Deitz, S. M. Current status of applied behavior analysis: Science versus technology. *American Psychologist*, 1978, *33*, 805–816.

Deluty, R. H. Children's Action Tendency Scale: A self-report measure of aggressiveness, assertiveness and submissiveness in children. *Journal of Consulting and Clinical Psychology*, 1979, *47*, 1061–1071.

Deluty, R. H. Alternative-thinking ability of aggressive, assertive, and submissive children. *Cognitive Therapy and Research*, 1981, *5*, 309–312.

DeMyer, M. K. *Parents and children in autism*. New York: Wiley, 1979.

Denicola, J., & Sandler, J. Training abusive parents in child management and self-control skills. *Behavior Therapy*, 1980, *11*, 263–270.

Dericco, D. A., & Garlington, W. K. The effect of modeling and disclosure of experimenter's intent on drinking rate of college students. *Addictive Behaviors*, 1977, *2*, 135–139.

DeProspero, A., & Cohen, S. Inconsistent visual analysis of intrasubject data. *Journal of Applied Behavior Analysis*, 1979, *12*, 573–579.

DeRubeis, R., Hollon, S., Evans, M., & Bemis, K. Can psychotherapies for depression be discriminated? *A systematic investigation of cognitive therapy and interpersonal therapy*. Unpublished manuscript, University of Minnesota, 1981.

DeSilva, P. & Rachman, S. Is exposure a necessary condition for fear-reduction? *Behaviour Research and Therapy*, 1981, *19*, 227–232.

Dewhurst, D. L. T., & Cautela, J. R. A proposed reinforcement survey schedule for special needs children. *Journal of Behavior Therapy and Experimental Psychiatry*, 1980, *11*, 109–112.

Diament, C., & Colletti, G. Evaluation of behavioral group counseling for parents of learning-disabled children. *Journal of Abnormal Child Psychology*, 1978, *6*, 385–400.

DiGiuseppe, R. A., Miller, N. J., & Trexler, L. D. A review of rational–emotive psychotherapy outcome studies. *Counseling Psychologist*, 1977, *1*, 64–72.

Doll, R., Gray, R., Hafner, B., & Peto, R. Mortality in relation to smoking: 22 years' observations on female British doctors. *British Medical Journal*, 1980, *280*, 967–971.

Donoghue, S. The correlation between physical fitness, absenteeism and work performance. *Canadian Journal of Public Health*, 1977, *68*, 201–203.

Douglas, V. I., Parry, P., Marton, P., Garson, C. Assessment of a cognitive training program for hyperactive children. *Journal of Abnormal Child Psychology*, 1976, *4*, 389–410.

Doyle, W. Paradigm for research on teacher effectiveness. In L. S. Shulman (Ed.), *Review of research in education*. Itasca, Ill.: Peacock, 1978.

Drabman, R. S., & Furman, W. Behavioral procedures in the classroom. In D. Glenwich & L. Jason (Eds.), *Behavioral community psychology*. Kalamazoo, Mich.: Behaviordelia, 1979.

Drenick, E. J., Bale, G. S., Seltzer, F., & Johnson, D. G. Excessive mortality and causes of death in morbidly obese men. *Journal of the American Medical Association*, 1980, *243*, 443–445.

Dubanoski, R. A., Evans, I. M., & Higuchi, A. A. Analysis and treatment of child abuse: A set of behavioral propositions. *Child Abuse and Neglect*, 1978, *2*, 153–172.

Dubey, D. R. The hyperkinetic child: Current status. *Comprehensive Therapy*, in press.

Dubey, D. R., & Kaufman, K. F. Home management of hyperkinetic children. *Journal of Pediatrics*, 1978, *93*, 141–146.

Dubey, D. R., & Kaufman, K. F. Training parents of hyperactive children in behavior management. *International Journal of Mental Health*, 1979, *8*, 110–120.

Dubey, D. R., O'Leary, S. G., & Kaufman, K. F. Training parents of hyperactive children in child management: A comparative outcome study, in press.

Dubos, R. *The mirage of health: Utopias, progress, and biological change*. New York: Doubleday, 1961.

Dubren, R. Self-reinforcement by recorded telephone messages to maintain nonsmoking behavior. *Journal of Consulting and Clinical Psychology*, 1977, *45*, 358–360.

Dudley, D. L., Aicken, M., & Martin, C. V. Cigarette smoking in a chest clinic population—psychophysiologic variables. *Journal of Psychosomatic Research*, 1977, *21*, 367–375.

Dunbar, J. M., & Stunkard, A. J. Adherence to diet and drug regimens. In R. Levy, R. Rifkind, B. Dennis, & N. Ernst (Eds.), *Nutrition, lipids and coronary heart disease*. New York: Raven, 1979.

Dunlap, G., & Koegel, R. L. Motivating autistic children through stimulus variation. *Journal of Applied Behavior Analysis*, 1980, *13*, 619–627.

Dunlap, G. Koegel, R. L., & Egel, A. L. Autistic children in school. *Exceptional Children*, 1979, *45*, 552–558.

Dunn, R. J. Cognitive modification with depression-prone psychiatric patients. *Cognitive Therapy and Research*, 1979, *3*, 307–317.

Durbeck, D. C., Heinzelmann, F., Schacter, J., Haskell, W., Payne, G., Moxley, R., Nemiroff, M., Limoncelli, D., Arnold, L., & Fox, S. The National Aeronautics and Space Administration–U.S. Public Health Service Health Evaluation and Enhancement Program. *American Journal of Cardiology*, 1972, *30*, 784–790.

Dutton, L. M., Smolensky, M., Leach, C., Lorimer, R., & Bartholomew, P. Stress levels of ambulance paramedics and fire fighters. *Journal of Occupational Medicine*, 1978, *20*, 111–115.

Dweck, C. S. The role of expectations and attribution in the alleviation of learned helplessness. *Journal of Personality and Social Psychology*, 1975, *31*, 674–685.

Dweck, C. S., & Reppucci, N. D. Learned helplessness and reinforcement responsibility in children. *Journal of Personality and Social Psychology*, 1973, *25*, 109–116.

D'Zurilla, T. J., & Goldfried, M. R. Problem solving and behavior modification. *Journal of Abnormal Psychology*, 1971, *78*, 107–128.

D'Zurilla, T., & Nezu, A. Social problem solving in adults. In P. C. Kendall (Ed.), *Advances in cognitive–behavioral research and therapy* (Vol. 1). New York: Academic Press, 1982.

Edelman, P., Herz, E., & Bickman, L. A model of behaviour in fires applied to a nursing home fire. In D. Canter (Ed.), *Fires and human behaviour*. London: Wiley, 1980.

Egel, A. L., Koegel, R. L., & Schreibman, L. Review of educational-treatment procedures for autistic children. In L. Mann & D. A. Sabatino (Eds.), *The fourth review of special education*. New York: Grune & Stratton, 1980.

Eisler, R. M., Miller, P. M., & Hersen, M. Components of assertive behavior. *Journal of Clinical Psychology*, 1973, *29*, 295–299.

Elder, J. P., Edelstein, B. A., & Narick, M. M. Adolescent psychiatric patients: Modifying aggressive behavior with social skills training. *Behavior Modification*, 1979, *3*, 161–178.

Ellenberger, H. F. The story of "Anna O": A critical review with new data. *Journal of the History of the Behavioral Sciences*, 1972, *8*, 267–279.

Ellis, A. Are cognitive behavior therapy and rational therapy synonymous? *Rational Living*, 1973, *8*, 8–11.

Ellis, A. Rational–emotive therapy and cognitive behavior therapy: Similarities and differences. *Cognitive Therapy and Research*, 1980, *4*, 325–340.

Ellis, A., & Harper, R. A. *A guide to rational living*. Hollywood, Calif.: Wilshire, 1961.

Ellis, N. R. The Pertlow Case: A reply to Dr. Rous. *Law and Psychology Review*, 1979, *5*, 15–49.

Emmelkamp, P. M. G. Relationship between theory and practice in behavior therapy. In W. DeMoor & H. R. Wijngaarden (Eds.), *Psychotherapy: Research and training*. Amsterdam: Elsevier/North Holland Biomedical Press, 1980.

Emmelkamp, P. M. G., & Kuipers, A. C. M. Agoraphobia: A follow-up study four years after treatment. *British Journal of Psychiatry*, 1979, *134*, 352–355.

Emmelkamp, P. M. G., Kuipers, A. C. M., & Eggeraat, J. B. Cognitive modification versus prolonged exposure in vivo: A comparison with agoraphobics as subjects. *Behaviour Research and Therapy*, 1978, *16*, 33–42.

Emmelkamp, P. M. G., van der Helm, M., van Zanten, B. L., & Plochg, I. Treatment of obsessive–compulsive patients: The contribution of self-instructional training to the effectiveness of exposure. *Behaviour Research and Therapy*, 1980, *18*, 61–66.

Emmelkamp, P., & van der Heyden, H. Treatment of harming obsessions. *European Journal of Behavioral Analysis and Modification*, 1980, *4*, 28–35.

Endler, N. S., Hunt, J. McV., & Rosenstein, A. J. An S-R inventory of anxiousness. *Psychological Monographs*, 1962, *76* (17, Whole No. 536).

Epstein, L. H., & Masek, B. J. Behavioral control of medicine compliance. *Journal of Applied Behavior Analysis*, 1978, *11*, 1–9.

Epstein, L. H., Thompson, J. K., & Wing, R. R. The effects of contract and lottery procedures on attendance and fitness in aerobics exercise. *Behavior Modification*, 1980, *4*, 465–480.

Epstein, L. H., & Wing, R. R. Aerobic exercise and weight. *Addictive Behaviors*, 1980, *5*, 371–388. (a)

Epstein, L. H., & Wing, R. R. Behavioral approaches to exercise habits and athletic performance. In J. Ferguson & C. B. Taylor (Eds.), *Advances in behavioral medicine*. Holliswood, N.Y.: Spectrum, 1980. (b)

Epstein, L. H., Wing, R. R., Koeske, R., Ossip, D., & Beck, S. *A comparison of lifestyle change and programmed aerobic exercise on weight and fitness measures in obese children.* Unpublished manuscript, University of Pittsburgh, 1981.

Epstein, L. H., Wing, R. R., Thompson, J. K., & Griffen, W. Attendance and fitness in aerobics exercise: The effects of contract and lottery procedures. *Behavior Modification*, 1980, *4*, 465–479.

Ericsson, K. A., & Simon, H. A. Verbal reports as data. *Psychological Review*, 1980, *82*, 215–251.

Erwin, E. *Behavior therapy: Scientific, philosophical and moral foundations.* New York: Cambridge University Press, 1978.

Evans, R. I., Hansen, W. B., & Mittlemark, M. B. Increasing the validity of self-reports of behavior in a smoking in children investigation. *Journal of Applied Psychology*, 1977, *62*, 521–523.

Eyberg, S. M., & Matarazzo, R. G. Training parents as therapists: A comparison between individual parent–child interaction training and parent group didactic training. *Journal of Clinical Psychology*, 1980, *36*, 492–499.

Eysenck, H. J. The conditioning model of neurosis. *The Behavioral and Brain Sciences*, 1979, *2*, 155–199. (a)

Eysenck, H. J. The place of theory in the assessment of the effects of psychotherapy. *Behavioral Assessment*, 1979, *1*, 77–84. (b)

Eysenck, H. J. Neobehavioristic (S-R) theory. In G. T. Wilson & C. M. Franks (Eds.), *Contemporary behavior therapy: Conceptual and empirical foundations*. New York: Guilford, 1982.

Eysenck, H. J., & Nias, D. K. B. *Sex, violence and the media.* London: Temple Smith, 1978.

Farber, P. D., Khavari, K. A., & Douglass, F. M. A factor analytic study of reasons for drinking: Empirical validation of positive and negative reinforcement dimensions. *Journal of Consulting and Clinical Psychology*, 1980, *48*, 780–781.

Farkas, G. M. An ontological analysis of behavior therapy. *American Psychologist*, 1980, *35*, 364–374.

Farkas, G. M. Social skills training of a blind child through differential reinforcement. *The Behavior Therapist*, 1981, *4*, 24–26.

Farkas, G. M., Evans, I. M., Sine, L. F., Eifert, G., Wittlieb, E., & Vogelmann-Sine, S. Reliability and validity of the mercury-in-rubber strain gauge measure of penile circumference. *Behavior Therapy*, 1979, *10*, 555–561.

Fawcett, S., Mathews, R. M., & Fletcher, R. K. Some promising dimensions for behavioral community technology. *Journal of Applied Behavior Analysis*, 1980, *13*, 505–518.

Feingold, B. *Why your child is hyperactive.* New York: Random House, 1975.

Feinstein, A. R. The measurement of success in weight reduction: An analysis of methods and new index. *Journal of Chronic Disease,* 1959, *10,* 439–456.

Felt, S. K., Montes, F., Irueste-Montes, A. M., & Eichengreen, L. *A "teaching skills" approach to the treatment and assessment of families affected by child abuse and neglect.* Paper presented at the fifth annual Conference on Child Abuse and Neglect, Milwaukee, April 1981.

Fensterheim, H. A behavioral method for improving sport performance. *Psychiatric Annals,* 1980, March, 1–6.

Ferguson, G. S., & Geller, E. S. Behavioral approaches to crime prevention: A critical review. *JSAS Catalog of Selected Documents in Psychology,* 1979, *9,* 57 (MS No. 1888).

Ferguson, J. M. *Learning to eat: Behavior modification for weight control.* Palo Alto, Calif.: Bull, 1975.

Ferguson, J. M., & Taylor, C. B. (Eds.). *The comprehensive handbook of behavioral medicine* (Vols. 1–3). New York: Spectrum, 1980.

Fiedler, F. E. The concept of an ideal therapeutic relationship. *Journal of Consulting Psychology,* 1950, *14,* 39–45.

Fielding, J. E. Preventive medicine and the bottom line. *Journal of Occupational Medicine,* 1979, *21,* 79–88.

Fielding, J. E. *Evaluation of work site health promotion programs.* Paper presented at the Institute of Medicine Conference on Evaluation of Health Promotion in the Workplace, Washington, D.C., June 1980.

Filipczak, J., Archer, M., & Friedman, R. M. In-school social skills training: Use with disruptive adolescents. *Behavior Modification,* 1980, *4,* 243–263.

Filipczak, J., Friedman, R. M., & Reese, S. C. PREP: Educational programming to prevent juvenile problems. In J. S. Stumphauzer (Ed.), *Progress in behavior therapy with delinquents.* Springfield, Ill.: Charles C Thomas, 1979.

Finch, A. J., & Kendall, P. C. The measurement of anxiety in children: Research findings and methodological problems. In A. J. Finch & P. C. Kendall (Eds.), *Clinical treatment and research in child psychopathology.* New York: Spectrum, 1979.

Finch, A. J., Kendall, P. C., Montgomery, L. E., & Morris, T. Effects of two types of failure on anxiety. *Journal of Abnormal Psychology,* 1975, *84,* 583–585.

Fine, M. J. (Ed.). *Handbook on parent education.* New York: Academic Press, 1980.

Finesmith, B. K. An historic and systemic overview of Wisconsin's behavior management guidelines. *The Behavior Therapist,* 1979, *2,* 3–6.

Finney, J. W., Moos, R. H., & Mewborn, C. R. Posttreatment experiences and treatment outcome of alcoholic patients six months and two years after hospitalization. *Journal of Consulting and Clinical Psychology,* 1980, *48,* 17–29.

Firestone, P., Kelly, M. J., Goodman, J. T., & Davey, J. Differential effects of parent training and stimulant medication with hyperactives: A progress report. *Journal of the American Academy of Child Psychology,* in press.

Firestone, P., & Martin, J. E. An analysis of the hyperactivity syndrome: A comparison of hyperactive, behavior problem, asthmatic, and normal children. *Journal of Abnormal Child Psychology,* 1979, *7,* 261–273.

Firestone, P., & Witt, J. E. Characteristics of families completing and prematurely discontinuing a behavioral parent training program, in press.

Firth, C. D. The effect of varying the nicotine content of cigarettes on human smoking behaviour. *Psychopharmacologia,* 1971, *19,* 188–192.

Fisher, J. D., & Baum, A. Situational and arousal-based messages and the reduction of crowding-stress. *Journal of Applied Social Psychology,* 1980, *10,* 191–201.

Fisher, R. A. *Statistical methods for research workers* (5th ed.). Edinburgh: Oliver & Boyd, 1934.

Fixsen, D. L., Phillips, E. L., Phillips, E. A., & Wolf, M. M. The teaching-family model of group home treatment. In W. E. Craighead, A. E. Kazdin, & M. J. Mahoney (Eds.), *Behavior modification: Principles, issues and applications.* Boston: Houghton Mifflin, 1976.

Flanagan, S., Adams, H. E., & Forehand, R. A. Comparison of four instructional techniques for teaching parents to use time-out. *Behavior Therapy,* 1979, *10,* 94–102.

Fleming, B. M., & Thornton, D. W. Coping skills training as a component in the short-term treatment of depression. *Journal of Consulting and Clinical Psychology,* 1980, *48,* 652–654.

Foa, E. Failure in treating obsessive–compulsives. *Behaviour Research and Therapy,* 1979, *17,* 169–176.

Foa, E., Steketee, G. S., & Milby, M. B. Differential effects of exposure and response prevention in obsessive–compulsive washers. *Journal of Consulting and Clinical Psychology,* 1980, *48,* 71–79.

Foa, E., & Tillmanns, A. The treatment of obsessive–compulsive neurosis. In A. Goldstein & E. Foa (Eds.), *Handbook of behavioral interventions.* New York: Wiley, 1979.

Folkins, C. H., Lynch, S., & Gardner, M. M. Psychological fitness as a function of physical fitness. *Archives of Physical Medicine and Rehabilitation,* 1972, *53,* 503–508.

Folkins, C. H., & Sime, W. E. Physical fitness training and mental health. *American Psychologist,* 1981, *36,* 373–389.

Forbes, W. F., Robinson, J. C., Hanley, J. A., & Colburn, H. N. Studies on the nicotine exposure of individual smokers: I. Changes in mouth-level exposure to nicotine on switching to lower nicotine cigarettes. *International Journal of the Addictions,* 1976, *11,* 933–950.

Ford, J. D. Therapeutic relationship in behavior therapy: An empirical analysis. *Journal of Consulting and Clinical Psychology,* 1978, *46,* 1302–1314.

Ford, J. D., & Kendall, P. C. Behavior therapists' professional behaviors: Converging evidence of a gap between theory and practice. *The Behavior Therapist,* 1979, *2,* 37–38.

Forehand, R., & Atkeson, B. M. Generality of treatment effects with parents as therapists: A review of assessment and implementation procedures. *Behavior Therapy,* 1977, *8,* 575–593.

Forehand, R., Griest, D. L., & Wells, K. C. Parent behavioral training: An analysis of the relationship among multiple outcome measures. *Journal of Abnormal Child Psychology,* 1979, *7,* 229–242.

Forehand, R., & King, H. Noncompliant children: Effects of parent training on behavior and attitude change. *Behavior Modification,* 1977, *1,* 93–108.

Forehand, R., Sturgis, E. T., McMahon, R. J., Aguar, D., Green, K., Wells, K., & Breiner, J. Parental behavioral training to modify child noncompliance. *Behavior Modification,* 1979, *3,* 3–25.

Forehand, R., Wells, K., & Griest, D. L. An examination of the social validity of a parent training program. *Behavior Therapy,* 1980, *11,* 488–502.

Foreyt, J. P. *The Methodist Hospital Weight Control Program.* Paper presented at the annual meeting of the American Psychological Association, New York, September 1979.

Foreyt, J. P., & Rathjen, D. P. (Eds.), *Cognitive behavior therapy: Research and application.* New York: Plenum, 1978.

Foreyt, J. P., Scott, L. W., & Gotto, A. M. Weight control and nutrition education programs in occupational settings. *Public Health Reports,* 1980, *95,* 127–136.

Forman, S. A comparison of cognitive training and response cost procedures in modifying aggressive behavior of elementary school children. *Behavior Therapy*, 1980, *11*, 594–600.

Foster, M. F., Horn, J. L., & Wanberg, K. W. Dimensions of treatment outcome: A factor analytic study of alcoholics' responses to a follow-up questionnaire. *Quarterly Journal of Studies on Alcohol*, 1972, *33*, 1079–1098.

Foster, S. L., & Cone, J. D. Current issues in direct observation. *Behavioral Assessment*, 1980, *2*, 313–338.

Foster, S. L., & Ritchey, W. L. Issues in the assessment of social competence in children. *Journal of Applied Behavior Analysis*, 1979, *12*, 625–638.

Four perspectives on the status of child abuse and neglect research. Springfield, Va.: National Technical Information Service, 1975.

Fox, R. A multidisciplinary approach to the treatment of alcoholism. *American Journal of Psychiatry*, 1967, *123*, 769–778.

Foxx, R. M., & Azrin, N. H. Restitution: A method of eliminating aggressive–disruptive behavior of retarded and brain damaged patients. *Behaviour Research and Therapy*, 1972, *10*, 15–20.

Foxx, R. M., & Brown, R. A. Nicotine fading and self-monitoring for cigarette abstinence or controlled smoking. *Journal of Applied Behavior Analysis*, 1979, *12*, 111–125.

Foxx, R. M., & Martin, E. D. Treatment of scavenging behavior (coprophagy and pica) by overcorrection. *Behaviour Research and Therapy*, 1975, *13*, 153–162.

Foy, D. W., Miller, P. M., Eisler, R. M., & O'Toole, D. H. Social skills training to teach alcoholics to refuse drinks effectively. *Journal of Studies on Alcohol*, 1976, *37*, 1340–1345.

Foy, D. W., & Simon, S. J. Alcoholic drinking topography as a function of solitary vs. social context. *Addictive Behaviors*, 1978, *3*, 39–41.

Frank, G. C., Berensen, G. S., & Webber, L. S. Dietary studies and the relationship of diet to cardiovascular disease risk factor variables in 10-year-old children: The Bogalusa Heart Study. *American Journal of Clinical Nutrition*, 1978, *31*, 328–340.

Frankel, F., & Simmons, J. Q. Self-injurious behavior in schizophrenic and retarded children. *American Journal of Mental Deficiency*, 1976, *80*, 512–522.

Franks, C. M. On behaviorism and behaviour therapy—not necessarily synonymous and becoming less so. *Australian Behaviour Therapist*, 1980, *7*, 14–23.

Franks, C. M. Introduction. In J. Kelly, *Social-skills training: A practical guide for interventions*. New York: Springer, 1981. (a)

Franks, C. M. Behaviour therapy in the year 2081: Will we be many or one—or none? *Behavioural Psychotherapy*, 1981. (b)

Franks, C. M., & Diament, C. What is child behavior therapy—and why a specialized new journal for this field? *Child Behavior Therapy*, 1979, *1*, 7–11.

Franks, C. M., & Diament, C. Child and family behavior therapy—broadening the compass of child behavior therapy while remaining on course. *Child and Family Behavior Therapy*, 1982, *4*.

Franks, C. M., & Rosenbaum, M. Behavior therapy: Overview and personal reflections. In M. Rosenbaum, C. M. Franks, & Y. Jaffe (Eds.), *Perspectives on behavior therapy in the eighties*. New York: Springer, 1982.

Franks, C. M., & Wilson, G. T. *Annual review of behavior therapy: Theory and practice* (Vol. 1). New York: Brunner/Mazel, 1973.

Franks, C. M., & Wilson, G. T. *Annual review of behavior therapy: Theory and practice* (Vol. 2). New York: Brunner/Mazel, 1974.

Franks, C. M., & Wilson, G. T. *Annual review of behavior therapy: Theory and practice* (Vol. 3). New York: Brunner/Mazel, 1975.

Franks, C. M., & Wilson, G. T. *Annual review of behavior therapy: Theory and practice* (Vol. 4). New York: Brunner/Mazel, 1976.

Franks, C. M., & Wilson, G. T. *Annual review of behavior therapy: Theory and practice* (Vol. 5). New York: Brunner/Mazel, 1977.

Franks, C. M., & Wilson, G. T. *Annual review of behavior therapy: Theory and practice* (Vol. 6). New York: Brunner/Mazel, 1978.

Franks, C. M., & Wilson, G. T. *Annual review of behavior therapy: Theory and practice* (Vol. 7). New York: Brunner/Mazel, 1980.

Frederiksen, L. W., Jenkins, J. O., Foy, D. W., & Eisler, R. M. Social skills training to modify abusive verbal behavior in adults. *Journal of Applied Behavior Analysis*, 1976/1977, *9*, 117-125.

Frederiksen, L. W., & Martin, J. E. Carbon monoxide and smoking behavior. *Addictive Behaviors*, 1979, *4*, 21-30.

Frederiksen, L. W., Martin, J. E., & Webster, J. S. Assessment of smoking behavior. *Journal of Applied Behavior Analysis*, 1979, *12*, 653-664.

Frederiksen, L. W., Miller, P. M., & Peterson, G. L. Topographical components of smoking behavior. *Addictive Behaviors*, 1977, *2*, 55-61.

Freeman, B. J., Ritvo, E. R., Guthrie, D., Schroth, P., & Ball, J. The Behavior Observation Scale for Autism: Initial methodology, data analysis, and preliminary findings on 89 children. *Journal of the American Academy of Child Psychology*, 1978, *17*, 576-588.

Fremouw, W. J., & Zitter, R. E. Individual and couple behavioral contracting for weight reduction and maintenance. *Behavior Therapist*, 1980, *3*, 15-16.

Fridgen, J. D. Environment–behavior research: Implications for the study of leisure and recreation behavior. In S. E. Iso-Ahola (Ed.), *Social psychological perspectives on leisure and recreation*. Springfield, Ill.: Charles C Thomas, 1980.

Friedling, C., & O'Leary, S. G. Effects of self-instructional training on second- and third-grade hyperactive children: A failure to replicate. *Journal of Applied Behavior Analysis*, 1979, *12*, 211-219.

Friedman, C. D., Dales, L. G., & Ury, H. K. Mortality in middle-aged smokers and nonsmokers. *New England Journal of Medicine*, 1979, *300*, 213-217.

Friedman, R. Child abuse: A review of the psychosocial research. In *Four perspectives on the status of child abuse and neglect research*. Springfield, Va.: National Technical Information Service, 1975.

Friedman, R., Sandler, J., Hernandez, M., & Wolfe, D. Child abuse. In E. J. Mash & L. G. Terdal (Eds.), *Behavioral assessment of childhood disorders*. New York: Guilford, 1981.

Fuchs, C. Z., & Rehm, L. P. A self-control behavior therapy program for depression. *Journal of Consulting and Clinical Psychology*, 1977, *45*, 206-215.

Furman, W., Geller, M. I., Simon, S. J., & Kelly, J. A. The use of a behavior rehearsal procedure for teaching job interviewing skills to psychiatric patients. *Behavior Therapy*, 1979, *10*, 157-167.

Galassi, J. P., DeLo, J. S., Galassi, M. D., & Bastien, S. The College Self-Expression Scale: A measure of assertiveness. *Behavior Therapy*, 1974, *5*, 165-171.

Galassi, J. P., Frierson, H. T., & Sharer, R. *Problems in cognitive assessment: Concurrent versus retrospective assessment in test anxiety.* Paper presented at the annual meeting of the Association for Advancement of Behavior Therapy, New York, November 1980.

Galassi, J. P., & Galassi, M. D. A comparison of the factor structure of an assertion scale across sex and population. *Behavior Therapy*, 1979, *10*, 117-128.

Galdston, R. Observations on children who have been physically abused and their parents. *American Journal of Psychiatry*, 1965, *122*, 440-443.

Gambrill, E., & Richey, C. An assertion inventory for use in assessment and research. *Behavior Therapy*, 1975, *6*, 550.

Garfield, S. L., & Kurtz, R. M. Clinical psychologists in the 1970s. *American Psychologist*, 1976, *31*, 1–9.

Garlington, W. K., & Dericco, D. A. The effect of modeling on drinking rate. *Journal of Applied Behavior Analysis*, 1977, *10*, 207–211.

Garrison, J. E., & Raynes, A. E. Results of a pilot management-by-objectives program for a community mental health outpatient services. *Community Mental Health Journal*, 1980, *16*, 121–129.

Gay, M. L., Hollandsworth, J., & Galassi, J. P. An assertion inventory for adults. *Journal of Counseling Psychology*, 1975, *22*, 340–344.

Geiss, S. K., & O'Leary, K. D. Therapist ratings of frequency and severity of marital problems: Implications for research. *Journal of Marital and Family Therapy*, in press.

Gelder, M., Bancroft, J., Gath, D., Johnston, D., Mathews, A., & Shaw, P. Specific and non-specific factors in behaviour therapy. *British Journal of Psychiatry*, 1973, *123*, 445–462.

Geller, E. S. Waste reduction and energy recovery: Strategies for energy conservation. In A. Baum & J. Singer (Eds.), *Advances in environmental psychology* (Vol. 3). Hillsdale, N.J.: Erlbaum, 1981. (a)

Geller, E. S. The energy crisis and behavioral science: A conceptual framework for large scale intervention. In A. W. Childs & G. B. Melton (Eds.), *Rural psychology*. New York: Plenum, 1981. (b)

Geller, E. S., Brasted, W. S., & Mann, M. F. Waste receptacle designs as interventions for litter control. *Journal of Environmental Systems*, 1979, *2*, 145–160.

Geller, E. S., Casali, J. G., & Johnson, R. P. Seat belt usage: A potential target for applied behavior analysis. Journal of Applied Behavior Analysis, 1980, *13*, 669–675.

Geller, E. S., Eason, S. L., Phillips, J. A., & Pierson, M. D. Interventions to improve sanitation during food preparation. *Journal of Organizational Behavior Management*, 1980, *2*, 229–240.

Geller, E. S., Johnson, R. P., & Pelton, S. L. Community-based interventions for encouraging safety belt use. *American Journal of Community Psychology*, in press.

Genest, M., & Turk, D. C. Think-aloud approaches to cognitive assessment. In T. V. Merluzzi, C. R. Glass, & M. Genest (Eds.), *Cognitive assessment*. New York: Guilford, 1981.

Genshaft, J. L., & Hirt, M. L. The effectiveness of self-instructional training to embrace math achievement in women. *Cognitive Therapy and Research*, 1980, *4*, 91–97.

Gentry, W. D. What is behavioral medicine? In J. R. Eiser (Ed.), *Social psychology and behavioral medicine*. New York: Wiley, 1982.

George, C., & Main, M. Abused children: Their rejection of peers and caregivers. In T. M. Field, S. Goldberg, D. Stern, & A. M. Sostek (Eds.), *High-risk infants and children: Adult and peer interactions*. New York: Academic Press, 1980.

Gibbs, L., & Flanagan, J. Prognostic indicators of alcoholism treatment outcome. *International Journal of the Addictions*, 1977, *12*, 1097–1141.

Gilbert, T. F. *Human competence: Engineering worthy performance*. New York: McGraw-Hill, 1978.

Girodo, M., & Roehl, J. Cognitive preparation and coping self-talk: Anxiety management during the stress of flying. *Journal of Consulting and Clinical Psychology*, 1978, *46*, 978–989.

Gittelman, M. Hyperactive children: Types and behavioral interventions. *International Journal of Mental Health*, 1979, *8*, 129–138.

Gittelman, R. Practical problems encountered in behavioral treatment with hyperactive children. In M. Gittelman (Ed.), *Intervention strategies with hyperactive children.* White Plains, N.Y.: Sharpe, in press.

Gittelman-Klein, R., Klein, D. F., Abikoff, H., Katz, S., Gloisten, A. C., & Kates, W. Relative efficacy of methylphenidate and behavior modification: An interim report. *Journal of Abnormal Child Psychology*, 1976, *4*, 361–379.

Glad, W., & Adesso, V. J. The relative importance of socially induced tension and behavior contagion for smoking behavior. *Journal of Abnormal Psychology*, 1976, *85*, 119–121.

Glasgow, R. E. Effects of a self-control manual, rapid smoking, and amount of therapist contact on smoking reduction. *Journal of Consulting and Clinical Psychology*, 1978, *46*, 1439–1447.

Glasgow, R. E., Lichtenstein, E., Beaver, C., & O'Neill, K. Subjective reactions to rapid and normal paced aversive smoking. *Addictive Behaviors*, 1981, *6*, 53–60.

Glass, C. R., & Arnkoff, D. B. Think cognitively: Selected issues in cognitive–behavioral assessment and therapy. In P. C. Kendall (Ed.), *Advances in cognitive–behavioral research and therapy.* (Vol. 1). New York: Academic Press, 1982.

Glass, C. R., Gottman, J., & Shmurak, S. Response acquisition and cognitive self-statement modification approaches to dating skill training. *Journal of Counseling Psychology*, 1976, *23*, 520–526.

Glenwick, D., & Barocas, R. Training impulsive children in verbal self-control by use of natural change agents. *Journal of Special Education*, 1979, *13*, 387–398.

Glenwick, D., & Jason, L. (Eds.). *Behavioral community psychology: Progress and prospects.* New York: Praeger, 1980.

Glogower, F. D., Fremouw, W. J., & McCroskey, J. C. A component analysis of cognitive restructuring. *Cognitive Therapy and Research*, 1978, *2*, 209–223.

Glueck, C. J. Dietary fat and atherosclerosis. *American Journal of Clinical Nutrition*, 1979, *32*, 2703–2711.

Glynn, T. A behavioural approach to teaching. In K. Wheldall & R. Riding (Eds.), *Psychological aspects of learning and teaching.* London: Crook Helm, 1981.

Gofman, J. W., Hanig, M., & Jones, H. B. Evaluation of serum lipoprotein and cholesterol measurements as predictors of clinical complications of atherosclerosis. *Circulation*, 1956, *14*, 691–742.

Golden, K., Twentyman, C. T., Jensen, M., Karan, J., & Kloss, J. D. Coping with authority: Social skills training for the complex offender. *Criminal Justice and behavior*, 1980, *7*, 147–159.

Goldfarb, T. L., & Jarvik, M. E. Accommodation to restricted tobacco smoke intake in cigarette smokers. *International Journal of Addictions*, 1972, *7*, 559–565.

Goldfried, M. R. Systematic desensitization as training in self-control. *Journal of Consulting and Clinical Psychology*, 1971, *37*, 228–234.

Goldfried, M. R. Behavioral assessment: Where do we go from here? *Behavioral Assessment*, 1979, *1*, 19–22.

Goldfried, M. R. Some views on effective principles of psychotherapy. *Cognitive Therapy and Research*, 1980, *4*, 271–306. (a)

Goldfried, M. R. Toward the delineation of therapeutic change principles. *American Psychologist*, 1980, *35*, 991–999. (b)

Goldfried, M. R. (Ed.). Special Issue: Psychotherapy process. *Cognitive Therapy and Research*, 1980, *4*, 269–306. (c)

Goldfried, M. R., & Davison, G. C. *Clinical behavior therapy.* New York: Holt, Rinehart & Winston, 1976.

Goldfried, M. R., Decenteceo, E. T., & Weinberg, L. Systematic rational restructuring as a self-control technique. *Behavior Therapy*, 1974, *5*, 247–254.

Goldfried, M. R., & D'Zurilla, T. J. A behavioral analytic model for assessing competence. In C. D. Spielberger (Ed.), *Current topics in clinical and community psychology* (Vol. 1). New York: Academic Press, 1969.

Goldsmith, J. R., & Aronow, W. S. Carbon monoxide and coronary heart disease: A review. *Environmental Research*, 1975, *10*, 236–248.

Goldstein, A. J., & Chambless, D. A reanalysis of agoraphobia. *Behavior Therapy*, 1978, *9*, 47–59.

Goldstein, A. P. *Psychotherapeutic attraction*. New York: Pergamon, 1971.

Goldstein, A. P., & Foa, E. (Eds.). *Clinical handbook of behavior therapy*. New York: Wiley, 1979.

Goldstein, A. P., & Sorcher, M. *Changing supervisor behavior*. New York: Pergamon, 1974.

Goldstein, I. L. The pursuit of validity in the evaluation of training programs. *Human Factors*, 1978, *20*, 131–144.

Goldstein, I. L. Training and organization psychology. *Professional Psychology*, 1980, *11*, 421–427. (a)

Goldstein, I. L. Training in work organization. *Annual Review of Psychology*, 1980, *31*, 229–272. (b)

Gordon, S. B. Multiple assessment of behavior modification with families. *Journal of Consulting and Clinical Psychology*, 1975, *43*, 917.

Gordon, S. B. & Davidson, N. Behavioral parent training. In A. S. Gurman & D. P. Kniskern (Eds.), *Handbook of family therapy*. New York: Brunner/Mazel, 1981.

Gordon, S. B., Lerner, L. L., & Keefe, F. J. Responsive parenting: An approach to training parents of problem children. *American Journal of Community Psychology*, 1979, *7*, 45–56.

Gordon, T. *Parent effectiveness training*. New York: Wyden, 1970.

Gordon, T., Castelli, W. P., Hjortland, M. C., Kannel, W. B., & Dawber, T. R. Diabetes, blood lipids and the role of obesity in coronary heart disease risk for women. *Annals of Internal Medicine*, 1977, *87*, 393–397.

Gordon, T., & Kannel, W. B. Obesity and cardiovascular disease: The Framingham study. *Clinics in Endocrinology and Metabolism*, 1976, *5*, 367–375.

Gori, G. B. Low risk cigarettes: A prescription. *Science*, 1976, *194*, 1243–1246.

Gorsuch, R. L. *Factor analysis*. Philadelphia: Saunders, 1974.

Gotlib, I. H., & Asarnow, R. F. Interpersonal and impersonal problem-solving skills in mildly and clinically depressed university students. *Journal of Consulting and Clinical Psychology*, 1979, *47*, 86–95.

Gotlib, I. H., & Asarnow, R. F. Independence of interpersonal and impersonal problem solving skills: Reply to Rohsenow. *Journal of Consulting and Clinical Psychology*, 1980, *48*, 286–288.

Gottman, J. Toward a definition of social isolation in children. *Child Development*, 1977, *48*, 513–517.

Gottman, J. Analyzing for sequential connection and assessing interobserver reliability for the sequential analysis of observational data. *Behavioral Assessment*, 1980, *2*, 361–368.

Gottman, J., Gonso, J., & Rasmussen, B. Social interaction, social competence, and friendship in children. *Child Development*, 1975, *46*, 709–718.

Grande, F. Predicting change in serum cholesterol from change in composition of the diet. In R. M. Lauer & R. B. Shekelle (Eds.), *Childhood prevention of atherosclerosis and hypertension*. New York: Raven Press, 1980.

Gravel, R., Lemieux, G., & LaDouceur, R. Effectiveness of a cognitive–behavioral treatment package for cross-country ski racers. *Cognitive Therapy and Research*, 1980, *4*, 83–89.

Graziano, A. M., De Giovanni, I. S., & Garcia, K. A. Behavioral treatment of children's fears: A review. *Psychological Bulletin*, 1979, *86*, 804–830.

Green, A. H. Child abuse. In B. J. Wolman, J. Egan, & A. O. Ross (Eds.), *Handbook of treatment of mental disorders in childhood and adolescence*. Englewood Cliffs, N.J.: Prentice-Hall, 1978.

Green, K. D., Beck, S. J., Forehand, R., & Vosk, B. Validity of teacher nominations of child behavior problems. *Journal of Abnormal Child Psychology*, 1980, *8*, 397–404.

Green, L. Training psychologists for work with minority clients: A prototypic model with black clients. *Professional Psychology*, 1981, *12*, 732–739.

Green, L. A learned helplessness analysis of problems confronting the black community. In S. M. Turner & R. T. Jones (Eds.), *Behavior modification in black populations: Psychosocial issues and empirical findings*. New York: Plenum, 1982.

Greenberg, D. J. Token economies: An intervention of the past or future. *Community Mental Health Review*, in press.

Greenwald, M. A., Kloss, J. D., Kovaleski, M. E., Greenwald, D. P., Twentyman, C. T., & Zibung-Huffman, P. Drink refusal and social skills training with hospitalized alcoholics. *Addictive Behaviors*, 1980, *5*, 227–228.

Greenwood, C. R., Walker, H. M., & Hops, H. Issues in social interaction withdrawal assessment. *Exceptional Children*, 1977, *43*, 490–499.

Greist, J. H., Klein, M. H., Eischens, R. R., Faris, J., Gurman, A. S., & Morgan, W. P. Running as treatment for depression. *Comprehensive Psychiatry*, 1979, *20*, 41–54.

Gresham, F. M. Misguided mainstreaming: The case for social skills training with handicapped children. *Exceptional Children*, in press. (a)

Gresham, F. M. Social skills training with handicapped children: A review. *Review of Educational Research*, in press. (b)

Gresham, F. M., & Nagle, R. J. Social skills training with children: Responsiveness to modeling and coaching as a function of peer orientation. *Journal of Consulting and Clinical Psychology*, 1980, *48*, 718–729.

Grey, S., Sartory, G., & Rachman, S. Synchronous and desynchronous changes during fear reduction. *Behaviour Research and Therapy*, 1979, *17*, 137–148.

Griffith, R. G. An administrative perspective on guidelines for behavior modification: The creation of a legally safe environment. *The Behavior Therapist*, 1980, *3*, 5–6. (b)

Griffith, R. G. On an administrative perspective on guidelines for behavior modification: The creation of a legally safe environment. *The Behavior Therapist*, 1980, *3*, 23. (a)

Gross, A. M., & Brigham, T. A. Behavior modification and the treatment of juvenile delinquency: A review and proposal for future research. *Corrective and Social Psychiatry*, 1980, *26*, 98–106.

Gross, A. M., Brigham, T. A., Hopper, C., & Bologna, N. C. Self-management and social skills training: A study with predelinquent and delinquent youths. *Criminal Justice and Behavior*, 1980, *7*, 161–183.

Group for the Advancement of Psychiatry. *A proposed classification of psychopathological disorders in children*. New York: Author, 1966.

Gruber, B., Reeser, R., & Reid, D. H. Providing a less restrictive environment for profoundly retarded persons by teaching independent walking skills. *Journal of Applied Behavior Analysis*, 1979, *12*, 285–297.

Gruber, J. J. Exercise and mental performance. *International Journal of Sport Psychology*, 1975, *6*, 28–40.

Gunderson, E. K. E., & Schuckit, M. A. Prognostic indicators in young alcoholics. *Military Medicine*, 1978, *143*, 168–170.

Gutin, B. Effect of increase in physical fitness on mental ability following physical and mental stress. *Research Quarterly*, 1966, *37*, 211–220.

Gutin, B., & DiGennaro, J. Effect of one-minute and five-minute step-ups on performance of simple addition. *Research Quarterly*, 1968, *39*, 81–85.

Gwinup, G. Effect of exercise alone on the weight of obese women. *Archives of Internal Medicine*, 1975, *135*, 676–680.

Hacker, N. F. Comment on Redd and Andresen, "Conditioned aversion in cancer patients," *The Behavior Therapist*, 1981, *4*, 2.

Hackett, G., Horan, J. J., Stone, C. I., Linberg, S. E., Nicholas, W. C., & Lukasi, H. C. Further outcomes and tentative predictor variables from an evolving comprehensive program for the behavior control of smoking. *Journal of Drug Education*, 1977, *7*, 225–229.

Hafner, R. J. Fresh symptom emergence after intensive behaviour therapy. *British Journal of Psychiatry*, 1976, *129*, 378–383.

Hafner, R. J. The husbands of agoraphobic women and their influence on treatment outcome. *British Journal of Psychiatry*, 1977, *131*, 289–294.

Hafner, R. J., & Marks, I. Exposure in vivo of agoraphobics: Contributions of diazepam, group exposure, and anxiety evocation. *Psychological Medicine*, 1976, *6*, 71–88.

Hagen, R. L., Foreyt, J. P., & Durham, T. W. The dropout problem: Reducing attrition in obesity research. *Behavior Therapy*, 1976, *7*, 463–471.

Haggerty, R. J. Changing lifestyles to improve health. *Preventive Medicine*, 1977, *6*, 276–289.

Hall, C., Sheldon-Wildgen, J., & Sherman, J. A. Teaching job interview skills to retarded clients. *Journal of Applied Behavior Analysis*, 1980, *13*, 433–442.

Hall, R. G., Sachs, D. P. L., & Hall, S. M. Medical risks and therapeutic effectiveness of rapid smoking. *Behavior Therapy*, 1979, *10*, 249–259.

Hall, R. V., & Copeland, R. E. The Responsive Teaching Model: A first step in shaping school personnel as behavior modification specialists. In F. W. Clark, D. R. Evans, & L. A. Hamerlynck (Eds.), *Implementing behavioral programs for schools and clinics*. Champaign, Ill.: Research Press, 1972.

Hamerlynck, L. A. (Ed.). *Behavioral systems for the developmentally disabled: I. School and family environments*. New York: Brunner/Mazel, 1979.

Hamerlynck, L. A. (Ed.). *Behavioral systems for the developmentally disabled: II. Institutional, clinic, and community environments*. New York: Brunner/Mazel, 1980. (a)

Hamerlynck, L. A. "When you pass the behavioral buck—make it contingent" or Reflection upon service in state government. *The Behavior Therapist*, 1980, *3*, 5–9. (b)

Hamilton, F., & Maisto, S. A. Assertive behavior and perceived discomfort of alcoholics in assertion-required situations. *Journal of Consulting and Clinical Psychology*, 1979, *47*, 196–197.

Hamilton, S. B., & Bornstein, P. H. Broad-spectrum behavioral approach to smoking cessation: Effects of social support and paraprofessional training on the maintenance of treatment effects. *Journal of Consulting and Clinical Psychology*, 1979, *47*, 598–600.

Hammen, C. L., Jacobs, M., Mayol, A., & Cochran, S. D. Dysfunctional cognitions and the effectiveness of skills and cognitive–behavioral assertion training. *Journal of Consulting and Clinical Psychology*, 1980, *48*, 685–695.

Hammet, V. B. Psychological changes with physical fitness training. *Canadian Medical Association Journal*, 1967, *96*, 764–768.

Hammond, E. C., Garfinkel, L., Seidman, H., & Lew, E. A. *Some recent findings concerning cigarette smoking*. Paper presented at symposium on The Origins of Human Cancer, Cold Spring Harbor Laboratory, 1976.

Hampson, R. B., & Tavormina, J. B. Relative effectiveness of behavioral and effective group training with foster mothers. *Journal of Applied Behavior Analysis*, 1980, *48*, 294–295.

Handleman, J. S. Generalization by autistic-type children of verbal responses across settings. *Journal of Applied Behavior Analysis*, 1979, *12*, 273–282.

Handleman, J. S., & Harris, S. L. Generalization from school to home with autistic children. *Journal of Autism and Developmental Disorders*, 1980, *10*, 323–333.

Hanna, C. F., Loro, A. D., Jr., & Power, D. D. Differences in the degree of overweight: A note on its importance. *Addictive Behaviors*, 1981, *6*, 61–62.

Hanson, J. S., & Neede, W. H. Preliminary observations on physical training for hypertensive males. *Circulation Research*, 1970, *26* (Suppl.), 49–53.

Hardy, A. *Agoraphobia: Symptoms, causes, treatment*. Menlo Park, Calif.: Terrap, 1976.

Hargis, K., & Blechman, E. A. Social class and training of parents as behavior change agents. *Child Behavior Therapy*, 1979, 1, 69–74.

Hargrave, G. E., & Hargrave, M. C. A peer group socialization therapy program in the school: An outcome investigation. *Psychology in the Schools*, 1979, *16*, 547–550.

Harley, J. P., Ray, R. S., Tomasi, L., Eichman, P. L., Matthews, C. G., Chun, R., Cleeland, C. S., & Traisman, E. Hyperkinesis and food additives: Testing the Feingold hypothesis. *Pediatrics*, 1978, *61*, 818–827.

Harris, D. V. *Involvement in sports: A somatopsychic rationale for physical activity*. Philadelphia: Lea & Febiger, 1973.

Harris, G., & Johnson, S. B. Comparison of individualized covert modeling, self-control desensitization, and study skills training for alleviation of test anxiety. *Journal of Consulting and Clinical Psychology*, 1980, *48*, 186–194.

Harris, S. L., & Ersner-Hershfield, R. Behavioral suppression of seriously disruptive behavior in psychotic and retarded patients: A review of punishment and its alternative. *Psychological Bulletin*, 1978, *85*, 1352–1375.

Harris, S. L., Wolchik, S. A., & Weitz, S. The acquisition of language skills by autistic children: Can parents do the job? *Journal of Autism and Developmental Disorders*, 1981, *11*, 373–384.

Hartmann, D. P. Considerations in the choice of interobserver reliability estimates. *Journal of Applied Behavior Analysis*, 1977, *10*, 103–116.

Hartmann, D. P., & Atkinson, C. Having your cake and eating it too: A note on some apparent contradictions between therapeutic achievements and design requirements in *n* = 1 studies. *Behavior Therapy*, 1973, *4*, 589–591.

Hartmann, D. P., & Gardner, W. On the not so recent invention of interobserver reliability statistics: A commentary on two articles by Birkimer and Brown. *Journal of Applied Behavior Analysis*, 1979, *12*, 559–560.

Hartmann, D. P., Gottman, J. M., Jones, R. R., Gardner, W., Kazdin, A. E., & Vaught, R. S. Interrupted time-series analysis and its application to behavioral data. *Journal of Applied Behavior Analysis*, 1980, *13*, 543–559.

Hartmann, D. P., Roper, B. L., & Bradford, D. C. Some relationships between behavioral and traditional assessment. *Journal of Behavioral Assessment*, 1979, *1*, 3–21.

Hartung, G. H., Foreyt, J. P., Mitchell, R. E., Vlasek, I., & Gotto, A. M. Relationship of diet to HDL-cholesterol in middle-aged marathon runners, joggers, and inactive men. *New England Journal of Medicine*, 1980, *302*, 357–361.

Haskell, W. L., & Blair, S. N. The physical activity component of health promotion in occupational settings. *Public Health Reports*, 1980, *95*, 109-118.

Haskell, W. L., Taylor, H. L., Wood, P. D., Schrott, H., & Heiss, G. Strenuous physical activity, treadmill performance and plasma high-density lipoprotein cholesterol. *Circulation*, 1980, *62* (Suppl. IV), 53-61.

Hawkins, R. P. The functions of assessment: Implications for selection and development of devices for assessing repertories in clinical, educational, and other settings. *Journal of Applied Behavior Analysis*, 1979, *12*, 501-516.

Hawkins, R. P., & Hawkins, K. K. Parental observations on the education of severely retarded children: Can it be done in the classroom? *Analysis and Intervention in Developmental Disabilities*, 1981, *1*, 13-22.

Hayes, S. C. Theory and technology in behavior analysis. *The Behavior Analyst*, 1978, *1*, 25-33.

Hayes, S. C. Single case experimental design and empirical clinical practice. *Journal of Consulting and Clinical Psychology*, 1981, *49*, 193.

Hayes, S. C., Rincover, A., & Solnick, J. V. Trends in applied behavior analysis. *The Behavior Analyst*, 1978, *1*, 25-33.

Hayes, S. C., Rincover, A., & Solnick, J. V. The technical drift of applied behavior analysis. *Journal of Applied Behavior Analysis*, 1980, *13*, 175-185.

Hayes, W. A. Radical black behaviorism. In R. L. Jones (Ed.), *Black psychology*. New York: Harper & Row, 1972.

Haynes, R. B., Sackett, D. L., Gibson, E. S., Taylor, D. W., Hackett, B. C., Roberts, R. S., & Johnson, A. L. Improvement of medication compliance in uncontrolled hypertension. *Lancet*, 1976, *1*, 1265-1268.

Haynes, R. B., Sackett, D. L., Taylor, D. W., Gibson, E. S., & Johnson, A. L. Increased absenteeism form work after detection and labeling of hypertensive patients. *New England Journal of Medicine*, 1978, *299*, 741-744.

Haynes, R. B., Taylor, D. W., & Sackett, D. L. (Eds.). *Compliance in health care*. Baltimore: Johns Hopkins University Press, 1979.

Haynes, S. N. Behavioral variance, individual differences, and trait theory in a behavioral construct system: A reappraisal. *Behavioral Assessment*, 1979, *1*, 41-49.

Haynes, S. N., Follingstad, D. R., & Sullivan, J. C. Assessment of marital satisfaction and interaction. *Journal of Consulting and Clinical Psychology*, 1979, *47*, 789-791.

Haynes, S. N., & Kerns, R. D. Validation of a behavioral observation system. *Journal of Consulting and Clinical Psychology*, 1979, *47*, 397-400.

Heimberg, R. G., & Harrison, D. F. Use of the Rathus Assertiveness Schedule with offenders: A question of questions. *Behavior Therapy*, 1980, *11*, 278-281.

Heimberg, R. G., Harrison, D. F., Goldberg, L. S., Desmarais, S., & Blue, S. The relationship of self-report and behavioral assertion in an offender population. *Journal of Behavior Therapy and Experimental Psychiatry*, 1979, *10*, 283-286.

Heinzelmann, F., & Bagley, R. W. Response to physical activity programs and their effects on health behavior. *Public Health Reports*, 1970, *85*, 905-911.

Helfer, R. E., & Kempe, C. H. (Eds.). *The battered child* (2nd ed.). Chicago: University of Chicago Press, 1976.

Hendricks, R. D., Sobell, M. B., & Cooper, A. M. Social influences on human ethanol consumption in an analogue situation. *Addictive Behaviors*, 1978, *3*, 253-259.

Henningfield, J. E., Stitzer, M. L., & Griffiths, R. R. Expired carbon monoxide accumulation and elimination as a function of the number of cigarettes smoked. *Addictive Behaviors*, 1980, *5*, 265-272.

Henshaw, D. *A cognitive analysis of creative problem solving*. Unpublished doctoral dissertation, University of Waterloo, 1978.

Heppner, P. H. A review of the problem-solving literature and its relationship to the counseling process. *Journal of Counseling Psychology*, 1978, *25*, 366–375.

Herman, C. P. External and internal cues as determinants of the smoking behavior of light and heavy smokers. *Journal of Personality and Social Psychology*, 1974, *30*, 664–672.

Herman, C. P. Restrained eating. *Psychiatric Clinics of North America*, 1978, *1*, 593–607.

Herman, C. P., & Polivy, J. Restrained eating. In A. J. Stunkard (Ed.), *Obesity*. Philadelphia: Saunders, 1980.

Hermansen, L. E., Pruett, E. D. R., Osnes, J. B., & Giere, F. A. Blood glucose and plasma insulin in response to maximal exercise and glucose infusion. *Journal of Applied Physiology*, 1970, *29*, 13–16.

Hersen, M. Do behavior therapists use self-reports as major criteria? *Behavioral Analysis and Modification*, 1978, *2*, 328–334.

Hersen, M. Limitations and problems in the clinical application of behavioral techniques in psychiatric settings. *Behavior Therapy*, 1979, *10*, 65–80.

Hersen, M., & Barlow, D. H. *Single-case experimental designs: Strategies for studying behavior change*. New York: Pergamon, 1976.

Hersen, M., & Bellack, A. S. (Eds.). *Behavior therapy in the psychiatric setting*. Baltimore: Williams & Wilkins, 1978.

Hersen, M., Turner, S. M., Edelstein, B. A., & Pinkston, S. G. Effects of phenothiazines and social skills training in a withdrawn schizophrenic. *Journal of Clinical Psychology*, 1975, *31*, 588–594.

Hertel, R. K. Application of stochastic process analyses to the study of psychotherapeutic processes. *Psychological Bulletin*, 1972, *77*, 421–430.

Heyden, S., Cassel, B. A., Tyroler, H. A., Hames, C. G., & Cornoni, J. D. Body weight and cigarette smoking as risk factors. *Archives of Internal Medicine*, 1971, *128*, 915–918.

Higgins, R. L., Alonso, R. R., & Pendleton, M. G. The validity of role-play assessments of assertiveness. *Behavior Therapy*, 1979, *10*, 655–622.

Higgins, R. L., & Marlatt, G. A. The effects of anxiety arousal on the consumption of alcohol by alcoholics and social drinkers. *Journal of Consulting and Clinical Psychology*, 1973, *41*, 426–433.

Higgins, R. L., & Marlatt, G. A. Fear of interpersonal evaluation as a determinant of alcohol consumption in male social drinkers. *Journal of Abnormal Psychology*, 1975, *84*, 644–651.

Hillner, K. P. *Conditioning in contemporary perspective*. New York: Springer, 1979.

Hingson, R., Scotch, N., & Goldman, E. Impact of the "Rand Report" on alcoholics, treatment personnel, and Boston residents. *Journal of Studies on Alcohol*, 1977, *38*, 2065–2076.

Hirsch, S. M., Von Rosenberg, R., Phelan, C., & Dudley, H. K., Jr. Effectiveness of assertiveness training with alcoholics. *Journal of Studies on Alcohol*, 1978, *39*, 89–97.

Hobbs, S. A., Moguin, L. E., Tyroler, M., & Lahey, B. B. Cognitive behavior therapy with children: Has clinical utility been demonstrated? *Psychological Bulletin*, 1980, *87*, 147–165.

Hodgson, R., & Rachman, S. Desynchrony in measures of fear: II. *Behaviour Research and Therapy*, 1974, *12*, 319–326.

Holcomb, W. *Coping with severe stress: A clinical application of stress inoculation therapy*. Unpublished doctoral dissertation, University of Missouri–Columbia, 1979.

Hollandsworth, J. G., Jr., Glazeski, R. C., Kirkland, K., Jones, G. E., & Van Norman, L. R. An analysis of the nature and effects of test anxiety: Cognitive, behavioral, and physiological components. *Cognitive Therapy and Research*, 1979, *3*, 165–180.

Hollenbeck, A. R., Susman, E. J., Nannis, E. D., Strope, B. E., Hersh, M. D., & Pizzu, P. A. Children with serious illness: Behavioral correlates of separation and isolation. *Child Psychiatry and Human Development*, 1980, *11*, 3–11.

Hollon, S. D., & Beck, A. T. Psychotherapy and drug therapy: Comparisons and combinations. In S. L. Garfield & A. E. Bergin (Eds.), *Handbook of psychotherapy and behavior change* (2nd ed.). New York: Wiley, 1978.

Hollon, S. D., & Beck, A. T. Cognitive therapy of depression. In P. C. Kendall & S. D. Hollon (Eds.), *Cognitive–behavioral interventions: Theory, research, and procedure*. New York: Academic Press, 1979.

Hollon, S. D., & Evans, M. *Self-monitoring of mood in depression: When is what you saw what you got?* Unpublished manuscript, University of Minnesota, 1978.

Hollon, S. D., & Kendall, P. C. Cognitive self-statements in depression: Development of an Automatic Thoughts Questionnaire. *Cognitive Therapy and Research*, 1980, *4*, 383–395.

Hollon, S. D., & Kendall, P. C. *In vivo* assessment techniques for cognitive–behavioral processes. In P. C. Kendall & S. D. Hollon (Eds.), *Assessment strategies for cognitive–behavioral interventions*. New York: Academic Press, 1981.

Holroyd, K. A. Effects of social anxiety and social evaluation on beer consumption and social interaction. *Journal of Studies on Alcohol*, 1978, *39*, 737–744.

Holroyd, K. A., & Andrasik, F. Coping and self-control of chronic tension headache. *Journal of Consulting and Clinical Psychology*, 1978, *46*, 1036–1045.

Hopkins, B. L., & Hermann, J. A. Evaluating interobserver reliability of internal data. *Journal of Applied Behavior Analysis*, 1977, *10*, 121–126.

Hops, H., Beickel, S. L., & Walker, H. M. *CLASS: Program for acting-out children*. Eugene: Center at Oregon for Research in the Behavioral Education of the Handicapped, 1976.

Hops, H., & Cobb, J. A. Survival behaviors in the educational setting: Their implication for research and intervention. In L. A. Hamerlynck, L. C. Handy, & E. J. Mash (Eds.), *Behavior change*. Champaign, Ill.: Research Press, 1973.

Horan, J., Hackett, G., Buchanan, J., Stone C. I., & Demchik-Stone, D. Coping with pain: A component analysis. *Cognitive Therapy and Research*, 1977, *1*, 211–221.

Horan, J. J., Hackett, G., Nicholas, W. C., Linberg, S. E., Stone, C. I., & Lucasi, H. C. Rapid smoking: A cautionary note. *Journal of Consulting and Clinical Psychology*, 1977, *45*, 341–343.

Horan, J. J., Linberg, S. E., & Hackett, G. Nicotine poisoning and rapid smoking. *Journal of Consulting and Clinical Psychology*, 1977, *45*, 344–347.

Hore, B. D., Life events and alcohol relapse. *British Journal of Addiction*, 1971, *66*, 83–88.

Horner, R. D. The effects of an environmental "enrichments" program on the behavior of institutionalized profoundly retarded children. *Journal of Applied Behavior Analysis*, 1980, *13*, 473–491.

Hugdahl, K. The three-systems model of fear and emotion—a critical examination. *Behaviour Research and Therapy*, 1981, *19*, 75–86.

Hughes, J. R., Frederiksen, L. W., & Frazier, M. A carbon monoxide analyzer for measurement of smoking behavior. *Behavior Therapy*, 1978, *9*, 293–296.

Hunt, G. M., & Azrin, N. H. A community-reinforcement approach to alcoholism. *Behaviour Research and Therapy*, 1973, *11*, 91–104.

Hunt, W. A., Barnett, L. W., & Branch, L. G. Relapse rates in addiction programs. *Journal of Clinical Psychology*, 1971, *27*, 455–456.

Hunter, R., & MacAlpine, I. *Three hundred years of psychiatry*. London: Oxford University Press, 1963.

Hussian, R. A. *Genetic psychology: A behavioral perspective*. New York: Van Nostrand Reinhold, 1981.

Hussian, R. A., & Lawrence, P. S. The reduction of test, state, and trait anxiety by test specific and generalized stress inoculation training. *Cognitive Therapy and Research*, 1978, *2*, 25–38.

Hutchison, W. R., & Fawcett, S. Issues in defining the field of behavioral community psychology and certifying (or *not* certifying) its members. *The Behavior Therapist*, 1981, *4*, 5–8.

Ilmarinen, J., Ilmarinen, R., Koskela, A., Korhonen, O., Fardv, P., Partenen, X., & Rutenfranz, J. Training effects of stair climbing during office hours on female employees. *Ergonomics*, 1979, *22*, 507–516.

Innes, J. M., & Owen, N. Social and behavioural dimensions of community health: An introductory course on psychology in health care settings. *Australian Psychologist*, 1980, *15*, 169–180.

Inouye, D. K. National health insurance—your destiny is in your hands. *The Behavior Therapist*, 1981, *4*, 8.

Intagliata, J. C. Increasing the interpersonal problem-solving skills of an alcoholic population. *Journal of Consulting and Clinical Psychology*, 1978, *46*, 489–498.

Isaacs, C. Behavioral and ecological modifications that have increased bus ridership. *The Behavior Therapist*, 1980, *3*, 19–22.

Isherwood, G. B., & Tallboy, R. W. Reward systems of elementary school principals: An exploratory study. *The Journal of Educational Administration*, 1979, *17*, 160–170.

Israel, A. C., Pravder, M. D., & Knights, S. A. A peer-administered program for changing the classroom behavior of disruptive children. *Behavioural Analysis and Modification*, 1980, *4*, 224–236.

Jackson, G. C. Is behavior therapy a threat to black clients? *Journal of the National Medical Association*, 1976, *68*, 362–367.

Jackson, L. A., & Larrance, D. T. Is a "refinement" of attribution theory necessary to accommodate the learned helplessness reformulation? A critique of the reformulation of Abramson, Seligman, and Teasdale. *Journal of Abnormal Psychology*, 1979, *88*, 681–682.

Jacobson, N. S. Specific and nonspecific factors in the effectiveness of a behavioral approach to the treatment of marital discord. *Journal of Consulting and Clinical Psychology*, 1978, *46*, 442–452.

Jacobson, N. S. Increasing positive behavior in severely distressed marital relationships: The effects of problem-solving training. *Behavior Therapy*, 1979, *10*, 311–326.

Jacobson, N. S., & Anderson, E. A. The effects of behavior rehearsal and feedback on the acquisition of problem-solving skills in distressed and nondistressed couples. *Behaviour Research and Therapy*, 1980, *18*, 25–36.

Jacobson, N. S., Elwood, R. W., & Dallas, M. Assessment of marital dysfunction. In D. H. Barlow (Ed.), *Behavioral assessment of adult disorders*. New York: Guilford, 1981.

Jacobson, N. S., & Margolin, G. *Marital therapy: Strategies based on social learning and behavior exchange principles*. New York: Brunner/Mazel, 1979.

Jacobson, N. S., Waldron, H., & Moore, D. Toward a behavioral profile of marital distress. *Journal of Consulting and Clinical Psychology*, 1980, *48*, 696–703.

Jaffe, J. H., Kanzler, M., Cohen, M., & Kaplan, T. Inducing low tar/nicotine cigarette smoking in women. *British Journal of Addiction*, 1978, *73*, 271–281.

Janis, I. L., & Hoffman, D. Facilitating effects of daily contact between partners who make a decision to cut down on smoking. *Journal of Personality and Social Psychology*, 1970, *17*, 25–35.

Jannoun, L., Munby, M., Catalan, J., & Gelder, M. A home-based treatment program for agoraphobia: Replication and controlled evaluation. *Behavior Therapy*, 1980, *11*, 294–305.

Jaremko, M. E. Cognitive behavior modification: Real science or more mentalism? *The Professional Record*, 1979, *29*, 547–552. (a)

Jaremko, M. E. A component analysis of stress inoculation: Review and prospectives. *Cognitive Therapy and Research*, 1979, *3*, 35–48. (b)

Jarvik, L. F., & Cohen, D. T. A biobehavioral approach to intellectual change with aging. In C. Eisdorfer & M. P. Lawton (Eds.). *The psychology of adult development and aging*. Washington, D. C.: American Psychological Association, 1973.

Jason, L. A. Prevention in the schools: Behavioral approaches. In R. H. Price, R. F. Ketterer, B. C. Bader, & J. Monahan (Eds.), *Prevention in mental health: Research, policy, and practice*. Beverly Hills, Calif.: Sage, 1980.

Jason, L. A. Training undergraduates in behavior therapy and behavioral community psychology. *Behaviorists for Social Action*, in press.

Jason, L. A., McCoy, K., Blanco, D., & Zolik, E. S. Decreasing dog litter: Behavioral consultation to help a community group. *Evaluation Review*, 1980, *4*, 355–369.

Jason, L. A., & Smith, T. The Behavioral Ecological Matchmaker. *Teaching of Psychology*, 1980, *7*, 116–117.

Jason, L. A., & Zolik, E. S. Follow-up data on two dog-litter reduction interventions. *American Journal of Community Psychology*, 1980, *8*, 737–741.

Jeffery, C. R. *Crime prevention through environmental design*. Beverly Hills, Calif.: Sage, 1977.

Jeffery, C. R. Criminology as an interdisciplinary behavior science. *Criminology*, 1978, *16*, 149–169.

Jeffery, R. W., & Wing, R. R. Frequency of therapist contact in the treatment of obesity. *Behavior Therapy*, 1979, *10*, 186–192.

Jeffery, R. W., Wing, R. R., & Stunkard, A. J. Behavioral treatment of obesity: The state of the art in 1976. *Behavior Therapy*, 1978, *9*, 189–199.

Jeffrey, D. B., & Katz, R. C. *Take it off and keep it off: A behavioral program for weight loss and healthy living*. Englewood Cliffs, N.J.: Prentice-Hall, 1977.

Jensen, R. E. *A behavior modification program to remediate child abuse*. Paper presented at the annual meeting of the American Psychological Association, Chicago, September 1975.

Jernstedt, G. C., & Forseth, K. C. Dedicated microcomputer systems as behavior therapy instruments. *Behavioral Engineering*, 1980, *6*, 135–142.

Johnson, B., & Morse, H. Injured children and their parents. *Children*, 1978, *15*, 147–152.

Johnson, R. P., & Geller, E. S. Engineering technology and behavior analysis for interdisciplinary environmental protection. *The Behavior Analyst*, 1980, *3*, 23–29.

Johnson, W. G., Wildman, H. E., & O'Brien, T. The assessment of program adherence: The Achilles' heel of behavioral weight reduction. *Behavioral Assessment*, 1980, *2*, 297–301.

Johnston, J. J., Duncan, P. K., Monroe, C., Stephenson, H., & Stoerzinger, A. Tactics and benefits of behavioral measurement in business. *Journal of Organizational Behavior Management*, 1978, *1*, 164–178.

Jones, R. R. Program evaluation design issues. *Behavioral Assessment*, 1979, *1*, 51–56.

Jones, R. R., Weinrott, M. R., & Vaught, R. S. Effects of series dependency on the agreement between visual and statistical inferences. *Journal of Applied Behavior Analysis*, 1978, *11*, 277–284.

Jones, R. T. The role of external variables in self-reinforcement. *American Psychologist*, 1980, *35*, 1002–1004.

Jones, R. T., & Evans, H. L. Self-reinforcement: A continuum of external cues. *Journal of Educational Psychology*, 1980, *72*, 625–635.

Jones, R. T., & Kazdin, A. E. Childhood behavior problems in the school. In S. M. Turner, K. S. Calhoun, & H. E. Adams (Eds.), *Handbook of clinical behavior therapy*. New York: Wiley, 1981.

Jones, R. T., Nelson, R. E., & Kazdin, A. E. The role of external variables in self-reinforcement: A review. *Behavior Modification*, 1977, *1*, 147–178.

Jones, S. L., Nation, J. R., & Massard, P. Immunization against helplessness in man. *Journal of Abnormal Psychology*, 1977, *36*, 75–83.

Jones, W. D., & Mawhinney, T. C. The interaction of extrinsic rewards and intrinsic motivation: A review and suggestions for future research. *Proceedings of the National Academy of Management Meetings*. Orlando, Fla., August 1977.

Jordan, H. A., Levitz, L. S., & Kimbrell, G. M. *Eating is okay: A radical approach to weight loss, the behavioral control diet*. New York: Rawson, 1977.

Josephson, S., & Rosen, R. The experimental modification of sonorous breathing. *Journal of Applied Behavior Analysis*, 1980, *13*, 373–378.

Kagan, J. Reflection–impulsivity: The generality and dynamics of conceptual tempo. *Journal of Abnormal Psychology*, 1966, *71*, 17–24.

Kalish, H. L. *From behavioral science to behavior modification*. New York: McGraw-Hill, 1981.

Kandel, H. J., & Ayllon, T. Rapid educational rehabilitation for prison inmates. *Behaviour Research and Therapy*, 1976, *14*, 323–331.

Kanfer, F. H. Assessment for behavior modification. *Journal of Personality Assessment*, 1972, *36*, 418–423.

Kanfer, F. H. A few comments on the current status of behavioral assessment. *Behavioral Assessment*, 1979, *1*, 37–39.

Kanfer, F. H., & Nay, W. R. Behavioral assessment. In G. T. Wilson & C. M. Franks (Eds.), *Contemporary behavior therapy: Conceptual and empirical foundations*. New York: Guilford, 1982.

Kannel, W. B., & Gordon, T. Physiological and medical concomitants of obesity: The Framingham study. In G. A. Bray (Ed.), *Obesity in America* (NIH Publication No. 79-359). Washington, D.C.: U.S. Department of Health, Education, and Welfare, 1979.

Kannel, W. B., McGee, D., & Gordon, T. A general cardiovascular risk profile: The Framingham study. *American Journal of Cardiology*, 1976, *38*, 46–51.

Kannel, W. B., & Thom, T. Implications of the recent decline in cardiovascular mortality. *Cardiovascular Medicine*, 1979, *4*, 983–997.

Kanter, N. J., & Goldfried, M. R. Relative effectiveness of rational restructuring and self-control desensitization in the reduction of interpersonal anxiety. *Behavior Therapy*, 1979, *10*, 472–490.

Kaplan, H. *The new sex therapy*. New York: Brunner/Mazel, 1974.

Karlin, R. A., & Epstein, Y. M. Acute crowding: A reliable method for inducing stress in humans. *Research Communications in Psychology, Psychiatry, and Behavior*, 1979, *4*, 357–370.

Karoly, P. Behavioral self-management in children: Concepts, methods, issues and directions. In M. Hersen, R. Eisler, & P. Miller (Eds.), *Progress in behavior modification* (Vol. 5). New York: Academic Press, 1977.

Karoly, P., & Rosenthal, M. Training parents in behavior modification: Effects on perceptions of family interaction and deviant child behavior. *Behavior Therapy*, 1977, *8*, 406–410.

Kasl, S. V., Gore, S., & Cobb, S. The experience of losing a job: Reported changes in health, symptoms and illness behavior. *Psychosomatic Medicine*, 1975, *37*, 106–122.

Katch, F. I., & McArdle, W. D. *Nutrition, weight control, and exercise.* New York: Houghton Mifflin, 1977.

Katz, E. R., Kellerman, J., & Siegel, S. E. Behavioral distress in children with cancer undergoing medical procedures: Developmental considerations. *Journal of Consulting and Clinical Psychology*, 1980, *48*, 356–365.

Kauffman, J. M. (Ed.). Are all children educable? Introduction. *Analysis and Intervention in Developmental Disabilities*, 1981, *1*, 1–3.

Kauffman, J. M., & Hallahan, D. P. Learning disability and hyperactivity (with comments on minimal brain dysfunction). In B. B. Lahey & A. E. Kazdin (Eds.), *Advances in clinical child psychology* (Vol. 2). New York: Plenum, 1979.

Kavanaugh, T., Shephard, R. J., Doney, H., & Randit, V. Intensive exercise in coronary rehabilitation. *Medicine and Science in Sports*, 1973, *5*, 34–39.

Kazarian, S. S., Howe, M. G., & Csapo, K. G. Development of the Sleep Behavior Self-Rating Scale. *Behavior Therapy*, 1979, *10*, 412–417.

Kazdin, A. E. *Behavior modification in applied settings.* Homewood, Ill.: Dorsey, 1975.

Kazdin, A. E. Statistical analysis for single-case experimental designs. In M. Hersen & D. H. Barlow, *Single-case experimental designs: Strategies for studying behavior change.* New York: Pergamon, 1976.

Kazdin, A. E. Advances in Child behavior therapy: Applications and implications. *American Psychologist*, 1979, *34*, 981–987. (a)

Kazdin, A. E. Fictions, factions, and functions of behavior therapy. *Behavior Therapy*, 1979, *10*, 629–654. (b)

Kazdin, A. E. Imagery elaboration and self-efficacy in the covert modeling treatment of unassertive behavior. *Journal of Consulting and Clinical Psychology*, 1979, *47*, 725–733. (c)

Kazdin, A. E. Situational specificity: The two-edged sword of behavioral assessment. *Behavioral Assessment*, 1979, *1*, 57–75. (d)

Kazdin, A. E. Covert and overt rehearsal and elaboration during treatment in the development of assertive behavior. *Behaviour Research and Therapy*, 1980, *18*, 191–201.

Kazdin, A. E. Drawing valid inferences from case studies. *Journal of Consulting and Clinical Psychology*, 1981, *41*, 183–192. (a)

Kazdin, A. E. Vicarious reinforcement and punishment processes in the classroom. In P. S. Strain (Ed.), *The utilization of classroom peers as behavior change agents.* New York: Plenum, 1981. (b)

Kazdin, A. E., & Wilson, G. T. *Evaluation of behavior therapy: Issues, evidence and research strategies.* Cambridge, Mass.: Ballinger, 1978.

Keefe, F. J., & Blumenthal, J. A. The Life Fitness Program: A behavioral approach to making exercise a habit. *Journal of Behavior Therapy and Experimental Psychiatry*, 1980, *11*, 31–34.

Keith, P. M. Life changes, leisure activities, and well-being among very old men and women. *Activities, Adaptation and Aging*, 1980, *1*, 67–75.

Kelly, G. A. *The psychology of personal constructs* (2 vols.). New York: Norton, 1955.

Kelly, J. A., Laughlin, C., Claiborne, M., & Patterson, J. A group procedure for teaching job interviewing skills to formerly hospitalized psychiatric patients. *Behavior Therapy*, 1979, *10*, 299–310.

Kelly, J. A., Wildman, B. G., & Berler, E. S. Small group behavioral training to improve the job interview skills repertoire of mildly retarded adolescents. *Journal of Applied Behavior Analysis*, 1980, *13*, 461–471.

Kendall, P. C. On the efficacious use of verbal self-instructional procedures with children. *Cognitive Therapy and Research*, 1977, *1*, 331–341.

Kendall, P. C. Assessment and cognitive–behavioral interventions: Purposes, proposals, and problems. In P. C. Kendall & S. D. Hollon (Eds.), *Assessment strategies for cognitive–behavioral interventions.* New York: Academic Press, 1981. (a)

Kendall, P. C. Assessing generalization and the single-subject strategies. *Behavior Modification*, 1981, *5*, 307–320. (b)

Kendall, P. C. Cognitive–behavioral interventions with children. In B. B. Lahey & A. E. Kazdin (Eds.), *Advances in clinical child psychology* (Vol. 4). New York: Plenum, 1981. (c)

Kendall, P. C. Stressful medical procedures: Cognitive–behavioral strategies for stress management and prevention. In D. Miechenbaum & M. Jaremko (Eds.), *Stress prevention and management: A cognitive–behavioral approach.* New York: Plenum, in press.

Kendall, P. C., & Braswell, L. On cognitive–behavioral assessment: Model, measures, and madness. In C. D. Spielberger & J. N. Butcher (Eds.), *Advances in personality assessment* (Vol. 1). Hillsdale, N.J.: Erlbaum, 1982.

Kendall, P. C., & Finch, A. J. A cognitive–behavioral treatment for impulsivity: A group comparison study. *Journal of Consulting and Clinical Psychology*, 1978, *46*, 110–118.

Kendall, P. C., & Finch, A. J. Reanalysis: A reply. *Journal of Consulting and Clinical Psychology*, 1979, *47*, 1107–1108. (a)

Kendall, P. C., & Finch, A. J. Changes in verbal behavior following a cognitive–behavioral treatment for impulsivity. *Journal of Abnormal Child Psychology*, 1979, *7*, 455–463. (b)

Kendall, P. C., & Finch, A. J. Developing nonimpulsive behavior in children: Cognitive–behavioral strategies for self-control. In P. C. Kendall & S. D. Hollon (Eds.), *Cognitive–behavioral intervention: Theory, research, and problems.* New York: Academic Press, 1979. (c)

Kendall, P. C., Finch, A. J., Mikulka, P. J., & Colson, W. Multidimensional assertive behavior: Conceptualization and empirical support. *Journal Supplement Abstract Service*, 1980, *10*, 15.

Kendall, P. C., & Hollon, S. D. (Eds.). *Cognitive–behavioral interventions: Theory, research, and procedures.* New York: Academic Press, 1979.

Kendall, P. C., & Hollon, S. D. (Eds.). *Assessment strategies for cognitive–behavioral interventions.* New York: Academic Press, 1981. (a)

Kendall, P. C., & Hollon, S. D. Assessing self-referent speech: Methods in the measurement of self-statements. In P. C. Kendall & S. D. Hollon (Eds.), *Assessment strategies for cognitive–behavioral intervention.* New York: Academic Press, 1981. (b)

Kendall, P. C., & Korgeski, G. P. Assessment and cognitive–behavioral interventions. *Cognitive Therapy and Research*, 1979, *3*, 1–21.

Kendall, P. C., & Nay, W. R. Treatment evaluation strategies. In W. R. Nay, *Multimethod clinical assessment.* New York: Gardner, 1979.

Kendall, P. C., & Norton-Ford, J. D. Therapy outcome research methods. In P. C. Kendall & J. N. Butcher (Eds.), *Handbook of research methods in clinical psychology.* New York: Wiley, 1982.

Kendall, P. C., Pellegrini, D. S., & Urbain, E. S. Approaches to assessment for cognitive–behavioral interventions with children. In P. C. Kendall & S. D. Hollon (Eds.), *Assessment strategies for cognitive–behavioral interventions.* New York: Academic Press, 1981.

Kendall, P. C., & Watson, D. B. Psychological preparation for stressful medical procedures. In L. A. Bradley & C. K. Prokop (Eds.), *Medical psychology: Contributions to behavioral medicine.* New York: Academic Press, 1981.

Kendall, P. C., & Williams, C. L. Behavioral and cognitive–behavioral approaches to outpatient treatment with children. In W. E. Craighead, A. E. Kazdin, & M. J. Mahoney (Eds.), *Behavior modification: Principles, issues and applications.* Boston: Houghton Mifflin, 1981.

Kendall, P. C., & Williams, C. L. Assessing the cognitive and behavioral components of children's self-management. In P. Karoly & F. Kanfer (Eds.), *Self-management and behavior change: From theory to practice.* New York: Pergamon, 1982.

Kendall, P. C., Williams, C. L., Pechacek, T. F., Graham, L., Shisslak, C., & Herzoff, N. Cognitive–behavioral and patient education interventions in cardiac catheterization procedures: The Palo Alto medical psychology project. *Journal of Consulting and Clinical Psychology,* 1979, *47,* 49–58.

Kendall, P. C., & Wilcox, L. E. Self-control in children: The development of a rating scale. *Journal of Consulting and Clinical Psychology,* 1979, *47,* 1020–1030.

Kendall, P. C., & Wilcox, L. E. Cognitive–behavioral treatment for impulsivity: Concrete versus conceptual training in non-self-controlled problem children. *Journal of Consulting and Clinical Psychology,* 1980, *48,* 80–91.

Kendall, P. C., & Zupan, B. A. Individual versus group application of cognitive–behavioral self-control procedures with children. *Behavior Therapy,* 1981, *12,* 344–359.

Kendall, P. C., Zupan, B. A., & Braswell, L. Self-control in children: Further analyses of the Self-Control Rating Scale. *Behavior Therapy,* 1981, *12,* 667–681.

Kent, R. N., & O'Leary, K. D. A controlled evaluation of behavior modification with conduct problem children. *Journal of Consulting and Clinical Psychology,* 1976, *44,* 586–596.

Kentala, E. Physical fitness and feasibility of physical rehabilitation after myocardial infarction in men of working age. *Annals of Clinical Research,* 1972, *4* (Suppl. 9), 1–84.

Kern, J. M., & MacDonald, M. L. Assessing assertion: An investigation of construct validity and reliability. *Journal of Consulting and Clinical Psychology,* 1980, *48,* 532–534.

Kernberg, O. F. Summary and conclusions of "Psychotherapy and psychoanalysis: Final report of the Menninger Foundation's psychotherapy research project." *International Journal of Psychiatry,* 1973, *11,* 62–77.

Kessler, M., & Albee, S. W. Primary prevention. *Annual Review of Psychology,* 1975, *26,* 557–591.

Kessler, M., & Gomberg, C. Observations of barroom drinking: Methodology and preliminary results. *Quarterly Journal of Studies on Alcohol,* 1974, *35,* 1392–1396.

Keve, P. *Prison life and human worth.* Minneapolis: University of Minnesota Press, 1974.

Keys, A. Atherosclerosis: A problem in newer public health. *Journal of the Mt. Sinai Hospital,* 1953, *20,* 118–139.

Keys, A. Is overweight a risk factor for coronary heart disease? *Cardiovascular Medicine,* 1979, *4,* 1233–1242.

Keys, A. *Seven countries: A multivariate analysis of death and coronary heart disease.* Cambridge, Mass.: Harvard University Press, 1980.

Kiesler, D. J. Some myths of psychotherapy research and the search for a paradigm. *Psychological Bulletin,* 1966, *65,* 110–136.

Kiesler, D. J. Experimental designs in psychotherapy research. In A. E. Bergin & S. L. Garfield (Eds.), *Handbook of psychotherapy and behavior change.* New York: Wiley, 1971.

Kiesler, D. J. *The process of psychotherapy: Empirical foundations and systems of analysis.* Chicago: Aldine, 1973.

Kiesler, D. J. Psychotherapy process research: Viability and directions in the 1980's. In W. DeMoor & H. R. Wijngaarden (Eds.), *Psychotherapy: Research and training.* Elsevier/North-Holland Biomedical Press, 1980.

Kihlstrom, J., & Nasby, W. Cognitive tasks in clinical assessment: An exercise in applied psychology. In P. C. Kendall & S. D. Hollon (Eds.), *Assessment strategies for cognitive–behavioral interventions.* New York: Academic Press, 1981.

Kim, N. S. Cognitive–behavioral treatment for students' adaptation to academic major departments and improvement of academic performances. *Behavior Therapy*, 1980, *11*, 256–262.

Kirsch, I. "Microanalytic" analyses of efficacy expectations as predictors of performance. *Cognitive Therapy and Research*, 1980, *4*, 259–262.

Kiveloff, B., & Huber, O. Brief maximal isometric exercise on hypertension. *Journal of the American Geriatric Society*, 1971, *19*, 1006–1012.

Klein, N. C., Alexander, J. F., & Parsons, B. V. Impact of family systems intervention on recidivism and sibling delinquency. *Journal of Consulting and Clinical Psychology*, 1977, *45*, 469–474.

Kleinman, J. C., Feldman, J. J., & Monk, M. A. The effects of changes in smoking habits on coronary heart disease mortality. *American Journal of Public Health*, 1979, *69*, 795–802.

Klepac, R. K., Hauge, G., Dowling, J., & McDonald, M. Direct and generalized effects of three components of stress-inoculation for increased pain tolerance. *Behavior Therapy*, 1981, *12*, 417–424.

Kloss, J. D., Christopherson, E. R., & Risley, T. R. A behavioral approach to supervision. *Security Management*, 1976, *20*, 48–49.

Knapp, J. R., & Delprato, D. J. Willpower, behavior therapy, and the public. *The Psychological Record*, 1980, *30*, 477–482.

Koegel, R. L., & Egel, A. L. Motivating autistic children. *Journal of Abnormal Psychology*, 1979, *88*, 418–426.

Koegel, R. L., Egel, A. L., & Williams, J. A. Behavioral contrast and generalization across settings in the treatment of autistic children. *Journal of Experimental Child Psychology*, 1980, *30*, 422–437.

Koegel, R. L., Gluhn, T. J., & Nieminen, G. S. Generalization of parent-training results. *Journal of Applied Behavior Analysis*, 1978, *11*, 95–109.

Koegel, R. L., & Rincover, A. Treatment of psychotic children in a classroom environment: I. Learning in a large group. *Journal of Applied Behavior Analysis*, 1974, *7*, 45–60.

Kolotkin, R. A. Situation specificity in the assessment of assertion: Considerations for the measurement of training and transfer. *Behavior Therapy*, 1980, *11*, 651–661.

Komaki, J. A behavioral view of paradigm debates: Let the data speak. *Journal of Applied Psychology*, 1981, *66*, 111–112.

Komaki, J., Barwick, K. D., & Scott, L. R. A behavioral approach to occupational safety. Pinpointing and reinforcing safe performance in a food manufacturing plant. *Journal of Applied Psychology*, 1978, *63*, 434–445.

Komaki, J., Blood, M. R., & Holder, D. Fostering friendliness in a fast food franchise. *Journal of Organizational Behavior Management*, 1980, *2*, 151–163.

Komaki, J., Collins, R. L., & Thoene, T. J. F. Behavioral measurement in business, industry, and government. *Behavioral Assessment*, 1980, *2*, 103–123.

Komaki, J., Heinzmann, A. T., & Lawson, L. Effect of training and feedback: Component analyses of a behavioral safety program. *Journal of Applied Psychology*, 1980, *65*, 201–270.

Koop, S., Martin, G., Yu, D., & Suthons, E. Comparison of two reinforcement strategies in vocational-skill training of mentally retarded persons. *American Journal of Mental Deficiency*, 1980, *84*, 616–626.

Kounin, J. S., & Gump, P. V. The ripple effect in discipline. *Elementary School Journal*, 1958, *59*, 158–162.

Kovacs, M., & Beck, A. T. An empirical clinical approach towards a definition of childhood depression. In J. G. Shulterbrandt & A. Raskin (Eds.), *Depression in children: Diagnosis, treatment and conceptual models*. New York: Raven Press, 1977.

Kovacs, M., Rush, A. J., Beck, A. T., & Hollon, S. D. Depressed outpatients treated with cognitive therapy or pharmacotherapy: A one-year follow-up. *Archives of General Psychiatry*, 1981, *38*, 33–39.

Krantz, D. S. A naturalistic study of social influences on meal size among moderately obese and nonobese subjects. *Psychosomatic Medicine*, 1979, *41*, 19–27.

Krantz, S., & Hammen, C. Assessment of cognitive bias in depression. *Journal of Abnormal Psychology*, 1979, *88*, 611–619.

Kranzler, G. *You can change how you feel: A rational–emotive approach*. Eugene, Ore.: RETC Press, 1974.

Krasnegor, N. A. (Ed.). *Behavioral approaches to analysis and treatment of substance abuse*. Washington, D.C.: National Institute on Drug Abuse, 1979.

Krasner, L. (Ed.). *Environmental design and human behavior: A psychology of the individual in society*. New York: Pergamon, 1980.

Krasnor, L. R., & Rubin, K. H. The assessment of social problem-solving skills in young children. In T. V. Merluzzi, C. R. Glass, & M. Genest (Eds.), *Cognitive assessment*. New York: Guilford, 1981.

Krassner, H. A., Brownell, K. D., & Stunkard, A. J. Cleaning the plate: Food left over by overweight and normal weight persons. *Behaviour Research and Therapy*, 1978, *17*, 155–156.

Kratochwill, T. R. (Ed.). *Single subject research: Strategies for evaluating change*. New York: Academic Press, 1978.

Kratochwill, T. R. Just because it's reliable doesn't mean it's believable: A commentary on two articles by Birkimer and Brown. *Journal of Applied Behavior Analysis*, 1979, *12*, 553–557.

Kratochwill, T. R., & Bergan, J. R. Training school psychologists: Some perspectives based on a competency-based behavioral consultation model. *Professional Psychology*, 1978, *9*, 71–82.

Kratochwill, T. R., & Wetzel, R. J. Observer agreement, credibility, and judgment: Some considerations in presenting observer agreement data. *Journal of Applied Behavior Analysis*, 1977, *10*, 133–140.

Kristein, M. Economic issues in prevention. *Preventive Medicine*, 1977, *6*, 252–264.

Krumboltz, J. D. A social learning theory of career decision making. In A. M. Mitchell, G. B. Jones, & J. D. Krumboltz (Eds.), *Social learning and career decision making*. Cranston, R.I.: Carroll, 1979.

Kuehnel, T., Marholin, D., Heinrich, R., & Liberman, R. Evaluating behavior therapists' continuing education activities: The AABT 1977 Institutes. *The Behavior Therapist*, 1978, *4*, 5–8.

Kuhn, T. S. *The essential tension: Selected studies in scientific tradition and change*. Chicago: University of Chicago Press, 1977.

LaDouceur, R., & Auger, J. Where have all the follow-ups gone? *The Behavior Therapist*, 1980, *3*, 10–11.

La Greca, A. M. Social skills intervention with learning disabled children: Selecting skills and implementing training. *Journal of Clinical Child Psychology*, 1979, *8*, 236–241.

La Greca, A. M., & Mesibov, S. B. Facilitating interpersonal functioning with peers in learning-disabled children. *Journal of Learning Disabilities*, in press.

La Greca, A. M., & Santagrossi, D. A. Social skills training with elementary school students: A behavioral group approach. *Journal of Consulting and Clinical Psychology*, 1980, *48*, 220–227.

Lahey, B. B., Delamater, A., & Kupfer, D. Intervention strategies with hyperactive and learning disabled children. In S. M. Turner, K. S. Calhoun, & H. E. Adams (Eds.), *Handbook of clinical behavior therapy*. New York: Wiley, 1981.

Lahey, B. B., & Drabman, R. S. Behavior modification in the classroom. In W. E. Craighead, A. E. Kazdin, & M. J. Mahoney (Eds.), *Behavior modification: Principles, issues, and applications* (2nd ed.). Boston: Houghton Mifflin, 1981.

Lahey, B. B., Green, K. D., & Forehand, R. On the independence of ratings of hyperactivity, conduct problems, and attention deficits in children: A multiple regression analysis. *Journal of Consulting and Clinical Psychology*, 1980, *48*, 566–574.

Lambert, M., de Julio, S., & Stein, D. Therapist interpersonal skills. *Psychological Bulletin*, 1978, *85*, 467–489.

Lancioni, G. E. Infant operant conditioning and its implications for early intervention. *Psychological Bulletin*, 1980, *88*, 516–534.

Lang, P. J. The mechanics of desensitization and the laboratory study of fear. In C. M. Franks (Ed.), *Behavior therapy: Appraisal and status*. New York: McGraw-Hill, 1969.

Lang, P. J. Self-efficacy theory: Thoughts on cognition and unification. *Advances in Behaviour Research and Therapy*, 1978, *1*, 187–192.

Lang, P. J., A bio-informational theory of emotional imagery. *Psychophysiology*, 1979, *16*, 495–512.

Lang, P. J., Melamed, B. G., & Hart, J. A psychophysiological analysis of fear modification using an automated desensitization procedure. *Journal of Abnormal Psychology*, 1970, *76*, 220–234.

Langseth, L., & Dowd, J. Glucose tolerance and hyperkinesis. *Food and Cosmetics Toxicology*, 1978, *16*, 129–133.

Lansky, D. A methodological analysis of research on adherence and weight loss: A reply to Brownell and Stunkard (1978). *Behavior Therapy*, 1981, *12*, 144–149.

Larson, L. D., Schnelle, J., Kirchner, R., Carr, A. F., Domash, M., & Risley, T. R. Reduction of police vehicle accidents through mechanically aided supervision. *Journal of Applied Behavior Analysis*, 1980, *13*, 571–581.

Latham, G. P., & Saari, L. M. The application of social learning theory to training supervisors through behavioral modeling. *Journal of Applied Psychology*, 1979, *64*, 239–246.

Latimer, P. Training in behaviour therapy. *Canadian Journal of Psychiatry*, 1980, *25*, 26–27.

Layman, E. M. Psychological effects of physical activity. In J. H. Wilmore (Ed.), *Exercise and sports sciences reviews*. New York: Academic Press, 1974.

Lazarus, A. A. The results of behaviour therapy in 126 cases of severe neurosis. *Behaviour Research and Therapy*, 1963, *1*, 65–78.

Lazarus, A. A. *Behavior therapy and beyond*. New York: McGraw-Hill, 1971.

Lazarus, A. A. *Multimodal behavior therapy*. New York: Springer, 1976.

Lazarus, A. A. Has behavior therapy outlived its usefulness? *American Psychologist*, 1977, *32*, 550–554.

Lazarus, A. A. *The practice of multimodal therapy.* New York: McGraw-Hill, 1981.

Lazarus, R. S. Cognitive behavior therapy as psychodynamics revisited. In M. J. Mahoney (Ed.), *Psychotherapy process: Current issues and future directions.* New York: Plenum, 1980.

LeBow, M. D. Can lighter become thinner? *Addictive Behaviors,* 1977, *2,* 87–94.

LeBow, M. D. *Weight control: The behavioural strategies.* New York: Wiley, 1981.

LeBow, M. D., Goldberg, P. S., & Collins, A. Eating behavior of overweight and non-overweight persons in the natural environment. *Journal of Consulting and Clinical Psychology,* 1977, *45,* 1204–1205.

Ledwidge, B. Cognitive behavior modification: A step in the wrong direction. *Psychological Bulletin,* 1978, *85,* 353–375.

Ledwidge, B. Cognitive behavior modification or new ways to change minds: Reply to Mahoney and Kazdin. *Psychological Bulletin,* 1979, *86,* 1050–1053. (a)

Ledwidge, B. Cognitive behavior modification: A rejoinder to Locke and to Meichenbaum. *Cognitive Therapy and Research,* 1979, *3,* 133–139. (b)

Ledwidge, B. A distinction worth preserving. *Behavioral Analysis and Modification,* 1979, *3,* 161–164. (c)

Lefkowitz, M. M., & Burton, N. Childhood depression: A critique of the concept. *Psychological Bulletin,* 1978, *85,* 716–726.

Lefkowitz, M. M., & Tesiny, E. P. Assessment of childhood depression. *Journal of Consulting and Clinical Psychology,* 1980, *48,* 43–50.

Leon, A. S., & Blackburn, H. The relationship of physical activity to coronary heart disease and life expectancy. *Annals of the New York Academy of Sciences,* 1977, *301,* 561–578.

Leon, G. R., Kendall, P. C., & Garber, J. Depression in children: Parent, child, and teacher perspectives. *Journal of Abnormal Child Psychology,* 1980, *8,* 221–236.

Lepper, M. R., & Greene, D. (Eds.). *The hidden costs of reward: New perspectives on the psychology of human motivation.* Hillsdale, N.J.: Erlbaum, 1978.

Leventhal, H., & Cleary, P. D. The smoking problem: A review of the research and theory in behavioral risk modification. *Psychological Bulletin,* 1980, *88,* 370–405.

Levine, D. W., O'Neal, E. C., Garwood, S. G., & McDonald, P. J. Classroom econology: The effects of seating position on grades and participation. *Personality and Social Psychology Bulletin,* 1980, *6,* 409–412.

Levis, D., & Hare, N. A review of the theoretical rationale and empirical support for the extinction approach of implosive (flooding) therapy. In M. Hersen, R. Eisler, & P. Miller (Eds.), *Progress in behavior modification* (Vol. 4). New York: Academic Press, 1977.

Levitz, L. S., Jordan, H. A., LeBow, M. D., & Coopersmith, M. L. *Maintenance of weight loss one to five years after a multicomponent behavioral weight control program.* Unpublished manuscript, Institute for Behavioral Education, 1980.

Lew, E. A., & Garfinkel, L. Variations in mortality by weight among 750,000 men and women. *Journal of Chronic Diseases,* 1979, *32,* 563–576.

Lewis, S., Haskell, W. L., Wood, P. D., Manoogian, N., Bailey, J. E., & Pereira, M. Effects of physical activity on weight reduction in obese middle-aged women. *American Journal of Clinical Nutrition,* 1976, *29,* 151–156.

Liberman, R. P. Review of "Psychosocial treatment for chronic mental patients" by Gordon L. Paul and Robert J. Lentz. *Journal of Applied Behavior Analysis,* 1980, *13,* 367–372.

Liberman, R. P., Ferris, C., Selgado, P., & Selgado, J. Replication of the Achievement Place model in California. *Journal of Applied Behavior Analysis,* 1975, *8,* 287–299.

Lichstein, K. L., & Sallis, J. F. Covert sensitization for smoking: In search of efficacy. *Addictive Behaviors*, 1981, *6*, 83–91.

Lichstein, K. L., & Stalgaitis, S. J. Treatment of cigarette smoking in couples by reciprocal aversion. *Behavior Therapy*, 1980, *11*, 104–108.

Lichtenstein, E. Modification of smoking behavior: Good designs—ineffective treatments. *Journal of Consulting and Clinical Psychology*, 1971, *36*, 163–166.

Lichtenstein, E., & Brown, R. A. Smoking cessation methods: Review and recommendations. In W. R. Miller (Ed.), *The addictive behaviors: Treatment of alcoholism, drug abuse, smoking, and obesity*. New York: Pergamon, 1980.

Lichtenstein, E., & Glasgow, R. E. Rapid smoking: Side effects and safeguards. *Journal of Consulting and Clinical Psychology*, 1977, *45*, 815–821.

Lichtenstein, E., & Penner, M. P. Long-term effects of rapid smoking treatment for dependent cigarette smokers. *Addictive Behaviors*, 1977, *2*, 109–112.

Lied, E. R., & Marlatt, G. A. Modeling as a determinant of alcohol consumption: Effect of subject sex and prior drinking history. *Addictive Behaviors*, 1979, *4*, 47–54.

Light, R. J. Abused and neglected children in America: A study of alternative policies. *Harvard Educational Review*, 1973, *43*, 556–598.

Lilienfeld, A. M. *Foundations of epidemiology*. New York: Oxford University Press, 1976.

Lindner, P. G., & Blackburn, G. L. An interdisciplinary approach to obesity utilizing fasting modified by protein-sparing therapy. *Obesity/Bariatric Medicine*, 1976, *5*, 198–216.

Linehan, M. M. Structured cognitive–behavioral treatment of assertion problems. In P. C. Kendall & S. D. Hollon (Eds.), *Cognitive–behavioral interventions: Theory, research, and procedures*. New York: Academic Press, 1979.

Lipscomb, T. R., Nathan, P. E., Wilson, G. T., & Abrams, D. B. Effects of tolerance on the anxiety-reducing function of alcohol. *Archives of General Psychiatry*, 1980, *37*, 577–582.

Lipsky, M. J., Kassinove, H., & Miller, N. J. Effects of rational–emotive therapy, rational role reversal, and rational–emotive imagery on the emotional adjustment of community mental health center patients. *Journal of Consulting and Clinical Psychology*, 1980, *48*, 366–374.

Lloyd, R. W., & Salzberg, H. D. Controlled social drinking: An alternative to abstinence as a treatment goal for some alcohol abusers. *Psychological Bulletin*, 1975, *82*, 815–842.

Locke, E. A. Behavior modification is not cognitive—and other myths: A reply to Ledwidge. *Cognitive Therapy and Research*, 1979, *3*, 119–125.

Locke, E. A. Latham versus Komaki: A tale of two paradigms. *Journal of Applied Psychology*, 1980, *65*, 16–23.

Locke, H. J., & Wallace, K. M. Short-term marital adjustment and prediction tests: Their reliability and validity. *Journal of Marriage and Family Living*, 1959, *21*, 251–255.

London, P. The end of ideology in behavior modification. *American Psychologist*, 1972, *27*, 913–920.

Loney, J., Langhorne, J. E., & Paternite, C. S. An empirical basis for subgrouping the hyperkinetic/minimal brain dysfunction syndrome. *Journal of Abnormal Psychology*, 1978, *87*, 431–441.

Lopez, A., Vial, R., Balart, L., & Arroyave, G. Effect of exercise and physical fitness on serum lipids and lipoproteins. *Atherosclerosis*, 1974, *20*, 1–9.

Lopez, M. A. Social skills training with institutionalized elderly: Effects of precounseling structuring and overlearning on skill acquisition and transfer. *Journal of Counseling Psychology*, 1980, *27*, 286–293.

Lopez, M. A., Hoyer, W. J., Goldstein, A. P., Gershaw, N. J., & Sprafkin, R. P. Effects of overlearning and incentive on the acquisition and transfer of interpersonal skills with institutionalized elderly. *Journal of Gerontology*, 1980, *35*, 403–408.

Loro, A. D., Jr., Fisher, E. B., Jr., & Levenkron, J. C. Comparison of established and innovative weight-reduction treatment procedures. *Journal of Applied Behavior Analysis*, 1979, *12*, 141–155.

Lovaas, O. I., Ackerman, A. B., & Taubman, M. T. An overview of behavioral treatment of autistic persons. In M. Rosenbaum, C. M. Franks, & Y. Jaffe (Eds.), *Perspectives on behavior therapy in the eighties*. New York: Springer, 1982.

Lovaas, O. I., Koegel, R. L., & Schreibman, L. Stimulus overselectivity in autism: A review of research. *Psychological Bulletin*, 1979, *86*, 1236–1254.

Lovaas, O. I., Young, D. B., & Newsom, C. D. Childhood psychoses: behavioral treatment. In B. J. Wolman, J. Egan, & A. O. Ross (Eds.), *Handbook of treatment of mental disorders in childhood and adolescence*. Englewood Cliffs, N.J.: Prentice-Hall, 1978.

Lovibond, S. H., & Caddy, G. Discriminated aversive control in the moderation of alcoholics' drinking behavior. *Behavior Therapy*, 1970, *1*, 437–444.

Lowe, M. R., Green, L., Kurtz, S. M. S., Ashenberg, Z. S., & Fisher, E. B., Jr. Self-initiated, cue extinction, and covert sensitization procedures in smoking cessation. *Journal of Behavioral Medicine*, 1980, *3*, 357–372.

Luiselli, J. K. Controlling disruptive behaviors of an autistic child: Parent-mediated contingency management in the home setting. *Education and Treatment of Children*, 1980, *3*, 195–204. (a)

Luiselli, J. K. Programming overcorrection with children. What do the data indicate? *Journal of Clinical Child Psychology*, 1980, *9*, 224–228. (b)

Luiselli, J. K., & Townsend, N. M. Effects of intermittent punishment in behavior modification progress with children: A review. *Corrective and Social Psychiatry*, 1980, *26*, 200–205.

Luyben, P. D. Effects of informational prompts on energy conservation in college classrooms. *Journal of Applied Behavior Analysis*, 1980, *13*, 411–417.

Luyben, P. D., Warren, S. B., & Tallman, T. A. Recycling beverage containers on a college campus. *Journal of Environmental Systems*, 1979, *9*, 189–202.

MacDonald, M. L. Measuring assertion: A model and method. *Behavior Therapy*, 1978, *9*, 889–899.

MacMahon, B., & Pugh, T. F. *Epidemiology: Principles and methods*. Boston: Little, Brown, 1970.

Maher, C. A., & Barbrack, C. B. On the advancement of behavioral school psychology. *Child Behavior Therapy*, 1979, *1*, 5–6.

Mahoney, M. J. *Cognition and behavior modification*. Cambridge, Mass.: Bollinger, 1974.

Mahoney, M. J. The obese eating style: Bites, beliefs, and behavior modification. *Addictive Behaviors*, 1975, *1*, 47–53.

Mahoney, M. J. A critical analysis of rational–emotive theory and therapy. *Counseling Psychologist*, 1977, *7*, 44–46.

Mahoney, M. J. Behavior modification in the treatment of obesity. *Psychiatric Clinics of North America*, 1978, *1*, 651–660.

Mahoney, M. J. (Ed.). *Psychotherapy process: Current issues and future directions*. New York: Plenum, 1980.

Mahoney, M. J. Cognitive and non-cognitive views in behavior modification. In P. O. Sjoden & S. Bates (Eds.), *Trends in behavior therapy*. New York: Academic Press, in press.

Mahoney, M. J., & Arnkoff, D. Cognitive and self-control therapies. In S. L. Garfield &

A. E. Bergin (Eds.), *Handbook of psychotherapy and behavior change* (2nd ed.). New York: Wiley, 1978.

Mahoney, M. J., & Kazdin, A. E. Cognitive behavior modification: Misconceptions and premature evacuation. *Psychological Bulletin*, 1979, *86*, 1044–1049.

Mahoney, M. J., & Mahoney, K. *Permanent weight control: A total solution to the dieter's dilemma.* New York: Norton, 1976.

Maisto, S. A., Connors, G. J., Tucker, J. A., & McCollam, J. B. Validation of the sensation scale, a measure of subjective physiological responses to alcohol. *Behaviour Research and Therapy*, 1980, *18*, 37–43.

Maisto, S. A., Sobell, L. C., & Sobell, M. B. Comparison of alcoholics' self-reports of drinking behavior with reports of collateral informants. *Journal of Consulting and Clinical Psychology*, 1979, *47*, 106–112.

Maisto, S. A., Sobell, M. B., & Sobell, L. C. Predictors of treatment outcome for alcoholics treated by individualized behavior therapy. *Addictive Behaviors*, 1980, *5*, 259–264.

Malamuth, Z. N. Self-management training for children with reading problems: Effects on reading performance and sustained attention. *Cognitive Therapy and Research*, 1979, *3*, 279–289.

Maloney, D. M., Fixsen, D. L., & Maloney, K. B. Antisocial behavior: Behavior modification. In B. J. Wolman, J. Egan, & A. O. Ross (Eds.), *Handbook of treatment of mental disorders in childhood and adolescence.* Englewood Cliffs, N.J.: Prentice-Hall, 1978.

Mann, G. V. Diet–heart: End of an era. *New England Journal of Medicine*, 1977, *297*, 644–650.

Mann, G. V., Garrett, H. L., Farhi, A., Murray, H., & Billings, F. T. Exercise to prevent coronary heart disease: An experimental study of the effects of training on risk factors for coronary disease in men. *American Journal of Medicine*, 1969, *46*, 12–27.

Manuso, J. S. J. Coping with job abolishment. *Journal of Occupational Medicine*, 1977, *19*, 598–602.

Margolies, P. J. Early infantile autism. In R. J. Daitzman (Ed.), *Clinical behavior therapy and behavior modification* (Vol. 2). New York: Garland STPM, 1981.

Marholin, D., Luiselli, J. K., & Townsend, N. M. Overcorrection: An examination of its rationale and treatment effectiveness. In M. Hersen, R. Eisler, & P. Miller (Eds.), *Progress in behavior modification* (Vol. 9). New York: Academic Press, 1980.

Marks, I. M. Behavioral psychotherapy of adult neurosis. In S. L. Garfield & A. E. Bergin (Eds.), *Handbook of psychotherapy and behavior change* (2nd ed.). New York: Wiley, 1978.

Marks, I. M. *Cure and care of neuroses.* New York: Wiley, 1981.

Marks, I. M., Stern, R., Mawson, D., Cobb, J., & McDonald, R. Clomipramine and exposure for obsessive–compulsive rituals: I. *British Journal of Psychiatry*, 1980, *136*, 1–25.

Marlatt, G. A. The drinking profile: A questionnaire for the behavioral assessment of alcoholism. In E. J. Mash & L. G. Terdal (Eds.), *Behavior therapy assessment: Diagnosis and evaluation.* New York: Springer, 1977.

Marlatt, G. A. *Relapse prevention: A self-control program for the treatment of addictive behaviors.* Unpublished manuscript, University of Washington, 1980.

Marlatt, G. A., & Gordon, J. R. Determinants of relapse: Implications for the maintenance of behavior change. In P. Davidson & S. Davidson (Eds.), *Behavioral medicine: Changing health lifestyles.* New York: Brunner/Mazel, 1980.

Marley, W. P. Asthma and exercise: A review. *American Corrective Therapy Journal*, 1977, *31*, 95–102.

Marmor, J. Recent trends in psychotherapy. *American Journal of Psychiatry*, 1980, *137*, 409–416.

Marmor, J., & Woods, S. M. (Eds.). *The interface between the psychodynamic and behavioral therapies*. New York: Plenum, 1980.

Marshall, W. L. Satiation therapy: A procedure for reducing deviant sexual arousal. *Journal of Applied Behavior Analysis*, 1979, *12*, 377–390.

Marshall, W. R., Epstein, L. H., & Green, S. B. Coffee drinking and cigarette smoking: I. Coffee, caffeine and cigarette smoking behavior. *Addictive Behaviors*, 1980, *5*, 389–394.

Marshall, W. R., Green, S. B., Epstein, L. H., Rogers, C. M., & McCoy, J. F. Coffee drinking and cigarette smoking: II. Coffee, urinary pH and cigarette smoking behavior. *Addictive Behaviors*, 1980, *5*, 395–400.

Marston, A. R. Behavior ecology emerges from behavior modification. *Behavior Modification*, 1979, *3*, 147–160.

Martin, A. S., & Morris, J. L. Training a work ethic in severely mentally retarded workers —providing a context for the maintenance of skill performance. *Mental Retardation*, 1980, *18*, 67–71.

Martin, G. L., & Osborne, J. G. (Eds.). *Helping in the community: Behavioral applications*. New York: Plenum, 1980.

Martin, J. External versus self-reinforcement: A review of methodological and theoretical issues. *Canadian Journal of Behavioural Science*, 1980, *12*, 111–125.

Martin, R. *Legal challenges to behavior modification*. Champaign, Ill.: Research Press, 1975.

Martin, R. Comments on the "Wisconsin Experience." *The Behavior Therapist*, 1979, *2*, 7.

Martin, R. The right to receive or refuse treatment. *The Behavior Therapist*, 1980, *3*, 8.

Marzillier, J. S. Cognitive therapy and behavioral practice. *Behaviour Research and Therapy*, 1980, *18*, 249–258.

Mash, E. J. What is behavioral assessment? *Behavioral Assessment*, 1979, *1*, 23–29.

Mash, E. J., & McElwee, J. Situational effects on observer accuracy: Behavioral predictability, prior experience, and complexity of coding categories. *Child Development*, 1974, *45*, 367–377.

Mash, E. J., & Terdal, L. G. (Eds.). *Behavioral assessment of childhood disorders*. New York: Guilford, 1981.

Masters, J. C., & Mokros, J. R. Self-reinforcement procedures in children. In H. W. Reese (Ed.), *Advances in child development and behavior* (Vol. 9). New York: Academic press, 1974.

Masters, W., & Johnson, V. *Human sexual inadequacy*. Boston: Little, Brown, 1970.

Mastria, E. O., Mastria, M. A., & Harkins, J. C. Treatment of child abuse by behavioral intervention. A case report. *Child Welfare*, 1979, *58*, 253–261.

Matarazzo, J. D. Behavioral health and behavioral medicine: Frontiers for a new health psychology. *American Psychologist*, 1980, *35*, 807–817.

Mathews, A. M., Johnston, D. W., Lancashire, M., Munby, M., Shaw, P. M., & Gelder, M. G. Imaginal flooding and exposure to real phobic situations: Treatment outcome with agoraphobic patients. *British Journal of Psychiatry*, 1976, *129*, 362–371.

Mathews, A., Teasdale, J., Munby, M., Johnston, D., & Shaw, P. A home based treatment program for agoraphobia. *Behavior Therapy*, 1977, *8*, 914–924.

Matson, J. L. Behavior modification procedures for training chronically institutionalized schizophrenics. In M. Hersen, R. M. Eisler, & P. M. Miller (Eds.), *Progress in behavior modification* (Vol. 9). New York: Academic Press, 1980. (a)

Matson, J. L. Preventing home accidents: A training program for the retarded. *Behavior Modification*, 1980, *4*, 397–410. (b)

Matson, J. L., Horne, A. M., Ollendick, R. G., & Ollendick, T. H. Overcorrection: A further evaluation of restitution and positive practice. *Journal of Behavior Therapy and Experimental Psychiatry*, 1979, *10*, 295–298.

Matson, J. L., Ollendick, T. H., & DiLorenzo, T. M. Time out and the characteristics of mentally retarded institutionalized adults who do or do not receive it. *Mental Retardation*, 1980, *18*, 181–184.

Matson, J. L., Ollendick, T. H., & Martin, J. E. Overcorrection revisited: A long-term follow-up. *Journal of Behavior Therapy and Experimental Psychiatry*, 1979, *10*, 11–13.

Matson, J. L., Stephens, R. M., & Horne, A. M. Overcorrection and extinction–reinforcement as rapid methods of eliminating the disruptive behaviors of relatively normal children. *Behavioral Engineering*, 1978, *4*, 89–94.

Matson, J. L., & Zeiss, R. A. The buddy system: A method for generalized reduction of inappropriate interpersonal behaviour of retarded–psychiatric patients. *British Journal of Social and Clinical Psychology*, 1979, 401–405.

Mattes, J., & Gittelman-Klein, R. A crossover study of artificial food colorings in a hyperactive child. *American Journal of Psychiatry*, 1978, *135*, 987–988.

Mausner, J. S., & Bahn, A. K. *Epidemiology: An introductory text.* Philadelphia: Saunders, 1974.

Mavissakalian, M., & Barlow, D. H. (Eds.). *Phobia: Psychological and pharmacological treatment.* New York: Guilford, 1981.

Mawhinney, T. C. Intrinsic × extrinsic work motivation: Perspectives from behaviorism. *Organizational Behavior and Human Performance*, 1979, *24*, 411–440.

Maynard, R. Omaha pupils given "behavior" drug. *The Washington Post*, June 29, 1970.

Mayhew, S. L., Enyart, P., & Cone, J. D. Approaches to employee management: Policies and preferences. *Journal of Organizational Behavior Management*, 1979, *2*, 103–111.

McArdle, W. D., Katch, F. I., & Katch, V. L. *Exercise physiology: Energy, nutrition, and human performance.* Philadelphia: Lea & Febiger, 1981.

McAuley, R. Success and failure in applying behavioural analysis. *Social Work Today*, 1980, *11*, 15–17.

McAuley, R., & McAuley, P. The effectiveness of behaviour modification with families. *British Journal of Social Work*, 1980, *10*, 43–54.

McClelland, L., & Cook, S. W. Promoting energy conservation in waste-metered apartments through group financial incentives. *Journal of Applied Social Psychology*, 1980, *10*, 20–31.

McDonald, R., Sartory, G., Grey, S., Cobb, J., Stern, R., & Marks, I. The effects of self-exposure instructions on agoraphobic outpatients. *Behaviour Research and Therapy*, 1979, *17*, 83–86.

McFall, M. E., & Wallersheim, J. P. Obsessive–compulsive neurosis: A cognitive–behavioral formulation and approach to treatment. *Cognitive Therapy and Research*, 1979, *3*, 333–348.

McFall, R. M. Effects of self-monitoring on normal smoking behavior. *Journal of Consulting and Clinical Psychology*, 1970, *35*, 135–142.

McFall, R. M., & Hammen, C. L. Motivation, structure, and self-monitoring: Role of nonspecific factors in smoking reduction. *Journal of Consulting and Clinical Psychology*, 1971, *37*, 80–86.

McFall, R. M., & Lillisand, D. B. Behavioral rehearsal with modeling and coaching in assertion training. *Journal of Abnormal Psychology*, 1971, *77*, 313–323.

McFall, R. M., & Marston, R. R. An experimental investigation of behavior rehearsal in assertion training. *Journal of Abnormal Psychology*, 1970, *76*, 295–303.

McGill, A. M. (Ed.). *Proceedings of the National Conference of Health Promotion Programs in Occupational Settings*. Washington, D.C.: U.S. Public Health Service, U.S. Government Printing Office, 1979.

McGill, H. C., Jr. The relationship of dietary cholesterol to serum cholesterol concentration and to atherosclerosis in man. *American Journal of Clinical Nutrition*, 1979, *32*, 2664–2703.

McGuire, F. M. The incongruence between actual and desired leisure involvement in advanced adulthood. *Activities, Adaptation and Aging*, 1980, *1*, 77–89.

McGuire, M. T., Fairbanks, L. A., & Cole, S. A. The ethological study of four psychiatric wards: Behavior changes associated with new staff and new patients. *Journal of Psychiatric Research*, 1977, *13*, 211–224.

McGuire, M. T., & Polsky, R. H. Behavioral changes in hospitalized acute schizophrenics: An ethological perspective. *Journal of Nervous and Mental Disease*, 1979, *107*, 651–657.

McLaughlin, T. F., Big Left Hand, P., & Cady, M. Effects of the Behavior Analysis Model of Follow Through on reading achievement of native American elementary school children. *Reading Improvement*, 1979, *16*, 314–316.

McLean, A. (Ed.). *Occupational stress*. Springfield, Ill.: Charles C Thomas, 1974.

McLean, A. *How to reduce occupational stress*. Lexington, Mass.: Addison-Wesley, 1979.

McLean, P. D. The effect of informed consent on the acceptance of random treatment assignment in a clinical population. *Behavior Therapy*, 1980, *11*, 129–133.

McLean, P. D., & Hakstian, A. R. Clinical depression: Comparative efficacy of outpatient treatments. *Journal of Consulting and Clinical Psychology*, 1979, *47*, 818–836.

McMahon, R. J., & Forehand, R. Self-help behavior therapies in parent training. In B. B. Lahey & A. E. Kazdin (Eds.), *Advances in clinical child psychology*. New York: Plenum, 1980.

McMahon, R. J., & Forehand, R. Suggestions for evaluating self-administered materials in parent training. *Child Behavior Therapy*, in press.

McNamara, J. R. Socioethical considerations in behavior therapy research and procedure. *Behavior Modification*, 1978, *2*, 3–24.

McNamara, J. R. (Ed.). *Behavioral approaches to medicine: Application and analysis*. New York: Plenum, 1979.

McNamara, J. R. Behavior therapy in the seventies: Some changes and current issues. *Psychotherapy: Theory, Research and Practice*, 1980, *17*, 2–9.

McNamara, J. R., & Andrasik, F. Behavioral intervention in industry and government. In L. Michelson, M. Hersen, & S. L. Turner (Eds.), *Future perspectives in behavior therapy*. New York: Plenum, 1981.

McNees, M. P., Gilliam, S. W., Schnelle, J. F., & Risley, T. R. Controlling employee theft through time and product identification. *Journal of Organizational Behavior Management*, 1979, *2*, 113–119.

McNees, M. P., Kennon, M., Schnelle, J. F., Kirchner, R. E., & Thomas, M. M. An experimental analysis of a program to reduce retail theft. *American Journal of Community Psychology*, 1980, *8*, 379–385.

McPherson, F. M., Brougham, L., & McLaren, L. Maintenance of improvements in agoraphobic patients treated by behavioural methods in a four year follow-up. *Behaviour Research and Therapy*, 1980, *18*, 150–152.

Meehl, P. Theoretical risks and tabular asterisks: Sir Karl, Sir Ronald, and the slow progress of soft psychology. *Journal of Consulting and Clinical Psychology*, 1978, *46*, 806–834.

Meichenbaum, D. Self-instructional methods. In F. M. Kanfer & A. P. Goldstein (Eds.), *Helping people change.* New York: Pergamon, 1974.

Meichenbaum, D. *Cognitive-behavior modification.* New York: Plenum, 1977. (a)

Meichenbaum, D. Dr. Ellis, please stand up. *Counseling Psychologist,* 1977, *7,* 43–44. (b)

Meichenbaum, D. Teaching children self-control. In B. B. Lahey & A. E. Kazdin (Eds.), *Advances in clinical child psychology* (Vol. 2). New York: Plenum, 1979.

Meichenbaum, D., & Asarnow, J. Cognitive–behavioral modification and metacognitive development: Implications for the classroom. In P. C. Kendall & S. D. Hollon (Eds.), *Cognitive–behavioral interventions: Theory, research and procedures.* New York: Academic Press, 1979.

Meichenbaum, D., & Cameron, R. *Stress inoculation: A skills training approach to anxiety management.* Unpublished manuscript, University of Waterloo, 1973.

Meichenbaum, D., & Cameron, R. Issues in cognitive assessment: An overview. In T. V. Merluzzi, C. R. Glass, & M. Genest (Eds.), *Cognitive assessment.* New York: Guilford, 1981.

Meichenbaum, D., & Cameron, R. Cognitive-behavior therapy. In G. T. Wilson & C. M. Franks (Eds.), *Contemporary behavior therapy: Conceptual and empirical foundations.* New York: Guilford, 1982.

Meichenbaum, D., Gilmore, J., & Fedoravicius, A. Group insight vs. group desensitization in treating speech anxiety. *Journal of Consulting and Clinical Psychology,* 1971, *36,* 410–421.

Meichenbaum, D., & Jaremko, M. (Eds.). *Stress management and prevention: A cognitive–behavioral perspective.* New York: Plenum, in press.

Meichenbaum, D., & Turk, D. The cognitive–behavioral management of anxiety, anger, and pain. In P. O. Davidson (Ed.), *The behavioral management of anxiety, depression, and pain.* New York: Brunner/Mazel, 1976.

Melamed, B. G., & Siegel, L. J. Reduction of anxiety in children facing hospitalization and surgery by use of filmed modeling. *Journal of Consulting and Clinical Psychology,* 1975, *43,* 511–521.

Melamed, B. G., & Siegel, L. J. *Behavioral medicine: Practical applications in health care.* New York: Springer, 1980.

Melamed, B. G., Yurcheson, R., Fleece, E. L., Hutcherson, S., & Hawes, R. Effects of film modeling on the reduction of anxiety-related behavior in individuals varying in level of previous experience in the stress situation. *Journal of Consulting and Clinical Psychology,* 1978, *46,* 1357–1367.

Melzack, R., & Wall, P. D. Pain mechanisms: A new theory. *Science,* 1965, *150,* 971.

Mercer, S. W., & Benjamin, M. L. Spatial behavior of university undergraduates in double-occupancy residence rooms: An inventory of effects. *Journal of Applied Social Psychology,* 1980, *10,* 32–44.

Merluzzi, T. V., Glass, C. R., & Genest, M. (Eds.). *Cognitive assessment.* New York: Guilford, 1981.

Metalsky, G. I., & Abramson, L. Y. Attributional styles: Toward a framework for conceptualization and assessment. In P. C. Kendall & S. D. Hollon (Eds.), *Assessment strategies for cognitive– behavioral interventions.* New York: Academic Press, 1981.

Metropolitan Life Insurance Company. Frequency of overweight and underweight. *Statistical Bulletin,* 1960, *41,* 4–7.

Meyer, V. Problems of selection of trainees considered from a behavioural viewpoint. In W. DeMoor & H. R. Wijngaarden (Eds.), *Psychotherapy: Research and training.* Amsterdam: Elsevier/North Holland Biomedical Press, 1980.

Meyers, A. W., & Craighead, W. E. Classroom treatment of psychotic children: Specificity of responses to operative contingencies. *Behavior Modification,* 1979, *3,* 73–96.

Meyers, A. W., & Craighead, W. E. (Eds.). *Cognitive behavior therapy for children*. New York: Plenum, in press.

Meyers, A. W., & Schleser, R. Behavioral community psychology. In W. E. Craighead, A. E. Kazdin, & M. J. Mahoney (Eds.), *Behavior modification: Principles, issues, and applications* (2nd ed.). Boston: Houghton Mifflin, 1981.

Meyers, A. W., Stunkard, A. J., & Coll, M. Food accessibility and food choice: A test of Schachter's externality hypothesis. *Archives of General Psychiatry*, 1980, *37*, 1133–1135.

Meyers, A. W., Stunkard, A. J., Coll, M., & Cooke, C. Obesity and activity choice. *Behavior Modification*, 1980, *4*, 355–360.

Mikulas, W. L. Buddhism and behavior modification. *Psychological Record*, 1981.

Milan, M. A. *When behavior modification fails*. Paper presented at the 10th annual meeting of the Association for Advancement of Behavior Therapy, New York, December 1976.

Milan, M. A. Personal communication, 1981.

Milan, M. A., & Long, C. K. Crime and delinquency: The last frontier? In D. Glenwick & L. Jason (Eds.), *Behavioral community psychology: Progress and prospects*. New York: Praeger, 1980.

Milan, M. A., Throckmorton, W. R., McKee, J. M., & Wood, L. F. Contingency management in a cellblock token economy: Reducing rule violations and maximizing the effects of token reinforcements. *Criminal Justice and Behavior*, 1979, *6*, 307–325.

Milan, M. A., Wood, L. F., & McKee, J. M. Motivating academic achievements in a cellblock token economy: An elaboration of the Premack principle. *Offender Rehabilitation*, 1979, *3*, 349–361.

Milan, M. A., Wood, L. F., Williams, R. L., Rogers, J. G., Hampton, L. R., & McKee, J. *Applied behavior analysis and the imprisoned adult fellow project: I. The cellblock token economy*. Montgomery, Ala.: Experimental Manpower Laboratory for Corrections, 1974.

Milby, J. B., Garrett, C., English, C., Fritschi, D., & Clark, C. Take-home methodone: Contingency effects on drug-seeking and productivity of narcotic adults. *Addictive Behaviors*, 1978, *3*, 215–220.

Milich, R. S., & Fisher, E. B., Jr. The effects of cue salience and prior training on the behavior of juvenile and adult-onset obese individuals. *Addictive Behaviors*, 1979, *4*, 1–10.

Miller, J. G. *Living systems*. New York: McGraw-Hill, 1978.

Miller, L. C., Schilling, A. F., Logan, D. L., & Johnson, R. L. Potential hazards of rapid smoking as a technique for the modification of smoking behavior. *New England Journal of Medicine*, 1977, *297*, 590–592.

Miller, L. K. *Behavior management*. New York: Wiley, 1978.

Miller, L. K., & Schneider, R. The use of a token system in project Head Start. *Journal of Applied Behavior Analysis*, 1970, *3*, 213–220.

Miller, N. E. Behavioral medicine: New opportunities but serious dangers. *Behavioral Medicine Update*, 1979, *1*, 508.

Miller, P. M. *Behavioral treatment of alcoholism*. New York: Pergamon, 1976.

Miller, P. M. Theoretical and practical issues in substance abuse and treatment. In W. R. Miller (Ed.), *The addictive behaviors: Treatment of alcoholism, drug abuse, smoking, and obesity*. New York: Pergamon, 1980.

Miller, P. M. Assessment of alcohol abuse. In D. H. Barlow (Ed.), *Behavioral assessment of adult disorders*. New York: Guilford, 1981.

Miller, P. M., & Eisler, R. M. Assertive behavior of alcoholics: A descriptive analysis. *Behavior Therapy*, 1977, *8*, 146–149.

Miller, P. M., Frederiksen, L. W., & Hosford, R. L. Social interaction and smoking topography in heavy and light smokers. *Addictive Behaviors*, 1979, *4*, 147–154.

Miller, P. M., Hersen, M., Eisler, R. M., & Hilsman, G. Effects of social stress on operant drinking of alcoholics and social drinkers. *Behaviour Research and Therapy*, 1974, *12*, 67–72.

Miller, P. M., & Sims, K. L. Evaluation and component analysis of a comprehensive weight control program. *International Journal of Obesity*, 1981, *5*, 57–66.

Miller, R., & Lewin, L. M. Training and management of the psychiatric aide: A critical review. *Journal of Organizational Behavior Management*, 1980, *2*, 295–315.

Miller, W. R. Behavioral treatment of problem drinkers: A comparative outcome study of three controlled-drinking therapies. *Journal of Consulting and Clinical Psychology*, 1978, *46*, 74–86.

Miller, W. R. (Ed.). *The addictive behaviors: Treatment of alcoholism, drug abuse, smoking, and obesity*. New York: Pergamon, 1980. (a)

Miller, W. R. (Ed.). *Recent advances in addictions research*. New York: Pergamon, 1980. (b)

Miller, W. R., & Caddy, G. R. Abstinence and controlled drinking in the treatment of problem drinkers. *Journal of Studies on Alcohol*, 1977, *38*, 986–1003.

Miller, W. R., Crawford, V. L., & Taylor, C. A. Significant others as corroborative sources for problem drinkers. *Addictive Behaviors*, 1979, *4*, 67–70.

Miller, W. R., & Hester, R. K. Treating the problem drinker: Modern approaches. In W. R. Miller (Ed.), *The addictive behaviors: Treatment of alcoholism, drug abuse, smoking, and obesity*. New York: Pergamon, 1980.

Miller, W. R., & Joyce, M. A. Prediction of abstinence, controlled drinking, and heavy drinking outcomes following behavioral self-control training. *Journal of Consulting and Clinical Psychology*, 1979, *47*, 773–775.

Miller, W. R., & Muñoz, R. F. *How to control your drinking*. Englewood Cliffs, N.J.: Prentice-Hall, 1976.

Miller, W. R., & Seligman, M. E. P. Depression and learned helplessness in man. *Journal of Abnormal Psychology*, 1975, *84*, 228–238.

Miller, W. R., & Taylor, C. A. Relative effectiveness of bibliotherapy, individual and group self-control training in the treatment of problem drinkers. *Addictive Behaviors*, 1980, *5*, 13–24.

Miller, W. R., Taylor, C. A., & West, J. C. Focused versus broad-spectrum behavior therapy for problem drinkers. *Journal of Consulting and Clinical Psychology*, 1980, *48*, 590–601.

Mills, J., Burke, J., Schreibman, L., & Koegel, R. L. *The social validation of behavior therapy with autistic children*. Paper presented at the annual meeting of the Association for Advancement of Behavior Therapy, San Francisco, November 1979.

Milton, F., & Hafner, J. The outcome of behavior therapy for agoraphobia in relation to marital adjustment. *Archives of General Psychiatry*, 1979, *36*, 807–811.

Minskoff, J. G. Differential approaches to prevalence estimates of learning disabilities. *Annals of the New York Academy of Sciences*, 1973, *205*, 139–145.

Mischel, W. *Personality and assessment*. New York: Wiley, 1968.

Mischel, W. A cognitive–social learning approach to assessment. In T. V. Merluzzi, C. R. Glass, & M. Genest (Eds.), *Cognitive assessment*. New York: Guilford, 1981.

Mitchell, A. M., Jones, G. B., & Krumboltz (Eds.). *Social learning and career decision making*. Cranston, R.I.: Carroll, 1979.

Mitchell, S. K. Interobserver agreement, reliability, and generalizability of data collected in observational studies. *Psychological Bulletin*, 1979, *86*, 376–390.

Moleski, R., & Tosi, D. J. Comparative psychotherapy: Rational–emotive therapy versus systematic desensitization in the treatment of stuttering. *Journal of Consulting and Clinical Psychology*, 1976, *44*, 309–311.

Moody, P. M. The relationships of quantified human smoking behavior and demographic variables. *Social Science and Medicine*, 1980, *14A*, 49–54.

Morgan, J. E. *University oars: Being a critical inquiry in the after health of the men who rowed in the Oxford and Cambridge boat race from the years 1829–1869*. London: Macmillan, 1873.

Morgan, S. B. *The unreachable child: An introduction to early childhood autism.* Memphis: Memphis State University Press, 1981.

Morgan, W. P. Exercise and mental disorder. In A. J. Ryan & F. L. Allman (Eds.), *Sports medicine*. New York: Academic Press, 1974.

Morgan, W. P., Roberts, J. A., Brand, F. R., & Feinerman, A. D. Psychological effect of chronic physical activity. *Medicine and Science in Sports*, 1970, *2*, 213–217.

Morris, A. F., & Husman, B. F. Life quality changes following an endurance conditioning program. *American Corrective Therapy Journal*, 1978, *32*, 3–6.

Morris, E. K. Applied behavior analysis for criminal justice practice: Some current dimensions. *Criminal Justice and Behavior*, 1980, *7*, 131–145.

Morris, J. N. *Uses of epidemiology* (3rd ed.). New York: Churchill Livingstone, 1975.

Morris, J. N., Adam, C., Chave, S. P. W., Sirey, C., & Sheehan, D. J. Vigorous exercise in leisure-time and incidence of coronary heart disease. *Lancet*, 1973, *1*, 333–339.

Morris, J. N., & Crawford, M. D. Coronary heart disease and physical activity of work. *British Medical Journal*, 1958, *2*, 1485–1496.

Morris, J. N., Everitt, M. G., Pollard, R., Chave, S. P. W., & Semmence, A. M. Vigorous exercise in leisure time: Protection against coronary heart disease. *Lancet*, 1980, *2*, 1207–1210.

Morris, J. N., Heady, J. A., Raffle, P. A. B., Roberts, C. G., & Parks, J. W. Coronary heart disease and physical activity of work. *Lancet*, 1953, *2*, 1111–1120.

Morris, R. J., & Suckerman, K. R. The importance of the therapeutic relationship in systematic desensitization. *Journal of Consulting and Clinical Psychology*, 1974, *42*, 147.

Mozer, M. H. Confessions of an ex-behaviorist. *The Behavior Therapist*, 1979, *2*, 3.

Mulhern, R. K., & Passman, R. H. The child's behavioral pattern as a determinant of maternal primitiveness. *Child Development*, 1979, *50*, 815–820.

Munby, M., & Johnston, D. W. Agoraphobia: The long-term follow-up of behavioural treatment. *British Journal of Psychiatry*, 1980, *137*, 418–427.

Munford, P. R., Alevizos, P., Reardon, D., Miller, W. H., Callahan, E., Liberman, R. P., & Guilani, B. A behavioral approach to behavior therapy training. *The Journal of Psychiatric Education*, 1980, *4*, 47–51.

Munford, P. R., & Wikler, L. Providing diagnoses and recommendations to parents: A behavioral training approach. *Journal of Medical Education*, 1976, *51*, 421–423.

Murray, D. C. Treatment of overweight: Relationship between initial weight and weight change during behavior therapy of overweight individuals: Analysis of data from previous studies. *Psychological Reports*, 1975, *37*, 243–248.

Naditch, M. P. The Control Data Corporation StayWell Program. *Behavioral Medicine Update*, 1980, *2*, 9–10.

Nasby, W., Hayden, B., & De Paulo, B. M. Attributional bias among aggressive boys to interpret unambiguous social stimuli as displays of hostility. *Journal of Abnormal Psychology*, 1980, *89*, 459–468.

Nathan, P. E. Etiology and process in the addictive behaviors. In W. R. Miller (Ed.), *The addictive behaviors: Treatment of alcoholism, drug abuse, smoking, and obesity.* New York: Pergamon, 1980.

Nathan, P. E., & Briddell, D. W. Behavioral assessment and treatment of alcoholism. In B. Kissen & H. Begleiter (Eds.), *The biology of alcoholism* (Vol. 5). New York: Plenum, 1977.

Nathan, P. E., & Goldman, M. S. Problem drinking and alcoholism. In O. F. Pomerleau & J. P. Brady (Eds.), *Behavioral medicine: Theory and practice*. Baltimore: Williams & Wilkins, 1979.

Nathan, P. E., & Lipscomb, T. R. Behavior therapy and behavior modification in the treatment of alcoholism. In J. H. Mendelson & N. K. Mello (Eds.), *Diagnosis and treatment of alcoholism*. New York: McGraw-Hill, 1979.

Naughton, J. P., Hellerstein, H. K., & Mohler, I. C. (Eds.). *Exercise testing and exercise training in coronary heart disease*. New York: Academic Press, 1973.

Nay, W. R. *Multimethod clinical assessment*. New York: Gardner Press, 1979.

Nelson, R. O. Realistic dependent measures for clinical use. *Journal of Consulting and Clinical Psychology*, 1981, *49*, 168.

Nelson, R. O., & Hayes, S. C. Some current dimensions of behavioral assessment. *Behavioral Assessment*, 1979, *1*, 1-16. (a)

Nelson, R. O., & Hayes, S. C. The nature of behavioral assessment: A commentary. *Journal of Applied Behavior Analysis*, 1979, *12*, 491-500. (b)

Nias, D. K. B. Desensitization and media violence. *Journal of Psychosomatic Research*, 1979, *23*, 363-367.

Nichols, A. B., Ravenscroft, C., Lamphiear, D. E., & Ostrander, L. D., Jr. Independence of serum lipid levels and dietary habits: The Tecumseh study. *Journal of the American Medical Association*, 1976, *236*, 1948-1953.

Nietzel, M. T. *Crime and its modifications: A social learning perspective*. New York: Pergamon, 1979.

Nisbett, R. E. Hunger, obesity, and the ventromedial hypothalamus. *Psychological Review*, 1972, *79*, 433-453.

Nisbett, R. E., & Ross, L. *Human inference: Strategies and shortcomings of social judgment*. Englewood Cliffs, N.J.: Prentice-Hall, 1980.

Nisbett, R. E., & Wilson, T. D. Telling more than we can know: Verbal reports on mental processes. *Psychological Review*, 1977, *84*, 231-259.

Noland, S. A., Arnold, J., & Clement, P. W. Self-reinforcement by under-achieving, under-controlled girls. *Psychological Reports*, 1980, *47*, 671-678.

Nord, W. R., & Peter, J. P. A behavior modification perspective on marketing. *Journal of Marketing*, 1980, *44*, 36-47.

Novaco, R. W. *Anger control: The development and evaluation of an experimental treatment*. Lexington, Mass.: Heath, 1975.

Novaco, R. W. Treatment of chronic anger through cognitive and relaxation controls. *Journal of Consulting and Clinical Psychology*, 1976, *44*, 681.

Novaco, R. W. A stress inoculation approach to anger management in the training of law enforcement officers. *American Journal of Community Psychology*, 1977, *5*, 327-346.

Novaco, R. W. The cognitive regulation of anger and stress. In P. C. Kendall & S. D. Hollon (Eds.), *Cognitive-behavioral interventions: Theory, research, and procedures*. New York: Academic Press, 1979.

Nowicki, S., Jr., & Strickland, B. R. A locus of control scale for children. *Journal of Consulting and Clinical Psychology*, 1973, *40*, 148-154.

Oberman, A., & Kouchoukos, N. T. Role of exercise after coronary artery bypass surgery. In N. K. Wenger (Ed.), *Exercise and the heart*. Philadelphia: Davis, 1978.

O'Brien, T. P., & Kelley, J. E. A comparison of self-directed and therapist-directed practice for fear reduction. *Behaviour Research and Therapy*, 1980, *18*, 573–580.

O'Connor, C. Effects of selected physical activities on motor performance, perceptual performance and academic achievement of first graders. *Perceptual and Motor Skills*, 1969, *29*, 703–709.

O'Connor, R. D. Treatment of race and sex discriminatory behavior patterns. In S. A. Harris (Ed.), *The group treatment of human problems*. New York: Grune & Stratton, 1977. (a)

O'Connor, R. D. *Status of initial training, change and prevention portion of SAO's antidiscrimination program* (Draft report to the General Accounting Office), December 1977. (b) (cited by Turner, 1982)

O'Dell, S. Training parents in behavior modification: A review. *Psychological Bulletin*, 1974, *81*, 418–433.

O'Dell, S., Mahoney, N. D., Horton, W. G., & Turner, P. E. Media-assisted parent training. Alternate models. *Behavior Therapy*, 1979, *10*, 103–110.

O'Donnell, C. R., & Tharp, R. G. Community intervention and the use of multidisciplinary knowledge. In A. S. Bellack, M. Hersen, & A. E. Kazdin (Eds.), *International handbook of behavior modification and therapy*. New York: Plenum, in press.

O'Donnell, C. R., & Worrell, L. Motor and cognitive relaxation in the desensitization of anger. *Behaviour Research and Therapy*, 1973, *11*, 473–481.

Oei, T. P. S., & Jackson, P. Long-term effects of group and individual social skills training with alcoholics. *Addictive Behaviors*, 1980, *5*, 129–136.

Ohlin, P., Lundh, B., & Westling, H. Carbon monoxide blood levels and reported cessation of smoking. *Psychopharmacology*, 1976, *49*, 263–265.

Oldenburg, F. A., McCormack, D. W., Morse, J.L.C., & Jones, N. L. A comparison of exercise responses in stairclimbing and cycling. *Journal of Applied Physiology*, 1979, *46*, 510–516.

Oldridge, N. B. Compliance of post myocardial infarction patients to exercise programs. *Medicine and Science in Sports*, 1979, *4*, 373–375.

Oldridge, N. B., Wicks, J. R., Hanley, C., Sutton, J. R., & Jones, N. L. Noncompliance in an exercise rehabilitation program for men who have suffered a myocardial infarction. *Canadian Medical Association Journal*, 1978, *118*, 361–364.

O'Leary, K. D. Behavioral assessment. *Behavioral Assessment*, 1979, *1*, 31–36.

O'Leary, K. D. Pills or skills for hyperactive children. *Journal of Applied Behavior Analysis*, 1980, *13*, 191–204.

O'Leary, K. D., Pelham, W. E., Rosenbaum, A., & Price, G. H. Behavioral treatment of hyperactive children. *Clinical Pediatrics*, 1976, *15*, 510–515.

O'Leary, K. D., Turkewitz, H., & Tafel, S. Parent and therapist evaluation of behavior therapy in a child psychological clinic. *Journal of Consulting and Clinical Psychology*, 1973, *41*, 289–293.

O'Leary, K. D., & Wilson, G. T. *Behavior therapy: Application and outcome* (2nd ed.). Englewood Cliffs, N.J.: Prentice-Hall, in press.

O'Leary, S. G., & Dubey, D. R. Application of self-control procedures by children: A review. *Journal of Applied Behavior Analysis*, 1979, *12*, 449–465.

O'Leary, S. G., & Pelham, W. E. Behavioral therapy and withdrawal of stimulant medication with hyperactive children. *Pediatrics*, 1978, *61*, 211–217.

Ollendick, T. H., & Cerny, J. A. *Clinical behavior therapy with children*. New York: Plenum, 1982.

Ollendick, T. H., & Elliott, T. H. *Locus of control as related to effectiveness in a behavior modification program for juvenile delinquents*. Unpublished manuscript, Indiana University, Terre Haute, 1978.

Ollendick, T. H., & Hersen, M. Social skills training for juvenile delinquents. *Behaviour Research and Therapy*, 1979, *17*, 547–554.

Ollendick, T. H., & Matson, J. L. Overcorrection: An overview. *Behavior Therapy*, in press.

O'Neill, P. M., Currey, H. S., Hirsch, A. A., Riddle, F. E., Taylor, C. I., Malcolm, R. J., & Sexauer, J. D. Effects of sex of subject and spouse involvement on weight loss in a behavioral treatment program: A retrospective investigation. *Addictive Behaviors*, 1979, *4*, 167–178.

O'Reilly, C. A., & Caldwell, D. F. Job choice: The impact of intrinsic and extrinsic factors on subsequent satisfaction and commitment. *Journal of Applied Psychology*, 1980, *65*, 559–565.

Ossip, D. J., & Epstein, L. H. Relative effects of nicotine and coffee on cigarette smoking. *Addictive Behaviors*, 1981, *6*, 35–40.

Ost, L., Jerremalm, A., & Johansson, J. Individual response patterns and the effects of different behavioral methods in the treatment of social phobia. *Behaviour Research and Therapy*, 1981, *19*, 1–16.

Ott, B. D. Advocacy and instruction in behavior therapy: Examination of productivity in current directions. *The Behavior Therapist*, 1980, *3*, 23–24.

Otto, M. L., & Smith, D. G. Child abuse: A cognitive behavioural intervention model. *Journal of Marital and Family Therapy*, 1980, *6*, 425–429.

Paffenbarger, R. S., Hale, W. E., Brand, R. J., & Hyde, R. T. Work-energy level, personal characteristics, and fatal heart attack: A birth-cohort effect. *American Journal of Epidemiology*, 1977, *105*, 200–213.

Paffenbarger, R. S., Wing, A. L., & Hyde, R. T. Physical activity as an index of heart attack risk in college alumni. *American Journal of Epidemiology*, 1978, *108*, 161–175.

Parke, R., & Collmer, C. Child abuse: An interdisciplinary analysis. In M. Hetherington (Ed.), *Review of child development research* (Vol. 5). Chicago: University of Chicago Press, 1975.

Parloff, M., Waskow, I., & Wolfe, B. Research on therapist variables in relation to process and outcome. In S. L. Garfield & A. E. Bergin (Eds.), *Handbook of psychotherapy and behavior change*. New York: Wiley, 1978.

Parrish, V., & Hester, P. Controlling behavioral techniques in an early intervention program. *Community Mental Health Journal*, 1980, *16*, 169–175.

Patterson, G. R. Interventions for boys with conduct problems: Multiple settings, treatments, and criteria. *Journal of Consulting and Clinical Psychology*, 1974, *42*, 471–481.

Patterson, G. R., & Fleischman, M. J. Maintenance of treatment effects: Some considerations concerning family systems and follow-up data. *Behavior Therapy*, 1979, *10*, 168–185.

Patterson, G. R., & Gullion, M. E. *Living with children: New methods for parents and teachers*. Champaign, Ill.: Research Press, 1971.

Patterson, G. R., Weiss, R. L., & Hops, H. Training of marital skills: Some problems and concepts. In H. Leitenberg (Ed.), *Handbook of behavior modification*. Englewood Cliffs, N.J.: Prentice-Hall, 1977.

Pattison, E. M. Nonabstinent drinking goals in the treatment of alcoholism. *Archives of General Psychiatry*, 1976, *33*, 923–930.

Pattison, E. M., Sobell, M. B., & Sobell, L. C. *Emerging concepts of alcohol dependence*. New York: Springer, 1977.

Paul, G. L., & Lentz, R. J. *Psychological treatment of chronic mental patients*. Cambridge, Mass.: Harvard University Press, 1977.

Paxton, R. The effects of a deposit contract as a component in a behavioural programme for stopping smoking. *Behaviour Research and Therapy*, 1980, *18*, 45–50.

Paxton, R. Deposit contracts with smokers: Varying frequency and amount of repaying. *Behaviour Research and Therapy*, 1981, *19*, 117–124.

Pearce, J. W., LeBow, M. D., & Orchard, J. The role of spouse involvement in the behavioral treatment of obese women. *Journal of Consulting and Clinical Psychology*, 1981, *49*, 236–244.

Pechacek, T. F. Modification of smoking behavior. In *Smoking and health: A report of the Surgeon General* (DHEW Publication No. [PHS] 79-50066). Washington, D.C.: U.S. Government Printing Office, 1979.

Pechacek, T. F., & Danaher, B. G. How and why people quit smoking. In P. C. Kendall & S. D. Hollon (Eds.), *Cognitive-behavioral interventions: Theory, research and procedures*. New York: Academic Press, 1979.

Pechacek, T. F., & McAlister, A. L. Strategies for the modification of smoking behavior: Treatment and prevention. In J. M. Ferguson & C. B. Taylor (Eds.), *The comprehensive handbook of behavioral medicine* (Vol. 3). New York: Spectrum, 1980.

Pelham, W. E. Hyperactive children. *Psychiatric Clinics of North America*, 1978, *1*, 227–245.

Pelham, W. E., Schnedler, R. W., Bologna, N. C., & Contreras, J. A. Behavioral and stimulant treatment of hyperactive children: A therapy study with methylphenidate probes in a within-subject design, *Journal of Applied Behavior Analysis*, 1980, *13*, 221–236.

Penk, W. E., Charles, H. L., & Van Hoose, T. A. Comparative effectiveness of day hospital and inpatient psychiatric treatment. *Journal of Consulting and Clinical Psychology*, 1978, *46*, 94–101.

Peters, R. K., Benson, H., & Peters, J. M. Daily relaxation response breaks in a working population: II. Effects on blood pressure. *American Journal of Public Health*, 1977, *67*, 954–959.

Peters, R. K., Benson, H., & Porter, D. Daily relaxation response breaks in a working population: I. Effects on self-reported measures of health, performance, and well-being. *American Journal of Public Health*, 1977, *67*, 946–953.

Petersen, R. Social class, social learning, and wife abuse. *Social Service Review*, 1980, September, 390–406.

Peterson, D. R. Is psychology a profession? *American Psychologist*, 1976, *31*, 572–581.

Peterson, D. R., Eaton, M. M., Levine, A. R., & Snepp, F. P. Development of Doctor of Psychology programs and experiences of graduates through 1980. *The Rutgers Professional Psychology Review*, 1980, *2*, 29.

Peterson, L., Hartmann, D. P., & Gelfand, D. M. Prevention of child behavior disorders: A lifestyle change for child psychologists. In P. O. Davidson & S. M. Davidson (Eds.), *Behavioral medicine: Changing health lifestyles*. New York: Brunner/Mazel, 1980.

Petitti, D. A., Friedman, G. D., & Kahn, W. Accuracy of information on smoking habits provided on self-administered research questionnaires. *American Journal of Public Health*, 1981, *71*, 308–311.

Phillips, J. S., & Ray, R. S. Behavioral approaches to childhood disorders: Review and critique. *Behavior Modification*, 1980, *4*, 3–34.

Picker, M., Poling, A., & Parker, A. A review of children's self-injurious behavior. *The Psychological Record*, 1979, *29*, 435–452.

Pierce, W. D., & Epling, W. F. What happened to analysis in applied behavior analysis? *The Behavior Analyst*, 1980, *3*, 1–9.

Pirie, P., Jacobs, D., Jeffery, R., & Hannan, P. Distortion in self-reported height and weight data. *Journal of the American Dietetic Association*, 1981, *78*, 601–606.

Platt, J. J., & Siegel, J. M. MMPI characteristics of good and poor social problem-solvers among psychiatric patients. *Journal of Psychology*, 1976, *94*, 245–251.

Polakow, R. L., & Doctor, R. M. A behavioral modification program for adult drug offenders. *Journal of Research in Crime and Delinquency*, 1974, *11*, 63–69.

Polakow, R. L., & Peabody, D. L. Behavioral treatment of child abuse. *International Journal of Offender Therapy and Comparative Criminology*, 1975, *19*, 100–103.

Pollack, E., & Gittelman, R. Practical problems encountered in behavioral treatment with hyperactive children. In M. Gittelman (Ed.), *Intervention strategies with hyperactive children*. White Plains, N.Y.: M. E. Sharpe, in press.

Pollock, M. L., Wilmore, J. H., & Fox, S. M., III. *Health and fitness through physical activity*. New York: Wiley, 1978.

Polsky, R. H., & Chance, M. R. An ethological analysis of long stay hospitalized psychiatric patients: Senders and receivers in social interaction. *Journal of Nervous and Mental Disease*, 1979, *107*, 669–674.

Polsky, R. H., & McGuire, M. T. An ethological analysis of manic–depressive disorder. *Journal of Nervous and Mental Disease*, 1979, *167*, 56–65.

Pomerleau, O. F. Behavioral factors in the establishment, maintenance, and cessation of smoking. In *Smoking and health: A report of the Surgeon General* (DHEW Publication No. [PHS] 79-50066). Washington, D.C.: U.S. Government Printing Office, 1979. (a)

Pomerleau, O. F. Behavioral medicine: The contribution of the experimental analysis of behavior to medical care. *American Psychologist*, 1979, *34*, 654. (b)

Pomerleau, O. F., Bass, F., & Crown, V. The role of behavior modification in preventive medicine. *New England Journal of Medicine*, 1975, *292*, 1277–1282.

Pomerleau, O. F., & Brady, J. P. (Eds.). *Behavioral medicine: Theory and practice*. Baltimore: Williams & Wilkins, 1979.

Pomerleau, O. F., Pertschuk, M., Adkins, D., & d'Aquili, E. Treatment for middle income problem drinkers. In P. E. Nathan & G. A. Marlatt (Eds.), *Alcoholism: New directions in behavioral research and treatment*. New York: Plenum, 1978.

Pomerleau, O. F., & Pomerleau, C. S. *Break the smoking habit: A behavioral program for giving up cigarettes*. Champaign, Ill.: Research Press, 1977.

Poole, A. D., Sanson-Fisher, R. W., German, G. A., & Harker, J. The rapid smoking technique: Some physiological effects. *Behaviour Research and Therapy*, 1980, *18*, 581–586.

Porteus, S. D. *The Maze test: Recent advances*. Palo Alto, Calif.: Pacific Books, 1955.

Potter, B. A. *Turning around: The behavioral approach to managing people*. New York: AMACOM, 1980.

Powell, R. R. Psychological effects of exercise therapy upon institutionalized geriatric mental patients. *Journal of Gerontology*, 1974, *29*, 157–161.

Prinz, R. J., Roberts, W. A., & Hantman, E. Dietary correlates of hyperactive behavior in children. *Journal of Consulting and Clinical Psychology*, 1980, *48*, 760–769.

Prue, D. M., Krapfl, J. E., Noah, J. C., Cannon, S., & Maley, R. F. Managing the treatment activities of state hospital staff. *Journal of Organizational Behavior Management*, 1980, *2*, 165–181.

Prue, D. M., Martin, J. E., & Hume, A. S. A critical evaluation of thiocyanate as a biochemical index of smoking exposure. *Behavior Therapy*, 1980, *11*, 368–379.

Quattrochi-Tubin, S., & Jason, L. A. Enhancing social interactions and activity among the elderly through stimulus control. *Journal of Applied Behavior Analysis*, 1980, *13*, 159–163.

REFERENCES   401

Rachman, S. The conditioning theory of fear-acquisition: A critical examination. *Behaviour Research and Therapy*, 1977, *15*, 375–388.

Rachman, S. *Fear and courage*. San Francisco: Freeman, 1978.

Rachman, S. Emotional processing. *Behaviour Research and Therapy*, 1980, *18*, 51–60.

Rachman, S., Cobb, J., Grey, S., McDonald, B., Mawson, D., Sartory, G., & Stern, R. The behavioural treatment of obsessional–compulsive disorders, with and without clomipramine. *Behaviour Research and Therapy*, 1979, *17*, 467–478.

Rachman, S., & Hodgson, R. *Obsessions and compulsions*. Englewood Cliffs, N.J.: Prentice-Hall, 1980.

Rachman, S., & Wilson, G. T. *The effects of psychological therapy*. Oxford: Pergamon, 1980.

Rahaim, S., Lefebvre, C., & Jenkins, J. O. The effects of social skills training on behavioral and cognitive components of anger management. *Journal of Behavior Therapy and Experimental Psychiatry*, 1980, *11*, 3–8.

Ramsay, R. W. Goals of a personal therapy for trainees considered from a behavioral viewpoint. In W. DeMoor & H. R. Wijngaarden (Eds.), *Psychotherapy: Research and training*. Amsterdam: Elsevier/North Holland Biomedical Press, 1980.

Randhawa, B. S. Do teachers shape the behaviour of students and vice versa? *Canadian Journal of Behavioural Science*, 1980, *12*, 187–193.

Rapp, D. J. Does diet affect hyperactivity? *Journal of Learning Disabilities*, 1978, *11*, 56–62.

Rapport, M. D., Murphy, A., & Bailey, J. S. The effects of a response cost treatment tactic on hyperactive children. *Journal of School Psychology*, 1980, *18*, 98–111.

Rathjen, D. P., & Foreyt, J. P. (Eds.). *Social competence: Intervention for children and adults*. New York: Pergamon, 1980.

Rathus, S. A. A 30-item schedule for assessing assertive behavior. *Behavior Therapy*, 1973, *4*, 398–406.

Redd, W. H., & Andresen, G. Conditioned aversion in cancer patients. *The Behavior Therapist*, 1981, *4*, 3–6.

Rehm, L. P. (Ed.). *Behavior therapy for depression: Present status and future directions*. New York: Academic Press, 1981.

Reichel, D. A., & Geller, E. Applications of behavioral analysis for conserving transportation energy. In A. Baum & J. E. Singer (Eds.), *Advances in environmental psychology* (Vol. 3). Hillsdale, N.J.: Erlbaum, 1981.

Reid, D. H., Schuh-Wear, C. L., & Brannon, M. E. Use of a group contingency to decrease staff absenteeism in a state institution. *Behavior Modification*, 1978, *2*, 251–266.

Reid, J. B. The study of drinking in natural settings. In G. A. Marlatt & P. E. Nathan (Eds.), *Behavioral approaches to the assessment and treatment of alcoholism*. New Brunswick, N.J.: Rutgers Center for Alcohol Studies, 1978.

Reiter, S. M., & Samuel, W. Littering as a function of prior litter and the presence or absence of prohibitive signs. *Journal of Applied Social Psychology*, 1980, *10*, 45–55.

Relinger, H., Bornstein, P. H., Bugge, I. D., Carmody, T. P., & Zohn, C. J. Utilization of adverse rapid smoking in groups: Efficacy of treatment and maintenance procedures. *Journal of Consulting and Clinical Psychology*, 1977, *45*, 245–249.

Repp, A. C., & Barton, L. E. Naturalistic observations of institutionalized retarded persons: A comparison of licensure decisions and behavioral observations. *Journal of Applied Behavior Analysis*, 1980, *13*, 333–341.

Reppart, J. T., & Shaw, C. G. A conceptual and statistical evaluation of a new obesity treatment program in a military population. *Military Medicine*, 1978, *143*, 619–623.

Reynolds, C. R. Concurrent validity of what I think and feel: The revised Children's

Manifest Anxiety Scale. *Journal of Consulting and Clinical Psychology*, 1980, *48*, 774–775.

Reynolds, C. R., & Richmond, B. O. What I think and feel: A revised measure of children's manifest anxiety. *Journal of Abnormal Child Psychology*, 1978, *6*, 271–280.

Rhoads, G. G., Gulbrandson, C. L., & Kagen, A. Serum lipoproteins and coronary heart disease in a population study of Hawaii–Japanese men. *New England Journal of Medicine*, 1976, *294*, 293–298.

Richardson, F. C., & Tasto, D. L. Development and factor analysis of a social anxiety inventory. *Behavior Therapy*, 1976, *7*, 453–462.

Riddle, K. D., & Rapoport, J. L. A 2-year follow-up of 72 hyperactive boys. *Journal of Nervous and Mental Disease*, 1976, *102*, 126–134.

Rie, E. D., & Rie, H. E. Recall, retention, and Ritalin. *Journal of Consulting and Clinical Psychology*, 1977, *45*, 967–972.

Rippere, V. What makes depressed people feel worse. *Behaviour Research and Therapy*, 1980, *18*, 87–97.

Risley, T. R., & Sheldon-Wildgen, J. Invited peer review: The AABT experience. *The Behavior Therapist*, 1980, *3*, 5–8.

Ritschl, E. R., & Hall, R. V. Improving MBO: An applied behavior analyst's point of view. *Journal of Organizational Behavior Management*, 1980, *2*, 269–277.

Ritson, B. The prognosis of alcohol addicts treated by a specialized unit. *British Journal of Psychiatry*, 1968, *114*, 1019–1029.

Roberts, L., & Kendall, P. C. *A new look into insight.* Unpublished manuscript, University of Minnesota, 1981.

Roberts, R. N., & Dick, M. L. Self-control in the classroom: Theoretical issues and practical applications. In T. R. Kratochwill (Ed.), *Advances in school psychology* (Vol. 2). Hillsdale, N.J.: Erlbaum, in press.

Robin, A. L., Kent, R., O'Leary, K., Foster, S., & Prinz, R. An approach to teaching parents and adolescents problem-solving communication skills: A preliminary report. *Behavior Therapy*, 1977, *8*, 639–643.

Robinson, J. C. Will behavior modeling survive the '80s? *Training and Development Journal*, 1980, January, 1–5.

Rodin, J. Environmental factors in obesity. *Psychiatric Clinics of North America*, 1978, *1*, 581–592.

Rodin, J. The externality theory today. In A. J. Stunkard (Ed.), *Obesity*. Philadelphia: Saunders, 1980.

Rodin, J. Current status of the internal–external hypothesis for obesity: What went wrong? *American Psychologist*, 1981, *36*, 361–372.

Rogers, T., Mahoney, M. J., Mahoney, B. K., Straw, M. K., & Kenigsberg, M. I. Clinical assessment of obesity: Evaluation of diverse techniques. *Behavioral Assessment*, 1980, *2*, 161–181.

Rohsenow, D. J. Comment on Gotlib and Asarnow's learned helplessness study. *Journal of Consulting and Clinical Psychology*, 1980, *48*, 284–285.

Romano, J. M., & Bellack, A. S. Social validation of a component model of assertive behavior. *Journal of Consulting and Clinical Psychology*, 1980, *48*, 478–490.

Rose, R. L. The functional relationship between artificial food colors and hyperactivity. *Journal of Applied Behavior Analysis*, 1978, *11*, 439–446.

Roseman, J. M., & Nelius, S. J. *Predictors of weight behavior in obese persons at least one year post discharge from a dietary program utilizing behavior modification techniques.* Unpublished manuscript, Duke University, 1980.

Rosen, A. C., Rekers, G. A., & Bentler, P. M. Ethical issues in the treatment of children. *Journal of Social Issues*, 1978, *34*, 122–136.

Rosen, S. M. Guidelines for the review of do-it-yourself treatment books. *Contemporary Psychology*, 1981, *26*, 189–191.

Rosenbaum, M. S. A schedule for assessing self-control behaviors: Preliminary findings. *Behavior Therapy*, 1980, *11*, 109–121. (a)

Rosenbaum, M. S. Individual differences in self-control behaviors and tolerance of painful stimulation. *Journal of Abnormal Psychology*, 1980, *89*, 581–590. (b)

Rosenbaum, M. S., & Drabman, R. S. ". . . But I'd rather do it myself": A review of self-control techniques in the classroom. *Journal of Applied Behavior Analysis*, 1979, *17*, 467–485.

Rosenbluth, J., Nathan, P. E., & Lawson, D. M. Environmental influences on drinking by college students in a college pub: Behavioral observation in the natural environment. *Addictive Behaviors*, 1978, *3*, 117–121.

Rosenthal, B., Allen, G. J., & Winter, C. Husband involvement in the behavioral treatment of overweight women: Initial effects and long-term follow-up. *International Journal of Obesity*, 1980, *4*, 165–173.

Rosenthal, B., & Marx, R. D. Modeling influences on the eating behavior of successful and unsuccessful dieters and untreated normal weight individuals. *Addictive Behaviors*, 1979, *4*, 215–221.

Rosenthal, B., & McSweeney, F. K. Modeling influences on eating behavior. *Addictive Behaviors*, 1979, *4*, 205–214.

Rosenthal, B. S., & Morse, R. D. Differences in eating patterns of successful and unsuccessful dieters, untreated overweight and normal weight individuals. *Addictive Behaviors*, 1978, *3*, 129–134.

Rosenthal, T. L. Social learning theory. In G. T. Wilson & C. M. Franks (Eds.), *Contemporary behavior therapy: Conceptual and empirical foundations*. New York: Guilford, 1982.

Ross, A. O. *Psychological aspects of learning disabilities and reading disorders*. New York: McGraw-Hill, 1976.

Ross, A. O. *Child behavior therapy*. New York: Wiley, 1981.

Ross, A. O., & Pelham, W. E. Child psychopathology. *Annual Review of Psychology*, 1981, *32*, 243–278.

Ross, D. M., & Ross, S. A. *Hyperactivity: Research, theory and action*. New York: Wiley, 1976.

Ross, J. The use of former phobics in the treatment of phobias. *American Journal of Psychiatry*, 1980, *137*, 715–717.

Rothman, D. J., & Rothman, S. M. The conflict over children's right. *Hastings Center Report*, 1980, *1*, 7–10.

Rothstein, R. N. Television feedback used to modify gasoline consumption. *Behavior Therapy*, 1980, *11*, 683–688.

Ruggles, T. R., & LeBlanc, J. M. Behavior analysis procedures in classroom teaching. In A. Bellack, M. Hersen, & A. E. Kazdin (Eds.), *International handbook of behavior modification*. New York: Plenum, 1982.

Rusch, F. R., & Mithaug, D. E. *Vocational training for mentally retarded adults: A behavior analytic approach for the behavior therapist*. Champaign, Ill.: Research Press, 1980.

Rush, A. J., Beck, A. T., Kovacs, M., & Hollon, S. D. Comparative efficacy of cognitive therapy and pharmacotherapy in the treatment of depressed outpatients. *Cognitive Therapy and Research*, 1977, *1*, 17–38.

Russell, M. A. H. Cigarette smoking: Natural history of a dependence disorder. *British Journal of Medical Psychology*, 1971, *44*, 1–16.

Russell, M. A. H., Wilson, C., Taylor, C., & Baker, C. D. General practitioners' advice against smoking. *British Medical Journal*, 1979, *2*, 231–235.

Russo, D. C., & Koegel, R. L. A method for integrating an autistic child into a normal public-school classroom. *Journal of Applied Behavior Analysis*, 1977, *10*, 579–590.

Rutter, M., & Schopler, E. (Eds.). *Autism: Reappraisal of concepts and treatment*. New York: Plenum, 1978.

Ryall, M. R., & Dietiker, K. E. Reliability and clinical validity of the Children's Fear Survey Schedule. *Journal of Behavior Therapy and Experimental Psychiatry*, 1979, *10*, 303–309.

Saccone, A. J., & Israel, A. C. Effects of experimenter versus significant other-controlled reinforcement and choice of target behavior on weight loss. *Behavior Therapy*, 1978, *9*, 271–278.

Sachs, D. P. L., Hall, R. G., & Hall, S. M. Effects of rapid smoking: Physiological evaluation of a smoking cessation therapy. *Annals of Internal Medicine*, 1978, *88*, 639–641.

Sachs, D. P. L., Hall, R. G., Pechacek, T. F., & Fitzgerald, J. Clarification of risk–benefit issues in rapid smoking. *Journal of Consulting and Clinical Psychology*, 1979, *47*, 1053–1060.

Sackett, D. L., Haynes, R. B., Gibson, E. S., Hackett, B. C., Taylor, D. W., Roberts, R. S., & Johnson, A. L. Randomized clinical trial of strategies for improving medication compliance in primary hypertension. *Lancet*, 1975, *1*, 1205–1207.

Safer, D. J., & Allen, R. P. *Hyperactive children: Diagnosis and management*. Baltimore: University Park Press, 1976.

Safran, J. D., Alden, L. E., & Davidson, P. O. Client anxiety level as a moderator variable in assertion training. *Cognitive Therapy and Research*, 1980, *4*, 189–200.

Saltin, B., Astrand, P. O. Maximal oxygen uptake in athletes. *Journal of Applied Physiology*, 1967, *23*, 353–362.

Sampson, E. E. Cognitive psychology as ideology. *American Psychologist*, 1981, *36*, 730–743.

Sandberg, S. T., Rutter, M., & Taylor, E. Hyperkinetic disorder in psychiatric clinic attenders. *Developmental Medicine and Child Neurology*, 1978, *20*, 279–299.

Sandler, J., Van Dercar, C., & Milhoan, M. Training child abusers in the use of positive reinforcement practices. *Behaviour Research and Therapy*, 1978, *16*, 169–175.

Sanger, M. R., & Bichanich, P. Weight-reducing program for hospital employees. *Journal of the American Dietetic Association*, 1977, *71*, 535–536.

Sanne, H. Exercise tolerance and physical training of non-selected patients after myocardial infarction. *Acta Medica Scandinavica*, 1973, Suppl. 551, 5–27.

Satterfield, J. H., Cantwell, D. P., & Satterfield, B. T. Multimodality treatment: A one-year follow-up of 84 hyperactive boys. *Archives of General Psychiatry*, 1979, *36*, 965–974.

Schachter, S. The interaction of cognitive physiological determinants of emotional state. In L. Berkowitz (Ed.), *Advances in experimental social psychology*. New York: Academic Press, 1964.

Schachter, S. Some extraordinary facts about obese humans and rats. *American Psychologist*, 1971, *26*, 129–144.

Schachter, S. Nicotine regulation in heavy and light smokers. *Journal of Experimental Psychology*, 1977, *106*, 5–12.

Schachter, S. Pharmacological and psychological determinants of smoking. *Annals of Internal Medicine*, 1978, *88*, 104–114.

Schachter, S., & Rodin, J. *Obese humans and rats*. Washington, D.C.: Erlbaum/Halsted, 1974.

Schaefer, C. E., & Millman, H. L. *How to help children with common problems.* New York: Van Nostrand Reinhold, 1981.

Scheuer, J., & Tipton, C. M. Cardiovascular adaptations to physical training. *Annual Review of Physiology,* 1977, *39,* 221-251.

Schlichting, P., Høilund-Carlsen, P. F., & Quaade, F. Comparison of self-reported height and weight with controlled height and weight in women and men. *International Journal of Obesity,* 1981, *5,* 67-76.

Schmahl, D. P., Lichtenstein, E., & Harris, D. E. Successful treatment of habitual smokers with warm, smoky air and rapid smoking. *Journal of Consulting and Clinical Psychology,* 1972, *38,* 105-111.

Schneider, F. W., Lesko, W. A., & Garrett, W. A. Helping behavior in hot, comfortable, and cold temperatures. *Environment and Behavior,* 1980, *12,* 231-240.

Schnelle, J. F., McNees, M. P., Thomas, M. M., Gendrich, J. G., & Beagle, G. P. Prompting behavior change in the community: Use of mass media techniques. *Environment and Behavior,* 1980, *12,* 157-166.

Schoenfeld, Y., Keren, G., Shimoni, T., Birnfeld, C., & Sohar, E. Walking: A method for rapid improvement of physical fitness: *Journal of the American Medical Association,* 1980, *243,* 2062-2063.

Schonfield, A. E. D. Learning, memory and aging. In J. E. Birren & R. B. Sloane (Eds.), *Handbook of mental health and aging.* Englewood Cliffs, N.J.: Prentice-Hall, 1980.

Schrag, P., & Divoky, D. *The myth of the hyperactive child.* New York: Pantheon, 1975.

Schreiber, F. R. *Sybil.* New York: Wagner, 1974.

Schreibman, L., & Koegel, R. L. A guideline for planning behavior modification programs for autistic children. In S. M. Turner, K. S. Calhoun, & H. E. Adams (Eds.), *Handbook of clinical behavior therapy.* New York: Wiley, 1981.

Schreibman, L., Koegel, R. L., Charlop, M. H., & Egel, A. L. Autism. In A. S. Bellack, M. Hersen, & A. E. Kazdin (Eds.), *International handbook of behavior modification and therapy.* New York: Plenum, in press.

Schreibman, L., & Mills, J. A. Infantile autism. In I. H. Ollendick & M. Hersen (Eds.), *Handbook of psychopathology.* New York: Plenum, in press.

Schulman, J. L., Stevens, T. M., & Kupst, M. J. The biomotometer: A new device for the measurement and remediation of hyperactivity. *Child Development,* 1977, *48,* 1152-1154.

Schulman, J. L., Suran, B. G., Stevens, T. M., & Kupst, M. J. Instructions, feedback, and reinforcement in reducing activity levels in the classroom. *Journal of Applied Behavior Analysis,* 1979, *12,* 441-447.

Schumaker, J., Hovell, M., & Sherman, J. *Managing behavior* (Pt. 9). Lawrence, Kan.: H & H Enterprises, 1977.

Schwab, J. J., Nadeau, S. E., & Warheit, G. J. Crowding and mental health. *Pavlovian Journal of Biological Science,* 1979, *14,* 226-233.

Schwartz, G. E. Behavioral medicine and systems theory: A new synthesis. *National Forum,* 1980, Winter, 25-30. (a)

Schwartz, G. E. Stress management in occupational settings. *Public Health Reports,* 1980, *95,* 99-108. (b)

Schwartz, G. E., & Weiss, S. M. What is behavioral medicine? *Psychosomatic Medicine,* 1977, *36,* 377-381.

Schwartz, G. E., & Weiss, S. M. Behavioral medicine revisited: An amended definition. *Journal of Behavioral Medicine,* 1978, *1,* 249-252. (a)

Schwartz, G. E., & Weiss, S. M. Yale Conference on Behavioral Medicine: A proposed definition and statement of goals. *Journal of Behavioral Medicine,* 1978, *1,* 3-12. (b)

Schwartz, M. L., & Hawkins, R. P. Application of delayed reinforcement procedures to the behavior of an elementary school child. *Journal of Applied Behavior Analysis*, 1970, *3*, 85–96.

Schwartz, R. M., & Gottman, J. M. Toward a task analysis of assertive behavior. *Journal of Consulting and Clinical Psychology*, 1976, *44*, 910–920.

Schwitzgebel, R. L., & Schwitzgebel, R. K. *Law and psychological practice*. New York: Wiley, 1980.

Scott, M. G. The contributions of physical activity to psychological development. *Research Quarterly*, 1960, *31*, 307–320.

Scovern, A. W., Bukstel, L., Kilman, P. R., Laval, R., Busemeyer, J., & Smith, V. Effects of parent counseling on the family system. *Journal of Counseling Psychology*, 1980, *27*, 268–275.

Seligman, M. E. P. *Helplessness: On depression, development and death*. San Francisco: Freeman, 1975.

Seligman, M. E. P., Abramson, L. Y., Semmel, A., & von Baeyer, C. Depressive attributional style. *Journal of Abnormal Psychology*, 1979, *88*, 242–247.

Seligman, M. E. P., & Hager, J. *Biological boundaries of learning*. New York: Appleton-Century-Crofts, 1972.

Sexton, M. M. Behavioral epidemiology. In O. F. Pomerleau & J. P. Brady (Eds.), *Behavioral medicine: Theory and practice*. Baltimore: Williams & Wilkins, 1979.

Shaffer, D., & Greenhill, L. A critical note on the predictive validity of the "hyperkinetic syndrome." *Journal of Child Psychology and Psychiatry*, 1979, *20*, 61–72.

Shahar, A., & Stravynski, A. Cognitive behavior modification: A case study in its appraisal. *Behavioural Analysis and Modification*, 1979, *3*, 152–160.

Shapiro, D. H., & Zifferblatt, S. M. Zen meditation and behavioral self-control: Similarities, differences, and clinical applications. *American Psychologist*, 1976, *31*, 519–532.

Sharpley, C. F., & Poiner, A. M. An exploratory evaluation of the Systematic Training of Parent Effectiveness (STEP) programme. *Australian Psychologist*, 1980.

Shaw, B. F. Comparison of cognitive therapy in the treatment of depression. *Journal of Consulting and Clinical Psychology*, 1977, *45*, 543–551.

Shaw, P. A comparison of three behaviour therapies in the treatment of social phobia. *British Journal of Psychiatry*, 1979, *134*, 620–623.

Shekelle, R. B., Shryock, A. M., Paul, O., Lepper, M., Stamler, J., Liu, S., & Raynor, W. J., Jr. Diet, serum cholesterol, and death from coronary heart disease. *New England Journal of Medicine*, 1981, *304*, 65–70.

Shoemaker, J., & Reid, D. H. Decreasing chronic absenteeism among institutional staff: Effects of a low-cost attendance program. *Journal of Organizational Behavior Management*, 1980, *2*, 317–328.

Shoemaker, J., & Reid, D. H. Increasing parental involvement with profoundly handicapped persons in an institutional setting. *Journal of Rehabilitation*, 1980, *8*, 42–46.

Shores, R. E., & Strain, P. S. Social reciprocity: A review of research and educational implications. *Exceptional Children*, 1977, *43*, 526–530.

Shorkey, C. T. Behavior therapy training in social work education. *Journal of Behavior Therapy and Experimental Psychiatry*, 1973, *4*, 195–196.

Shure, M. B., & Spivack, G. Means–ends thinking, adjustment, and social class among elementary-school-aged children. *Journal of Consulting and Clinical Psychology*, 1972, *38*, 348–353.

Sidman, M. *Tactics of scientific research: Evaluating experimental data in psychology*. New York: Basic Books, 1960.

Sillett, R. W., Wilson, M. B., Malcolm, R. E., & Ball, K. P. Deception among smokers. *British Medical Journal*, 1978, *2*, 1185–1186.

Simpson, R. L. Behavior modification and child management. In M. R. Fine (Ed.), *Handbook on parent education*. New York: Academic Press, 1980.

Singh, R., & Oberhummer, I. Behavior therapy within a setting of Karma Yoga. *Journal of Behavior Therapy and Experimental Psychiatry*, 1980, *11*, 135–141.

Sloane, R. B., Staples, F. R., Cristol, A. H., Yorkston, N. J., & Whipple, K. *Psychotherapy versus behavior therapy*. Cambridge, Mass.: Harvard University Press, 1975.

Smart, R. G., & Gray, G. Minimal, moderate and long-term treatment for alcoholism. *British Journal of Addiction*, 1978, *73*, 35–38.

Smith, E. R., & Miller, F. O. Limits on perception of cognitive processes: A reply to Nisbett and Wilson. *Psychological Review*, 1978, *85*, 355–362.

Snyder, J. J., & White, M. J. The use of cognitive self-instruction in the treatment of behaviorally disturbed adolescents. *Behavior Therapy*, 1979, *10*, 227–235.

Sobel, H. J. (Ed.). *Behavior therapy in terminal care: A humanistic approach*. Cambridge, Mass.: Ballinger, 1981.

Sobell, M. B. Alternatives to abstinence: Evidence, issues, and some proposals. In P. E. Nathan & G. A. Marlatt (Eds.), *Alcoholism: New directions in behavioral research and treatment*. New York: Plenum, 1978.

Sobell, M. B., & Sobell, L. C. Individualized behavior therapy for alcoholics. *Behavior Therapy*, 1973, *4*, 49–72. (a)

Sobell, M. B., & Sobell, L. C. Alcoholics treated by individualized behavior therapy: One year treatment outcome. *Behaviour Research and Therapy*, 1973, *11*, 599–618. (b)

Sobell, M. B., & Sobell, L. C. *Behavioral treatment of alcohol problems: Individualized therapy and controlled drinking*. New York: Plenum, 1978.

Sobell, M. B., & Sobell, L. C. Nonproblem drinking as a goal in the treatment of problem drinkers. In J. M. Ferguson & C. B. Taylor (Eds.), *The comprehensive handbook of behavioral medicine* (Vol. 3). New York: Spectrum, 1980.

Sobell, M. B., Sobell, L. C., & VanderSpek, R. Relationships among clinical judgment, self-report, and breath-analysis measures of intoxication in alcoholics. *Journal of Consulting and Clinical Psychology*, 1979, *47*, 204–206.

Soloff, P. H., & Turner, S. M. Patterns of seclusion: A prospective study. *Journal of Nervous and Mental Disease*, 1981, *169*, 37–44.

Sommer, R. The isolated beer drinker in the Edmonton beer parlor. *Quarterly Journal of Studies on Alcohol*, 1965, *26*, 95–110.

Sorlie, P., Gordon, T., & Kannel, W. B. Body build and mortality: The Framingham Study. *Journal of the American Medical Association*, 1980, *243*, 1828–1831.

Spanier, G. B. Measuring dyadic adjustment: New scales for assessing the quality of marriage and similar dyads. *Journal of Marriage and the Family*, 1976, *38*, 15–28.

Spence, A. J., & Spence, S. H. Cognitive changes associated with social skills training. *Behaviour Research and Therapy*, 1980, *18*, 265–272.

Spielberger, C. D. *Manual for the State-Trait Anxiety Inventory for Children*. Palo Alto, Calif.: Consulting Psychologists Press, 1973.

Sprague, R. L., & Gadow, K. D. The role of the teacher in drug treatment. *School Review*, 1976, *85*, 109–140.

Sprague, R. L., & Sleator, E. K. Methylphenidate in hyperkinetic children: Differences in dose effects on learning and social behavior. *Science*, 1977, *198*, 1274–1276.

Spring, C., & Sandoval, J. Food additives and hyperkinesis: A critical evaluation of the evidence. *Journal of Learning Disabilities*, 1976, *9*, 565–569.

Spring, F. L., Sipich, J. F., Trimble, R. W., & Goeckner, D. J. Effects of contingency and non-contingency contracts in the context of a self-control-oriented smoking modification program. *Behavior Therapy*, 1978, *9*, 967–968.

Staats, A. W., Minke, K. A., & Butts, P. A token-reinforcement remedial reading program administered by black therapy techniques to problem black children. *Behavior Therapy*, 1970, *1*, 331–353.

Stalonas, P. M., Johnson, W. G., & Christ, M. Behavior modification for obesity: The evaluation of exercise, contingency management, and program adherence. *Journal of Consulting and Clinical Psychology*, 1978, *46*, 463–469.

Stamler, J. Lifestyles, major risk factors, proof and public policy. *Circulation*, 1978, *58*, 3–19.

Staples, F. R., Sloane, R. B., Whipple, K., Cristol, A. H., & Yorkston, N. Differences between behavior therapists and psychotherapists. *Archives of General Psychiatry*, 1975, *32*, 1517–1522.

Starr, R. A. Child abuse. *American Psychologist*, 1979, *34*, 872–878.

Stason, W. B., & Weinstein, M. C. *Hypertension: A policy perspective*. Cambridge, Mass.: Harvard University Press, 1976.

Steele, B. F., & Pollock, C. B. A psychiatric study of parents who abuse infants and small children. In R. E. Helfer & C. H. Kempe (Eds.), *The battered child* (2nd ed.). Chicago: University of Chicago Press, 1974.

Steffen, J. J., Nathan, P. E., & Taylor, H. A. Tension-reducing effects of alcohol: Further evidence and some methodological considerations. *Journal of Abnormal Psychology*, 1974, *83*, 542–547.

Stein, T. J. Some ethical considerations of short-term workshops in the principles and methods of behavior modification. *Journal of Applied Behavior Analysis*, 1975, *8*, 113–115.

Stern, R. S., & Marks, I. Contract therapy in obsessive–compulsive neurosis with marital discord. *British Journal of Psychiatry*, 1973, *123*, 681–684.

Stevenson, C. L. Socialization effects of participation in sports: A critical review of the research. *Research Quarterly*, 1975, *46*, 287–301.

Stewart, R. D. The effect of carbon monoxide on humans. *Annual Review of Pharmacology*, 1975, *15*, 409–425.

Stine, J. J. Symptom alleviation in the hyperactive child by dietary modification: A report of two cases. *American Journal of Orthopsychiatry*, 1976, *46*, 637–645.

Stires, L. Classroom seating location, student grades, and attitudes: Environment or self-selection? *Environment and Behavior*, 1980, *12*, 241–254.

Stolz, S. B. Comments on "An administrative perspective on guidelines for behavior modification": A legally safe environment is not necessarily an ethical one. *The Behavior Therapist*, 1980, *3*, 7. (a)

Stolz, S. B. Who do guidelines protect? A rejoinder to Griffith and Coral. *The Behavior Therapist*, 1980, *3*, 24. (b)

Straus, M. A., Gelles, R. J., & Steinmetz, S. K. *Behind closed doors: Violence in the American family*. Garden City, N.Y.: Doubleday, 1979.

Strossen, R. J., Coates, T. J., & Thoresen, C. E. Extending generalizability theory to single-subject designs. *Behavior Therapy*, 1979, *10*, 606–614.

Strupp, H. H. A psychodynamicist looks at modern behavior therapy. *Psychotherapy: Theory, Research and Practice*, 1979, *6*, 124–131.

Strupp, H. H. Clinical research, practice, and the crisis of confidence. *Journal of Consulting and Clinical Psychology*, 1980, *49*, 216.

Strupp, H. H., & Hadley, S. W. A tripartite model of mental health and therapeutic outcomes: With special reference to negative effects in psychotherapy. *American Psychologist*, 1977, *32*, 187–196.

Stuart, R. B. Weight loss and beyond: Are they taking it off and keeping it off? In P. O. Davidson (Ed.), *Behavioral medicine: Techniques for promoting life style change.* New York: Brunner/Mazel, 1979.

Stuart, R. B., & Davis, B. *Slim chance in a fat world; Behavioral control of obesity.* Champaign, Ill.: Research Press, 1972.

Stuart, R. B., & Jacobson, B. Sex differences in obesity. In E. S. Gomberg & V. Franks (Eds.), *Gender and disordered behavior: Sex differences in psychopathology.* New York: Brunner/Mazel, 1979.

Stuart, R. B., & Stuart, F. *Marital Precounseling Inventory.* Champaign, Ill.: Research Press, 1972.

Stumphauzer, J. S. Behavior modification with delinquents and criminals. In W. E. Craighead, A. E. Kazdin, & M. J. Mahoney (Eds.), *Behavior modification: Principles, issues, and applications.* Boston: Houghton Mifflin, 1981.

Stunkard, A. J. From explanation to action in psychosomatic medicine: The case of obesity. *Psychosomatic Medicine,* 1975, *37,* 195–236.

Stunkard, A. J. Behavioral medicine and beyond: The example of obesity. In O. F. Pomerleau & J. P. Brady (Eds.), *Behavioral medicine: Theory and practice.* Baltimore: Williams & Wilkins, 1979.

Stunkard, A. J. (Ed.). *Obesity.* Philadelphia: Saunders, 1980.

Stunkard, A. J., & Albaum, J. M. The accuracy of self-reported weights. *American Journal of Clinical Nutrition,* 1981, *34,* 1593–1599.

Stunkard, A. J., & Brownell, K. D. Behavior therapy and self-help programs for obesity. In J. F. Munro (Ed.), *The treatment of obesity.* London: MTP, 1979.

Stunkard, A. J., & Brownell, K. D. Work site treatment for obesity. *American Journal of Psychiatry,* 1980, *137,* 252–253.

Stunkard, A. J., Coll, M., Lundquist, S., & Meyers, A. Obesity and eating style. *Archives of General Psychiatry,* 1980, *37,* 1127–1129.

Stunkard, A. J., & Kaplan, D. Eating in public places: A review of reports of direct observation of eating behavior. *International Journal of Obesity,* 1977, *1,* 89–101.

Stunkard, A. J., & Penick, S. B. Behavior modification in the treatment of obesity: The problem of maintaining weight loss. *Archives of General Psychiatry,* 1979, *36,* 801–806.

Stunkard, A. J., & Rush, A. J. Dieting and depression reexamined: A critical review of reports of untoward responses during weight reduction for obesity. *Annals of Internal Medicine,* 1974, *81,* 526–533.

Sturgis, E. T., Calhoun, K. S., & Best, C. L. Correlates of assertive behavior in alcoholics. *Addictive Behaviors,* 1979, *4,* 193–197.

Sue, S., & Zane, N. Learned helplessness theory and community psychology. In M. Gibbs, J. Lachenmeyer, & J. Sigal (Eds.), *Community psychology: Theoretical and empirical approaches.* New York: Gardner, 1980.

Suinn, R. M. (Ed.). *Psychology in sports: Methods and applications.* Minneapolis: Burgess, 1980.

Sulzer-Azaroff, B. Behavioral ecology and accident prevention. *Journal of Organizational Behavior Management,* 1978, *2,* 11–14.

Sulzer-Azaroff, B., & De Santamaria, M. C. Industrial safety hazard reduction through performance feedback. *Journal of Applied Behavior Analysis,* 1980, *13,* 287–295.

Susskind, D. J., Franks, C. M., & Lonoff, R. Desensitization program with third- and fourth-grade teachers: A new application and a controlled study. In R. D. Rubin, H. Fensterheim, A. A. Lazarus, & C. M. Franks (Eds.), *Advances in behavior therapy.* New York: Academic Press, 1971.

Sussner, M. *Causal thinking in the health sciences: Concepts and strategies of epidemiology.* New York: Oxford University Press, 1973.

Sutton, S. R. Interpreting relapse curves. *Journal of Consulting and Clinical Psychology,* 1979, *47,* 96–98.

Sutton-Simon, K. Assessing belief systems: Concepts and strategies. In P. C. Kendall & S. D. Hollon (Eds.), *Assessment strategies for cognitive-behavioral interventions.* New York: Academic Press, 1981.

Swan, G. E. On the structure of eclecticism: Cluster analysis of eclectic behavior therapists. *Professional Psychology,* 1979, *10,* 732–739.

Swan, G. E., & MacDonald, M. L. Behavior therapy in practice: A national survey of behavior therapists. *Behavior Therapy,* 1978, *9,* 799–807.

Swan, G. E., Piccione, A., & Anderson, D. C. Internship training in behavioral medicine: Program description, issues, and guidelines. *Professional Psychology,* 1980, *11,* 339–346.

Swanson, J. M., & Kinsbourne, M. Food dyes impair performance of hyperactive children in a laboratory learning test. *Science,* 1980, *207,* 1485–1487.

Swanson, J. M., Kinsbourne, M., Roberts, W., & Zucker, K. Time-response analysis of the effect of stimulant medication on the learning ability of children referring for hyperactivity. *Pediatrics,* 1978, *61,* 21–29.

Tager, I. B., Weiss, S. T., Rosner, B., & Speizer, F. E. Effect of parental cigarette smoking on the pulmonary function of children. *American Journal of Epidemiology,* 1979, *100,* 15–26.

Tavormina, J. B. Relative effectiveness of behavioral and reflective group counseling with parents of mentally retarded children. *Journal of Consulting and Clinical Psychology,* 1975, *43,* 22–31.

Taylor, C. B. Editorial. *Behavioral Medicine Abstracts,* 1980, *1,* 1.

Taylor, C. B., Ferguson, J. M., & Reading, J. C. Gradual weight loss and depression. *Behavior Therapy,* 1978, *9,* 622–625.

Taylor, F. G., & Marshall, W. L. Experimental analysis of a cognitive-behavioral therapy for depression. *Cognitive Therapy and Research,* 1977, *1,* 59–72.

Taylor, H. L., Buskirk, E. R., & Remington, R. D. Exercise in controlled trials of the prevention of coronary heart disease. *Federation Proceedings,* 1973, *32,* 1623–1627.

Taylor, H. L., Kleptar, E., & Keys, A. Death rates among physically active and sedentary employees of the railroad industry. *American Journal of Public Health,* 1962, *52,* 1697–1707.

Taylor, J. G. *The behavioral basis of perception.* New Haven, Conn.: Yale University Press, 1962.

Teasdale, J. D., & Fogarty, S. J. Differential effects of induced mood on retrieval of pleasant and unpleasant events from episodic memory. *Journal of Abnormal Psychology,* 1979, *88,* 248–257.

Teasdale, J. D., Taylor, R., & Fogarty, S. J. Effects of induced elation–depression on the accessibility of memories of happy and unhappy experiences. *Behaviour Research and Therapy,* 1980, *18,* 339–346.

Tharp, T. F., & Wetzel, R. J. *Behavior modification in the natural environment.* New York: Academic Press, 1969.

Thelen, M. H., Fry, R. A., Fehrenbach, P. A., & Frantschi, N. M. Therapeutic videotape and film modeling: A review. *Psychological Bulletin,* 1979, *86,* 701–720.

Thomas, D. R. Moral guidelines for the review of behavior treatment programs. *The Behavior Therapist,* 1980, *3,* 23.

Thomas, D. R., & Murphy, R. J. Practitioner competencies needed for implementing behavior management guidelines. *The Behavior Therapist,* 1981, *4,* 7–10.

Thompson, M. S. *Benefit-cost analysis for program evaluation.* Beverly Hills, Calif.: Sage, 1980.

Tinsley, H. E. A., & Weiss, D. J. Interrater reliability and agreement of subjective judgments. *Journal of Counseling Psychology,* 1975, *22,* 358-376.

Tomaszewski, R. J., Strickler, D. P., & Maxwell, W. A. Influence of social setting and social drinking stimuli of drinking behavior. *Addictive Behaviors,* 1980, *5,* 235-240.

Tryon, W. W., Ferster, C. B., Franks, C. M., Kazdin, A. E., Levis, D. L., & Tryon, G. S. On the role of behaviorism in clinical psychology. *Pavlovian Journal of Biological Science,* 1980, *15,* 12-20.

Tucker, J. A., Vuchinich, R. E., Sobell, M. B., & Maisto, S. A. Normal drinkers' alcohol consumption as a function of conflicting motives induced by intellectual performance stress. *Addictive Behaviors,* 1980, *5,* 171-178.

Turkat, I. D. The image of behavior therapy. *The Behavior Therapist,* 1979, *2,* 17.

Turkat, I. D., & Brantley, P. J. On the therapeutic relationship in behavior therapy. *The Behavior Therapist,* 1981, *4,* 16.

Turkewitz, H., & O'Leary, K. D. A comparative outcome study of behavioral marital and communication therapy. *Journal of Marital and Family Therapy,* in press.

Turner, S. M. The behavioral model and black populations. In S. M. Turner & R. T. Jones (Eds.), *Behavior modification in black populations: Psychosocial issues and empirical findings.* New York: Plenum, 1982.

Turner, S. M., & Jones, R. T. (Eds.). *Behavior modification in black populations: Psychosocial issues and empirical findings.* New York: Plenum, 1982.

Turner, S. M., & Luber, R. F. The token economy in day hospital settings: Contingency management or information feedback. *Journal of Behavior Therapy and Experimental Psychiatry,* 1980, *11,* 89-94.

Ulmer, R. A. Noncompliance problems of pediatric and adolescent patients. *Child Behavior Therapy,* in press.

United States Department of Agriculture. Consumption of food in the U.S. in 1909-1952, Supplement-1961. *Agricultural Handbook,* No. 62, 1962.

United States Department of Health, Education, and Welfare (USDHEW), Public Health Service. *Smoking and health: A report of the Surgeon General* (DHEW Publication No. [PHS] 79-50066). Washington, D.C.: U.S. Government Printing Office, 1979.

United States Department of Health and Human Services (USDHHS), National Institutes of Health, National Cancer Institute. *Smoking programs for youth* (NIH Publication No. 80-2156). Washington, D.C.: U.S. Government Printing Office, 1980.

United States Public Health Service. *Adult use of tobacco, 1975.* Atlanta: Center for Disease Control, 1976.

Urbain, E. S., & Kendall, P. C. Review of social-cognitive problem-solving interventions with children. *Psychological Bulletin,* 1980, *88,* 109-143.

Van Hasselt, V. B., Hersen, M., & Milliones, J. Social skills training for alcoholics and drug addicts: A review. *Addictive Behaviors,* 1978, *3,* 221-233.

Van Houten, R. *Learning through feedback: A systematic approach for improving academic performance.* New York: Human Sciences Press, 1980.

Van Itallie, T. *Testimony before Senate Select Committee on Nutrition and Human Needs.* Washington, D.C.: U.S. Government Printing Office, 1977.

Van Itallie, T. B. Obesity: Adverse effects of health and longevity. *American Journal of Clinical Nutrition,* 1979, *32,* 2723-2733.

Van Itallie, T. B. Dietary approaches to the treatment of obesity. In A. J. Stunkard (Ed.), *Obesity.* Philadelphia: Saunders, 1980.

Vardin, P. A., & Brody, I. N. (Eds.). *Chldren's rights: Contemporary perspectives.* New York: Teachers College Press, 1979.

Varni, J. W., & Henker, B. A self-regulatory approach to the treatment of three hyper-active boys. *Child Behavior Therapy*, 1979, *1*, 171–192.

Vogler, R. E., Compton, J. V., & Weissbach, T. A. Integrated behavior change techniques for alcoholism. *Journal of Consulting and Clinical Psychology*, 1975, *43*, 233–243.

Vogler, R. E., Weissbach, T. A., Compton, J. V., & Martin, G. T. Integrated behavior change techniques for problem drinkers in the community. *Journal of Consulting and Clinical Psychology*, 1977, *45*, 267–279.

Vogt, T. M., Selvin, S., Widdowson, G., & Hulley, S. B. Expired carbon monoxide and serum thiocyanate as objective measures of cigarette exposure. *American Journal of Public Health*, 1977, *67*, 545–549.

Volkmar, F. R., Stunkard, A. J., Woolston, J., & Bailey, R. A. High attrition rates in commercial weight reduction programs. *Archives of Internal Medicine*, 1981, *141*, 426–428.

Wade, T. C., Baker, T., & Hartmann, D. P. Behavior therapists' self-reported views and practices. *The Behavior Therapist*, 1979, *2*, 3–6.

Wahler, R. G. The insular mother: Her problems in parent–child treatment. *Journal of Applied Behavior Analysis*, 1980, *13*, 207–219.

Wahler, R. G., & Afton, A. D. Attentional processes in insular and noninsular mothers: Some differences in their summary reports about child behavior problems. *Child Behavior Therapy*, 1980, *2*, 25–41.

Wald, N., & Howard, S. Smoking, carbon monoxide, and arterial disease. *Annals of Occupational Hygiene*, 1975, *18*, 1–14.

Walker, H. M., & Hops, H. Increasing academic achievement by reinforcing direct academic performance and/or facilitative nonacademic responses. *Journal of Educational Psychology*, 1976, *68*, 218–225.

Wall, S. M., & Bryant, N. D. Behavioral self-management of academic test performances in elementary classrooms. *Psychology in the Schools*, 1979, *16*, 558–567.

Walton, D., & Mather, M. The application of learning principles to the treatment of obsessive–compulsive states in the acute and chronic phases of illness. *Behaviour Research and Therapy*, 1963, *1*, 163–174.

Walton, R. G. Smoking and alcoholism: A brief report. *American Journal of Psychiatry*, 1972, *128*, 1455–1459.

Wardlaw, S. Premack theory and applied behavioural analysis. *Australian Psychologist*, 1980, *15*, 85–93.

Warshaw, P. R. Predicting purchase and other behaviors from general and contextually specific intentions. *Journal of Marketing Research*, 1980, *17*, 26–33.

Washington Business Group on Health. *A survey of industry sponsored health promotion, prevention, and education programs.* An interim report prepared for the DHEW Conference on Health Promotion Programs in Occupational Settings, Washington, D.C., 1978.

Waters, J. E. Evaluating correctional environments: The social ecological perspective. *Corrective and Social Psychiatry*, 1980, *26*, 45–52.

Waters, L. K. Social reinforcement of the working behaviour of retardates in a rehabilitation centre. *Australian Journal of Psychology*, 1979, *31*, 201–211.

Watson, D., & Friend, R. Measurement of social-evaluative anxiety. *Journal of Consulting and Clinical Psychology*, 1969, *33*, 448–457.

Watson, L. S. Issues in behavior modification of the mentally retarded individual. In I. Bialer & M. Sternlicht (Eds.), *The psychology of mental retardation: Issues and approaches.* New York: Psychological Dimensions, 1977.

Watzlawick, P. The psychotherapeutic technique of "reframing." In J. Claghorn (Ed.), *Successful psychotherapy.* New York: Brunner/Mazel, 1976.

Watzlawick, P., Weakland, J. H., & Fisch, R. *Change: Principles of problem formation and problem resolution.* New York: Norton, 1974.

Weiman, C. G. A study of occupational stressor and the incidence of disease/risk. *Journal of Occupational Medicine,* 1977, *19,* 119–122.

Weingarten, G. Mental performance during physical exertion: The benefit of being physically fit. *International Journal of Sport Psychology,* 1973, *4,* 16–26.

Weiss, G., Kluger. E., Danielson, E., & Elman, M. Effect of long-term treatment of hyperactive children with methylphenidate. *Canadian Medical Association Journal,* 1975, *112,* 159–165.

Weiss, S. M. News and developments in behavioral medicine. *Journal of Behavioral Medicine,* 1978, *1,* 135–139.

Weissman, A., & Beck, A. T. *Development and validation of the Dysfunctional Attitude Scale (DAS).* Paper presented at the annual meeting of the Association for Advancement of Behavior Therapy, Chicago, November 1978.

Weisz, G., & Bucher, B. Involving husbands in the treatment of obesity: Effects on weight loss, depression, and marital satisfaction. *Behavior Therapy,* 1980, *11,* 643–650.

Wells, K. C., & Forehand, R. Childhood behavior in the home. In S. M. Turner, K. S. Calhoun, & H. E. Adams (Eds.), *Handbook of clinical behavior therapy.* New York: Wiley, 1981.

Wells, K. C., Griest, D. L., & Forehand, R. The use of a self-control package to enhance temporal generality of a parent training program. *Behaviour Research and Therapy,* 1980, *18,* 347–353.

Wenger, N. K. (Ed.). *Exercise and the heart.* Philadelphia: Davis, 1978.

Werry, J. S. (Ed.). *Pediatric psychopharmacology: The use of behavior modifying drugs in children.* New York: Brunner/Mazel, 1978.

Werry, J. S., Sprague, R. L., & Cohen, M. N. Conners' Teacher Rating Scale for use in drug studies with children—an empirical study. *Journal of Abnormal Child Psychology,* 1975, *3,* 217–229.

Wetherby, B., & Baumeister, A. D. Mental retardation. In S. M. Turner, K. S. Calhoun, & H. E. Adams (Eds.), *Handbook of clinical behavior therapy.* New York: Wiley, 1981.

Whalen, C. K., & Henker, B. Psychostimulants and children: A review and analysis. *Psychological Bulletin,* 1976, *83,* 1113–1130.

Whalen, C. K., & Henker, B. (Eds.). *Hyperactive children: The social ecology of identification and treatment.* New York: Academic Press, 1980.

Whalen, C. K., Henker, B., Collins, B. E., Finck, D., & Dotemoto, S. A social ecology of hyperactive boys: Medication by situation interactions. *Journal of Applied Behavior Analysis,* 1979, *12,* 65–81.

White, P. D. The role of exercise in the aging. *Journal of the American Medical Association,* 1957, *165,* 70–71.

Whitehead, A. Psychological treatment of depression: A review. *Behaviour Research and Therapy,* 1979, *17,* 495–509.

Wicker, A. W. Ecological psychology: Some recent and prospective developments. *American Psychologist,* 1979, *34,* 755–765. (a)

Wicker, A. W. *An introduction to ecological psychology.* Monterey, Calif.: Brooks/Cole, 1979. (b)

Wicker, A. W. Assessing the settings of human behavior: Recent contributions from the ecological perspective. In P. McReynolds (Ed.), *Advances in psychological assessment* (Vol. 5). San Francisco: Jossey-Bass, 1981.

Wilbur, C. S. The Johnson & Johnson Live for Life program. *Behavioral Medicine Update,* 1980, *2,* 7–8.

Wiley, J. A., & Camacho, T. C. Life-styles and future health: Evidence from the Alameda County Study. *Preventive Medicine*, 1980, *9*, 1–21.

Wilhelmsen, L., Sanne, H., Elmfeldt, D., Grimby, G., Tibblin, G., & Wedel, H. S. Controlled trial of physical training after myocardial infarction. *Preventive Medicine*, 1975, *4*, 491–508.

Williams, C. L. Assessment of social behavior: Behavioral role play compared with *Si* scale of the MMPI. *Behavior Therapy*, 1981, *12*, 578–584.

Williams, G. J., & Money, J. (Eds.). *Traumatic abuse and neglect of children at home*. Baltimore: Johns Hopkins University Press, 1980.

Williams, J. I., & Cram, D. M. Diet in the management of hyperkinesis: A review of the tests of Feingold's hypothesis. *Canadian Psychiatric Association Journal*, 1978, *23*, 241–248.

Williams, J. I., Cram, D. M., Tausig, R. T., & Webster, E. Relative effects of drugs and diet on hyperactive behaviors: An experimental study. *Pediatrics*, 1978, *61*, 811–817.

Williams, R. B., Jr., & Gentry, W. D. (Eds.). *Behavioral approaches to medical treatment*. Cambridge, Mass.: Ballinger, 1977.

Williams, S. L., & Rappoport, J. A. *Behavioral practice with and without thought modification for agoraphobics*. Unpublished manuscript, Stanford University, 1980.

Williamson, G. A., Anderson, R. P., & Lundy, N. C. The ecological treatment of hyperkinesis. *Psychology in the Schools*, 1980, *17*, 249–256.

Wilson, D. D., Robertson, S. J., Herlong, L. H., & Haynes, S. N. Vicarious effects of time-out in the modification of aggression in the classroom. *Behavior Modification*, 1979, *3*, 97–111.

Wilson, G. T. Booze, beliefs and behavior: Cognitive processes in alcohol use and abuse. In P. E. Nathan & G. A. Marlatt (Eds.), *Alcoholism: New directions in behavioral research and treatment*. New York: Plenum, 1978. (a)

Wilson, G. T. Methodological considerations in treatment outcome research on obesity. *Journal of Consulting and Clinical Psychology*, 1978, *46*, 687–702. (b)

Wilson, G. T. On the much discussed nature of the term "behavior therapy." *Behavior Therapy*, 1978, *9*, 89–98. (c)

Wilson, G. T. Behavioral therapy and the treatment of obesity. In W. R. Miller (Ed.), *The addictive behaviors: Treatment of alcoholism, drug abuse, smoking, and obesity*. New York: Pergamon, 1980. (a)

Wilson, G. T. Behavior therapy for obesity. In A. J. Stunkard (Ed.), *Obesity*. Philadelphia: Saunders, 1980. (b)

Wilson, G. T. Toward specifying the "nonspecifics" in behavior therapy. A social learning analysis. In M. J. Mahoney (Ed.), *Psychotherapy process*. New York: Plenum, 1980. (c)

Wilson, G. T. Behavior therapy as s short-term therapeutic approach. In S. H. Budman (Ed.), *Forms of brief therapy*. New York: Guilford, 1981. (a)

Wilson, G. T. Some comments on clinical research. *Behavioral Assessment*, 1981, *3*, 217–226. (b)

Wilson, G. T. Adult disorders. In G. T. Wilson & C. M. Franks (Eds.), *Contemporary behavior therapy: Conceptual and empirical foundations*. New York: Guilford, 1982.

Wilson, G. T. Psychotherapy process and outcome: The behavioral mandate. *Behavior Therapy*, in press.

Wilson, G. T., Abrams, D. B., & Lipscomb, T. R. Effects of intoxication levels and drinking pattern on social anxiety in men. *Journal of Studies on Alcohol*, 1980, *41*, 250–264.

Wilson, G. T., & Brownell, K. D. Behavior therapy for obesity: Including family members in the treatment process. *Behavior Therapy*, 1978, *9*, 943–945.

Wilson, G. T., & Brownell, K. D. Behavior therapy for obesity: An evaluation of treatment outcome. *Advances in Behaviour Research and Therapy*, 1980, *3*, 49–86.

Wilson, G. T., & Davison, G. C. Aversion techniques in behavior therapy: Some theoretical and meta-theoretical considerations. *Journal of Consulting and Clinical Psychology*, 1969, *33*, 327–329.

Wilson, G. T., & Evans, I. M. The therapist–client relationship in behavior therapy. In A. S. Gurman & A. M. Razin (Eds.), *The therapist's contribution to effective psychotherapy: An empirical approach*. New York: Pergamon, 1977.

Wilson, G. T., & Franks, C. M. (Eds.). *Contemporary behavior therapy: Conceptual and empirical foundations*. New York: Guilford, 1982.

Wilson, G. T., & O'Leary, K. D. *Principles of behavior therapy*. Englewood Cliffs, N.J.: Prentice-Hall, 1980.

Wilson, W., & Calhoun, J. F. Behavior therapy and the minority client. *Psychotherapy: Theory, Research and Practice*, 1974, *11*, 317–325.

Winett, R. A. Parameters of deposit contracts in the modification of smoking. *Psychological Record*, 1973, *23*, 49–60.

Winett, R. A. Behavioral community psychology: Integrations and commitments. *The Behavior Therapist*, 1981, *4*, 5–8.

Winett, R. A., & Winkler, R. C. Current behavior modification in the classroom: Be still, be quiet, be docile. *Journal of Applied Behavior Analysis*, 1972, *5*, 499–504.

Wing, R. R., Epstein, L. H., Ossip, D. J., & LaPorte, R. E. Reliability and validity of self-report and observers' estimates of relative weight. *Addictive Behaviors*, 1979, *4*, 133–140.

Wing, R. R., & Jeffery, R. W. The effect of two behavioral techniques and social context on food consumption. *Addictive Behaviors*, 1979, *4*, 71–74.

Winkler, R. C. New directions for behaviour modification in homosexuality, open education and behavioural economics. In P. W. Sheehan & K. D. White (Eds.), *Behaviour modification in Australia*. Brisbane: Australian Psychological Society, 1979.

Winkler, R. C. Behavioral economics, token economies and applied behavior analysis. In J. E. R. Staddon (Ed.), *Limits to action: The allocation of individual behavior*. New York: Academic Press, 1980.

Winkler, R. C. The contribution of behavioral economics to behavior modification. In M. Rosenbaum, C. M. Franks, & Y. Jaffe (Eds.), *Perspectives on behavior therapy in the eighties*. New York: Springer, 1982.

Wirt, R. D., Lachar, D., Klinedinst, J., & Seat, P. D. *Multidimensional description of child personality: A manual for the Personality Inventory for Children*. Los Angeles: Western Psychological Services, 1977.

Wolfe, B. Behavioral treatment of childhood gender disorders. *Behavior Modification*, 1979, *3*, 550–575.

Wolfe, D. A., Sandler, J., & Kaufman, K. A competency-based parent training program for child abusers, in press.

Wolpe, J. *Psychotherapy by reciprocal inhibition*. Stanford, Calif.: Stanford University Press, 1958.

Wolpe, J. Cognition and causation in human behavior and its therapy. *American Psychologist*, 1978, *33*, 437–446.

Wolpe, J. Cognitive behavior: A reply to three commentaries. *American Psychologist,* 1980, *35,* 112–114.

Wolpe, J. Behavior therapy versus psychoanalysis. Therapeutic and social implications. *American Psychologist,* 1981, *36,* 159–164.

Wolpe, J., & Lazarus, A. A. *Behavior therapy techniques.* New York: Pergamon, 1966.

Wolpe, J., & Rachman, S. Psychoanalytic evidence: A critique based on Freud's case of Little Hans. *Journal of Nervous and Mental Disorders,* 1960, *131,* 135–145.

Wolraich, M., Drummond, T., Solomon, M. K., O'Brien, M. L., & Sivage, C. Effects of methylphenidate alone and in combination with behavior modification procedures on the behavior and academic performance of hyperactive children. *Journal of Abnormal Child Psychiatry,* 1978, *6,* 149–161.

Wood, P. D., Haskell, W., Klein, H., Lewis, S., Stern, M. P., & Farquhar, J. W. The distribution of plasma lipoproteins in middle-aged male runners. *Metabolism,* 1976, *25,* 1249–1257.

Woods, K. M., & McNamara, J. R. Confidentiality: Its effect on interviewee behavior. *Professional Psychology,* 1980, *11,* 714–721.

Woodward, R., & Jones, R. B. Cognitive restructuring treatment: A controlled trial with anxious patients. *Behaviour Research and Therapy,* 1980, *18,* 401–407.

Wooley, S. C., Wooley, O. W., & Dyrenforth, S. R. Theoretical, practical, and social issues in behavioral treatments of obesity. *Journal of Applied Behavior Analysis,* 1979, *12,* 3–26.

Workman, E. A., & Hector, M. A. Behavioral self-control in classroom settings: A review of the literature. *Journal of School Psychology,* 1978, *16,* 227–236.

Wynder, E. L., & Hoffman, D. Tobacco and health: A societal challenge. *New England Journal of Medicine,* 1979, *300,* 894–903.

Wysocki, T., Hall, G., Iwata, B., & Riordan, M. Behavioral management of exercise: Contracting for aerobic points. *Journal of Applied Behavior Analysis,* 1979, *12,* 55–64.

Yates, B. T. *Improving effectiveness and reducing costs in mental health.* Springfield, Ill.: Charles C Thomas, 1980.

Yates, B. T., & Newman, F. L. Approaches to cost-effectiveness analysis and cost–benefit analysis of psychotherapy. In G. R. VandenBos (Ed.), *Psychotherapy: Practice, research, policy.* Beverly Hills, Calif.: Sage, 1980. (a)

Yates, B. T., & Newman, F. L. Findings of cost-effectiveness and cost–benefit analyses of psychotherapy. In G. R. VandenBos (Ed.), *Psychotherapy: Practice, research, policy.* Beverly Hills, Calif.: Sage, 1980. (b)

Yelton, A. R., Wildman, B. G., & Erickson, M. T. A probability-based formula for calculating interobserver agreement. *Journal of Applied Behavior Analysis,* 1977, *10,* 127–132.

Young, R. J. The effect of regular exercise on cognitive functioning and personality. *British Journal of Sports Medicine,* 1979, *13,* 110–117.

Zajonc, R. Feeling and thinking. *American Psychologist,* 1980, *35,* 151–175.

Zarit, S. H. *Aging and mental disorders: Psychological approaches to assessment and treatment.* New York: Free Press, 1980.

Zeiss, A. M., Lewinsohn, P. M., & Muñoz, R. F. Nonspecific improvement effects in depression using interpersonal skills training, pleasant activity schedules, and cognitive training. *Journal of Consulting and Clinical Psychology,* 1979, *47,* 427–439.

Zentall, S. S. Optimal stimulation as theoretical basis of hyperactivity. *American Journal of Orthopsychiatry,* 1975, *45,* 549–563.

Zentall, S. S. Behavioral comparisons of hyperactive and normally active children in natural settings. Journal of Abnormal Child Psychology, 1980, *8*, 93–100.

Zentall, S. S., & Shaw, J. H. Effects of classroom noise on performance and activity of second-grade hyperactive and control children. *Journal of Educational Psychology*, 1980, *72*, 830–840.

Zettle, R. D., & Hayes, S. C. Conceptual and empirical status of rational–emotive therapy. In M. Hersen, R. M. Eisler, & P. M. Miller (Eds.), *Progress in behavior modification* (Vol. 9). New York: Academic Press, 1980.

Zilbergeld, B., & Evans, M. The inadequacy of Masters and Johnson. *Psychology Today*, 1980, *14*, 28–43.

Zitrin, C. M. Combined pharmacological and psychological treatment of phobias. In M. Mavissakalian & D. H. Barlow (Eds.), *Phobia: Psychological and pharmacological treatment*. New York: Guilford, 1981.

Zitrin, C. M., Klein, D., & Woerner, M. Unpublished manuscript, Hillside Hospital, Glen Oaks, New York, 1980.

Zorn, E. W., Harrington, J. M., & Goethe, H. Ischemic heart disease and work stress in West German sea pilots. *Journal of Occupational Medicine*, 1977, *19*, 762–765.

Zukow, P. G., Zukow, A. H., & Bentler, P. M. Rating scales for the identification and treatment of hyperkinesis. *Journal of Consulting and Clinical Psychology*, 1978, *46*, 213–222.

AUTHOR INDEX

SUBJECT INDEX